AGENTS 2/e
OF POWER

THE MEDIA AND PUBLIC POLICY

J. HERBERT ALTSCHULL

Longman *Publishers USA*

Agents of Power: The Media and Public Policy, second edition

Longman, 10 Bank Street, White Plains, N.Y. 10606

Associated companies:
Longman Group Ltd., London
Longman Cheshire Pty., Melbourne
Longman Paul Pty., Auckland
Copp Clark Longman, Ltd., Toronto

Acquisitions editor: Kathleen M. Schurawich
Production editor: Dee Amir Josephson
Text design adaptation: Betty Sokol
Cover design: David Levy
Cover photos: Top left, AP/Wide World Photos; bottom left,
    reprinted with permission of Fredrick Shook; right, AP/Wide World Photos
Production supervisor: Richard Bretan

Library of Congress Cataloging-in-Publication Data

Altschull, J. Herbert.
    Agents of power : the media and public policy / by J. Herbert
Altschull.—2nd ed.
        p.   cm.
    Includes bibliographical references and index.
    ISBN 0-8013-0776-7
    1. Journalism—Social aspects.   2. Press—United States.
I. Title.
PN4731.A388   1994
302.23'0973—dc20   93-42400
                                                        CIP

1 2 3 4 5 6 7 8 9 10-MA-9998979695

For Joy, with love

Contents

Preface *xi*

Introduction *xvii*

PART I THE PRESS AND AMERICAN DEMOCRACY   **1**

CHAPTER 1 **The Mission of the American Press**   **3**

The Democratic Assumption *3*
Those Spare Forty-five Words *8*
The "City Upon a Hill" *14*

CHAPTER 2 **The Gigantic Engines of Publicity**   **21**

The Penny Press and the Rise of Advertising *21*
The American Press Becomes Big Business *28*
News Managers and Social Control *31*

PART II   THE NEWS MEDIA AND SOCIAL CONTROL   **43**

CHAPTER 3   **Freedom of the Press**   **45**

   The Free Press Model   *45*
   Limits to Press Freedom   *52*

CHAPTER 4   **The "Power" of the Press**   **62**

   The Special Case of "Objectivity"   *62*
   Where Is the Independent Power of the Press?   *70*

CHAPTER 5   **Henry Luce and the Competitive
                Marketplace   81**

   The Wedding of Capitalism and the American Press   *81*
   The Incredible Shrinking Reader   *90*

CHAPTER 6   **TV and Cable: The Fabulous Rise
                of Ted Turner   102**

   TV Comes of Age   102
   CNN: Something New Under the Sun   *109*

CHAPTER 7   **"We Don't Have News on TV;
                We Have Entertainment"   122**

PART III   THE POLITICAL ARENA IN MARKET SOCIETY   **135**

CHAPTER 8   **Power, Politics, and the Media
                in the United States   137**

   Accountability and Manipulation   *137*
   The Boundaries of Acceptable Dissent   *144*

CHAPTER 9 **Spin Doctors and Media Managers** **152**

Political Campaigns and the News Media *152*
President, Pollsters, and Modern News Managers *159*
The Iran-Contra Affair *170*

CHAPTER 10 **Diversity: Minorities, Women, and the Media** **180**

PART IV **THE POLITICAL ARENA IN COMMUNITARIAN**
AND ADVANCING SOCIETIES **193**

CHAPTER 11 **The Communitarian Press:**
The Role of Karl Marx **195**

Marx's Press Philosophy *195*
The Job of the Press Is to "Change the World" *201*

CHAPTER 12 **From Lenin to Glasnost** **209**

Lenin's Three Roles for the Press *209*
Glasnost and Communitarianism *216*

CHAPTER 13 **The Advancing Press:**
The Old Order Changes **227**

The Press: A Shortcut to Development? *227*
The "Twin Agents" of Progress *235*

CHAPTER 14 **The Advancing Press:**
Africa, Asia, and Iran **242**

Africa East and West *242*
Asia and the Money Men *251*
Iran and the New Minimedia *257*

CHAPTER 15   **The Advancing Press: Peru   267**

A Revolutionary Press Experiment   *267*
The Sendero Luminoso and the News   *274*
The Reporter is "A Reporter . . . Not a Politician"   *282*

PART V   FREE FLOW AND BALANCE IN THEORY AND PRACTICE 291

CHAPTER 16   **The World Challenge for Fairness
                in Expression   293**

The Quarrel Over "Free Flow of Information"   *293*
New Agencies and "Cultural Imperialism"   *305*

CHAPTER 17   **The Attempt to Find
                a World Information Order   316**

The MacBride Commission and the Declaration of Talloires   *316*
The Perilous Push for International Cooperation   *325*

CHAPTER 18   **Learning and Training for a Free
                and Balanced Press   336**

The Education of Journalists   *336*
International Influences on Third World Training   *344*

CHAPTER 19   **Ethics and the Explosion of Knowledge   353**

Communication Research: A Variety of Paradigms   *353*
The Ethics of Journalism   *362*

**PART VI   PAYMASTERS AND PIPERS:
                THE SYMPHONY OF THE PRESS   371**

CHAPTER 20   **The Lords of the Global Village   373**

The Boundaries of Journalistic Autonomy   *373*
Transnationals, Conglomerates, and Media Moguls   *382*

CHAPTER 21 **Whither the Information Society?** **396**

The Time Warner Story *396*
The Choice: Gossip or Analysis? *407*

CHAPTER 22 **Politics, Power, and Perceptions** **418**

A Symphonic Classification System *418*
Purposes and Articles of Faith *423*
Can the Public Be Participants in Journalism? *433*

Epilogue: The Seven Laws of Journalism *440*

Appendix *444*

The Absurdity of "Social Responsibility" *444*

Svetlana Starodomskaya's Comments on the Soviet Code *448*

Will Irwin's View of 1911 Advertising *449*

Charles Dickens's Comments on the American Press in 1842 *450*

Index *451*

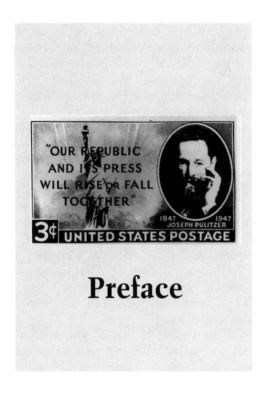

Preface

This is an integrated book: The whole is greater than the sum of its interlocking parts. The news media processes are inevitably dynamic, for the media never stand still. They are always in motion. What was completely true yesterday is today at best only partially true and at worst completely false.

So when I create a classification system for the news media by applying the metaphor of a symphony, I recognize I am not describing a perfectly stable system, since change is part of the system. The chapters that make up this book cannot be appreciated or understood separately. Even though the chapters are related to one another in a "macro" system we can identify as *the* news media, they may also be examined in their various "micro" forms.

In order to be effective, the wielders of power, the shapers of public policy, must maintain control over their populations in the macro arena of ideas and beliefs *and* in the micro arena composed of the channels of communication—newspapers, radio, and television. The sum of the structural, environmental, political, and economic aspects of the news media does not equal the *power* of the media. That power is, in the largest sense, impossible to state in mere words; no collection of verbal symbols can contain all the variables that, taken together, comprise power.

The narcotic of power is eternal. As Lord Acton and others have correctly observed, power tends to corrupt. Yet it is in the nature of us human beings to seek power, to seek to have control over our lives. In order to control our own lives, however, we must also control the lives of others. The history of human relationships is a history of power. From the beginning of time, men—however unjustly—have exercised power over women, as adults have over children. These seem to be natural power relationships. Then there are political relationships: monarchs over subjects, lawmakers over citizens, coaches over athletes, teachers over students. And economic relationships: the rich over the poor, bankers over depositors, shop foremen over workers. And military relationships: officers over troops. And legal relationships: judges over the accused. At some point in time, the powerless rebel in the conviction that the powerful are abusing their power; the powerless seek to turn the tables, to find for themselves a modicum of the power that has been exercised over them. It is like a musical round that goes on and on, a symphony with unlimited encores.

History has shown us the unstable nature of power relationships. Uprisings and rebellions have occurred again and again. We have witnessed for ourselves a racial revolt in the white-dominated nations of the Western world. Africans and African-Americans have demanded their share of power. So have Hispanics and native Indian populations in North and South America. Asians have rebelled, too; an Asian nation, Japan, has achieved the power to challenge the might of the long-dominant white nations. We have also witnessed a rebellion by women against male oppression. And there will be more rebellions.

It is *resources* that permit power to maintain and strengthen itself. Without resources, power cannot survive. When it declines, groups and states and organizations that were once top dog fall from the pinnacle. History is full of the rise and decline of empires—from Babylon to Tenochtitlan to Rome to Moscow.

Some of the required resources that must be controlled are easy to identify: arable land, mineral and fuel deposits, the requisite tools, and the technical skills. Some cannot be identified so easily. The resource addressed in this book is one of those: *information and the mesmerizing uses made of information*. Svengali and Houdini used it; the prophets and teachers of the Bible and Koran used it; Hitler and Stalin used it. And now the modern mass media use it.

Power itself is neutral, however corrupt its wielders may be. Power may be used for good or for ill. Differences exist between those who hold power and those who *appear* to hold and exercise power. In the end, it is power over people that counts.

My original plan in writing this book was to prepare a second edition of *Agents of Power: The Role of the News Media in Human Affairs*. The first edition was a macro study offering a theory of the role played by news media in various parts of the planet. I recognized early on, however, that what was needed now was a book that combined practice with theory, that showed *how* the social control function of the news media plays itself out in actual micro political, economic, and cultural settings. Moreover, the world has changed substantially since that book went to press in late 1983.

Shifts of power have occurred. The focus of public policy issues has changed. We have witnessed what to many appears to be the victory of commercial forces over communist doctrine. It is the suggestion here that the appearance of victory is premature. Like the processes of power, the processes of history are dynamic and always subject to change. The closing years of the twentieth century hint at weaknesses in the market economic system and at dislocations in the Northern Hemisphere power base. The sovereignty of nations is threatened by global technologies. Dissonance in the melodies of the symphony of the press are easily audible despite the collapse of the Soviet Union and the rise of what George Bush mistakenly identified as the new world order. National borders and the old ideologies may indeed by altering, but of order there is none. The wielders of power, the moderators of public policy, need the news media as profoundly as ever, perhaps even more than ever before.

This book is composed of six parts. Part One covers the essence of what is frequently thought of as the mission of the American press, a mission that is codified in the First Amendment to the Constitution and today influences the news media around the world. Part Two explores the social control function carried out in the development of public policy by the mass news media, primarily in the United States, where mass media have achieved their highest level of prominence. For all their prominence and *apparent* power to shape and influence policy, the news media do not, as demonstrated in these chapters, play an independent role in policy formation. Policy is set not by the media but by those who control the media's purse strings. These paymasters are the real wielders of power. In Part Three, we examine the principle of the news media as agents of power at theoretical and practical levels in both the newspaper and the television industries. The career of Henry R. Luce of *Time* magazine illustrates the critical role of the print media in the marketplace of the competitive, commercial world of the capitalist social order. The career of Ted Turner of CNN advances the story into the even more lucrative world of television, cable, and satellites. Later chapters examine the increasing importance of entertainment values in the media, exemplified by the open manipulative political campaigns for the office of president of the United States.

In Part Four, the emphasis shifts to the role of the news media in a variety of places. I have made no effort to encompass the entire world but have chosen representative nations whose media melodies appear in the other two movements of the metaphorical symphony of the press, to which I have given the names communitarian and advancing. This is a symphony in the process of becoming: It has no ending and might be considered an unfinished symphony. The story of the rise and fall of the Soviet Union's model of a useful press demonstrates both the might and the weakness of a communitarian media belief system. The changing face of the communitarian ideology can be seen in the transition from Marx to Lenin to Gorbachev and Yeltsin. Despite the collapse of the Soviet Union, communitarian ideology remains a viable alternative to the commercial market belief system, as shown not only in China and Cuba and the survivor nation-states of Eastern Europe but also in a number of Third World lands, among them Peru, Iran, and certain other nations identified here as the advancing nations.

Ideas about the appropriate role of the news media have taken a different form in much of the Third World, and these ideas are encompassed in Part Five, which examines the bitter battles around the world over such abstractions as freedom and ethics in political, academic, and professional arenas. The challenge to gain and hang on to freedom and fairness in the news media is immense and still elusive. The struggle inside the United Nations and its cultural arm, Unesco, over the role of the news media illustrates the interplay of the melodies of the symphony of the press. This interplay can be seen in both practice and theory in the education of journalists, the turnings and twistings of scholarly research about the news media, the ethical values that are increasingly drawing the attention of the public at large, and the amazing changes that technological advances are bringing about in education, research, and ethical values.

Part Six demonstrates the boundaries that constrain the news media inside the political economy and shows that the media exercise at best only limited autonomy in all elements of the communication process. Ultimately, information autonomy is in the hands of the paymasters who use the media as their most powerful instruments of social control. In addition, the tale that began with Luce's *Time* magazine is brought to a conclusion with the story of Luce's successor, Time Warner, the world's largest communications conglomerate, inextricably linking news and entertainment in one massive organization. Finally, Part Six describes the metaphor of the symphony, offering the theoretical framework of the book contrasted and compared with the principles and ideas that underlie the unfinished symphony.

Certain qualifications are in order, and they need to be made at the start. Even though I emphasize that the media are not independent actors, I do not mean to say they are mere lapdogs of the wielders of power. The opportunity is always available for journalists to try to counter power, to do their best to be revolutionary forces driving for change in the fabric of society and the structure of institutions. The press is an institution that thrives under the existing system whether that system be market, communitarian, or advancing. My point, as argued at many places in the book, is that the opportunity to push for systemic change is taken very rarely, and then only under the most unusual of circumstances. As profit-making institutions, the media dare not go far beyond the fundamental belief system on which the social order rests. To pursue the metaphor to its far reaches, I can say that while journalists are not lapdogs, they are sitting ducks for political and public relations strategists and media managers who are adept at manipulating them. It is also true that readers and viewers are not necessarily passive receivers of news, for they have the opportunity to demand that the press resist manipulation. To do so, however, is to challenge the social order, and audiences are as subject as journalists to skillful manipulation.

Readers who have delved into my earlier works or are well versed in the history of journalism are advised that it is not necessary for them to read the first two chapters. Those readers might just as well start with Chapter 3, which begins in the pivotal year 1917, when the modern world began to take shape.

ACKNOWLEDGMENTS

Many friends and students have contributed to the work on this book, and I would like to express my deep thanks to them all. A number of students at Johns Hopkins

University provided valuable research assistance; I would like to single out Alexandra Pham, Steven Kotler, Rob Porcarelli, Jeff Pruzan, and Patricia O'Brian for special thanks. I appreciate also the preliminary reading of certain sections of this book by Olatunji Dare, Anthony Giffard, Sara Castro Klaren, John Lent, John Merrill, Hamid Mowlana, Kaarle Nordenstreng, Judith Norwood, and Elisabeth Schillinger, and their valuable suggestions for revisions. In compiling the artwork, I had valuable assistance in creating the graphics and charts from Wes Harvey, Connie Naden, and Peter Shayotovich. Mike Lane of the Sunpapers in Baltimore, MD, kindly permitted me to make use of some of his excellent cartoons; so did Robert Grossman, an artist for the *Nation*. Marsden Epworth gave her generous permission to reproduce a photograph. I have discussed the work in progress with many colleagues and students, too numerous to mention, and thank them all for listening and offering valuable opinions. The following reviewers' comments were also helpful.

Steve Barker, University of Maryland

Donald Brenner, University of Missouri

John Busterna, University of Minnesota

Bruce Garrison, University of Miami

Sharon Hartin Iorio, Wichita State University

Stephen Lacy, Michigan State University

Robert Logan, University of Missouri

Mercedes Lynn de Uriarte, University of Texas at Austin

Robert Picard, California State University, Fullerton

Stephen Ponder, University of Oregon

Thomas Schwartz, Ohio State University

Kenneth Starck, University of Iowa

Leonard Ray Teel, Georgia State University

Frederic Belle Torimiro, Ferrum College

There is no way I can convey strongly enough the hard work and useful commentary by Lou Telich, who assisted with the editing of the book and saved me from some egregious errors. My thanks also to the scores of scholars, journalists, and news sources who cheerfully submitted themselves to intensive interviews, and to Kathy Schurawich, Dee Josephson, and the late Tren Anderson of Longman for their enthusiastic assistance. Finally, I would like to express my deep appreciation to Joy Naden, who shared with me all the anxieties I felt as I worked through the book, and whose support got me past some very tough times.

Johannes Gutenberg creates a revolution: an engraving of the inventor of movable type takes the first proof. (Bettmann)

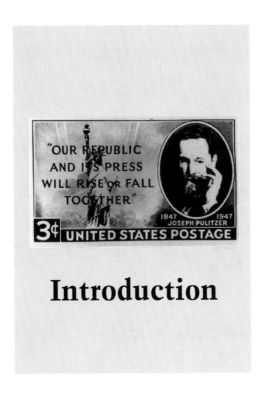

Introduction

THE FIRST JOURNALISTS

It is only human to view the past through the eyes of the present. After all, these are the only eyes we have. The most dedicated historians have similar problems, and the history of history is shot through with illustrations of the fallacy of anachronism. Certainly, our view of the origins of the press is subject to this fallacy. We are likely to conceive of the earliest press as a device designed to provide "news" to the "public." To do so, however, is to apply modern meanings for these verbal symbols to a historical setting in which the words, if they existed at all, referred to something quite different.

If, as the Scottish historian-philosopher David Hume suggested, "our ideas are copy'd from our impressions," then our ideas about the press are derived from what we see, hear, and experience. Perhaps the most important word in that sentence is *we*, for the modern press, which began in Belgium in 1605, has developed for "us" in different ways in different parts of the world. Our impressions are likely to be based on our experiences with our hometown newspapers, local network television stations, and weekly newsmagazines.

Although movable type appeared originally in eleventh-century China, printing remained undeveloped for centuries; in the West, it followed quickly on the heels of Gutenberg's press four centuries later. Before that time, the ability to read and write was confined to the great merchants and to the first two estates—the nobility and, primarily, the clergy; a merchant class was slow in developing, and the nobility was devoted to warfare and statecraft rather than to the gentler arts. It was the invention of the printing press more than any other event that shattered the medieval world and gave rise to modernism. The growth of a reading public led inevitably to the spread of ideas, including the philosophical and technological innovations that ultimately destroyed the power of the clergy and the nobility; it also led to new forms of political, economic, social, cultural, and religious systems. The press was never separate from these developments, but a part of them. To forget this is to fail to understand the history of the press.

When did journalism originate? Certainly, journalism did not spring full blown from Gutenberg's machine. In fact, intelligence about what was taking place at the seats of power dates back to the earliest days of recorded history. Shakespeare's accounts of ancient Rome in the days of Coriolanus and Caesar are filled with tales of messengers delivering written intelligence. Indeed, the "correspondent" was an important figure in Rome. It is not insignificant that the earliest news media in the Western world were devoted to supplying information about the economy of the Roman Empire.

Marshall McLuhan said of the process of communication that the "medium is the message."[1] More important, the media may be said to be the economy. Try to imagine the American economy without the media. Although political information may or may not be of utility to the public, commercial information—intelligence about goods—is indispensable to that public because it is within the media that the individual learns what goods are for sale in the commercial marketplace and indeed in the marketplace of ideas.

It was principally as factors in the distribution of goods that the news media emerged as instruments of communication. In Roman days, news traveled via messengers on foot in the form of letters. The Roman elite who resided in the provinces dispatched one or more personal correspondents to the capital to send back written reports of the events of the day, especially about the commercial and political transactions that affected life in the provinces. Most often, these correspondents were intelligent slaves who learned rather quickly they could pick up extra money by sending their letters to additional provincial residents. The money earned through these journalistic exploits was sometimes used to buy their freedom. The journalists who supplied the information were personal slaves; later, many came to look on themselves as wage slaves—that is to say, captives of the market.[2] Indeed, today's journalists work for what might be called "news factories" financed not by owners or even by employers but rather by commercial interests the journalists never meet and whose existence they often do not recognize.

Harold Lasswell identified "surveillance of the environment" as one of three communication activities that must be conducted by any society (the others involve information gathering and transmitting).[3] Information is not a matter of societal responsibility or desire but a matter of *need*, Lasswell said, as if a society were a biological organism that had to survey the environment in order to make sure of surviving as a species. Now substitute for the abstraction "society" a concrete portrait of that society's individuals in a position of power over their environment, and you can see that those individuals cannot continue to assert their power unless they are able to keep an eye and ear on the world they inhabit. The significance of Lasswell's insight is difficult to overstate; it places the abstraction "press responsibility" in its proper position, subordinate to the need for survival. In other words, press responsibility is an intellectual cosmetic coating over the raw power needs of those in a position to control their environment. As has often been said, information is power—or better, perhaps, control over information is necessary for the gaining and maintenance of power. It is obviously necessary for the powerful to know about the threats and opportunities that affect their interests; it is equally necessary that the channels of information be used to ward off the threats and to safeguard the opportunities affecting those in positions of power. *In other words, the media must be used as agencies of social control.*

Thus, the provincial entrepreneurs of the Roman Empire saw the utility of dispatching correspondents to Rome—to do their surveying for them, to be their eyes and ears for their life savings—and their power bases were directly involved. Surveillance of this nature in one form or another continues. Even the arrival of the printing press did not give the journalistic system its modern form. It was not until the rise of a mass market in the nineteenth century that a modern press came into being. All through that period, however, it retained its importance as an agency of social control in the hands of the powerful, surveying the environment for threats and opportunities.

It was the arrival of the printing press that made possible for the first time a reading "public." It was no longer necessary for written material to be copied laboriously by hand, and no longer could the clergy, who had been occupied in this copying process for a thousand years, claim a monopoly on written information. With the printing press, information became available to a greater number of people, but information had been flowing in limited circles throughout the fifteen centuries between the fall of Julius Caesar in Rome and the triumph of Gutenberg in Mainz.

The preprinting press served *first* as an agency of communication among princes and statesmen and, as towns and medieval guilds developed, among the political leaderships of the towns. Information had flowed between rulers even before the rise of Rome, but the agents of communication then were messengers and heralds who reported directly to the rulers and then broadcast carefully selected "news" in public announcements from the towers of buildings. The masses received no other news. The flow of information served as an early warning about potential threats and as a kind of tip sheet about potential opportunities.

The *second* group among which information circulated was the clergy. In more than a few instances, the monks and bishops briefed illiterate statesmen on the contents of received intelligence and used their monopoly in reading skills to influence political decisions and indeed to color the information passed out in their schools. For centuries the clergy maintained control over education in universities. Until the

Reformation, all the great European universities were organized by the Roman Catholic Church. As education spread, of course, direct control became more difficult.

With the growth of towns and commerce, opportunities arose for the acquisition of great wealth. Then a *third* group developed for which information was a device for both social control and the acquisition of power: the merchants and financiers. By the sixteenth century, the House of Fugger in Augsburg had its own news agency in full operation, a kind of Renaissance Associated Press. Throughout the previous two centuries, the news-gathering systems of the great financial houses had been expanding, so it is not surprising that the earliest news center was Venice, the capital of the world of commerce. It was essential for merchants of Venice to know the location of their vessels and the value of the jewels and spices they carried. The word *gazeta*, which was used in Italy as the name for the early, irregularly published information sheets, derived, not surprisingly, from the name of a small Venetian coin. The association of press with the world of commerce was as natural as the flow of rain from heaven.

These "information sheets," a direct translation of the Italian *fogli d'avvisi*, were being compiled even before the invention of printing. The Council of Venice not only ordered the collection of information and the dispatch of "news" to ambassadors, consuls, ship captains, and merchants but also demanded information from them. Occasionally, the merchants relayed the *fogli d'avvisi* to friends and business acquaintances abroad in the form of newsletters. The newsletter phenomenon was remarkable in the American colonies as well as across Europe. With the spread of these newsletters came wider dissemination of information to the masses and the incorporation of political information.

Like their fellows in ancient Rome, enterprising Venetians discovered the potential profit to be made in the exchange of news, in the gathering and dissemination of information. By the mid-sixteenth century in Venice, a veritable guild of *scrittori d'avvisi* (newswriters) had developed, selling their information sheets on the Rialto bridge across the Grand Canal to anyone possessing enough ducats to pay for news about the arrival and departure of ships; the dangers of the pirates and highwaymen; trade news; and, most threatening of all to established authority, news of political events. In Rome scribes became known as *novellanti* (feature writers) and *gazettani* (newsmen or journalists). Two popes went so far as to ban the writing of *avvisi* on pain of branding or sentence to the galleys. As with later journalists, the threats were ineffective. The business of news gathering and dissemination continued to expand, moving across the continent of Europe and across the seas. It was only among the elite that the newsletters circulated; not until the nineteenth century would modern journalism with its mass circulations make its appearance.

Still, the confluence of the Protestant Reformation and the growth of the business of printing doomed the medieval social order and tumbled the great principalities as well as the immense power of the Roman Catholic Church. The printing press allowed the Protestant leadership to transmit to the emerging "public," especially the intelligentsia, information about the excesses of the Catholic Church. The intelligentsia then used their own persuasive powers to move the masses to support their causes. Although the percentage of those among the public who could read or write remained small, their influence in spreading information was great. There developed an even greater desire among the masses as well as the intelligentsia for direct information, rather than for information filtered through the Church.

Our "thirst for news" has been well established. Who can dispute that men and women are interested in hearing about what is going on, that in all parts of the world people read their newspapers, listen to their radios, and tune in their televisions? Yet it may be that the world public has never had an active interest in accurate information about public affairs. No one can sustain the argument that the public really wants from the press accurate information about public affairs. There is evidence of a need for and/or interest in information, but the key question remains: Information about what? It is relevant to ask whether the information needed or desired relates to complex public issues, to life-threatening situations, to humorous occurrences, or to mere gossip.

Human beings have always needed and desired information about life-threatening situations. Long before Gutenberg's press, communications on the Asian plains, the African savannas, the forests of Central Europe, the deserts of the Middle East, and the American continents passed along through primitive channels information about the impending arrival of hostile armies or stampeding animals or thunderstorms. Such information constituted news of genuine significance to all who received it. In the traditional world, such "news" often was crucial for survival. In a social setting where daily survival is a challenge, interest in the external world is necessarily limited. It was only after commercial transactions had moved out of the neighborhood that an audience was created for news about external events. Not surprisingly, the earliest intelligence from distant places was commercial. The "thirst for news" was experienced first by the nobility, the clergy, and the tradesmen. The function of the media of communication before the rise of printing was to provide information of utility to the politically and economically powerful.

The final centuries of the Middle Ages were marked by the slow, painful growth of a middle class that began to challenge the dukes and the royal houses for what it perceived to be its fair share of power. Frustrated after a serious challenge in Flanders in the fourteenth century, tradesmen, artisans, and political rebels turned to the printed page to fuel the revolutionary fires that flamed after the Reformation. The flames boiled up into a conflagration with the startling advances in technology and the companion rise in the rate of literacy. As more people were able to read, they began to clamor for more information. The first "newspapers" followed. In the early seventeenth century, periodicals appeared almost simultaneously from one end of Europe to the other. It would be an error, however, to assume that these periodicals were available to the masses or that there was a ground swell of interest in public issues. The growth of the press kept pace with the explosion of ideas that accompanied the collapse of the old medieval order, but it would be centuries before those ideas would interest the masses, if such has ever been the case.

During the seventeenth and eighteenth centuries, as a popular press emerged throughout Europe and the New World, the periodicals were agencies of social control, powerful forces surveying their environment for threats and opportunities.

They appeared to be serving four functions. First, the clergy found in the new week-ly popular journals an avenue for the spread of religious doctrine. Second, shipping and other commercial operators saw the utility of the press as a means of providing speedy information about the market. Third, the entrenched political forces, as well as the rising challenges of political orthodoxy, turned to the printed page as an instrument to disseminate their forms of political persuasion. Fourth, gradually the press came to be recognized as a potential tool to educate the people. It can be said that the clergy, the commercial interests, and the political forces all sought to use the press for purposes of education, which to them meant to propagandize target audiences. For the first time, it became significant to the powerful to use information to win over the masses; and for the first time, the press was seen as carrying out the role of an agent or an instrument designed to accomplish specific objectives.

In no way were the periodicals of the seventeenth and eighteenth centuries newspapers in the modern sense. The earliest publications that can properly be identified as newspapers appeared only in the second third of the nineteenth centu-ry, originating, appropriately enough, in New York City. The origin of the word *newspaper* is lost in the mists of time; the word evidently had its origin in the *diur-na*, the etymological ancestor of *journal*, and the word *journalist* seems to have made its first appearance in seventeenth-century England as a synonym for *writer* or *mercurist*. The reference to the messenger of the gods of Greece indicates the function of journalists as the agents of their employers, commissioned to transmit messages.

These early publications in Europe did not print "news" as we know it. Often, they were called newsletters, as printers made use of the new technology of print-ing to pass information from one place to another. News pamphlets were employed by many seventeenth-century writers; the most notable in terms of influence on the ideology or folklore of the press was John Milton, whose 1644 pamphlet *Aeropagitica* argued in ringing phrases for free expression in print. In fact, Milton's assertion of the "self-righting principle" has stood for more than three centuries as moral justification for a free press system as that system is understood in the capital-ist West. Truth, Milton wrote, will always conquer falsehood: "Let her and falsehood grapple: who ever knew truth put to the worse in a free and open encounter?"[4]

It is from this passage that the concept of a "free marketplace of ideas" origi-nates, although it was not until 1919 that this particular combination of words appeared from the pen of Justice Oliver Wendell Holmes of the U.S. Supreme Court. The idea that "truth" would triumph over "falsehood" in a free and open encounter is an idea that thrilled the great experimenters who followed Milton in the eigh-teenth century and who drafted the American Bill of Rights and Constitution, both of which gave the self-righting principle the legitimacy that comes from being codi-fied into what, for Americans at least, is honored as sacred writ. In Marxist society and the Third World, however, Milton's maxim has been assigned a different inter-pretation by press theorists who have spoken out against the self-righting principle. So have certain iconoclastic Western thinkers, including John Stuart Mill, who cau-tioned: "The dictum that truth always triumphs over persecution is one of those pleasant falsehoods which men repeat after one another till they pass into common-place, but which all experience refutes."[5]

Although the self-righting principle originated in English thought, it was in the United States that the principle achieved the stature and veneration usually reserved only for revealed truth. Jefferson and Madison preached it in the days of the American Revolution; Justices Holmes and Brandeis added to its glory from their seats on the Supreme Court; and the contemporary fraternity of practicing journalists and journalism teachers has placed after it the exclamation point, that embellished dot of finality. Yet in other parts of the world, where the American Constitution has not been accepted as dogma, that principle has not been viewed as the pinnacle of morality in a lofty marketplace of ideas but rather as part of a semantic con game whose objective is the acquisition of dollars in the grubby marketplace of the exchange of goods.

All through the eighteenth-century Age of Enlightenment, passionate speech and stirring letters rang with a fierce praise of free expression and unlimited circulation of information. The Americans who enshrined free speech and a free press in the First Amendment to the Constitution were guided by Milton's rhetoric but were stirred also by two dedicated Englishmen writing under the name Cato, who proclaimed in a widely circulated series of messages to the colonies that free speech is "the right of every man, as far as by it he does not hurt and control the right of another."[6]

Yet the questions remain: What kind of information? For what purpose? One would search in vain for an advocate of free speech within the establishment who would use that speech to undermine the fundamentals of the society's belief system. The same Milton who expressed contempt for censorship of his ideas was to become himself a censor who would suppress ideas that to him were unacceptable. The same Jefferson who at one point elevated the press to a position more honored than that of government would come to urge prosecution of newspapers that published licentious matter.

It is clear that while free expression was glorified, little agreement—indeed, little discussion—occurred over what kind of information ought to be authorized. Nor was "free expression" closely defined. The American revolutionaries clearly sought license to say and write what they wished about the wickedness of their British masters; they were less enthusiastic about permitting similar grants to Tory sympathizers. Rebellion against Britain was condoned, but nowhere was there agitation for free expression against the prevailing economic system or accepted ethical values. Charles Beard later declared the Constitution to be a conservative defense of the property holdings of the Founding Fathers.[7] Beard's analysis no doubt went too far, yet we cannot deny his argument that the Founders managed to secure their own economic well-being and did nothing to encourage free expression of revolutionary *economic* doctrine. It is appropriate to keep in mind that financial embarrassment can force even prominent defenders of press freedom to deny in the real world some of the lofty principles they promoted in the realms of theory and philosophy.

Journalists are not independent figures. They write as did the Roman slaves at the Forum, as agents for others—others who pay their salaries, determine their working conditions, and possess the power to force him them to shift directions when they decide the journalists have become a threat to their power.[8] Exceptions to this rule arise from time to time, but the power of journalistic mavericks is inevitably limited. One of the authors of *Cato's Letters* accepted a government position under a man he had earlier reviled as hostile to a free press, this despite his having written a widely quoted passage that if men are not allowed "to communicate their Opinions and Improvements to one another, the World must soon be overrun with Barbarism, Superstition, Injustice, Tyranny, and the most stupid Ignorance. They will know nothing of the Nature of Government beyond a servile submission to Power."[9]

On the continent of Europe, phrases such as those that flowed from the pen of Cato were almost unknown. In Germany and France, we do not find editors and writers like those in England who were struggling to win the right to criticize political authorities in print. The rulers of Prussia and France, like those of Britain and the royal governors of the American colonies, insisted on unequivocal support from the press. In Prussia and France, until the heady days of the French Revolution, journalists seem to have accepted the directives of the crown without apparent protest. Frederick the Great, after his 1740 accession to the Prussian throne, not only demanded unconditional loyalty from the Prussian journalists but also went so far as to write some of the very reports published in the Prussian press. Frederick launched two newspapers of his own and composed a column that appeared irregularly under the heading "Journal of a Prussian Officer."[10] Frederick, a man who understood the utility of myths, appears also to have been the first Prussian ruler to recognize the potential importance of newspapers in exerting pressure on his enemies abroad and in furthering his policies at home.

In France, the Bourbon kings pursued a press policy not dissimilar to that of Frederick the Great. As might have been expected, however, the passionate applause for reasonable discourse and free expression that accompanied the French Revolu-tion brought demands for a free press. Frankly acknowledging his debt to Milton, Count Mirabeau implored the Estates General in 1789: "Let the first of your laws consecrate forever the freedom of the press. Of all freedoms, this is the most untouchable, the most unlimitable. Without it, other freedoms can never be secured."[11] Sweeping laws guaranteeing a free press were enacted, and all across the country journals and gazettes sprang into being, applauding the triumph of the Jacobins. In 1788, the year before the Revolution, only 4 newspapers were listed as being published in Paris, but by 1790 the number had increased to 355!

As seems to be the universal experience, those heady days endured but briefly. The laws that had proclaimed the freedom of the press were already being amended by August 1791, when France's Constituent Assembly enacted a law banning "voluntary slander against the probity of civil servants, or against their rectitude in carrying out their duties." Publications were censored and seized, editors flung into prison, their presses smashed. With the assertion of power by Napoleon, the presses became once again the organs of the ruling forces.

Borrowing from Frederick the Great, Napoleon converted the French press into agents of propaganda. Foreign governments and journalists abroad saw the Napoleonic press as mouthpieces of the government failing (as is common enough) to detect comparable practices at home. Metternich's comment is justly renowned:

"The French press is worth three hundred thousand men for Napoleon."[12] So distorted were the French accounts of Napoleon's military victories that his fall would come not merely as surprising but as quite unbelievable to the French public. Indeed, throughout modern history, the domestic press has so frequently failed to discuss military disaster that rarely has the public been prepared for defeat on the battlefield.

NOTES

1. Marshall McLuhan, *Understanding Media: The Extensions of Man* (New York: McGraw-Hill, 1964), 7, 9.

2. Carl Bucher, "The Genesis of Journalism," in *Industrial Revolution* (New York, Henry Holt, 1901), 215-43.

3. Harold Lasswell, "The Structure and Function of Communication in Society," in Bernard Berelson and Morris Janowitz, eds., *Reader in Public Opinion and Communication*, 2nd ed. (New York: Free Press, 1966), 179.

4. John Milton, *Aeropagitica* (1644), reprinted in *Great Books of the Western World* (Chicago: Encyclopedia Britannica, 1932), vol. 32, p. 23: "Who knows not that truth is strong next to the Almighty? She needs no policies, nor stratagems, nor licensings to make her victorious; those are the shifts and the defences that error uses against her power. Give her but room and do not bind her when she sleeps."

5. John Stuart Mill, *Essay on Liberty* (1859), reprinted in Max Lerner, ed., *Essential Works of John Stuart Mill* (New York: Bantam, 1961), 280.

6. The two were John Trenchard and Thomas Gordon, who over a ten-year period dating from 1720 penned a series of essays published in London newspapers under the byline of Cato, a Roman statesman-writer of the first century B.C. celebrated for impeccable honesty and renowned as a stubborn foe of the imperial Caesar. Circulated in the American colonies under the title of *Cato's Letters*, these essays extolled what would later come to be known as "the free flow of information." Clinton Rossiter in *Conservatism in America: The Thankless Persuasion* (New York: Knopf, 1955), 46, called *Cato's Letters* "the most popular, quotable, esteemed sources of political ideas of the colonial period" in the United States. See also Frederick Seaton Siebert, *Freedom of the Press in England from 1476 to 1776* (Urbana: University of Illinois Press, 1965), 333-45.

7. Charles Beard, *An Economic Interpretation of the Constitution of the United States* (New York: Macmillan, 1929).

8. Lasswell, "Structure and Function of Communication," 179, notes that the holders of power regularly survey their environment for threats to their "value position," another way of speaking of power.

9. Arthur Schlesinger, *Prelude to Independence: The Newspaper War on Britain 1764-1776* (New York: Vintage, 1957).

10. For an interesting account of Bismarck's press policies, see Erich Eyck, *Bismarck and the German Empire,* 3rd ed. (London: Allen & Unwin, 1968), 18, 104, 149-50.

11. For a study of the French press at the time of the Revolution, see especially Henri Avenel, *Histoire de la press française* (Paris; Flammarion, 1900). For further studies of French press history during that period, see Irene Collins, *The Government and the Newspaper*

Press in France, 1814-1881 (London: Oxford University Press, 1959); Charles Ledré, *La presse à l'assaut de la monarchie, 1815-1848* (Paris: Armand Colin, 1960); and Frederick B. Artz, *France Under the Bourbon Restoration 1814-1830* (New York: Russell and Russell, 1931).

12. The citation is usually attributed to Count Metternich at the time of the Treaty of Vienna in 1814. Efforts to produce the precise source have been unsuccessful, and the citation may be apocryphal. Napoleon was also quoted as saying at one point, "If I lost control of the press, I wouldn't last three months." See Anthony Smith, *The Geopolitics of Information: How Western Culture Dominates the World* (New York: Oxford University Press, 1980), unnumbered page prior to the Contents.

PART I

THE PRESS AND AMERICAN DEMOCRACY

Chapter

1

"OUR REPUBLIC
AND ITS PRESS
WILL RISE OR FALL
TOGETHER"

1847   1947
JOSEPH PULITZER

3¢ UNITED STATES POSTAGE

The Mission of the American Press

THE DEMOCRATIC ASSUMPTION

For two centuries, the First Amendment to the U.S. Constitution has stood stalwart and firm, glittering in the sunlit splendor of hope in a chapel of freedom atop a mountain of liberty, toward which men and women and their nations have struggled. To reach the top of that mountain, many have died and many more have suffered torture and imprisonment.

For most Americans the mountain has not been distant. It has, as it were, been a gift from the Founding Fathers, handed down from generation to generation as a part of what they saw as the American Dream. Not for all Americans, however. When the First Amendment went into force in 1791, free expression was denied to Native Americans, African-Americans, and most women. Nor was freedom of the press available for illiterates or those without the means to gain access to a printing press. It is not asked of legends, however, that they be consistent; and the mythology of the First Amendment has endured from its inception, so much so that it can be said to be an inseparable element in what might be called the dogma of the press. In the United States, belief in the idea of the First Amendment is as fixed as is belief in religious doctrine: The First Amendment is extolled as a crucial ingredient of the American way of life. Throughout the rest of the world, the liberty of the press codified in the First Amendment has served as an ideal to be attained. Not

The Associated Press newsroom—New York City, 1934.

SOURCE: Associated Press

everywhere, however, has it been accepted that the American ideal of press free-dom has been matched by reality. In capitalist Europe, the American press has often been seen as self-serving rather than noble. In the Marxist world and in the newer countries, doubts have been expressed about the extent of *real* freedom in a press system largely financed by advertising and committed to earning profits for its own-ers. Among the disenfranchised in the United States as well, the belief has not been universal. For example, when Martin Luther King, Jr., preached the doctrine of "free at last," he was expressing the hope that blacks as well as whites might climb the mountain of liberty.

To confront the press in its American context, we must recognize it as the most tangible and apparent of all institutions. The news media are everywhere. It is said the average citizen watches television five to seven hours a day. Supermarkets, drugstores, record shops, and department stores display newspapers, magazines, and books about persons in the news. Radios wake up millions and can be heard on street corners as well as in automobiles; some Americans walk along city streets and beaches with transistor earphones clamped to their heads.

The news can be found everywhere, and it is also everywhere respected. We must search long and hard to find an American who will say that news is not good for him or her: Who would deny it is an American's duty to be informed? This point is critical to an understanding of the role and the meaning of the news media in American life. Of course, the news media are unpopular in many American homes—or so the pollsters are informed. However, the American public distinguishes between the news media and the news itself; the media themselves may be despised but not the "news." We can say with a large measure of certainty that one of the primary assumptions held by American citizens is that democracy thrives in part *because* of the information disseminated by the news media.

This is the basic assumption: In a democracy, it is the people who rule, and their voices are heard in the voting booths. The decisions made by the people in the voting booths are based on the information made available to them. That information is provided primarily by the news media. Hence, the news media are indispensable to the survival of democracy. To carry the assumption a bit further: A democracy is a free society. In no other form of government are citizens free. Hence, for a society to be free, the flow of information to the citizens must come from news media that are free. By now this is a central assumption not only to Americans but also to most other citizens in the capitalist world.

It is but a short step from proclaiming the overwhelming importance of a free press or free media (the words *press* and *media* are usually interchangeable) to asserting their power. Controversies over the power of the press predated the First Amendment. Medieval clergy and rulers, as well as the governors of all the countries of the Western world, sought to place that power at their disposal; the idea of a free people presupposed the liberty of their press to pronounce their sovereignty over that of kings and bishops. Small wonder that journalists as a class have tended to the deadly sin of pride that haunts all who proclaim power, for power corrupts.

Proclamations of press (or media) power have become commonplace. Metternich spoke of the printed word in France as an agency in the service of Napoleon, and the propagandists of the twentieth century developed a reliance on radio and television as agencies of social and political control while advertisers relied on a "media mix" to gain their ends. Power, of course, is implied in all these cases. The point to remember as we examine the folklore of the press is that the flow of information has been widely viewed over the centuries as of transcendent importance with regard to both liberty and power. Of course, there is great strength in language; words are indeed mighty instruments. The error, we shall see, is to proclaim the *independence* of the press, to fail to recognize that *the news media are agencies of someone else's power*. The folklore, in fact, blinds us to the reality; and if on occasion evidence is assembled to direct our attention to it, the temptation (as with all legends) is to ignore the existence of that evidence.[1]

In the United States and elsewhere in the capitalist world, it is difficult to find a person prepared to argue against a "free press." The assumption about the centrality of the press in a democratic society is believed almost universally even though grousing about "press abuses" also is not uncommon. To be noted here, however, is that support for a free press may be more ritual than belief. Studies have shown that many among those who express themselves in support of a free press do not in fact want anything of the sort. It is more likely that what they desire is a press that presents not a portrait of the world as it really is but rather a portrait of the world as they would like it to be. A study made public in 1960 illustrated the point definitively. Residents of Ann Arbor, Michigan, and Tallahassee, Florida, two university communities in which highly educated and thoughtful individuals are liberally represented, produced the anticipated heavy support for abstract declarations in support of free speech and other democratic principles. More than 90 percent of the respondents supported the abstract declarations, but much of that support vanished when concrete situations were cited. For instance, only 63 percent would have authorized a person to make a speech "against churches and religion," and a mere 44 percent would have agreed to allow an admitted Communist to speak in favor of communism. The authors concluded that "consensus in a meaningful sense" does not exist with regard to cases of concrete behavior that endorses minority views—"even among those with high education."[2]

The study's findings have been confirmed in subsequent surveys dealing with similar questions. Even so, they do not appear to have received the attention they deserve. Although it is clear that many who say they believe in the democratic assumption do not actually believe in it, the fact they say they do is of great significance. Americans cling to the idea, the *perception*, of the democratic assumption with ferocious tenacity. The assumption is linked and intertwined with the search for truth.

Representatives of the American press and those who share with them a common faith in the democratic assumption often find in the phrase "a marketplace of ideas" an excellent metaphor to describe the assumption, because it postulates an open quest for the truth in a public arena. The origin of the metaphor is unknown, but it was given expression by Greek philosophers (Aristotle once said, "Plato is dear to me, but truth is dearer still") and by Jesus ("Know ye the truth and the truth shall make ye free"). Indeed, Socrates and Jesus, we are told, lost their lives in defense of that very metaphor. With specific reference to modern democratic theory, the concept is most dramatically expressed in John Milton's *Areopagitica* essay.

The marketplace image was added to the self-righting principle only in the twentieth century, when capitalism had been firmly established in the United States. No one gave it clearer, more vivid expression than Oliver Wendell Holmes, the distinguished Supreme Court justice, who wrote that "the ultimate good" is best reached by the "free trade in ideas" and "the best test of truth is the power of thought to get itself accepted in the competition of the market. . . . That at any rate is the theory of our Constitution."[3] Holmes's position, implying the transfer into the U. S. Constitution of Milton's self-righting principle, has by today emerged as part of the American dogma of conservative as well as of liberal philosophies.

The road from Milton to Holmes was the road also traveled by the American economy as the institutions of capitalism became more deeply linked with the belief system of political liberalism. That Holmes spoke correctly when he described the self-righting principle or the marketplace metaphor as "the theory of our Constitution" cannot be doubted. The Founding Fathers were themselves men of the Enlightenment. The English Bill of Rights, the earliest of the codes of the rights of man from which the basic concepts of the American Bill of Rights sprang, endorsed free expression only for members of Parliament, not for the citizenry at large, implying that free expression, orally or in print, was a grant only to the privileged, those who would make wise use of that right.

The American Founding Fathers, following in the footsteps of the Enlightenment philosophers, preached the triumph of reason in the affairs of man and the right of the majority to make political decisions. For if right will inevitably triumph when challenged by error, that right will be recognized and shared by the same majority. Majority rule is, in fact, an extension to the people of Milton's self-righting principle. Only through free expression could the people be granted access to the truth or to right thinking. It need not be considered strange that the American Founders endorsed a free press. Indeed, the glorification of a free press in the colonies came much earlier than the Bill of Rights.

Early declarations of freedom of expression did not claim any kind of absolute right. In fact, the attorney who defended John Peter Zenger in 1735 acknowledged that the right "of exposing and opposing arbitrary Power . . . by speaking and writing Truth" might be denied to those speaking falsehood (just as Milton sought to censor Catholics he believed were preaching falsehood) and when applied in parts of the world other than the American colonies.[4] Thus the earliest declarations of press freedom contain an element of patriotism and xenophobia, as indeed they do today. Totally free expression has never been practiced anywhere.

The Zenger case has been the most widely discussed over the years, but it was not the only or even the first time that free expression in print had become a public issue in the United States. Ben Franklin's older brother, James, came under heavy attack a generation before Zenger for condemning the medical policy of the powerful clergy of colonial Boston during a smallpox epidemic. Franklin's paper was ordered closed down, and he was forced to flee despite his published declaration that it was "injudicious" and "wicked" and contrary to democratic principle "to anathemize a printer for publishing the different opinions of men."[5] The central point of a free society, Franklin was saying, was that controversy must be aired in public, that it was *essential* the collision between truth and falsehood take place in public print. The line from James Franklin to Oliver Wendell Holmes is a direct one. Characteristically, the twentieth-century metaphor is an economic one—the marketplace; that of the eighteenth century was religious, with its emphasis on virtue and wickedness. The part James Franklin plays in history is a small one; not so that of his brother, Benjamin, who moved from Boston to Philadelphia and launched a career that brought him honor as a journalist, a statesman, an armchair philosopher, and a businessman. In Boston, he had received a powerful message: A journalist might write articles criticizing the holders of political, economic, and religious power, but if he was not careful, the criticism might well bring ostracism, imprisonment, debts, and even bankruptcy. Ben thoughtfully ran his presses within the system for commercial profit, engaging in cautious criticism but never straying past the boundary beyond which such criticism became unacceptable to those in power. His endeavors permitted him to rise to the most revered position ever enjoyed by an American journalist.

It was Ben Franklin who first asserted the commercial realities of a free press; in short, he raised a question about "the price of Truth." Although his question was not put in such terms, he was examining the fundamental dilemma of a capitalist press. *The dilemma can be characterized as the "central tension" in a capitalist press system.* On the one hand, there is the ideal of which legends have been sung for more than two centuries: The model goal of the press is to provide information for the good of humankind and a free society, to serve as a beacon to illuminate wickedness and abuse of power and thus hasten their end. On the other hand, there is the drive for private profit in the commercial world of the free market-place. In the second half of the equation, truth and the exposure of the untrustworthy are assigned a position inferior to that of financial gain. There is much of religious symbolism in the first half of the equation; this is not so, of course, in the second. Ben Franklin did not shy away from the commercial.

In his personal statement in the first issue of his *Pennsylvania Gazette* and in his well-known "Apology for Printers," Franklin, like his brother, endorsed the journalistic ethic of presenting all sides of controversial issues so readers could decide for themselves which was true and which was false. Franklin also observed that he might realize higher profits if he were to present sensationalized information but said he would not stoop to the lowest common denominator. His portrait of the heavy demands placed on the editor is also in keeping with the dogma that asserts the weighty burdens on the conscientious journalist. Yet Franklin the businessman went on to tell his readers that his newspaper would not be ponderous and dull but, in fact, "as agreeable and useful Entertainment as . . . Nature . . . will allow." It was one of the earliest public linkages of news and entertainment, about which we will have much to say later. Not only would Franklin's papers serve all sides to a dispute, but also they would pay well those who expressed those views. Even though truth is the highest calling, Franklin avoided "printing such things as usually give offense to Church or State."[6] He had no intention of going to jail as his brother had done; thus, he would not undertake a direct assault on the authorities of Pennsylvania. There was not in Ben Franklin a fanatical devotion to great principles. To him, there were clearly limitations on the freedom of the press, and he had no intention of pursuing a challenge that might lead beyond those limits to a confrontation with civil authority.

THOSE SPARE FORTY-FIVE WORDS

The revolutionary idea embodied in the First Amendment has frequently summoned to the barricades men and women who believe that no liberty is genuine unless it contains the right to express one's opinion, however unpopular, hated, or inflammatory. No doctrine announced by the new republic has been more widely cheered around the world than the declaration of free expression. It has fueled the fires of every revolutionary movement for two centuries. It is doubtful in the extreme that the drafters of those spare forty-five words could have imagined their impact, for, after all, there was nothing new in an assertion of the right of free expression. What was to be new, however, was the wide circulation of the declaration and the broad interpretation that came to be placed on the right, as well as the universal adulation that was to be heaped upon it.

The great code of the press embodied in the First Amendment declares, with deceptive simplicity, that "Congress shall make no law . . . abridging the freedom of speech, or of the press." The language was largely the work of James Madison, whose assignment in the first Congress was to analyze the dozens of proposals advanced by the states for inclusion in a Bill of Rights. In order to win approval of the Constitution of 1787, the framers found it necessary to agree to a formal bill that would enshrine in the positive law the major elements of the English Bill of Rights and the accumulated wisdom of eighteenth-century thought. Madison's original draft followed the constitution of his own state of Virginia with reference to the press. The third article of Madison's draft of a federal Bill of Rights guaranteed religious freedom; the fourth declared: "The people shall not be deprived or abridged of their right to speak, to write, or to publish their sentiments; and the freedom of the press, as one of the great bulwarks of liberty shall be inviolable."[7]

Congress submitted twelve amendments to the states for ratification. The first two were rejected.[8] The third, grouping religious liberty with guarantees of free speech and press and the right to assemble peaceably for redress of grievances, was approved and became the First Amendment. Although some later jurists were to assign this amendment preeminence over the others because it is first among the ten amendments of the Bill, what is now first was, in fact, third in Madison's original draft. Madison believed in a plural society where a multitude of factions would serve as a check on any one faction, even that of a majority. One of the most important such factions would inevitably be the press—the more newspapers, pamphlets, and broadsheets the better.[9]

Few Americans have been more forceful than Madison in asserting the centrality of the press in the democratic assumption. Within seven years of the adoption of the Bill of Rights, the threat of war with France induced President John Adams to secure congressional approval of the Sedition Act, which threatened journalists with prison for writing material that cast aspersions on the political leadership of the country. Well aware of the abusive language and sensationalism to which a licentious press was tempted, Madison, in responding to the Sedition Act, issued a ringing declaration of the importance of press freedom. Yes, Madison said, any good thing can be abused, even the press. However, "it is better to leave a few of its noxious branches to their luxuriant growth, than by pruning them away, to injure the vigour of those yielding the proper fruits." After all, he said, it is "to the press alone, chequered as it is with abuses, [to which] the world is indebted for all the triumphs which have been gained by reason and humanity over error and repression."[10] The democratic assumption Madison advanced holds that the press may be noxious, abusive, sensational, and even inaccurate, but its freedom is vital to the survival of American society.

Its freedom has never been absolute, as it indeed was not intended to be by the Founding Fathers, who were pragmatists, not absolutists. The goal of "objectivity" was one that did not even occur to the Founders, for there did not exist in the press of their era any publisher or editor who did not see his journal as an instrument for spreading good, or truth, and not merely as a catalog of points of view. What was desired, not only by the American Founders but also by the thinkers of the Enlightenment, was open discussion in the pages of public print. To Madison as well as to others, there apparently was nothing, at least in theory, that ought to be excluded from the pages of public print.

Yet from the very beginning, the practice did not coincide with the theory. The same Thomas Jefferson who could write the most ringing support for a free press could also condemn journalists as a pack of liars and argue, at least once, that they ought to be thrown in prison for what they printed. In 1787, years before he took office as president of the United States, Jefferson wrote that, because the American government was based on "the opinion of the people," he would choose a newspaper without governments over a government without newspapers.[11]

So attractive are those words to the practitioners of journalism that samplers and printed reproductions have been framed and hung in newspaper offices across the United States. Few newspaper offices note other words that Jefferson wrote years later when he was president and beleaguered by waves of vitriol in the Federalist press. In 1803, when Jefferson was so dismayed by what opposition presses were saying about him, he wrote that "nothing in a newspaper is to be believed." He said he had concluded that "a few prosecutions of the most prominent offenders would have a wholesome effect in restoring the integrity of the presses."[12]

Clearly, the revolutionary message of the First Amendment was not entirely acceptable to the most celebrated of the libertarian heroes among the Founders, at least after he had attained the pinnacle of power. To President Jefferson, the Federalist press was not serving as a proper vehicle of social control. Jefferson worried that the masses were in danger of being polluted by the lies he believed were being spread by the Tory newspapers. It was a troublesome theme for Jefferson, who found his *abstract* endorsement of a totally free press in dangerous collision with his *practical* desire to develop the kind of society he believed was needed to build the new nation. The problem confronting Jefferson was markedly similar to that faced two centuries later by libertarian thinkers in the new nations of, for example, Africa. Still, however impractical the revolutionary idea of the First Amendment, it had now become a powerful force in the world of practical politics. In office, nevertheless, libertarians have found the revolutionary idea unsuitable. It must be remembered that the drafters of the First Amendment were members of a social and cultural elite; they were fearful of the potential excesses of democratic government, for they believed the masses to be unlettered, culturally apathetic, and intellectually incapable of steering the ship of state. Rather than envisaging the average man as a participant in power, they perceived him as a cooperating consumer prepared to turn over the direction of the state to his cultural and intellectual betters. To ensure such cooperation on the part of the reading public was, in their view, the task of the press.

The Founding Fathers, it is to be remembered, anticipated that the press would serve their political cause. The newspapers of their day spoke for and were read by the social and cultural elite: those who regularly read books and pamphlets and newspapers and who had the financial resources to pay the price, in those days about six cents a copy for the newspapers. The ideas expressed in the newspapers were, not surprisingly, the ideas of the social and cultural elite. If the publications were read by the masses, it was assumed the masses would be influenced by the ideas and political principles supported by the press. In this way, the press was seen as an instrument of social control, an agency for the improvement and benefit of society.

During the presidencies of Jefferson and his Virginia allies, Madison and Monroe, the great experiment in democratic government spawned by the French Revolution ran its course with Napoleon's brief empire followed by the restoration of the Bourbon monarchy. With an eye on the doctrine of free expression let loose in the world by the First Amendment, factions in France fought out the most bitter of their battles over the issue of freedom of the press. The sides of the struggle were similar to those faced in Milton's England and Jefferson's America: How might the philosophical abstraction of a free press as a social good be made acceptable practically when that free press seemed to be undermining legal authority? (It was also a question that would bedevil constitutional Germany when the Nazi press was demanding its overthrow.) Jean Baptiste de Villèle, the prime minister to whom the ailing, gout-ridden Louis XVIII delegated his power, responded with the *loi de tendance*, adopted in 1822, a measure similar to the Bad Tendency guideline proposed in Blackstone's 1769 Commentaries, which held that "to punish any dangerous or offensive writing . . . of a pernicious tendency is necessary for the preservation of peace and good order, or government, and religion, the only solid foundations of civil liberty"[13] and later to become the official position of the U. S. Supreme Court in 1917. To Villéle it was necessary, if he could not conciliate his political foes, to "silence them," as he said, by subjecting the opposition press to punishment for printing articles that sought to frustrate his legislative program or even to challenge the hereditary right of the monarch to rule. Villèle remained in power when Charles X succeeded to the throne in 1824.

When his restrictive laws proved ineffective, drawing criticism not only from the opposition press but also from some loyalist papers and from political foes of both left and right, Villèle turned to outright bribery, a practice by no means unusual in Europe, especially in England. In fact, the French king received a better press in England than in his own country. One contemporary wrote that the correspondence of the three leading London journals was composed in the office of the French minister of police.[14] Anti-Royalist forces won the approval of Jefferson's old friend, the Marquis de Lafayette, who backed an unsuccessful coup attempt to overthrow the king. Hearing of the efforts to censor the French press, Jefferson, in retirement at Monticello, wrote to Lafayette yet another stirring declaration in support of a free press: In keeping government honest and unoppressive, he said, "the only security of all is in a free press. The force of public opinion cannot be resisted, when permitted freely to be expressed."[15] That letter was written in 1823; yet, a year earlier, Jefferson had written Lafayette that his opinion of the American press had sunk so low he was content to read but one newspaper—the *Richmond Enquirer*—because none of the rest could be believed.[16] Jefferson (and every other president) never was able to resolve either his love-hate affair with the press or his dilemma in choosing between free expression and the national good.

In France, Villèle responded to press opposition to the French invasion of Spain with an even more stringent proposal; the arch-conservative minister of justice, Count Charles Ignace de Peyronnet, gave the measure its unfortunate identification.[17] Criticized for introducing a measure its foes called a plan to annihilate the press, Peyronnet responded that the bill was conceived as "a law of justice and love." And so it was named, with consummate Gallic irony, by its enemies. It never did become law but went far toward forcing Charles from office and ending the Bourbon restoration. However, it evoked the most extensive public debate the world has ever experienced on the nature of the press and its role in the political and cultural life of society.

The debate occupied nearly the total attention of the Chamber of Deputies for a full month and dominated public life in the French capital as have few issues before or since.[18] Every day, fascinated crowds gathered outside the chamber to jeer the parliamentarians and to vent their collective anger against the law that would have imposed a stamp tax on all printed matter and required all political manuscripts to be cleared by government censors.

Among the speeches in opposition to the Law of Justice and Love, the most widely applauded was that of the intellectual leader of the liberals, Pierre-Paul Royer-Collard, one of the most gifted orators in French history. So celebrated in the charged political atmosphere was his speech that its printed circulation was said to have reached a million copies. Even allowing for hyperbole, Royer-Collard's words must have struck a nerve throughout the country. Writing over a hundred years later, Guillaume de Bertier de Sauvigny pronounced the address "one of the high points of political eloquence" in the nineteenth century.[19] To what must have been stormy applause in the chamber, Royer-Collard derided the law as at last "lifting mankind to the happy innocence of the brute." It would never work, he said, for to prevent the people from speaking out through the press against tyranny and oppression would not succeed unless all industry, all agriculture, all transportation, all activity were destroyed along with the books, pamphlets, and newspapers. "If your plows do not bury all of civilization," he taunted the Royalists, "you will not overcome our efforts."[20] The response of Minister of Justice Peyronnet was curiously modern. The press was being blindly critical, he said, and in its negativism was tearing down all the institutions of society; it was "intolerant, engaging in persecution for its own sake."[21]

Interestingly, the words of no less a libertarian than Thomas Jefferson were invoked on the side of the censors. On Jefferson's death in 1826, not long before the start of the debate, a letter written during his presidency a score of years earlier attacking the excesses of a licentious press was introduced to support the restrictions proposed by the Law of Justice and Love. Dismayed, Lafayette wrote Madison to ask whether the reported words of Jefferson were true; Madison responded sadly that they were, but that they did not represent Jefferson's true convictions.[22] It is impossible to know how influential the citation of Jefferson was, but it could not have damaged the cause of the censors for Jefferson was held in high esteem in France. In any case, the law was approved by the chamber by a vote of 233 to 134.

It was, however, a Pyrrhic victory because the public outcry was substantial, and the Chamber of Peers, to which the measure was referred, allowed the draft law to expire without a vote. When the peers adjourned, the irritated Villèle issued an executive order imposing censorship on the French press. Opponents took to the streets in protest; and in the elections that followed six months later, the Royalists suffered severe losses. Villèle resigned in January 1828, and Charles was cast from power after two days of revolution in 1830, an event royalists had foreseen as inevitable unless the press were checked.

Historians have assigned the press a key role in the 1830 overthrow of the Bourbon monarchy and by and large have credited the press with being responsible for it. A. J. Tudesq, for example, said the liberal press was "the principal author of the Revolution." Daniel Rader, in the only full-fledged English-language treatment of the period, assigned to the press the primary role in the overthrow of the monarchy and in directing "the reality of history."[23] Journalists in England as well as in France proudly proclaimed their power and immodestly draped around their shoulders the mantle of defenders of freedom and scourges of abusive power. At another time and in another place, the press would drape a similar mantle around its shoulders, asserting it was the press that had cast from power President Richard Nixon, sending his chief assistants to jail and condemning him to political exile.

Both explanations described the press as an independent force that was successfully confronting the power of entrenched industrial and political forces. It cannot be doubted that the press was a significant element in the struggle for power in both the France of 1830 and the Washington of 1974; yet it was but one element in those struggles, and indeed some members of the press could in both instances be found on the side of entrenched power as well as on the revolutionary side. It is more correct to assert that the press participated in the power struggle and that the revolutionary press, financed and prodded by the merchants, artisans, and growing middle class, as well as by powerful allies in the courts and among parliamentarians, aided the cause of revolt. The historian David Pinkney pointed out that by concentrating his attention on a single element in the fall of the Bourbon monarchy in 1830, Rader exaggerated the role of the press. The revolution, Pinkney noted, had "more fundamental origins" rising from Charles's alienation of deputies in the chamber; his failure to reward deserving politicians; and, above all, his economic measures, which were threatening both merchants and peasants with repressive taxes while the cost of living mounted ever higher.[24]

That journalists were very influential in the revolt is not to be questioned, but to say they were responsible oversimplifies a complex pattern of influences. The revolution against Charles would have occurred without the journalists, although perhaps not in that year. The same conclusion can be reached about the events of the 1974 fall of Richard Nixon.

Historians, but, more important, the journalists themselves, have popularized the avowal of press power incorporated in the claim it was the press that overthrew Charles X and Richard Nixon. It is not to be wondered that the journalists of 1830, as well as the journalists of 1974, pronounced themselves responsible for the overthrow of wickedness and the triumph of virtue. Historians are not infrequently overwhelmed by journalistic explanations and are sometimes channeled into narrow explanations of complex events by the pressures they feel to assign "causes" to events. Sober reflection compels us to recognize that the press, then as now, charts no independent course but serves the interests of those who own and operate it. The enemies of Charles X and of Richard Nixon were powerful in their own right, and inasmuch as both leaders had acted in sharp opposition to the revolutionary ideology of the First Amendment, they were clearly going to be opposed by the majority of the press, the journalists thus inevitably serving *as willing allies of the opposing political forces*—hence agents of a different social group.

THE "CITY UPON A HILL"

The press has always been an instrument of information, although it has been less clear what kind of information readers have desired. In nineteenth-century America, the expansion of literacy, the development of technology, and the growth of the mass market affected the expectations of both producer and consumer of news with increasing importance assigned to the commercial and political role of the press. The early character of the press as disseminator of religious doctrine all but disappeared in the nineteenth century, at least as far as the mass press was concerned, and while people everywhere continued to speak of the press as an instrument of education, its educational role became largely associated with the distribution of commercial and political information.

The growth of the newspaper paralleled the growth of the advertising industry. It was the first get-rich-quick age humankind had experienced. For that remarkable development, it was necessary that there be a remarkable confluence of facilitating factors, and only rarely in the annals of humankind had there been such a remarkable confluence.

Of the utmost importance was the Industrial Revolution itself, born in eighteenth-century Britain and quickly spreading across Europe and into the American colonies. As industry grew and flourished, lightning advances appeared in technology, trade, and transportation systems. For the first time, it became possible for farmers and the urban working classes to move from place to place. The immigration of large numbers of Europeans to the United States helped expand the Atlantic coastal towns into incipient urban centers, especially New York City. With the companion rise in the rate of literacy, increasing numbers were able to read and to clamor for information. It is important to remember that mass media developed simultaneously with urban centers. In fact, it is difficult to separate the two developments: Without urban centers, mass media were unlikely; and without mass media, the continued growth of urban centers were unlikely.

In addition, the character of the political environment underwent a significant change, accompanying the shifts in the worlds of science, industry, commerce, transportation, and the mass media. The political leadership of the American colonies and of the United States in its first half-century derived from members of the social and economic elite. The first six presidents were aristocrats from coastal Virginia and Massachusetts. By the 1830s, however, the social and cultural elite's dominance of the political world had been shattered—permanently, as it turned out. The American public had elected Andrew Jackson to the presidency and had moved the seat of political power from the landed aristocracy represented by Jefferson, Madison, and Monroe to the commercial entrepreneurs represented by Jackson, Van Buren, and their successors. The brokers had replaced the squires; the "democrats" had turned out the "gentry."[25] And a simple political truth was learned: Among political voters there are more "common men" than "aristocrats." With a minimum of modesty, Jackson ushered in what he and his agents identified variously as the Age of the Common Man and the Age of Democracy. In 1829, Jackson's Democratic party thoroughly defeated the supporters of John Quincy Adams, many of whom were remnants of the aristocratic Federalist party. With the arrival of Andrew Jackson, there came also a new ideology—one that in time was to spread around the world—to Latin America and the Orient as well as in the countries of Europe. The new ideology was the ideology of the common man, a democratic figure, to be sure, but a figure quite different from the democrat imagined by the French revolutionaries a generation earlier. The American democrat was not a democrat at all in the fraternal sense dreamed of by Robespierre and his compatriots. The American democrat was, in fact, an incipient capitalist, a man who dreamed of "rising by his own bootstraps" to a higher economic and social class, a man obsessed not with the idea of fraternity but with that of equality. The social order proclaimed by the Jacksonians was egalitarian, where every man would be the equal of every other, even his social betters. The American environment, with its happy mixture of what seemed to be unlimited land and opportunity, made the dream possible and raised in the overcrowded class-ridden society of Europe a vision, which persists in many places to this day, of "a land of unlimited opportunity."

As millions of immigrants streamed into America, writers and editors of the new mass media served as "advance men" for the American dream; they spread the message of equality and opportunity from coast to coast. Among those media barons were penniless Europeans, men such as James Gordon Bennett and Joseph Pulitzer, profound believers in the dream and chief among its publicists. Even in the face of depression and the tragedy of urban despair and blight that struck the cities of the United States, the leaders of society in politics and press continued to spread the message of optimism, for they, too, believed in the dream of equality and bounty.[26]

The dream was also to spread the good tidings across the continent, later around the world. The militant nationalism that flowered during the age of Jackson has indeed been a key ingredient in the American experience ever since. Not surprisingly, the press was a powerful agent in the expansionist impulses.[27] The urge for expansion derived in large measure from one of the most persistent elements in the belief system of Americans, the conviction that Providence had bestowed on the happy citizens of the country a special role to be played: to lead the nations of the world to the blessedness of the freedom and equality that were the inevitable products of self-determination. The idea originated in powerful form in the words of John Winthrop, the most celebrated of the early governors of the colony of Massachusetts, within a decade of the landing of the *Mayflower*: "We shall," Winthrop asserted, "be as a city upon a Hill, the eyes of all people upon us."[28]

The spread of American power from coast to coast and into foreign lands was carried out under the banner of Manifest Destiny, a term originated by the founder of *The New York Morning News*, John L. O'Sullivan, a journalist and political activist writing in the pages of *The Democratic Review*. A *News* editorial called it the mission of the United States to rescue "a vast portion of the globe, untrodden save by the savage and the beast, and . . . to render it tributary to man." The historian Frederick Merk said it was the mood of mid-nineteenth-century America to extend the geographical boundaries of the "city upon a hill" beyond the Rio Grande.[29] Whether the crusading zeal that is inherent in a sense of mission would be manifested in the Mexican war in 1846 or somewhere else a bit later is less important than that the people could be so easily persuaded to rally round the flag in transporting the blessings of liberty south of the border.

Because the press participated in—and often led—the rally round the flag, it should not be imagined that the press was the cause—or the originator—of Manifest Destiny. As in every similar situation, the press acted as agency for those who wished for the war: those, for instance, who were eager to extend the cotton-growing area of the nation into the vast, inviting area of Texas; and those for whom Texas might be yet another slave state to counter the new states clamoring for admission to the Union from the north. A number of political figures and newspapers spoke out against war with Mexico. The abolitionist *New Englander*, for instance, decried the war as "wasting millions of capital which stalwart labor must pay" and for raising "a few into the rank of a purse-proud aristocracy, vulgar and odious."[30] It was difficult for the press to resist the emotional fervor of the time. Horace Greeley, in his *New York Tribune*, gave lukewarm support to the war, although he was opposed to it; and he contented himself with applauding the end of the fighting. Rather than leading in moments of crisis, the press finds itself drawn into the fray on the popular side. Only occasionally do editors rise to oppose the popular will.

In the increasingly hostile moods of both northern and southern states, the press played its customary role. Southern papers condemned northern ideas and practices; northern papers performed a like service with regard to southern papers. The historian Avery Craven labeled the hostile campaign waged in the pages of the press as the first cold war. Indeed, during the Reconstruction period that followed the Civil War and lasted until 1877, northern and southern newspapers continued to endorse sectional interests, often in inflammatory terms. With the conquest of the continent assured, the people, their leaders, and their press turned their eyes beyond national borders. The same sense of mission that had served as motivation for the invasion of Mexico served also as motivation for the invasion of Cuba—to free her from Spanish rule. Modesty played little part. The publisher of *The New York Journal*, William Randolph Hearst, announced that it was he who had "furnished the war" with Spain.[31]

The history of the settlement of the West, as well as that of the territorial and economic expansion of white Europeans—especially punitive against Native Americans and African-Americans—was violent in the extreme. This violence was chronicled by the rising popular press, the so-called yellow press. Late in the nineteenth century, Hearst and his chief competitor, Joseph Pulitzer, challenged each other daily in an effort to present the most dramatically violent of acts and, in so doing, amassed vast wealth as their circulations soared. The Spanish-American War presented the most striking opportunity of all, and Hearst and Pulitzer rose to the occasion. Hearst, an amazing personality of monumental arrogance, went so far as to charter a tramp steamer off the coast of Cuba, the hold of which contained a printing press and composing room; he based himself and a staff of reporters on the steamer, often going ashore to observe battles, sometimes even to participate in the fighting. Pulitzer contented himself with sending an array of distinguished reporters, including the novelist Stephen Crane, to cover the war, their mission driven by the wish to extend the "City on the Hill" to every place in the hemisphere.[32]

The yellow designation that has come to describe the sensationalistic press of the late nineteenth century as well as current practices derived from "Hogan's Alley," a comic strip published in Pulitzer's *World*, in which there appeared the "yellow kid," a small child whose dress contained a dab of yellow. Hearst and Pulitzer, and those who followed them, invoked both the new "human interest" formula designed to expand circulation and to wage social campaigns to improve the lot of the "common man." These were, in short, sensational crusades, or perhaps crusading sensationalizers. In whichever case, circulation achieved astronomical heights.

The folklore of the press is part of a larger folklore, one that was dispatched into the wide world by those with a nineteenth-century vision of human development: an unending upward path for Americans that led across turbulent streams and rocky pinnacles to a pleasant plateau where brotherhood was preached and practiced, where the American Way would be adopted as the way of peace and plenty. On this plateau each man (some would add *woman*, but not many) would be educated and informed about events near and far, prepared to participate in democratic practices for the greatest good of the greatest number. The plateau was also envisioned as desired by the Christian God, who looked below with a special benevolence for his American children, the Chosen to lead the Others to the plateau. The nineteenth century was a time of almost unbounded optimism, when it was believed American men (and perhaps women) might lift themselves up by their bootstraps to attain the rewards of peace, prosperity, and power. The twentieth century has recognized the deficiencies of that view and has largely abandoned the dream of the great plateau in the sky; yet the folklore remains, a curious hangover rather like the dinosaur or the Neanderthal man, unable to survive or to overcome developmental deficiencies.

Advertising was not a new phenomenon, but it did not generate great wealth for the publisher until he was able to solicit for commercial notices among retailers and manufacturers. The press in all industrialized societies developed a similar pattern. Whatever its role as a political force or as an instrument for public education, it was expected above all to serve as an agent for the supply of information about products available to readers for purchase, as an agent of commerce, or, more precisely, as itself a commodity.

Interestingly, many journalists, in the nineteenth as well as the twentieth centuries, have spoken out, sometimes in violent terms, against debasement of the press from an educational instrument to a crass commercial enterprise. But there is an anomaly here, one that journalists themselves have rarely recognized, for they of course are working inside a commercial enterprise and tasting of the rewards therefrom while at the same time condemning the very commercialism that is providing those rewards. It is a paradox inherent in the nature of the commercial press, that, on the one hand, it is an institution devoted to the lofty ideals of the First Amendment, while, on the other, it is itself a commodity in the marketplace.

NOTES

1. We find ourselves in a position similar to the perhaps apocryphal position of the woman in an often-told English tale. In the story, the canon of Worcester Cathedral is informing his wife about Darwin's theory of evolution. This is her response: "Descended from the apes! Let us hope, my dear, that it is not true. But if it is, let us pray that it will not become generally known."

2. James W. Prothro and Charles M. Grigg, "Fundamental Principles of Democracy: Bases of Agreement and Disagreement," *Journal of Politics* 22 (May 1960): 276–94, ref. 293.

3. Holmes's opinion was filed in dissenting from the view of the Court majority, which ruled in *Abrams v. United States* (250 U.S. 616, 1919) that the conviction of five Russian nationals on charges of sedition during World War I was within constitutional limitations. Holmes argued that the conviction was unconstitutional on the grounds that the free expression of ideas, even hated ideas, was proper. Holmes's argument was later endorsed by the Court.

4. In the celebrated case of John Peter Zenger in 1735, attorney Andrew Hamilton argued with memorable persuasiveness that free expression by American printers of information about tyrannical acts of the mighty not only was an important goal for colonial society but also was, in fact, "the best Cause. It is the Cause of Liberty." See Leonard Levy, *Freedom of the Press from Zenger to Jefferson* (Indianapolis, IN: Bobbs-Merrill, 1966), 59.

5. The case was that of *The New-England Courant*, printed in 1721 under the leadership of a group scornful of the mighty Calvinist theocracy of Massachusetts. These men defied the policy of Increase and Cotton Mather, who endorsed inoculation as a means of easing the ravages of a smallpox epidemic. The Boston power structure forced *The Courant* out of existence, but not before it had laid the groundwork for the declared critical role of the American press in carrying out the democratic assumption. See, for instance, Carolyn Garrett Cline, "The Hell-Fire Club: A Study of the Men Who Founded *The New-England Courant* and the Inoculation Dispute They Fathered," unpublished thesis (Bloomington: Indiana University, 1976).

6. Benjamin Franklin, "Apology for Printers," in *The Selected Works of Benjamin Franklin, Including His Autobiography* (Boston: Phillips, Sampson, 1856), 172–79.

7. Bernard Schwartz, ed., *The Bill of Rights: A Documentary History*, vol. 2 (New York: Chelsea House, 1971), 1164.

8. Leonard W. Levy, *Emergence of a Free Press* (New York: Oxford University Press), 264-66. It was not until 1992 that the second of the original twelve amendments became law, a measure that refuses to allow pay raises for members of Congress to take effect before an intervening election.

9. James Madison, "Federalist No. 10," in Jacob E. Cooke, ed., *The Federalist Papers* (Cleveland: World Publishing Co., 1955), 55-65.

10. James Madison, *The Virginia Report of 1799-1800, Touching on the Alien and Sedition Laws; Together with the Virginia Resolutions of December 21, 1798, the Debate and Proceedings Thereon in the House of Delegates of Virginia, and Several Other Documents* (Richmond, VA: J. W. Randolph, 1850), 222. For a brief examination of the history of the Bill of Rights and Madison's role in it, see J. Herbert Altschull, *From Milton to McLuhan: The Ideas Behind American Journalism* (White Plains, NY: Longman, 1990), 109-26.

11. Letter from Thomas Jefferson to Edward Carrington, January 16, 1787, in Paul L. Ford, ed., *The Writings of Thomas Jefferson* (New York: Putnam, 1892-99) vol. 6, 357-61.

12. Letter from Thomas Jefferson to Thomas Kean, February 19, 1803, in Ford, *Writings of Thomas Jefferson*, vol. 8, 218-19.

13. Sir William Blackstone, *Commentaries on the Laws of England*, 4 vols. (Oxford: Clarendon Press), 1765-69; the specific passage can be found in vol. 4, chap. 11, 151-54.

14. The most complete account written in English of the controversy over the press in France in the early years of the nineteenth century is contained in Daniel L. Rader, *The Journalist in the July Revolution in France; The Role of the Political Press in the Overthrow of the Bourbon Restoration, 1827-1830* (The Hague: Nijhoff, 1973).

15. Letter from Thomas Jefferson to the Marquis de Lafayette, November 4 1823, in Ford, *Writings of Thomas Jefferson*, vol. 10, 279-83.

16. Letter from Thomas Jefferson to the Marquis de Lafayette, October 28, 1822, in Ford, *Writings of Thomas Jefferson*, vol. 10, 227-34.

17. Irene Collins, *The Government and the Newspaper Press in France 1814-1881* (Oxford: Oxford University Press, 1959).

18. In the debate, thirty-two deputies spoke out in favor of the Law of Justice and Love and forty-six in opposition. The entire text of the fascinating 1827 debate in the Chamber of Deputies is included in *Le Moniteur*, the government newspaper. The intriguing exchange of correspondence among Jefferson, John Norvell, Lafayette, Madison, and Nicholas Trist can be found in the collected *Works* of Jefferson and Madison; and in the Trist papers, some of which are in the library of the University of North Carolina and some in the Virginia Historical Society Collections.

19. Charles Ledré, *La presse à l'assaut de la monarchie, 1815-1848* (Paris: Armand Colin, 1960), 70.

20. Henri Avenel, *Histoire de la presse français* (Paris: Flammarion, 1900), 286-87.

21. *Le Moniteur Universel*, February 15, 1827. The *Moniteur*, a government publication, reported the entire debate.

22. James Madison, *Letters & Other Writings of James Madison* (Philadelphia: J. B. Lippincott, 1865), vol. 3, 618-19.

23. Daniel Rader, *The Journalists and the July Revolution* (The Hague: Nijhoff), 1973. See also André Jean Tudesq, *La Presse et l'evenement: Recueil de Travaux Publies* (Paris: Mouton, 1973).

24. David H. Pinkney, "The Media and the Monarchy in France, 1827-1830," *Reviews in European History* 1 (March 1975): 519-25.

25. The words *democrats* and *gentry* are enclosed by quotation marks to emphasize the point that the Jacksonians were no more democrats than were the Jeffersonian gentry, perhaps less so. Yet many historians have been kind enough to the Jacksonians to accept their definitions.

26. Readers desiring to pursue this point with additional details are referred to J. Herbert Altschull, *Agents of Power: The Role of the News Media in Human Affairs* (New York: Longman, 1984), 39-44, 311-13.

27. This spirit of nationalism led to war with Mexico; the acquisition of Texas, California, and the Southwest; indirectly to the Civil War; then to the purchase of Alaska; and by the end of the century to an imperialistic war wrestling Cuba and the Philippine islands from Spain. In all these ventures, the American press played a major role.

28. John Winthrop, "A Modell of Christian Charity," Winthrop Papers (Boston: Massachusetts Historical Society, 1931), 293-95. A century and a half later, in 1782, Benjamin Franklin bestowed his weighty endorsement on the metaphor with these words: "Establishing the liberties of America will not only make the people happy, but will have some effect in diminishing the misery of those, who in other parts of the world groan under despotism, by rendering it more circumspect, and inducing it to govern with a lighter hand."

29. Frederick Merk, *Manifest Destiny and Mission in American History: A Reinterpretation* (New York: Knopf, 1963), 24-25. Merk describes the expansionist zeal of the American press in detail, ref. 107-112 and 121-28.

30. *New Englander*, cited by Merk in *Manifest Destiny*. On page 262 he also quotes Albert Gallatin, who had served as Jefferson's secretary of treasury and was eighty-five years old in 1847, as saying the contemporary idea of conquest was all wrong. "America's mission," Gallatin said, was "to improve the state of the world," not to "abandon the lofty position which your fathers occupied, to substitute for it the political morality and heathen patriotism of the heroes and statesmen of antiquity."

31. Hearst's claim was documented in James Creelman, *On the Great Highway* (Boston: Lothrop, 1901), 177-78. See also W. A. Swanberg, *Citizen Hearst* (New York: Scribner's, 1964). However absurd, Hearst's claim was accepted as historical truth by scores of historians and, of course, by most journalists, for what could better assert the independent power of the press than the launching of a national war!

32. See, for instance, Stephen Crane, "God Rest Ye, Merry Gentlemen," in *Wounds in the Rain* (London: Methuen, 1900), 137-54.

Chapter
2

"OUR REPUBLIC AND ITS PRESS WILL RISE OR FALL TOGETHER"

1847 1947
JOSEPH PULITZER

3¢ UNITED STATES POSTAGE

The Gigantic Engines of Publicity

THE PENNY PRESS AND THE RISE OF ADVERTISING

We will not be far from the mark by assigning the date of September 3, 1833, as the beginning of the mass media. That was the date on which Benjamin Day, the publisher of *The New York Sun*, achieved success with a daily newspaper priced so low it could, for all practical purposes, be purchased by anyone in the city. The one-cent price marked the start of the "penny press." Day was straightforward about his intentions. He told his readers *The Sun* would "shine for all."[1] Day's reasoning was flawless: The standard price for a New York daily had been six cents, and only the well-to-do could afford to buy. By reducing prices, Day was able to attract more readers and increase his profits on the basis of circulation. Such reasoning came, in the twentieth century, to be recognized as deriving the benefits of the economy of scale. Day's penny press exceeded even his own expectations. Because his circulation soared to unimaginable heights, his New York City competitors soon were forced to slash their prices to a penny in order to compete. Provincial newspapers followed the lead; and for the first time, price competition entered the world of the press. Technological improvements followed rapidly, reducing the costs of the printers and increasing the space for information in the news columns and especially for advertisements.

The producers of the penny press knew full well that the human spirit craves information. But what is it that we want to know? The moguls of the penny press decided that what a mass audience desired was excitement and gossip: What they achieved was a new and enduring—if questionable—definition of "news," a concept that, while by no means universal, has spread around the planet.

It is instructive to examine the first issue of Ben Day's *Sun* as it cast its rays lightly on light subjects: a tale of an Irish captain, a poem titled "August Noon," a paragraph about the delights of very small objects, police-court proceedings, advertisements, and other short items. No report demanded of the reader more than a brief moment; the paper made no effort at all to report political events. Its purpose, Day wrote, was "to lay before the public, at a price within the means of everyone, all the news of the day, and at the same time afford an advantageous medium for advertising." To present "all the news," as Day put it, he would devote a small volume of space to a large number of items, and most of those items were what later came to be known in the world of journalism as "human-interest stories."[2] Clearly, the pattern of *The Sun* and the papers that appeared almost at once as competitors was one that found ready acceptance among the new readership, the workers whose social class had been virtually ignored by the older commercial press. These were the "democratic men" to whom Jackson appealed and who were now developing a sense of identity as citizens in the American democratic experiment; these were the urban proletarians, and now they were being made part of the system, insiders instead of outsiders. In short, they had been co-opted into the belief that they were significant elements in the decision-making process of the social order.

The penny press, an excellent instrument for social control, served a variety of purposes: For the printer, it was a source of potential wealth; for the working-class reader, it was a source of entertainment, a glimpse into the lives of both peers and leaders, an instrument to help soften the hard, boring life of the new urban centers; for the political leader, it was a potential instrument for propaganda, for swaying readers to support for himself or opposition to his foe; and for the commercial entrepreneur, it was a device for reaching a large group of potential buyers. When Ben Day sold *The Sun* to his brother-in-law in 1838, the price was $40,000; he had launched the paper with no capital at all. Day was the first of many who would make fortunes, small and large, from publishing newspapers.

The appeal to "human interest" was not an American invention. English periodicals began experimenting with inexpensive publications in the early nineteenth century. Those periodicals combined popular fiction and brief news items in packets that sold for a penny; their success was built largely on short articles on the proceedings of the Bow Street police court. Crime played a crucial part in the fiction they printed and also in their "news" items. *The Sun*'s world was the world of brevity, the vernacular of the streets, simplification, crime, gossip. The writing was sharp and crisp, filled with colorful phrases, clearly inimical to the publishers of the older papers, which were marked by verbosity and dullness; predictably, those editors sneered at *The Sun* as vulgar and degraded; but they soon came to accept the vulgarization and to adopt it themselves.

One of Day's rivals, *The New York Evening Post*, whose publisher-editor was the poet William Cullen Bryant, had more serious pretensions; its news pages consisted for the most part of information about the arrival and departure of ships, other commercial information, and the proceedings in Congress. It had no intention of providing news for the masses; but its editor, the romantic poet-essayist William Leggett (whose life is fictionalized in Gore Vidal's historical novel *Burr*), soon spoke out in support of the penny press because, as he wrote, it "communicates knowledge to those who had no means of acquiring it." The man who writes for the masses, Leggett wrote, has readers whose opinions are unformed and "whose minds are ductile and open to new impressions, and whose characters he, in some measure, moulds."[3]

The idea that it was in their power to mold the minds and opinions of their readers has motivated many thousands of journalists over the years. As immigrants flooded into the new land, creating thousands of villages and towns, enterprising printers and editors founded newspapers, printing information about political and economic activities and seeking to spread the message of union and community. It was a message that would be repeated across the land and repeated a century and more later in the new nations of Africa and Asia.

The lure of progress has attracted into the field of journalism many thousands of young men and women with an itch to reform society, to direct and implement social change. That many among those thousands were doomed to passionate disappointment has been well recorded; and yet the idea continues to fire the minds of men and women all over the world. As historian Leo Rosten commented in his excellent study, *The Washington Correspondents:* "Scratch a journalist and you will find a reformer."[4]

The evolution of the press from an instrument of information for the elite to a product for consumption by a mass audience transformed its nature. Thus, it can be said that before the rise of the penny newspapers in the United States, there was no press in any contemporary sense of that term. This is because the penny press altered the shape of "news" to make it more dramatic and more appealing to a mass audience and because the newspaper itself was changing from a source of intelligence for those engaged in commerce to a commodity for use by the entire market. A commodity is an article of trade or commerce that can be transported. Commodities are most often conceived as agricultural or mining products; the mass newspapers, on the other hand, supplied information not only about agricultural and mineral products but also about all items available for purchase in the market. It is not surprising, then, that simultaneously with the growth of the mass media, there arose the modern advertising industry.

If the newspaper was a commodity, it was widely assumed to be a form of public utility supplying the needs of the public for information about political issues and goods for sale, just as the barge and the train supplied the public need for transportation. The courts later ruled that the newspaper is not a public utility (and not required to accept material sent it for publication). In any case, whatever the readers may have thought, newspaper owners never acted as if they were producing a public utility. The press has operated less in terms of what the reading public wanted of it than in terms of what the merchants who supplied the advertising revenue desired. However, it is grossly unfair to characterize journalists as ignoring the question of public interest. Even as writers and editors surrendered financial control of their newspapers to business managers and advertising solicitors, they insisted on their independence as servants of the public. And disputes between journalists and the mass media's business managers have by no means subsided.

Reformers and charlatans were among the editors of the penny press; yet each of them was motivated by a desire for profit and the power that would come with prominence. Horace Greeley, the prototype of Horatio Alger's rags-to-riches heroes, came from New England to New York to find his fortune. Young Horace is said to have arrived in New York City in 1831 at the age of twenty carrying over his shoulder the traditional stick and bandanna containing his entire fortune: ten dollars. He became the most prominent editor of his day, gaining such fame that in 1872 he was nominated as Democratic-party candidate for president (defeated, of course, by Ulysses S. Grant). A self-educated printer, Greeley earned enough in ten years as a journeyman printer to buy *The New York Tribune*. Unlike other editors, he promised to elevate the taste of the masses, pledging that his paper would "advance the interests of the people, and promote their Moral, Political and Social Well-being."[5] On the other hand, his chief rival, James Gordon Bennett, offered no literary pretensions. His promise to his readers was to attack "all damned rogues" and "kick all politicians and parsons to the devil."[6] Although Greeley's paper did seek out more uplifting fare than Bennett's *New York Herald,* Greeley nevertheless published crime news and gossip as well as substantial political information.

As circulation increased and more and more Americans became readers, newspapers played a larger role in the political process. The lesson Jackson learned and parlayed into his political successes was adopted by those who followed him. Leaders of all political groups used the papers and their editors for their own electoral purposes. The government openly used financial reward to win support. Occasionally, as was the case of Thomas Gordon, a co-author of *Cato's Letters,* a pioneering advocate of a free press, high government office was held out as an enticement. More often, such direct rewards were not necessary. The editors were devoted to particular political causes long before they and their papers had achieved prominence.

Bennett's *Herald* was the most typical and most successful of the penny press. A Scot, Bennett came to the United States in 1819, worked as a journalist in South Carolina and New York, and then—failing to land a job with Day's *Sun*—invested $500 and launched *The Herald* in 1835. He was the first to proclaim "objectivity" as his goal. "We shall," he told his readers, "endeavor to record the fact, on every public and proper subject, stripped of verbiage and coloring."[7] In a passage that may have seemed arrogant to his contemporaries but that expressed an attitude shared by generations of journalists yet to come, Bennett wrote, "Books have had their day—the theatres have had their day—the temple of religion has had its day. A newspaper can be made to take the lead of all these in the great movements of human thought and human civilization."[8]

While Bennett, Day, and Greeley spoke openly of their interest in profit, it was Adolph Ochs of *The New York Times* who gave the clearest expression to the drive for profit of the early journalistic entrepreneurs. If the others gave impetus to the

Horace Greeley makes it from rags to riches: The publisher makes his way to the big city to found *The New York Tribune*.

SOURCE: Bettmann

sensational press, it was Ochs who spoke of the potential conservative impact of the press. The nineteenth century was a world of industrial expansion—of budding commercial empires, of fortunes made and lost in grain, railroads, shipbuilding, mining, and ranching. It was not an era for unblushing pretense of disinterest in wealth. The announcement of the origin of the species by Darwin in 1859 was followed by the rapid growth of Social Darwinism in the United States with its emphasis on the acquisition of money and power in what Andrew Carnegie blithely defined as "the gospel of wealth." The press, that *nonpareil* instrument of social control, spread the gospel across the land, participating equally in its message and its rewards.

Ochs's most important contribution to the history of the press was his return to the principle, begun centuries ago by the *scrittori* of Venice, that "news" was itself a highly salable commodity. Gay Talese made the point tellingly in *The Kingdom and the Power*, his entertaining history of *The Times*: "Ochs had something to sell—news—and he hoped to sell it dispassionately and with the guarantee that it was reliable and unspoiled and not deviously inspired."[9]

Few editors were so saintly as to fail to take advantage of the great advertising bonanza that came their way. Some were naive enough or frank enough to express openly their devotion to the advertiser above the reader. Bennett's *Herald* went so far as to reject public outcries against the quackery of patent-medicine announcements; he gave this picturesque response in 1836 to a reader's protest about the qualities of an elixir advertised by one Dr. Brandeth: "Send us more advertisements than Dr. Brandeth does—give us higher prices—we'll cut Dr. Brandeth dead—or at least curtail his space. Business is business—money is money . . . we permit no blockhead to interfere with our business."[10] Business is business, Bennett said, and the order of the day was *caveat emptor*—let the buyer beware. However, as the Civil War drew to an end in 1865, *The Herald* modified its own position and joined *The New York Times* in refusing to accept patent-medicine advertising.

It was clear in the 1830s from comments by Bennett and others that, although they espoused the cause of the common man and were—at least in theory—performing a public service for him, the editors saw themselves not as servants to that public but rather as its teachers. The early editors did not shy away from offering moral as well as political advice to readers. At best, editors reluctantly acknowledged the qualifications of the reader to speak with authority equal to the journalist's. The practice of commenting with open arrogance or contempt about readers' opinions has largely disappeared, but a clearly implied distance between the convictions and understanding of the journalist on the one hand and those of readers or viewers on the other remains. It is a state of mind that on a loftier plane has been characterized by Third World representatives as a "one-way flow of communication," from the top down.[11]

In the early years of the penny press, display advertising closely resembled what is now known as classified advertising. It flowed as the financial lifeblood of penny-press publishers, for reducing the price of their wares sixfold demanded of them a massive increase in the number of subscribers or an alternative source of revenue—or, best of all, both. It was both sources that provided the required capital. At the same time, public notices were crucial sources of revenue, less so for the wildly successful sensational press than for the more sedate small-town newspapers.

Advertising in one form or another has been an ingredient of printed periodicals from their earliest days. In England, the publication of a new book was announced in a paper as early as 1625; the notice stirred a flurry of criticism, however, from printers who did not consider such information to be news. It remained for the next generation to publish the second recorded advertisement, and this one was for an agricultural commodity: coffee.[12] Even so, the incidence of advertising was small throughout the seventeenth century and during the early eighteenth century in England, the countries of Europe, and the American colonies. The elite readership complained frequently that such insertions took space away from the commercial and political items in which it was interested, and many publishers concurred. Moreover, early advertisements were roundly condemned on the grounds they were untrue and publicized quack remedies. For more than two centuries, patent medicines remained the chief items advertised in American newspapers.

By the mid-eighteenth century, advertising revenues were beginning to play an important role in the financing of newspapers; but subscriptions remained the largest factor until the late nineteenth century. By 1750, opposition to advertising began to wane, no doubt because it became increasingly clear that commerce among the colonies helped assure independence and well-being. Benjamin Franklin openly endorsed the practice and regularly published two columns of ads per issue. Still, it was not until the nineteenth century that advertising began to be an element of major significance in the operation of newspapers. The fact that the early press served primarily the interests of the upper classes gave rise to a special motivation for newspapers to publish commercial notices. Advertisements confirmed the business community's support for individual papers, just as the earlier proud pronouncements that certain newspapers were issued on the authority of government were a source of confirmation of the worth of the product.[13]

There is no certain causal connection between the penny press and the expansion of the advertising industry; each was a phenomenon whose time had come, and each needed the other in order to prosper. In the decade that preceded the appearance of Ben Day's *Sun*, the pages of newspapers devoted to commercial messages increased steadily.[14] By 1835, the pages of *The Sun* were so filled with ads that it had room for only five columns of reading matter in a paper with a total of twenty columns. The small-town provincial press was even more overloaded with ads. The space devoted to ads in *The Pittsburgh Gazette* in 1833 consumed 74 percent of the paper; by 1860, the high mark of the advertising cornucopia, *The Gazette's* ad content was up to 83 percent. Meanwhile, a new commercial enterprise had appeared on the scene to fill the advertising needs of the penny press: the department store, itself a product of the developing consumerism. Before the department store entered the advertising lists, the space assigned to commercial notices was limited; now more space was needed to promote a larger volume of wares, and the brief classified items began to be replaced by larger display ads.

The development was mutually beneficial to advertisers and publishers. The demand for advertisement space meant more pages were needed to accommodate the ads and also to provide more room for the dramatic articles that filled the news pages. The press industry indulged in a binge of expansion with almost guaranteed circulation as readers eagerly paid their pennies to receive their daily dose of sensational news items and advertising messages. Publishers no longer had to scrounge for subscribers, and they did not need to depend on patronage from government or political parties. The newspaper now represented a way to take quick advantage of the expanding capitalistic economy. Power had been vested in a new economic force: the advertiser. For it was now the advertiser who was paying the greatest share of the cost of producing newspapers, and the press was suddenly depending for its financial success mainly on advertising.

THE AMERICAN PRESS BECOMES BIG BUSINESS

Few writers in a capitalist society have spoken out against the influence of advertisers with less equivocation than Will Irwin, one of the leaders of the muckraking school of journalists in the early twentieth century. Irwin wrote that advertising was "the main handicap on American journalism in its search for truth."[15] It was, he said, greedy newspaper publishers who had allowed their product to become commercial enterprises. He decried the shift of power from the editorial offices to the boardrooms and the growth of a breed of newspaper editors indistinguishable from the captains of industry who played golf at the same country clubs and whose news values were identical to those of the directors of Standard Oil. Irwin's essays, together with *The Brass Check*, a graphic attack on the press industry by another muckraker, Upton Sinclair, exerted for a while a powerful impact on the newspaper industry.[16]

Theorists who endorse a financial underpinning of the press through advertising argue, as Irwin noted, that the profits gained from advertising revenue have led to substantial growth in salaries and technological devices, which in turn have improved the quality of the American press. Others would prefer some form of public financing for the press.

With the growth of advertising revenues, whether for good or for ill, the American press became big business. By 1879, advertising revenue in the printing industry had risen to nearly $40 million; and in the next decade, advertising passed subscriptions and sales as the chief source of income in the industry, amounting to more than 54 percent of the total. By 1919, the figure exceeded 65 percent. The Sunday edition, which Joseph Pulitzer pioneered in the 1880s, became the most lucrative resting place for commercial messages and ballooned to unimaginable dimensions. The twenty-fifth-anniversary edition of Pulitzer's *New York World* appeared on Sunday, May 10, 1908, and boasted 200 pages, with more than 116 devoted to advertisements. Meanwhile, the per-capita consumption of newsprint in the United States rose from 6 pounds to 16 pounds in the 1890s and reached 25 pounds by 1910.[17]

New fields of employment opened up for advertising agents and for dealers in public relations and the manufacture of images. Press agents became almost as familiar in the corridors of newspapers as the journalists themselves; all, of course, were selling something. The sociologist Alfred McClung Lee speaks of "gigantic engines of publicity," observing, mildly enough, that they "enabled newspapers to become stable business ventures, and they changed drastically the nature of editorial content."[18]

The engine metaphor was not new. It had been used, with utter scorn, by the English novelist Charles Dickens, one of a number of distinguished Europeans who came to see for themselves how the new republican experience was working. Of all the institutions that distressed Dickens, none exceeded the press. It was, he said, a "frightful engine which was poisoning American society," arrogant, full of gossip, censoring itself by excluding anything good from its pages. No one, Dickens said, in his widely read travelogue, can enjoy freedom of opinion or think for himself "without humble reference to a censorship by the press which, for its rampant ignorance and base dishonesty, he utterly loathes and despises in his heart." In short, Dickens attacked the credibility of the press and, in a curiously modern image, complained that it portrayed only the seamy side of life without giving credence to the good impulses in American life. He portrayed a sensationalistic press contributing more to ignorance than to understanding.[19]

An earlier, more analytical European observer, Alexis de Tocqueville, had seen that the New York City newspapers were composed of 75 percent advertising;[20] the remaining quarter, de Tocqueville wrote, was devoted to "political intelligence or trivial anecdotes." The journalist, de Tocqueville found, occupied "a very humble position, with a scanty education and a vulgar turn of mind." Moreover, he wrote, "the characteristics of the American journalist consist in an open and coarse appeal to the passions of his readers; he abandons principles to assail the characters of individuals, to track them into private life, and disclose all their weaknesses and vices."[21]

It was the aristocrat de Tocqueville who spoke most tellingly of the potential "tyranny of the majority," and while he applauded the principles of democracy, he expressed grave concern for the emphasis in the United States on equality rather than on freedom. In this praise of equality, the press, he observed, was an indispensable factor, especially because it seemed to speak with a single voice: "When many organs of the press adopt the same line of conduct, their influence in the long run becomes irresistible."

The word *socialization* was unfamiliar in de Tocqueville's day, but the phenomenon was recognized at least by that thoughtful visitor. He saw how a press that reflected popular values reinforced those values and contributed to a pattern historian Richard Hofstadter identified more than a century later as the antiintellectual impulses in American life.[22] In the twentieth century, press theorists in Asia and Africa applied the U.S. experience to their own societies as they sought to use the press to build nations of many diverse ethnic and religious elements.

Of all the colorful pressmen of the nineteenth century, none were noisier or more prominent than Pulitzer and Hearst, who lifted sensationalism to its apogee in the great war for circulation and profit that characterized the age of yellow journalism. In the firmament of heroes and villains, Pulitzer is usually cast as the good guy, although, like a true tragic hero, with distinct character flaws; and Hearst is clearly the desperado in a black hat damned for all time by the portrait in Orson Welles's *Citizen Kane*. In truth, the two men were dissimilar; yet there were also significant points of commonality.

Hearst came from the West and wealth, the son of a mineowner-politician who was at one time a U.S. senator from California; Pulitzer was a poor Jewish immigrant from Hungary who made it to the land of unlimited opportunity by enlisting in the Union army during the Civil War. Both came to New York City after learning the newspaper business in provincial centers—Pulitzer in Saint Louis and Hearst in San Francisco. By 1880, each of these cities was a flourishing journalistic center whose newspapers were already pursuing the sensational patterns, soon to dominate the American press scene. Pulitzer arrived in New York in 1883; Hearst a dozen years later, when he launched the most dramatic circulation war in press history. The pursuit of great circulations was made possible by the revolutionary discovery in the late 1880s of a process for extracting web paper from wood pulp, creating a cheap, easily produced form of paper called newsprint. The circulation of Hearst's *Journal* and Pulitzer's *World* soared past a million and a half.

The yellow formula was an expansion of the penny-press formula, making profitable use as well of the new technological possibilities. Pulitzer introduced the Sunday edition, Hearst the banner headline that occupied a quarter of the space on the front page. Cartoons and reproductions of photographs were displayed lavishly. The incident that gained the greatest public attention was the war with Spain over Cuba. In that war, both Hearst and Pulitzer applauded American imperialism and the triumph of the country of the common man over the forces of aristocracy. It was a democratic crusade following the dogma pronounced by historian George Bancroft in the days of Andrew Jackson: "The popular voice is all powerful with us; this . . . is the voice of God."[23] The American mission and its execution at San Juan Hill sent millions of editions rolling off the presses of *The Journal* and *The World*.

Circulation was chosen as the advertiser's unit of measurement. The greater the circulation of the newspaper, the more eager the advertiser was to announce his wares in that publication. Higher rates were demanded when more readers were guaranteed to receive the messages. It was apparent to the managers of the press that their news columns had to present material of the widest possible public appeal if high circulations were to be maintained and large numbers of advertisers attracted. Demand for weighty articles all but disappeared, although *The World*, *The Times*, and *The Tribune* sought to direct a significant portion of their appeal to an elite audience. On the whole, however, the press that expanded and grew wealthy in the great surge of advertising and vast circulations concentrated its efforts on the formula originated in the days of the penny newspapers: heavy emphasis on "human-interest stories," on crime and romance, on gossip and entertainment. The increasing use of photographs and changes in format to render the product more "readable" led to a packaging of information resembling that in display cases in department stores with local news occupying a separate package—or aisle—from state, national, and international news, while "sports" news was distinct from "business" or from "women's" news. Speed became crucial. Relationships were blurred, and information came in discrete dosages designed more to please the reader than to induce thought.[24]

Many editors, then as now, campaigned strenuously to limit the influence of commercial forces. They found themselves struggling against puffery, inflating claims about the qualities of merchandise, as well as against outright lies and clever manipulation of journalists on the part of press agents who provided free trips, tickets, and products in return for articles about their merchandise.[25]

The inventiveness of pioneer press agents was boundless. With no limitations on their imaginations, they created the concept of "shopping notes," which were free, often quite well written articles about items for sale, distributed to newspapers to use as filler copy or sometimes even as front-page articles. So advanced did puffery become that advertising agents succeeded in sneaking notices past editors even when they were on the lookout for hidden messages. The extravagance of the advertising industry ultimately led to a federal requirement that all paid insertions sent through the mail carry the label of advertisement in the pages of the newspapers.

Many journalists continued to follow their star, to pursue the ideals inherent in the democratic assumption, to resist the seductive blandishments of press agents and promoters, and to maintain a press free of the excesses of sensationalism. Years of struggle against the wild claims of patent-medicine manufacturers finally brought an end to the advertising of the mysterious elixirs in the press; the most effective instrument in this campaign was Samuel Hopkins Adams's series of muckraking articles in *Collier's* in 1905 and 1906. *The New York Times* in 1910 published what it called an *Index Expurgatorius* identifying advertisers purged for making false claims and warning the public about additional offenders. The heyday of quackery and blatantly false advertising came to an end, but subtler forms of puffery persisted. Not only misleading advertising came under attack by serious editors. Greeley, for example, had urged his fellow editors and publishers as early as 1850 to reject voluntarily special pleading, however lucrative, and to strive for what he called "the public good." Adolph Ochs of *The New York Times* pledged to publish only news and advertisements that were "fit to print." Pulitzer demanded honesty and accuracy. Muckrakers such as Will Irwin, Upton Sinclair, and Lincoln Steffens penned hundreds of articles storming against misuse of the press for personal profit, and the widely respected William Allen White, editor of the *Emporia Gazette*, wrote tirelessly of the need for the American press to seek truth wherever it lay at whatever cost.[26] The purpose here is not to disparage advertising as an evil force but to demonstrate the weaknesses in the folklore of the press as a fearless seeker of truth that tramples on those who would lead it into temptation.

NEWS MANAGERS AND SOCIAL CONTROL

Not only commercial interests tempted editors and publishers with financial rewards; so did political forces. In a practice long familiar in Europe, those in power in the American republic used the expectation of financial gain to seduce the press into helping sustain their personal and political appetites. The value of a supportive press in nineteenth-century America was underscored by Martin Van Buren, a New York political leader who later became president of the United States. In an 1823 letter to a political ally, Van Buren observed that without a paper on their side "we may hang our harps on the willows." But, he added, "with it, the party can survive a thousand such convulsions as those which agitate and probably alarm most of those around you."[27]

The use of the press for political ends was extensively practiced. Attention has been directed to the techniques employed by European and American leaders to promote public backing for their policies. In the United States, it is obvious that the power of incumbents to use the press for political gain is vastly superior to that of challengers. Incumbents are able to make use of indirect inducements and of the legal machinery, too.

In 1789, for instance, Congress gave the federal government authority to choose certain newspapers to publish the laws and resolutions enacted by Congress, providing a form of financial control over the press for nearly a century.[28] The race was on, especially after James Madison, as Thomas Jefferson's secretary of state, openly adopted a system of rewards for those papers that supported the Jeffersonian program.

The inescapable effect was a press establishment in debt to the government; financial survival might very well depend on government largesse. The most significant subsidy provided to the press was in terms of postal rates. Between 1792 and 1845, rates assigned for letters ranged from six cents to twenty-five cents depending on the distance; but the maximum for a newspaper, whatever the distance, was a penny and a half. Even more beneficial to the newspaper was the provision of a fixed rate for papers however much the product weighed. The rate for letters rose sharply as their weight increased. The same 1792 act that fixed postal rates also authorized newspaper publishers to send their papers free of charge to other publishers. Whenever a newspaper challenged the government, it was, its publisher knew, courting fiscal suicide. Fear of financial loss did not, however, always deter editors and publishers from attacking the government; but the practice of seeking favor was far more common, especially in the scramble to win contracts as official printers of government documents.

The appearance of the Government Printing Office in 1860 signaled the end of formal government patronage of the newspaper industry. The end of the patronage system came after millions of dollars in windfall profits had been received by printers. Corruption and scandal were widespread, and wild disorder marked congressional debate on the issue.[29] A great many newspapers had grown strong financially under the old system of subsidies for printing; and in a number of instances, journalists were rewarded with high office. In fact, hundreds of journalists moved from their newspapers to government positions. The most effective instrument of presidential influence, however, was neither the direct subsidy nor the promise of office. It was the practice begun by President Jackson of "management" of the news. It was not until well into the twentieth century that the concept of news management came to be recognized, but it had long been widespread.

News management refers to the practice, typically employing some form of duplicity, of seeing to it that what is printed is what the news manager wants printed. For example, if a president desired, as Andrew Jackson did, to have newspapers report his veto of the extension of the Second Bank in 1836 as an action taken on behalf of the Common Man, the lower classes, in opposition to the vested interests of rapacious bankers, then it was the task of the president and his press agents to make sure this was how the veto message was reported. It would have been far more difficult for Jackson to sell his veto to the public if it were reported in the press as motivated by a desire to crush the power of Nicholas Biddle, the president of the bank, who was a formidable political foe and a leader of the urbane eastern aristocracy that represented the chief opposition to Jackson's "democratic revolution." In short, news management is a form of skillful press agentry; it can be—and is—practiced quite as deftly by resourceful politicians as it is by accomplished public-relations specialists.

Put another way, news management is a form of social control. The president, the advertiser, the circus promoter, or whoever it is who is seeking to manage the news is attempting to evoke in print an image of reality that is of benefit to him. The president may want to win public endorsement of a policy; the advertiser may want to sell a product; the circus promoter may want to convince readers to pay their way into the big tent—in whichever case, the news manager is seeking to manipulate the press into serving his ends. In such situations, the press as an institution is serving as an instrument for the gaining of certain ends, sometimes public, sometimes private. The same opportunity for manipulation is available to others less powerful than presidents, advertisers, or circus promoters; but it is far more difficult for them to use the press to achieve their private ends than it is for presidents, advertisers, or circus promoters who have special claims on the attention of journalists by virtue of their position or their wealth.

According to the folklore of the press, the news media, by exposing graft and corruption, may change the direction of public policy. Beyond that, the press, by pointing out wickedness in high places, also can cause the wicked to be brought to grief, so the forces of good may prevail. An illustration of this belief is the enforced resignation of President Nixon as the result of articles about the Watergate break-in. The belief is remarkably widespread; it is associated with the "watchdog" role of the press—the theory that the press keeps a watchful eye on government or on other mighty institutions so as to remedy abuses of power. Yet if the press is not an independent institution, it is not of itself capable of remedying abuses of power. It can participate in the remedy but cannot be the causal agent. The folklore is of advantage not only to journalists, whose status is thereby elevated, but also to those who may make use of the press for their own political objectives—the powerful, for example. Those who believed Nixon to be wicked and sought to overthrow him were able to make clever use of the mythology and to manipulate the press into doing their work for them. This is not to say that journalists are without power. In fact, more than a few journalists have achieved prominence and power through their writings and have sought to exercise that power in the political arena. However, only when the goals of journalists coincide with the goals of the society they inhabit can the journalist achieve his or her ends. All of Hearst's efforts to promote war with Spain would have been wasted were not the Congress, the president, and the general public ready to fight.

No time frame was more important in the flowering of the legend of press power than the age of the muckrakers, which made its appearance in the midst of a widespread reaction against the dogma of Twain's Gilded Age, when Social Darwinism adapted the message of natural selection and applied it to the social order. It was linked to the Protestant work ethic and condemned the poor as unfit, unable to survive in a competitive setting. Surprisingly, many among the poor and the intellectual community embraced the message of Social Darwinism; its accompanying laissez-faire economics; and, perhaps most significant of all, its glorification of rugged individualism, a glorification that was accompanied by an outpouring of books, plays, and newspaper articles elevating the exploits of the heroic loner, captured especially in the image of the laconic Western hero who took his own fate in his hands at high noon. The muckraking journalist cast himself in the same mold as the marshal at Dodge City.

The image of the lonely battler struggling against immense odds was given lasting expression by one of the most prominent of the muckraking writers, Ray Stannard Baker, in a December 1903 *McClure's* article titled "The Lone Fighter." It related the tale of a union member who reformed his union by winning it away from control by the bosses and of a politician who remained honest under heavy pressure. "It has rather an odd sound, a hero in politics," Baker wrote, "but I want to tell of just such a hero."[30] In a sentence Baker summed up the belief system of the muckrakers and the essence of the watchdog imagery: "If this republic is saved, it must be saved by *individual effort.*" His ultimate hero was the lonely journalist fighting against insuperable odds, identical to the lonely sheriff fighting against the mob of outlaws or the lonely politician battling against the mighty machine.

Baker also dabbled in poetry. He painted his image in sharp lines, especially in "The Lone Rider":

> Lone rider on the gray cayuse—
> Gray shadow in an empty land—
> And overhead the burning sky,
>   And underneath. the sand.
> Look sharp to the spur, my bronc, my bronc,
> Look sharp to the spur, I say,
> For long lies the trail, the canteens fail.
>   And we ride for our lives this day.[31]

The political hero of the muckrakers was Theodore Roosevelt. No American appeared to be a more vivid incarnation of the lone fighter or the lone rider than Roosevelt, who fought big game on the African plains, the wicked Spanish at San Juan Hill, and the mighty corporations in Washington, D.C.

If muckraking is defined as using the press to battle entrenched power, it was not a new phenomenon. The practice is cited many times in these pages, occurring in Europe as well as in the United States. Where the crusading failed to coincide with prevailing belief, it was unsuccessful, for the powerful were able to muffle the opposition press through intimidation, persuasion, bribery, or incarceration. The opposition press in all cases was part of a social movement directed by individuals who were enemies of those in power; the establishment press, however, was run by individuals determined to remain in power. Where the opposition was able to overturn the establishment, the "watchdog" press was applauded as a cause of the overthrow, often by itself, as in the Watergate or American Revolution examples. In the muckraking era, the watchdog press was part of a large social movement, one that embraced the progressive political platform of reform.

Among the nineteenth-century political leaders who recognized the utility of a favorable press was Otto von Bismarck, the chief architect of modern Germany. Press freedom, as exemplified in the First Amendment, achieved vast popularity in all the countries of Europe, even though many among them were under the tight control of strong monarchs. Earlier, we saw how in France the issue of press freedom generated political upheaval. In the revolutionary decade of the 1840s in both France and Prussia, free expression was one of the most passionately sought revolutionary demands. The reformist intellectuals who drafted a Prussian constitution at Frankfurt-am-Main in 1848 adopted a proposal that is one of the clearest and most unequivocal ever drawn on press freedom: "Every German has the right to express his opinions freely in word, handwriting, print, photographs, and the graphic arts. The freedom of the press shall under no circumstances and in no way be limited, suspended, or prohibited."[32]

Unfortunately, for Germans as well as much of the rest of the world, the Frankfurt draft never became German policy, but it did enable opposition newspapers to spring up all over the country in the mid-nineteenth century, including the *Neue Rheinische Zeitung* established in Cologne in 1848 by Karl Marx. The opposition newspapers sought unceasingly to play the role of watchdog and to call attention in public print to the authoritarian excesses of the Prussian rulers. When Bismarck was elevated to power as chancellor of Prussia in 1862, he began one of history's most successful efforts to manipulate the press. One year after he was named chancellor, he induced the king to deny the press the right to criticize the government.[33] The crown prince's English-born wife, Victoria, in proper English fashion characterized Bismarck's views of the press as "medieval," especially after he ordered troops to arrest the editor of a newspaper in a part of Prussia that was then under Austrian suzerainty. At that time, Prussia was building up for war against Austria, and Bismarck was not prepared to tolerate dissident views in the press.

Victory in the Austrian war enabled Bismarck to proclaim the modern German state, with Wilhelm I assuming the title of emperor. Under the empire, Bismarck's usage of the press shifted directions: No longer would he throw dissidents into prison; no longer would he engage in acts of physical repression. Now he adopted the more modern tactic of "news management." As a news manager, Bismarck knew few peers. He was assisted in this campaign by a substantial volume of money at his sole disposal, a source of money that was labeled by the liberal press as *Reptilien-Fonds*, or "reptile fund." Bismarck used the money to bribe the press to propagandize for his policies and for other political objectives; a number of journalists grew wealthy thanks to the reptile fund. Bismarck did not hesitate to use his "press dogs" to gain his political ends—some internal, some external.[34] In 1875, even though he was not in favor of war with France, Bismarck induced journalists to suggest that preventive war was imminent in articles that agitated Europe. In 1884, he turned his journalists loose on Britain as part of a successful campaign to induce Prime Minister Gladstone to agree to German colonization in Southwest Africa. Bismarck was a master at guiding the German public, although he was careful, especially in his later career, not to veer too far in his public utterances from what he considered the prevailing public opinion. It was under Bismarck that the German press became a factor in power politics as it had already become in the United States. Bismarck was the first German political leader to be faced with an opposition that appealed to the people over the head of the government. To Bismarck, the press was a necessary evil; he sought, with considerable success, to subvert it to his own ends. *Realpolitik* was his creed.

The "reptile" phrase stuck. The journalist-philosopher Walter Lippmann was to apply it to U.S. press policies half a century later. The occasion was the threat on the part of the Coolidge administration in 1926 to intervene in Mexico, which seemed on the verge of nationalizing the oil and mineral holdings of U.S. companies. Lippmann, then chief of the editorial page of *The New York World*, had been speaking out against intervention; so had other journalists. An angered President Coolidge demanded that reporters submit all stories about Mexico for approval, and an equally angry Lippmann condemned any attempt on the part of the government to edit newspapers:

> There is a name for the kind of press Mr. Coolidge seems to desire. It is called a reptile press. This is a press which takes its inspiration from government officials and from great business interests. It prints what those in power wish to have printed. It suppresses what they wish to have suppressed.[35]

It is the duty of the watchdog press to oppose such a policy; and on this occasion, at least, Lippmann found himself a steadfast adherent of the watchdog doctrine, forgetting that a few years earlier he had without critical examination printed what his earlier political heroes had wished to have printed. The pattern of behavior is one that has ensnared journalists throughout history. They have stood ready to take their inspiration from government officials and great business interests when they were expertly manipulated, but they have spoken out vigorously in opposition to those policies when the manipulative practices were less skillful or when those practices ran counter to the folklore of the press. In this sphere, contradictions abound.

The muckrakers, the magazine and book equivalent of the yellow press, were outstanding writers and skillful investigators operating in an age that was reacting against the gospel of social Darwinism and its laissez-faire economics. Some among the critics of big business, like their ideological comrades throughout Europe, were socialists, followers of the ideas of their spiritual leader, Karl Marx. Most, however, were reformers, bred in the more pragmatic American model seeking not revolution but curative legislation. Chief among their specific goals was the regulation of government monopolies; they were solidly in the camp of the reform wing of the Republican party, whose hero was Theodore Roosevelt, famed to this day as a buster of trusts. Astute politician that he was, Roosevelt succeeded in harmonizing and arranging the muckraking sonata.

There was much that was similar in the formulae adopted by the magazine muckrakers and the yellow press. Although both the yellow press and the muckrakers lauded the common man, they were also hero worshipers, demanding an American Napoleon to lead the fight against the giant monopolies and the corrupt politicians they saw as smoothing the way for the excesses of big business. The excessive freedom enjoyed by the captains of industry and banking in the United States was indeed collapsing in the 1890s, and collective ideologies were on the tongues of many seeking to hasten that collapse. It was also an age when personal fame beckoned, when the writer of exposés could achieve wealth and glory. Small wonder that Roosevelt invoked the image of the *Pilgrim's Progress* in his renowned declaration about the muckrakers.

It was not until 1906 that Roosevelt applied the term *muckraker* to the crusading journalists, and by that time, the movement was already on the decline. Its most spectacular period came in the preceding four years in a period marked by the appearance of perhaps the most remarkable magazine issue in publishing history, the January 1903 issue of *McClure's*, a periodical that had been providing exposés and critiques of laissez-faire excesses for a decade. S. S. McClure, an ambitious young man who had a clear eye on both political and publishing developments, launched his magazine in 1893 in the spirit of Ben Day by cutting prices. The same war for circulation that marked competition between Hearst and Pulitzer hit the magazine industry, and magazine readership soared. *McClure's* circulation leaped from 120,000 in August 1895 to 307,000 in 1900 and to nearly half a million by 1907 before the decline set in. Similar gains were registered by other magazines.

In the famed January 1903 issue of *McClure's*, readers eager to read about scandal, heartlessness, and graft in high places were treated to the second article in Lincoln Steffens's enduring account of municipal corruption, "The Shame of the Cities," this one about Minneapolis. Even more titillating to the public was the open attack on John D. Rockefeller in Ida Tarbell's "The History of the Standard Oil Company: The Oil War of 1872." It was Ida Tarbell who coined a phrase to dramatize the motive of the muckrakers; she was speaking out, she said, in "righteous indignation." The third of the three outstanding features of that issue was Ray Stannard Baker's "The Right to Work," an attack on the inhumanity of the coal-mining industry in the great miners' strike and a stirring argument for unionization. *McClure's* plays a substantial role in the folklore of the press as the perfect model of a crusading magazine devoted to careful documentation of its charges. It, too, was guilty of many excesses but less so than its chief competitors, *Cosmopolitan* and *Munsey's*, whose crusading arms flailed out in all directions and whose publishers, like McClure, grew wealthy.

Not all the muckrakers grew rich. The socialist agitator Upton Sinclair was one who didn't. In *The Brass Check*, an unabashed attack on the press industry itself,

Sinclair snarled at the advertising and public relations industries, demanded public ownership of the means of newspaper production, and called for news agencies to be designated as public utilities under public control. *The Brass Check* and other Sinclair writings contain interpretations that foreshadowed those of Lenin in his analysis of the role of the press.

Few among the muckrakers were prepared to travel Sinclair's path. Their more modest goal was government regulation, especially of railroad rates and of industries directly affecting public health and safety. Roosevelt, who advanced from vice president to president on the assassination of William McKinley in 1901, won wide support among the press as a trust buster, as the man who used the powers of government for the first time to see to it that avaricious industrial lords were forced by a benevolent government to work in the common interest for the benefit of all citizens.

In truth, the press's muckraking campaign was orchestrated by President Roosevelt himself, a practice he had begun a score of years earlier when, as police commissioner of New York City, he had sought out journalists and made personal friends of them as a device to put his name and his ideas before the public and those in political power.[36] Indeed, Roosevelt launched the most celebrated public attack on the reformers offering the crusading journalists the unwanted label of muckrakers. The term was first used in an off-the-record speech to a society of journalists—the Gridiron Club—but Roosevelt developed his idea further in a speech at the cornerstone laying of the first office building for members of the House of Representatives.[37] Roosevelt turned to the image in John Bunyan's *Pilgrim's Progress* of the "Man with the Muckrake [who can] look no way but downward," who refuses to see anything good but who "fixes his eye with solemn intentness only on that which is vile and debasing."[38] In Roosevelt's imagery, it was essential to scrape up the filth on the floor with the muckrake; it was equally important to recognize the good in life: "But the man who never does anything else, who never thinks or speaks or writes save of his feats with the muckrake, speedily becomes not a help to society, not an incitement to good, but one of the most potent sources of evil."[39]

Roosevelt thus established himself as one in an unbroken line of presidents who delighted in a press that served their interests but despised a press that worked on behalf of their enemies. In his speech about muckrakers, he chastised "the wild preachers of unrest and discontent, the wild agitators against the entire social order" who were publicly condemning the institutions of capitalism; these troublemakers, he said "were the most dangerous opponents of real reform." In other words, a press in the service of Rooseveltian reform was a good press, but one that did not go far enough or went too far was not to be trusted. Rarely has there been a clearer expression of the agency role of the press in a capitalist society.[40]

The irony is telling, for the muckrakers were not at all men and women who saw only the base and wicked, who were motivated to sort out the dirty linen for its own sake; their goals were romantically lofty. As Baker said in his memoirs, "We 'muckraked' not because we hated our world but because we loved it. We were not hopeless, we were not cynical, we were not bitter."[41] The lone rider they envisaged, a man much like Theodore Roosevelt, had betrayed their trust.

In the late nineteenth and early twentieth centuries, the press in the United States and, to a somewhat lesser degree throughout the industrialized world, had waxed powerful and profitable. Thanks to increasing revenues from advertising, publishers had raked in the dollars. Thanks to the advancing circulations that accompanied yellow newspapers and muckraking magazines, they had raked in more dollars. The press and the journalists who wrote for it, many now achieving a high level of personal fame, were playing a more and more significant role in the political process, not generally cognizant, however, of how significant that role was. It remained for the dramatic events that began in the pivotal year of 1917 to bring a larger awareness of that significance and to generate the ideological division that dominated discussions of the press for years to come in all parts of the world.

NOTES

1. *New York Sun*, September 3, 1833.
2. Edward and Michael Emery, *The Press and America: An Interpretive History of Mass Media* (Englewood Cliffs, NJ: Prentice-Hall, 1954), 120-21.
3. Gore Vidal, *Burr: A Novel* (New York: Random House, 1973).
4. Leo C. Rosten, *The Washington Correspondents* (New York: Anno Press, 1937), 6.
5. Horace Greeley, *Recollections of a Busy Life* (New York: J. B. Ford, 1869), 137.
6. *New York Herald*, September 25, 1835.
7. *New York Herald*, May 6, 1835, quoted in William Bleyer, *Main Currents in the History of American Journalism* (Boston: Houghton Mifflin, 1927), 186.
8. *New York Herald*, August 18, 1836.
9. Gay Talese, *The Kingdom and the Power* (New York: Laurel, 1966).
10. *New York Herald*, June 26, 1836.
11. The issue has come up repeatedly at conferences of Unesco, the United Nations Educational, Scientific, and Cultural Organization. See chapters 17 and 18.
12. *The Publick Advisor*, on May 19-26, 1657, urged its readers to buy coffee, which it described as a kind of miracle elixir; according to the insertion, the product "helpeth the digestion, quicketh the spirits . . . is good against eyesores, coughs, or colds, rhumes, consumptions, head-ache, dropsie, gout," and assorted ailments.
13. *New York Morning Courier*, one of the leaders of the traditional press in the years just prior to the appearance of the penny press, summed up the attitude succinctly in its January 24, 1828, issue: "Commercial patronage is best, safest, and most unstraying of any, and less affected by prejudice, whim, or petulance than any others. Merchants are ever ready to bestow their confidence and their support on those who exhibit zeal, industry and vigilance in their service and devotedness to their interests."
14. In 1829, when *The Morning Courier* merged with *The New York Enquirer*, the new publication printed so many ads that it was able to issue four-page supplements on

Saturdays and occasionally two-page inserts on other days. See Robert A. Rutland, *The Newsmongers* (New York: Dial Press, 1973), 98.

15. Will Irwin, *The American Newspaper*, ed. Clifford F. Weigle and David Clark (Ames: University of Iowa Press, 1969). Irwin's work appeared originally as a fifteen-part series in *Collier's* in 1911.

16. Upton Sinclair, *The Brass Check* (Muscatine, IA: Norman Baker, 1928), 224. Original publication was in 1919.

17. Alfred McClung Lee, *The Daily Newspaper in America: The Evolution of a Social Instrument* (New York: Farrar, Straus and Giroux, 1973).

18. Lee.

19. Charles Dickens, *American Notes for General Circulation*, ed. John S. Whitley and Arnold Goldman (Baltimore: Penguin Books, 1966). Original publication was in 1842.

20. New York City counted 11 dailies with a total circulation of 30,000 in 1832, a year before Day gave birth to the penny press.

21. Alexis de Tocqueville, *Democracy in America*, ed. Phillips Bradley, vol. 1 (New York: Vintage Books, 1945), 193–94.

22. Richard Hofstadter, *Anti-Intellectualism in American Life* (New York: Knopf, 1963).

23. George Bancroft, *History of the United States from the Discovery,* abridged and edited by Russel B. Nye (Chicago: University of Chicago Press, 1966).

24. A popular "how-to" book that appeared in 1901 illustrates the formula: "As an aid to securing advertising, the paper should make the most of every opportunity to demonstrate its progressiveness, be the first to bulletin news and the first to print it, and always endeavor to convey the impression that it is growing continuously and rapidly." See O. F. Bixbee, *Establishing a Newspaper* (Chicago: Inland Printer, 1901), 100.

25. Many editors railed against such practices in speeches, in leading articles, and sometimes in the pages of trade publications, the first of which, *The Journalist: A Magazine for All Who Read and Write*, appeared in 1884. In an 1887 issue, the poet Eugene Field parodied the practice of newspapermen accepting free tickets from railroads in exchange for favorable articles by reporting an imaginary schedule of advertising rates: "For the setting forth of virtues (actual or alleged) of presidents, general managers, or directors, $2 per line for the first insertion, and $1 for each subsequent insertion. . . . For complimentary notices of the wives and children of the railroad officials, we demand $1.50 per line. . . . We are prepared to supply a fine line of heptameter puffs, also a limited number of sonnets and triolets, in exchange for 1,000 mile tickets. Epic poems, containing descriptions of scenery, dining cars, etc., will be published at special rates."

26. White occupies a special place in U.S. press history as a symbol of integrity. In 1905, when the Standard Oil Company was offering heavy bribes for articles favorable to its campaign against restrictive legislation in Kansas, White refused to publish the tables and calculations that the oil company sent to all state editors, inviting them to publish the material "at their own figure." The muckraking magazine *McClure's* wrote that the offer meant as much as $1,000 to Kansas papers whose total annual profits might be no more than $2,500. According to the article, White's paper refused "the fruit," but "there were more which looked and ate." See Arthur Weinberg and Lila Weinberg, eds., *The Muckrakers: The Journalists Who Opened the Public's Eyes to Corruption Everywhere and Shocked America into an Era of Reform* (New York: Capricorn Books, 1964), 57.

27. William MacDonald, ed., *The Jackson and Van Buren Papers*, (Worcester, MA: American Antiquarian Society, 1907), 271–88.

28. In 1799, Congress amended the law to obligate the secretary of state to choose at least one newspaper in every state and as many as three if one did not seem adequate.

29. For a detailed account, see Culver Smith, *The Press, Patronage and Politics* (Athens: University of Georgia Press, 1977).

30. Ray Stannard Baker, *American Chronicle: Autobiography of Ray Stannard Baker* (New York: Scribner's, 1935), 122–23.

31. Ray Stannard Baker, "The Lonely Rider," reprinted in Robert C. Bannister, *Ray Stannard Baker: The Mind and Thought of a Progressive* (New Haven, CT: Yale University Press, 1966) 78.

32. Hans A. Muenster, *Geschichte der deutschen Presse in Ihren Grundzeugen Dargestellt* (Leipzig: Bibliographisches Institut, 1940), 21.

33. Erich Eyck, *Bismarck and the German Empire*, 3rd ed. (London: Allen & Unwin, 1968), 104.

34. Eyck, *Bismarck*, 150.

35. Cited in Ronald Steel, *Walter Lippmann* (New York: Vintage Books, 1981), 239.

36. Among that group was the crusading writer-photographer Jacob Riis, author of *How the Other Half Lives: Studies Among the Tenements of New York* (Cambridge, MA: Belknap Press of Harvard University, 1970). Original publication was in 1890.

37. The speech was made on April 14, 1906.

38. Quoted in Harvey Swados, ed., *Years of Conscience: The Muckrakers*, (Cleveland: World, 1962) 10.

39. Weinberg and Weinberg, *The Muckrakers*, 67.

40. In his private correspondence, Theodore Roosevelt went even beyond his muckraker speech. A decade later, in 1915, he wrote the American novelist Winston Churchill that even "the more honest muckrakers," Baker and Steffens, had rarely written statements of fact that Roosevelt could trust. See William Allen White, *Autobiography* (New York: Macmillan, 1946).

41. Baker, *American Chronicle*.

PART II

THE NEWS MEDIA AND SOCIAL CONTROL

Chapter
3

"OUR REPUBLIC AND ITS PRESS WILL RISE OR FALL TOGETHER"

1847 1947
JOSEPH PULITZER

3¢ UNITED STATES POSTAGE

Freedom of the Press

THE FREE PRESS MODEL

As the twentieth century approaches its end, the earth is in turmoil. Massive political and economic changes are taking place, and in the patterns that are emerging, the news media has become the world's most visible mechanism of social control. No one can predict with certainty what specific forms the news media of the future will take, but it seems clear that whoever controls the news media will wield the greatest share of power in the new century. Tennyson had seen the death of King Arthur's Camelot a millennium and a half ago as marking the changing of the old order, yielding place to a new one. Now another old order is changing, and Tennyson's puzzler is still alive. God fulfills himself in many ways, Tennyson wrote, lest one good deed corrupt the world.

God and technology are indeed being fulfilled in many ways at the dawn of the twenty-first century. The socialist empire of Eastern Europe has collapsed; new financial empires are rising; the emerging countries of the Southern Hemisphere are struggling to find their identity; and new forms of technology are integrating and fragmenting the nations of the world. Of good and bad deeds there are many, and the news media chronicles these events.

Some see the crumbling of orthodox socialism in the Soviet Union and its client states as a triumph for the forces of democracy, as if, among other things, it signals the triumphant end of a long struggle for a press free of government control.

45

Others see the collapse of newspaper readership and the trivialization of television fare in the United States and its partners in the market economy as the death rattle of a press under the control of commercial forces. Voices of gloom and doom are raised, though so are the voices of those proclaiming a new and meaningful democratic order.

Will the end of the century-long struggle between the forces of capitalism and the forces of socialism turn out to be another metaphorical passing, like that of King Arthur, and might that good deed corrupt the world? Or will it steer humankind on a path to a future of sunny new horizons? Many opinions are expressed, many judgments are made; but the mass media in all parts of the world seems to be locked with rising levels of passion in the embrace of entertainment. News is becoming a by-product in an age that is, paradoxically, referred to as both the Age of Entertainment and the Age of the Information Society.

At this point, it is well to look more closely at the twentieth century and how we have arrived at the place where we now find ourselves. The remarkable prevision of Alexis de Tocqueville gives us a good starting place.

The year 1917 was pivotal in the history of humankind. It marked the beginning of a tidal shift in the seat of power away from Western Europe, which had dominated the Western world, indeed the entire planet, since the days of the Roman Empire. The shift was both westward and eastward, fulfilling de Tocqueville's prophecy of nearly a century earlier. All other nations, de Tocqueville wrote, "seem to have reached their natural limits," but the United States to the west and Russia to the east "are proceeding with ease and celerity along a path to which no limit can be perceived." According to de Tocqueville, American strength was based on freedom and Russian strength on servitude: "Their starting point is different and their courses are not the same; yet each of them seems marked out by the will of Heaven to sway the destinies of half the globe."[1]

In April 1917, the United States declared war on Germany, ending its preoccupation with its own frontiers, and, as the saying went, America "entered Europe." Despite a brief attempt to retreat into an isolationist posture during the 1920s, the United States was in Europe to stay and steadily increased its military and economic strength until it assumed a dominant role on both sides of the Atlantic. Surprisingly, and despite its insular cultural development, it also took over a leading role in the arts and letters, including the sphere of the press.

Six months after the United States entered World War I, a second and equally significant event occurred. Far to the east in St. Petersburg, the Bolshevik Revolution propelled the Soviet Union into a position as dominant as that of the United States in terms of military and economic strength and in the arts and letters. A struggle matched the U.S. politicoeconomic system against that of the Soviet Union. The role assigned to the press in Soviet ideology was quite different from that assigned to the press in the American model, which by 1917 had become so popular it was viewed as a global model of an ideal press. The folklore of the First Amendment had, by the start of World War I, spread across the Western world.

The crumbling of the Soviet empire that began in the mid-1980s signaled a severe weakening in the strength of the Russian ideas about the role of the press as they had been enunciated by Marx and Lenin, but it by no means destroyed those ideas. We will turn to the Soviet ideas later; for now, it is important to stress that despite the strength of the First Amendment ideal, the free-press model has not been widely practiced *anywhere*.

The deepest significance of the free-press model lies in the central position it has occupied in the folklore of the press. In Western Europe throughout the century, even under legal guarantees of press freedom, newspapers were often pressured, manipulated, and even forced to practice deception in the interests of *realpolitik*. Similar practices have been illustrated in the United States. In much of Africa and Asia, an indigenous press was slow to develop and tended to follow the models provided by colonial rulers. In China, perhaps because of the complexity of the written languages, newspapers for a reading public did not appear until the twentieth century, even though movable type had been invented in China in the mid-eleventh century and the first extant book appeared there as early as 868.[2] In Latin America, the early press was patterned almost entirely on that of the United States, and the first significant newspapers were established by American printers. Of the press in all the countries outside the United States, the press in Great Britain was subjected to the fewest official controls, and the British press system was more influential than that of the United States in the development of press patterns on the continent. The British press, as the model for the American press, published under legal guarantees almost as extensive as those of the United States. Until the Bolshevik Revolution, the ideal press system was seen, almost universally, as that of the Anglo-Saxon model, born in Britain but developed and enshrined in the United States. In the Soviet Union after the Revolution of 1917, of course, the ideal press was seen as something quite different.

In Britain, in the United States, and on the continent of Europe, the political opposition tended to condemn the majoritarian press for accepting the role of Bismarck's reptiles. On the other hand, it was equally clear that the opposition would have preferred a supportive press, one that could be identified by *its* opponents as reptilian. The ideal type was identical everywhere: a free press conjured up in the spirit of the First Amendment, a fearless seeker of the truth, however formidable the obstacles cast in the path of the seekers.

The struggle over press rights was inherent in the 1830 fall of Charles X of France. In the decades that followed, under the monarchy of Louis Philippe, the issue of press rights never subsided completely; and a revolutionary press was an integral element in the activities of the new Jacobins in the February 1848 uprising that toppled Louis Philippe and paved the way for the Second Empire, which collapsed in 1871 when France at last became an enduring republic. Between 1830 and 1848 were years of *Sturm und Drang*, turbulence and ferment. During the same period in the United States, the penny press rose to herald the appearance of the "common man" on the stage of history and to help the cause of Jacksonian democracy.[3] In Britain, a popularized press indulged itself in articles about the Bow

Street Runners and, in the spirit of Charles Dickens, found much to write about the English common man, his problems and his pleasures. In Prussia, challenges to the entrenched power of the military and the landed aristocracy led to the revolutionary assembly in Frankfurt-am-Main.

All across the Western world, the abstract image of a free and outspoken press gained popularity. So highly was the idea of free expression praised that few persons were willing to speak out against it. Even the despots who imposed restrictions on the liberty of the press represented themselves as friends of free expression. No thought was given, of course, to free expression in the traditional societies that made up the colonial empires of Africa and Asia. Moreover, in the Russia whose vast potential was envisaged by de Tocqueville, the czars saw no reason to permit hostile intellectuals to speak out against their rule. Despite the extent of the lip service, in most parts of the world the powerful had little sympathy with the idea of untrammeled freedom of expression.

It may be that however lofty their abstract convictions, the powerful have never been comfortable with the idea of a free press. Complete openness has always been contrary to their objectives. We have seen how even the great journalistic hero Thomas Jefferson found secrecy more satisfying than openness when his goals were practical. A docile press or, even better, a press in the service of power was a useful instrument in carrying out anyone's policies. It ought not to be really surprising this was so—and remains so today. In the world of practicality, openness can at best be a *means* toward a desired end; it cannot be the end itself.

Those who demanded openness had their agenda, too. Entrenched power was their enemy, for it was power that was preventing them from gaining their contrary ends. The seekers after openness could be found on all sides of issues, but because power was usually held by the Right, the seekers tended to be of the Left. In the authoritarian social order of Hohenzollern Germany, a young radical humanist, Karl Marx, inveighed against the evils of censorship in the name of human decency for the poor and the downtrodden. In the mercantile social order of industrial England, a young radical humanist, James Mill, went even further. He set about trying to convert reporters into what today we call investigative journalists as instruments working to frustrate the antilabor social policy of the British government. From one end of Europe to the other in the mid-nineteenth century, the struggles between secrecy and openness were primarily political.

The same struggle was going on in the United States, though the flavor of the quarrel was decidedly commercial. We have already seen the fabulous rise of advertising in the United States in the nineteenth century and its influence on the development of the press. In fact, it was the phenomenal growth and influence of commercial forces in the United States that induced the struggle between secrecy and openness there to take on a different cast from the struggle in other parts of the world where political factors were at the heart of the struggle. By the close of the twentieth century, however, the distinctions had blurred substantially. Perhaps they were gone forever.

One of the major differences between the news-media system in the United

States and the systems in other industrialized nations lay in the fact that the content of U.S. broadcasting has from the beginning been controlled by commercial forces, while in the rest of the world it has been subject, in greater or lesser degree, to government direction.

We ought not to mistake these patterns for something they are not. There is an inevitable linkage between governments and commercial forces. It may not matter very much whether the news media are agents of governments or agents of commercial forces. In either case, openness is cramped, if not altogether eliminated. Certainly, one of the hallmarks of the modern world is the continuing increase in the power of commercial forces and the continuing decline in the independent might of governments, the traditional sources of political power. In the pages that follow we will explore this matter with considerable care.

What exactly does it mean to speak of the news media as instruments of social control? Let us say at the outset that *control* is a word capable of many interpretations. It can conjure up many images, perhaps that of a sorcerer maneuvering his manikin or of a puppeteer working the arms and legs of his marionette. That is not the sense in which the word is being used here. Substitute for *to control* the verb *to manage* or *to direct*, and you will be close to the meaning we are assigning here.[4] As you can see, there is no sinister connotation implied. To control can be a good or a bad thing; it all depends on how and why control, or management, is exercised. It is important to recognize that all of us try to control the environment in which we find ourselves. No natural phenomenon is more terrifying than an earthquake. How frightening to imagine an environment where everything is random and haphazard, where the earth might shift under our feet at any moment. When we speak of *social* control, of course, we are referring to control over people, not over nature. Control can be defined simply as "purposive influence toward a predetermined goal," whatever our goal may be.[5] Obviously, these purposes must be communicated, illustrating the central position of communication in the process of control. The modern science of cybernetics has been created in order to study communication and control as interdependent.[6]

Our need to control our environment is simply part of our humanity. But how extensive is the environment we want to control? For most of us, for those of us who follow the leader, our environment is severely limited. The environment of leaders, the wielders of power, is far more extensive, for their environment includes us. The law, for example, demands we abide by it. If we break the law, there are police and judges to see to it we are punished. The lawmakers, the police, and the judges exercise power and harness or manipulate the society of people they must control if the system of law is to work. Here is social control in practice. It is institutional rather than individual. It may be exercised for the good of the people, or it may be exercised for the private benefit of the wielders of power. In a democratic society, the citizens yield up to the exercisers of power the instruments of social control. We violate their controls at our own peril. To do so could cost us our fortunes, our liberty, our lives. Sometimes the controls are exercised by rewards rather than by punishment. Teachers control their students as judges of a

different sort. Students who abide by the teacher's rules and directions are rewarded with A's. Violators are punished with failing grades; they might even be dismissed from the society altogether by being expelled.

Pleasure is another form of reward. Mass media offer a great deal of pleasure.
We are entertained, made to laugh, and made to enjoy what is placed before us by
television, by novels, by newspapers, by theater, by recordings, and by comic
books. We are also rewarded by news reports, which satisfy our desire for information as well as entertainment. Many of us simply enjoy being able to converse about
the day's events—it makes us feel good to be in command of our environment.
When we know what is going on, we have a stronger sense of control over our
environment. When we are told there is a traffic tie-up at Fifth and Market streets,
we can control our environment to the extent that we can take an alternate route
to reach our destination.

Politicians who are elected to office try to control the votes of their constituency. Sales executives try to control the behavior of consumers. They seek
out whatever instrument, whatever mechanism, whatever agency will help them
gain their ends. Advertising is, of course, the first mechanism that springs to
mind, but there are others: speeches, appearances on television, articles in newspapers and magazines, the release of public-opinion polls. These instruments are
all agents—words, pictures, charts, and tables—and whoever is in command of
these instruments, whoever can put these agents to work for him or her is exercising social control.

The psychologist William Stephenson distinguishes between social control,
which he says takes form in our inner beliefs and values, and what he calls "convergent selectivity," which he uses to refer to the "fads and fancies" we select for ourselves.[7] In Stephenson's imagery, the individual is not completely under the social
control of a person or an organization so long as he or she can choose what to read
or what to do. Advertising, in his view, is based not on social control but rather on
convergent selectivity because we may choose for ourselves whether to read the ad
or view the commercial.[8] This distinction suggests an either/or conception of
"social control," as if it would cease to exist if individuals could think for themselves. In our view, there are many degrees of social control.

Language has been the chief instrument of social control as long as human
beings have communicated with one another. It was quite early in the human experience, in preindustrial Mesopotamia, Egypt, and China, that administrators, the exercisers of power, began to create language-using bureaucracies to establish control
over large numbers of people. The early bureaucracies were made up of secretaries
and notaries, scribes and lawyers, priests and judges, all in the employ of religious and
secular leaders, all agents of social control. Before the surge of liberating new technologies in the Industrial Revolution, social control was relatively uncomplicated; it
was exercised by primitive bureaucracies in a generally straightforward fashion.
These agents, all dabblers in the printed word, were in a way primitive journalists.
Max Weber, who in 1910 spoke for the first time about "a sociology of journalism,"
predicted that journalists liberated from the control of kings and parliaments would

soon be exercising control of their own. Merely by threatening not to publish speeches by lawmakers, Weber said, journalists could force Parliament to its knees.[9]

No journalists existed at the dawn of Western civilization, unless we want to count the official scribes and priests who worked for princes, kings, and pharoahs. Perhaps it is because of the dearth of genuine reporters that the wondrous skills of antiquity were for millennia so surprisingly lost. When the ancient Egyptians who had directed the construction of such startling monuments as pyramids and sphinxes succumbed to civilizations far less advanced than theirs, the secrets of their scientific know-how vanished with them. The priesthood, those bureaucrats in the service of the pharoahs, had kept their secrets locked in their own heads; they had in a sense managed the news, for they had failed to broadcast their information, and their ill-informed followers were no match for the military might of the Greeks and Romans.

Questions about the power of journalists compared with that of political leaders is by no means a new topic, yet Weber may have been the first to give it a twentieth-century slant. He saw the twentieth-century press in the service of a new wave of bureaucrats as a powerful instrument to bring order to a modern economy, one that seemed otherwise to be in a state of anarchy. Order is always demanded by the public; and thus, Weber wrote, it was highly probable that bureaucratization would master capitalism.[10]

The temptation to manage the news seems to be irresistible, whether it be by governments, advertisers, circus promoters, or any other mighty interest group. Since it has been for some 5,000 years that bureaucracies have been charged with controlling the flow of news, it is not surprising that the techniques of news management have by now been refined and perfected to an astonishing degree. American presidents have from the very beginning tried to control the flow of information, but the art has now reached a level unimagined by George Washington or Thomas Jefferson. As we shall see later, the capability of such presidents as Ronald Reagan and George Bush to induce the news media to put out the kind of reports they wanted was overwhelming. The men and women they employed as public-relations specialists, pollsters, media managers, and spin doctors were themselves bureaucrats who were fabulously skilled at their jobs, far superior to the ancient scribes and priests or the merchants of information who fascinated the great English liberal philosopher John Stuart Mill a century and a half ago. At that time, Mill saw operating under the French monarchy a bureacuracy that was "a vast network of administrative tyranny" leaving no one free "except the man at Paris who pulls the wires."[11]

The technologization of the press has certainly been phenomenal. In the 100 years that began in the 1830s, consider the introduction of these new devices and developments: photography, telegraphy, rotary-power printing, the typewriter, transatlantic cable, the telephone, motion pictures, wireless telegraphy, magnetic tape recording, the radio, and rudimentary television.[12]

Each of these devices enabled the holders of power to maintain and extend their social control through the application of the mechanisms of persuasion and propaganda, market research, polling activity, and advertising.

LIMITS TO PRESS FREEDOM

It is the central thesis of this book that the content of the news media inevitably reflects the interests of those who pay the bills. The argument, in other words, is that the financiers—or the paymasters, as we can call them—or the group they represent will not allow their media to publish material that frustrates their vital interests. This form of control is often subtle, and we will develop this thesis in some detail later. For now, it is useful to note four basic patterns of relationships between the paymasters and the content of the news. We will call these relationships official, commercial, interest, and informal. Rarely is the relationship a pure one; overlapping is quite common. So are exceptions. Still, the four basic patterns are clear enough.

In the *official* pattern, the content of the newspaper, magazine, or broadcasting outlet is determined by government rules, regulations, and decrees. Some news media may be themselves state enterprises, some may be directed through government regulations, and some may be controlled under a network of licensing arrangements. All dictatorships, whether run by one person or by a group, follow the official pattern. No nation is free of official controls; the variations come in the degree of autonomy permitted. In the *commercial* pattern, the content reflects the views of advertisers and their commercial allies, who are usually found among the owners and publishers. The means of control are advertising and public relations. Even under planned economies, commercial influences can be detected, although for the most part these are exerted only indirectly. In the *interest* pattern, the content of the medium echoes the concerns of the financing enterprise— a political party, a trade union, a religious organization, or any other body pursuing specific ends. In the *informal* pattern, media content mirrors the goals of relatives, friends, acquaintances, or lobbying groups who supply money directly or who exercise their influence to ensure that the desired reports are circulated. The less heavily industrialized a country, the more apparent the impact of informal patterns will be.

We must be careful not to stumble into the trap here. We must not force the press into a classification system that is national in nature. Freedom House and other organizations that rate the press of one country as free and the press of another as controlled are simplifying highly complex patterns. To be sure, we can set forth plausible arguments, as Freedom House has done, that the press has a greater degree of political autonomy in some places than in others; but there are forms of control that are not purely political. Equally controlling are economic or religious or cultural factors. Rating systems establish the fiction that the press of one country is a monolith. The newspapers and magazines within the borders of a nation are not identical.

No newspaper, magazine, or broadcasting outlet exceeds the boundaries of autonomy acceptable to those who meet the costs that enable them to survive. These boundaries, it must be remembered, are not carved in stone. They are very flexible; and in every place on earth, the boundaries have changed over time. Measuring sticks that seek to classify the dynamic are necessarily flawed, as are

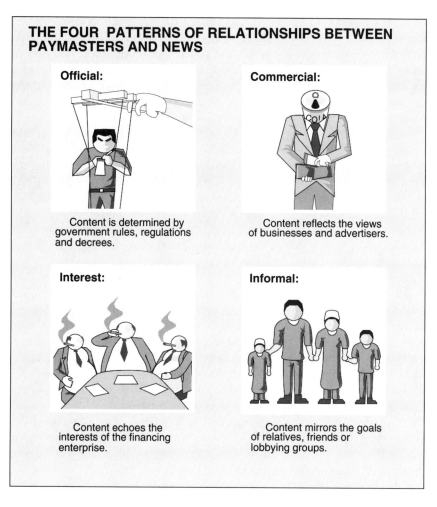

THE FOUR PATTERNS OF RELATIONSHIPS BETWEEN
PAYMASTERS AND NEWS

Official:

Content is determined by
government rules, regulations
and decrees.

Commercial:

Content reflects the views
of businesses and advertisers.

Interest:

Content echoes the
interests of the financing
enterprise.

Informal:

Content mirrors the goals
of relatives, friends or
lobbying groups.

SOURCE: L. W. Harvey

those that place national labels on the measuring sticks. The imperfect best we can do is deal in degrees. For example, we can say with some confidence that the political system in a country derives from the economic power structure and that the press of that country by and large will reflect the ends of those who manage the economy. Those ends may be openly stated; or they may be concealed. When the ends are openly stated, the press is likely to be subjected to a large measure of official control. When they are concealed, the press is likely to be directed through either commercial channels or informal arrangements. In all cases, for whatever their purpose, interest groups (both those that support the objectives of power and the dissidents who oppose those ends) make use of media, sometimes the mass media, and sometimes in forms that we can speak of as minimedia.

Revolutions do not take place often; when they do, the identity of the holders of power changes rapidly. Old patterns are shattered. During periods of transition, control of the news media is crucial, and sound logic supports the seizure of control over the news media by revolutionaries. During the failed 1991 coup in the Soviet Union, the role of the media was decisive; but, it is interesting to note, whichever side did the controlling, the official pattern held firm. We will turn our attention to the ups and downs of Marxist press ideology later.

However, the 1980s had already seen major changes in the pattern of relationships between the news media and the Soviet power structure. At the beginning of the decade, before Mikhail Gorbachev's program of perestroika brought on the collapse of the Soviet empire and its highly structured forms of press control, the distinction between the official and the commercial patterns was clear and vivid. In the Soviet Union and its client states, the media were governed by an all-powerful regime that administered strict and fixed rules. In the capitalist world, especially in the United States, commercial interests that were less obtrusive dominated the content of the media, although by means of silken gloves rather than iron fists.

Commercial forces were on the march everywhere, not only in the industrialized world. Aided by the remarkable expansion of communication technology, the media industry moved into countries still struggling to achieve a viable industrial base. With that movement, commercial forces, often allying themselves with fragile governments, began to gain a dominant position challenging the traditional command of interest groups and informal patterns. We will examine these developments more closely later when we turn our attention to parts of the world only recently penetrated by the ideology associated with capitalism.

As the twenty-first century approached, it certainly looked as if capitalism were going to sweep aside all challengers. Yet we should remember that claims of total victory for this or that ideological construct have been made again and again only to be frustrated by the unpredictable march of history.

When we speak of capitalism we are speaking of a system of economics where the marketplace is central. In theory, everyone has an equal chance to gain in the marketplace simply by claiming just compensation for his or her product or services. The desire for profit is what drives human behavior. No one is going to profit if his or her product or service isn't top of the line or doesn't serve the needs of a large segment of the buying public. Therefore, in this ideological construct, the marketplace works for the benefit of everyone by guaranteeing quality products and services and guaranteeing reasonable prices, because reasonable people know if they charge too much for their goods or services, they will drive away the potential buyers who enable them to make their profits.

It may not always work the way it is supposed to work in theory; however, there is little doubt at this stage of history that this ideological construct has captured the applause even of those who, like the leaders of the Soviet Union, had just a few years earlier been condemning capitalism as an evil system. In much of Western Europe, even as late as the start of the 1980s, *capitalism* was still a dirty word, evoking images of the age of robber barons, sweatshops, and rapacious monopolies. There, the acceptable phrase was *market economy*, which was seen as kinder and gentler than *capitalism*. By the end of the decade, however, the word *capitalism* had been freed of its uglier connotations.

The word *capitalism* has in many places come to be equated with the blessed words *freedom* and *democracy*. This linkage is not only incorrect but also dangerous in any attempt to understand the role played by the news media or any institution. Capitalism is indeed rooted in belief in free interplay of buyers and sellers in the marketplace, though buyers and sellers do not enter the marketplace with equal freedom to buy and sell. Some have fewer assets than others in terms of money or talent and hence are not as "free" as those with greater assets. Freedom is not an absolute term; some people are freer than others. Therefore, we may not simply equate capitalism with freedom.

It is just as inaccurate to equate capitalism with democracy. The essence of democractic *theory* is of course freedom, but in the *practice* of democracy, freedom has been a limited commodity. In a pure democracy, all political decisions are made by the total population. In a representative democracy, decisions are made by the deputies the people have elected to a decision-making legislature. Power is not shared equally; certainly some people have greater financial and other resources than others. Those with the greater power also have the means to influence and manipulate others, whether the general public or their representatives. The existence of unequal power is perhaps the fatal flaw in the abstract idea of democracy.

What does all this have to do with the role played by the news media in public affairs? Everything. Claims that the press is automatically free and democratic under a capitalist system (or indeed under any economic or political system) are false. To understand the role the news media play in any society, then, we must face the hard reality that they are not, and cannot be, independent actors in the process of life.

None of this discussion is meant to suggest that capitalism is a bad economic system or that democracy is a poor form of government. It is to suggest, rather, that the issues are enormously complex and that the careful student of the news media must set aside his or her political or economic assumptions and examine the role of the media as it is played out in the real world of money and power rather than in the comfortable abstractions of freedom and democracy.

Traditionally, political institutions have been separated from one another by what is thought of as their end or their purpose. Institutions are not absolute forms but means toward particular ends. In democratic theory, the end of government is the freedom and welfare of the *individual*. In collectivist theory, as carried out for seven decades by the Soviet Union under the banner of Marxism-Leninism, the end was perceived to be the welfare of the *society*. If we imagined scales weighted by human beings and placed society on one side and the individual on the other, our political philosophy would be determined by how we balanced the scales. The more we tilt toward the group, the greater the weight we assign to society; the more we tilt toward the lone person, the greater the weight we give to the individual. Some level must be found—there is no absolute. It is on the scale that we find our own view of institutions. Because the individual and society are good, our balance lies somewhere between the two extremes so that we tilt toward belief

THE GOAL OF GOVERNMENT

Society:
In collectivist theory the aim of government is the welfare of society.

Individual:
In market theory the aim of government is the freedom and welfare of the individual.

SOURCE: L. W. Harvey

either in a society created for the benefit of the individual or one in which the rights of the individual are limited by the needs of society.

We usually divide the political Right from the political Left by placing the Right on the side of the individual, the Left on the side of society. This distinction may sound new or modern, yet this division has been drawn since earliest history. It did not begin with the French Revolution, when the Right and Left were marked off by their seats in the Assembly, although this made for a neat little model for a tough abstraction. The rights of individuals have always had to be balanced against the rights of the society they inhabit. Many illustrations come from the Bible. For example, Moses limited the freedom of individuals to worship as they wished when he forced the Israelites to quit revering the golden calf. The Israelites would never have reached the Promised Land if the individuals hadn't conformed.

Limiting the freedom of the individual in the interest of society was at the very center of the philosophical Enlightenment that produced the idea of the social con-

Pierre Sarrazin directs a Canadian film in Florida: A different look at society by Canadians and Americans.

SOURCE: *MIAMI HERALD*/PAT FARRELL

tract and, indeed, the Mayflower Compact, the first practical instrument of democracy in the United States. All political constructs have been based on the argument that the society they created was designed to provide the greatest degree of freedom for the individual. This argument is part of the capitalist doctrine of the Western democracies, as is the Marxist doctrine of socialist lands and the ideologies of the new societies of the developing world, no matter how authoritarian they may be.

It is clear then that freedom has *always* been limited and that the interests of collectives have *always* been safeguarded. Even so, human beings, their political economy, and their social systems tend to tilt one way or the other, toward emphasis on the individual or on the collective. We may call these collectives many things. The extreme seems to be some form of communitarian society in which the individual's wishes and desires are sacrificed for the benefit of the collective. Jean-Jacques Rousseau spoke of this collective in terms of the "General Will." Karl Marx and his followers spoke of it as a socialist or communist order. In the United States and other capitalist lands, it has often been spoken of as the community. Perhaps the difference is easiest to see if we speak in a primitive sense of the individual and the tribe. The Canadian movie director Pierre Sarrazin made the point succinctly.

Conjuring up a scenario that contrasts directors writing satirical film scripts about a war between adjoining American and Canadian towns, he asserted: "In Canada we stress the tribe more, not your rampant individualism. We finance a huge social security net; yours is more every-man-for-himself."[13]

In other words, the choice of the individual or the tribe is basic. It can be seen in situations far less dramatic than the collision between capitalism and Marxism. It is, of course, a critical factor in any examination of the role of the news media. Journalists may plead the case of the individual with conviction, but they are rarely if ever anarchists; every man for himself is not a journalistic value. The question, therefore, is not whether a journalist supports a collective, a tribe if you will, but rather which one and to what extent.

Belief in the centrality of the individual somehow survived and even strengthened itself during the 1980s, despite the actual weakening of the influence of individuals and the increasing fragmentation of the social order that accompanied the decade's fabulous leap in the power of commercial forces. New, hitherto unheard-of technological advances forged a quiet revolution in communications and gave the commercial forces just what they needed to dominate the news media in all parts of the world: entertainment. It was a weapon that had always lain at hand, but technological advances gave that weapon incalculable influence. News had always contained an entertainment component. Readers did not turn to their newspapers or magazines to be bored. They had thrilled to the sensational copy put out by the Pulitzers and Hearsts. Now, more dramatic vehicles for entertainment emerged—in television, in videotapes, in computer-generated games. What at one time we spoke of soberly as news media were no longer primarily news media. They were, more important, vehicles for entertainment and instruments of the vast profits that accompany the world of entertainment. News can no longer be separated from entertainment.

When the press is discussed here, the word stands for broadcasting as well as the print media. As far as ideas are concerned, there is no difference among the news media. In handing down ideas about the role of the press in public affairs—ideology, that is—the importance of schools of journalism cannot be ignored. The word *ideology* has a somewhat sinister connotation in the United States, although it is more acceptable elsewhere. In any case, the education of journalists is obviously an important factor in the building of a framework of ideas about what role the dissemination of news plays in society. In the United States, ideology is transmitted by other names; hence, the school of journalism with its emphasis on *practical* training is an American invention. For many years, emphasis on the practical did not establish a strong foothold in other nations, though the custom is changing. The American school of journalism has by the final years of the twentieth century become a model for schools in all parts of the world.

Those schools will be examined in due course. At the moment, it is useful to explore the underlying belief system expressed in U.S. schools of journalism: that unlimited years of progress lie ahead for the United States and its politicoeconomic system, that the press plays a leadership role in bringing about that glorious future, that the financial structure of the American press assures economic health and political independence for the news media, and that this healthy future can be ensured best of all by following the path of objectivity.

This press ideology is rarely as explicitly expressed as was the official socialist doctrine under Lenin's clearly spelled-out press code. American practitioners and scholars often disagree about the role of the press. To some, the very idea of a role for the press is unthinkable. "Our job," journalists often say, "is to get out the news." The idea of role somehow smacks to them of government interference or of sociological jargon. Still, there does exist an ideology composed of four articles of faith: (1) The press is free of outside interference, be it from the government or from advertisers or even from the public; (2) the press serves "the public's right to know"; (3) the press seeks to learn and present the truth; and (4) the press reports facts objectively and fairly. These canons are listed here in declarative form; they might also be construed as moral imperatives—that is to say, instead of characterizing what the press *is*, they might declare what the press *should* be.

Confusion over the "is" and the "ought," over description and prescription, permeates all discussion of the press. In the hope of avoiding the morass into which this confusion always threatens to plunge the analyst, we will make no effort to separate the "is" and the "ought" and will instead assume that the capitalistic press ideology encompasses both. These four articles of faith are intrinsic in all interpretations of the press in the United States, Western Europe, and other industrial states with market economies, however their interpretations may vary in detail and whatever contradictions may arise over the "is" and the "ought."

Most analysts of the capitalist press have identified *three*—and sometimes *four*—expectations of the news media. They tend to agree that the media are expected to inform, to entertain, and to serve as watchdogs of the powerful. Others insist on a fourth expectation: to advertise what is available in the marketplace. In the United States, the educative role is usually not mentioned, although it is sometimes seen as part of the informative role. In France, the distinction between information and education is given explicit expression. Most important, the American—or capitalist—analysis of the press is rooted in what we speak of as the democratic assumption; the press provides the information that enables citizens to make appropriate democratic decisions. It is this assumption that provides the philosophical foundation for the four articles of faith—as well as for the three (or four) expectations—held for the press. The belief system, or ideology, dealing with the press is held with the same kind of dogmatic conviction as are all ideologies of the press. Capitalist and socialist, follower of the market (or corporate) economy and the planned economy, are equally trapped in dogma. And each dogma—or folklore—is false. Nevertheless, the dogma is spread by newspapers and broadcasting outlets themselves and by those who train future practitioners. Some may point to the pluralism within schools and American departments of journalism that may harbor an occasional Marxist and more than a few opponents of principles of the free-enterprise system. Islands of dissent exist; yet few craft end up moored at these islands; the pressures to accept the folklore are irresistible. Young journalists have no difficulty finding like thinkers among their newspaper friends, among the folklore-addicted faculties, and among the public at large. It is an enticing myth, this myth of the heroic press fighting the overwhelming power of the mighty and corrupt in the interests of the grateful citizen. It is a charming fairy tale, and it is accepted in one form or another by almost everyone who has practiced the craft of journalism in the United States in the twentieth century.

Even though this fairy tale is unbelievable, discarding all the elements of the romance is unnecessary. Certainly, much good can be wrought by the press. However, it is not independent; it operates as an instrument of power. It is an agent, but it is not a secret agent as in a spy thriller. The output of the press is in the open. It is public, but its director may be in the shadows. Whatever form power takes—government, party, or corporation—it may well wish to conceal its relationship with the press. When the relationship is obscure, when the press itself operates in the shadows, there is little likelihood the press will perform any important public service; instead, it will simply be quietly serving the bidding of its paymaster. It is when the agency role of the press is exposed to daylight that it can work in the interests of all.

NOTES

1. Alexis de Tocqueville, *Democracy in America*, abridged and edited by Richard D. Heffner (New York: Mentor Books, 1945), 142.

2. Thomas Francis Carter (revised by L. Carrington Goodrich), *The Invention of Printing in China and Its Spread Westward* (New York: Ronald Press Co., 1955), 247-49. See also Anthony Smith, *The Newspaper: An International History* (London: Thames and Hudson, 1979).

3. Marvin Olasky in *Central Ideas in the Development of American Journalism: A Narrative History* (Hillsdale, NJ: Lawrence Erlbaum, 1991) points correctly to the great significance among early American editors of their desire to promote the cause of Puritan religious values during this period; these editors were less committed to the material welfare of the "common man" than to saving his soul.

4. Here are some other possible synonyms for *to control*: command, direct, dominate, govern, master, modify, rule, regiment, regulate, restrain, subdue, sway, verify.

5. James R. Beniger, *The Control Revolution: Technological and Economic Origins of the Information Society* (Cambridge, MA: Harvard University Press, 1986), 7.

6. See, for instance, Norbert Wiener, *Cybernetics: Or, Control and Communication in the Animal and the Machine* (New York: Wiley, 1948), 3-5.

7. William Stephenson, *The Play Theory of Mass Communication* (Chicago: University of Chicago Press, 1967), 1-3.

8. Stephenson holds that our ability to decide for ourselves whether to buy "this or that toothpaste, car, or cookie" provides for us conditions that "tend to be self-developing and self-enhancing—an enrichment of individual aspects of self rather than the reverse" (Stephenson, *The Play Theory*, 2). The reader will note as this book unfolds that I disagree on this point. Moreover, I find that although Stephenson's theory offers much that

is clear and sound, it has a fundamental weakness in that he tends to ignore the powerful influence of the drive for profits in the news-media business, especially in advertising.

9. Max Weber, "The Press," a 1910 report at a congress of German sociologists, cited in J. P. Mayer, *Max Weber and German Politics* (London: Faber and Faber, 1944), 67–68.

10. Mayer, *Max Weber*, 70–71. For further information on Weber and bureaucracy, see Beninger, *Control Revolution*, 14.

11. Cited in Beniger, *Control Revolution*, 14. See also Laverne Burchfield, *Our Rural Communities* (Chicago: Public Administration Service, 1947).

12. Beninger, *Control Revolution,* 7.

13. Quoted in Richard L. Barton, *Ties That Blind in Canadian/American Relations: Politics of News Discourse* (Hillsdale, NJ: Lawrence Erlbaum, 1990), 138. The quote is taken from a *New York Times* article of November 27, 1988.

Chapter

4

"OUR REPUBLIC AND ITS PRESS WILL RISE OR FALL TOGETHER"

1847 1947 JOSEPH PULITZER

3¢ UNITED STATES POSTAGE

The "Power" of the Press

THE SPECIAL CASE OF "OBJECTIVITY"

One of the weightiest moral weapons in the quest for social control is what we know as the code of objectivity. The idea of the disinterested journalist is, of course, quite old. The word *objectivity* is as slippery as an eel; no matter how you seize it, it is difficult to hold on to it. Nor is the origin of the term as it applies to journalism any easier to handle. It appears to have quite different meanings to different people. For many Marxists, for example, the problem of definition is resolved by dividing the term in two, distinguishing between "to be objective" and "to objectify." In the case of objectivity, we are dealing in reality, with the way things really are; objectification *pretends* to reality while it propagates a false ideology. The distinction is useful, at least in theory. To describe a dog as a four-legged carnivorous creature with an anticipated life span of ten or twelve years is to be "objective"; describing that same dog as man's best friend is "objectifying." The first statement represents reality; it is scientific. The second, however, is propaganda and hence ideological.

Absolute objectivity is impossible to achieve, a fact that has led to interminable, useless discussions. At best, it is a relative concept. Some analysts argue it is not meant to be thought of as attainable, that rather than a reality, it is a process, an attitude, a way of thinking. The sociologist Michael Schudson, for example, identifies objectivity in journalism as a belief system about what kind of knowledge is reliable. Moreover, he says, it is a moral philosophy—"a declaration of what kind of thinking one should engage in, in making moral decisions."[1] It does not, then, seem contradictory to believe that while objectivity is unattainable, it is still good and should therefore be sought anyway; it is a way of joining the "is" and the "ought."

Certainly an aura of the lofty and the noble surrounds the idea of objectivity. To be disinterested, to be dispassionate, to avoid prejudgment, to abandon illusion, to seek painstakingly for the real and the verifiable—these are inseparable elements in the search for scientific truth. From Bacon and Descartes, to Watt and Edison, to Fermi and Einstein, the concept of the scientific method was defined and refined; it passed from the world of natural science to the social sciences and the humanities. The revelation by physicist Werner Heisenberg that scientific truth was unattainable, that even in the most precise of measurements there exist areas of uncertainty where differences must be tolerated, stirred the community of natural scientists but made less headway among social scientists. The "sciences" of politics and economics and the newer "science" of communications seemed sometimes to proceed with disregard for Heisenberg's findings, as if correct answers could be found if only the correct measuring instruments were discovered. Faith in technology has seemed boundless in the modern world, and scientific methods have often been thought to be capable of solving the riddles of politics, economics, the social order, and indeed the press and other means of communication.

Dispassionate analysis, in which the seeker of explanations struggled to free himself or herself of bias, was considered the hallmark of the scientific method. The closer the investigator could approach the stance of objectivity, the more empirical the research, the more likely it would lead to true resolutions. The aim of the social scientists was to adapt the method to their own research. Their tragic flaw was *hubris*, the presumptuous arrogance that destroyed Agamemnon and Lear. It was in this framework that the code of objectivity flowered. How could it be a false code? Its purpose was noble: the presentation of facts. Moreover, it squared with the goals of science itself. That it also served the interests of the capitalist system was not at first recognized, and it is not acknowledged even today. Objectivity tended to act as what Lenin described as a mechanism of collective organization, a quality the Russian leader demanded of the Soviet press.

In the capitalist world, as well as in the Marxist, the code of objectivity helps power to maintain social order and to fix limits to departures from ideological orthodoxy. As it operates in the market society of the United States and other industrialized nations, objectivity turns out on close examination to be anything but scientific; rather, *it hallows bias, for it safeguards the system against the explosive pressures for change.* So long as "both sides" are presented, neither side is glorified above the other, and the status quo remains unchallenged. Dissent is permitted, even encouraged, under the code of objectivity; however, its limits are proscribed, and the counterbalancing orthodoxy is assured a voice—not only a voice but the most powerful voice, because orthodoxy is represented by the powerful, whose command of financial resources and of newsworthy authority assures it of dominance in the press.

As a further guarantee, the code of objectivity requires that open persuasion be limited to the editorial pages and that the news columns be free of "opinion." Because few persons read editorial pages, their influence is minimal. The American press condemned the witch hunts of Senator Joseph McCarthy on its editorial pages but presented his harangues "objectively" on its front pages.[2] It was only when the power of the political system was directed against McCarthy, whose excesses threatened to disrupt the system, that McCarthy was vanquished. The code of objectivity then may be used to bring evil or good; it may at one time serve the ends of a McCarthy and at another the ends of those who would destroy him. In either case, the press is an agent of power, lacking in independence. Objectivity bestows on the conductor the baton with which to conduct the symphony of the press.

Recognizing that absolute objectivity is impossible, many practitioners and students of journalism have proposed that other words be substituted. If one cannot be objective, one can certainly be fair. Or balanced. Or truthful. Yet substitute words have not resolved the muddle over definitions, for the goals of "fairness" and "balance" incorporate the same bias as does the word *objectivity*.[3]

Gaye Tuchman has attempted to bring clarity to the muddle by suggesting that objectivity is useful to journalists as a defense against anyone who would accuse them of slanting or distorting their output. What is involved, she says, is "strategic ritual." Tuchman writes in the spirit of a growing number of sociologists who have been studying the media as social institutions that behave in much the same manner as other occupational institutions—with their own bureaucratic structures and value systems. The pioneer in this movement was Warren Breed, who in 1955 first discussed the social pressures for conformity in the newsroom. Edward Jay Epstein and Herbert Gans confirmed similar pressures at the television networks.[4] The evidence amassed by Breed, Tuchman, Epstein, Gans, and others is formidable. It substantiates the value the code of objectivity holds for the mass media.

In analyzing the code, Tuchman identifies four "strategic procedures" the journalist follows in order to separate facts from feelings: (1) presenting both sides of a dispute, thus identifying the truth claims of the antagonists in conflictual situations; (2) presenting corroborating statements on behalf of these truth claims; (3) using direct quotations to indicate it is the source and not the journalist who is speaking; and (4) organizing stories in such a way as to present the most material facts first. In addition, Tuchman points out, the journalist practicing objectivity is careful to distinguish facts from opinions by identifying interpretive material as "news analysis." Tuchman writes that objectivity enables newspeople to lay "professional claim to objectivity, especially since their special professional knowledge is not sufficiently respected by news consumers and may indeed be the basis of critical attack."[5]

Others offer an economic explanation for the rise of the cult of objectivity, maintaining the idea of objectivity grew out of the economic imperatives of the news agencies. Indeed, it is often said—although the statement cannot be confirmed—that the goal of objectivity was created by the Associated Press (AP). That this explanation was first offered by an AP representative raises some questions as to its validity; but the historical account presented in 1938 by Oliver Gramling, an

Why objectivity is a myth.

SOURCE: L. W. Harvey

AP executive, in his book *AP: The Story of News* has been remarkably long-lived. Gramling cited a comment by Lawrence Gobright, an early AP writer during the Civil War. "My business," Gobright was quoted as saying, "is to communicate facts; my instructions do not allow me to make any comment upon the facts which I communicate."[6] Kent Cooper, who served for twenty-five years as general manager of the AP, preached the code of objectivity from one end of the land to the other, defining it as "true and unbiased news." Not one for understatement, Cooper proclaimed objective news "the highest original moral concept ever developed in America and given the world." It was Cooper, too, who enunciated for the first time in 1945 a doctrine he identified as "the public's right to know."[7]

Cooper died in 1965. Six years later, a reading room named for him was dedicated at Indiana University, which he had attended, by Wes Gallagher, then the Associated Press general manager. In eulogizing Cooper, Gallagher also delivered a eulogy to the code of objectivity:

> It seems to me that all men and women must have a Holy Grail of some kind, something to strive for, something always just beyond our fingertips even with the best of efforts. To the journalist that Holy Grail should be objectivity. To have anything less would be demeaning and would result in the destruction of the profession.[8]

The crucial point about objectivity, Gallagher said, was to separate thought from emotions and to distinguish facts from feelings. The objective journalist, he said, "must not let his ego overpower his conscience or good sense. He should try to shed a cold, clear light of fact and reason where fogs of prejudice and partnership envelop so many issues. He must not make concessions to the cult of irrationality that is widely prevalent today." Gallagher's critique of "irrationality" was directed at political dissidents, especially those manning the so-called underground press that openly condemned the code of objectivity.

It is not surprising the chief exponent of the code of objectivity has been the Associated Press. Almost from its inception, the AP has interested itself in multiplying its subscribers, those who use its services. Technically, the AP is a cooperative owned by its members, the thousand or more newspapers that receive AP news wires. But the AP also sells its services directly to subscribers, among whom are numbered radio and television stations; magazines; governments; colleges and universities; and many newspapers, broadcasters, and wire services abroad. Its chief competitor, the United Press International (UPI), which has been declining steadily, is a privately owned organization that sells directly to subscribers. The output of these two services is barely distinguishable. The AP and UPI compete fiercely for subscribers; they are also in competition with foreign news agencies—such as Reuters—as well as with syndicated news services operated by the most powerful American newspapers—*The New York Times, The Washington Post*, and *The Los Angeles Times*. In this competition, political advocacy of any sort is disadvantageous since it is likely to limit the lists of subscribers. Foes of any political stance would not look with sympathy at joining forces with its friends. In other words, it *pays* to practice objectivity; political neutrality is a commercial benefit. To maximize the number of subscribers, it is necessary to avoid taking sides politically, to give equal weight to the truth claims of Democrats and Republicans or Ralph Nader and General Motors.

The goal of journalistic objectivity has been spread and accepted so widely that by now it has become a part of the public's belief system in all parts of the world. In the United States, for example, the goal is disseminated and stamped as good not only in schools of journalism but also in classes in history, political science, and civics. So deeply has the notion of journalistic objectivity been implanted that it has become suicidal for a news service or indeed a newspaper to publicly espouse subjectivity or persuasion in its news columns. Objectivity is financially valuable to the all-purpose newspaper that seeks to expand its profitability through its advertising revenue and subscription lists. The same applies, of course, to radio and television. In presenting both sides of issues, wire services, newspapers, and broadcasting outlets often present ideas that are anathema to the government, to the advertisers, and to the industrial and commercial elite; yet this practice is accepted, sometimes reluctantly, as part of the code of objectivity. After all, its perimeters are circumscribed. Moreover, journalism operates, as do all institutions, under a set of conventions that dictate what is to be published.[9] It is well known, for instance, that the unusual is chosen over the usual: It is not news when a dog bites a man, but it is news when a man bites a dog. What happens today is more newsworthy than what happened yesterday; what happens close to home is more newsworthy than what happened thousands of miles away. What is said by a prominent person, a "celebrity," is more newsworthy than what is said by an unknown. Whatever is more dramatic and conflictual is more newsworthy than the routine or cooperative. All these—the unusual, the topical, the near at hand, the voice of the celebrity, the conflictual—are journalistic conventions; these are what define "news." No clear definition exists; professional journalists smell it out with their nose for news. They define it based on their news judgment. Thus, even the concept of news is subjective. As David Brinkley often correctly pointed out, "News is what I say it is."

The code of objectivity and the conventions of news limit dissent in the mass media largely to criticism of individuals. The fundamental institutions are beyond the frontiers of censure. In all the noisy criticism of President Nixon and his administration in the Watergate affair, the press shied away from charges against fundamental institutions. It was the president who was condemned, not the presidency. So long as both sides were heard, it was the anti-Nixon crowd versus the Nixon people. The repeated use of "Watergate" to symbolize corruption contributed to misunderstanding of the situation; it also helped many Americans to hold there was nothing in the behavior of the Nixon administration that was different from the behavior of all administrations. How serious, after all, was a break-in at the Democratic National Committee offices in the Watergate complex in Washington? The decisive issue, however, did not center on the Watergate break-in but rather on the debasement of power at the highest levels of the system; on attempts to establish a secret police force answerable only to the president; on the use of the Internal Revenue Service to bring ruin to political opponents; and on the positioning of the president and his advisers in a state of absolute power, answerable to no one. The essential evil lay in a system that allowed itself to be so easily corrupted by corrupt people, not altogether in the character of Richard Nixon or H. R. Haldeman. The charge was that Nixon had corrupted the institution.

Nixon recognized the nature of the criticism and sought to ride out the attacks by cloaking himself in the majesty of his office and by seeking to portray his critics as challenging the institution of the presidency. His defense might even have worked if he had not been foolish enough to permit the tapes of White House conversations to be preserved. The Watergate case confirms that under the code, fundamental institutions may not be attacked. They may be tinkered with but never directly challenged. We may bash Congress, for example, but not the American system of mixed government. We may not condemn the symbols of those fundamental institutions either—for example, the flag, democracy, freedom of the press, freedom of speech or religion, or the presidency. Enemies of the system may not be applauded, nor symbolic representation of those enemies. Atheism may be tolerated yet not ever endorsed; freedom of religion does not extend that far. Patriotism may not be questioned. No symbol of animosity to "family" may be supported. Homosexuality may be tolerated, but it may not be advocated. Motherhood may not be condemned. Communism may not be defended. Nor, for that matter, is it acceptable within the parameters of the system to attack the code of objectivity.

Moreover, the code of objectivity appears to be operative only within the geographical limits of the United States. When the United States is in collision with another nation, it is not necessary to give equal attention to both sides to the dispute; to do so is to be unpatriotic. It has been exceedingly rare to find the views of Fidel Castro given equal weight with those of his enemies; and when Castro's stance has been presented, it usually has been reported in such a way as to illustrate clearly the wrongheadedness of his views. The situation has been similar with regard to the views of Soviet and Chinese leaders as well as those of Iraq's Saddam Hussein and the chieftains of the Palestine Liberation Organization. One would have had to seek long and hard to find the position of the Ayatollah Khomeini presented in a balanced fashion in the American press during (and after) the holding of the American hostages in Iran.[10]

There are—and always have been—individual journalists who flout the code of objectivity and present views beyond the normal parameters of ideological expression. These are, however, the exception and not the rule. The pluralist structure of the United States permits and indeed encourages dissident individual voices, though these voices are drowned out effectively by the noises raised by the institutions and the loyalist defenders of the system. Sociologist Robert Paul Wolff likened the territory of American politics to a plateau with steep sides rather than a pyramid. On that plateau, he says, are all the interest groups that have been recognized as legitimate: "The most important battle waged by any group in American politics is the struggle to climb onto the plateau."[11]

According to the logic of democratic pluralism, visibility for groups depends on the willingness of the press to accord them a place on the plateau. When deciding whether to grant this privilege, the press does not behave independently, however. In this activity, the press operates under the rigid rules of its unwritten network of conventions. Let there be authoritative voices speaking for the dissident group, and it will be allowed on the plateau; let its objectives be perceived as operating within the boundaries of the accepted belief system, and the plateau will be open to it. When there are no authoritative voices speaking for it and when its goals are outside those boundaries, access to the plateau is denied. Unless, of course, the group is able to make so much noise that its existence cannot be denied.[12] Civil-rights activists learned this lesson in the 1960s, and other dissident and outlaw groups have sought to manipulate the press into providing coverage of their activities by defying the law or behaving in a fashion so outrageous the press cannot ignore the unusualness and conflictual nature of their behavior. Even then, the group may not be granted the comfortable cloak of legitimacy. Communists and atheists have long fallen into the illegitimate category; so have those labeled sexual deviates. In short, a group that threatens the social order or the politicoeconomic system is rejected. Thus do the mass media serve as significant instruments of social control operating as agents of the system itself. In this sense, the code of objectivity is itself a mechanism of social control.

The political left in the United States has frequently condemned the press as being conservative and even reactionary. Referring to the fact that the overwhelming majority of American newspapers support the Republican party, critics have spoken of a "one-party press." Such was the comment of Adlai Stevenson when, as the 1952 Democratic candidate for president, he found the newspapers supporting his opponent, Dwight Eisenhower, by 83 percent. Yet a dozen years later, the press endorsed the candidate of the Democratic party, Lyndon Johnson, against Republican Barry Goldwater, who was thought to be so extreme in his rightist views he might upset the carefully constructed social market system and perhaps even induce a disruptive movement on the left. When Nixon succeeded to the White House in 1968, he seemed determined to attempt to whip the press into docility and seemed unwilling to accept a press role as agent of the system and insisted it become a full-fledged servant of the government. Predictably, the press responded angrily by rejecting the efforts of Nixon and Vice President Spiro Agnew to impose restraints on press behavior.[13] In this response, the press was joined not only by liberals already predisposed to opposition to Nixon but also by many conservatives, among them Goldwater, who wished for adherence to the status quo and maintenance of power by the commercial and industrial forces that dictated the social order.

Fighting back against the Nixon campaign, the press naturally turned for support to the First Amendment. Perhaps surprisingly, it also called on the code of objectivity that had been officially embraced by the press industry as early as 1937. In a 1970 article, I. William Hill, associate editor of *The Washington Evening Star*, identified his cause with the rhetoric of Lincoln's Gettysburg Address: "Nine score and five years ago, our forefathers brought forth upon this continent the daily newspaper, conceived in objectivity and dedicated to the proposition that all men are entitled to impartial facts. Now we are engaged in a great media debate, testing whether this newspaper or any medium so conceived and so dedicated can long endure." In the following issue, Derek Daniels, executive editor of *The Detroit Free Press*, constructed a different interpretation of history: "If my understanding of history is correct, it was just the opposite—that the press in America was born of advocacy and protest—that opinion and activism were the cornerstones which the Constitution is designed to protect."[14]

Hill and Daniels gave expression to two different ingredients in the folklore of the press: On the one hand, its mission is to present "facts" impartially, and on the other, it is a watchdog to guard against the abuse of power. For each man and woman, there is a magic password to open the golden gates into the promised land where the press is free of government restraint and free to serve humankind. For Hill, the password is objectivity; for Daniels, the password is watchdog—or, to use Douglass Cater's colorful phrase, the press is "the fourth branch of government." Neither Hill nor Daniels spoke of a more fundamental role for the press: an instrument to help preserve the social order.

WHERE IS THE INDEPENDENT POWER OF THE PRESS?

Much is said and written about the power and influence of the press—especially the television journalists—on the course of contemporary events. This argument's assumption is that this "power" of the press is an *independent* power, that it can be and is used in adversarial fashion against governments and the politicians and statesmen who run them. It is an easy assumption to make. There is great potential for power in the press, and the American news media do *seem* to be operating independently; they do *seem* to be challenging power—as a kind of fourth branch of government. On closer investigation, however, it is apparent that *belief* in the exercise of independent power by the press is a formidable weapon in the hands of those who seek to use the press for their own purposes. Governments and the politically and economically powerful have been manipulating newspapers throughout history. The opportunity for manipulating of television journalists is one that has not been lost on the powerful.

Each of the four articles of faith of press independence noted earlier turns out to be useful for the manipulators: that the press is free of outside interference, serves the public's right to know, seeks to learn and present the truth, and reports facts objectively and fairly. Yet not one of these articles of faith squares with reality. It is the widespread belief in them, however, that makes the task of the manipulators easier and assists in the maintenance of the fundamental ideology that keeps them in power. This ideological construct even has a name: the doctrine of social responsibility.

Shortly after the end of World War II, a commission under the direction of Robert Hutchins, chancellor of the University of Chicago, concluded that the mass media had become so important an element in American life that, if left unchecked, they were a threat to the democratic fabric of the country, even the world. The press (television was at that time still in its infancy), the commission declared, had become a "vital necessity" in the transaction of public business; its scope was increasing, and so was its power. The commission termed the modern press "a new phenomenon" that might "facilitate thought or thwart progress," that might, in fact, debase and vulgarize mankind and endanger peace:

> If the press is inflammatory, sensational and irresponsible, it and its freedom will go down in the universal catastrophe. On the other hand, it can help create a new world community, by giving men everywhere knowledge of the world and one another by prompting comprehension and appreciation of the goals of a free society.[15]

Such assertions about the power of the mass media have by now become common. So extensively have these assertions been spread it is safe to say that today most people assume the press has enormous power. This assumption has become so firmly fixed in press dogma that people everywhere believe in the power of the press with the same assurance with which they revere the public's right to know. In 1970, for instance, a prominent magazine editor wrote this:

> After 200 years of fixed tradition and accepted practice, American journalists are now facing a new situation: If knowledge is power, it is no longer concentrated in the hands of the powerful. . . . By shaping our picture of the world on an almost minute-to-minute basis, the media now largely determine what we think, how we feel and what we do about our social and political environment.[16]

Similar avowals of an immense press power are broadcast almost daily by journalists, politicians, media scholars. and the public whenever queried (as in opinion surveys). The perception of vast power is sobering for many journalists. As Frederick Kempe wrote in *The Wall Street Journal*, "We Western journalists . . . have an enormous power to influence events. More than most of us would like to admit."[17] It no longer seems astonishing that a spokesperson for the news department of a Minnesota television station could remark: "We are the most powerful men in the history of the world, and I'm happy to say that, on the whole, I think that power is being used in the best interests of everybody." The comment was made in a study surveying broadcasters' attitudes about the part played by television news in reporting the Watergate scandal. The author of the study, Marvin Barrett, saw the power of the press in equally hyperbolic terms, maintaining that President Nixon's confrontation with the press marked the first time since the medieval confrontation of the crown with the papacy that there had been "a comparable encounter of power with equal but disparate power." In twentieth-century America, Barrett wrote, "the press seemed to be assuming the role of the medieval papacy."[18] Thomas R. Dye, a long-time student of the mass media, has asserted the media have "established themselves as equal in power to the nation's corporate and governmental leadership."[19] Such comments could be multiplied endlessly.

The assumption of prodigious power held by the press is derived largely from the visibility of newspapers, magazines, and especially television. It is drawn also from the perception of the majority of the population that it receives its information about the world from the news media. "Where do you get most of your information?" is a simplistic question. Information and news are not the same thing. Often we don't know where most of our information comes from. Information, whether of "news" or of anything else, rarely arrives in our consciousness through a single channel. We read, listen, speak, hear—in all these ways we receive information. The way in which we process that material is rarely discrete. For example, information about an airplane crash may reach us first in a conversation with another person. Then we may tune in a radio, check an evening newspaper, watch an evening news program on television, and acquire additional scraps of intelligence from others. Yes, much of what we have seen and heard has originated in "news" reports, but it has gone through many filters, including what we learned as children at home and in school, what we read and heard earlier—from all the forces of socialization we have encountered in our lives. It is from packages that we receive our information. Thus, to assert we receive most of our information from television or from newspapers is to assert a pattern of learning that is at the very best misleading and at the very worst thoroughly erroneous. In fact, the most clearly visible "power" of the press turns out to be a misleading power. To claim, with Stein, Barrett, Dye, and the others, that the press has the power to instruct is even more questionable, since our attitudes about our perceptions and experiences have been formed long before we watch a television program or read a newspaper article. Undeniably, we are informed and instructed by the news media, yet it is a logical absurdity to assign an exclusive role, or even primacy, to the news media in these processes.

No television program has been cited more frequently in support of the notion the news media possess great power than the CBS show "60 Minutes." It has been, without question, the most profitable and influential "news" program on television, earning the network in the neighborhood of $2 million a week—or, as its executive producer, Don Hewitt, said, "a net profit for CBS of over $1 billion" in its first twenty-five years of operation.[20] CBS producer Perry Wolff called it "the most successful [news] show in the history of television."[21] The tale of the success of "60 Minutes" is truly astounding. By 1994, it had ranked in the top 10 of A. C. Nielsen's influential ratings for fifteen consecutive years, a ranking stronger than that achieved by any competing comedy show. Very likely, more American citizens have watched "60 Minutes" than any other "news" program. On the average, "60 Minutes" has reached an audience of nearly 32 million viewers each Sunday, more than any other single news form in the history of American journalism.[22]

There is, however, a very large question to be examined—and that is whether "60 Minutes" is in fact a news program. The investigator is certainly led to wonder why "60 Minutes" is so successful. Harry Reasoner, one of the original interviewers, offered his audience an explanation when the first program aired in 1968: "All art," he said, "is the rearrangement of previous perceptions, and we don't claim this is anything more than that, or even that journalism is an art, for that matter. But we do think this is sort of a new approach."[23]

Dozens of other magazine-type shows have copied "60 Minutes," and while some have achieved success, none has equaled the original. The closest has been "20/20," an ABC show that by 1994 was averaging an audience rating of 15.6. By

" '60 Minutes' is on."

SOURCE: Drawing by Shanahan: copyright 1992 The New Yorker Magazine, Inc.

contrast, "60 Minutes" gained an average rating of 18.7. For the networks, it was financially lucrative to deal in magazine shows because the networks owned them themselves and did not have to buy the shows from producers of entertainment shows.

A major reason for the success of "60 Minutes" can probably be found in the criticisms leveled at it, some by targets of the show but others also by serious critics, including myself, it must be said. Many of the show's segments fit comfortably into a well-known pattern of fiction, the good guy in the white hat besting the bad guy in the black hat—in this case not by means of gunfire and violence but by reason and evidence, the essence of investigative journalism. In fact, "60 Minutes" proudly dons for itself the rewarding raiment of the investigating journalist. But it also stacks the deck in favor of the investigator by selecting material favorable to the cause and suppressing material likely to help the other side. Hewitt and his producers frankly acknowledge they edit their shows selectively to promote their own "story line." The show makes no real pretense to seeking "objectivity" or fairness but rather to documenting a particular line. In whatever case, it has been a strong supporter of popular American values and, therefore, like objectivity, an endorsement of the status quo. Hewitt, who was not a college graduate, credits the program's success on its abandonment of elitist pretensions and its open appeal to a middle-class audience. A colleague called him "a $5-million Joe-Sixpack." Instead of dealing with issues, Hewitt said, "we tell stories" and "package news as well as Hollywood packages fiction."[24] Hewitt and his star interviewer, Mike Wallace, speak of "60 Minutes" as a series of "morality plays" in which they merge reporting practices with the detective story. The interviewer has emerged as a kind of reporter-detective.

Its list of exposés is long and impressive; its list of targets is equally lengthy. It has been especially tough on businesses, some of them advertisers on television. It has also gone after politicians, church groups, professional organizations, environmental polluters, auto manufacturers, used-car dealers, and many others. Hewitt is proud of his accomplishments: "I have," he once said, "the best show on television."[25] Peter Jennings, anchorman on the competing ABC network, credited the show's success to Hewitt's imagination and editing. Jon Katz, media critic for *Rolling Stone*, said that Hewitt "has some sort of sorcerer-like skills in the editing room." Katz said also that "60 Minutes" represents a shift from the early modern Old News to the post-modern New News, which he describes as "dazzling, adolescent, irresponsible, fearless, frightening, and powerful." In the New News world, according to Katz, "talk-shows, entertainment shows, and music are as likely to provide public discourse about important issues as the Old News.[26]

It was through the editing skills of Hewitt and his highly paid staff of producers that "60 Minutes" turned out to be more an entertainment show than a news program. It did not hesitate, by cutting, trimming, splicing, and altering context, to make its targets sound as if they had said something quite different from what they had in fact said. It also made use of hidden cameras and what came to be known in the trade as "ambush" interviews.[27]

Claims of immense power for "60 Minutes" and other television programs that take strong positions on issues of public concern are fortified by the defensive stances of those on the receiving end of bullets fired by these shows. In late 1991, for instance, when word leaked out that "60 Minutes" was preparing a report on the food additive monosodium glutamate, the industry reacted with a massive damage-control campaign. Bruce Ingersoll wrote in *The Wall Street Journal* that to learn "60 Minutes" was going to do a report on a particular business had become the worst nightmare a business executive could face.[28]

Some critics argue that "60 Minutes" has made a significant contribution to American democracy. Professor David Thorburn of the Massachusetts Institute of Technology says the show brings American people together by telling stories that "articulate the culture's central mythologies." This is achieved, Thorburn says, by providing an inheritance of "shared stories, plots, character types, cultural symbols, and narrative conventions."[29] However, Jay Rosen, a journalism professor at New York University, says the "60 Minutes" formula creates heroes of the tough omniscient reporter-detectives, making them, rather than "the real powers that be," the focus of attention.

The "60 Minutes" formula fits comfortably into what media critic Edward Jay Epstein has written on the television industry's "basic assumptions" about news. TV newsmen and newswomen, he wrote in a study of NBC news procedures, assume that viewer interest, which is maintained through easily recognized images, is likely to wander if the images become confusing. After all, the attention span of viewers is seen as limited, so it can be prolonged mainly through action or subjects in motion. Complex issues, then, are presented in terms of human experience rather than abstract ideas. Not only that: It is clear, he concluded, that scenes of potential conflict are assumed to be more interesting than placid scenes.

At all events, the conviction that the press enjoys remarkable power is part of the belief system held not only by Americans but by people everywhere. The conviction has obtained as much in Japan and Europe, in the poorer nations of the Southern Hemisphere, and in the far-reaching regions once dominated by Moscow as it has in the United States. International discussions of the press confirm the overwhelming acceptance of the conviction: We human beings simply take for granted that the power of the press to inform and instruct is vast, greater than that of any other institution. The implication, then, is that the responsibility of the press is to inform and instruct. As the Hutchins Commission phrased it, to the press belongs the power to "facilitate thought or thwart progress." Moreover, the public has every right to expect this role to be carried out faithfully and truthfully.[30]

Political partisanship inevitably invades any discussion of press power. Interestingly, political Right and political Left each assumes the press enjoys great power, and each argues this power is used for the benefit of the other. Spokespeople for the Media Research Center, a conservative group in Alexandria, Virginia, have claimed that "Big Media" (meaning the television networks and the nationally circulated newspapers) distort the news (often unintentionally) toward liberal causes and liberal political figures.[31] At the same time, liberal press researchers argue that the news media slant their reports in favor of conservatives and corporate interests.[32]

Many analysts have joined the fray, some on the side of the Right, some on the side of the Left. Marvin Olasky, a conservative professor at the University of Texas, has endorsed the Right's attack on leftist journalists who defend what he calls "an inherently flimsy position."[33] For, he argued, leading media representatives not only have been captured by the Left but also have joined forces with the federal government to promote ever-increasing federal power.[34] On the other hand, Edward Asner, a liberal actor with a long history of portraying journalists, has applauded liberal researchers for producing proof of the media's conservative bias. These researchers, Asner said, have shown that certain stories are "effectively censored, made unavailable to the average citizen." Americans, he said, ought to be "outraged" that they hadn't heard about those stories.[35] Jeane Kirkpatrick, ambassador to the United Nations under President Reagan, has spoken of "colossal concentrations of media power [used] to manipulate images as well as ideas," all in the interests of liberal or left-wing causes. She spoke also of "a kind of self-indulgence" among the mass media, whereby they make use of *anonymous* sources to promote such liberal shibboleths as the argument that it is poverty that brings on revolutions. "The power of the media," she wrote, "is much greater with regard to politics than with regard to experiences that are more subject to reality testing." The directors of the Media Research Center have said that by serving as instruments for the manipulation of culture, liberal media are controlling the nation's agenda and using their vast power not only to "make winners look like losers and vice versa" but also to wreck political careers and "greatly influence the political direction of the country."[36] Leftist analysts such as Edward Herman and Noam Chomsky have countered that, rather than relying on anonymous sources backing liberal causes, the giant media organizations are utterly dependent on *official* sources, who make them vehicles for the communication of "systematic propaganda" defending concentrated wealth against the interests of the working class.[37]

The one area on which critics of both Right and Left agree is that the mass media possess enormous power and that this power is used for the wrong ends—in other words, not in the service of the public but rather for the political advantage of someone else. Like many other journalism educators, William Hachten invokes the principles of social responsibility to argue that the news media's obligations of public service run so deep they "transcend moneymaking."

> . . . in the Western concept the media have a positive responsibility to provide reliable and essential information from around the world. By so doing, journalists help protect political liberty by providing information that a democratic society requires if it is to govern itself.[38]

The irony here is that while both Right and Left scoff at the idea of journalistic objectivity, they agree that journalism's proper role is to provide the reliable information a democratic society needs to govern itself. Although it may be comforting to imagine that news media can carry on their frail shoulders such a heavy burden, it is quite unrealistic to do so. Such great expectations place impossible burdens on both the press and the public. They ignore the truth that the press is an instrument rather than an independent actor. They fail to recognize the reality that the capitalist press is part of the apparatus of private profit regulating the economy and the political system.

Some writers find other reasons to question the power of the press. A study of media coverage of the territorial war Britain fought with Argentina over the Falklands Islands (called the Malvinas by the Argentines) questioned the "scientific belief" that the media, television in particular, had a tremendous effect on attitudes and behavior. The study sought to "dispel some myths about media and war" for its authors saw no evidence that any reporting "of horrors of war or supposed horror of nuclear war will stop war."[39] A conclusion of such sweeping magnitude is unusual for commentators as well as journalists. The authors observed that the media were only part of a person's social world and argued they were not "a primary influence" over attitudes and behavior. Walter Lippmann, often named the most influential American journalist of the twentieth century, also questioned the assumption of sweeping power for the press. He learned his lesson the hard way when as the quintessential Washington columnist he failed to influence President Lyndon Johnson to change directions in his Vietnam War policies. Disappointed, Lippmann unleashed the full force of his vindictiveness against Johnson. The biographer Ronald Steel maintained that Lippmann's influence was perhaps the greatest of all American journalists and that although he did not change Johnson's policies, he was ultimately vindicated and Johnson lost the White House.[40]

It is more dangerous to overestimate the power of the media than it is to understate it. The economist John Kenneth Galbraith suggested how persuasive the perception of media power can be on both viewers and journalists, constructing this ironic illustration:

> The self-esteem of the Washington reporter or network correspondent is admirably served by meditation on the power he or she exercises. The sense of this power is then reflected not only in a solemnity of mien but in much equally sober public writing and confession, and it is further enhanced by the attention and the efforts at social and like subornation of reporters, editors, columnists, and commentators by politicians, lobbyists, and professionally righteous citizens who seek access to the media.[41]

We will turn soon to a detailed examination of these efforts at subornation by all the groups Galbraith mentioned. In any case, viewing the media as agents of power rather than as wielders of power brings us closer to actuality, as Lippmann and so many others have discovered late in their careers.

NOTES

1. Michael Schudson, *Discovering the News: A Social History of American Newspapers* (New York: Basic Books, 1978), 8.

2. Edwin P. Bayley, *Joseph McCarthy and the Press* (New York: Pantheon, 1981), 113–18. See also Fred W. Friendly, *Due to Circumstances Beyond Our Control* (New York: Random House, 1967). For a summary of the press and the McCarthy phenomenon, see J. Herbert Altschull, *From Milton to McLuhan: The Ideas Behind American Journalism* (White Plains, NY: Longman, 1990), 312–18.

3. See J. Herbert Altschull, "Fairness, Truth, and the Makers of Image," *Media Studies Journal* (Fall 1992): 1–15.

4. Warren Breed, "Social Control in the Newsroom," *Social Forces* vol. 33 (May 1955): 326–35; Edward Jay Epstein, *News from Nowhere: Television and the News* (New York:

Random House, 1973); Herbert J. Gans, *Deciding What's News: A Study of CBS Evening News, NBC Nightly News*, Newsweek and Time (New York: Vintage Books, 1980). See also Dan Schiller, *Objectivity and the News: The Public and the Rise of Commercial Journalism* (Philadelphia: University of Pennsylvania Press, 1981) and W. Lance Bennett, *The Politics of Illusion*, 2nd ed. (White Plains, NY: Longman, 1988).

5. Gaye Tuchman, "Objectivity as Strategic Ritual: An Examination of Newsmen's Notions of Objectivity," *American Journal of Sociology* vol. 5, no. 4 (January 1972): 660-79.

6. Oliver Gramling in *AP: The Story of News* (New York: Scribner's, 1938), 36, quotes Gobright as saying: "My dispatches are sent to papers of all manner of politics, and the editors say they are able to make their own comments upon the facts which are sent to them. I therefore confine myself to what I consider legitimate news. I do not act as a politician belonging to any school, but try to be truthful and impartial. My dispatches are merely dry matters of fact and detail. Some special correspondents may write to suit the temper of their organs. Although I try to write without regard to men or politics, I do not always escape censure."

7. Kent Cooper introduced the "right to know" phrase in a speech at a meeting of B'nai B'rith in New York. See *New York Times*, February 19, 1945. See also Kent Cooper, *Kent Cooper and the Associated Press* (New York: Random House, 1965).

8. Wes Gallagher, "Ego Journalism versus Objectivity," unpublished speech delivered at the dedication of the Kent Cooper Room at the Indiana University library, Bloomington, May 16, 1971. Along the way, Gallagher said this: "The critics say no man can be objective. It is of course true that all men are fallible. To be otherwise would make men saints. And the world seems to be devoid of saints nowadays. But a journalist is no more fallible in his profession than a jurist or a doctor in the pursuit of theirs. He can subordinate his feelings to his profession just as the jurist must, or a doctor in treating a patient or a lawyer representing a client."

9. For a discussion of journalism conventions, see Walter Lippmann, *Public Opinion* (New York: Macmillan, 1922). Douglass Cater in *The Fourth Branch of Government* (Boston: Houghton Mifflin, 1963) offers a contrary view. For a more modern discussion of these conventions, see Leon V. Sigal, *Reporters and Officials* (Lexington, MA: Heath, 1973).

10. Altschull, *Milton to McLuhan*, 254-60.

11. Robert Paul Wolff, "Beyond Tolerance," in Robert Paul Wolff, Barrington Moore, Jr., and Herbert Marcuse, *The Critique of Pure Tolerance* (Boston: Beacon House, 1965), 45.

12. For additional commentary and analysis of these points, see especially Sigal, *Reporters and Officials*, and Gans, *Deciding What's News*.

13. For a review of the Agnew phenomenon, see Altschull, *Milton to McLuhan*, 325-31.

14. I. William Hill, "Some Objective Jottings on Objectivity," *Bulletin of the American Society of Newspaper Editors* (January 1970): Derek Daniels, "Separating Fact, Emotion, by Edict or Example?," *Bulletin of the American Society of Newspaper Editors* (February 1970):

15. Commission on Freedom the the Press, *A Free and Responsible Press: A General Report on Mass Communication* (Chicago: University of Chicago Press, 1947). The principal findings of the commission first appeared in print in *Fortune* magazine as a supplement to its April 1947 issue. An abridged version appeared in *Nieman Reports*, ed. Louis Lyons (Autumn 1976), 18-25. The citations here, identified as Hutchins, come from that article, ref. 19.

16. Robert Stein, *Media Power: Who Is Shaping the Picture of the World?* (Englewood Cliffs, NJ: Prentice-Hall, 1970), xii.

17. Quoted by Freedom Forum, Arlington, Virginia, May 10, 1992.

18. Martin Barrett, ed., *Moment of Truth? The Fifth Alfred I. du Pont Columbia University School of Broadcast Journalism Lecture* (New York: Thomas Y. Crowell, 1975).

19. Thomas R. Dye, *Who's Running America? The Reagan Years*, 3rd ed. (Englewood Cliffs, NJ: Prentice-Hall, 1983), 119.

20. Bill Carter, "'60 Minutes,' a Success Story and Still Counting," *New York Times*, September 15, 1990.

21. Judy Flander, "Hewitt's Humongous Hour," *Washington Journalism Review* (April 1991): 28.

22. Richard Campbell, "Don Hewitt's Durable Hour: A Pioneering News Magazine Hits 5," *Columbia Journalism Review* (September/October 1993): 25. Campbell, a professor of communications at the University of Michigan, is the author of *60 Minutes and the News: A Mythology for Middle America* (Urbana: University of Illinois Press, 1991).

23. Campbell, "Don Hewitt's Durable Hour," 26.

24. Campbell, "Don Hewitt's Durable Hour," 27.

25. Flander, "Hewitt's Humongous Hour," 29.

26. Cited in Flander, "Hewitt's Humongous Hour," 28.

27. Ben A. Franklin, "Some '60 Minutes' Targets Feel Run Over," *Washington Journalism Review* (April, 1991): 30. The account deals with a "60 Minutes" show in December 1990 titled "Is There Poison in Your Mouth?," which suggested that American dentists had been using certain amalgam dental fillings that contained mercury and may have, therefore, contributed to cases of multiple sclerosis.

28. Bruce Ingersoll, "Food Industry Awaits with Queasy Stomach a '60 Minutes' Show," *The Wall Street Journal*, October 17, 1991.

29. Campbell, "Don Hewitt's Durable Hour," 28.

30. Hutchins. The Commission said the people have a right to expect the press to present them with not only the facts but also the "truth about the facts."

31. L. Brent Bozell III and Brent H. Baker, eds., *And That's the Way It Isn't: A Reference Guide to Media Bias* (Alexandria, VA: Media Research Center, 1990).

32. Martin A. Lee and Norman Solomon, *Unreliable Sources: A Guide to Detecting Bias in News Media* (Secaucus, NJ: Carol Publishing Group, 1990).

33. Bozell and Baker, *And That's the Way It Isn't*, inner flap. They go on to say that reading about the bias of "Big Media" is like "watching all the episodes of *Friday the 13th* or some other horror movie back-to-back."

34. Marvin Olasky, *Central Ideas in the Development of American Journalism: A Narrative History* (Hillsdale, NJ: Lawrence Erlbaum, 1991), esp. 109-23. Olasky is an especially sharp critic of what he considers a leftist slant in the leading news media. He identifies what he sees as an enduring bias among leading news media in support of the idea that social institutions cause evil in the world rather than the sinfulness of man.

35. Lee and Solomon, *Unreliable Sources*, xii.

36. Jeane Kirkpatrick, foreword in Bozell and Baker, *And That's the Way It Isn't*, xiv-xvii.

37. Edward E. Herman and Noam Chomsky, *Manufacturing Consent: The Political Economy of the Mass Media* (New York: Pantheon Books, 1988), 1-3. I find the analysis of Herman and Chomsky to be remarkably on target, especially in their clear portrait of the limits on the media's capacity to withstand the pressures of corporate interests. The influence of Ben H. Bagdikian's painstaking work is apparent.

38. William Hachten, *The World News Prism: Changing Media, Clashing Ideologies*, 1st ed. (Ames: Iowa State University Press, 1981), 66.

39. David E. Morrison and Howard Tumber, *Journalists at War: The Dynamics of News Reporting during the Falklands Conflict* (London: Sage, 1988), 346-48.

40. Ronald Steel, *Walter Lippmann and the American Century* (New York: Vintage Books, 1980), 557-72.

41. John Kenneth Galbraith, *The Anatomy of Power* (Boston: Houghton Mifflin, 1983), 179.

Chapter
5

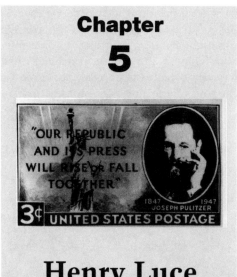

"OUR REPUBLIC
AND ITS PRESS
WILL RISE OR FALL
TOGETHER"

1847 1947
JOSEPH PULITZER

3¢ UNITED STATES POSTAGE

Henry Luce
and the Competitive Marketplace

THE WEDDING OF CAPITALISM
AND THE AMERICAN PRESS

The triumph of capitalism in twentieth-century America was accompanied by the appearance and expansion of new forms of mass media: the all-purpose news agency, the newsmagazine, radio, television, the videocassette, and, as the twenty-first century approached, ever more advanced and miniaturized channels of communication. Whereas the newspaper and the general-interest magazine predated the victory of both laissez-faire and progressivism, each of the newer mass-media forms arose in an environment saturated in corporate capitalism, an environment in which the ideology of the market economy had already taken root. It was also an age in which the Soviet Union's Communist ideology was present as a rival and challenge. If the American ideology was "good," then the Soviet ideology was "bad."

We will turn later to the rise of a noteworthy television entrepreneur, Ted Turner, creator of CNN (Cable News Network), but for now consider the remarkable career of the father of the newsmagazine, Henry R. Luce, of *Time* magazine. Together with his equally precocious fellow student at Yale University, Briton Hadden, Luce invented in 1923 a new phenomenon in the world of journalism—a slick weekly periodical whose pretense (and selling point) was that it would serve up in cogently written, easy-to-digest form a summary of the week's news that clarified for its readers what it all meant. The two young men, seizing an idea whose time had clearly come, were each twenty-four on the magazine's date of birth; and by the time they had reached thirty, they had become millionaires. They understood, with intuitive shrewdness, the American reading public was less interested in receiving "objective" news than was popularly believed—or at least the readers eagerly desired an antidote to the dull, dry phrases that were pouring from the news-agency teletypes. It was as if they understood a salable commodity lay between the hyped-up sensationalism of the tabloids and the pallid paragraphs of the news agencies.

Henry R. Luce, the man who founded *Time.*
SOURCE: *Time*

Of even greater importance was that these young men were clearly tuned in to the developing ideology of the twentieth century's market press system. It was Luce who was to proclaim in a remarkable 1941 pamphlet that the twentieth "must be to a significant degree the American Century."[1] A man who before World War II thought Mussolini and Hitler may themselves have been the wave of the future, Luce became a dedicated foe of fascism. He proclaimed the American Century, over and above any claims to the contrary that might be made by the Germans. "The sneers, groans, catcalls, teeth-grinding, hisses and roars of the Nazi Propaganda Ministry are of small moment" in combating American hegemony, Luce said. At the end of the war, the identity of the enemy was to change, and Luce was for the remainder of his life to lead the American troops in an all-out ideological struggle against the Soviet Union and against communism everywhere.

It is perhaps not accidental that the two most powerful and outspoken anti-communists in the United States were sons of Presbyterian ministers: Luce and the author of the doctrine of "massive retaliation," John Foster Dulles, secretary of state during the Eisenhower administration. Luce and Dulles were following in the footsteps of another son of a Presbyterian minister, Woodrow Wilson, whose moralistic pretensions set the stage for the "crusades" that were to follow and figure prominently in the kind of journalism that emerged during the American Century. Wilson, Dulles, and Luce were moral thoroughbreds, utterly convinced of the purity of free enterprise America; they dedicated themselves to assisting the rest of the world to partake of the same purity through the intervention of the political Holy Ghost, the United States. Satan, who appeared to Wilson as the embodiment of Metternich and the nineteenth-century balance-of-power theorists, was transmuted by Dulles and Luce into godless communism.

The model Luce and Hadden introduced was characterized by brevity, subjectivity, and simplicity. To *Time*, the problems of the world were not insoluble or even painfully difficult; all questions had answers. As one analyst put it, Luce "resisted complexity."[2]

Additionally, Luce and Hadden introduced the idea of group journalism. Articles were unsigned, produced by a series of editors who sharpened and polished and tuned their ears to the music of the hyphenated adjective. Subjects of the articles were "lantern-jawed," "spy-infested," "high-powered." The man (or woman) was characterized instantly and simplistically by the hyphenated adjective. It was a clean, uncluttered, uncomplicated world *Time* presented to its readers—and that world glorified the United States and its economic system. The target audience was Middle America or, as Luce put it, "the gentleman from Indiana."

Hadden died in 1929, and at thirty one, Luce took over sole direction of *Time* and of its children, beginning in 1930 with *Fortune* and expanding later to include *Life, Sports Illustrated*, and others. In all his publications, Luce paid homage to free enterprise and extolled the virtues and wisdom of commercial and industrial tycoons; it was Luce who adapted the Japanese word *tycoon* and applied it to the Babbitts of the United States. He went so far as to identify himself with the Sinclair Lewis character and to urge his readers to express pride in their quest to make money. Luce was a brilliant businessman who converted almost everything he touched into profit; small wonder he admired the tycoon—he was the greatest press tycoon of his Time.

In his self-anointed role of communism's enemy, Luce combined progressive admiration for a capitalist economy with a theological hatred of a planned economy and the atheistic element in communism in the Soviet Union and the emerging People's Republic of China. Luce's enemies—and there were many, especially those who enthusiastically supported Franklin Roosevelt's New Deal—accused him, not without reason, of being the leading member of the "China lobby." This was the name given to the business leaders, anti-Communist writers, and intellectuals who ceaselessly attacked Roosevelt for "selling out" to communism in China. Luce's image of the world, narrow and parochial, he no doubt inherited from his missionary father, a nineteenth-century jingoist in the tradition of those American patriots who supported wars in Mexico and Cuba in order to export white American virtue to the less developed darker-skinned races in Latin America. That same patriotism and jingoism were to influence intervention in Vietnam, designed to bring American virtue to the yellow races of Asia.

The singular success of *Time* influenced the ideology of the U.S. press in important ways. Many American newspapers copied the language style and story structure of *Time*. An increasing volume of "analytical" stories appeared in the daily press, stories that followed the pattern of *Time*'s—in the moralizing manner of the crusader with heavy infusions of anti-Communist explanations of events and shallow analysis that implied ready answers to complex questions. No part of this ideological orientation was new; it had always represented an element in the American press. What was new was the emphasis. The economic strength of *Time* had not

The first issue of *Time*—March 23, 1923.

SOURCE: Copyright 1923 Time, Inc.

been lost on the press industry, and imitation was indeed sincere flattery. Moreover, the industry had observed the widespread acceptance of the *Time* formula among the public, especially the upper middle class, from whose ranks arose the politically powerful. Overlooked, perhaps, was the tone of religiosity in *Time*'s pages that has now been adopted by its imitators. Here, Luce was following in the footsteps of generations of early American journalists who had been deeply committed to combating the corruption of godless political leaders.[3] The journalistic crusade, the all-out moral assault on devils and malefactors, later swept into the press net such figures as Joseph Stalin, Richard Nixon, Bruno Richard Hauptmann (kidnapper/murderer of the Lindbergh baby), Bert Lance, and Gary Hart. *Time* influenced the tone and content of the European press as well, and newsmagazine imitators sprang into existence in France and Germany, in Belgium and Italy, across the Continent, and ultimately in Africa, Asia, and Latin America.

After Luce's death in 1967, the face of *Time* changed slowly. Bylines began to appear, and with them came an end to the uncritical glorification of capitalism. Writers and editors, many of whom had not shared Luce's vision, were now able to criticize the excesses of laissez-faire and to move away from adulation of Chiang Kai-shek and the corrupt leadership of South Vietnam. It became almost impossible to distinguish *Time* from its chief competitor, *Newsweek*, which was under the management of *The Washington Post*, whose left-liberal views were anathema to Luce. In 1992, *Time,* now merged into the largest media conglomerate in the world, Time Warner, moved even farther away from Luce's brainchild when it turned to the latest in typography to streamline its product, relying on a relatively few pages of hard news and concentrating on splashy but brief analytical articles and cultural reviews. Managing editor Henry Muller said the publication was redefining the newsmagazine "in an era of instant communications."

Two-thirds of the magazine was now original rather than derivative, he said.[4] But even with modifications, *Time* (and *Newsweek*) continued to give its readers "the answers." Some acknowledgment was now made of the complexity of public questions, and an increased volume of criticism of American leadership emerged. Still, rarely did there appear criticism of the institutions on which the economy rested; the virtue of these institutions was taken for granted. While more balanced analysis appeared of the Soviet Union and communism, it was clear, at least until the collapse of the Soviet empire in the last years of the twentieth century, that these remained the enemy. Profits remained high for the older *Time* publications (aside from the weekly *Life*, which succumbed to the fate of all general-circulation magazines unable to compete succesfully with television for advertising revenue), but the corporation expanded into a new arena, that of the gossip sheet—in the form of the enormously profitable *People* magazine. The newsmagazine was not selling as well as it had in the simpler, preatomic days of the 1920s; it was entertainment that was selling now in the age of video. *Time* was now part of the Time Warner conglomerate, which included book publishing, television and radio operations, cable and video, and extended into the broad arena of pure entertainment.

By the twentieth century the press had become essential to the capitalist economy. Marshall McLuhan said the media are the message. It might also be said the media are the economy. Anyone interested in abstract intellectual exercises might ponder the American economic system without the media; it would be a difficult exercise.

It is in the distribution of goods—intellectual as well as material—that the media's position in the American system (as in all capitalist systems) is central. Advertising was an important factor in the development of the American press. In the modern capitalist state whose locus is the marketplace, advertising is an essential element because consumers seeking to buy goods must know something about the goods' quality and price and where to find them. The economic process consists of production, distribution, and consumption. In modern mass society, the news media more than any other institution facilitate the distribution of goods. In primitive societies and in much of the traditional world today, prospective buyers travel short distances to the sometimes makeshift marketplaces to test and sample the wares, then buy them or pass along to the next stall. By word of mouth, prospective buyers learn whose products are the most reliable; sometimes the producers send out criers to proclaim the worth of their goods, but the lack of easy transportation limits the distances these criers can travel. As modern society developed, as farmers moved into towns and even distant cities, as technology exploded the old social and economic order, the traditional marketplace largely disappeared to be replaced by the modern mass market.

The sociopolitical order of the United States as well as its economy is rooted in the philosophical principles of classical liberalism, in which it is virtuous to seek and make a profit. It is good to work hard; it is good to earn a substantial income. Borrowing from John Calvin and the Puritans, the capitalist ethic holds that it is good to use your income to aid the needy and thereby to earn your just reward to heaven. Not all Americans believe in the Protestant work ethic any longer, yet it is a value system that dies hard. In the mass media the rewards of hard work continue to be applauded along with the basic tenets of classical liberalism and capitalism, which see individuals rousing themselves from apathy when they reason their way to an activity they perceive to be of value to themselves. Advertising fits comfortably into this system. The producer informs the prospective buyer about goods available in the marketplace, be it in a store or a mail-order catalog. It is in the mutual interests of producer and buyer to fix a balanced price for the benefit of both of them because each is following his or her own self-interested ends. If the producer fixes the price too high, the buyer will go elsewhere. So Adam Smith's invisible hand fixes a price that is best for both producer and consumer.

For the system to work, people must know where goods are available, of what quality they are, and at what price they are offered. Newspapers, magazines, radio, and television provide the most efficient mechanism for furnishing this kind of information. Of course, other media of advertising are available. A growing advertising device is the use of direct mail, as is the unsolicited catalog or letter; others include shoppers' guides, billboards, and signs. In a mass society, however, the mass media still provide the most efficient mechanism for producer and consumer. The

Let the buyer beware: Newspaper advertisements, old style.

media become, in fact, the marketplace. Thus, 60 to 70 percent of the daily newspaper is made up of advertisements, and television programs are interrupted every few minutes for commercial messages. If advertising were eliminated from the mass media, they would be forced out of business or forced to operate on handouts from government or the great corporations or even contributions from the public.

Marxists (and some capitalist critics) maintain the search for advertising dollars converts the media into simple instruments in the hands of producers and advertising agencies seeking to induce customers to buy what they don't need for money they don't have. It is held by a substantial body of economists it is not advertising that brings producers and consumers together in the market but the actual price of goods. To them, it is the price and not the advertisement that represents information. They may be right, but the system of advertising is so deeply entrenched in the United States and other capitalist nations it has become a crucial element in their economies. And the mass media are crucial. Without them, people would have little information about what was available in the market.

It is no accident the word *market* turns up in the traditional picture of the media in the democratic assumption of the press as a marketplace of ideas. The media are not described as a *sample* of ideas or a *source* of ideas or a *conflict* of ideas; the media are markets to which news consumers go to learn what ideas and opinions are being expressed and by whom and under what circumstances. In the television industry, areas in which broadcast operations compete are officially described as "markets." We do not hear of the top twenty cities in the country, but we do hear of the top twenty markets. The image of the marketplace of ideas that Mr. Justice Holmes presented in 1919 has, appropriately, replaced the self-righting principle enunciated by John Milton three centuries earlier. That same image was invoked by Edward Bernays, one of the founding fathers of the industry that has come to be known as public relations, as his rationale. "In the struggle among ideas," Bernays wrote in 1923, "the only test is the one which Justice Holmes of the Supreme Court pointed out—the power of thought to get itself accepted in the open competition of the market."[5]

Luce's devil included the socialist ideas, theories, and doctrines embodied in the Russian revolution and the native radical movement in the United States that grew out of the Populist and Progressive protests against the excesses of an unchecked free-enterprise system. Lincoln Steffens was a socialist who later exulted in the accomplishments of Soviet Russia; his friend John Reed, another American journalist, joined the revolution and was rewarded with burial inside the walls of the Kremlin near the tomb of Lenin. The writer Upton Sinclair called for rebellion against the misdeeds of the great capitalists. In the early twentieth century, even Walter Lippmann identified himself as a socialist. In other words, the same seeds that flowered in the planned economy of the Soviet Union were planted in the United States, but the flowers that sprouted from the American seeds bore little resemblance to those that blossomed in the Soviet Union. Whenever similar blossoms appeared in the United States, they were cut down (as, for example, in the Pacific Northwest, where lumbermen preached the gospel of Marxism and were smashed by lawmen).

At the same time, the American press, without benefit of Leninist dogma, was becoming the chief cheerleader for the policies and practices of American leaders and their by now well-established economic system. What had begun as laissez-faire had been modified into a system of free enterprise and, by the end of the nineteenth century, into the modern corporate industrial state. Although the economic system of capitalism had been substantially revised and pure laissez-faire was no longer practiced after the Civil War, the belief system was handed down almost intact well into the twentieth century. Despite the practical end of free enterprise, the 1920s represented an Indian summer apotheosis of laissez-faire as the American public convulsively pursued a variety of get-rich-quick schemes. The pattern repeated itself in the 1980s.

Few spokespeople for capitalism defend any longer the idea that the marketplace should be allowed to operate free of outside controls. The rise of corporations and the regulatory instruments forged by the Progressives undid laissez-faire in the nineteenth century, and the New Deal experiment in "scientific capitalism" restructured Adam Smith quite as thoroughly as Lenin and others revised Marxism. In fact, the New Deal brought with it many elements of socialism and the planned economy; interference by the federal government became commonplace in efforts to restrain uncontrolled capital forces and to protect the weak, much as Marx himself had urged. In West Germany following World War II, economics minister Ludwig Erhard coined a new expression to describe the modifications in the theory of capitalism: He spoke of "a social market economy." It was with reluctance the press came to tolerate the modifications; in the United States, publishers responded with overt hostility to the New Deal. Despite an unfavorable press, however, Franklin D. Roosevelt was elected president four times. Publishers got the message and abandoned their open warfare against the modified system. But the hostility remained, mostly undercover. Voices emerged from time to time over the next half-century to call for a return to the "good old days" of free enterprise, when there was, it was said, no government interference with a free press. The economic policies of Ronald Reagan sought to restore something of the laissez-faire world that predated the Great Depression.

The New Deal reforms of the 1930s were never quite able to conquer the Depression, but they were wildly successful in combating fear and restoring Progressive optimism to the public. Science became an article of faith—countering the ideas of Marx and those of Darwin and Freud, who had rocked traditional values by making manifest the animal nature of humankind and the unconscious, irrational nature of much of its behavior. Humans and their institutions could be understood only through the use of the scientific method, through dispassionate observation and the assembly of verifiable data. Old values were cast in doubt in those troubled days; fundamental assumptions had to be confirmed. Even the old gods were suspect in a world that no longer seemed to be playing by the rules; this accounted for the search for heroes who would somehow find a way out and restore the sanity of an ordered world. The fascination of Americans with Mussolini, even of such enlightened editors as Luce, can be explained in this search for heroes. For many, Roosevelt was deified, elevated to the stature of a god among men—yet for many others, he was the embodiment of the anti-Christ, and counter-Roosevelt heroes had to be found. Stability, above all, was sought.

The press was buffeted by the same winds of change, searching out a role that seemed to fit the altered human environment. In this period of turbulence, as scientific advances spurred expanding technological growth, the gaining and maintenance of political and economic power demanded more pervasive instruments of social control. None was more readily available than the media of mass communications. Roosevelt found a mighty weapon at hand in the new technology of radio, turning to "fireside chats" to promote public support for his policies. Across the Atantic in Germany, Hitler's chief propagandist, Josef Goebbels, was at the same time converting the radio into a sinister instrument of Nazi propaganda.

THE INCREDIBLE SHRINKING READER

Sound, pictures, and digital combinations have overtaken books, newspapers, and magazines in popularity in our information society. The optimistic Marshall McLuhan has characterized this new society as the age of the global village, but this is a premature conclusion. In any case, despite its relative decline, the printed word is very much with us, still a major source of information and entertainment and also an indispensable tool for the wielders of power to use in controlling the world around them.

In the early twentieth century, both before and after the pivotal year of 1917, the newspaper was the chief instrument of public information, occupying a central position in the market economy and attracting the advertisers who were in the forefront of the rising consumer society. The great circulation contest between Pulitzer and Hearst had come to an end, but the struggle to boost newspaper readership continued, less to increase the number of readers than to deliver to advertisers a healthy audience for their products. The emergence of a feisty tabloid press following World War I sent circulation soaring to ever-greater heights. By 1920, adult readership of daily newspapers in the United States had climbed to an estimated 32 million.[6] The total reached 115 million half a century later; it was estimated that some 63 percent of American adults were daily newspaper readers.[7] Yet, as the final decade of the century arrived, circulation and readership were on a steadily declining slope, although the decline seemed to have bottomed out by 1993.[8] Average daily readership was up by about one-half of 1 percent; Sunday circulation declined slightly. Something similar was happening to advertising revenues. The fantastically lucrative years of the advertising industry boom had vanished in the 1990–92 recession. Agencies discovered they could downsize without serious injury to their operations.

Somewhere around the beginning of the twentieth century, circulation was overtaken by advertising as the primary source of income for the American press.[9] Advertising was no longer a mere adjunct to a business operation; it was itself a big business. In 1880, it was still a $200-million-a-year industry, but that figure had increased to $3.5 billion by the time of the 1929 stock-market crash.[10] As the twenti-

ATLAS JOE;

OR, THE FEARFUL RESPONSIBILITIES OF A SELF-APPOINTED MANAGER OF THE UNIVERSE.

Joseph Pulitzer runs the World.

SOURCE: Bettmann

eth century drew to a close, advertising had assumed a decisive role in just about every country on earth, including even those one-time bitter foes of capitalism in the communist world.

Just how important is the advertising dollar to the mass media today? A few statistics will suffice: Four-fifths of the income of American daily newspapers comes from advertising.[11] In 1992, dailies logged nearly $31 billion in advertising receipts, down from the $32.3-billion figure achieved a year earlier.[12] At the close of World War II in 1946, that figure had been only slightly more than $1 billion.

Despite the prominence gained by television in the mass media market, newspapers were still hanging on to their position as the leading vessel for the advertising dollar, with 24.1 percent of the total investment, compared with 21.7 percent for television. Direct mail produced 19.3 percent, magazines 5.2 percent, and radio 6.7 percent of the total.[13]

Although voices were raised from time to time challenging the ethics and business practices of the advertising industry, by the end of the twentieth century, only a handful of critics were questioning the institution itself. Condemnation of advertising "excesses" was common enough, but "excesses" are hard to define, and we don't usually find the complaints accompanied by a call for regulation or policing of advertising practices.

In any case, the question that had nagged at the soul of Horace Greeley midway through the nineteenth century—"once one allows himself to be subsidized by the unscrupulous advertisers, what becomes of the independence of journalism?"—was rarely being asked.[14] One who was deeply concerned about the influence of the advertising industry was Ben Bagdikian, a long-time journalist and journalism educator who had become the leading spokesperson for idealists complaining that the news media had become mere appendages of the nation's corporate power structure. "The media," he wrote, "are no longer neutral agents selling space and time for merchants to promote their wares but are now vital instruments needed by major corporations to maintain their economic and political power."[15]

Bagdikian's analysis was well known among students of the mass media, and he was justifiably revered in circles critical of the excesses of a market economy; though flying as he did in the face of the wielders of political and economic power, he was sometimes dismissed as a kind of crank. Yet the main thrust of his argument was scarcely to be disputed. He called attention, for example, to statements by media-acquisition experts who pointed out that investment in the mass media brought not only profit but also power and influence in high places.[16]

However we sliced it, it was supremely clear that fewer and fewer people were reading the daily newspaper. This development was a source of grave concern to the workers in the vineyard—the publishers, editors, and reporters—and to advertisers and readers who were interested in the news. The ramifications of what we can call the age of "the shrinking newspaper reader" are stunning. What, for example, is to become of that most basic of all democratic articles of faith—that it is on the basis of information citizens vote and otherwise play their part in the democratic process? If the daily newspaper dies or ceases to be an important factor in public life, what will replace it as a source of information, as an educational tool, or as a mechanism of social control? Can citizens rely on television to provide the information they need to carry out the requirements of the "democratic assumption"? What will become of the advertising industry if the daily newspaper disappears?

It is facile to blame the decline in newspaper readership and circulation on television. Obviously, the presence of television has had an impact on reading; but it is by no means clear that the time we now spend on viewing television would otherwise have been devoted to reading newspapers, magazines, or books. Furthermore, a case can be made that watching television actually induces us to read. Consider how avidly the sports enthusiast who has watched a game on TV reaches for his morning newspaper to check out whether the sportswriter saw the game the way he or she did.

The news media do not operate in a vacuum. They are creatures of their own time and their own social order. We cannot legitimately speak of the eighteenth-century press as newspapers in the same way we speak of today's. Nor, as a matter of fact, can we place the nineteenth-century press in the same basket as today's newspapers. The urban daily at the dawn of the twenty-first century is a giant industrial enterprise, prepared and delivered by individuals carrying out a wide variety of duties. No longer is there a Ben Day writing his articles, printing them, running his presses, and dashing out to the street corner to sell them. In fact, the marketing function of the newspaper has become decisive. Editors and publishers are saying it is only through that marketing function the daily newspaper might survive.

As the population of the country rose through the 1970s and 1980s, the circulation of daily newspapers stood still, locked in place at between 62 and 63 million copies, fixed as if someone had painted those figures on the hands of time and thrown away the brush. For Albert E. Gollin, research director of the Newspaper Advertising Bureau, the operative word was "stagnant."[17] The best course for survival, Gollin said, giving voice to a view shared by virtually all editors, publishers, and media analysts, was to pursue "a more market-driven strategy" in which newspapers became more sensitive to the needs and the wants of the reader.

The question of needs and wants was critical. For their role in carrying out the democratic assumption, it was the "needs" that counted. In this role, the function—indeed the very purpose—of the newspaper was to serve up the information readers simply had to have if they were going to play their part as citizens of a democratic society. What they *wanted* to read was not a crucial factor. They might want to read tidbits of gossip, whispers about what kind of sexual games celebrities were playing, about shocking crime and soap-opera romance and sideshow freaks; but about these matters they *needed* to know very little in order to play their part as democratic citizens.

Was it necessary in order for newspapers to regain readers, increase circulations, and raise their appeal to advertisers that they abandon their goal of providing needed information and make their appeal to the basest interests of the public, to what has often been spoken of as the lowest common denominator?

Gollin was one who said it wasn't necessary to abandon the high road, though at the same time he spoke of a need for changes in the corporate structure of newspapers and for breaking down the barriers that have always existed between the newsroom and the business office. Joseph Pulitzer had set a pattern for the separation a century earlier when he insisted on the necessity of keeping the business office out of the newsroom.[18]

Other newspaper doctors were even more insistent on change if the patient were going to survive. Steven Rattner, vice president of the investment firm Lazard

Frères, took the position that it made no financial sense to "give the people what they need and expect them to buy."[19] In turning away from the traditional daily press, Rattner said, the public had voted: "They don't want long analytical pieces."

The newspaper industry already had its model for a future of wants, not needs: *USA Today*, created by Al Neuharth, president of the Gannett Company, the largest newspaper chain in the country.[20] Directly challenging the most influential papers in the United States, Neuharth promised a national newspaper that offered a "new journalism of hope" in contrast with *The New York Times* and *The Washington Post*, which he said produced the "old journalism of despair . . . the derisive technique of leaving readers discouraged, or mad, or indignant."[21]

Anticipating Rattner's comment, Neuharth abandoned long analytical pieces; not only did *USA Today* place great emphasis on color, on easy-to-read layout, and on sections dealing with sports, weather, and money matters, but also it turned hard news into a series of short, punchy stories bolstered by bold and dramatic headlines. Neuharth defined his goal as covering "all of the news, with accuracy, but without anguish, with detail but without despair."

Not surprisingly, journalists and journalism scholars spoke out scornfully about Neuharth's concept. Jokes abounded. *USA Today*, it was said, would win a Pulitzer Prize for the best paragraph. Others called it McPaper, "the fast food of the newspaper business," tasty but without substance. The *New Republic* called it "expert marketing and mediocre journalism." Bagdikian said the paper represented a serious blow to journalism, giving readers a flawed picture of the world and showing "the primacy of packagers and market analysts in a realm where the news judgment of reporters and editors had traditionally prevailed."[22]

The goal, based on market research that depicted harried American workers unwilling to devote more than a fraction of their valuable time to reading newspapers, was to offer in newspaper pages a structure similar to 20- or 30-second television news reports with their even briefer sound bites from interviews.

Despite the criticism, *USA Today* flourished and soon was distributed worldwide. Even though it remained unprofitable for a decade, it ate in decreasing degree into Gannett's profits. By the 1990s, Gannett was averaging a profit margin of 11 percent.[23] The journalism of hope was paying off.

So was the sound-bite structure and the upscale layout promoted by *USA Today*. By 1991, the largest metropolitan newspaper in the country, *The Los Angeles Times*, flagship of the *Times Mirror* conglomerate, had replaced its emphasis on long analytical articles with shorter items stressing what its editors called "literary journalism." In addition, the editors put a new face on the newspaper, promoting it as a new and more entertaining "faster format" that featured packaged news shorts, bright graphics, and a Sunday magazine very much like a newsmagazine or *USA Today*.[24] The goal was to appeal to a national readership and to reach Los Angeles readers of diverse educational and ethnic backgrounds. By 1993, even the good gray *New York Times* was promoting color layouts.

As editors gathered in 1991 to discuss the future, their planning for the changes needed to combat declining readership emphasized Gollin's market-driven strategy. They were sobered by the results of an American Society of Newspaper

Editors (ASNE) survey showing that only 55 percent of the adult population could be counted as loyal readers of daily newspapers.[25] The report, appropriately titled "Keys to Our Survival," identified many of the others who remain potential readers as "at risk." Those persons and even a good number of the loyal readers were demanding items that were entertaining to read, went beyond the headlines, and focused on people rather than events. The "at-risk" group included busy, overburdened people prepared to read a daily only when it served as "a coping medium" to help them deal with the world around them rather than as a medium of information.[26] What was particularly worrisome to editors was the future, because a large percentage of the nonreaders were under thirty-five.[27]

The media analyst Kenneth T. Berents spoke to the 1992 ASNE convention about the approaching end of "the golden era of the newspaper business, but that didn't mean it was not still a good business." The daily press was packaging its news stories so readers in a hurry could keep up, mainly with local news. One popular convention workshop called itself "Fix Local News or Die!"[28] The session was in keeping with the move by editors to techniques downplaying the traditional function of informing or educating readers and stressing entertaining news reports and design that would lure audiences away from television.

Bill Kovach, curator of the Nieman Foundation, wondered whether such newspapers were relevant: "The more they devote to entertainment," he said, "the easier it is to pass the paper up." He sounded an even more ominous note: "I think the notion of giving people what they want in order to have an ever-growing market of consumers in order to boost your profit—well, I don't believe that's the reason the press is protected in this nation."[29]

Editors and publishers have consistently endorsed Kovach's appeal for newspapers to continue to provide the information people need to execute their democratic duties; at the same time, they have called attention to shrinking readership and pointed out that in order for them to carry out their democratic responsibilities it was necessary for them to survive economically. A blue-ribbon team studied the state of affairs for a year on behalf of the American Newspaper Publishers Association (ANPA) and issued a report offering its members a grab bag of ideas designed to counter the trends.[30]

Advertisers were going to seek out different markets if newspapers didn't provide the numbers they needed. Similar concern was expressed by the magazine industry, which was witnessing a switch in advertiser spending from print to billboards, direct mail, radio, and television.[31] The ANPA panel maintained that in order to survive and thrive, newspapers had to perform a balancing act that satisfied the needs of both readers and advertisers, needs that were sometimes in concert, sometimes in conflict: "The better newspapers satisfy the needs of both groups. They balance their First Amendment obligations and social responsibility with the pressures of competition, advertiser wishes and profitability. But the two needs are intertwined: Newspapers cannot serve the public interest unless they are managed efficiently and are profitable."[32]

The report offered a wide variety of suggestions based on a strategy of keeping a clear eye on both the market and the needs and wants of readers. Individual editors

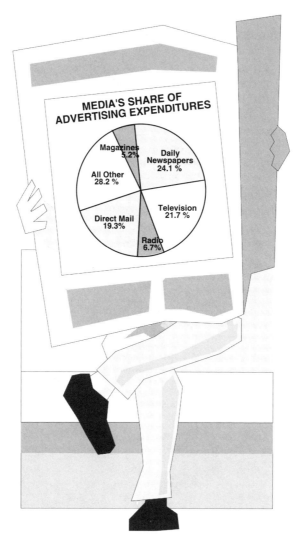

SOURCE: Newspaper Association of America

and advertisers came up with additional strategies. Some of them sounded bizarre, like that of *The Syracuse News-Journal*, which tried to cope with the sharp decline in readership among teenagers by issuing weekly sections on youth, including special pages captioned "Hi" and "Yo knucklehead."[33] Other papers have introduced weekly sections on topics ranging from skateboarding to safe sex, but the youth crowd is a tough nut to crack. Some editors complained of teenage illiteracy. Teenagers countered that newspapers were boring. Judy McGrath, executive vice president of MTV, the music video channel, said the feeling among teenagers was that newspapers were "written and produced by and for a bunch of old white people."[34]

Editors, publishers, and researchers were pushing some exotic solutions: These included suggestions from a think tank at the University of Missouri, whose proposals included a news digest wrapped around papers and even a newspaper that smelled like baked bread. *The Minneapolis Star-Tribune* launched a news digest distributed to businesspeople by fax. "We've got to experiment with other ways of delivering information than dropping dead trees on people's porches," commented business editor Larry Werner.[35]

Television was a factor, although not the only one in the shrinking newspaper readership. The printed press was confronted with a variety of changes that amounted to a kind of social reorganization. These changes, said Al Gollin of the Newspaper Advertising Bureau, meant the medium was "changing its character."[36] The flight of affluent Americans to the suburbs changed readership patterns and caused advertisers to rethink ways of reaching their markets. Moreover, young women—the primary shoppers in American homes, at one time easy targets for advertisers—and mothers who once had time to read the paper, clip the ads, and go to the store were now out of the house and on the job. Eighty percent of women from twenty-five to forty-five had jobs out of the home, a factor that resulted in a more pronounced decline in readership among women than men. High-income white men are considered the most loyal daily newspaper readers in the country.

Afternoon newspapers were vanishing altogether, victims of competition from the evening TV news and the complexity of making home deliveries through jammed city streets. Sunday circulation climbed sharply until leveling off in 1992. Advertising inserts boosted Sunday newspaper profits. Weeklies, with local shopping ads, made early increases but foundered against opposition from cable television, direct mail, and zoned editions put out by metropolitan dailies. A 40-percent decline in advertising revenue over three years forced Chicago's Pulitzer Publishing Company to give up on 15 of its suburban weeklies, a move that cost 150 jobs.[37] The main sufferer among newspapers, however, was the all-purpose daily. Some analysts thought it was on the way out altogether. Major newspapers cut their staffs sharply. Inducing early retirement, papers paid staffers to surrender their jobs through a "buyout" process. *The Los Angeles Times*, the largest daily in the country, suffered a 16.5 percent decline in advertising revenue between 1991 and 1993 and launched a major buyout, paying $16 million to buy up contracts of 668 of its 7,500 employees.[38]

Certainly, profits were down.[39] Earnings fell steadily during 1992 but began to level off as the deep recession receded. More than a few newspapers went out of business altogether, among them the century-old *San Diego Tribune*, an afternoon paper that merged into the city's morning paper, both owned by the Copley Press. Among the other 1991 failures were afternoon papers in Richmond, Roanoke, and Newport News, all in Virginia, and Charleston, South Carolina.[40] Even with the failures of afternoon papers, the prophets of gloom and doom were exaggerating. Profits were down from their high mark, but the daily newspaper was still a paying proposition.

Magazines shared the difficulties encountered by daily newspapers. Three-fourths of magazines tracked by the Publishers Information Bureau declined in the number of ad pages sold between 1989 and 1990; the decline continued into 1991 and 1992.[41] Magazine editors, their backs against the wall, according to Betsy Carter, editor in chief of *New York Woman* magazine, were also seeking out new strategies for survival. *Time* changed its format abruptly in 1991, cutting its staff, adding the most modern graphics techniques, reducing the length of its stories, and in general turning to more "human interest" stories than ever appeared in Luce's day. The chairman of the publishing division of Time Warner, successor to the Luce empire, said *Time* and its sister publications were now more "interesting and full of energy and full of all the reasons that people buy magazines."[42] One disturbing ploy on the part of some magazines was to accept payments from advertisers for promoting products in supposedly objective news and editorial columns. After looking into the ploy for the American Society of Magazine Editors, Betsy Carter concluded, "There's a sense in the industry of trying to please advertisers, and that stretches into areas that are questionable." Furthermore, she said, "advertisers know they've got us."[43]

The advertising industry was having troubles of its own. After sixteen years of unparalleled growth, including widespread expansion from national to international operations, advertising agencies began to retrench in 1991. The U.S. Department of Labor reported there were 6,300 fewer ad agency jobs in June 1991 than a year earlier, a drop of 3.7 percent.[44] Still, 137,000 people were at work in ad agencies and 223,400 in the industry as a whole. The recession was given as one explanation, but it wasn't the only factor; clients were benefiting from technological changes that enabled them to turn to computers rather than human help. Moreover, they were not only reducing their budgets for advertising but also turning away from paying hefty 15-percent commissions to agency staffers and going in for quick-hit promotions like coupons and sweepstakes.

The changes in the social order did nothing to weaken the power of commercial forces in the world of newspapers and magazines and, as we shall see shortly, among broadcast media as well. In fact, these changes solidified the power base of commercial forces in all corners of the world, for the changes occurring in the United States were occurring everywhere, even in less heavily industrialized countries. The behavior of some magazines was especially blatant, openly presenting commercial material as if it were news; other media were more circumspect but nonetheless dependent on revenues from advertisers.

The pattern is not a new one. It is simply clearer than ever before that the media of communications are vital instruments to be used by the wielders of power. At the close of the century, corporations were less direct about their ideological and power imperatives than they had been a generation earlier. In 1936, Proctor & Gamble, the largest U.S. advertiser, acknowledged its ads were promoting not only its products but its ideological viewpoints as well. It said this at government hearings called to check into how much influence advertisers were exerting on the noncommercial content of radio and television.[45]

In the 1990s, when advertising was reaching saturation levels, especially in television, marketers came up with a new slant to attract customers: so-called point-of-purchase politics. In this effort, certain products were linked with certain causes, many of them politically liberal, in order to gain credibility with socially conscious readers and viewers. For instance, a new vodka imported from Georgia by Heublein was introduced in ads announcing sponsorship of an AIDS Danceathon organized by the Gay Men's Health Crisis; and a chain of cosmetics stores, Body Shop International, displayed ads criticizing the testing of cosmetics on animals. Some critics condemned point-of-purchase politics as cynical and opportunistic; yet others, such as Dan Osheyack, promotion director for the Time Warner magazine *Entertainment Weekly*, which links its programs to fighting AIDS, called it "the right thing to do" on behalf of the interests of the magazine's readers.[46]

Marketers were clearly striving for sincerity and new ways of inducing customers to buy. But the campaigns could backfire. Sears, Roebuck, for instance, encountered a problem after it had pledged 8 percent of its proceeds from catalog sales of certain stuffed animals to the Humane Society of the United States. The National Rifle Association protested, and Sears stopped selling the animals.

NOTES

1. W. A. Swanberg, *Luce and His Empire* (New York: Scribner's, 1972), 181–82. Quotations from Luce in this paragraph are drawn from Swanberg. His account is breezier if less authoritative than the standard examination of Luce and the growth of *Time* magazine or the two-volume unauthorized work by Robert T. Elson, *Time Inc.: The Intimate History of a Publishing Enterprise 1923–1960* (New York: Atheneum, 1968 and 1973).

2. Swanberg, *Luce and His Empire*, 430–43, cites this among a number of assessments of Luce.

3. For a thorough examination of this period of American journalism, see Marvin Olasky, *Central Ideas in the Development of American Journalism* (Hillsdale, NJ: Lawrence Erlbaum, 1991). See also David R. Nord, "Teleology and the News: The Religious Roots of American Journalism, 1630–1730," *Journal of American History* (June 1990).

4. "One More Time: Magazine Is Reborn," *New York Times*, April 13, 1992.

5. Edward Bernays, *Crystallizing Public Opinion* (New York: Boni and Liveright, 1923).

6. Alfred McClung Lee, *The Daily Newspaper in America: The Evolution of a Social Instrument* (New York: Farrar, Straus & Giroux (Octagon Books, 1973), 726.

7. *Facts About Newspapers '92: A Statistical Summary of the Newspaper Business,* (Washington, D.C.: American Newspaper Publishers Association, 1993), 5. Sunday readership had reached 68 percent of adult population. Hereafter cited as *Facts*.

8. Albert H. Gollin, interview with the author, New York, February 22, 1993.

9. William J. Thorn, *Newspaper Circulation: Marketing the News,* (White Plains, NY: Longman, 1987), 44–45. The best historical account of the newspaper as a business can be found in Lee, *The Daily Newspaper in America*.

10. Ben H. Bagdikian, *The Media Monopoly*, 3rd ed. (Boston: Beacon Press, 1980), 149. He draws these figures from the Bureau of the Census, *Historical Statistics*, vol. 2, 855. The depression toll was heavy. By 1933, advertising revenue had fallen 45 percent. But it regained its health and strengthened itself as the impact of the depression declined. See

Edwin Emery and Henry Ladd Smith, *The Press and America*, 1st ed. (New York: Prentice-Hall, 1954), 665.

11. Thorn, *Newspaper Circulation*, 45.

12. *Facts*, 10.

13. *Facts*, 10. Other areas included farm publications, business publications, billboards, and the yellow pages of the telephone directory. National advertising accounted for 57.5 percent of the total and local advertising 42.5 percent.

14. Gamaliel Bradford, "Horace Greeley," in *As God Made Them: Portraits of Some Nineteenth-Century Americans* (Port Washington, NY: Kennikat Press, 1929), 121-53. Despite accepting advertising in his paper, Greeley considered advertisers among a band of social oppressors who resisted progress and especially Greeley's program of social reforms. In contrast, a contemporary editor, Henry Raymond of *The New York Times*, argued the market system was a safeguard against the social evils that resulted from the corruption in man's heart. The "Great Debate" fought between Greeley and Raymond in the pages of their newspapers in 1846 and 1847 is described in Olasky, *Central Ideas*, 70-78. For additional information on Greeley's views, see J. Herbert Altschull, *From Milton to McLuhan: The Ideas Behind American Journalism* (White Plains, NY: Longman, 1990), 209.

15. Bagdikian, *Media Monopoly*, 151.

16. Bagdikian, 11. Bagdikian quotes Christopher Shaw, a Wall Street acquisitions expert, as making this assertion to potential media investors in 1986. I can confirm similar statements made in the 1990s.

17. Albert E. Gollin, interview with the author, March 21, 1991.

18. George Juergens, *Joseph Pulitzer and the World* (Princeton, NJ: Princeton University Press, 1966).

19. Steven Rattner, interview with the author, March 20, 1991. Rattner, who specialized in media acquisitions, was influential in arranging the sale of the troubled *New York Daily News* to the late British media mogul Robert Maxwell in the spring of 1991.

20. For an in-house account of the birth and rise of *USA Today*, see Peter Prichard, *The Making of McPaper: The Inside Story of USA Today* (Kansas City, MO: Andrews, McMeel, & Parker, 1987).

21. Prichard, *Making of McPaper*, 293. In his October 1983 speech a year after launching *USA Today*, Neuharth defined his "journalism of hope" as offering an approach that "chronicles the good, the bad, and the otherwise, and leaves readers fully informed and equipped to judge what deserves their attention and support."

22. Prichard, *Making of McPaper*, 8, 22.

23. *Forbes*, January 7, 1991, 155.23.22.

24. Susan Tifft, "Hello, Sweetheart! Get Me Remake!," *Time*, April 15, 1991, 46-47.

25. Thomas B. Rosenstiel, "Editors Debate Need to Redefine America's Newspapers," *Los Angeles Times*, April 13, 1991.

26. Cameron Barr, "Newspaper Goals: Editor Sees Ways to Gain Readers," *The Christian Science Monitor*, April 11, 1991.

27. Rosenstiel, "Editors Debate."

28. James Bock, "Editors Ponder Future of Newspapering," *The Evening Sun*, Baltimore, March 31, 1993.

29. Eleanor Randolph, "Extra! Extra! Who Cares?," *Washington Post*, April 1, 1990.

30. American Newspaper Publishers Association, *A Way to Win: Strategies to Evaluate and Improve Your Readership and Circulation* (Washington, D.C., 1990). The report was sponsored jointly by the ANPA and the Newspaper Advertising Bureau. The organization has since renamed itself the American Newspaper Association.

31. *New York Times*, February 13, 1991. The article "Magazines Hurt by Shift in Ad Plans" reported a gloomy study by Myers Marketing and Research of Parsippany, NJ. The study, based on interviews with leading executives and researchers, held that the pressures on the magazine industry were systemic and not the result of the recession.

32. *New York Times*, February 13, 1991.

33. Randolph, "Extra! Extra!"

34. Bock, "Editors Ponder Future of Newspapering."

35. Randolph, "Extra! Extra!"

36. Gollin interview, March 21, 1991. Gollin said it was crucial for the newspaper industry to recognize that all institutions had to change to operate successfully in a reorganized society. Since, Gollin said, there are no more general readers, editors must learn to appeal to diverse interests to reach both mass and target audiences so that these audiences can be made available to advertisers.

37. Alex S. Jones, "Suburban Weeklies Hit by Rivals and Recession," *New York Times*, August 24, 1992.

38. Calvin Sims, "Ads Down, *Los Angeles Times* Again Cuts Staff," *New York Times*, February 1, 1993.

39. Net income declines that had marked the newspaper scene in 1990 continued into 1991 and 1992, sharpened by the persistent recession.

40. *New York Times*, September 23, 1991. Neil Morgan, editor of *The Tribune*, said the action was "a dollar and cents move."

41. Lloyd Shearer, "World of Magazine Advertising," *Parade*, December 23, 1990; Joanne Lipman, "Hurt by Ad Downturn More Magazines Use Favorable Articles to Woo Sponsors," *The Wall Street Journal*, July 30, 1991. Shearer listed the top five in the number of advertising pages sold in 1990 as *Business Week, People, Forbes, Bride's,* and *Fortune*.

42. *New York Times*, September 23, 1991.

43. Joanne Lipman, "Number of Jobs in Advertising Declines 3.7%," *The Wall Street Journal*, August 5, 1991. For example, according to the article, *Gaming Monthly*, published by the Sendai Publishing Group, claimed its revenue from ad pages had increased by 500 percent in less than a year partly because it began selling article lookalikes to advertisers.

44. Lipman.

45. Bagdikian, *Media Monopoly*, 156–59.

46. Stuart Elliott, "When Products Are Tied to Causes," *New York Times*, April 18, 1992.

Chapter
6

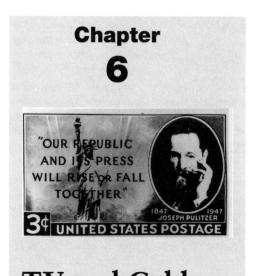

"OUR REPUBLIC AND ITS PRESS WILL RISE OR FALL TOGETHER"

1847 1947
JOSEPH PULITZER

3¢ UNITED STATES POSTAGE

TV and Cable:
The Fabulous Rise of Ted Turner

TV COMES OF AGE

In the contemporary world, the newspaper has been forced to yield primacy to its newer, gaudier cousin: broadcasting. As instruments of social control, radio and television are perhaps the most effective ever conceived. It has become common-place to say that most people get most of their information or "news" from televi-sion. Although this may not be strictly accurate—most people probably get most of their news from other people—it is correct that the broadcasting media dominate the lives of human beings more than any previous medium of communication. Small wonder that those who wield power try to control or regulate the broadcast media in their territory or those who seek to wrest power strike first at radio and television outlets. Small wonder also that advertisers pour ever-increasing resources into trumpeting their messages over the air.

Television's share of the money that goes into advertising in the United States has risen steadily over the years. By 1992, it had reached $27.4 billion, nearly 22 percent of the amount spent on advertising in the country. The total had not yet eclipsed that of newspapers, but it was coming steadily closer.[1]

By the 1990s, the pattern of sharp increases in growth and profitability of net-works and their affiliates had leveled off. Advertising revenues of local television stations was advancing, but at a rate slower than that of advances by syndicated shows.[2] Major networks were barely holding their own. Agencies were downsizing. The industry had never been constant. The greatest threat to their stability and profitability was coming from advances in technology, which were threatening their very existence. High-tech developments promised new and remarkably lucrative opportunities for programming fed along coaxial cable lines under ground, by distant signals from satellites in space, and through digital messages streaking through unimaginably thin strands of fiber optics. Telephone companies were moving in as competitors.

Those newspapers that survive fierce competition from both the electronic media and their own colleagues strengthen their position in the economy and in political influence. Still, among the media, it is broadcasting that has hastened the triumph of capitalism in the United States, Japan, and Western Europe, as well as in many of their less-developed client states in Africa and Asia.

New opportunities for advertisers arose in the expanding economies of the Third World. The collapse of the Soviet empire and the breakaway from Soviet domination of the countries of eastern Europe seemingly offered immense promise to advertisers eager to move into wholly new markets; it offered the same to those capitalist ideologues who had learned to use broadcast outlets as tools of incalculable power in promoting and expanding support for the market system of economics and beliefs. That is not to say the capitalist journalists who report news for television were pliant mouthpieces for commercial enterprises and their advertising agencies. It is to say, however, that as members of a market society they subtly, often unwittingly, served as agents for transmission of the economic and political values of that society. Third World journalists were joining their colleagues from the industrialized world as boosters of a free-market social order.

In the United States, the model of capitalism, the radio and television industries developed differently from the broadcasting industries of other industrialized countries. When radio appeared early in the twentieth century, the governments of Western Europe placed the new medium under their control. In some instances, government officials were in direct charge of media financing and content. In others, notably Great Britain, control was placed in the hands of public corporations ultimately responsible to the government but with a substantial degree of latitude, especially in programming content. In the socialist world, radio financing, distribution, and programming came under ministerial direction. Governments of the scores of new nations that emerged when colonial empires tumbled after World War II found it prudent to take complete control of their radio and television facilities.

By contrast, in the United States, private commercial interests were permitted to develop and profit from broadcasting as they wished. The result was one of the most lucrative financial channels to wealth ever to appear in America. Those who got in on the ground floor of radio and television made fortunes and established a pattern of programming that was to stress attracting the maximum audiences. These audiences were then delivered to the advertisers, who promoted their wares in what soon came to be a national marketplace. It was obvious from the outset that entertainment in the form of programs featuring comedy, popular music, vaudeville, quizzes, and light drama drew the maximum audience. More and more listeners and viewers tuned in also to news shows, but news was always treated more superficially there than in the printed press, and the personalities delivering the news bulletins rapidly emerged as celebrities. Radio and television networks soon became the most visible instruments of communication and the most widely heeded. A new name was applied to the press—media, which included the broadcasting networks and stations.[3]

The three networks that emerged victorious in the years of financial skirmishing, ABC, CBS, and NBC, operated programming empires and also owned a number of radio and television stations in the nation's largest, richest "markets." Challengers emerged in time. The most striking was from the world of cable television, especially Ted Turner's Cable News Network (CNN). Other pretenders took on the big guys, including the Fox system, operated by the Australian media baron Rupert Murdoch.

The profits of all television-franchise owners were substantial, but those of the network-owned stations were the greatest of all. Each of the stations owned and operated by the networks regularly returned profits of more than a million dollars a year before taxes. In 1980, a network affiliate in mid-sized Dayton, Ohio, was sold for $40 million; one in the somewhat larger market of Sacramento, California, went for $65 million. By 1990, a network affiliate in Baltimore, Maryland, was sold at a figure between $125 million and $154.7 million.[4]

Jokesters found TV station profits amusing. One witticism had it that ownership of a television station was "a license to print money." The money could be "printed" from the immoderate fees charged for advertising messages. A thirty-second spot during the 1992 Super Bowl went for $800,000; 42 million homes were tuned in. A half-minute commercial on network prime time that year cost $106,400.

Murdoch launched his Fox Broadcasting enterprise in 1986 as an irritant to the networks, linking a small coterie of independent stations and offering primarily warmed-over entertainment fare. By the mid-1980s, however, Fox had entered legitimate claims as a fourth network. And that wasn't all. In late 1993, Paramount Communications and Warner Brothers announced they, too, were creating broadcast networks. Like Fox, Paramount and Warner planned networks around a dozen or so independent stations and their substantial supply of old movies. We will turn later to a close examination of the new global media giants and their multibillion-dollar takeover maneuvering, all of it posing new threats or challenges (depending on your way of looking at it) to the business of news and the establishment of public policy. In any case, the traditional networks presented a brave face. They pointed to their continuing—if declining—dominance in rating points. And Audrey Steele, a researcher for Saatchi & Saatchi, a dominant global advertising firm, observed wryly that the death of the networks had been long hyped, but they were "still the only medium that [could] deliver a mass audience."[5] She was referring to the pattern of "niche" programming delivered by cable to narrow and specialized audiences, comparable to the appeal of local FM radio stations and special-interest magazines.

Traditional network news programs, however profitable they may have been over the years, were never able to compete on the level of the top entertainment shows. Still, historically, the most profitable time periods for *local* programming were the local news shows, especially the late programs at eleven o'clock. Audience research showed that typical viewers of local news programs on network affiliates were among the best-educated and most prosperous people in town. Because local stations could offer advertisers their favorite customers during the news-show time periods, those stations were also able to demand their highest prices for commercial messages at those times. Even with the 1990–92 advertising slump, local shows continued to pull in the dollars. In the Washington, D.C., market, one of the nation's most lucrative, the top-rated station sold thirty seconds of commercial time on its late news show for $2,600; its total advertising take for the eleven o'clock show for a week came to $208,000. The recession took its toll, however. Marketing experts said profit margins for commercial TV stations fell in a decade from 40 percent into single figures.[6]

Operators of the publicly owned television networks in other capitalist countries could only shake their heads in wonder at the volume of money changing hands in the U.S. broadcasting business, whose profits exceeded even those of heavy industry. The head shaking was being replaced by smiles, however, as more and more of the public television systems became privately owned in all parts of the world. Even while ownership of television facilities was passing into the hands of private investors and corporations in much of the capitalist world, broadcasting continued to be financed largely by revenue from taxes paid by owners of the receivers. Those who defended public financing argued persuasively that relying on commercial advertisers lowered the cultural level of the product; they insisted public ownership is in the public interest. However, before the end of the 1970s, nearly all television systems in the capitalist world had been forced to permit some commercial advertising to supplement their incomes.

Meanwhile, the U.S. television product came under steady and unrelenting attack. In 1961, Newton Minow, chairman of the Federal Communications Commission (FCC), the agency charged with regulating television, called television "a vast wasteland." Thirty years later, Minow lamented that, despite its promise, television had become "a severely distorting influence" on American life. He said it gave off only "a dim light in education," that it had failed to benefit the lives of children and had cast "a dark shadow" over the nation's electoral process. Like others, Minow said it had dropped the level of communication to "the lowest common denominator in the marketplace."[7] From one end of the country to the other, and indeed around the globe, it became popular to blame television for almost everything from lowered scholastic achievement by high-school students to the reported increase in crime rates. All these assertions were exaggerated, for television was only a part, albeit a critical one, of the world's social environment. What was not exaggerated, however, was the profitability of television and the role the medium had come to play in the capitalist economic system and in its ideological orientation. In fact, the conquest of other ideologies by the marketplace was due in no small degree to the ubiquity of television.

When Reed E. Hundt was sworn in as the new FCC chairman in 1993, he did not repeat Newton Minow's gloom over the course of U.S. television, but he did issue a veiled warning to the corporate ownership. That ownership, he said, builds networks to a point where they are economically optimal, but "market mechanisms will not lead to networks being built to the optimal social point."[8] The implication was that the government would step in if it must in order to promote broader social goals.

Not surprisingly, viewers grumble over the frequency of commercials and complain about the simplistic content of many TV programs. It is doubtful, however, viewers are prepared to eliminate commercials in favor of government or direct corporate control of the medium. As media managers have pointed out, they need significant advertising revenues if they are to turn out distinguished products. Without substantial profit, they have argued, they would be forced to depress salaries so severely the media could ill afford to hire the best people for the jobs; moreover, they could not purchase the most modern cameras and sophisticated electronic gear.

Critics of the system have often acknowledged the rationale but complained the profits were unnecessarily high and so much attention was paid to profits that sight was lost of genuine concern about the public interest. No one expressed this viewpoint more poignantly than the late Edward R. Murrow, often revered as the greatest of all television journalists, especially for his tough and courageous exposé of the methods and behavior of Senator Joseph McCarthy. Speaking to the Radio and Television News Directors Association in 1958, Murrow, who was then quarreling with his network, CBS, argued that the public interest should carry greater weight than the demand for private profits: "There is no suggestion here that networks or individual stations should operate as philanthropies. But I can find nothing in the Bill of Rights or the Communications Act which says they must increase their profits each year, lest the Republic collapse." Murrow said television had the opportunity to "teach, illuminate . . . even inspire." Failure to do so, he maintained, would mean the industry was nothing but "wires and lights in a box."[9] Thirty-five years later, CBS anchorman Dan Rather censured news directors for failing to fight for Murrow's dream. "We all should be ashamed," he told the Radio and Television News Directors Association.[10]

Murrow's argument was not with making profit or with the free-enterprise system. His objection was to *maximization* of profit at the expense of the public interest. Like Murrow, other critics of television in capitalist societies complained the search for advertising dollars pushed the broadcasting medium into filling consumers with unnecessary and unrealistic desires in order to sell the advertised products. Because products advertised on television so often resembled one another closely, advertisers were convinced that success or failure depended primarily on the effectiveness of the commercial messages seen on television. The more interesting, the more entertaining the message, they believed, the greater the sales potential. The same was true of news programming. The popularity or entertainment quotient of the anchorperson became a stronger selling point than the quality of the news reports.[11]

Rather spoke nothing but the truth when he called the news directors cowardly for permitting network news to switch its emphasis from serious information to crime, violence, sex, and celebrity gossip. That kind of emphasis promoted profits yet did little to serve the needs of the public. He recognized that challenging the bottom line could cost them their jobs, and he said he wasn't asking for that—just to "make noise" and take chances by choosing substance over "sleaze and glitz." It was, Rather said to enthusiastic applause, "showbizzification" that resulted. "Just to cover our ass," he said, "we give the best slots to gossip and prurience."[12]

The news directors may have agreed with Rather and Murrow, though like all supporters of the commercial marketplace, they recognized advertising as a powerful democratic force leading to a society of abundance. From this perspective, it was the consumers who called the tune, and the advertisers and news media followed the public lead by putting on the market what the consumers really wanted, to their own benefit. In this sense, the argument went, the consumers were the "voters" in a democratic system casting their ballots at the cash register. This form of "balloting" materialized in the ratings systems of A. C. Nielsen and others.

Established rules required the FCC to see to it that holders of radio and television licenses used those licenses "in the public interest, convenience, and necessity." Under the regulations, a station owner had to convince the FCC he or she intended to operate the radio or TV station in the public interest in order to receive a license. When the license was up for renewal, the owner had to demonstrate he or she had actually operated in the public interest. At first, licenses had to be renewed every three years; later, the time was extended to seven years. Only rarely has the FCC refused to renew a license; and in nearly all those cases, the refusal was ordered because of false statements in applications or other flagrant behavior. The most dramatic case of revocation was ordered not by the FCC but by a federal court and only after the FCC had twice refused the federal court's "suggestions" to act. The case involved WLBT-TV of Jackson, Mississippi, which had operated its license in utter disregard of the interests of African-Americans in its viewing area.[13] Whether broadcasting programs catered to the lowest tastes or whether they offered nothing but a vast wasteland to their viewers was not considered in renewal applications. The content of the specific programming was outside FCC control. Control of programming content belonged to the owners of licenses as part of their First Amendment protection.

The free-press guarantees of the First Amendment were not extended in wholesale fashion to broadcasters. By law, the finite broadcasting spectrum is considered to be owned by the public; hence, no one may operate on a piece of that spectrum without a license from the government.[14] Since the owners of broadcasting facilities, unlike the owners of newspapers and magazines, could not operate without an FCC license, they did not receive the same free-press guarantees possessed by their brethren in the print media. The rationale was the scarcity principle: Because there were physical restraints on the number of broadcasting outlets, not all Americans had an equal opportunity to acquire a radio or TV station. For decades, broadcasters viewed this status as second-class citizenship, a demon to be exorcised. In particular, broadcasters resented the Fairness

Doctrine, first enunciated in 1949, which required that broadcasters air contro-versial public issues and make sure their coverage of those issues was fair to all points of view.

The requirement was rarely enforced partly because the FCC staff was too small to police the requirement. More significantly, the FCC (like most government regulatory agencies) cooperated with more than policed the industry it was empowered to regulate. The columnist Jack Anderson spoke of the FCC as "little more than a retriever for the networks. The network executives soothingly stroked its fur, confident that Congress would keep the watchdog from biting."[15]

Few doubt the influence of the television networks on members of Congress, who were required regularly to run for reelection and whose "images" on the screen were thought to represent one of the decisive factors in voters' decisions. Congress had the power, if it chose to use it, to increase the authority of the FCC and direct it to enforce rigorously the Fairness Doctrine and the requirement that broadcasters operate in the public interest. To do so, however, would have sub-jected those Congress members who voted to extend the FCC grip on the industry to criticism on the air. Few of them could be expected to take this risk. By limiting the restraints on broadcasters, Congress members reasonably might have expected to receive favorable attention on television. A kind of three-cornered manipulation mechanism was at work here, with pressures generated by broadcasting execu-tives, the FCC, and Congress. The interests of the public came last.

However powerful broadcasters may have been in other areas, they were for decades unsuccessful in attacking the Fairness Doctrine, which required an "objec-tivity" not required of print media. Broadcasters found allies in President Reagan and deregulation. In 1987 Reagan-appointed FCC members threw out the doctrine, arguing that the rules had frustrated the original purpose of the doctrine and had caused broadcasters to shy away from covering controversial issues.[16]

The Reagan FCC agreed with broadcasters who had been pointing out for years that because the rules had forced them to air all sides of issues, they had often avoided controversial issues and instead limited their editorial observations for the most part to the tried and true: urging highway safety, condemning criminals, pro-moting clean air and clean water. Television stations had from time to time endorsed candidates for office and attacked the wicked; but, under FCC rules, they were required to give all those condemned or criticized an opportunity for fair reply, an opportunity that inevitably ate into the profits of the stations, for such programming could not be sold. The end result, as the FCC concluded in its 1987 decision, was that the content of TV programming was notably bland. The thrust of television had been inevitably toward the middle, toward the safe, toward the prof-itable. As Newton Minow observed in his 1991 speech, television, rather than aim-ing to lead the country in the direction of the public interest as it was obligated to do, was instead operating as "a reactive mirror" of that society.

The case that led the FCC to overthrow the Fairness Doctrine involved an appeal by the Syracuse (New York) Peace Council, which argued that a Syracuse TV station had failed to follow the doctrine when it aired a series of advertisements supporting a nuclear power plant and refused to balance those ads with reports critical of the plant. In repealing the doctrine, the FCC ruled the policy violated the free-speech guarantees of the First Amendment; moreover, the FCC held that in an age when many voices could now be heard in broadcasting, the Fairness Doctrine no longer served the public interest.

Congress, which had long been reluctant to overturn the Fairness Doctrine through legislation, now acted to save it. By a hefty but not veto-proof margin, Congress passed legislation that would have written the Fairness Doctrine into law. As expected, President Reagan vetoed the measure, denouncing it as "antagonistic to the freedom of expression guaranteed" by the Constitution.[17] Congress failed to muster the two-thirds vote necessary to override the veto.[18] When Democrat Bill Clinton moved into the White House in 1993, a number of members spoke of reviving the Fairness Doctrine, though the body as a whole seemed unwilling to challenge the news industry.

Despite the growth of interest in investigative journalism, political and economic realities contributed to timidity and lack of adventurousness on the part of television. At times broadcasters acted contrary to their economic interests when they took on vested power and risked their own profitability.[19] Networks and broadcast stations do occasionally bite the hand that is feeding them, but the cases are few and seem not to interfere markedly with industry profitability.

CNN: SOMETHING NEW UNDER THE SUN

The networks, holdovers from the days when radio held sway in the United States, had the nationwide TV airwaves all to themselves until technological advances made it cheap enough for cable- and antenna-driven communications to challenge them, just as frequency-modulated (FM) facilities had taken on standard radio broadcasters following World War II. Turmoil over potential collision between positions on the broadcast spectrum caused the FCC to "freeze" television frequency allocations in 1948, and until those positions were unfrozen six years later, the enterprising entrepreneurs who had acquired licenses early in the game enjoyed monopoly ownership in their local markets.

The potential for profit was almost unimaginable. By 1960 in the United States, no fewer than nine households in ten could boast at least one television set. When the freeze went into force, the FCC had issued only 160 permits to construct television facilities. Thirteen years later, 531 stations were in operation. TV was slower to invade other countries. Everywhere other than in the United States, governments retained control of the television spectrum rather than licensing segments of it to private, profit-making companies.[20]

The technology of broadcasting also advanced rapidly, and by 1951 it was possible to air programs across the entire country by relaying signals electronically from one local station to another. The networks needed the local network affiliates, and the local affiliates needed the networks. The mutually profitable arrangement enabled the networks and their affiliates to dominate the television landscape completely—until fresh technology allowed network competitors to move into the market, drawing on the narrow spectrum that had made FM radio broadcasts possible. In 1962, the launching of Telstar, the first communications satellite, paved the way.

The cable industry emerged shortly afterward, but its beginnings were halting, and few investors were willing to risk their money on the new scheme. The Community Antenna Television System (CATV) aimed at relaying signals to remote areas not easily reachable by the familiar over-the-air radio signals. It was found, however, that coaxial cables, used at first as telephone relay mechanisms, could carry hundreds of narrow signals. Later technology established that fiber-optic systems could use even narrower beams of light as transmission tools, and the number of potential signals rose geometrically. Despite the slowness of cable development, the networks remained fearful of the incipient competition.

And well they might. By 1992, no less than 62 percent of TV households including more than 57 million homes in the United States were able to receive cablecasts; pay cable, composed largely of recent films and sports events, could be received in 30 percent of those households.[21] Of the total television advertising pie, the cable share came to 9 percent. At the same time, the networks' share of

The global village.

SOURCE: Robert Grossman, *The Nation*

the advertising revenue from the television market slumped precipitously. As a result, their standing in the competition for rating points tumbled. The future promised more gains for cable and further declines for the networks. Viewership of syndicated programs, largely old sitcoms, and including the product of Fox Broadcasting, a division of Rupert Murdoch's conglomerate empire, were also on the rise. By the beginning of 1994, viewership on network affiliates and on cable-casts was virtually identical.[22]

The FCC at first protected the over-the-air networks and stations from cable competition, but in 1972 it issued new rules allowing cable systems to import signals from far away to augment their services. Within four years, pay television had arrived, pioneered by *Time*, Henry Luce's brainchild, in the form of Home Box Office (HBO). Dozens of other cable operators dreamed of challenging the mighty networks. And soon they were on the air. As the end of the century approached, the average television household in major markets was offering the viewer thirty-seven channels, most of them cable channels.

The most remarkable of the cable entrepreneurs was Robert Edward (Ted) Turner III, a cocky, adventurous businessman who successfully defied the networks, which had hitherto been thought to be impervious to challenge. It is testimonial to the difference between print and broadcast journalism that what the patrician recluse Henry Luce had been to print, the self-made bombast Ted Turner should be to broadcasting. Between Luce and Turner, news per se had been replaced by news as entertainment. Luce and Turner were visionaries; each imagined and then pioneered a future in the news media that revamped the underlying structure of news. Luce introduced ensemble journalism; Turner introduced the concept of global news. In 1991, *Time* magazine, now merged into the media conglomerate Time Warner, proclaimed Turner the magazine's "man of the year." His Cable News Network (CNN), *Time* declared, had "changed the way the world does its business."[23] Journalism scholars also acclaimed Turner and his work. In 1992, the organ of journalism scholars, the Association for Education in Journalism and Mass Communication (AEJMC), chose Turner for its prestigious Common Wealth award, a citation that in the past had gone primarily to practicing newspersons.

Ted Turner was born to a middle-class family that was forced to rebuild itself after the Great Depression. His father went from owning a cotton farm to being a salesman and ultimately to owning a billboard company in Georgia. Ted, a rebel from his childhood (he was sent to military school for structure and later was expelled from Brown University for bringing females to his dormitory room), went into business for himself after his much-beloved father committed suicide. At first, he operated the billboard enterprise but was fascinated by the seemingly limitless opportunities of television and borrowed the money to buy an independent facility in Atlanta. This was Channel 17, a money-losing operation whose ratings were fifth in a five-station market. Advice that he was acquiring a losing property spurred him on. "I just love it when people say I can't do anything," he recalled later. "There's nothing that makes me feel better, because all my life people have said I wasn't going to make it."[24]

In 1970, its first year of operation, the station lost half a million dollars. Within three years, however, Channel 17's profits had reached $2 million, and Turner had acquired a second UHF (ultra-high frequency) station in Charlotte, North Carolina. Ironically, considering Turner's future in the broadcasting industry, his original strategy in Atlanta was to stay as far away from news as he could. When the local ABC affiliate began carrying the network's evening news program at 6 P.M., Turner challenged it with "Star Trek" reruns and thereby began his climb in the ratings scale. Sid Pike, general manager of the Atlanta facility originally known as WCTG-TV but later dubbed by Turner "the SuperStation" (with the call letters TBS for Turner Broadcasting System), recalled that the station avoided news shows and actually provided counter-news programming with shows such as "Leave It to Beaver" and "Gilligan's Island." News loses money, Pike said; "We make money."[25] Turner acknowledged frankly that when he entered the business, he knew nothing about news and nothing about television.

Turner began relaying movies and sports programming from his Atlanta facility along a land-linked network of independent stations in the Southeast. To make certain he could maintain his generally successful sports programming, Turner borrowed again and purchased Atlanta's major-league baseball team, the Braves. He also acquired a controlling interest in Atlanta's professional basketball team, the Hawks. With these acquisitions Turner made sure the sports franchises would not move away from his TV station. As his limited network began to thrive, Turner saw greater profits ahead. He watched the rise of *Time*'s Home Box Office and began to envision an expansion of his little network nationwide. When that became possible with RCA's launching of its satellite SATCOM 1 in 1975, Turner made his move. HBO was a step ahead, leasing one of the satellite's twenty-four transponders (a device that on receiving certain radio signals from earth automatically transmits another signal back to earth) as soon as it became available. For three-quarters of a million dollars, he made a down payment on an "earth station," from which he could relay satellite signals onto cable for distribution across the country. His SuperStation was at hand. Buoyant and boastful as usual, Turner announced in a *Playboy* magazine interview that he was "going to destroy television and cause the motion-picture industry to collapse."[26]

Turner was now a celebrity. Where Luce had operated in the lofty circles inhabited by diplomats, politicians, and academics, Turner had become a staple of gossip columns and entertainment magazines.[27] By 1978, his SuperStation was worth an estimated $100 million.[28] It was then he announced his intention to begin a nationwide all-news television network that would one day expand to broadcast around the planet. His vision was never small. It was also canny. He wanted passionately to challenge the power and profit of the three networks, and he imagined four choices: movies, sports, sitcoms and other series, and news. HBO had beaten him in movies, the all-sports network ESPN had occupied the sports beat, and the networks were dominant in sitcoms and series. "All that's left is news." That was what he told Reese Schonfeld, whom he asked to join him in launching CNN.[29] Schonfeld, a veteran of television news programming, had operated several independent cable systems and had himself proposed an all-news operation but had never been able to gain the necessary financing.

When Turner announced the launching of CNN at a 1978 cable show at the Disneyland Hotel in Anaheim, California, cable was clearly on the upswing, having

Ted Turner, leader of the global revolution: The CNN chief holds
the Emmy he won in 1992.
SOURCE: AP/Wide World Photos

reached an audience of 13 million, 18 percent of television homes. HBO, the pay-television operation, had 2 million subscribers.

Turner lambasted the networks whenever the opportunity arose. In 1983 he borrowed heavily to launch a hostile takeover bid to buy CBS for himself. The bid failed, but it cost CBS heavily to withstand it. The subsequent downsizing of CBS News and other network news operations can be said to date from that point. In a National Press Club speech at the height of his takeover maneuver, Turner attacked CBS for doing what he said was a poor job of news coverage and for wasting money. He even went after "60 Minutes," saying that if and when he took over, he would "try and increase the objectivity of it."[30]

The effort put Turner into a deep financial hole, though he found himself in a position to recover when he spotted a chance to buy up a lucrative division of the motion-picture firm Metro-Goldwyn-Mayer. He was $1.4 billion in debt at the time, and the takeover bid cost him so much he couldn't afford tbe purchase price. Determined to avoid taking a step backward, Turner sold off a third of TBS. It was a painful deal. It forced him to surrender some of his iron control. The bailout money came from two conglomerates that later assumed a commanding position in the jockeying for media power, one of which was the successor to the empire built by Henry Luce, Time Warner, Inc. The other was the largest cable operator in the world, Telecommunications, Inc. Between them, they gained seven seats on the fifteen-member TBS board of directors and a pledge from Turner to make no deal costing more than $2 million without their approval.[31] Turner was no longer an absolute boss. He now had to deal with a board of directors, although he maintained a majority holding.

What he got for that price, however, was a bonanza: a library of more than 3,000 movies, many of them classics, which he could distribute to cable and over-the-air television stations at a handsome profit. He could, in short, finance his burgeoning news operation with proceeds from the very epitome of the entertainment business. Moreover, he antagonized many film aficionados by colorizing old black-and-white movies. Turner was always antagonizing somebody.

The technology was available for rapid expansion of cable television around the globe. What cable had done in making use of the capability of satellites to transmit information to the most remote places on earth was to join in, perhaps even to lead, the astonishing fragmentation that was taking place in human society.

The paradox was remarkable. New financial giants, supergiants in fact, were rising in the fabulously lucrative world of the information society. Conglomerates, multimedia and multinational, rose to the surface, operations so vast in their holdings and structure they were beyond the capacity of single governments to control. The old family newspaper was largely gone, replaced by conglomerates run from out of town. The late controversial media magnate Robert Maxwell, of whom we'll say more later, said in the midst of the new giantism that it wouldn't be long before a handful of firms would run all the media of the world.[32] That was in 1984, seven years before his mysterious death and the collapse of his empire.

The pace of fragmentation was speeding up. The old political empires were beginning to totter, to be succeeded by ever smaller units, each claiming for itself the status of nationhood. The greatest of the communication giants overreached themselves and began to disintegrate, none more dramatically than the conglomerate constructed by Maxwell. The economy of scale that had helped the giants grow and prosper, it seemed, was not going to work. Even as the Soviet Union was falling apart and reconstituting itself as a series of less unwieldy units, so were the communications giants splitting into more workable units. We will return to the world of conglomerates and multinational structures later, but let us note here how Ted Turner seized his greatest opportunity in the 1990–91 conflict in the Persian Gulf.

His response there helped change the face of television news. For the first time in human affairs, a news organization was able to deliver the same news reports simultaneously to both sides in a military confrontation. Information released by the Iraqi government was reported by CNN's Peter Arnett from his base in Baghdad while at the same time other CNN journalists were sending out information released by the U.S. military from Washington and Saudi Arabia. In other words, TV viewers in Iraq and the United States were able to hear the same reports at the

The man of Bau Bang and Baghdad: In Vietnam, Peter Arnett
tests a flame thrower.
SOURCE: AP/Wide World Photos

same time. So indeed could viewers all over the world, for by that time CNN reports could be seen by untold millions on six continents.

This development provoked a political uproar. How, it was asked, could Turner, a loyal American, sanction the broadcast of news that conceivably could be of aid and comfort to Iraq, an enemy of the United States? Some members of Congress hinted darkly that Turner, Arnett, and the entire CNN crew might be guilty of treason.

CNN's defense of its reportage was in keeping with the traditional values of a free press: It was putting out the news without fear or favor; it was letting the people know what both sides were saying and giving to them the choice of who and what to believe. Turner would point later to the indisputable fact that most people around the world seemed to believe CNN was doing nothing more than laying out the facts. "We just put it all out there," Turner said with an acid dismissal of his competition. "Our readers are news readers." His anchorpersons, he said, did not "mix it all together the way the other guys do."[33]

CNN's live on-the-scene coverage of the Gulf War was a financial bonanza. All across the country, viewers who had not signed up for the CNN service flooded cable companies with requests for Turner's news operation. Some companies had to go on overtime to handle all the requests. Even the glum networks praised the operation.

Good news arrived for the networks a year later. The FCC let it be known it was thinking of relaxing its 1970 ruling barring the networks from owning cable systems. At that time, 90 percent of the viewing public was tuning it to the networks during prime-time hours. By 1993, that figure had fallen to slightly more than 60 percent.

Turner had great expectations not only of himself but also of his cable network. He seemed convinced he could put into practical being a the new world of Marshall McLuhan's global village.[34] CNN, Turner said, had become an international or global news operation: "We try to be two-sided." Morever, CNN had directed its staff no longer to refer to nations other than the United States as "foreign." In fact, Turner said, the regime of Iraqi dictator Saddam Hussein "was the enemy of the United States, not of CNN."[35]

Turner's missionary impulses were easily to be seen. He acknowledged them himself. He said his hope was that CNN would eventually eliminate war and "I think it is doing that." He went so far as to credit the news media relaying information around the world with reducing the number of wars between nations. If international news media had been in Germany during the rise of Adolf Hitler, Turner said, the horrors unleashed on the world by the National Socialists would never have occurred. He would gladly have based CNN staffers in Berlin in the 1930s, he said, just as he had based newspeople in Baghdad half a century later.

It was not only war Turner saw as his target. His mission for CNN was to help humankind "to understand, to study, to grow," to work on behalf of the global environment, for population control: "Let's learn to live in peace and harmony with each other." In his earlier years, Turner said, he had been stimulated by the desire to compete as a yachtsman, as a businessman, as a broadcasting pioneer, and as a "rampant nationalist." But he had, he said, put those days behind him and was dreaming now of "doing the impossible."

Still, a part of Turner sulked like Achilles in his tent. He was not happy being forced to share power. Seven years after he struck the deal with Time Warner and TCI, he told an interviewer he felt "hemmed in" because he was no longer in a position to wheel and deal as the mood struck him.[36] To abandon his dream of directing a vast vertical media empire was not in Turner's character. What he really wanted was an empire that combined the production of programs with the distribution of the products. And six months after that interview, he announced he was buying a majority share in Castle Rock Entertainment, the largest independent movie studio in Hollywood, and New Line Cinema Corporation, a publicly traded independent film company.[37] Martin Shafer, one of Castle Rock's founding partners, said Turner had assured him Castle Rock would maintain its creative control, but he said Turner's input would be welcome nonetheless. "He's a visionary," Shafer said. "We'd be pretty stupid not to listen."[38]

In any case, Shafer observed, "Ted's plan is to have a full-fledged media empire."[39] Time Warner, which owned 21.9 percent of the Turner Broadcasting

Company, agreed to the deal in the apparent belief it was strengthening its own competitive position. Of such strange bedfellows is the media news and entertainment business constructed. Before the end of the century, all of them—Turner, Time Warner, and their competitors—were looking forward to occupying the crucial stretch along what had come to be called the global data superhighway. They were all in competition with the telephone and computer industries pushing for digital interactive TV communication.

Nevertheless, Turner rejected a chance to forge an alliance with the newspaper industry. This idea came from Leland Schwartz, who runs a news organization that supplies reports from the capital to some 300 newspapers. Turner said he didn't want to be in the newspaper business.[40] Meanwhile, Turner and other cable operators aimed toward constructing a national data highway partly because that would keep them competive with the fast-moving computer industry that was pushing for digital interactive television communication.

Challenges of various types came to Turner and CNN, but would-be American competitors found it difficult to get off the ground. The cost of moving into the global-news delivery business was prohibitively expensive. NBC, for instance, began and then dropped plans to compete.[41] Challenges from abroad, notably from Europe and Japan, looked more promising. The most likely came from the BBC (British Broadcasting Corporation), which had pioneered international broadcasting half a century earlier with its widely admired external radio service. Despite its advocacy of "objective," dispassionate reporting, however, it was clearly a British enterprise, and it was limited to radio transmissions.

In 1991, the BBC established a World Service Television system and promised to deliver fewer live news reports and to concentrate not on hard news but, as with the older radio service, on a good deal of news analysis. The system's chief executive, Christopher Irwin, was direct and cutting in speaking of the difference between CNN and what the British intended: "One danger is if you go to a press conference and turn on a camera and think that's journalism. It's not." Moreover, Irwin said, "CNN is brilliant reportage; I'm more dubious about its journalism." And, in an aside to Turner, he remarked, "Historically, the Atlanta world view is narrower than the BBC world view."[42] Pushing itself further along with its challenge, the BBC moved toward a global linkup with ABC.

At the time of Irwin's remarks, CNN was sending its televised reports, all in English, to more than 125 countries; it estimated 75 million households could receive its reports. The BBC's international radio service, broadcast in 37 languages, could be heard by some 120 million listeners.[43]

In the astonishing surge of new technology, the development of yet another medium of communication, the videocassette recording (VCR) does not seem to have the sex appeal of global television systems, but it may not be ignored, and it may turn out in fact to exert an even more striking impact on the conduct of human affairs. The remarkable thing about the VCR is that it can be used as an instrument of political communication in virtual defiance of detection. The wielders of power in nations may be able to censor out electronically—by jamming or still-to-be discovered new techniques—unwanted big-media news reports (or coded espionage messages or pornography), but they find it extraordinarily difficult to keep out the minimedia, the small, portable videocassettes, which are capable of subverting the very idea of national sovereignty. As we will see later, VCRs have already been used to import revolution.

Wielders of power remain, however, in control of the news production of the big media—as Turner and all his competitors came to realize during the Persian Gulf War. Not only could Saddam Hussein assure that his messages got out to the world via CNN, but so indeed could the American military assure their own version of the war story went out to all news consumers on earth.

As Turner later acknowledged in a televised interview, "we knew we were being used" by both Saddam Hussein and the United States. Gazing through unblinking and contemplative eyes, he told his interviewer, David Frost, "Everybody uses us. Everybody uses everybody else. You use your wife. Your wife uses her husband. Intelligent self-interest is what the world's all about."[44]

Turner's reference was to the fact that U.S. military rules denied journalists unrestricted access to the troops or to military engagements, so all information was given out at carefully controlled "briefings" and all photographic handouts were carefully preselected.[45] "We were," Turner said, "manipulated just as much by the United States government, the United States military, as by the Iraqis—the whole media, not just CNN."[46]

CNN International was not only providing information to its viewers but also was returning a substantial profit to Turner and his stockholders. Even with its success in covering the Gulf War, the Turner Broadcasting System's news operation trailed its entertainment programming in profits by a wide distance. The same fiscal reality describes the operations of all news media; they all live in the same environment. CNN and the competing networks illustrated the point vividly by presenting their war reports in the form of football games or adventure movies opening with colorul graphics and dramatic music. The war was, as one commentator observed, "the first full-scale video logo war."[47] It was an apt harmonization of the print graphics techniques of *USA Today* and the sophisticated video-game technology of television entertainment fed willy nilly around the globe.

NOTES

1. *Trends in Advertising Volume* (New York: Television Bureau of Advertising), 5/92, 1. Hereafter identified as TBA. See also *Facts About Newspapers 92* (Reston, VA: Newspaper Association of America, 1993), 10. Television's ad revenues in the third quarter of 1992 increased 16 percent over the same figure for 1991. See "Television Ad Revenue for Third Quarter Up 16% Hiking Yearly Increase to 7% over 1991," TBA press release, December 15, 1992.

2. TBA Ad Revenues, 3. Local gains from January through September came to 8 percent. Syndicated shows advanced 10 percent.

3. The volume of books and articles about broadcasting history has been increasing geometrically. There is no standard work, although many scholars approve the three-

volume Erik Barnouw, *Tube of Plenty: The Evolution of American Television* 2nd ed. (New York: Oxford University Press, 1990). See also works by Sidney Head, including *Broadcasting in America: A Survey of Television and Radio*, 3rd ed. (Boston: Houghton Mifflin, 1976). Among more specialized works, see Ken Auletta, *Three Blind Mice: How the TV Networks Lost Their Way* (New York: Random House, 1992).

4. The larger figure was reported by *The New York Times*, September 30, 1990, the lesser one by *The Baltimore Sun*, September 13, 1991.

5. Ian Johnson, "TV Networks Defy Portents of Doom," *Baltimore Sun*, December 5, 1993. See also Bill Carter, "Long Ratings Climb Ends for Cable Television," *New York Times*, November 15, 1993.

6. Paul Farhi, "The Great Big Broadcast of 1991: Advertising Slump, TV Station Economics Create an Explosion of Local News," *Washington Post*, Business Supplement, March 11, 1991. Farhi was citing David Smith, manager of television consultation for Frank N. Magid Associates, Inc., Marion, Iowa.

7. Minow's first remark was made in a speech to the National Association of Broadcasters, Washington, D.C., May 9, 1961, the second in a speech at the Gannett Foundation Media Center, New York City, May 9, 1991.

8. Edmond L. Andrews, "New F.C.C. Chief Looks Beyond the Corporations," *New York Times*, December 6, 1993.

9. Murrow's speech is reprinted in Fred W. Friendly, *Due to Circumstances Beyond Our Control . . .* (New York: Random House, 1967), 252.

10. Dan Rather, address to RTNDA convention, Miami Beach, Florida, September 29, 1993. See also J. Herbert Altschull, "Merely Wires and Lights in a Box," *The Evening Sun*, Baltimore, November 1, 1993.

11. For many years, the standard view in the Soviet Union was of private commercial television as dominated and controlled by blind commercial forces. American TV critics who looked at the domestic TV scene in the same way were not usually aware that they were, in a sense, echoing communist rhetoric.

12. Rather, address to RTNDA convention.

13. For a fascinating account of the case, see Charles W. Clift, *The WLBT-TV Case, 1964–69: An Historical Analysis*, unpublished dissertation, Indiana University, 1976. See also Huntington Williams, *Beyond Control: ABC and the Fate of the Networks* (New York: Atheneum, 1989).

14. The FCC was set up originally in order to referee disputes among potential broadcasters claiming the same piece of the spectrum.

15. Barnouw, *Tube of Plenty*, 124.

16. "FCC Votes Down Fairness Doctrine in a 4-0 Decision," *New York Times*, August 5, 1987.

17. *New York Times*, June 21, 1987.

18. For accounts of the actions by the FCC and Congress, see 1989 articles in the *New York Times*, February 11, April 18, October 4. Congress resurrected the plan to save the Fairness Doctrine two years later. Representative John Dingell, Michigan Democrat and chairman of the House Commerce Committee, argued: "It is only fair that when broadcasters own that wonderful right to use the money machine, which they are given by the FCC, that they should use it in the public interest." Presidential intransigence, with

George Bush following Reagan's lead in supporting broadcasters' claim the Fairness Doctrine violated free-speech guarantees, ultimately forced Congress to surrender.

19. One of the more dramatic such documentaries was "Migrant," a 1970 NBC production that attacked a leading advertiser, the Coca-Cola Company, exposing the wretched living conditions of migrant workers employed in Florida citrus groves that were owned by Coca-Cola. The company failed to have the documentary suppressed but induced the network to make some minor changes that proved unsatisfactory. The company canceled commercials on NBC in the next quarter after spending $2.5 million for spots in the previous quarter. Later, however, Coca-cola returned to NBC, evidently deciding it needed the network despite the poor image it had been given in the documentary.

20. Many books cover the history of broadcasting; many journal articles deal with specific aspects of that history. Among the landmark works, especially on the early years of broadcasting, none is superior to the second edition of Barnouw's *Tube of Plenty*. See Asa Berger, ed., *Television in Society* (New Brunswick, NJ: Transaction Press, 1986) for a collection of interesting essays and articles. For an examination of the rise of cable, see, among others, Timothy Hollins, *Beyond Broadcasting: Into the Cable Age* (London: BFI Publishing, 1984).

21. These figures are drawn from 1992 data supplied by TBA, which collects reports from a variety of sources, chief among them being the A. C. Nielsen Company and the advertising firms of McCann Erickson and Paul Kagan Associates.

22. The three leading cable companies each were projected to show increases, ESPN up $29 million to $289.2 million, CNN up $24 million to $239.2 million, and USA up 39 percent to $236.4 million. These estimated revenues, published by TVB in June 1991, were drawn from Paul Kagan. At the same time, TVB reported total broadcast television revenues down 4.9 percent in the first half of the year, with the network advertising revenues falling a whopping 7.1 percent to $4.8 billion.

23. William A. Henry III, "History As It Happens," *Time*, January 6, 1992, 24.

24. Hank Whittemore, *CNN: The Inside Story* (Boston: Little, Brown, 1990), 14.

25. Whittemore. The quotation from Pike is on p. 18.

26. *Playboy*, November 1978, cited in Whittemore, 26.

27. A devotee of sailing, Turner had won the America's Cup, the world championship in ocean racing.

28. Whittemore, *CNN: The Inside Story*, 2-3.

29. Whittemore, *CNN: The Inside Story*, 34.

30. The account of Turner's takeover bid and MGM purchase is taken from Whittemore, *CNN: The Inside Story*, 265-79.

31. Priscilla Painton, "The Taming of Ted Turner," *Time*, January 6, 1992, 37.

32. Ben Bagdikian, "Cornering Hearts and Mind: The Lords of the Global Village," *The Nation*, June 12, 1989, 814.

33. Ted Turner interview with David Frost on Public Broadcasting System, October 27, 1993.

34. See, for instance, Marshall McLuhan, *Understanding Media: The Extensions of Man* (New York: McGraw-Hill, 1964).

35. Turner's comments here and in subsequent passages were made in the interview with David Frost. Turner acknowledged the staff of his news organization was at the time composed mostly of American citizens and therefore, "you've got to be somewhat of an American, but we try to give the news an international slant." He said he hoped the time

would come when all the non-American bureaus of CNN would be manned by nationals of the countries where the bureaus were located.

36. Bill Carter, "Ted Turner's Time of Discontent," *New York Times*, June 6, 1993. Turner told Carter his partners were his "close friends," and he credited them with helping his company more than double its revenues in 1992, to nearly $1.8 billion.

37. Geraldine Fabrikant, "Turner Buys Castle Rock and New Line Cinema," *New York Times*, November 18, 1993. See also Claudia Eller, "Castle Rock Entertainment Heads Happily for Turner Empire," *Los Angeles Times*, reprinted in *The Sun*, Baltimore, MD, November 10, 1993. Another media empire, the Sony Corporation was the chief distributor of Castle Rock films, illustrating the complexity of the conglomerate mix.

38. Eller, "Castle Rock Entertainment."

39. Eller, "Castle Rock Entertainment."

40. William Glaberson, "Press Notes," *New York Times*, June 7, 1993.

41. Hollins, *Beyond Broadcasting*, 154.

42. Steven Prokesch, "BBC's Global Challenge to CNN," *New York Times*, October 28, 1991.

43. Prokesch, "BBC's Global Challenge."

44. Turner interview with David Frost.

45. Journalists did manage to move into the field after American troops had landed in Kuwait and Iraq, but even then their access to actual events was severely limited. For a thorough examination of the media control exercised by the U.S. government, see John R. MacArthur, *Second Front: Censorship and Propaganda in the Gulf War* (New York: Hill & Wang, 1992).

46. Turner, when asked whether he thought humanity would survive the various world pressures, concluded he did not but would continue to behave as if he did. "The odds are we won't make it," he said. "The exciting thing is doing the impossible." Interview with David Frost; see Note 33.

47. MacArthur, *Second Front*, 80.

Chapter
7

"We Don't Have News on TV; We Have Entertainment"

The poet William Butler Yeats once asked this question: "How can we know the dancer from the dance?"[1] The same question might now be posed about news, for it has grown increasingly clear that with the decline in newspaper readership and the companion increase in television viewing we can no longer know the news from entertainment.

Nothing illustrates this point more clearly than the docudrama. This is a form of television theater that purports to tell the documented story of a historical event. In other words, it is supposed to be dramatized reality. Like all drama, it must be entertaining. So it is at best a distorted documentation of reality. The now defunct National News Council, an independent agency designed to judge the quality and ethical content of the American mass-media elite, denounced the very concept of the docudrama, holding that it uses the form of television news to present entertainment or a political point of view, thereby damaging the credibility of legitimate news broadcasts.[2] Condemnation of the docudrama form comes from both ends of the political spectrum. The critic Michael Parenti, who has said television operates under "a politics of entertainment," has maintained that the docudrama blinds its audience to the harsh realities of life. He called it "make-believe history [that] reinforces historical illiteracy fostered in the schools and in political life in general."[3] A survey of the "television elite" leads the Right to agree that docudramas are inaccurate but to blame the inaccuracies on what three writers identify as "the social liberalism" of TV writers and producers. Two out of three members of the TV elite, they say, believe televised entertainment should be a major force for social reform.[4] The question of social control is addressed though not pinpointed.

There is nothing new about entertainment in news. Certainly, no one writing the news ever set out deliberately to make his or her report unentertaining and dull. When Henry Luce launched *Time* in 1923, his goal was to lure readers to his magazine by entertaining them, by appealing, as he said, to "the gentleman from Indiana." The appeal to the "average" reader had already become a routine appeal in journalism. It was with the ascendance of television, however, that the clear connection between news and entertainment became obvious. Show-biz treatment of news reached new levels. It was not surprising, as Professor Ben Bagdikian has reminded us, that business interests found the news media to be "vital instruments" for maintaining their economic and political power.[5] The media have always served the economic interests of those who paid the bills; they have always promoted the values of their paymasters. The precipitate rush toward more and more entertainment has led to a boom in the field of advertising as well as to massive shifts in popular culture and to a giant amusement industry that provides the fodder served up by cable, antenna, and satellite systems. News, as we have seen, has not been immune to these developments.

Does this suggest that the media are immoral purveyors of wicked values? Certainly not. It does, however, suggest the *amoral* character of the news media. I have written elsewhere that the overriding moral imperative of today's editors seems to be to publish the news—with little attention paid to the consequences of publication.[6] The only exceptions considered by American editors were stories in questionable taste and stories whose publication threatened the lives of citizens. Even in these cases, editors felt great pressure to publish, to "get out the news," for the edification and interest of readers. Ethical questions were indeed raised, but almost always *after* the story had been published. The reading and viewing public must be reached; they must be entertained. It is certainly not fair to journalists, however, to suggest that in the effort to entertain readers and viewers they tend to make *unethical* choices. Quite the contrary. They have almost always been able to find what they considered moral explanations. Still, given a choice between publishing and not publishing, the inclination was to publish, and it grew increasingly clear that the kind of news that most attracts readers and viewers is news that is entertaining, appealing more to the emotions than to the mind. That road is the path to reader and viewer interest, hence to greater attractiveness to those who want to use newspapers and television to sell their products.

It was by no means only in the United States where the pressures for entertainment and profit were pushing toward trivialization of the content of newspapers and especially television, in both entertainment shows and news programming. In Russia, for instance, money troubles forced *Pravda,* the long-time Communist party newspaper, to suspend publication in 1992, to return only as a thin three-times-a-week publication. *Izvestia*, once the mouthpiece for the Soviet government, introduced direct advertising, even real-estate notices, in an effort to survive. Newspapers and television turned to what a Ukrainian media expert spoke of as "pop music and the worst kind of trash."[7] In the Czech republic, President Václav Havel, a poet and former journalist, appealed for financial help to underwrite qual-ity writing in newspapers and even in books. Only sure-fire best-sellers were hitting the market.[8] Sensational tabloid newspapers were springing up all over eastern Europe. In Africa, newspapers were imitating the worst excesses of the yellow press in Britain. Quality television was declining in Britain as a result of sharp cost increases. Independent television and the publicly financed BBC were in trouble. So profound were the British media's financial woes that fears were expressed the government might be driven to cancel the BBC's special status and open it up to private interests. Independent, privately financed television (ITV) cut back its quality programming. The producer Derek Granger warned the climate for quality broadcasting in Britain was growing "ferociously cold."[9] Similar warnings came from all over the European continent.

We have seen how the shrinkage in newspaper readership forced editors to move toward closer harmony with their business and advertising departments, to the extent of overruling Joseph Pulitzer's brave (if unrealistic) demand that his business people stay out of his papers' news offices. Space salespeople know all too well that readers read news reports that are entertaining and refrain from reading those that aren't. The connection between news and entertainment is simply there. And few, if any, broadcasting executives, many of them veterans of business and advertising departments, argue for Pulitzer's announced policy. Many working journalists, are, on the other hand, reluctant to accept the—for them—depressing idea that the quest for profits can interfere with the integrity of their reporting.

In the broadcasting industry, where the potential for huge money making is manifestly clear, the connection between news and entertainment was obvious to one and all. So involved a person as Michael Deaver, who once served as President Reagan's right-hand man, stated the case quite simply: "We don't have news on television; we have entertainment."[10]

Indeed, when the entertainment operator Capital Cities, in one of the decade's more spectacular takeovers, took control of ABC in January 1986, it made it clear entertainment would take precedence over news on the network that was then marking its thirty-second year. One writer observed laconically that Capital Cities "barely knew the difference" between news and entertainment.[11] All three major networks that had once been independent operators had by the beginning of the century's last decade become segments of giant multimedia enterprises, all committed primarily to profit. News operations were consolidated. The networks fired many dozens of news writers and reporters.

Faced with declining revenues, network news programs moved away from their traditional hard-news format in search of longer, in-depth reports and softer human-interest features. An organization that monitors evening news programs reported, for instance, that the time on news shows devoted to arts and entertainment features jumped from thirty-eight to sixty-eight minutes a month between the first half of 1988 and the same period of 1990.[12] Nothing was more disturbing to

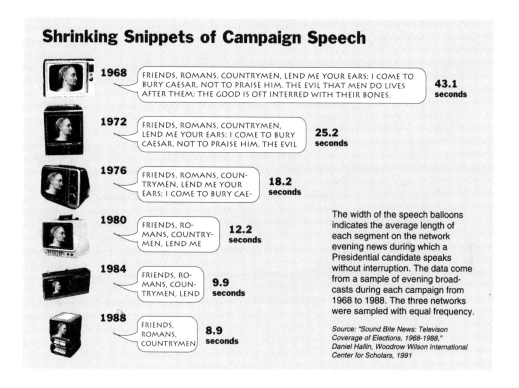

Shrinking Snippets of Campaign Speech

1968 — FRIENDS, ROMANS, COUNTRYMEN, LEND ME YOUR EARS; I COME TO BURY CAESAR, NOT TO PRAISE HIM. THE EVIL THAT MEN DO LIVES AFTER THEM; THE GOOD IS OFT INTERRED WITH THEIR BONES. — **43.1 seconds**

1972 — FRIENDS, ROMANS, COUNTRYMEN, LEND ME YOUR EARS; I COME TO BURY CAESAR, NOT TO PRAISE HIM. THE EVIL — **25.2 seconds**

1976 — FRIENDS, ROMANS, COUNTRYMEN, LEND ME YOUR EARS; I COME TO BURY CAE — **18.2 seconds**

1980 — FRIENDS, ROMANS, COUNTRYMEN, LEND ME — **12.2 seconds**

1984 — FRIENDS, ROMANS, COUNTRYMEN, LEND — **9.9 seconds**

1988 — FRIENDS, ROMANS, COUNTRYMEN — **8.9 seconds**

The width of the speech balloons indicates the average length of each segment on the network evening news during which a Presidential candidate speaks without interruption. The data come from a sample of evening broadcasts during each campaign from 1968 to 1988. The three networks were sampled with equal frequency.

Source: "Sound Bite News: Televison Coverage of Elections, 1968-1988," Daniel Hallin, Woodrow Wilson International Center for Scholars, 1991

SOURCE: "Sound Bite News: Television Coverage of Elections, 1968-1988," Daniel Hallin, Woodrow Wilson International Center for Scholars, 1991. Copyright 1992 by the New York Times Company

broadcast journalists than the rise of a news-driven phenomenon that was soon labeled tabloid TV. Syndicated programs such as "A Current Affair," "Hard Copy," and "Inside Edition" appeared as copycats of "60 Minutes," specializing, however, in lurid reports on crimes, sex, and scandal. The tabloid TV shows did not hesitate to pay sources for interviews and insider tips. They did not demonstrate the traditional journalistic values, but they were indeed entertaining, especially to audiences fascinated by scandal, gossip, and celebrities, standard fare for the supermarket newspaper tabloids. Their ratings continued to climb.[13]

Tabloid news was like Gresham's Law, the bad driving out the good, said Hodding Carter, president of MainStreet Television Productions and a veteran media critic. It was not that he was in favor of censoring the tabloids, he told U.S. broadcast news directors; it was rather that he feared television was allocating its resources not for the kind of news a democratic public needed but for scandal. "TV itself is a scandal." he said. "If you believe your only mandate is to make a buck, that's a scandal." David Bartlett, president of the organization, acknowledged that "flashy presentations" could be seen but that there were also plenty of good programs. The Reverend Donald W. Shriver, president emeritus of Union

Theological Seminary, said what was required were stories that Americans need to know about if the country were going to remain a democracy: "I fear people have sold themselves to the market."[14]

The heated debate took place in late 1993 at the annual convention of RTNDA, the Radio and Television News Directors Association. The location was Miami Beach, which was fitting since Channel 7 in Miami is often pointed to as the zenith of tabloid television. There, on its 10 P.M. "news" show, images flash past the viewer with blinding speed. Sound bites are rarely more than two or three seconds long, and a new story begins before the viewer can grasp the sense of the story just reported. The great bulk of the stories are, not surprisingly, about sex and violence and the exploits of celebrities. One tabloid news show called the child-abuse allegations against entertainer Michael Jackson "the scandal of the decade."

Bartlett said it was improtant to deliver "choice" to the American viewer, providing both "Hard Copy" and the "McNeil-Lehrer News Hour" on public television. John Lippmann, former news director of KCBS-TV, Los Angeles, agreed that such choice was in the public interest. Bartlett predicted the future would bring more tabloid news but also more quality news. "The bulk of the segments on TV now," he said, "are important to the public. I believe that journalism has a responsibility to serve the public." Jane Hall, media reporter for *The Los Angeles Times,* replied the discussion was not about choice but about the *illusion* of choice. She said she found less difference between the news on tabloid shows and regular news shows. "It's true of print as well," she said. "It's the whole style of journalism. Are the tabloids driving the agenda?"

As Michael Deaver made clear, cloaking information in the format of television entertainment is crucial for politicians seeking maximum exposure. Deaver's job in the Reagan administration was to gain maximum publicity for his boss and to place Reagan in the best possible light in order to ensure ongoing public support. That meant creating images that would put Reagan in the very center of the television box, in a position that tugged at the viewers' heartstrings. One illustration will suffice.

In 1982, early in Reagan's first term, the country was mired in a troublesome economic recession, one that did nothing positive for the presidential image. Reagan's handlers, Deaver chief among them, cast about hopefully for the slightest sign the recession was easing. When it turned out a slight improvement was occurring in the housing market, Deaver and his people seized on the development immediately. Aware the viewing public turns to television more for light entertainment than for hard news, they rejected any idea of suggesting to Reagan he simply summon the TV cameras to his office to report the favorable changes in the housing market. Instead, they searched for—and found—a way to present that news as visual entertainment. Turning their researchers loose, they learned that Fort Worth, Texas, was among the cities with the most favorable housing patterns. What an opportunity! They ordered up Reagan's plane, Air Force One, flew him to Fort Worth, and staged the "photo opportunity" they were looking for. They called in the TV cameras for Reagan's announcement of the housing upturn. The visual was just what the spin doctors ordered, with Reagan standing at a construction site, decked out in a Stetson, the perfect image of a man who really cared about the common folk who wanted a decent place to live.

That image, Deaver recalled later, was "the story line" he was looking for.[15] The idea of a "line of the day" went back a dozen years to an orchestrated White House strategy using "tricks of puffery and calumny" that the presidential adviser David Gergen said was "how the game is played."[16] In the particular announcement Deaver was recounting, the president was the commodity being sold and, as Deaver knew full well, entertainment was what sells. The information, with the requisite visual, did not appear on any sitcom or entertainment program. It appeared on evening news programs across the country. Richard Cohen, at that time a producer for CBS News, said Deaver had played television newspeople "like a Stradivarius." Deaver said he hadn't been slanting anything, that what he had been doing in providing entertainment was "capitalizing on the truth." Cohen said his technique was more properly identified as "slanting the news," whereupon Deaver suggested that CBS had done plenty of "news-twisting" itself. He recalled the controversial 1985 visit of President Reagan to a German military cemetery at the town of Bitburg, a visit that came under heavy criticism not only from Jewish survivors of Nazi concentration camps but also from American religious leaders, political parties, and even journalists. It developed that among the graves at the Bitburg ceremony were those of forty-nine members of the hated Waffen SS. According to Deaver, in order to heighten the visual impact of photos of the Bitburg ceremony, CBS people placed little Nazi flags on some SS graves, an act making that evening's news program more dramatic, more interesting, and more entertaining.[17]

There is nothing wicked or evil about entertainment. It has been part of the human experience since the beginning of time. Life without entertainment, private and public, is impossible to imagine. Life is, after all, a tragedy, ending in sickness and death. To bear the tragic condition of life, we must be diverted from endless contemplation of how life is going to end and the pain and suffering that accompany it. Religious institutions divert the faithful with rituals and crusades and promise of eternal glory. The irreligious Karl Marx called religion the opiate of the people; we all need opiates of one kind or another to survive in a hostile world. States divert the people with flags, patriotic songs, noble causes, and sometimes wars. The Greeks diverted the citizens with running and discus throwing, the Romans with circuses, the medieval barons with jousting and tournaments. Human beings have always found entertainment and distraction in beauty: painting, sculpture, singing, and dancing. How tragic can life appear when beholding a glorious sunset or when listening to the magic of Mozart?

Reading is the most private of all forms of entertainment. Sitting in our chair alone, we can read the words of others and forget the tragedy of life; we can relax, we can be amused, we can even experience joy. Like the motion picture, television adds yet another dimension to entertainment, for in front of the screen we are able to experience two- or even three-dimensional entertainment. Unlike sitting in a movie theater, however, watching television from our favorite armchair is a private experience. Small wonder those who wish to reach us seek to accomplish the connection through providing us with entertainment over whatever medium of communication is chosen.

Small wonder, too, that control of the communications media offers the holder what some Marxist social theorists speak of as "hegemony."[18] This means predominance, the ruling principle; the hegemony of ancient Greece was said to be in the hands of the Athenian rulers. Hegemony means power. This in turn means whoever dominates the media of communications gains prestige and wields power, thereby exercising a critical measure of social control. Marketing the television programs that entertain the audience thus becomes a major step toward prestige, power, and wealth. The marketers, the imagemakers like Michael Deaver, are in heavy demand. Their task is to market news as other entertainment is marketed, so in the end the viewer cannot tell the dancer from the dance, so through entertainment the viewer is led to choose his or her leader, party, and beliefs. Without judging the content of the entertainment, we can nevertheless identify it as propaganda.

There is a vast literature on the news as entertainment, much of it written by harsh critics. No criticism is more pointed than that of media specialist Neil Postman, who calls the television era "the age of show business."[19] Television, he writes, has made entertainment "the natural format for the representation of all experience." In addition, he says, newscasters tell viewers to tune in tomorrow for more "fragments of tragedy and barbarism," thereby letting us know the "news" is not to be taken seriously.[20] Some of Postman's assault seems to be overstated in order to make his case—he says news has been packaged as vaudeville, political discourse has been rendered empty, and American viewers no longer talk to one another—but he is persuasive when he argues that television is at its best in presenting entertainment (he calls it "junk entertainment") and "serves us most ill when it co-opts serious modes of discourse . . . and lumps them into entertainment packages."[21]

The critic W. Lance Bennett labels the age of television "an information system based on mind-numbing stereotypes."[22] Another critic, Edwin Diamond, speaks of "disco news" and "news hype" on television and says that even before 1980, the country had approached "a model of journalism that was practically all entertainment and zero information."[23] Ben Bagdikian speaks of a "spread of fluff," not only in television but also in newspapers and other competing news media.[24] Not all commentators condemn the concept of television news as entertaining. Virtually all TV journalists maintain, sensibly enough, that TV news programming must be presented in an interesting—that is to say, entertaining—manner or viewers would tune out.[25] In the end, the debate was really over whether entertainment values have superseded traditional news values. Some, such as TV news directors, said the public was being served by a widening choice of news programs. Others said there was only drab sameness, just an illusion of choice. Hodding Carter called attention to the lack of journalism traditions in television: "TV ownership has no tradition like newspapers."[26]

As most research shows, audiences use the news for a number of different reasons. Readers and viewers are particularly attracted by what can be identified as "service" stories—information about the weather, about new products, about developments in medical care, and so on.[27] The sociologist Herbert J. Gans, who has

The "Tailhook" scandal and the Navy: The news media as entertainment media.

SOURCE: Mike Lane, *Evening Sun*

made an exhaustive study of the news production process at CBS and NBC, says journalists have "struck a bargain" with their audience, especially viewers who lack a serious interest in the news. Under it, journalists supply important news about what is going on in the world that they believe the public ought to know about, and in return the audiences are provided "interesting stories to please them"[28]—in other words, stories that offer entertainment to the audiences. Under this contract, he says, "with some simplification, it would be fair to say that the news supports the social order of public, business and professional, upper-middle-class, middle-aged, and white male sectors of society." Moreover, Gans adds, journalists in the United States emphasize people over groups and "enduring social values."[29]

Most, but not all, critics hold that the entertainment ingredient in the news supports social values, although explanations vary. In any case, spokespeople for both Left and Right see the media's fare—news and otherwise—as propaganda.[30] The leftist critic Roger Smith says that "when we watch the [Persian Gulf] war and the politics on TV, it becomes just another show, a continuing docudrama on all stations."[31] George Gerbner perceives modern journalists as prophets and priests, storytellers and mythtellers; he describes television as a secular religious institution.[32]

The most passionate censure of television fare has been directed at the excessive levels of sex and violence on both entertainment and news programming. Many voices have been raised to accuse television of responsibility for increasing levels of violent crime around the world, especially in the United States. No scholar has been able to prove a direct causal connection between television programs and rising crime rates, but it can be said that most individuals do see a clear relationship between TV and crime. The U.S. Surgeon General linked television with aggressive behavior as early as 1972. Over the years, Congress has conducted hearings on the topic, and a growing number of members have demanded the industry cut back sharply on the number of action shows depicting graphic violence, blood, and gore. Attorney General Janet Reno warned the industry in late 1993 that if it did not itself stem the tide of such programs, the president and Congress would consider laws to do it for them.[33] She did not blame television alone for the rise of violence—it was the entire society that was responsible, she said—but she demanded the industry air shows that repudiated violence and guns. The industry, countering threats of "censorship," responded it had been busy for years replacing hard-core action shows with sitcoms and blander fare. Neither side in the dispute said much about the material aired on news shows, but it was clear to all viewers that local news stations, like Channel 7 in Miami, were busy copying the hard-core sex and violence format of the tabloid shows.

Staff changes on television were having their own impact on the rising tide of entertainment in TV news. Like Hodding Carter, media critic Edwin Diamond saw the appearance of a "new generation" of TV journalists on network and local news programs, replacing the distinguished pioneers who came from newspaper or magazine news backgrounds. The news men and women, Diamond wrote, "act as if they were standing above and beyond print journalists with their fussy, too-literal regard for the facts and sober reportage."[34]

Fascination with the electronic gadgetry produced by technological innovation has also been a factor. Colorful visuals often take the place of sober reporting; the "talking head," a face speaking without benefit of pictures, is shunned by producers and directors as if it represented the dinosaur age of television. Statistics, especially the results of polls and surveys, have become a daily staple of TV news fare. Critic Todd Gitlin has said these developments lead to simplistic reporting and to confusing statistics with knowledge. In sports reporting as well as war journalism, he says scornfully, "everything is technique and know-how."[35]

On the other hand, journalists themselves take sharp exception to the idea that their news selection is dominated by entertainment considerations. In a national survey of journalists working for various news media, only one-fifth said they considered it to be "extremely important" to provide their audiences with entertainment and relaxation. Interestingly, many more newspaper journalists than those in the television field said they placed extreme importance on entertainment: 26 percent of newspaper journalists compared with 10 percent among television journalists. In reporting the results of their study, David Weaver and G. Cleveland Wilhoit found the response ironic; perhaps, they said the TV newspersons were responding defensively.[36] Editors were far more prepared than their reporters to see "extreme importance" in providing entertainment to audiences (64 to 49 percent). The journalists rated "proximity, impact, and prominence" the most salient of their news values, stating that "the news is, by definition, timely and out of the ordinary."[37]

However valid the sharp criticisms of entertainment journalism or the newspersons' self-portrait may be, it is certainly true that many hard-working journalists remain highly committed to fulfilling their role in the democratic assumption. Even such critics of contemporary journalism as Gitlin, Diamond, and Bagdikian also called attention to high-quality reporting, especially in digging behind official pronouncements. Gitlin spoke of "traditions of real though limited journalistic independence, traditions whose modern extension causes businessmen, indeed, to loathe the press."[38] Bagdikian says in recent years, "daily journalism has shown more initiative in probing social forces that affect people's lives." But he found certain "taboo subjects" that only a handful of news organizations were prepared to enter—for example, "abuse of land planning in cities, harmful real-estate developments, the auto lobby's crippling of public transportation."[39] They were speaking of what is identified in this book as the boundaries of acceptable dissent.

NOTES

1. The line appears at the close of Yeats's 1927 poem, "Among School Children," reprinted in the *Norton Anthology of Poetry* (New York: W. W. Norton, 1970), 918.
    O chestnut-tree, great-rooted blossomer,
    Are you the leaf, the blossom or the bole?
    O body swayed to music, O brightening glance,
    How can we know the dancer from the dance?
2. Patrick Brogan, *Spiked: The Short Life and Death of the National News Council* (New York: Priority Press, 1985), 50–51.
3. Michael Parenti, *Make-Believe Media: The Politics of Entertainment* (New York: St. Martin's, 1991), 61–68.
4. Linda Lichter, S. Robert Lichter, and Stanley Rothman, "Hollywood and America: The Odd Couple," in L. Brent Bozell III and Brent H. Baker, eds., *And That's The Way It Isn't: A Reference Guide to Media Bias* (Alexandria, VA: Media Research Center, 1990), 273–83.
5. Ben H. Bagdikian, *The Media Monopoly, Revised and Expanded with the Latest Information on the Expansion of Global Media Giants*, 3rd ed. (Boston: Beacon Press, 1990), 151.
6. J. Herbert Altschull, "The Amoral Morality of Editors," in Anne van der Meiden, ed., *Ethics in Journalism* (Utrecht: University of Utrecht Press, 1987), 89–107.
7. Henrikas Yushkiavitshus, assistant director-general, Unesco, letter to the author, March 11, 1992.
8. *New York Times*, February 17, 1991.
9. Suzanne Cassidy, "Profits vs. Programs for British TV," *New York Times*, February 10, 1992.
10. Deaver made this comment to a class taught by Stephen Cohen in the Writing Seminars program at the Johns Hopkins University, Baltimore, MD, on March 26, 1991. The author attended the class and took notes.

11. Ken Auletta, "Why ABC News Survived Best," in *New York Times Magazine*, July 28, 1991, 20-28. Auletta later expanded his article into a book, *Three Blind Mice: How the TV Networks Lost Their Way* (New York: Random House, 1992). He relates numerous accounts of the clash between news and entertainment specialists but concludes that the entertainment entrepreneurs learned to try for leadership in TV news as well as in entertainment.

12. Walter Goodman, "Nightly News Look Beyond the Headlines," *New York Times*, July 7, 1991. The monitoring organization was identified as the newsletter *Tyndall Report*.

13. Bill Carter, "Now It Can Be Told: Tabloid TV Is Booming," *New York Times*, December 23, 1981.

14. The comments in this and the following two paragraphs were made during a session at a convention of the Radio and Television News Directors Association (RTNDA), Miami Beach, Florida, September 30, 1993. The session was titled "'Flash or Trash': The Impact, Credibility and Fairness of Tabloid News."

15. Ibid. Deaver remarked the visual appealed to the vision that the people wanted to have, both of themselves and the country, as well and healthy. "TV ate it up," he said.

16. Michael Kelly, "David Gergen, Master of the Game: How Image Became the Sacred Faith of Washington, and How This Insider Became Its High Priest," *New York Times Magazine*, October 31, 1993, 68.

17. See note 14.

18. See especially Antonio Gramsci, *Selections From the Prison Notebook*, Quintin Hoare and Geoffrey Nowell, eds. (New York: International Publishers, 1971).

19. Neil Postman, *Amusing Ourselves to Death: Public Discourse in the Age of Show Business* (New York: Penguin, 1985), 83-98. The media treatment of the sexual harassment by Naval officers at the "Tailhook" convention in 1991 is a case in point.

20. Postman, 87.

21. Postman, 92, 111, 136, 159.

22. W. Lance Bennett, *The Politics of Illusion*, 2nd ed. (White Plains, NY: Longman, 1988), 176.

23. Edwin Diamond, *Sign Off: The Last Days of Television* (Cambridge, MA: MIT Press, 1982), 3-25.

24. Bagdikian, *The Media Monopoly*, 136. For other critics of television news as entertainment, see Herbert I. Schiller, *The Mind Managers* (Boston: Beacon Press, 1977), Michael R. Real, *Mass-Mediated Culture* (Englewood Cliffs, NJ: Prentice-Hall, 1977), and Michael Parenti, *Inventing Reality: The Politics of the Mass Media* (New York: St. Martin's, 1986).

25. See, for instance, Reuven Frank, *Out of Thin Air: The Brief Wonderful Life of Network News* (New York: Simon & Schuster, 1991). See also Hank Whittemore, *CNN: The Inside Story* (Boston: Little, Brown, 1990), among others.

26. Carter spoke at the RTNDA convention, September 30, 1993.

27. Herbert J. Gans, *Deciding What's News: A Study of CBS Evening News, NBC Nightly News, Newseek and Time* (New York: Vintage Books, 1960), 214-48.

28. Gans, 241.

29. Gans, 61. On page 48, he identified these values as ethnocentrism, altruistic democracy, responsible capitalism, small-town parochialism, individualism, moderation, order, and national leadership.

30. See, for instance, Herbert Marcuse, *One-Dimensional Man* (Boston: Beacon Press, 1964), and Jacques Ellul, *Propaganda* (New York: Vintage Books, 1973).

31. Roger Smith, "The TV War As a Game Show," *Propaganda Review* 8 (Fall 1991): 32.

32. George Gerbner, "Television: The New State Religion," *Et cetera* (June 1977): 2145-50: "Television is the new state religion run by a private Ministry of Culture (the three networks), offering a universal curriculum for all people, financed by a form of hidden taxation without representation. You pay when you wash, not when you watch, and whether or not you care to watch."

33. Michael Wines, "Reno Chastises TV Executives Over Violence," *New York Times*, October 21, 1993.

34. Diamond, *Sign Off*, 9-10.

35. Todd Gitlin, "Prime Time Ideology: The Hegemonic Process in Television Entertainment," *Social Forces* 26, 3 (February 1979): 440-41.

36. David H. Weaver and G. Cleveland Wilhoit, *The American Journalist: A Portrait of U.S. News People and Their Work*, 2nd ed. (Bloomington: Indiana University Press, 1991), 123.

37. Weaver and Wilhoit, 209.

38. Gitlin, "Prime Time Ideology," 449.

39. Bagdikian, *The Media Monopoly*, 167.

PART III

THE POLITICAL ARENA IN MARKET SOCIETY

Chapter
8

"OUR REPUBLIC AND ITS PRESS WILL RISE OR FALL TOGETHER"

1847 1947
JOSEPH PULITZER

3¢ UNITED STATES POSTAGE

Power, Politics, and the Media in the United States

ACCOUNTABILITY AND MANIPULATION

The news media are not isolated actors. They play a central role in the economic and political lives of cities and nations, of the world itself. They are an institution, with all the qualities of other institutions. They have their own structures, their own bureaucracies, and their own belief systems. In short, they can't be imagined in isolation from other institutions. How, then, does the press interact with the political institutions of the United States, especially the presidency? An examination of this interaction allows us to illustrate the social control role the news media play in societies generally, for, although the presidency is a peculiarly American institution, the pattern of interaction appears everywhere. Some elements in the media's belief system have already been noted, particularly belief in the code of objectivity. Another, equally important part of that belief system is what we call the doctrine of social responsibility.[1]

The term surfaced as a model for American institutions following World War II, and in short order it swept the world as a standard to seek. The model quickly gained wide acceptance in the press, perhaps because of the press's tenuous state as the only commercial institution in the country to be guaranteed under the First Amendment freedom from government interference in its private operations. The social reforms of the New Deal had severely limited the freedom of action of the business community, and the press had no reason to assume these limitations would not be extended to the media, the First Amendment notwithstanding.

Traditionally, conservative publishers took nervous notice of the increasing criticism of the press by Democratic party leaders, by the rising trade-union movement in the press industry, and by President Franklin Roosevelt. The criticism took two forms: The press was unfair and slanted in its political coverage, and in its news columns it was presenting gossip, trash, and trivia rather than information useful to the public. If this criticism were to go too far, many publishers believed, it might lead to governmental restraints. In this situation, Henry Luce of *Time* magazine decided it was prudent to develop a counterstrategy. He provided the financing for a commission of scholars to study the state of the press and come up with recommendations for improving the quality of the press in an effort to head off any government intervention.

Thus the Hutchins Commission was established in 1946, a year after the end of the war, under Robert Hutchins, the "boy wonder" of academe and a man with impeccable credentials among liberals. Luce was determined the commission would not be made up entirely of persons of his own political persuasion; the University of Chicago's Hutchins was an ideal choice. Twelve others, all experts in their own fields, were named to the study group, and *Time* provided a $200,000 grant. *Encyclopedia Britannica* gave an additional $15,000. The commission's report, published a year later, not only wrote the term *social responsibility* into the world of the U.S. media but also came to dominate the discussions of press philosophy and ethics that followed, up to the present, all over the world. The carefully written, concise report, titled *A Free and Responsible Press*, concluded that freedom of the press was in actual danger for three reasons: (1) In the modern world, the press had increased in importance and visibility; (2) the few who ran the press had not provided a service adequate to the needs of society; and (3) the few had sometimes engaged in society-condemned practices that, if continued, would lead inevitably to government regulation or control. The remedy, the commission announced, was a greater assumption of responsibility by the press and action by the informed public to see to it the press lived up to its responsibility. The commission minced few words in its condemnation of press practices, calling press output meaningless, flat, and distorted, leading to "the perpetuation of misunderstanding." The press's emphasis on "the exceptional rather than the representative; the sensational rather than the significant," it said, means that "the citizen is not supplied the information and discussion he needs to discharge his responsibilities to the community."[2]

The commission painted its picture of an irresponsible and sensational press with a broad brush, condemning the concentration of press ownership in the hands of a few representatives of "big business" and spoke of "exaggerated drives for power and profit" as leading toward monopoly, and "a common bias" of the large investors and employers. The commission recommended a five-point program on what a free press ought to provide, urged the creation of councils to review the performance of the press, and reproved schools of journalism for failing to set standards for the press. It fell short of proposing enforcement powers for the press councils, but it did emphasize a need for "vigorous mutual criticism" within the press. If the press (the commission studied both newspapers and radio) did not reform itself, the commission said, then the government would. It declared that freedom of the press is "essential to political liberty" but freedom is in danger unless it becomes "an accountable freedom"—accountable to conscience and the common good.

The commission clearly spelled out its view of the role of the press in contemporary society. The public, it said, had a right to expect of the press five basic services: (1) an accurate, comprehensive account of the day's news; (2) a forum for exchange of comment; (3) a means of projecting group opinions and attitudes to one another; (4) a method of presenting and clarifying the goals and values of the society; and (5) a way of reaching every member of society. The public had a right to expect not only the fact to be presented in a meaningful context but also "the truth about the fact"—in other words, not merely objective reality but objective reality clarified and explained.

The press was expected, as called for in the fourth service, to state and clarify the goals and *values* of society, a heavy responsibility indeed because society's values may not be identical among men and women, rich and poor, white and black, native-born and immigrants, Christians and Jews. Such superhuman expectations contribute to the often furious debates and confusions that continue to take place over precisely what role the press plays and ought to play in human affairs.

If Luce expected widespread approval by the U.S. press community, he was mistaken. Wilber Forrest, president of the American Society of Newspaper Editors, accused the commission of condemning the entire U.S. press because of the "dereliction of the comparative few." Other editors spoke out in similar vein. So did journalism scholars. In an article in *Journalism Quarterly*, a publication of journalism educators, Robert Desmond challenged the commission for failing to conduct systematic research and especially for its harsh criticism of journalism schools. *The New York Times*, in a cautiously balanced commentary, complained the commission "holds to standards of perfection in an evolving medium and is too impatient because we have not caught up yet with these standards."[3] Still, while the initial reaction was cool if not overtly hostile, within a decade the U.S. press community had adopted the social-responsibility thesis as if it, like freedom of the press and the public's right to know, had been handed down from some journalistic Mount Sinai.

The fundamental role the Hutchins Commission demanded of the press was rooted in the *democratic assumption*, which holds that democracy is nurtured and furthered when an informed citizenry make wise judgments in choosing their government representatives. To work toward this end is to be responsible. In carrying out this role, the press must be accountable to the public it serves. This, then, is the central theme of the Hutchins Commission report. The standards it assigned to the press are similar to those all institutions assign to themselves. The code of the medical profession is identified in the oath of Hippocrates. Similar codes have been developed by lawyers, engineers, teachers, and representatives of other institutions. The code of social responsibility for the press was identified and publicized by the Hutchins Commission. The ideas behind that code had been in circulation for centuries throughout the world. Marx had written of the duties of the press a century earlier, and before Marx there had been Cato and Franklin, Voltaire and Milton, and many others. When Pulitzer proposed a school of journalism at Columbia University, he proclaimed its purpose to be to help the journalist become more responsible in gathering and reporting news. The school would "mark the distinction between real journalists and men who do a kind of newspaper work that requires neither culture nor conviction but only business training."[4] It was not until 1956, with the publication of *Four Theories of the Press* by Theodore Peterson, Wilbur Schramm, and Fred S. Siebert, that the term *social responsibility* became a shortcut phrase to stand as a symbol for the ideal of a "democratic" press.

In their renowned book, the authors identified the "social responsibility" doctrine as one of four theories of the relationship between the press on one hand and government or society on the other as to "concepts of what the press should be and do."[5] In the history of humankind, they wrote, there had been no more than two, or four, basic theories of the press. They identified the basic two as authoritarian and libertarian and said that the remaining two were but developments and modifications of the first two. The authoritarian theory had been modified into the Soviet communist doctrine and the libertarian into the social-responsibility concept.

The basic difference between libertarian and social-responsibility ideas was that in the libertarian concept, the press was totally free, altogether unfettered; whereas the social-responsibility doctrine recognized the peril of unrestrained liberty. According to the authors of *Four Theories*, libertarianism demanded two duties of the press: to serve as a watchdog, "as an extralegal check on government," and to serve as an instrument of adult education, since "the success of democracy was posited upon an intelligent and informed electorate." To carry out these duties, the press "had to be completely free from control or domination by those elements which it was to guard against." The idea of social responsibility developed, they wrote, when people recognized there were weaknesses and inconsistencies in libertarianism, mainly because it had failed to supply "rigorous standards for the day-to-day operations of the mass media—in short, a stable formula to distinguish liberty and abuse of liberty." It had served a noble purpose, nonetheless, for it had "struck off the manacles from the mind of man" and "opened up new vistas for humanity."[6]

The vision of a press world offered by *Four Theories* was riven by colliding doctrines of social responsibility and Soviet communism; it was possible only in a war of ideologies where, as was said by Winston Churchill, perhaps the chief cold warrior of all, a great battle was being fought for the minds of men. Time has shown that if ever such a battle took place, it was no more than a skirmish in the history of the press. The fall of the Soviet empire has demonstrated the fragility of ideological analyses of press history. If the "theory" of one-half of the theoretical contest, that of Soviet communism, can be shown to be illusory, what can be said of the validity of the other half of the theoretical equation?

The authors were on more solid footing in their examination of some of the historical factors that led to the rise of the social-responsibility doctrine. In the Western world, faith in progress had declined, and the increasing complexity of social and political issues had muddled public understanding. The simple rural life of harmony with nature had all but vanished with the growth of cities and the appearance of the megalopolis. The alienation recognized by Hegel and Marx had become the suicidal anomie identified by Durkheim. Belief in rationality had evaporated with the expansion of psychological and psychiatric insights. Economic power was increasingly vested in distant and anonymous corporations. The mass media had become big business. Newspapers and magazines were now competing for attention with comic books, motion pictures, and radio; television had already appeared as a reality. Computers were just over the horizon.

Moreover, the world of faith—in God, in one's fellow man, in the future—had disintegrated and been replaced by a world dominated more by fear of the future than by confidence in it. Institutions were on the defensive. The age of the muck-rakers had been one of persistent assault on all institutions. Will Irwin, Upton Sinclair, and the others had cast so much doubt on the validity of the old assumptions it was no longer possible to perceive the press simply as the servant of the people, as their eyes and ears in alerting them to incipient tyranny. Moreover, there was increasing concentration of the ownership of the mass media. Newspapers ceased to multiply in number as the population increased, and the roster of owners decreased. Mergers and joint-stock agreements resulted in lessened competition. Cities in which small-circulation newspapers could manage to eke out a living declined. Only the mighty were able to survive in the great cities. The age of "giantism" was at hand. Newspapers owned by absentee landlords could not hope to maintain the same kind of loyal readership as might the small-town publisher whose interests were identical to those of other local entrepreneurs. In this situation, it was only natural the press would slip in public esteem and would cease to be revered as an ally of the people. It was also only natural there would arise a new word to express an overriding need of the institution of the press: *credibility*.

If only the newspapers and the broadcasters could retain their image as the ally of the people, they might preserve their position in the social and economic firmament. To maintain that image, they had to be believable; their reports had to be perceived to be accurate and fair, serving the interests of the public at large. The press could not be considered to possess credibility if it did not practice social responsibility, if it did not cease insisting on unchecked liberty. Instead, the press must itself condemn transgressions of the institution and proclaim it would no longer deserve its privileged freedom under the First Amendment if it did not link that freedom with responsibility to all members of society.

The call of the Hutchins Commission was less for a poorly defined sense of responsibility than for the more demanding aim of *accountability*. Freedom, the commission wrote, was in danger unless it became accountable to "conscience and the common good." To monitor press accountability, the commission proposed "a new and independent agency" that would appraise and report annually on press performance. If no such independent body were set up, the commission warned, the government might take unto itself the power to appraise and perhaps even regulate press performance. From this proposal developed the concept of the press council, an institution that would be composed of experts from within and outside the world of journalism to keep an eye on both the press and the government to protect against inroads on press freedom. Despite the high reputation of the Hutchins Commission members and despite agitation by many individual journalists and professors of journalism, the kind of press council envisaged by the Hutchins group did not materialize in the United States, although a National News Council, lamentably short-lived, was created in 1973.

On the other hand, a press council in Britain established a powerful beach-head, serving as model for similar institutions elsewhere—in Germany, Sweden, Switzerland, Canada, Italy, and India, among other places. The impetus for a British council came at the same time as the movement in the United States, fired by charges by Socialist members of Parliament that concentration of ownership and sensational news treatment had "degraded . . . the honorable profession of journalism." Haydn Davis, a journalist and Socialist party member of Parliament, raised this question: "Can we or can we not have real freedom of the press in a system of combines and chain newspapers?" Even though a royal commission was set up in 1946, it took twenty years for a viable, independent British council to gain support from public and Parliament. Composed of twenty press members and five public members, it accepted the challenge of preserving press freedom and at the same time reviewing the industry in order to maintain "the highest professional and commercial standards." The council was given no enforcement powers, but newspapers were required to publish its findings on the theory that the glare of publicity would shame offenders into desisting from questionable practices. H. Phillip Levy, author of a history of the council, held that it was intended to be an educator, not an inquisitor, and its appeal was to conscience and fair play.[7] The council, as Levy has noted, has become "feared, respected, and obeyed" in the British media community. Still, sensationalism is as alive as ever in the narrowing English press spectrum, as it is in all parts of the world. The raucous, unreliable *Bild Zeitung* is, for instance, the most widely read newspaper in Germany. Imitators can be found everywhere.

The major impetus in England (as in the United States) was to improve the news media's level of credibility, to do something to make the product of newspapers and broadcasters more believable. In the view of Patrick Brogan, a student of press councils, the British council was wise to limit itself to questions of accuracy and fairness, thereby avoiding questions of taste or news judgment, aiming instead at keeping the press honest and politicians off its back, not at eliminating trivia from the news pages or at elevating the level of public taste.[8] The push for councils in the United States came with an outburst of public rage over a "credibility gap" between what was true and what it was being told during the Vietnam War. Contempt for sensationalism and the trivializing of the news always had played a powerful role on the American scene, but questions about a credibility gap magnified a decline in the prestige of the press.[9]

In that period, the credibility of all large and visible institutions was called into question. In 1973, the columnist David Broder of *The Washington Post* observed the public had "more faith in the competence of people who run local trash collection" than in those who controlled television or the press or even the Supreme Court or Congress.[10] Insistence that the watchdog be watched emerged everywhere, especially following the open attack on the behavior of the press by President Nixon and Vice President Agnew.[11] The vice president drew widespread public applause and outraged criticism from the press for implying possible government action to restrict its "independence." Arguing that unparalleled power had been seized by a handful of television and print journalists, Agnew said the public would not long tolerate such concentration of power in the hands of television anchormen and producers. "Is it," he asked, "not fair and relevant to question its concentration in the hands of a tiny and closed fraternity of privileged men, elected by no one, and enjoying a monopoly sanctioned and licensed by government?"[12]

In such an environment, it was not surprising that news councils sprang up in communities from coast to coast; that one state, Minnesota, established a statewide council; or even that the National News Council was brought into existence. The National News Council was, however, in trouble from the start. The mass media gave it only lukewarm support, arguing newspapers and broadcasters were better equipped to judge flaws in press behavior than any kind of quasi-official body that might seek to impose regulations on a free press. Still, many papers did agree to cooperate with the council, and more than thirty news organizations contributed financially (the British council was financed by levies assessed on all media on the basis of circulation). The American council limited itself to examining "national" news reporting—meaning the product of the news agencies; news magazines; television networks; and a handful of leading newspapers, such as *The New York Times*, *The Washington Post*, and *The Wall Street Journal*.

The failure of the American council can be attributed to a number of factors, among them inadequate financing, lukewarm support from media leaders, and weak management, although the prime factor was its failure to win over the public. Few Americans seemed even to have heard of the council. This ignorance was enhanced by the limited publicity given by the news media to council decisions. In Britain, the rule was for news media to give prominent mention to council action. Not so in the United States. As Patrick Brogan has pointed out, the council spent more time trying to win favor with the media than in criticizing its behavior. Such a council would never win friends among journalists and editors, he said, so it ought to recognize that its proper constituency is the public, not the professionals.[13]

Many journalists and editors as well as journalism educators saw and continue to see considerable merit in the concept of a news council, and it remains at least possible that the council will one day be revived and made to work. In order to achieve higher credibility, some newspapers have adopted the ombudsman technique widely used in the Scandinavian countries, where the public lodges complaints against official actions and the ombudsman investigates for them. Two dozen American newspapers, beginning with *The Louisville Courier-Journal and Times* in 1967, have followed the ombudsman technique, with varying success. A similar function is carried out by the "house critic" of *The Washington Post*, whose assignment is to guard against "creeping bias, laziness, inaccuracy, and the sins of omission." Ombudsmen and house critics have made serious efforts to represent the public in their challenges to the performance of the press, but it has been a lonely job that has rarely resulted in more than cosmetic change.[14] The chief difficulty confronted by ombudsmen has been the hostility of their fellow workers on newspapers, who resent, as do journalists everywhere, being second-guessed about their work. Social responsibility remains the unofficial doctrine of the press, yet it remains a vaguely worded model whose perimeters are ill defined and in practice largely ignored.

THE BOUNDARIES OF ACCEPTABLE DISSENT

Every social order—regardless of its economic, social, or political system—confers on the press, particularly in market societies such as the United States and its traditional capitalistic allies, the obligation to behave "responsibly." In the years when Marxist-Leninist doctrines held sway in the Soviet empire, capitalist analysts such as the authors of the *Four Theories* accused the Marxist press of irresponsible behavior; at the same time, socialist theorists condemned the capitalist press as irresponsible. In the less industrialized nations, the charge of irresponsibility was directed against both capitalist and socialist mass media. In short, everyone accused the other guy of the wickedness of irresponsibility and exhorted his or her own press to live up to the virtue of responsibility. The adjective *social* was not always employed, but it was clear that the benefits of a responsible press were to accrue to the people, to the public, and to society. These troublesome terms—*people*, *public*, *society*—were never clearly defined. Under repressive programs in force in China, South Africa, Indonesia, Iraq, Paraguay, and elsewhere, the news media were nonetheless required to be "responsible."

The image is inevitably that of the press serving the needs of society. Yet it has also been true that no authority has wanted its press to practice just any kind of social responsibility; what was wanted was the kind of social responsibility that suited a particular conception of the social order and acted as a medium of social control. Soviet rulers were not prepared to accept as virtuous the American model of social responsibility, and the U.S. government was not ready to accept the Soviet idea of social responsibility. In the same way, the leaders of many arriving nation-states rejected both the Soviet and the American models. Despite tolerance of a modest number of critical voices, each system allowed only those news media that were prepared to live in comfortable companionship with the leadership to flourish and prosper.

It is important for leaders in all nation-states to see to it their press behaves in an acceptable fashion. The most painless method for ensuring this has proved to be manipulation, the gentle direction of publishers, editors, and reporters into the promotion of the status quo. Where mere manipulation has failed, the wielders of power have found themselves compelled to resort to less genteel practices: to rigid rules and regulations; to censorship; or, if necessary, to repression, prison sentences, torture, or even death. Each of these practices has been carried out in the name of protecting society and ensuring the press behaves "responsibly" in reporting to society. The press in all instances is an agent of political and economic power.

The sociologist Max Weber recognized the agency role of the press in the early twentieth century. He argued that "so-called public opinion" in a modern democratic state was for the most part stage-managed by political leaders luring the press into manipulating the masses to accept the social order with good cheer.[15] The notion of freedom of the press, Weber wrote, is a convenient vehicle for charismatic leadership. Believing this, Weber nonetheless pursued a career as a political journalist, imagining that he might somehow break the rules and exert an independent influence over the course of events. In this, Weber was behaving like many journalists and writers before and since, among them Karl Marx and Walter Lippmann.

Even more than Weber, Ferdinand Tönnies, another influential German sociologist, recognized the vulnerability of the press to manipulation. Writing before the advent of television and the highly sophisticated technical equipment of the modern mass media, Tönnies said that in the press, "judgments and opinion are wrapped up like grocers' goods and offered for consumption in their objective reality."[16] Newspapers, he said, provide "the quickest production, multiplication, and distribution of facts and thoughts, just as the hotel kitchen provides food and drink in every conceivable form and quantity." Thus, Tönnies wrote:

> The press is the real instrument of public opinion, a weapon and tool in the hands of those who know how to use it and have to use it; it possesses universal power as the dreaded critic of events and changes in social conditions. It is comparable and, in some respects, superior to the material power which the states possess through their armies, their treasuries, and their bureaucratic civil service.[17]

In Tönnies's analysis, public opinion was the expression not of the masses but of the elite of the social order; hence the press, when it gave voice to public opinion, was in reality expressing the viewpoint of the elite. No government would be likely to object to that kind of public opinion. After all, it would be socially irresponsible not to deliver such reports.

Those journalists who refused to be manipulated and were determined to be independent of authority—who were, in short, revolutionary thinkers and writers—followed the time-honored tradition of going underground. Many names have been applied to a revolutionary press of this nature. In modern times, we have heard of the new journalism, the underground press, the alternative press, the advocacy press, and the investigative press. Significant differences exist among these groups. Not all are revolutionary, though all share the belief that a press can be revolutionary and free to the extent it raises challenges to the politically and economically powerful who normally control the press. According to Narindar Aggarwala of India, an executive in the United Nations Development Program, the duty of a journalist in a developing society is similar to the duty revolutionary journalists have identified for themselves: to examine public figures and issues critically and call attention to the differences between what government officials claim and how they really execute their programs.[18] Interestingly, revolutionary journalists, unlike those who operate in the mainstream of their trade, disclaim any kind of pro-

I. F. Stone defies the boundaries: a columnist who could not be manipulated.

SOURCE: UPI/Bettmann

fessional status. Only they, the revolutionary journalists say, constitute the truly socially responsible press.

It was in the United States that the new journalism and the other modern forms of revolutionary press originated, reaching their zenith during the social upheaval of the 1960s. Those in power were convinced it was necessary to neutralize these journalists to prevent them from exercising their potential to influence the public or to effect changes not desired by the leadership. It is for this reason presidents and other political leaders have appealed to the patriotic public to help trim the sails of the runaway press. Failing to produce legal controls, they have nevertheless succeeded in raising serious doubts about the credibility of the press, especially those elements critical of the powerful. Although television networks and the most influential newspapers condemned Vice President Agnew's assault on their freedom of movement, many newspapers and television stations across the country agreed with him. Some elements of the press had, they said, grown too powerful and needed to exercise greater social responsibility—meaning they needed to assent to the status quo. Even political foes of Nixon and Agnew rallied to their side. Daniel Patrick Moynihan, a Harvard professor who had served as a diplomat under Nixon and who later became a Democratic senator from New York, complained of a "culture of disparagement" in the U.S. press, in which an adversarial media threatened the future of democratic institutions. Journalists, he said, referring not to the revolutionary press but to the mainstream reporters in Washington, were not engaging in serious inquiry and were guilty of "an almost feckless hostility to power."[19]

The impact of the underground periodicals that sprang up across the United States in the 1960s was significant. The editors and journalists blithely disregarded profit and demonstrated contempt for those in power. In a romantic vein they embarked on a quest for Truth. As one of their leaders, Ray Mungo, put it: "Facts are less important than truth and the two are far from equivalent . . . for cold facts are nearly always boring and may even distort the truth, but Truth is the highest achievement of human expression."[20] Most mainstream journalists ridiculed such claims, accusing Mungo and his fellows of distorting the truth to pursue their political objectives. The real path to truth in their view was through the time-honored tradition of dispassionate observation and objective reporting. The new journalists rejected objectivity altogether. Truth, according to Tom Wolfe, Norman Mailer, and the others, could be discovered only if the writer or journalist were subjectively involved in his or her research. While the principles advocated by the revolutionary journalists were being publicly disavowed by the traditional press, some of their practices were being taken over. The layout, graphics, and design of the mainstream press became splashier and easier to read, following the patterns of the underground press. Attacks on the powerful increased; emboldened columnists and editorial writers stepped up their criticism of the political leadership and its programs. While the underground press failed to gain the readership and advertising necessary for survival, it had an impact on the mainstream press, which ultimately drove it away by coopting some of its practices, although in a severely modified form.[21]

With the virtual disappearance of the underground press came the rise of investigative journalists. Whereas underground editors and reporters adopted as a creed the quest for truth, investigative journalists aimed to unearth evidence of wickedness in high places and to publish indictments so scathing the evil perpetrators would be brought to justice, either in the courtroom or—as it was often said—in the court of public opinion. The quest was no longer for truth but for victory over evil. The "adversary culture" of which Moynihan had spoken had arrived. British scholar Anthony Smith wrote that the Western journalist in Europe as well as the United States came to see his or her role "as a kind of institutionalized permanent opposition, always looking critically askance at the doings of those who hold official positions of power."[22]

Investigative journalists claimed they were sounding their drumbeat of opposition for the benefit of society and therefore they were true upholders of the doctrine of social responsibility. On the other hand, critics held the investigators were so biased by their very nature they were not using their power responsibly when they sapped the ability of their leaders to govern effectively. Walter Annenberg, a veteran publisher and diplomat, put it this way: "The difference is that the President has power with responsibility; the press has power without responsibility."[23]

Of all the paradoxes, none is more intriguing than the inconsistency in the principle of watchdoggery. Anyone who studies the press finds himself or herself confronted almost with a belief system that accepts the press as an institution whose reason for existence is wrapped up in the idea that it serves the public by acting as a watchdog, a German shepherd whose glittering eye is eternally fixed on Wotan and his henchmen to make certain they do not abuse their power. Such declares an article of faith in the capitalist press system, a system sometimes described as adversarial. The idea of an adversarial press conjures up an image of the press playing prosecuting attorney, charging power—usually identified as government—with violations of law or moral rectitude. In this picture, power functions as the defendant, with the reading or viewing public as judge and jury. The principle of watchdoggery notwithstanding, the literature about the press is also filled with recognition the relationship between press and power is less adversarial than symbiotic.

The watchdog news media.

SOURCE: Mary Miller

What a difference! What a remarkable paradox! If in fact press and power need each other, cannot exist without each other, what becomes of the principle of watchdoggery? What becomes of the concept of prodigious independent power on the part of the press?

A sharp increase in critical articles about those who hold or seek political power is obvious. Consider the rash of scatological articles about the private, sexual lives of political candidates. This outpouring of behind-closed-doors articles has led such commentators as Larry Sabato to speak of a feeding frenzy among American journalists, and while it is true criticism of *individuals* has heightened markedly, one must search long and hard to find serious criticism of the political and economic systems that have furthered public venality. For example, many journalists have written articles exposing greed and corruption among individuals in high places, but very few articles have taken on the *systemic* weaknesses that have fostered the behavior. The systemic boundaries of dissent criticism of such mainstays of the society as a market economic system, the iconic symbols of motherhood and the flag, formal religion, or adherence to the societal virtues of reverence, faithfulness, loyalty, and the sanctity of the family. Individuals have indeed been wounded by investigative journalism, yet the values expressed in these investigative articles have been the icons of the social order.

The French philosopher Jacques Ellul has presented a thoughtful explanation in his concept of "sociological propaganda," which operates at a subtler and deeper level than political propaganda and produces "a certain general conception of society, a particular way of life. . . . When an American movie producer makes a film, he has certain definite ideas he wants to express, which are not intended to be propaganda. Rather, the propaganda element is the American way of life with which he is permeated and which he expresses in his film without realizing it."[24]

Sociological propaganda goes out via the same media that are devices for airing political propaganda: advertising, movies, education, social agencies, technological devices, and, of course, the news media. Here we reach the boundaries of acceptable dissent in any social order, not of individuals but of the society's basic belief system. Media criticism of the social order does not extend to an abstraction such as "the American way of life." In fact, the sociological propaganda broadcast over media channels is virtually identical in essence to the messages distributed by a government's public-relations industry.[25]

In recent years, the power claims advanced for the press have pursued a new path, drawing on an assertion by political scientist Bernard C. Cohen that the press "may not be successful much of the time in telling people what to think, but it is stunningly successful in telling its readers what to think *about*."[26] Cohen's comment was instrumental in leading to an area of research its creators identified as the agenda-setting function of the mass media.[27] Douglass Cater went a step further by declaring the media "have a vast power to shape government" in the very act of selecting which information to report and which to ignore. "Those words that fail to get projected might as well not have occurred," he said.[28] Editor Robert Stein injected a variation on the agenda-setting theme by arguing the power to select gives the media "a new kind of power over us all" because they are able to select which group to make visible to the public and which to condemn to some limbo simply by inattention.[29] Indeed, according to Stein, it is this "power" that has intensified an adversarial relationship between the press and politicians, who see the media as usurping their prerogative to shape the public agenda. I refer to this spurious role for the news media as their AWA role—as adversary, watchdog, and agenda setter.

NOTES

1. For a discussion of the term *social responsibility* and its philosophical significance, see the Appendix.

2. *A Free and Responsible Press* (Chicago: University of Chicago Press, 1947). The text of the commission report appeared in Luce's *Fortune* (April 1947) issue, 1-4. In an accompanying article, *Fortune* expressed a few reservations, calling the report difficult to read and saying that in many cases it used "exasperatingly cryptic" expressions. On the whole, it said, the report was meaty and important. An interesting summary of the Hutchins Commission report, together with certain criticisms, appeared in *Nieman Reports* (Autumn 1976), 18-25, in an article written by Louis Lyons, the curator of the Nieman Foundation. No better summary of the report and its findings is available anywhere. Among other things, Lyons criticized the report for failing to provide for policing of rulings of the news councils that are recommended by the commission.

3. Wilbur Forrest, address at convention of American Society of Newspaper Editors, April 17, 1947, reprinted in *Problems of Journalism*, 19; Robert Desmond, "Of a Free and Responsible Press," *Journalism Quarterly* 24, 2 (June 1947): 188-92.

4. Joseph Pulitzer offered his rationale for starting the school in "The College of Journalism," *North American Review* 178 (May 1904): 164-80. See also Richard Terrill Baker, *A History of the Graduate School of Journalism* (New York: Columbia University Press, 1954).

5. Theodore Peterson, Wilbur Schramm, and Fred S. Siebert, *Four Theories of the Press: The Authoritarian, Libertarian, Social Responsibility and Soviet Communist Concepts of What the Press Should Be and Do* (Urbana, IL: University of Chicago Press, 1956).

6. Peterson, Schramm, and Siebert, *Four Theories*.

7. H. Phillip Levy, *The Press Council: History, Procedure and Cause* (New York: St. Martin's, 1967). The cited quotations in this paragraph are drawn from Levy. For a report on an intriguing British Press Council case, see J. Herbert Altschull, "'Moment of Truth' for the BBC," *Columbia Journalism Review* (November/December 1971) 43-50. See also *Mass Media, Codes of Ethics and Councils*, (Paris: Unesco, 1980).

8. Patrick Brogan, *Spiked: The Short Life and Death of the National News Council* (New York: Priority Press, 1985), 104-8.

9. The *APME News*, official publication of the Associated Press Managing Editors Association, reported in 1969 that a questionnaire of editors and public officials had shown a wide acknowledgment of a credibility gap. Katharine Graham, publisher of *The Washington Post*, told an APME meeting: "The American people do not seem at all happy with their press. . . . The nation's publishers are acutely aware of the general indictment."

10. David Broder, *Washington Post*, October 11, 1973.

11. Brogan, *Spiked*, 10-11.

12. See *New York Times*, November 4, 1969, 24, for the text of Agnew's speech.

13. Brogan, *Spiked*, 92.

14. The most celebrated case in which a house critic has been involved in the case of Janet Cooke, a Pulitzer Prize winner for *The Washington Post*, who was later found to have manufactured her story. For details, see J. Herbert Altschull, *From Milton to McLuhan: The Ideas Behind American Journalism* (White Plains, NY: Longman, 1990), 361-63. See also Brogan, *Spiked*, 68-70, in which he accuses the *Post* house critic of "pulling his punches" in his lengthy report on the case.

15. Max Weber, "Politik als Beruf," in Johannes Winckelmann, ed., *Max Weber: Staatssoziologie* (Berlin: Drucker & Humboldt, 1966), 83. The article, originally delivered as a lecture in Munich in 1918, has often been reprinted. For an excellent discussion of Weber's writings on journalism, see Hanno Hardt, *Social Theories of the Press: Early German & American Perspectives* (Beverly Hills, CA: Sage, 1979), 159-86.

16. Quoted in Hardt, *Social Theories of the Press*, 150-51. The original passage appears in Werner Tönnies, *Community & Society*, trans. Charles P. Loomis (New York: Harper Torchbooks, 1963), 221.

17. Hardt, *Social Theories*, 151.

18. Quoted in Anthony Smith, *Geopolitics*, 99.

19. Daniel Patrick Moynihan, "The President and the Press," *Commentary* (March 1971): 43.

20. Raymond Mungo, *Famous Long Ago: My Life and Hard Times with Liberation News Service* (Boston: Beacon Press, 1970), 75-76.

21. See, among others, Robert J. Glessing, *The Underground Press in America* (Bloomington: Indiana University Press, 1970).

22. Smith, *Geopolitics*, 154.

23. Walter Annenberg, "The Fourth Branch of Government," *TV Guide*, May 15, 1982.

24. Jacques Ellul, *Propaganda: The Formation of Men's Attitudes* (New York: Vintage Books, 1973), 65.

25. Ellul.

26. Bernard C. Cohen, *The Press and Foreign Policy* (Princeton, NJ: Princeton University Press, 1957), 38.

27. Donald L. Shaw and Maxwell E. McCombs, *The Emergence of American Political Issues; The Agenda-Setting Function of the Press* (St. Paul, MN: West, 1977).

28. Douglass Cater, *The Fourth Branch of Government* (Boston: Houghton Mifflin, 1953), 14.

29. Robert A. Stein, *Media Power: Who Is Shaping the Picture of the World* (Englewood Cliffs, NJ: Prentice-Hall, 1970), xii.

Chapter

9

"OUR REPUBLIC AND ITS PRESS WILL RISE OR FALL TOGETHER"

1847   1947
JOSEPH PULITZER

3¢ UNITED STATES POSTAGE

Spin Doctors and Media Managers

POLITICAL CAMPAIGNS AND THE NEWS MEDIA

As an objective, disinterested observer, the press is essentially a transmitter of information. In spite of appearances, the press is not an independent voice either in its AWA role or as an "objective" observer. Because the vision of journalists is clouded by the folklore, they are themselves more easily *used* as AWA. In that role journalists find it increasingly difficult to recognize they are being manipulated. All press systems operate in similar ways, however "free" the system may be. Manipulation of the press is more open in rigidly controlled political societies, as in China today or in the Soviet Union for more than seventy years. Each press model officially endorses a doctrine of social responsibility—and in each system, the effort is made to manage the press. It is hard to sever the silken cords of the folklore that enmesh the press in the market system. The news reporting of U.S. presidential campaigns illustrates the practice.

The doctrine of social responsibility charges the press in its AWA role with "watching" everybody, searching always for defects and weaknesses, and bringing those defects and weaknesses to the attention of the public. On the other hand, the challenge for candidates seeking political office is to maneuver the news media into watching what *they* want watched and into closing their eyes to what the candidates wish to remain unseen.

With each new advance in media technology, manipulation of the news media has grown in importance in contests for the presidency. Candidates and their managers aim to organize the information the electorate receives so the candidate appears the best possible choice for the office. If the contest were over automobiles or aspirins or hair spray, the aim would be to sell the desired product by extolling it while bad-mouthing competing products. Image has become the decisive factor in presidential politics.

The process resembles theater or motion-picture production, where the images you see are on the stage or on the screen. The key players in what we can speak of as the image industry are the directors, here identified as the media managers; the script writers, the set designers, the art directors, the costumers, the makeup people, the lighting experts, and the researchers, in this case meaning the pollsters. The image industry works for two things: power and profit. The mass media are the vehicles used to gain these objectives. To manipulate the media, to use them as agents in this quest for power, is the central task of the image industry. Its job is to present a winning image that evokes the aura of success.

Because the promotional and advertising activities of political candidates are now well known to everyone, much of the selling program is devoted to disguising the very existence of the campaign. The image industry works at manipulating images while the candidate appears to stand above such practices. Perhaps the strongest ally of the media managers has been the existence of the folklore of the press that depicts the news media as adversaries, watchdogs, and agenda setters.

The targeted vessels, the media, are used for "socialized propaganda" on all levels—through direct, paid advertisements in newspaper and magazine displays; paid commercials on radio and television; planted passages in TV comedy shows; hints in newspaper columns; talk shows; TV commemtary; and public statements by celebrities. For little-known candidates, the goal may simply be to be mentioned at all; for the better known, it is to be seen in the favorable light of the wished-for image. The most desirable platform of all is the news. However heavily criticized the news may be, it is inescapable that what is billed as news is regarded as more reliable than what is patently an ad or commercial or what is obviously a planted blurb.

In news sections of newspapers; on news shows on television, cable, and radio; and in news articles in magazines, the image is often decisive. There is nothing new in image building. Abraham Lincoln won fame as a rail splitter and yarn weaver; William Henry Harrison, Zachary Taylor, Ulysses S. Grant, and Dwight Eisenhower as heroic military leaders; Theodore Roosevelt as a Rough Rider in Cuba. What is new, however, is the technology available to the image industry. Stump speeches, self-serving interviews, posed photographs, published white papers—these cannot compete with electronically enhanced docudramas, carefully prepared comments on talk shows and at town meetings, live speeches, interviews, or the carefully doled out reports on public opinion-polls.

Something else new and of great value to the image industry are the vast numbers of journalists in Washington, D.C. Journalism is one of the city's great industries, with the number of journalists ranking just behind those of government employees and lobbyists. In other words, an imagemaker need not travel far to find a journalist to manipulate. Where Franklin Roosevelt could gather the entire White House press corps around his desk in the Oval Office, thousands of journalists now roam the corridors of Washington in search of "news." Newspaper and broadcast journalists based in the capital now total nearly 5,000. The number of nongovernment news sources has soared even more spectacularly. No fewer than 6,000 lobbying organizations were registered in 1993, and that total included not only individual lobbyists but also lobbying firms, many of which counted dozens of public-relations agents on their payrolls.[1] The competitive nature of the journalism business makes life easy for the news source. Journalistic reputations are built by getting in first with the story; so are getting the inside story, getting out the facts behind the headlines. Beating the opposition is a goal built into the journalism business. An imagemaker can offer just what the journalist thirsts for: a news beat, the inside story. Serious, honorable journalists are determined not to surrender to the blandishments offered by the image industry and rather search for what the Hutchins Commission demanded, the true facts behind the apparent facts. But they are frustrated by the reality that their numbers are so great. The image industry has thousands of journalists to whom the apple can be offered. And, in the competitive world of journalism, where life or death depends on advertising revenue, even the best among reporters

A half century of symbiosis between politicians and journalists: a youthful Walter Lippmann and a youthful Franklin D. Roosevelt, two men who knew about wielding power, with Frank Alpine at a 1917 labor-relations board meeting in Washington, D.C.

SOURCE: LIBRARY OF CONGRESS

and editors find themselves bound to compete once the imagemaker's story has found its way into print or on the air.

It is at this point we come to the heart of the question of media power, for it is widely believed the media have the power to shape public opinion and the creation of policy. Many writers and commentators have said so; the vast majority of the public believes it. After all, have not the news media brought down presidents? Have they not shaped public attitudes about sex, race, and public policy? Writers, the public, and students of government preach the same sermon. In a book about the media and foreign policy, Patrick O'Heffernan says "it is obvious" the mass media operating "independent of the government" have "become a significant force shaping our cultural and political future."[2] Michael Kelly, in an examination of the career of the masterful imagemaker David Gergen, writes of "the irresistible rise of news-media power."[3]

My argument is, however, that this belief is a faulty one. It is not the *media* that shape public opinion. It is rather the holders of power who shape public opinion by using the media as their agents. If the media were to attempt to move public opinion into a position contrary to what is desired by the holders of power, the power holders would counterattack. We have seen how Nixon tried to manipulate the press by claiming that in attacking him, they were going beyond the limits of acceptable dissent: They were not contenting themselves with criticizing him; they were attacking the very institution of the presidency, an institution so revered it is secure from condemnation in the press. Nixon, like other presidents and political figures before and after him, sought to coopt the media by rewarding those journalists prepared to play his game and by ostracizing or demonizing those who refused. Nixon's failure was the exception that proved the rule. The press surely called attention to his crimes, but it was not the press that brought him down. Rather, it was his partners in the American system of mixed government: the Congress and the courts.

Gergen, who did his spinning for presidents from Richard Nixon to Bill Clinton, says it was under Nixon that the formula for marketing the president and his policies made its mark. Gergen called it "a systematic program of propaganda." In the end, he said, he viewed his career with "feelings of sadness and guilt."[4]

The role of the spin doctor is similar to that of the "sociological propagandist" as described by Ellul. It is both "to hide political reality by talking about it" and to give the public the opposite impression—"that it understands everything clearly." He or she, Ellul wrote, "must give the public distorted news and intentions, knowing clearly beforehand what conclusions the public will draw from them."[5]

The "independent" power of the news media cannot equal that of the government; the First Amendment is neither carved in stone nor sacrosanct. It is subject to change or revision by that very government, which of necessity pays heed to the voice of the people, the voters. Alexander Hamilton spoke the simple truth in declaring a free press can be secure only if its freedom is backed by public opinion.[6] The final choice rests with the public; and it, too, is subject to the lure of the image industry.

This is a hard truth, perhaps, but one that must ultimately be faced. So long as the news media in a market economy are profit-making institutions, they are sub-

The uncrowned king of spin doctors: President Bush's campaign manager, Lee Atwater, mobbed by reporters at the 1988 Republican campaign.
SOURCE: AP/Wide World

ject to market forces. They must make profit, or they die. It is a credit to the many thousands of honorable journalists that they so often seek to overcome the laws of the marketplace.

Few journalists speak fondly of the image industry. In fact, a new, pejorative name emerged in the 1980s to identify the imagemakers as *spin doctors*. The term arose to describe the behavior of the candidate's staff who made it a practice to interpret the results of elections or polls for journalists, offering them a "spin" favorable to their candidate. Although journalists spoke with some contempt about spin doctors, they nonetheless reported their interpretations for their audiences. In a competitive world, they had to. If they ignored the spin doctors, some other news organization wouldn't, and they knew they would be asked by their desks to "match the opposition."

Journalists regularly speak critically of the image industry's manifest efforts to slant the news in its favor, but at the same time they report what the image industry provides. They are offered "photo ops," where officials permit photographers to snap carefully staged scenes and allow journalists to shout questions that can easily be dodged. They use but object to "packaging" of information and the reliance on short, punchy "sound bites" from speeches and interviews rather than longer, duller, and more heavily qualified though more accurate reports. The journalism industry goes along with what is available. The market forces are at work. That journalists are well aware of the skill with which imagemakers maneuver

SOURCE: Mike Lane, *Evening Sun*

them is clear enough. At its 1992 convention, the Radio and Television News Directors Association (RTNDA) drew its largest crowd to a session on "Handling the Handlers."

According to critic Daniel C. Hallin, the power of television journalists has increased during the last years of the twentieth century. He has said the journalist has become "the primary communicator," replacing the candidate or other "newsmaker."[7] This idea suggests a shift in power from content to form. Thus, "mediated news reporting" came about because of a weakening of political consensus in the United States. In Hallin's view, journalists have definitely become adversaries of those in power, for they have moved away from the earlier traditions of "objective" reporting to more analytical journalism where they package the news in ways that interpret for the viewer what political figures, presidents chief among them, really mean in those sound bites that appear on the air. There has indeed been a sharp increase in the *appearance* of an adversary role for the news media, but the idea is suspect. It is important to keep in mind that what is negative for one candidate is positive for his or her opponent. What "mediated" journalism has brought more than anything else has been a cheapening of the political process, as form has increasingly replaced content and trivialization of political information has become more and more apparent.

Moreover, as the manipulative efforts of imagemakers became painfully obvious to journalists, many reporters determined to fight back. Media specialist Michael Robinson has spoken of this mind set as "fear of flacking."[8] Hallin saw this fear as one explanation for what politicians often speak of as negative reporting. These changes in form can be attributed also to the pressure put on TV news divisions to make their product more salable and hence more profitable, like "60 Minutes."

Here, then, is another noteworthy kind of irony of journalism, for while the news media have called more and more attention to the spin doctors and their image-making campaigns, they have at the same time given more time and greater space to those campaigns. "There are moments," Hallin has said, "when it is hard to distinguish the journalists from the political technicians they are interviewing."

Much of the assertion of great power on the part of the news media comes in the context of the political arena. Journalists, as we have seen, are sometimes likened to roving packs of beasts with a bloodthirsty urge to destroy their prey. "If it bleeds," media analyst Larry Sabato has written, "try to kill it."[9] I have written elsewhere about the "jackal syndrome," under which journalists wait about for a lion among them, often *The New York Times*, to interpret events and then move in quickly to adopt the lion's interpretation as their own.[10] Pack journalism certainly is a reality. When a "big story" emerges, reporters descend on it in droves, with such intense concentration that the story rapidly becomes the nation's chief topic of conversation, and other "news" disappears from the television screen and the front pages. The celebrated case of Gary Hart's sexual peccadilloes is an example; so is the struggle in the Senate over the nomination to the U.S. Supreme Court of Clarence Thomas; so is the move to war in the Persian Gulf. The frenzy over undocumented allegations that Bill Clinton had engaged in an affair with one Gennifer Flowers drove journalists to hitherto unimagined mountains of copy and photographs during the 1992 primary campaign. Never before had reputable news organizations such as NBC and *The New York Times* given credence to a report that originated in a tabloid article for which the accuser was paid, a figure said to be $50,000. The emphasis inevitably was on whatever seemed scandalous or melodramatic; the stories were indeed the stuff of fiction, and gossip and innuendo dominated public attention. This trend was by no means limited to American journalism. Similar scandal and melodrama appeared on TV screens and front pages around the world. In these situations, as the veteran television journalist Sandor Vanocur said, a number of "young reporters" display "a quality of the avenging angel," determined to sanitize American politics.[11]

The widely accepted premise was that public preoccupation with scandal and melodrama ought to be credited (or charged) to the news media, especially television. The error was to jump from this premise to the assertion of media power. Robert Woodward and Carl Bernstein found a gold mine for investigative journalists when they uncovered the image-making efforts of the "dirty tricks" campaign waged on behalf of Richard Nixon in 1972. Although especially blatant, this campaign was only marginally different from efforts made on behalf of all candidates who seek to portray opponents as weak or ineffective. Much has been written also about Franklin Roosevelt's use of radio in his "fireside chats" and of Nixon's "selling of the president" by the use of television in his 1968 campaign.[12] These efforts were by no means unique. Indeed, exposure of false image-making comes almost always *after* the images have been generated. Lamentably, as all editors are aware, corrections never catch up with accusations.

David Paletz and Robert Entman, political scientists and media specialists, have documented the successful campaign waged on behalf of Jimmy Carter to use the folklore and the conventional definitions of news employed by the media to gain an unlikely victory in 1976.[13] Carter's success in winning the presidency can be contrasted with the 1972 failures of Edmund Muskie and George McGovern, where the candidates were far less adept than Carter in manipulating the press and wound up paying for that ineptitude.[14]

It does not follow that McGovern or Muskie would have won the 1972 election if the press had behaved differently. However, in neither the case of Muskie nor that of McGovern did the press operate independently. It was maneuvered into watching first Muskie, then McGovern, by the Nixon strategists, who understood full well the ways of the press, and it was also maneuvered by those very ways that serve the interests of the politicoeconomic system. These assertions cannot be proved; yet the evidence cited by Woodward and Bernstein and validated by many journalists (including myself, in my reportorial career) tends to confirm that imagemakers can and do set the agenda for presidential election campaigns. They are aided in this process by their understanding of the conventional ways in which journalists define news. Make it moving, dramatic, and headline grabbing, mix in hints of sex and corruption, and you can just about guarantee a spot on the front page.

Nixon in 1972, Carter in 1976, Ronald Reagan in 1980 and 1984, and George Bush in 1988 all used the press effectively, succeeding in projecting their images and tarnishing that of their opponents. And they all won. This fact does not suggest that the images in the news media *caused* their election; causation is a far too complex process for that. Concrete factors such as the state of the economy and public content or discontent are always present. No one can state authoritatively these images are the decisive factor in the final outcome, but it is evident the contestants believe they are and dedicate more time and money to creating and promoting images than to any other goal—and to making use of the news media as their chief agents in this quest.

PRESIDENTS, POLLSTERS, AND MODERN NEWS MANAGERS

The political successes of Ronald Reagan and George Bush were phenomenal, even in an era where manipulation of information was widespread. The imagemakers were doing their jobs well; and despite the continual assertion of the media's AWA role, despite grumbling and sniping in commentary and on editorial pages, despite the *appearance* of independent press power, the news media joined in a symbiotic partnership that served the power interests of both presidents, especially in their early years in office when rival claimants to power failed, for the most part, to gain the attention of the news media.

Reagan was an ideal client for the imagemakers, for he did not choose to play in the journalists' ball park. The journalist, as has often been noted, is the very model of the empiricist—that is to say, he or she deals in facts, in reality, in logic, and in inductive reasoning, collecting pieces of information and drawing conclusions based on facts and on research.[15] The aura the imagemakers cast about Reagan had virtually nothing to do with facts or hard reality. Reagan's image was that of the visionary, the man with his eyes and especially his heart fixed on a glorious future for the country he led. To such a man, facts were unimportant; it was the dream, the vision, that counted.[16] He was made to appear to be the master in complete charge of the world around him. The task of the imagemakers was eased a great deal because Reagan seemed to believe the myth himself and could appear to be in command of both foreign and domestic policies even when the reasoned views of many experts in the field differed from his. That Reagan had been an actor was an additional boost for the imagemakers, for he was skillful at portraying the role of commanding leader. So consummate in playing this role was he that he was able to triumph over actual evidence to the contrary. The remarkable Iran-Contra affair, discussed later, illustrates this point clearly.

Although the image industry was equally successful in its handling of George Bush, its strategy was markedly different. Here was no visionary to sell, no dreamer, no lack of inductive reasoning; yet the imagemakers were able to cast an aura that was almost equally effective. In the end, however, the era of successful manipulation came to an at least temporary halt because by the close of Bush's term, the news media had begun to fulfill their AWA role. Bush found himself under sharp criticism both in newspapers and on the air, and his popularity with media audiences plunged to new depths. In a matter of months, public approval of his record fell from nearly 90 percent to less than 50 percent. Richard B. Wirthlin, a professional pollster who had been a central figure in promoting the Reagan image, had a ready answer to what at first glance may seem an inconsistency. Public support, Wirthlin said, is never based entirely on images but on a mix of image, policies, and the consequences of those policies.[17] In other words, imagemakers need to be also shrewd long-range analysts of the consequences of any policy.

One illustration may suffice. Among the most telling images that had been established for Reagan was that of the man who had restored pride to America. His predecessor, Jimmy Carter, had been condemned severely for his failure to gain the release of fifty-two hostages seized by the Iranian militants who overran the U.S. Embassy in Teheran. In the 1980 election campaign, Carter was reviled for having permitted American prestige to decline. People, it was said, no longer felt proud to be Americans.

Reagan's announced aim was to restore that pride. His imagemakers scored with a portrait of Reagan as the leader restoring American pride and confidence. The press was a willing co-conspirator in promoting that image, for stories about Reagan's tough stance on foreign policy made good copy. Readers eagerly turned to the prideful pages; viewers of TV news shows tuned in. Reagan's foreign policy was very popular with the American public. The newly popular media talk shows made the point supemely clear. His rhetoric with regard to the enemy, the Soviet Union, was strong and colorful. He called it the "evil empire" and pledged to stand firm against any Soviet inroads, especially in Latin America and the Caribbean. He issued harsh warnings to Fidel Castro's Marxist government in Cuba. He underwrote military support for anti-Castro movements in El Salvador and Nicaragua. He sent war planes over Libya to bomb its two major cities and, it was hoped, to destroy the rule of its leader, Moammar Kaddafi, who had long ago been condemned as a terrorist by the American government and public. He ordered troops into Grenada to oust what he called a drive for a Cuban takeover. He sent Marines into Lebanon to prevent Arab assaults on Israel. He broke off diplomatic relations with Iran and threatened retaliation for the hostage taking.

So powerful was the strong leader image that emerged from his gunboat diplomacy that when the 1988 Bush election campaign promoted the idea that he was as tough on foreign policy as Reagan, the Democratic candidate, Michael Dukakis, was dismissed as an inadequate novice.

Like Reagan, Bush fit his policy to the image. Shortly after taking office, Bush sent American troops into Panama in an announced attempt to seize Manuel Noriega, the very unpopular Panamanian strongman who had been indicted in the United States on charges of violating the American anti-drug laws and laundering money. He was later convicted and sentenced to prison. The American people once again rallied behind their president in a foreign military venture. Less than two years later, Bush moved again, this time against Iraq, towing the United Nations along with him. Few American military actions have been so carefully orchestrated or so overwhelmingly popular with the public. Approval for Bush's war policy shot up to 90 percent.[18] His failure to accomplish one of his implied aims, the dislodging of the Iraqi dictator Saddam Hussein, ultimately cost him a great deal of popular applause, however, confirming Wirthlin's observation that image alone is inadequate if the consequences of policy are not equally popular.

In its early stages, the news media played the precise role desired by Bush and his imagemakers in the government-policy apparatus, joining in the outpouring of praise for a policy described as just and tough in its stand against aggression and also as overcoming what Bush called "the Vietnam syndrome," a feeling that the United States no longer commanded the world's respect for its power and devotion to international justice. The imagemakers in the Persian Gulf affair were not, of course, electoral-campaign media managers but the skilled public-relations professionals playing on those "enduring" American values, especially appeals to patriotism.[19] The image was fashioned with great skill. The news media were kept at arm's length, screened off from access to battlefields and direct contact with American military forces. Censorship was complete (aside from the CNN access to Baghdad), and for many weeks all news that reached the public came from briefings by the U.S. military, which, of course, presented only carefully selected information that gave the desired positive public-relations slant to the American cause.[20] Later, however, when it became clear the information received had been less than entirely accurate, a substantial minority of the public began to speak out against the policy of censorship. Among the news media themselves, a sense of discomfort, sometimes of sharp criticism, emerged, clouding the image of a just war.

Directing images in the desert: General Norman Schwarzkopf lets the press in on U.S. troop moves in the gulf.

SOURCE: AP/Wide World

What ingredients went into the image-making mix that gained such remarkable advantage for Reagan and Bush? Why was this mix more successful than any blend of ingredients had achieved before? If the news media surrendered their avowed role as adversary, watchdog, and agenda setter, why did they? More than a few among the journalists working for the distinguished national press, the "big media," were not so blind as all that to the manipulative efforts of power. The problem was that even these savvy and knowledgeable journalists were prisoners of the system in which they operated. The imperatives of a commercial press system dictate that in order to survive, a news operation must generate a profit; and profit requires success in the marketplace. Thus, it is only by taking an immense (and virtually unthinkable) risk that a news organization can resist the seductions of power and refuse to play by the ground rules set by news sources. For this reason, the spectrum of American media reported to the public the distorted image of the Gulf War drawn by military briefers. Ergo, the imagemakers succeeded in sketching the precise image of the war they knew would attract the widest public support. After the brief ground war began in January, newsmen and newswomen were permitted to roam relatively freely and developed a number of stories showing the earlier Pentagon reports had been sometimes distorted and sometimes wrong.

In the Gulf War (and, to a lesser extent, the interventions in Libya, Grenada, and Panama earlier in the 1980s), the task of the imagemakers was both uncomplicated and irresistible, for the appeal was to patriotism; no other message packs the wallop of an appeal to the flag, to duty to country. Throughout the Gulf War, especially in its early stages, the American media—and indeed the media of all countries allied with the United States—served as actual cheerleaders for the war effort.[21]

Patriotism and boosterism are very much a part of the political process. In the 1988 election campaign, one of the most telling bits of Bush image making was to present himself as wholly and completely devoted to the American flag while at the same time depicting his opponent, Michael Dukakis, as less than protective of the flag and thereby possibly lacking patriotism. The issue arose when the Supreme Court, by a vote of 5 to 4, ruled that burning the American flag was protected by the First Amendment's guarantee of free speech. Responding to public dismay over this ruling, Bush's imagemakers took him for a photo opportunity at a flag-manufacturing plant; he literally wrapped himself in the flag. What a contrast to the portrait of Dukakis driving a tank, an ill-fitting helmet strapped under his chin, looking lost and diminished in the bowels of the tank. His campaign manager acknowledged later that Bush's flag message out-imaged Dukakis's tank image. The Dukakis people were left with little more than a shot at damage control.[22] Their error lay in permitting a potentially unfavorable image to be broadcast. Their opposition seized the opportunity to prepare TV spots contrasting the patently absurd portrait of Dukakis as a uniformed tank rider with an image of Bush as strong and sturdy in supporting the cause of America. It all made a good story for the swarming, competitive legions of journalists covering the campaign.

A ploy that played poorly in Peoria: Democratic presidential candidate Michael Dukakis presents the wrong image in 1988.

SOURCE: UPI/Bettmann

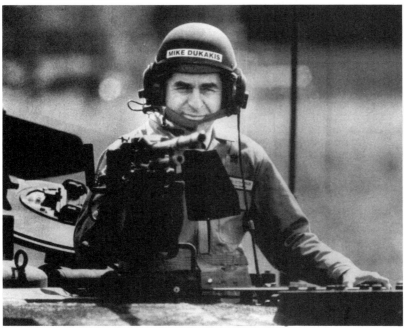

An image of Dukakis that tapped into racial prejudices lying just below the surface of American society damaged him even more severely. This powerful negative image served up in another televised political advertisement accused Dukakis of granting a temporary release to Willie Horton, an African-American imprisoned in Massachusetts on rape charges who was arrested on rape and murder charges while on release. The unspoken implication was that Dukakis, a champion of civil rights, was foolishly soft on crime and, if elected, would condone potentially dangerous prison-release programs, especially those involving black convicts. After the election, Bush's media adviser, Lee Atwater, on his deathbed said he was sorry the Willie Horton spot had been aired and acknowledged the image had been a scurrilous one.[23]

This is not to say Bush defeated Dukakis *because* his imagemakers were skillful manipulators of the mass media and thus of their viewers and readers. No such clear causal connection can be proved. Obviously, many factors went into Bush's victory. Still, it is clear from public-opinion polls that Dukakis was rated as high as Bush, sometimes even higher, prior to the start of the actual two-man campaign when the production of marketable images went into full swing. It has often been argued quite correctly that voters cast their ballots based more on their *perceptions* of a candidate's policies and experience than on the candidate's positions on actual issues and actual experience. Perceptions are derived from images—some accurate, some inaccurate, some true, some false. The news media provide the mechanism for the promoters, the creators, and the distributors to supply those images.

In his foreign adventures as well as in his domestic policies, Bush's imagemakers candidly sought to bask in the aura that had surrounded Reagan during his remarkable popular eight-year run in the White House. Few presidents have been as popular during their tenure. Much of that popularity can be attributed to the success of his imagemakers in promoting him as the Great Communicator, the spokesman for the American Dream on the domestic front and in foreign affairs. The term *Reaganomics* was invented, probably by journalists, to describe his economic policy, one designed to boost profits for entrepreneurs while benefits—as the saying went—would "trickle down" to consumers. In 1980, while challenging Reagan for the Republican nomination, Bush labeled these policies "voodoo economics"; yet when the extent of Reagan's popularity became clear to Bush and his advisers, they bought into the Reagan no-taxes policy, and Bush was portrayed as even more of a hard-liner on economics. His "read my lips" image—standing for no new taxes—became his chief slogan. However, powerful images can backfire, and Bush's became a classic case of the backfiring image. In his losing 1992 campaign against Bill Clinton, he had to admit publicly he had broken his promise.

It was apparent to the journalists reporting on the economic policies of both Reagan and Bush that their announced economic policies were self-contradictory, for a substantial increase in military spending without providing the tax money to pay for it inevitably leads to vast budget deficits and economic decline. While this pattern was apparent, broadcasters and newspaper reporters continued to spread the word of the two presidents' popularity and not point out the fundamental contradictions. To be sure, critical commentary appeared on editorial pages and in analytical broadcasts, but these commentaries were dwarfed by the repetitive "hard news" emanating from the White House. Once again, the code of objectivity served the power wielders and converted the news media into agents for those in power. Giving "both sides" meant giving equal weight to the reasonable and the unreasonable. When equal weight is assigned to those in power and those out of power, the weight is not really equal. Power inevitably comes out ahead, and the imagemakers who know how to manipulate that power for their clients are the winners. When an economic decline hit in the 1990s, Bush's popularity tumbled with it, and even the reputation of the Great Communicator went into a slide.

While concrete factors such as the 1990–92 economic decline and recession contributed heavily to Bush's loss to Clinton, he was also a victim of the same kind of media strategy that had propelled Reagan and himself to power. The power equation and news-management processes are two-edged swords. The spin-doctor weapon can be triumphant or vanquished. In short, Clinton's media managers outwitted Bush's. After the election, Republican strategists uniformly applauded the Clinton campaign. It didn't begin well for the Arkansas governor, who was battered and bruised by the allegations of sexual infidelity that surfaced in the paid-for interview aired on "A Current Affair." He was damaged even further by charges of draft dodging in the Vietnam War and truth dodging in his response to accusations of marijuana smoking. Early on, Bush's spin doctors had Clinton reeling from an image that portrayed him as shifty and slick, waffling, glib, and fast-talking. Clinton's media managers recognized that if he were going to win, he would need some powerful image modification. Accordingly, the pollster Stan Greenberg, the strategist James Carville, and the media consultant Frank Green came up with what may have been the most skillful image campaign of them all.[24] After all, Clinton had not started out with the favorable movie-star image that had launched Reagan.

Clinton's media team, aware that the Bush strategists were building a campaign around Clinton's negative image, produced a plan outlined in a fourteen-line single-spaced memorandum to replace what they believed was a false image of the candidate with an image of the "real Clinton." Accordingly, Clinton moved around the news media that were airing the negative images and began telling his story on talk shows and at staged town-hall meetings. In his first talk-show appearance, on the Arsenio Hall program, he donned dark glasses and played the saxophone, projecting a portrait of a modern young man who was determined to replace old, tired candidates and ideas with change that was forward-looking and willing to take risks. Clinton pursued the same strategy on policy issues, presenting himself as an aggressive, honest, plain-folks agent of change ready to stand up to the interest groups.[25]

A third candidate, the wealthy Texan Ross Perot, won 19 percent of the presidential vote largely through presenting himself on talk shows and at staged town-hall meetings. Bush found himself forced to join Clinton and Perot in scurrying almost daily to appear on the before-breakfast network shows. Whatever dividing line there may have been between news and entertainment was gone forever. The record turnout of voters reflected the fact that what had at first been perceived as a boring campaign had gained the appeal of Arsenio Hall, Larry King, Phil Donahue, and the other talk-show hosts. The imagemakers had a new strategy at hand.

How to win elections against fearful odds: Bill Clinton's media director, George Stephanopoulos, passes the word.

SOURCE: Reuters/Bettmann

Public-opinion polling had come to play an increasingly critical role in the political process. From a small and insecure business started in the 1930s, polling had long before the close of the twentieth century become as significant as any other ingredient in the image-making process. It didn't start that way, nor are today's experts on polling prepared to accept such a questionable interpretation of their work. Pioneer George H. Gallup was convinced when he launched his Institute for Public Opinion in 1935 that he would provide the public with a powerful tool to learn what the American people truly believed, not, he said, the lies they were being fed by vested interests. Forty-four years later, Gallup remained confident the data compiled by pollsters offered the citizen "access to the same sources of information as a member of Congress."[26] He was giving voice to the democratic assumption, of which we have spoken before, and he was crediting pollster reports of public-opinion surveys with enabling the people "to make wise judgments [from] the mountain of polling data collected."[27] Appropriately, Gallup credited the mass media with distributing the polling information the public needed if it were to make those wise decisions in the voting booth.

Gallup's view is not shared by everyone in the field. Philip E. Converse, for instance, has argued that it is difficult to show that "a greater sensitivity to public opinion populist style has necessarily improved the quality of governance in the republic."[28]

Some of the early flubs by pollsters are memorable. In 1936, *The Literary Digest* predicted from its survey of readers that Alfred E. Landon would defeat Franklin D. Roosevelt in his reelection campaign; Landon captured only Maine and Vermont as FDR won the most sweeping election victory gained up to that time.[29] In 1948, anticipating a result predicted by pollsters and unimpressed by early returns showing the reverse, some incautious newspapers reported that Thomas E. Dewey was triumphing over Harry S Truman. A photo of a rejoicing Truman holding up a front page that claimed victory for Dewey has become a classic of its genre. Gross errors of that nature are no longer likely, because pollsters have learned much more about the possibility of sampling error and of improper timing in their surveys. *The Literary Digest* had polled only its largely Republican readership to arrive at its spectacularly faulty conclusion, and 1948 pollsters had made the fatal error of quitting their surveys two weeks before the election. Indeed, predicting election results based on opinion surveys has become so accurate it has taken on the aura of a "science."

Polling has become so central to the election process that one of the first decisions a candidate makes is which polling organization to hire to help him in his bid for office. His "pollster" has become one of his foremost advisers, sometimes his chief adviser, during the election campaign and afterward, when the elected presi-

Ah, to savor victory at the polls and over the press: President Truman flashes the headline that haunted *The Chicago Tribune* in 1948.

SOURCE: AP/Wide World

dent seeks to maintain the favorable image he has gained during the campaign. Patrick Cadell not only helped Jimmy Carter in his campaign but remained on as a key adviser. Richard Wirthlin played a similar role for Ronald Reagan.

During campaigns, a strong showing in the polls is taken as proof the candidate is electible. Surely, no more reliable proof is available. Potential backers watch the polls carefully for guidance on where to place their financial support. "When the polls go good for one," President Nixon was once quoted as saying, "the cash register really rings."[30]

Pollsters play two or three roles in the election process. First, they learn, as best they can, where their candidate stands with the public: Have you heard of X? Would you vote for X? Against Y? Against Z? Where do you stand on his tax policy? On his foreign policy? And so on. Questions of this sort are posed by the candidates' pollsters and by private polling agencies, especially those employed by news organizations. The television networks have joined forces with major newspapers in conducting periodic polls. Other polling groups, some reliable, some not, also publish results. The target is inevitably the news media. If a poll is taken and not reported, it might as well never have existed. These polls are pretty much straightforward, with responses that are simple and easily placed into categories. Interpretation of these polls, on the other hand, is not at all straightforward. It is in the interpretation that the possibility of manipulation is extremely strong. Leo Bogart, a veteran student of polling, has been particularly critical of what he calls the one-question survey. Opinion, he notes, is not a simple matter but "multifaceted, multilayered, and intricate."[31] Furthermore, yes or no answers to questions fail to take into account specific contexts that change from day to day, sometimes from hour to hour. Cantril agrees that poll results are inexact, dynamic, and subject to rapid change: "People hold opinions with varying levels of intensity, base their opinions on varying amounts of information, and are affected in varying degrees by sentiments that are in conflict with each other."[32]

The critical use of polling in the electoral process lies not in mere data collection but in image making because the images generated on the basis of polling information can be decisive. The pollster Louis Harris has said that polling results can influence election results by as many as four points. Wirthlin, who was wildly successful on behalf of Reagan during and between campaigns, agrees with Harris; he adds that to accomplish such a big gain, one needs not only good polling and good strategy but also a good candidate.[33]

The challenge for political pollsters is to use the information they collect in order to establish a favorable image for their candidate and to raise questions about the image of their opponent. Wirthlin said it isn't easy to deceive the media, but that may be a matter of definition. As he correctly pointed out, the media's purpose in conducting polls is different from the goals of pollsters for politicians. "Their purpose is to provide news," Wirthlin said. "Our concern is to predict movement and how to make the movement occur in whatever direction we want them to move and to attenuate movement in the wrong direction."

In other words, the goal of political pollsters is not to find *facts* but to create *images* and thereby shape opinion. It is often a matter of "political symbolism,"

The Great Communicator communicates: President Reagan meets reporters—including UPI's Helen Thomas—in the White House.
SOURCE: UPI/Bettmann

Wirthlin said. He cited as an example the poor symbol created in Michael Dukakis's ride in a tank in the 1988 campaign. "Symbols can backfire," Wirthlin affirmed. Dukakis's problem, he said, did not lie in being seen riding in a tank but with the particular image he created. While campaigning for reelection in Britain, Prime Minister Margaret Thatcher, for whom Wirthlin once served as pollster, also appeared on television riding a tank. Instead of being seen hunched down *under* the cannon in a cramped space with a helmet fastened to her chin, she was shown riding on top of the tank as it rolled down a road, dust swirling in her path, her face clearly visible and riding *above* the cannon.

The data collected in polls directed by the news media are reliable, Wirthlin said, but the news organizations have problems in analyzing that data. They need material to support the leads they have chosen; they are always on the lookout for the unusual, and they rarely have time to analyze the results their computers provide for them. "You must," Wirthlin said, "never rush to judgment."

That advice may be fine for the news media, but pollsters are always ready to rush to judgment if those judgments are deemed to benefit their candidate. They can provide excellent fodder for spin doctors.

Thoughtful journalists have long been concerned about what they consider to be overemphasis on polling results. They recognize the potential for manipulation. They are, in fact, worried that emphasizing poll results reinforces the horse-race image of elections. Reporting every poll that becomes available simply increases the volume of news about the process of elections and emphasizes the question of "who is ahead" while downgrading the issues in the campaign.

On occasion, news organizations have suppressed poll results for fear of losing contact with what the election is all about. For example, in 1988, NBC's Ken Bode recommended that his network refrain from reporting polling results in the last month of the campaign, keeping those results only for NBC staffers' use as guidelines but avoiding any perception of influencing results. Other reporters, including Dan Rather of CBS, have at various times recommended a halt in the reporting of poll results. The stress on polling has gone on nonetheless. Rather lamented it: "The problem with these polls," he said, "is it comes out in black and white; and it all looks authoritative—and it isn't."[34]

One instructive incident illustrates the remarkably important place that polling has come to occupy in political reportage. Bush and Dukakis engaged each other in two televised debates during the 1988 campaign. In advance, most journalists billed the second debate as decisive to Dukakis's chances. On ABC stations, political analysts immediately offered their interpretations of how the debate went. Twenty minutes after the analytical session began, anchorman Peter Jennings broke in to report on an instant ABC poll. It showed, Jennings said, that Bush was the winner in the eyes of 49 percent of the respondents, with Dukakis scoring only 33 percent.[35] Here, the media had, as Wirthlin warned against, rushed to judgment. On the whole, according to Wirthlin, the news media do adopt a skeptical stance when confronted by pollsters' information as well as word from the spin doctors. The news media possess great power, he said, giving voice to conventional wisdom; but he acknowledged that the media *can* be moved because the imagemakers know full well what makes news and have at the same time the capability of making news. "The president," he said, "can create an event to encourage media attention."

Still, Wirthlin noted that the "most dangerous thing" a pollster can do with the media "is to try to fool them." Greeted by a quizzical look from the interviewer, Wirthlin broke into a smile and acknowledged that it was also "a considerable asset to convince the media that the other side has been fooling them."

THE IRAN-CONTRA AFFAIR

While the imagemakers for presidents Reagan and Bush scored a substantial success on economic policy in the 1980s, what was arguably their most striking victory came in the area of foreign policy. Reagan's ascension into the White House came simultaneously with the release of the hostages held by Iran for fifteen months. The news media reported the Iranian leader Ayatollah Khomeini as negatively as Reagan was treated positively. When further Western hostages were seized by Iranians and their friends in Syria and Lebanon, the president, the public, and the press spoke out firmly in support of a policy of refusing to "deal" with the hostage takers. The heavily cheered bombing of Libya, ordered after a questionable report that Libyans were responsible for a nightclub bombing in Berlin, was in pursuit of the same "get tough with Arab leaders" policy.

The global geopolitical policies followed by Reagan and Bush were in keeping with the long-standing hostile Cold War stance against the Soviet Union, a contest already thirty-five years old when Reagan came to power in 1981. Verbal assaults on the Soviet Union and on communism continued throughout the Reagan years, increasing in tempo in the face of revolutionary movements in Central America. This is not the place to go deeply into these conflicts, though it is important to note the role of the news media as agents of power in disputes linking the United States not only to revolutionary Cuba, Nicaragua, and El Salvador but also to the hostage takers in Iran. As with journalistic shortcuts such as Watergate, this complex situation has come to be known as the Iran-Contra affair.

Evidence now indicates, as it appeared to more than a few persons at the time, that the misuse of executive power during the Iran-Contra affair constituted impeachable offenses no less virulent than those carried out during the Watergate goings on.[36] Legislation had barred the White House from providing military assistance to Nicaraguan rebels known as the Contras, who were waging a civil insurrection to unseat the revolutionary, later elected, Sandinista government headed by President Daniel Ortega. At the same time, Reagan had pledged not to make a deal with the Iranians that would give them benefits for freeing American hostages held by Arab insurgents backed by Iran. Nevertheless, an obscure lieutenant colonel, backed by the president's national-security advisor, engineered a deal that sent arms to Iran in exchange for money that was in turn supplied to the Contras for their civil-war effort, which Reagan had again and again publicly endorsed. Lieutenant Colonel Oliver L. North and security chief Admiral John M. Poindexter later acknowledged they had swung the deal in what they had hoped would bring about the release of hostages.

Such a scam would be certain to rouse news media playing their AWA role to heights of tough investigative journalism. It didn't.[37] The government kept the operation closely guarded. Even the political opposition was unaware of what was going on. It was the "imperial" presidency in action, illustrating the extent of its power and the limitations on the alleged power of the news media.

Although some U.S. newspapers had noticed and written a smattering of articles, it wasn't the American news media that broke the story. The breakthrough came in an article published by an inconspicuous Lebanese journal, *al-Shiraa*. The source for the story was one Manucher Ghorbanifar, a middleman in the arms-for-hostages deal. He had already informed William Casey, director of the Central Intelligence Agency, that he would make the transaction public if he weren't fully paid for his work in the deal.[38] The middleman tipped the journal that U.S. officials had visited Iran to discuss trade. North and his colleagues had kept a tight rein on that information, and reports of the visit had only been hinted at in the American press but not in the news capitals of Washington and New York. It was, ironically, on the very day the Lebanese story was published, November 3, 1986, that an article by John Wallach, foreign editor of the Hearst Newspapers, appeared in Hearst papers reporting that secret negotiations with Iran had been going on for a year.[39]

Once word of the visit to Iran by U.S. officials got out, opposition to Reagan and his foreign policy exploded in Congress. Intelligence committees summoned North and Poindexter to Capitol Hill to testify in closed-door hearings. Now reporters scurried about to try to verify the leaked information about what the witnesses had said. It was apparent to most analysts that lies were being told, and the Reagan people were forced to respond. On November 25, 1986, three weeks after the article appeared in Lebanon, Attorney General Edward Meese called a news conference to disclose publicly for the first time that weapons for the Contras had been purchased with proceeds from the sale of arms to Iran. Details of the illegal transaction continued to come to light during the remaining two years of Reagan's presidency, especially during hearings before a joint Senate-House committee investigating the Iran-Contra affair.

Whole volumes have been devoted to information about the hearings that took place during Reagan's administration and about the criminal trials of North and Poindexter during Bush's term, but we will confine ourselves to illustrating how limited in power the news media were in carrying out their avowed role as adversary, watchdog, and agenda setter. Perhaps the most lamentable product of the spin doc-

The colonel refuses to take the hot seat lying down: Lieutenant Colonel Oliver North, on the griddle before a congressional committee, plays to the House.
SOURCE: AP/Wide World

tors' success story in directing the flow of news has been just this: the relative impotence of the mass media in serving as a counterforce to the massive power of the media manipulators, thus limiting the information available to their audiences, to the people. The agency role may be a sturdy support for social stability, yet it does little to safeguard democratic institutions. The social-responsibility doctrine invoked by the Hutchins Commission called for more, for the truth behind the facts.

It is clear that secret and illegal acts were taking place from the time the Reagan administration took office; and, for the most part, the news media failed to inform the public about them until the first public information came out in the form of a leak from a news source. Some journalists had been working hard to try to track down evidence of behind-the-scenes wheeling and dealing in both Iran and Central America, but their efforts were frustrated at every turn. When the news broke and the actors involved began talking, journalists swarmed onto the story, a further illustration of Larry Sabato's intriguing metaphor of a "feeding frenzy" at work.

Even then, the journalists were not concentrating on the real issue involved: a question of abuse of power by those entrusted with that power by the people. In this, the reporting of the media was quite similar to the reporting of the Watergate affair. *Instead of zeroing in on the frightening question of abuse of official power, media concentration was on individual behavior, not institutional behavior.* This is not to say questions were not raised, primarily in editorials and commentary, about usurpation of power by the executive or legislative branches, about the separation of powers decreed by the Constitution, or about the weakness of Congress or possible crimes in the executive branch; however, the emphasis was always elsewhere, and few, if any, of the news media questioned the system that had given rise to the Iran-Contra affair.

Journalists devoted column after column, news show after news show, to stories of mysteries and high drama. How was it, for example, that an unknown lieutenant colonel could run a multimillion-dollar covert operation from a basement office in the White House? Who knew what North was doing? The question that seemed to fascinate the news media more than any other was "Did the president know?" Or, perhaps, further paralleling the Watergate case, "When did the president know?" Some commentators consider the question of what the president knew and when he knew it of foremost importance because it represents a major prerequisite to a serious examination of presidential power. The question is certainly important, but a review of the reports in newspapers and especially on television illustrates that the overriding emphasis was on the *personal* integrity of the president rather than on the *systemic* question.

The threat posed by the Iran-Contra affair was the same threat posed by the Nixon administration in the Watergate affair. It was a threat to democratic institutions and to constitutional government. To concentrate on personal drama and on who was gaining and who was losing politically was to play the role long carved out for a news-media institution serving power as a mechanism of social control. The conventions of journalism ensured it. Seeking to practice objectivity and thereby giving equal weight to lies and truth, the news media did not challenge the holders of power but provided them with news space to advance their case. For all practical purposes, then, the press served as an important element of the power structure. Might there not be a fatal danger in a system that allows such abuse of executive power? Might there be a way in which those charged with being watchdogs can get at the reality of abuse of executive power? A review of the role of the news media in the Iran-Contra affair illustrates how the holders of power, the defenders of economic stability and the status quo, make use of their media to preserve their own power base. A statement of their pleading is guaranteed in any policy debate. At best, only limited space is available for dissenting voices. In any case, the holders of power inevitably argue their case on the basis of the society's traditional values.[40] Audiences are not necessarily passive recipients of the official position, but their access to opposing voices is sharply restricted.

There is nothing weak or morally wrong in the media's pursuit of its role of reporting whatever information they can track down, even though the greatest share of their sources are spokespeople for entrenched power. It is the way the system works. We can, however, see here a clear illustration of the relative power of the news media and those who hold real power. The wielders of financial power continued to support Reagan and Bush throughout the entire Iran-Contra affair.

The relative power of government and media can be seen also in the curious case of a Dan Rather interview, an event of apparent insignificance but one that, on closer examination, can tell us much about the extent of the media's "independent" power. The interview took place on January 25, 1988, as Vice President Bush's campaign to win his party's nomintion for president was warming up. It was a critical junction, for Bush's media managers were well aware of the potential dangers that lay ahead. Political analysts recognized that critics were trying to tag Bush as a kind of faceless nobody, as a "wimp." They recognized also that the fallout from the Iran-Contra affair could be troublesome because Bush's role in the operation was still unclear. In an authoritative account of the campaign, Peter Goldman and Tom Mathews described a plan of action directed by Roger Ailes, Bush's chief imagemaker, after CBS News requested a live interview in which Bush was certain to be questioned about his role in the Iran-Contra affair.[41] The interview offered a golden opportunity to show the electorate this candidate was no wimp and was in fact a hard, tough bargainer who could dish it out as well as take it.

CBS anchorman Rather also was ready to go all out. Bush's response seemed to come as a huge surprise to him. Rather demanded answers. He insisted they talk about "the record"; when Bush replied by demanding "the full record," Rather said he didn't want to be argumentative.

Bush's reply was, "You do, Dan," and when Rather said he didn't, Bush accused him of unfairness. "It's not fair to judge my whole career by a rehash on Iran. How would you like it if I judged your career by those seven minutes when you walked off the set in New York City?"

The counterattack was directed at an incident that had taken place several months earlier, when Rather's news report came from Miami. Angry when the report was being delayed by a tennis match, Rather walked off camera to telephone his New York office to complain. The tennis match ended during his absence, and CBS was forced to go to black, an empty screen.

President Bush and Dan Rather mix it up: The president and the anchorman go head to head.

SOURCE: L. W. Harvey

Bush did not let up after the interview with Rather ended. He pulled out his earpiece, threw it over his shoulder, and said, "Well, I had my say, Dan." A CBS sound man advised that the mike was live, but Bush went on anyway: "The worst time I've had in twenty years of public life; but it's going to help me, because that bastard did not lay a glove on me." Bush later apologized for his language, but the point was that his ratings in the polls jumped and, most analysts agreed, the wimp image was gone. Writing in *The National Journal* a week later, commentator Dom Bonafede said Bush appeared to have gained politically largely because "his public image [was] reinforced as a standup guy willing to take on the powerful national news media, no less than the sometime king of television news himself."[42]

It is by no means with regard only to elections that attention has been directed to the "independent power" of the press. The press has been credited (or charged, depending on the point of view) with bringing an end to the war in Vietnam, undermining Nixon's presidency, inducing social change, combating crime, improving race relations, challenging appointments to the Supreme Court, defending the environment against predatory encroachment, and even promoting warfare in the Persian Gulf and a race riot in Los Angeles. In all these situations, as with electoral politics, close examination demonstrates the independent power of the press was illusory. The continuation of the war in Vietnam was not threatened until the number of casualties mounted so high that patriotic Americans began asking themselves the unusual question: For what were their husbands, sons, and friends dying? *Press criticism of the conduct of the war followed rather than led to public disaffection or simply reflected the same disaffection.* The undoing of Nixon was accomplished not by the press but by the congressional Republicans who were outraged by the disclosures of Nixon's behavior in open court and open committee rooms. By arousing the public to clamor for action, press reports about the Vietnam War and the Watergate affair played a major role in bringing about the end of the war and the resignation of President Nixon, but this fact does not show it was the press that *caused* the outcome. The news media carried out their symbolic role in the execution of power.

Attention to crime and violence in the news media has increased since the days of the penny press, but it was always there. It was and is the dramatic, the unusual, and the heart warming that is emphasized. The criminals given the most space are those who violate the conventional social order, not those who break the law in an acceptable manner, such as merchants who overcharge customers, restaurateurs who water the wine or the ketchup, mechanics who fail to repair what they promise to fix, or journalists or academics who accept gifts or free trips from those about whom they are expected to write critically.

NOTES

1. As of April 21, 1993, the total number of registrants with the Office of Records and Registration at the House of Representatives totaled 6,088. The Press and Radio-TV Galleries of the House and Senate counted about 2,200 print journalists and 2,500 TV journalists. Of the 4,165 members of the National Press Club, some 60 percent are considered working journalists. The precise total cannot be found, but the fact that there are many lobbyists and journalists on the scene in Washington is clear.

2. Patrick O'Heffernan, *Mass Media and American Foreign Policy: Insider Perspectives on Global Journalism and the Foreign Policy Process* (Norwood, NJ: Ablex, 1991), xi. O'Heffernan limits his analysis of media power to the area of foreign policy and argues it is because of the appearance of global issues, which he characterizes as "a new category of issue," that the news media and other "nonstate players," such as terrorists and nongovernmental organizations, have taken on an independent role in the shaping of foreign policy.

3. Michael Kelly, "David Gergen, Master of the Game: How Image Became the Sacred Faith of Washington, and How This Insider Became Its High Priest," *New York Times Sunday Magazine*, October 31, 1993, 66.

4. Kelly, "David Gergen," 57, 97. Kelly's carefully written and deeply felt article is must reading for students of the spin-doctor syndrome.

5. Jacques Ellul, *Propaganda* (New York: Vintage Books, 1973), 59. He gives credit for this concept to Alfred Sauvy, *L'opinion publique* (Paris: Presses Universitaires de France, 1956).

6. Alexander Hamilton, "Federalist 84," in Jacob E. Cooke, *The Federalist* (Cleveland: World, 1965), 580.

7. Daniel C. Hallin, "Whose Campaign Is It, Anyway?" *Columbia Journalism Review* (January/February 1991): 43.

8. Cited in Hallin,"Whose Campaign Is It, Anyway?" 44.

9. Larry J. Sabato, *Feeding Frenzy: How Attack Journalism Has Transformed American Politics* (New York: Macmillan, 1991), 6. Sabato cautions that not all journalists ought to be placed among those with feeding frenzies but remarks that "veteran journalists will recognize more press behavior in this passage than they might wish to acknowledge."

10. J. Herbert Altschull, "The Journalist and Instant History: An Example of the Jackal Syndrome," *Journalism Quarterly,* 50, 3 (Autumn 1973): 489-96, and "Khrushchev and the Berlin 'Ultimatum': The Jackal Syndrome and the Cold War," *Journalism Quarterly,* 54, 3 (Autumn 1977): 545-51, 565.

11. Sabato, *Feeding Frenzy,* 4.

12. See, for instance, Joseph McGinniss, *The Selling of the President, 1968* (New York: Trident Press, 1969). See also the series by Theodore H. White titled *The Making of the President*, published by Atheneum, New York.

13. David L. Paletz and Robert M. Entman, *Media Power Politics: A Timely, Provocative Look at How the Media Affect Public Opinion and Political Power in the United States* (New York: Free Press, 1981).

14. For a detailed account of the Muskie and McGovern campaigns, see J. Herbert Altschull, *Agents of Power: The Role of the News Media in Human Affairs* (New York: Longman, 1984), 196-99.

15. Sidney Blumenthal, "Reagan the Unassailable," *The New Republic*, September 12, 1983, 11-16, quotes a frustrated Washington journalist, Lou Cannon, as saying, "The conventions of journalism don't allow you to get close to Reagan. All the appalling and appealing things about him are outside the realm of what we do well. They require people to make judgments of what he means, what he understands. . . . You have to go outside the conventions too because Reagan is unconventional."

16. Michael Schudson in *Discovering the News: A Social History of American Newspapers* (New York: Basic Books, 1978), 6, describes the philosophical stance of early journalists as the direct opposite, that of "naive empiricists." Schudson maintains this stance has grown more sophisticated over the years but empiricism rather than intuition remains the lodestar of news judgment. See also Herbert J. Gans, *Deciding What's News: A Study of CBS Evening News, NBC Nightly News, Newsweek and Time* (New York: Vintage Books, 1980).

17. Richard B. Wirthlin, interview with the author, McLean, Virginia, April 16, 1991.

18. *Washington Post*, February 26, 1991, citing a poll conducted by the *Post* and ABC News. Approval of Bush's handling of his job reached 87 percent, according to a *New York Times*/CBS News survey reported in the *Times* on the same day; it was, the *Times* said, the highest approval percentage ever achieved by a president. Only once before had a president's approval level reached that height, in early June 1945, shortly after the unconditional surrender of Germany in World War II, when the Gallup Poll recorded the same approval rating for President Harry Truman.

19. For a discussion of the media and patriotic causes, see J. Herbert Altschull, *From Milton to McLuhan: The Ideas Behind American Journalism* (White Plains, NY: Longman, 1990), 254-60.

20. A substantial literature on the successful image-making efforts of President Bush's Pentagon has emerged. See, for instance, John R. MacArthur, *Second Front: Censorship and Propaganda in the Gulf War* (New York: Hill & Wang, 1992). See also Mark Crispin Miller, "Operation Desert Storm," *New York Times,* June 24, 1992.

21. MacArthur, *Second Front,* 105. *Los Angeles Times* bureau chief Jack Nelson said, "If you look at it from the outset, the press was reflecting the views of the government, and it never really changed." MacArthur, *Second Front,* 111.

22. The acknowledgment by Dukakis's campaign manager Susan Estrich was made during a television symposium that brought together eight campaign managers on a Public Broadcasting System report, January 17, 1992.

23. Atwater made his apology on January 12, 1991, to interviewers from *Life* magazine. He died two months later.

24. The story of Clinton's remarkable media strategy is detailed by Michael Kelly in an authenticated article, "The Making of a First Family: A Blueprint," *New York Times,* November 14, 1992.

25. Kelly, "The Making of a First Family."

26. George H. Gallup and Saul Rae, *The Pulse of Democracy* (New York: Simon & Schuster, 1940), and George H. Gallup, "Preserving Majority Rule," in Albert H. Cantril, ed., *Polling on the Issues* (Cabin John, MD: Seven Locks Press, 1980), 172–73. For a first-rate look at polling history and modern developments, see Albert H. Cantril, *The Opinion Connection: Polling, Politics, and the Press* (Washington, D.C.: Congressional Quarterly, 1991).

27. In one of his earliest pronouncements, Gallup asserted his belief that survey results indicated "we can place great faith in the collective judgment and intelligence of the people." He quoted the distinguished nineteenth-century historian James Bryce as saying that public genius was "a real force, impalpable as the wind . . . which we all are trying to discover and nearly all to obey." George A. Gallup and Saul Forbes Rae, *The Pulse of Democracy: The Public Opinion Poll and How It Works* (New York: Greenwood Press, 1940), 9, 14.

28. Philip E. Converse, "Assessing the Accuracy of Polls and Surveys, in *Science,* 234 (1986): 1094–1098.

29. An embarrassed *Literary Digest* found itself forced to abandon publication. The poll had been based on postcards sent to the magazine by its readers. The pollsters here had failed to notice that the great majority of the magazine's readers were Republicans and hence not likely to support FDR.

30. James R. Beniger and Robert J. Giuffra, Jr., "Public Opinion Polling: Command and Control in Presidential Campaigns," in Alexander Heard and Michael Nelson, eds., *Presidential Selection* (Durham, NC: Duke University Press, 1987), 200.

31. Leo Bogart, *Editorial Research Reports,* 456.

32. Cantril, *Polling on the Issues,* 37.

33. Richard B. Wirthlin, interview with the author, McLean, Virginia, April 10, 1991. All the quoted passages from Wirthlin are from the same interview.

34. Martin Schram, *The Great American Video Game: Presidential Politics in the Television Age* (New York: William Morrow, 1987), 136–37.

35. Cantril, *Polling on the Issues,* 47.

36. For a thoroughly documented account of the Iran-Contra affair and the role of the press in coverage, see Theodore Draper, *A Very Thin Line: The Iran-Contra Affair* (New

York: Hill & Wang, 1991). An earlier version of Draper's work appeared in a two-part series in *The New York Review of Books*, March 1 and May 17, 1990, under the title "The Constitution in Danger." Draper's version of these events displeased the White House enormously; letters contradicting Draper's account, written on White House stationery and signed by Lawrence J. Block, senior attorney-adviser in the Office of Public Development of the Department of Justice, and David B. Rivkin, Jr., legal adviser to the Counsel to the President, appeared in the second article in *The New York Review*, pages 50-52, followed by further commentary by Draper. In his articles and books, Draper relied heavily on *Report of the Congressional Committees Investigating the Iran-Contra Affair* (Washington, D.C.: U.S. Government Printing Office, 1987), and *Iran-Contra Investigation, Joint Hearings*, 1986, a multivolume official transcript of public hearings held by the Senate and House Select Committees.

37. Scott Armstrong, "Iran-Contra: Was the Press Any Match for All the President's Men?" *Columbia Journalism Review* (May/June 1970): 27-35.

38. Armstrong, 28. The *al-Shiraa* article appeared in print on November 3, 1986.

39. Armstrong, 29.

40. See the persuasive discussion of these enduring values in Gans, *Deciding What's News*, 39-69.

41. Peter Goldman and Tom Mathews, *Quest for the Presidency* (New York: Simon & Schuster, 1989), 197-201. The account of the incident is taken from this book.

42. Dom Bonafede, "Call It a Draw," *National Journal*, February 6, 1988, 357. There was some disagreement among journalists at first as to who "won" the encounter, but as the campaign wore on, more and more analysts concluded that Bush had gained by demonstrating a new image. Bonafede concluded: "Most TV viewers have a mental picture of network TV anchors as being as smooth as olive oil, unflappable in a storm, gracious to a fault and, above all, always in control. For many, that illusion has now been shattered. That may be one of the rewarding legacies of the Bush-Rather shout-down."

Chapter

10

"OUR REPUBLIC AND ITS PRESS WILL RISE OR FALL TOGETHER"

1847 1947 JOSEPH PULITZER

3¢ UNITED STATES POSTAGE

Diversity: Minorities, Women, and the Media

In the last half century in the United States, few issues have been more significant or have generated higher drama than the struggle between the races. Both friends and foes of racial equality have condemned the press for failing to practice social responsibility in its treatment of news items about racial issues. More recently, the criticism has broadened into sharp attacks on the news media for not encouraging "diversity" in their hiring practices. Diversity means employing more African-Americans, more Hispanics, more Native Americans, and more women. Critics accuse the news media of bias in their treatment of all groups except heterosexual white American men. A press that practiced the doctrine of social responsibility would have served the interests of whites and all minorities. After all, a pluralistic "society" must be color blind and gender blind. Yet before 1954, when a Supreme Court ruling set the civil-rights struggle in motion, the majoritarian U.S. press had by and large ignored the issue of race. A black press had existed, almost unknown, for a century and a half.[1]

White journalists wrote and broadcast about racial matters before the 1960s riots but rarely within the larger context of civil liberties. News about black citizens was confined mainly to crime reports and stories about the need of African-Americans for welfare or unemployment benefits. Faces of blacks, Hispanics, Asians, and women were barely visible among the sea of white male faces on television, and only a smattering of women worked as newspaper reporters. The number of African-American journalists employed by mainstream news media was minute. Racial and ethnic minorities had only the most limited access to the news columns. The presidential Kerner Commission that investigated the causes of the 1960s racial disturbances concluded, "The media report and write from the standpoint of a white man's world . . . their failure to convey the ills of the ghetto, the difficulties of life there, and the Negro's burning sense of grievance [was] inexcusable in an institution that has the mission to inform and educate the whole of our society."[2]

More forceful even than the Kerner Commission report was a statement by Stokely Carmichael, then chairman of the Student Nonviolent Coordinating Committee, that contrary to the folklore of social responsibility, the white press had little concern for representing the interests of blacks. Instead, he wrote, the white press's chief interest was in "sensationalism and race-warmongering," so much so that white newspersons were "incapable of objective observation and reporting of racial *incidents*, much less the analysis of *ideas*." The white journalist's failure to gain the vision necessary to tell the story of racism accurately, Carmichael said, was the "inevitable consequence of the dictatorship of definition, interpretation, and consciousness along with the censorship of history the society has inflicted upon the Negro—and itself."[3]

If Carmichael was correct, then the mainstream press felt most responsible to the society of whites, those who defined and interpreted history. Certainly, in dealing with racial issues, the press failed to carry out its AWA model. It served neither as adversary of racist practices or sexual harassment, nor as watchdog of government abuses, nor as setter of an agenda of public concern among the white male population about racial matters or gender issues. Instead, the press served the interests of the social order that had for hundreds of years practiced racial and gender discrimination either in the form of slavery or in the kinds of prejudices perpetuated by white male society and its institutions. Foes of the civil-rights movement went out of their way to accuse the mainstream press of stirring up trouble with its reports about racial issues. To do so, they argued, was a violation of social responsibility.

Stung especially by accusations of racism, the American news media changed directions in the generation that followed the 1960s riots. News organizations actively recruited African-Americans as reporters and sharply increased their coverage of racial issues. Many turned out distinguished reports that included in-depth newspaper analyses and television documentaries about the complex racial questions facing the country. After a 1978 survey showed 3.95 percent of a newspaper's "professional positions" were held by minorities, the American Society of Newspaper Editors (ASNE) promoted a vigorous recruitment campaign; by 1992, the percentage had risen to 5 percent; of new hirings, 23 percent were minority, although this figure included clerical and other workers as well as news personnel.[4] However, 45 percent of the nation's newspapers employed no African-Americans. The figures continued to generate antagonism among minority groups. The 1990 U.S. Census showed the African-American population totaled 12.1 percent (Hispanics numbered 8 percent, Asian-Americans 2.9 percent, and Native

Americans 8 percent, for a total of 24.8 percent).[5] The ASNE set a "Year 2000" goal, at which point the target for percentage of minorities in the newsrooms of each paper was to equal the percentage of the total minority population in that paper's circulation area. Although minority percentages went up substantially on small papers in communities with small minority populations, newsroom minority percentages actually decreased in areas with large minority populations. Of the nation's major newspapers, only *The Boston Globe* was reaching the goal.[6] Even so, a study by the journalist Kirk Johnson showed that 85 percent of the news about Boston's predominantly black neighborhoods in the city's "major media"— two dailies, three TV channels, and a radio station—reinforced "negative stereotypes of blacks and the poor" and in no way reflected "the true diversity of the black community."[7]

A 1993 survey of the 2,400-member National Association of Black Journalists (NABJ), the first ever conducted by the country's largest organization of minority journalists, painted a bleak picture of the news industry and race relations, which was "too often a picture of despair." The association's president, Dorothy Gilliam, said the survey found "the news industry resisting the diversity on which its economic survival depends." African-American journalists complained of "gross misrepresentation in management, chronic problems of promoting and retention and few black journalists in plum assignments."[8]

Mainstream newspapers encountered serious difficulties in seeking to change the face of what the Kerner Commission had called a journalistic profession "shockingly backward in seeking out, hiring, training and promoting Negroes."[9] Twenty-five years later, things hadn't changed much, the NABJ's Gilliam said. Roosevelt University, an essentially black school in Chicago, created a program aimed at correcting statistics that showed a 25 percent minority population in the United States yet fewer than 8 percent employed in newsrooms.[10] *Newsweek* wrote in 1986 that despite gains in minority hiring, fewer than 1 percent of management jobs in the news media were held by minorities. The ASNE said in 1992 that 6.3 percent of managerial posts in newspapers were in the hands of minorities.[11] Both white and black editors called again and again for raising the number of black reporters and managers; but the pace remained slow, and in city after city, minority groups rose to complain.[12] The ASNE broke new ground in 1993, installing its first African-American president, William A. Hilliard, editor of the *Oregonian* in Portland. Under the leadership of its president, Arthur Ochs Sulzberger, Jr., *The New York Times* launched a campaign to redouble its efforts to hire and promote minority editors and reporters. Sulzberger told the NABJ in 1991 that he considered diversity the single most important issue faced by the *Times*. A year later, he told the National Gay and Lesbian Journalists Association that his newspaper would "no longer offer our readers a predominantly white, straight, male vision of events."[13]

Indeed, the ASNE joined the Newspaper Association of America at the end of 1992 in a "diversity summit meeting" that William McGowan, a former editor of *The Washingtion Monthly*, wrote "had the air of a tent revival, full of jeremiads, calls for repentance, and holy roller zeal."[14] The goal of diversity in both newspaper newsrooms and in their coverage of news events was an acknowledgment of what

SOURCE: L. W. Harvey

Carmichael and others had seen as the arrogance of a white press. That goal took the shape of political correctness, or what McGowan called "fashionable nostrums." *The Philadelphia Inquirer* went so far as to announce a five-year plan of hiring "quotas," under which minorities would represent 50 percent of all new hires; half the new hires, white or minority, would also be women.[15]

Despite these proposals, the respondents to the NABJ survey found only begrudging tolerance of minorities in newsrooms. Sixty-seven percent of the respondents said the management of their newsrooms were not committed to retaining and promoting African-American journalists. Eighty-nine percent of the African-American journalists spoke of a newsroom problem caused by a lack of black mentors and role models. Two-thirds of the respondents said black journalists spent more time in entry-level jobs than did whites. The survey included a sample not only of the African-American journalists but also of the white managers, and differences between the responses of the workers and their managers was sharp. For instance, while two-thirds of the African-American journalists reported a lack of commitment on the part of their white managers, only 5 percent of the managers perceived that to be the case.

Differences in perception were striking. In fact, the perceptions about diversity of blacks and whites on American newspapers is overwhelming and accounts in considerable measure for the continuing racial tension in many newsrooms. Thomas Kochman, an expert in cross-cultural communication, said the NABJ survey findings illustrated the depth of the "cultural disparities." The cultural style of African-Americans, he said, "is much more parental" than that of self-reliant, self-promoting white males. "Take the person under their wings and make sure they know what they have to know to succeed. In Anglo self-reliance, the editor feels the failure is not their fault." Kochman offered a proposal that was startling in the context of the long-standing set of American values. The perceptions and cultural differences were so profound, he said, that "we have to put aside the concept of objectivity, because that is a pretense."[16]

While the ASNE established a hoped-for numerical ratio system for minorities, none was considered for women, but the U.S. Commission on Civil Rights concluded after a thorough study of television stations in the mid-1970s that white males dominated the nation's newsrooms, particularly at management levels. Among those who appeared on network news programs, the report said, white males outnumbered black and female journalists by nine to one.[17]

Following that report, the number of women hired by the networks and major newspapers rose quickly, though chiefly to lower-level jobs. Contemporary studies show that women make up nearly 40 percent of journalists working on newspapers, half of them in their thirties.[18] Nearly all women encounter the "glass ceiling," a metaphor long used by blacks to describe the invisible barrier that stops minorities from advancing beyond a certain point up the artificial ladder of success imposed by the white male "power structure" in the news media. While 39 percent of newsroom employees are women, only 18 percent of news executives are women, and only 8.5 percent of publishers are women.[19] In television, women make up 34 percent of all news staffs, chiefly in the largest markets, but only 16.5 percent are news directors. Those figures have changed little since the mid-1980s.[20] A 1991 survey showed 63 percent of women journalists believe a glass ceiling exists, contrasted with 35 percent of the men.[21] Women journalists complained of encountering the glass ceiling, especially in television. Christine Craft, who was fired as a co-anchor by a Kansas City television station because, she said, she didn't look young enough, look pretty enough, or act deferential enough to men, continued to hammer at that theme years later. In her third year of law school in 1993, Craft told a convention of news directors they were still hiring people for cosmetic purposes and, therefore, had to take the blame for what she called "the dumbing down of America."

ABC correspondent Carole Simpson said television seemed to be trading experience, qualifications, and maturity "for pretty and cheap."[22] *New York Times* executive editor Max Frankel countered that most major political decisions were made by men, so that "bean counting is not a constructive operation."[23] *Times* reporter Maureen Dowd blamed the infusion of young male blood into the ranks of leading journalists. Howard Kurtz, *Washington Post* media critic, said it was the rise to prominence of some female reporters that had changed the scene. Dowd, with tongue perhaps in cheek, said that wasn't true at all; she blamed male reporters for the changes, especially the new breed of young father types. "It's guys who are ruining political journalism," she said, and labeled them "New Age stiffs" who were filling the business "with a bunch of 30-something touchy-feely guys, tying up all cellular phone circuits trying to call home to talk baby talk with their wives and kids."[24]

As columnist Barbara Reynolds put it, "How can you have a democracy and a free press . . . when 95 percent of all the decisions made in the media are made by white males?"[25] She spoke before a panel that evaluated the coverage given women at the two 1992 political conventions.

During the 1992 election campaign, coverage of Hillary Rodham Clinton, the Democratic candidate's wife, did nothing to improve the balance. That coverage provided, as Maureen Beasley wrote, "a glaring example of media mistreatment of women." Male contempt for the outspoken, politically savvy future First Lady seemed to know no bounds. Some journalists likened her to Lady Macbeth. *U.S. News & World Report* went to the extreme of tagging her "an overbearing yuppie wife from hell"[26]

The feminist author Betty Friedan spoke of a "male blind spot" that led the news media to preoccupation with candidates' personal lives, "namely who slept with whom. . . . The media turn women into sex objects." A study of the front pages of twenty newspapers showed the number of photographs of women increased from 1989 to 1990 by 32 percent; but the number of women quoted as sources averaged only 14 percent (up from 11 percent), and only 28 percent of the bylines were women's.

Achieving newsroom diversity is a challenge not only for indifferent editors but also for those who are seeking to achieve it. For instance, one complicating factor has been the determination of a number of minority members to refuse employment with mainstream newspapers or television operations out of conviction that they were being disloyal to their own community. This motive was fed by continuing criticism of news coverage of racial affairs in mainstream media. The complaint was that a focus on crime, poverty, and aberrant behavior failed to treat minority members as the "human equal" of whites. Many white commentators agreed with the charges of distortion in news coverage leveled by the African-American press.[27]

Newspapers were not, however, the chief culprit. That distinction went to television, despite the fact that the rate of minority employment in the broadcast media was higher than that on newspapers. Figures for 1992 showed minorities made up 18.5 percent of TV news personnel, a 5 percent increase over the total twenty years earlier; the rate of Hispanic hires was the highest among minorities. Among news directors, however, the percentage of minorities remained low, totaling only 8.7 percent, half of those Hispanic. "While broadcasting has outpaced print," wrote Vernon A. Stone, who conducted the survey, "newsrooms in all media still have catching up to do to reflect the diversity of the American people."[28]

As for coverage of minority affairs, *The Journal of Broadcasting & Electronic Media* reported a study that found little change in the way minorities and women were covered in television network news during the twenty-eight years that had elapsed since the publication of the Kerner Commission report.[29] Rob Sierra, a Latino reporter on the news staff of WGN, the powerful Chicago radio and television outlet, didn't find that surprising. He said only 4 percent of newsroom staffers were Latin American, and Hispanic enrollment in journalism schools was also only 4 percent while the national percentage stood at 10 percent.[30] Spokespersons for Asian-American and homosexual journalists also reported a lack of balance in both newsrooms and journalism schools. The sharpest lack of diversity on staffs was reported in small Midwest markets. "You have to have a life too," one African-American journalism school graduate told the meeting, noting the small number of minority residents in those places. A white manager asked why minority journalists could not put off their social lives for a bit.

The political scientist Robert Entman blamed television for feeding negative emotional feelings towards blacks, mainly by denying the continued existence of racial discrimination and by rejecting blacks' political agendas.[31] African-American columnist Clarence Page wrote in *The Chicago Tribune* that television, which loves pictures of "cops and robbers, people getting arrested, blood and guts and shootouts," concentrates on teeming urban centers where crime is highest. As a consequence, he wrote, "you wind up with a lot of pictures on TV of black and Hispanic people getting busted for crime. The problem in the public is the mentality that confuses crime with blacks and Hispanics. . . . Too often crime is portrayed with a minority face on it."[32]

The question of news reports on racial affairs sprang to front and center once again in 1992 with the sensational coverage, especially on television, of the beating of black motorist Rodney King by four white Los Angeles police officers and the rioting and looting that followed the acquittal of three of those officers. TV news came under heavy attack, sometimes for sensational reporting and sometimes for biased reporting that, it was held, exacerbated racial tensions.[33]

Lamentably, the focus remained on racial "troubles" and their political consequences. Leading newspapers struggled to complement their news stories about beatings, rioting, and looting with analytical "sidebars" pointing to the social factors that gave rise to the turmoil. So, to some degree, did television. The social factors, poverty and discontent, were not ignored, not at all; but they tended to get lost in the dramatic pictures of police officers beating a black driver, of blacks beating white motorists, of looting and fires raging out of control. The holders of political and economic power in the country seemed unable to achieve social stability. The press coverage reflected the nervousness in both Caucasian and minority neighborhoods and invoked a sense of panic that sent thousands of frightened men and women to dealers in firearms. An agenda of reconciliation might have helped dispel the fear and panic; however, neither the holders of power nor their agents in the news media prepared such an agenda. It is unrealistic in the real world to expect the press to calm its audiences when the holders of power cannot calm the people. Once again, we can see the limits of the "power" of the press and recognize its lack of independent power.

Very likely as a result of the kind of coverage in mainstream newspapers, black readership has fallen sharply. Sulzberger seemed to be referring to the fact when he told the NABJ that another sound reason for promoting diversity in the newsroom was that it was good business. The decline of black readership has, not surprisingly, led newspapers faced with generally shrinking readership to devote ever more reportage to information about white elites, those who can be counted on to read the papers. The researchers Ted Pease and Frazier Smith wrote newspapers "run the risk of becoming more elite and increasingly narrow in their content focus as they try to retain what readers they can."[34]

Interestingly, the portrait of African-Americans on news programs has been in sharp contrast to their portrait on entertainment programs. The sociologist Herman Gray noted that mainstream fictional television fare features "idealized black middle-class families living the American Dream" while news shows depict primarily the black underclass.[35] The diversity is there all right, Gray points out; but this pattern of treatment only aggravates the nation's racial hostilities and the "split image" Dates and Barlow wrote about. Editor at large Audrey Edwards of *Essence* magazine also spoke of split images, calling the dramatic confrontation on live television between Supreme Court nominee Clarence Thomas and Professor Anita Hill an introduction to the white audience of a different TV image: the "polished professional, cool under fire, smart and articulate . . . in a way never quite dramatized before."[36]

A split image seems to exist in the press as well. All mainstream news media are working hard to recruit journalists of color. More minority members than ever before have begun working for the news media, even though the glass ceiling continues to shunt the great majority into second-class citizenship in the newsrooms. Many African-American journalists who responded to the NABJ survey applauded radio and television management for making overt efforts to hire a larger number of blacks, but motivations were often suspect. They said they were convinced the "immediate assumption" of white managers was that a black journalist got his or her job not out of merit but because of the color of his or her skin. One nonmanagement journalist offered an observation that seemed to be widely shared: "We've never had blacks or any other minorities in decision-making positions," he said. "It may not be a racist shop in the harshest sense of the word—it is a callous shop which lacks sensitivity." A minority reporter in his thirties said that in the nation's newspaper newsrooms, minority journalists are largely "still the invisible people."[37]

Resolution of the diversity issue to the satisfaction of both whites and blacks was clearly extraordinarily difficult to achieve. McGowan and others have called attention to the slumping morale in newsrooms long accustomed to nearly all white faces. Veteran white staffers are uneasy over the threat diversity poses to their power and prestige. The decline in morale is illustrated by the enthusiasm with which journalists accepted *The Los Angeles Times's* 1992 buyout offer during the advertising slump that happened to occur simultaneously with the street riots in south-central Los Angeles. Following the riots, which were set off by the initial acquittal of the police officers charged with beating black motorist Rodney King, the paper's management increased efforts to recruit minority staffers. Meanwhile, 88 percent of the newsroom staff was accepting the offer—four times the number management had expected.[38] Howard Kurtz, *Washington Post* media reporter, wrote that the exodus was a reflection of plummeting morale; one departing Metro staff member told him "factionalism at work at this paper that I think is extremely counterproductive."

Despite its steps to achieve greater diversity, the press has in the years since the 1967 Kerner Commission report come no closer, as Pease and Smith wrote, to fulfilling its "social responsibility . . . to cover completely all segments of the society."[39] Their conclusion is worth repeating:

> The country's demographic character will change more radically in the next few decades than ever before in its history. How newspapers adapt and prepare for those changes will determine how well they'll survive as participants within the economic marketplace and the democratic marketplace of ideas.[40]

The doctrine of social responsibility assumes independent power for the news media. However questionable, this doctrine has become so ingrained in public consciousness it is invoked across the country—and throughout the world—wherever discussions about the press are encountered. In their analysis, the authors of *Four Theories of the Press* held that the doctrine operates in the interests of "society," by which they meant the entire population. Coverage of racial issues has failed to ease the country's racial trauma or to work for the benefit of minority Americans. Nor has coverage of gender questions ameliorated the tensions between men and women. News reports about political and economic events and trends serve the interests of the powerful far more than those of the powerless. Challenges are raised in the media to individuals who stray from the norm, presidents among them, so much so the press enjoys the reputation of being a kind of loyal opposition to power. Yet that opposition extends only so far, and not beyond the boundaries of acceptable dissent—aside from a handful of periodicals that circulate to small audiences, usually unprofitably. Individuals are attacked freely by the mainstream press, but institutions are not. These are defended. It is ironical that in this activity the press is dutifully carrying out one of the five roles assigned to it by the Hutchins Commission: to present and clarify the goals and values of society. The doctrine of social responsibility, in fact, excludes those goals and values that lie beyond the ideological boundaries established by the social order. The limits of investigative journalism are precisely those boundaries. The advice of India's Neville Jayaweera is admirable:

> The last thing media people can do is to come alive to the historical processes in which they are inextricably caught up and adapt their styles and priorities within them. Theirs has always been and will continue to be

only a supportive role—supportive of values and systems that are not theirs to prescribe. Those values and systems are fashioned by economic and social forces much larger and more fundamental than themselves. The media ego must learn to diminish gracefully.[41]

Journalists have rarely been accused of humility. It is not easy for them to accept the reality they cannot separate themselves from a society in which racism is rampant. If they are ever to develop a clear understanding of what they do and how what they do fits into the social order around them, it will be necessary for them to surrender their arrogance—or, as Jayaweera says, to diminish it gracefully—and to remove the motes from their eyes. They will need, for instance, to reflect deeply about the comment made by a respondent to the NABJ survey that while his television station might not have been racist in the harshest meaning of that word, it was nevertheless a racist shop that lacked sensitivity. A vast gulf lies between getting out the news and being sensitive to the total context in which the news story took place. They are not the same thing. Journalistic actions are followed by public consequences.

NOTES

1. See, for example, Jannette L. Dates and William Barlow, eds., *Split Image: African Americans in the News Media* (Washington, D.C.: Howard University Press, 1990). The notes at the end of each chapter are outstanding. The literature on the black press has been expanding in recent years. Among the best still is Roland E. Wolseley, *The Black Press U.S.A.* (Ames: Iowa State University Press, 1971). See also Herman Gray, "Television, Black Americans, and the American Dream," in *Critical Studies in Mass Communication* 6 (December 1989): 376–386.

2. Kerner Commission, *Report of the National Advisory Commission on Civil Disorders* (Washington, D.C.: U.S. Government Printing Office, 1986), 362–89.

3. Stokely Carmichael, "Toward Black Liberation," *The Massachusetts Review* 7 (Autumn 1966): 639–51.

4. "ASNE's 1992 Survey Shows Small Gain in Minority Employment," ASNE news release, April 2, 1992.

5. *Statistical Abstracts* (Washington, D.C.: Bureau of the Census, 1993).

6. While the 1990 minority population in its circulation district stood at 8 percent of the total, the percentage of minority members in the *Globe* newsroom had reached 13.9 percent in 1990. Here are comparable figures for the papers with leading circulations: *New York Daily News*, 45 percent and 16 percent; *Los Angles Times*, 45 percent and 12.6 percent; *New York Times*, 41 percent and 11.8 percent; *Washington Post*, 37 percent and 16.2 percent. Dick Haws, "Minorities in the Newsroom and Community: A Comparison," *Journalism Quarterly*, 68, 4 (Winter 1991): 764–71. The data themselves were compiled by the ASNE from responses to questionnaires.

7. Kirk A. Johnson, "Black and White in Boston," *Columbia Journalism Review*, 26 (May/June 1987): 50–52. Johnson also reviewed the content of four black-owned media

and found 57 percent of the stories "suggested a black community thirsty for educational advancement and entrepreneurial achievement, and eager to remedy poor living conditions made worse by bureaucratic neglect."

8. *Muted Voices: Frustration and Fear in the Newsroom* (Washington, D.C.: The National Association of Black Journalists, 1993), 3.

9. Kerner Commission, *Report of the National Advisory Commission*, 211.

10. *Chicago Defender*, July 17, 1991, 5.

11. ASNE news release, April 2, 1992.

12. See, for instance, *Denver Post*, March 11, 1992; *Los Angeles Times*, December 13, 1991; *St. Louis Post-Dispatch*, July 20, 1989.

13. William McGowan, "The Other Side of the Rainbow," *Columbia Journalism Review* (November/December 1993): 53.

14. Ibid.

15. Ibid., 54. Editor Maxwell King was quoted as speaking of this move to diversity as "the most aggressive plan" at any newspaper in the country.

16. *Muted Voices*, 14–15. Kochman is the author of *Black and White Styles in Conflict* (Chicago: University of Chicago Press, 1981).

17. U.S. Commission on Civil Rights, *Window Dressing on the Set: Women and Minorities in Television* (Washington, D.C.: U.S. Government Printing Office, 1977). See also a 1979 update.

18. Ted Pease and J. Frazier Smith, "The Newsroom Barometer: Job Satisfaction & the Impact of Racial Diversity at U.S. Daily Newspapers," *Ohio Journalism Monographs* 1 (July 1991): 9–10.

19. Kay Mills, "The Media and the Year of the Woman," *Media Studies Journal* (Winter/Spring 1993): 25.

20. Vernon A. Stone, "Good News, Bad News," *Communicator* (August 1993): 68–69. Stone was research director for the Radio and Television News Directors Association, which funded the study.

21. Pease and Smith, "The Newsroom Barometer," 39.

22. Simpson spoke to a session of the 1993 convention of the Radio and Television News Directors Association in Miami Beach, September 30, 1993. Craft addressed the same session via satellite from Sacramento, California.

23. Judy Southworth, "Women Media Workers: No Room at the Top," *Extra!* (March/April 1991): 16.

24. Maureen Dowd, "Requiem for the Boys on the Bus," *Media Studies Journal* (Winter/Spring 1993): 99–100.

25. Barbara Reynolds. "Women on the Media: Still Not Getting It," *Washington Journalism Review* (September 1992): 5.

26. Maurine H. Beasley, "Myths, Media and Women," *Media Studies Journal* (Winter/Spring 1993): 243.

27. See, for instance, *Amsterdam News* July 28, 1991, and *Chicago Defender*, December 31, 1991. On January 13, 1991, the *Defender* cited a study that showed television news coverage of criminal and political news among blacks and whites were treated in a manner that created racial fears among white audiences.

28. Stone, "Good News, Bad News," 69.

29. Dhyana Ziegler and Alisa White, "Women and Minorities on Network News: An Examination of Correspondents and Newsmakers," *Journal of Broadcasting and Electronic Media* 34, 2 (Spring 1990): 215-3. A similar conclusion was drawn at a conference at the Harvard University School of Government. See *Boston Globe*, May 5, 1990, 23.

30. Sierra spoke at a session of the RTNDA in Miami Beach on October 1, 1993.

31. Robert M. Entman, "How TV News Promotes Anti-Black Stereotyping," *Los Angles Times*, February 17, 1992.

32. Clarence Page, interview with Paula Kamen, September 9, 1989, in Martin A. Lee and Norman Solomon, eds., *Unreliable Sources* (Secaucus, NJ: 1990), 244. See also commentary by Clarence Page, "The Good Thing About Riots," *Chicago Tribune*, May 19, 1992, in which he writes there was at least one thing the riots in Los Angeles accomplished: They got the attention of the presidential candidates, the news media, and all Americans to focus on the problems of racial equality.

33. See, for instance, articles in *The San Francisco Chronicle* May 8 and 20, 1992, reporting criticism especially from Korean and other Asian-American communities.

34. Pease and Smith, "The Newsroom Barometer," 7.

35. Herman Gray, "Television", 384, cited in Dates and Barlow, *Split Images*, 458, comment that "these two seemingly disparate black representations are linked, because they tell opposite sides of the same mythical story of African American success and failure."

36. Audrey Edwards, "From Aunt Jemima and Anita Hill: Media's Split Image of Black Women," *Media Studies Journal* (Winter/Spring 1993): 221-22.

37. *Muted Voices*, 8.

38. McGowan, "The Other Side of the Rainbow," 54.

39. Pease and Smith, "The Newsroom Barometer," 34-35.

40. Pease and Smith.

41. Neville Jayaweera, "Political Access to the Media in Sri Lanka," *World Association for Christian Communication Journal* 22, 1 (1975): 3-6.

PART IV

THE POLITICAL ARENA
IN COMMUNITARIAN
AND ADVANCING SOCIETIES

Chapter
11

The Communitarian Press:
The Role of Karl Marx

MARX'S PRESS PHILOSOPHY

The fall of the Communist party has been widely heralded, especially in the market societies of the West, as meaning the death of communism; and it certainly has demonstrated the demise of *Soviet* communism as well as of the Soviet Union itself, but it is at best premature to consign the ideology of communism to the grave. Eulogies have been pronounced over many ideologies throughout history, including conservatism and liberalism, but they have nevertheless survived. The ideal of a communitarian society dates back a long way. Few movements have been more intensely dedicated to a communitarian ideal than early Christianity. That ideal has by no means disappeared. In its essence, communism is communitarian, a world without classes, with each person contributing to the community to the best of his or her ability and drawing from it according to his or her need. The ideal of the French Revolution was equally communitarian, with "citizens" exercising power just as "comrades" were meant to do under the Communist Revolution. Neither revolution produced such an idealized society, and both fell in part because their expectations were beyond the reach of mortal men and women. The failure of Soviet communism was long evident beyond the Soviet borders; by the 1990s, when it was toppled in a relatively bloodless coup, that failure had become equally clear to the people of the Soviet empire.

The communitarian ideal—or, as indicated in the guiding metaphor of this book, the second movement of a symphony—is as alive as ever. In this reshaping of a model developed earlier,[1] the name of the movement has been changed from "Marxist" to "communitarian." With the alteration of name have come some modifications in description, though the melodies remain basically unchanged.[2] We have turned away from "Marxist" because the designation has become too ambiguous. As Marx himself once observed, perhaps in playful mood, *"Je ne suis pas marxiste."*[3] So, "communitarian" is the choice. Later in these pages, we will return to the topic of names and their importance in understanding.

Journalism schools throughout the Soviet empire made a point of teaching "Marxist journalism." Whatever that phrase meant, the idea that "Marxist journalism" began with Karl Marx was a central element of Soviet press doctrine. Yet this is not a valid idea; it is folklore that was politically useful in the Soviet Union just as the folklore of an adversary press is politically useful in the United States. In truth, Marx is as difficult to pin down as Jefferson, who can be found on all sides of the issue of press freedom at different periods of his life.

The communitarian concept can be found in all corners of the earth today, often in areas of the Third World and the market social order. In the United States, commitment to shared communities has stirred political movements from its beginnings to the present. In the 1990s, the American political philosopher Amitai Etzioni spearheaded a movement seeking "a communitarian perspective" that avoided particular policies and instead aimed at strengthening families.[4]

For many but not all supporters, communitarianism means the open use of the press as an avowed instrument of propaganda. It is an old idea, long part of the intellectual mainstream when Marx was born in 1818. The press has played a central role in the circulation of attitudes and beliefs in all systems. We have seen its role in the capitalist system in providing information about the availability of goods in the marketplace. In the "socialist" system that evolved in the nineteenth century and was to be codified by Vladimir Ilyich Lenin and the Bolsheviks in the twentieth century, the position of the press was equally central. It is fascinating to note the key men and women who participated in the evolution of socialism were all journalists: Marx and Engels, Lenin, Rosa Luxemburg, Trotsky, and even Stalin.

Unquestionably, however, the dominant figure in the evolution of socialist thought was Marx. It was Marx who was the chief theorist of a set of ideas that challenged the dominant Western beliefs about all its institutions, including the press; it was he who advanced new social and economic theories that challenged the dominant capitalist ideology. In so doing, he converted the world (and its presses) into conflict so perilous it threatened the continued existence of humankind. This characterization of Marx and socialist ideology is in no way meant to assign blame. Marxist theory holds that the peril is the inevitable consequence of historical factors, that capitalism, when threatened, will inexorably launch warfare to preserve its position of power against the challenge of the rising class of workers. For their part, adherents of capitalism assigned the blame to the socialists for recklessly risking war in order to achieve world domination. Analysis of the rights and wrongs

Karl Marx, the man who said he wasn't a Marxist.
SOURCE: Library of Congress

of the planned economy and capitalism is not within the scope of this study; it is sufficient to point out the danger lying in the conflict model preached by the theology of both socialists and capitalists.

As with many theories, that of Marx is incomplete. He was more the scholarly analyst than the fiery revolutionary. His most thorough work is his study of history and the sociological, philosophical, and economic elements that went into the development of the capitalist world in which he lived. It remained for Lenin to adapt—and to modify—Marxist ideas into the revolutionary social and political system of the Soviet empire. Still, even though Marx's theory is incomplete, in his writings many clues can be found that cast light on the revolutionary social and political system that survives under his name. It is the very fact that Marx's theory is incomplete that has made it possible for so many different interpretations to emerge about his writings and ideas. Marxism is by no means a monolithic philosophy; to many it is not a philosophy at all but a description of objective reality.

In any case, Marxism does not equal communitarianism. Far from it. But Marxism, as blended with Leninism and institutionalized in the Soviet Union, is the most highly developed form of communitarianism yet to have been practiced. Central to communitarianism and as stated directly under Marxism is the idea that institutions are (and ought to be) structured to work for the benefit of a selfless collective, tribal community rather than for the benefit of egoistic, personally motivated individuals. In both cases, the individual is required to yield his or her selfish freedom for the benefit of the community.

In the classification system we will discuss in detail later, the communitarian movement of the symphony of the press is one with many variations, as is Marxism. Another book might be written that would merely examine the variations, but it was the dominant melody of this movement that was, by and large, played for the tens of thousands of students who studied at the school of journalism at the Moscow State University in the heyday of Marxism-Leninism. It is important to recognize that what was conveyed to the students were the strains of Marxism-Leninism, not communitarianism or even Marxism.

The press theory developed in the Soviet Union, heavily laden with ideological dogma, became an integral ingredient in the education of future journalists throughout the Soviet empire. Vladimír Hudec, then dean of the faculty of journalism at Charles University in Prague, gave voice to the basic lines of that theory in a sketch of the growth of journalism:

> *During the bourgeois democratic revolution in Germany in 1848-1849, Karl Marx and Friedrich Engels founded and edited in Cologne the "Neue Rheinische Zeitung"—which was actually the beginning of the history of Marxist journalism*. This paper was a tribune for proletarian policy in the bourgeois democratic revolution, promoting this policy in the spirit of the famous "Manifesto of the Communist Party," also published in 1848. It was for the first time that the spontaneously developing proletarian movement gradually shifted from *"utopia to science,"* and this was fully reflected also in journalism.[5]

The first job Marx held after completing his university studies in Berlin was as a contributing writer for a newspaper begun in Cologne in 1842 by Moses Hess, a devotee of the radical socialist ideas then popular in France. Within ten months of the founding of the paper, the *Rheinische Zeitung*, Hess elevated Marx to the position of editor in chief. Hess had the deepest admiration for his young protégé, who had already won a reputation as a scholar and writer. Hess once described Marx in these words: "He combines the deepest philosophical seriousness with the most biting wit. Imagine Rousseau, Voltaire, Holbach, Lessing, Heine and Hegel fused into one person—I say fused, not thrown together in a heap—and you have Dr. Marx."[6]

Under Marx's iron leadership—he was never a man to shun assertiveness—the *Rheinische Zeitung* opened a full-scale attack on Prussian rule. Marx attacked the Prussian leadership and the landowning class in general, and the paper's circulation grew rapidly. For a time, the Prussian authorities treated the paper with restraint, even though tough censorship rules provided the authorities with almost limitless opportunities to suppress it. The Rhineland territories only recently had been annexed by Prussia, and the authorities were reluctant to stir public opposition by censoring the paper. Still, Marx drew the ire of the political censors by attacking the government's failure to improve the living conditions of the vine-growing peasantry and its imposition of heavy penalties on the poor who stole decayed timber in the forests for fuel. Marx, whose way with words has rarely been equaled among political writers, managed for a time to outwit the censors and publish material that appeared on the surface to be properly attentive to the interests of the Prussian crown but disseminated its democratic messages to those who could read between the lines.[7] Apparently Marx went too far when he publicly called on the Prussian rulers to go to war against the oppressive Russian regime of Czar Nicholas I. The *Rheinische Zeitung* was promptly suppressed, and Marx was out of a job; but he had learned well the skills of political journalism.

Perhaps the most remarkable article Marx wrote during that period was "Comments on the Latest Prussian Censorship Instruction,"[8] composed for yet another political journal launched by fellow journalist Arnold Ruge. The publication was to have appeared in Paris, though censors shut it down before the first edition could appear. Ruge then went to Switzerland and published Marx's article in a journal he called the *Anekdota*; it was the first and last issue. In November 1843, Marx left Prussian territory for Paris, then the center of radical activity. It was in those years that Marx, secretly discussing the writings of Proudhon and Saint-Simon by night in flats and cafés, became radicalized, shifting from the libertarian humanism of his early years to the fiery revolutionary rhetoric that led to his reputation as the "red terrorist doctor."

Marx's article was based on an 1841 Royal Cabinet Order ostensibly designed to lift some of the more repressive censorship rules handed down twenty-two years earlier.[9] Marx wrote with power, demanding the abolition of the "bad institution" of censorship. Institutions, he argued, "are more powerful than men."[10] As Marx pointed out in his closely reasoned article, the modification in censorship was more apparent than real and came to be used as a device to stifle philosophical dissent, whereas the earlier rule had been directed against the expression of religious differences. Of even greater concern to Marx was the introduction in the 1841 Instruction of a rule similar to what was later to become a part of U.S. press law, the Bad Tendency test. Writings that criticized administrators and laws or proposed improvements were to be free of censorship, the Instruction said, "so long as their form [was] decent and their tendency [was] well-intentioned." Good intentions were to be measured in terms of being free of spite or malice. Censors were directed to pay close attention to the form and tone of the language used and to prohibit "publication of writings if their tendency is harmful because of passion, violence, and presumptuousness."

Responding with scathing wrath, Marx declared: "According to this statement, the writer is subject to *the most horrible terrorism, to jurisdiction based on suspicion. Tendentious* laws, without objective norms, are laws of terrorism."[11] Such rules, Marx wrote, imposed penalties on citizens not for their action but for their thoughts; they denied the citizen his or her existence: "I may turn and twist myself as much as possible—the evidence is not important. My existence is suspect; my innermost being, my individuality, is considered to be *evil*, and I am *punished* for that. The law does not penalize me for wrongs I commit but for wrongs I do not commit."[12]

An ethical state, Marx said, leveling his heaviest artillery on the Prussian authorities, may not claim for itself exclusive possession of reason and morality. To drive home a point that was even more distasteful to the Prussian ruler, Marx declared the Instruction "aims to protect religion, but it violates the most universal of all religions: the sacredness and inviolability of subjective conviction. It replaces God as the judge of the heart with the censor."[13]

The Bad Tendency test concerned itself not only with content but also with tone, and the censors were directed to combat a tendency on the part of the newspapers to play "on the curiosity of their readers by printing gossip, insinuations, and meaningless reports taken from foreign newspapers and written by malevolent and poorly informed correspondents."[14] In other words, Marx commented, the censors were to decide what made for good journalism and what were the proper qualifications for editors. Marx, whose capacity for invective and acid sarcasm is legendary, turned his pen on the censors themselves. Under the Instruction, the censors were made to pass judgment on the "scientific qualifications" for editors. But where, Marx asked, did these "universal geniuses" acquire the scientific qualifications to make such judgments? He asked further:

> Why don't these encyclopedic minds come out as writers? If these officials, overwhelming in number and so powerful by knowledge and genius, would rise all of a sudden and by sheer weight crush those wretched writers who are active in one genre of writing only, and even there without officially tested qualifications, the confusion in the press could be terminated better than can be done by censorship. Why are these skilled men so silent when they could act like Roman geese saving the Capitol by their cackle? They must be men of great reserve. The scientific public does not know them, but the government does.[15]

The basic premise of Marx's essay was that free inquiry is good and censorship—in whatever form—is not only wicked but counterproductive. The purpose of journalism, he said, was the search for truth. The entire society would be the better for the search. In language drawn from Aristotle and echoed by democrats and libertarians for two millennia, Marx asserted:

> All purposes of journalistic activity are subsumed under the one general concept of "truth." Even if we disregard the subjective side, namely that one and the same object appears differently in different individuals and expresses its various aspects in as many various intellects, shouldn't *the character of the object* have some influence, even the slightest, on the inquiry? Not only the result but also the route belongs to the truth. The pursuit of truth must also be true; the true inquiry is the developed truth, whose scattered parts are assembled in the result.[16]

It was while editing and writing articles for the *Rheinische Zeitung* that Marx became intrigued by socialism and communism; in fact, he launched his study of communism only after his paper was accused of "flirting with communism." Not so, he wrote in a formal reply, adding he did not know enough about the doctrines of Fourier and Proudhon "to hazard an independent judgment" of communism.[17] His concern at the time he was writing for the paper—and throughout his life—was with specific issues; his general conclusions and laws grew out of his analysis of existing matters, what he identified as "objective factors." One of those objective factors was the wretched life of the vine-growing peasants in the Moselle Valley, where he had been born in the frontier city of Trier. The censorship laws were directed against the *Rheinische Zeitung* for its attacks on government disinterest in the plight of the Moselle peasants. His examination of the state of these peasants led to Marx's lifelong fascination with the economic factors in oppression. To assist in countering the oppression, in Marx's view, a free press was indispensable. Many of his *Rheinische Zeitung* articles concentrated on this theme. In response to the censors who were repeatedly assailing him for the Moselle articles, Marx identified both external and internal limitations on a free press. The external limitations were easy to see; they were official censorship, prior or ex post facto restraints. Internal limitations, he wrote, were more complex and philosophically more serious.

Internal limitations on the press were historical and intangible; they involved the political and cultural atmosphere inhabited by the press. Where journalists despaired of their power and influence, where they believed whatever they wrote would make no difference and dissident reports would lead to punishment, they lost their courage and contented themselves with simply reporting "the news"— that is to say, the correct facts as interpreted by the authorities. The next step in such an environment was the public's loss of interest in participating in public affairs. With this loss came the disappearance of "the creative force for a free and open press, as well as the condition of popular acceptance of a free and open press, the atmosphere without which the press is hopelessly sick."[18] In other words, for there to be a free press, there had to be public desire for a free press; and that desire was killed by internal limitations on the press. The oppressed public would sink into apathy where there was no free and open discussion—and without the support of the people, such free and open discussion was impossible. Marx clearly saw his paper as seeking "the truth" about the plight of the Moselle peasants and attempting to lift the public out of its apathy to demand social change. The press, in his view, ought never to be a mere reporter of "the news." From this conviction emerged the central theme in the socialist analysis of the press.

THE JOB OF THE PRESS IS TO "CHANGE THE WORLD"

In Marx's analysis of capitalism, the press was a central element of the superstructure, the *Überbau*, which the ruling classes erected as their literary, political, and ideological mechanism for maintaining power. The concept of a ruling class in a classed society is pivotal in Marx's theory. Like all communitarians, Marx had contempt for the idea of a society focused on the rights of individuals and not the welfare of society. Human emancipation is possible, Marx wrote, only in union forged in a social and political order.[19] The French philosopher Jean-Jacques Rousseau, from whom both Marx and Jefferson took important insights, wrote that a nation was valid only when it was able to transform each individual into something greater than his selfish self.[20] Marx argued that in a capitalist society rooted in the "so-called rights of man," those who enjoyed actual rights, the ruling class, used the superstructure to prevent the oppressed from finding their true identity and their true rights.

Although the word *superstructure* is the accepted translation of *Überbau*, it can be somewhat misleading. The structure of a society, in particular that of a capitalist society, Marx held, derives from material production—that is, the producing of goods; those who own the means of producing the goods constitute the ruling class. These are the capitalists, and they maintain their power by owning the means of production not only of material goods but also of "intellectual goods." Thus they control not just the farms and the factories but also the governments, churches, schools, and presses. These institutions—governments, churches, schools, and presses—are the chief components of the *Überbau*, the mechanisms established for the purpose of enabling the ruling class to maintain its power.[21] In English, *superstructure* suggests something built on top of something else; it is not included in the foundation and hence is not necessarily a part of the building. To Marx, the *Überbau* is not something built on top of the social order; it is, in fact, a critical part of that social order. Its job, its function, is to facilitate the maintenance of power by the ruling class, to enable the capitalists to exploit the workers, the proletariat. Without the *Überbau*, the capitalist structure would collapse of its own internal weaknesses—or, as Marx put it, of its contradictions.

In Marx's analysis of capitalist society, the press is crucial for the ruling class's capacity to maintain power. After his 1843 arrival in France, Marx wrote nothing further of significance about the press directly, but his view of the press and of its centrality was implicit in all his work.

He never entirely abandoned his career as a journalist. For ten years he and his friend and associate Friedrich Engels wrote articles from London for Horace Greeley's *New York Tribune*, an activity that provided American readers with insightful articles about world political affairs and also helped Marx, on the edge of poverty in London, to provide for himself and his family in their English exile. It was Charles Dana, then managing editor of the *Tribune*, who offered the position to Marx. Dana had met Marx while on a trip to Cologne and had been thoroughly impressed; he misread Marx as being a utopian Socialist in the vein of Charles Fourier or Robert Owen, the English industrialist who founded a commune in New Harmony, Indiana. But few Americans were knowledgeable about the intricacies of European socialism. Marx and Engels wrote 487 articles for *The Tribune* from 1852 to 1862, for the sum of one pound (about five dollars) an article. Marx's articles, all written in English, were largely composed of analyses of European political events; they were, on the whole, free of the invective so common in Marx's philosophical and sociological writings. His reports were among the best examples of interpretive journalism of the age.

The press was to Marx an indispensable weapon in the arsenal of the capitalists. As for the working class, those who were exploited by the ruling class, the capitalist system condemned them to a life of alienation, a state of incompleteness or
dehumanization. Socialism would restore to the alienated proletariat not only their
economic well-being and a share of political power but also even more important,
freedom and fulfillment in a productive community. Working-class men and women
would have their "existence" returned to them. And in that process of restoration,
the press was to play a decisive role.

Few aspects of Marx's thinking are as hotly debated today as the quality and
significance of the concept of "alienation," or *Entfremdung*. In fact, the way Marx
is understood will depend substantially on the interpretation of this concept. To
some, Marx's thinking on the subject of alienation is religious, if not mystical; to
others, it is economic; and to still others, it is political. There is some validity in all
three interpretations. Since the concept is so important in understanding the socialist press model, it is worth exploring in some detail.

Marx's fullest examination of alienation is in his early writings, especially in
Economic and Philosophical Manuscripts, written in 1844.[22] At that time, Marx
was twenty-six years old and had not yet embarked on his career as journalist and
revolutionary; he was still very much under the influence of the philosopher Georg
W. F. Hegel, from whom he borrowed his fundamental analytical tool, the dialecti-
cal method of analysis. The dialectic preached conflict: History was a chronicle of
struggle between opposing forces, between thesis and antithesis. The resultant synthesis itself formed the next thesis in the eternal round of conflicts that for Hegel
would ultimately conclude with the realization of the Idea, a mystical concept that
may well have been, in Hegel's mind, the realization of the Prussian state. For Marx,
as he stood Hegel "on his feet," the ultimate was to be the realization of communism, in which the *Überbau* would no longer be necessary since all classes would
be equal, and there would no longer be a ruling class to require the existence of
governments and instruments of persuasion and exploitation. All these would
"wither away." In the state of communism, alienation would no longer exist either,
and the self-realization of man would become complete.

Some would accuse Marx of presenting a utopian view of humankind and its
institutions, and there is some truth in this accusation. Yet Marx saw his analysis as
scientific, and over and over he expressed contempt for "utopian socialism" or
"crude socialism." To Marx, communism was the solution to what he called the
"riddle of history," and its arrival could be objectively predicted through the application of the theory of scientific materialism. Anyone approaching communism
would cease to be alienated, as in the capitalist world. In Marx's ideal, communitarian state, society would represent a social, unselfish bonding of individuals.

Whatever else Marx may have meant by alienation, it clearly had a pyschologi-
cal reality for him. He looked about him, in Prussia, in France, in England, and saw
factory workers barely surviving in long hours on the job, in unhealthy and degrading conditions. The capitalists, who owned the factories and the machinery in
them, to all intents and purposes owned the workers as well. The workers, in that

situation, were "alienated"—estranged not merely from worldly goods but also from their life force, from their potential. Workers were commodities to be used by capitalist employers for their own gain. The very language held them in bondage because it was the language of the capitalists. The workers therefore were not even masters of their own consciousness. For to Marx, consciousness—awareness of self—came only through the use of language.[23] If you couldn't talk about something in your own terms or write about it, then you could not be aware of yourself. In that case, in a certain sense you did not even exist. The words themselves and the meanings assigned to them were part of the *Überbau*, whose task it was to keep the lower classes in their place and to keep people unaware of their existence as human beings. Those who were denied the awareness of self were obviously alienated. This state would change, Marx theorized; the collapse of capitalism would signal the beginning of the end of man's alienation.

Many Marxists, chief among them Lenin, argue that Marx's early writings are unimportant, maintaining that as he matured, he dismissed the romanticism of much of his early, humanistic writing. And Marx himself appears to have given some weight to this reasoning. In his famous preface to *The Critique of Political Economy*, written fifteen years after his *Economic and Philosophical Manuscripts*, Marx said he and Engels were prepared "to settle accounts with our former philosophical conscience."[24] This phrase was enough to persuade Lenin (and many others) that nothing Marx had written prior to 1859 was to be taken as "Marxist." Yet it is doubtful Marx meant to suggest any such thing in his preface. What Marx was doing was rejecting his philosophical conscience—in other words, he was no longer even dealing in philosophy. For everything that went under the name of "philosophy," he was saying, was bourgeois. The language of philosophy was the language of the ruling class and had to be replaced by what Marx called "scientific socialism." Karl Korsch, one of the most astute analysts of Marx's thought, has said that from 1859 on, Marx turned to philosophical topics only in order either to illustrate his own analysis or to attack his enemies in the socialist camp. The aim of Marxist socialism remained, as before, to free man from his alienation.[25] Erich Fromm, who sees Marx as a messianic visionary, says that to Marx the contradiction in capitalist production that would ultimately be its downfall was that man was alienated, the slave of things and circumstances, a powerless appendage in a world that seemed beyond his power to combat.[26] The values of that world—"gain, work, thrift, and sobriety"—failed to lead to any moral values, such as a good conscience or virtue. In the socialist revolution, the alienated would rise against their oppressors; they would have nothing to lose, as Marx and Engels wrote in the *Communist Manifesto* of 1848, but their chains.

In this world, the capitalist world of the alienated, the press assumed an important task in the *Überbau*, together with governments, schools, and churches. It concealed from people the true nature of the world they inhabited; it made them content with their lot as members of the exploited proletariat. Religion was, Marx said, "the opiate of the masses." States and governments were tools of the ruling class, established in order to perpetuate its power. Marx did not assign to the press directly a function as dominant as those of government, school, and church, because in the mid-nineteenth century newspapers were not widely read by peasants and factory workers. The modern concept of the "two-step flow" is, however, consistent with Marx's analysis. Newspapers would certainly influence the ideology of the intelligentsia, civil servants, shopkeepers, and tradespeople—and these in turn would pass along to the underclass the "truths" they had read in the papers. Marx did not speak of propaganda; it remained for Vladimir Ilyich Lenin half a century later, when newspaper readership had expanded enormously, to accord the press its central position in Marx's *Überbau*. But even in the mid-nineteenth century Marx envisioned the press, directed and buffeted by official censors, as a significant agency of social control. It was also a target for subversion, and throughout his life, Marx sought to use the printed page as a device to challenge his capitalist foes. Journalists, in Marx's view, were themselves members of the proletariat, but like civil servants, teachers, and priests they were compensated for their function in the *Überbau* by being lifted from the lower strata of the social order, the *Lumpenproletariat*, and permitted entry to the lofty coteries of the ruling class; they were allies of the bourgeoisie in the maintenance of its power, particulalry through deceiving the people into failure to recognize their state of alienation.

Such a portrait of the press was diametrically opposite to the image of the press in capitalist lands, where it was viewed as a watchdog; as a force arrayed against those in power; or as an instrument of education, information, and enlightenment. In the last of his *Eleven Theses on Feuerbach*, Marx dealt indirectly with one of the most sacred of the canons of journalism in a capitalist society: objectivity. Philosophers, Marx wrote—referring not only to those who called themselves philosophers but also to historians and all those who communicated in words about the beliefs of their society—have previously offered various interpretations of the world. His business, Marx said, was to *change* it.[27] The goal of Etzioni's communitarianism was also change, but it was not the world he was out to change; it was public policy.[28]

Marx was convinced all interpretations are partisan offered on behalf of one point of view or another. The historians of the past, he said, including the journalists who have been identified appropriately as the first historians, have examined only the surface of things. When they referred to "objective" reality, they were supplying the theoretical weapons the ruling class needed to maintain power. In *The German Ideology*, Marx called this kind of objectivity "reactionary," since whenever we object reality, we are defending it. The press, in short, was serving as a decisive instrument of social control: By practicing a code of objectivity, it was denying the possibility of change. It is only in actions, Marx held, that a human being or society expresses true beliefs. For words to be true, they must be interchangeable with action; if not, the words are a lie. It is, in short, ideology, not truth.

In Marx's analysis, the press was charged with carrying out the most important assignment of all: to overthrow capitalism, restore people to their true identities, and make words and actions identical. Marx himself undertook to carry out that assignment. It was to thwart the efforts of the capitalists to deceive the workers and instead make the workers aware of the true character of their exploited, alienated existence. The job of the journalist (and of all other members of the revolutionary vanguard—or "advance section") was to make known to the proletariat that it was enslaved, a human commodity; it was alienated; and it was being systematically deprived of its true existence. Put in Marx's phrasing, the job was to transform false consciousness into true consciousness. It was to reveal to people their true human needs. The mechanism was the pen, not the sword. The revolutionary Lenin later modified Marx by placing greater emphasis on the sword, but Marx himself was foremost an intellectual and teacher, and the instrument of education was for him the word. To overcome the *Überbau*, Marx held, people must be made aware, must come to recognize how easily they can be deceived by mere words, by the ideology of capitalism.

One commentator has spoken of the *Überbau* as the secret weapon in the class struggle, "the fountain of false consciousness."[29] The state, standing for the power of the dominant class, is in business primarily to maintain the status quo and the existing power base. Marx himself wrote: "The state is the executive committee of the bourgeoisie."[30] The press, for its part, worked hand in hand with the state. Before the proletarian class could overthrow its exploiters, it was necessary it be made aware of the existence of its class. Marx's "advance section," composed of working-class intellectuals and journalists, was assigned the task of developing class consciousness and ultimately revolutionary consciousness. The novelist Arthur Koestler, who believed the modern Soviet state betrayed the earlier idealism of Marxism, challenged the idea of the *Überbau* as being vague and capable of many conflicting interpretations. "Marxist society," Koestler wrote, "has a basement—production—and an attic—intellectual production; only the stairs and lifts are missing."[31] In Marx's view, the press, before it could join in or lead the "advance section," must come to recognize its own true nature; its goal must be no longer to interpret, to present an objective view of "both sides," but to work instead for change. Of course, Marx did not actually speak in these terms—the value system of objectivity had not yet been identified, and no one spoke of presenting "both sides" of an issue in seeking objectivity. Still, he was addressing the precise point in his analysis.

Consciousness itself, Marx said, existed only through communication. Before there could be communication, society was necessary. People experienced themselves through their interaction with others in the community, and the primary means of their interaction was language. Those who controlled the language controlled society and could bring humankind to slavery or to freedom. The creators of words were the state, the schools, the churches—their transmitter was the journalist. Those who controlled the press controlled the ideology and the social order. The press, then, can be seen as central in both the capitalist and the socialist theories. The melodies that make up the symphony of the press in both market and communitarian (or planned) economies are similar. In fact, we sometimes need a carefully tuned ear to recognize the differences. Each melody is one of turbulence, of conflict directed not only internally, against domestic discord and challenges to harmony, but also externally, against one another. The struggle has sometimes been portrayed as a battle or war, sometimes unto death.

NOTES

1. See J. Herbert Altschull, *Agents of Power: The Role of the News Media in Human Affairs* (White Plains, NY: Longman, 1984), 279-99.

2. Several other names might have been used. *Collective* is one, because the ideal places far greater emphasis on the well-being of the collective—or society—than on the individual. But to many people, the connotation of collective is negative; it suggests to them the worst excesses of the Soviet dictatorship. The word *tribal* was another possibility because the ideal chooses the welfare of the tribe over the welfare of the individual. But to many, *tribal* sounds primitive, and the communitarian ideal is in no way hostile to growth or technology. Marx saw himself as preaching the cause of *scientific* socialism. A third possible name was *socialist*, but it, too, carries with it the baggage of Soviet dictatorship. Moreover, there are so many different kinds of socialists that a simple use of the designation is meaningless.

3. Robert Kilroy-Silk, *Socialism Since Marx* (Hammondsworth, England: Penguin, 1972), 5.

4. Amitai Etzioni, *Rights, Responsibilities, and the Communitarian Agenda* (New York: Crown, 1993).

5. Vladimír Hudec, *Journalism, Substance, Social Functions, Development* (Prague: International Organization of Journalists, 1978), 22 (italics in original).

6. Isaiah Berlin, *Karl Marx: His Life and Environment*, 3rd ed. (New York: Oxford University Press, 1963), 73.

7. Some of the outwitted censors were publicly reprimanded and replaced by stricter officials.

8. Marx's "Comments on the Latest Prussian Censorship Instruction," written for *Anekdota zur neuesten deutschen Philosophie und Publicistik* (1842), is reproduced by Lloyd D. Easton and Kurt H. Guddat, ed. and trans., *Writings of the Young Marx on Philosophy and Society* (Garden City, NY: Doubleday, 1967), 67-92. Hereafter referred to as Marx, Comments.

9. The ruling was issued by Frederick William III. It was his successor, Frederick William IV, who issued the new censorship Instruction and who was later to smash the liberal uprising of 1848-49.

10. Marx, Comments, 92.

11. Marx, Comments, 79. Italics in original.

12. Marx, Comments, 80.

13. Marx, Comments, 81.

14. Marx, Comments, 86-87.

15. Marx, Comments, 86.

16. Marx, Comments, 72. Italics in original.

17. Erich Fromm, *Marx's Concept of Man* (New York: Frederick Ungar, 1961), 38-39.

18. Patrick J. Daley and John Soloski provide an interesting analysis of Marx's views on the power of language in "Marxism and Communication," an unpublished paper presented at a session of the Qualitative Studies Division of the Association for Education in Journalism, Seattle, Washington, 1978.

19. Karl Marx, "On the Jewish Question," in Eugene Kamenka, ed., *The Portable Karl Marx* (New York: Penguin, 1983), 114. The essay appeared originally in February 1844 in *Deutsch-französischer Jahrbücher*.

20. Jean-Jacques Rousseau, "The Social Contract" in John Somerville and Ronald E. Santoni, eds., *Social and Political Philosophy: Readings from Plato to Gandhi* (Garden City, NY: Doubleday Anchor Books, 1963), 205–38. See especially book 1, chap. 6, 213–15.

21. Marx's class theory is detailed most thoroughly in the book he wrote jointly with Friedrich Engels, *The German Ideology*, which appeared in 1846. The first part of *The German Ideology* is reprinted in Karl Marx and Friedrich Engels, *Feuerbach: Opposition of the Materialist and Idealist Outlooks* (London: Laurence Wishart, 1973). The editor is not identified, but a subtitle states that the material was published in accordance with the text and arrangement of the original manuscript. For a brief encapsulation of the theory, see Somerville and Santoni, *Social and Political Philosophy*, 342–80. See also Philip Corrigan, Harve Ramsay, and Derek Sayer, *Socialist Construction and Marxist Theory: Bolshevism and Its Critics* (New York: Monthly Review, 1978).

22. *Economic and Philosophical Manuscripts of 1844 by Karl Marx*, Dirk J. Struik, ed. and intro., Martin Milligan, trans. (New York: International Publishers, 1964), 9–56.

23. Daley and Soloski, "Marxism and Communication."

24. Kamenka, *Portable Karl Marx*, 161.

25. Karl Korsch, *Marxism and Philosophy* (New York: Monthly Review Press, 1970), 48. Korsch, whose four essays were published in German in 1923, observes that Marx and Engels were not really abandoning "philosophy" but "bourgeois philosophy," which they saw as part of the *Überbau*.

26. Fromm, *Marx's Concept of Man,* 43–58.

27. Marx and Engels, *Feuerbach*, 92–93. The eleventh thesis says this: "The philosophers have only *interpreted* the world in various ways; the point, however, is to *change* it" (emphasis in original). The theses were written in 1845 but were not published until 1888 in Engels's appendix to his *Ludwig Feuerbach und der Ausgang der klassischen deutschen Philosophie*.

28. Etzioni, *Rights, Responsibilities, and the Communitarian Agenda*. See also Edward Schwartz, "The Spirit of Community," *New York Times Book Review*, April 11, 1993, 10.

29. Kilroy-Silk, *Socialism Since Marx,* 10.

30. Korsch, *Marxism and Philosophy*, 53.

31. Arthur Koestler, *The Yogi and the Commissar* (New York: Macmillan, 1945), 70.

From Lenin to Glasnost

LENIN'S THREE ROLES FOR THE PRESS

Marxist theory was transformed by Vladimir Ilyich Lenin, who found it necessary to rechannel many of Marx's concepts to make them fit the social conditions in Russia. Marx was convinced that before a "feudal" society such as that in Russia could even aspire to a socialist revolution, it had first to pass through the capitalist stage of development. It was in Lenin's interest to portray Marx as a dedicated revolutionary, and yet Marx himself was uncertain on the subject. In fact, he was always more at home in the cloistered corridors of a library than at the barricades.

While Marx wrote little about the press directly, especially in his later years, Lenin's literary output on the subject was prolific throughout his life; he was more decisive in developing a socialist theory of the press than his mentor. Moreover, Lenin loaded a good deal of the rhetoric of leftist collectivism on top of Marx's more communitarian views. Since Marxism-Leninism was official ideology in the Soviet Union, it was there its analysis of the role of the press was carefully codified.

When Marx died in 1883, Lenin was thirteen years old. Twice exiled to Siberia for revolutionary activities against the czarist regime, Lenin turned to the press as his principal instrument for stirring up support for revolution, much as the colonial rebels had done in eighteenth-century America.

V. I. Lenin as communicator.

SOURCE: Bettmann

In the conflictual political model that dominated most of the twentieth-century world—a world that often seemed bipolar, in ideology if not in practice—the image of the other side was simple and monolithic. In one image, virtue and capitalism were destined to triumph; in the other, virtue and communism would emerge victorious—and each side aimed its sharpest attacks at the wickedness of the other. In truth, neither model was simple or monolithic. There was never just one model of capitalism, nor was there ever only one model of communism. The variations were extensive, perhaps limitless.

There was not, for instance, a clear line from Marx to Lenin, nor was there agreement on the "correct road to socialism." Lenin was reacting against interpretations of Marx that had led in the late nineteenth century to a reformist adaptation of socialism, in which mass political movements led by trade unions sought political power through traditional electoral processes developed under capitalism. To Lenin the revolutionary, this approach was futile and doomed to failure. He scorned mass political movements and turned instead to a plan wherein a small cadre of leaders, patterned to some degree on Marx's "advance section," would direct the workers under the tightly controlled machinery of the Communist party. The Bolshevik doctrine ultimately prevailed in Russia, but that victory was not without a bitter internal struggle. Although it triumphed in the Soviet Union, it was not adopted by socialist movements everywhere. In fact, the struggle still goes on in China, in the developing world, and among the nations carved from the defunct Soviet Union, even in the countries of Western Europe. In his *Philosophical Notebooks*, Lenin asserted: "After half a century, not a single Marxist had understood Marx!"[1]

For Lenin, equally at home as a writer and an orator, the role of the press was vital if his Bolshevik party was to defeat its internal Marxist opposition and if the capitalists were to be overcome. In this program, Lenin was following Marx's insistence on the necessity of raising the level of class consciousness. Yet Lenin went beyond anything Marx had suggested and developed a full-blown theory of the role of the press. Operating underground inside Russia, Lenin was among the founders of the Bolshevik newspaper *Iskra (The Spark)*. And in a 1901 article headlined "Where to Begin" in the fourth issue of *Iskra*, Lenin wrote a paragraph that became as much sacred dogma in the Soviet Union as the First Amendment became in the United States:

> The role of a newspaper . . . is not limited solely to the dissemination of ideas, to political education, and to the enlistment of political allies. A newspaper is not only a collective propagandist and a collective agitator: It is also a collective organizer. In this last respect it may be likened to the scaffolding around a building under construction, which marks the contours of the structure, and facilitates communication between the builders, enabling them to distribute the work and to view the common results achieved by their organized labor. With the aid of the newspaper, and through it, a permanent organization will naturally take shape that will engage, not only in local activities, but in regular general work, and will train its members to follow political events carefully, appraise their significance and their effect on the various strata of the population, and *develop effective means for the revolutionary party to influence those events*.[2]

There was no pretense to "objectivity" here; to Lenin, it was the duty of the journalist, as Marx had said, to "change the world." He identified three roles for the newspaper: collective propagandist, collective agitator, and collective organizer. As part of the superstructure, Lenin held, newspapers and the journalists who wrote for them played key roles in training those who would lead the society in influencing the course of events—in other words, to educate into class consciousness not only the working classes but also the leaders themselves. Therefore, the training of socialist journalists, at the Moscow State University School of Journalism and at all journalism schools and institutes throughout the socialist world, included instruction in propaganda, agitation, and organization.

To the capitalist eye, the terms seem inconsistent with truth and liberty, further testimony to the political character of language. Lenin commanded the professors at the journalism schools of the Soviet empire to teach that each of these—propaganda, agitation, and organization—was a vital cog in pursuit of truth and human liberty. If Jefferson might have preferred newspapers to government, Lenin, at least in 1901, sounded as if he might have preferred newspapers to the Communist party. Neither man, of course, believed what he said, but each man was an activist, sometimes swept away by his own emotional nature into making exaggerated declarations. Nonetheless, both Jefferson and Lenin were convinced believers in the potential power of the press, and each believed the end he sought was virtuous.

It was in an article published in September 1917, six weeks before the Bolshevik Revolution, that Lenin presented his most thorough analysis of freedom of the press.[3] The article has been cited frequently by socialist critics in their analyses of the capitalist press. At the time, Russia was under the rule of Alexander Kerensky's provisional government, and the leading Russian newspapers were under capitalist control. Lenin's *Pravda* (*Truth*) was struggling for circulation, hampered by a lack of funds. Those newspapers with the greatest circulation were filled with advertising, much as were the leading newspapers of Europe. To Lenin, this situation did not demonstrate freedom but rather exploitation. What the capitalists call freedom of the press, he said, "is not freedom of the press, but freedom for the rich, for the bourgeoisie, to deceive the oppressed and exploited mass of the people."[4]

It was not only the capitalists who perverted the concept of freedom of the press, Lenin wrote angrily, but also his rivals in the socialist movement, who, he said, followed the definition of the capitalists "either from stupidity or from inertia." The bourgeois Russian press was dependent on advertising inserted by wealthy capitalists, who were thus able to control the content of the papers. The remedy was to prohibit private advertising and provide a government subsidy to pay for official advertising in all Soviet papers. Only when "the opinions of *all* citizens may be freely published," he said, can there be genuine freedom of the press. The issue, he continued, was not really freedom of the press, but rather "the exploiters' sacrosanct ownership of the printing press and stocks of newsprint they have seized!" And, he thundered: "Just why should we workers and peasants recognize that sacred right? How is that 'right' to publish false information better than the 'right' to own serfs?"[5]

Only when printing presses and newsprint were made available to all political movements might there be genuine press freedom, Lenin said, asserting that under Bolshevik rule such distribution "could be effected easily enough." Such a move, he said, "would be real freedom of the press *for all*, and not for the rich. It would be a break with that accursed, slavish past which compels us to suffer the usurpation by the rich of the great cause of informing and teaching the peasants."[6]

In power, however, Lenin elected not to make printing presses and newsprint available to holders of all opinions. In fact, the Bolsheviks established the same kind of monopoly Lenin had been decrying. His justification was that his party was not oppressing or exploiting anyone but was representing the interests of the poor and oppressed. Of course, in Lenin's view, the Bolsheviks' monopolistic practices were virtuous. Lenin no doubt believed what he said, as do those who believe virtue lies in the use of private advertisements and a free press based on the First Amendment. All press ideologues claim their models and practices are being carried out in the interests of the people, that they are practicing the doctrine of social responsibility. Interestingly, in the Soviet Union, great stress was placed on the value and significance of letters to the editor, which occupied many columns in every publication. It was the responsibility of the newspaper, as "collective agitator," to respond to the letter writers and thus to provide a distinct social service. TASS, the Soviet news agency, listed as its primary duty provision to the people of information that was "topical," "truthful," and "socially meaningful"—that is to say, information that was useful.

Trying to give capitalism a bad name: Lenin claims
you cannot have a free press in a capitalist society.
SOURCE: Library of Congress

In explaining "Marxist journalism," the Czech educator Vladimír Hudec said
journalists might adopt one of two attitudes in order to influence public opinion.
They might identify themselves as protagonists for a particular set of ideas and try
to convince their readers to adopt those ideas, or they might act as "professionals"
and be prepared to advocate ideas for money, whatever their own judgment about
those ideas. In the first case, the journalists were being objective; in the second,

they were being objectivist, or making a pretense of being fair and balanced while in reality serving paid propagandists for their employers. It was in the first case, where the journalists stood among "the bearers of progressive ideas, that they became an active force in the conscious efforts to carry out historical transformations benefiting society."[7] Hudec and the journalism teachers of the Soviet empire were clearly following the fundamental ideas of Marx and Lenin, training future journalists to change the world for the better.

The fall of the Soviet empire and the official banishment of communist ideology from Russia and the other successor states brought a rash of bitter criticism of both Marx and Lenin. Statues and icons tumbled, and Communist parties lost their power base. Marxism-Leninism may have been cast out, but in no way were all Marxist or even Leninist theories rejected. The names of the theorists were often ridiculed, but not everywhere. We will return to this topic later, but for now it is important to keep in mind that although street and city names were changed (Leningrad to St. Petersburg, for instance) and statues toppled, Lenin's ideas, especially those dealing with the press, remained very much alive.

As we carefully examine Lenin's three goals for the press, we see a remarkable similarity between his goals and those of the journalist and politician Horace Greeley.[8] *To learn* is closely associated with the verb *to inform*. *To propagandize* is closely associated with the verb *to teach*. As for *to organize*, that is a bit more complex and can be set aside for a moment. The remaining two roles, information and education, have been accepted worldwide. Everyone speaks of informing and educating as among the roles of the press. Sometimes, in fact, those two roles are telescoped into one. Can we indeed differentiate clearly between information and education? One person's information may be another's education. Perhaps the distinction can be seen in the often-heard advice to put "the news on the news page and the editorials on the editorial page." In this case, news would be information and editorials would be education.

Lenin spoke of the press as having a "collective" role, a formulation that can easily be understood if "collective" is defined as that which is assembled or accumulated into a whole. Lenin pictured the newspaper as providing information and education not to individuals as single units but to them as part of a whole, as a "collection of individuals." Since American journalists also see their audiences as collective, as groups of individuals, the concept is not exclusively communitarian. At schools throughout the Soviet empire, the Leninist role model for the journalist was carefully taught, and collective agitation was defined as "presenting information on everyday events." This definition was provided by Yassen Zassursky, longtime dean of the Moscow State University School of Journalism.[9]

As for the basic question, "Information for what?," Zassursky held that the information had to provide for the objective needs of the reader. "Any information or commentary contributes to behavior and actions," he said.[10] The first role was simply to supply information; the behavior and actions were generated under the third role, that of "collective organizer." Zassursky maintained that the capitalist model insisted not only on supplying information about events but also about what was for sale in the market—advertisements. Readers were lured into buying newspapers for news but were in fact given information about what they didn't need: unnecessary products and useless gossip. Soviet theoreticians saw two different types of information: primary and secondary. The primary dealt with information that met needs; the secondary dealt with unnecessary material: advertisements, gossip, entertainment. Both types fell into the category of collective agitation. To Hudec, the information role properly called for "disseminating positive experiences and criticism of everything that hinders society in its development."[11] If we examine the language carefully, avoiding emotionally charged political reactions, we can see much that is similar in the goals in the Marxist and capitalist models. The press in each system was designed to criticize all aberrations and work for the good of society. Indeed, we can find a similarity between capitalist press analysis with the socialist primary and secondary types of information: Primary is that which readers need to know in order to carry out their democratic duties; secondary is information they want out of curiosity or a desire to be entertained. Such secondary functions, Soviet journalists were taught, involved artificial needs as opposed to objective needs, which were defined as food, clothing, housing, and essentials. "There is," Zassursky said, "a relationship between needs and interests."

The second role, "collective propagandist," presents few problems. To Zassursky, it involved "explanation of the mechanics of the work of society, and of the reasons for events." In addition, it provided "timely interpretation." There is little difference between this role in the Marxist model and the persuasion role in the capitalist system: the writing of editorials, leading articles, and columns.

More complex is the role of the press as "collective organizer." To Marx and Lenin and to all communitarian theorists, to those who would change the social order, the press is a vehicle for manipulating public opinion and stirring the public to action. Zassursky characterized the goal as molding "one's views and thus [modifying] behavior." He cited the weather report as an elementary example: Information about an impending rainstorm will cause readers to carry umbrellas. "We are talking about a direct appeal to action," he said. Organization was the centerpiece of all Marxist-Leninist society; it is critical in the communitarian movement of the symphony of the press. The press and the public become one. As Hudec put it, "A collective organizing function is characteristic for progressive journalism which develops in a broad way for the popular masses."[12] He added:

> Reactionary journalism, defending the exploiting minority, naturally cannot have such links with the popular masses and find support in them. It works for the disorganization of progressive movements, tries to divert the exploited and oppressed people and nations from the political struggle for liberation. It carries out its function through manipulation. . . . Progressive publications . . . utilize letters of the working people, win over for cooperation outside authors, organize themselves with the popular masses political campaigns to try to achieve the stipulated objectives. Such participation of the popular masses in progressive journalistic activities is valuable not in itself; it is essential for the broad

integration of their collective experience and wisdom to solve problems of social development, in the fight against vestiges of the past and reactionary elements.[13]

GLASNOST AND COMMUNITARIANISM

It is premature at best to proclaim the death of communism or at least of Marxist socialism. Long before the fall of the Soviet empire, scholars, journalists, and political theorists were reflecting and writing about what might replace a collapsed Soviet empire and the political, economic, and moral forces that shaped Marxist ideology. But neither before nor after that fall was it possible to know the future. Certainly, the kind of overt, blatant, and rigid social controls maintained by the Kremlin had fallen into disrepute, at least in the industrialized world dominated by the nations of the Northern Hemisphere and perhaps everywhere. Despite its severe wounds, however, collectivism, the communitarian concept, survived, even where it had been tried and failed—the former Soviet Union and its client states. Some foresaw a new political model labeled "socialistic capitalism," but perhaps that was the same thing as "capitalistic socialism."[14] In any case, as the twentieth century drew to a close, capitalism had still not won the hearts and minds of all humankind, and more than a few were wondering whether it was possible for the individualist model of a market society to wrestle with the inexorable demands of the earth's ecological system. A threat to the planet did not fit comfortably into a world where economic growth was revered as a necessity for the well-being of humankind.

The coups in the Soviet Union and Eastern Europe were fired by popular uprisings marked by demands for greater freedom and the principles of democracy, yet the successor regimes continued to place heavy restrictions on freedom and democracy. Indeed, it was not at all clear the population of these countries really wanted to be free. After all, freedom brought an end to government-guaranteed jobs and wages. The collective social order had not permitted individuals freedom to speak as they wished, but it provided security and abolished unemployment and homelessness. Moreover, it kept under control the bloody impulses of unrestrained nationalism and claims of ethnic purity. Opportunities for individuals increased with the fall of the Soviet state, though so did uncertainty.

As in all revolutionary eras, the press played a key role in the fall of the Soviet empire. As the rigid bonds of Kremlin control loosened in the 1980s, newspapers began to criticize the regime openly, increasing their fervor the longer they got away with their complaints. The director of ITAR-TASS said that with its greater freedom to express diverse viewpoints, "the press in turn helped shape the events that led to the demise of the Communist party."[15] Like all journalists, the men and women of the Soviet and Eastern European press wanted to report and write what they themselves considered newsworthy; they did not want to be told what to report and what to write. Both before and after the fall of the Soviet empire, however, they knew there were rules to be played by. Those rules were clear when the Soviet Union existed; they were Lenin's. After the collapse of the Soviet Union, the rules were more subtle and more difficult to follow. By no means were all journalists content to follow the Soviet code as laid down by Lenin. They had to adapt, said Svetlana Starodomskaya, a television interviewer and documentarian dubbed by American correspondents in the Soviet Union as "the Barbara Walters of Russia."[16]

We have seen how the press in capitalist societies has been manipulated by powerful political and economic forces. It was equally evident the press in the Soviet Union and among her allies was manipulated by powerful political and economic forces. Once again we are confronted with the politics of language, for clearly *manipulation* meant different things to press analysts and theoreticians in socialist and capitalist societies.

Lenin's rationale for the Soviet press system remained in force until the failed coup of the diehard Soviet bureaucracy in 1991, but it had been eroding for decades. Modest criticism of the ruling powers began to appear in the Soviet media shortly after Stalin's death in 1953, though under Leonid Brezhnev's tough social-control measures, even such modest criticism was suppressed. It was not until the emergence of Mikhail Gorbachev and his glasnost (or "openness") program in the mid-1980s that the Leninist model crumbled, ever so slowly. What would ultimately replace it could not be known, and it is certainly not our task here to forecast the future. Suffice it to say the communitarian movement of the symphony of the press, which is heard today and will no doubt increase in volume with the passage of years, embodies the heart of the collectivist melodic structure imposed on it by Marx and Lenin.

It can be said that Marxism-Leninism is a system of ideas used to provide a rational foundation for communitarianism, just as capitalism is a system of ideas used to provide a rational foundation for the individualism enshrined in the market belief system.[17] Each system represents a strategy, either out front or under cover, to guarantee its leaders control of the social order or at least a clear structure of social organization bolstering their power. The media are agents in either case. The range of communitarian beliefs is far broader than that of Marxism-Leninism, but it comfortably accommodates the views of Marx and Lenin.

Glasnost was not intended to shatter altogether the press rules laid down by Lenin, but openness is rarely constrained once it is set in motion. Under Stalin, every publishing house and publication in the Soviet Union was in the hands of the Communist party. Despite the shifts in policy that marked the next generation, party control remained secure until Gorbachev. Then the gradual loosening of controls slowly began to bring changes to the face of journalism in the Soviet Union and its client states in Eastern Europe.[18]

All this changed abruptly with the fall of the Soviet Union. Dozens, perhaps hundreds, of formerly frustrated writers and editors scrambled to launch new publishing ventures, mostly weekly newspapers and magazines with a limited number of pages; some expanded radio and television offerings. Many failed. The pressure to stir reader and viewer interest was so intense that the formerly dull and bland communist press turned to melodrama and sensationalism.

A pattern of startling change began even before the fall of the Communist party. Writers and editors, especially in Hungary, Poland, and East Germany, began courting Western media moguls in a hunt for investments that might help them operate newspapers free of government direction. Media magnates in Berlin and Paris were attracted. By December 1990, the major European publishers had bought up some 40 percent of the leading national dailies in Hungary. The British multimedia financier Rupert Murdoch, a Hungarian by birth, started his own tabloid in Budapest. "This whole region of eastern Europe," said Murdoch, the quintessential media capitalist of his age, "is the most exciting and important part of the world today."[19] The glasnost-inspired Soviet press began castigating its leaders and even publishing articles about the Soviet economic and political problems. By the time Gorbachev fell in 1991, the former "Marxist" press was publishing daring articles assailing the Soviet brand of communism itself. One new Moscow publisher called for American-style investigative reporting. The American commentator David Remnick chortled that "Moscow has become the most exciting newspaper city since New York after the Second World War."[20]

Still, in a social order that had been rigidly controlled in the Leninist model, habits and tradition die slowly. Despite the promises, governments were reluctant to surrender their control over information. Money was in dazzlingly short supply; and the rush to appeal to readers troubled those who were committed to Western concepts of press freedom. One Ukrainian commentator objected that some new media were financed by industrial enterprises that had been military in the past. He called for legislation to cover questions of media ownership and editorial freedom.[21] The Soviet Union did enact a press law in 1991, and Russia modified it a year later, but there remained an uncertain legal distinction between "pure" and "impure" media.[22] New media founded by government organizations were spoken of as pure, while others were considered impure, meaning they had "to prove themselves" through their performance before they could be granted access to information made available to pure editors. In any case, media were required to register with the government, an obvious mechanism for imposing some government controls.

By 1993, no fewer than 4,000 publications had received licenses from the Press Ministry.[23] Many of these were, however, not newspapers in the strict sense of the word. Included in that roster were advertising circulars and sex magazines peddled by vendors in subway tunnels of Moscow and St. Petersburg. The most successful publication, *Moskovsky Komsomolets* (*The Moscow Young Communist*), enjoyed a handsome circulation of 1.2 million in greater Moscow, and as a result sold the most advertising in the country. Even so, the O'Kei ad agency had to find more customers than the newspaper in order to survive, so it operated a side business promoting paper dolls and desk calendars. The old giants of the Soviet press slipped badly, unable to master the rough-and-tumble of the capitalist marketplace. The once-mighty *Pravda*, which had boasted a circulation of 11 million under the old order, now sold a mere 570,000 copies a day; by 1994, it had become the chief organ of opposition to the reformist president Boris Yeltsin. *Ogonyok*, a glossy magazine that at the height of Gorbachev's power specialized in tough, once-banned topics, declined after Gorbachev fell in 1991. Within two years, its circulation plummeted from 4.5 million to 300,000. Lev Gushin, the editor of *Ogonyok*, said its readers were "tired of politics, tired and disappointed with the political changes that have not brought about any real changes for the better."[24]

There was no end to pressures from above. Underpaid reporters were easily tempted by publicity-hungry businesses and by the politicians they were supposed to be covering. State and local governments still owned the printing presses. Criticism of the government and its leaders was for the most part permitted, though only up to a point. When Boris Yeltsin's position of power was threatened, he did not hesitate to reimpose censorship. "Our Russian press is as unfree now as before the coup," a Russian journalism told a 1992 colloquium of editors and scholars from the United States and the new nations that once formed the Soviet Union. An American, who described the Russian law as a mine field, said that as a journalist, he "would be proud to be labelled impure."[25]

The members of the colloquium concluded journalists and politicians were making progress in the new Russia. Still further reform was needed, the delegates said, demanding government officials recognize it was beneficial to have a press that was sometimes adversarial and did not always support the government. They called also for an end to official monopoly control over paper, production facilities, and distribution networks. To accomplish this, they suggested further development of a market economy where the drive for profit would push businesspeople to develop a powerful media infrastructure free of direct government control. They also encouraged "innovative joint ventures and/or investment relationships" linking states of the former Soviet Union and foreign organizations.[26] It is not surprising the American delegates to the colloquium were more committed to advertising as the major sources of revenue than the Russians, or that the Americans were more committed to localized newspapers while the Russians were committed to national newspapers. Russians were long used to massive-circulation newspapers that were not likely to be of great interest to advertisers seeking smaller, highly targeted audiences. For a long time, American newspapers have kept their "newsholes" at 30 percent or less compared with the Russian press, which in the past has been almost totally free of advertising.

On the whole, intervention by multimedia corporations and media magnates from the West did not thrill the Russian journalists who helped spark the overthrow of the Communist party. Members of Moscow's intellectual community were especially critical. Indigenous Russian culture was at risk, they said. One commentator put it strongly: "The new millionaires of the bourses sponsor nothing but pop music and the worst sort of trash on television. Artists, writers, and musicians . . . are being forced into a new and largely unwilling wave of emigration by unsympathetic governmental policies and swinging taxation."[27]

Media executives from Russia and the other new republics were less interested in joint ventures than in receiving loans and investments from Western governments and entrepreneurs, but these were not likely to be made, at least in the short run, partly because of the unsettled state of the currency and government restrictions on taking money out of the country.[28] A Ukrainian media authority said it was imperative the West act positively to help the cause of a free press in the former

Soviet Union: "It is strange," he said, "that after spending billions of dollars in the past on the arms race against the Soviet regime, the West is not willing to use even a small part of that amount to support those intellectuals and journalists who fought for democracy and liberalization."[29] Similar comments were heard from journalists in the Third World.

An intriguing dispute arose at the colloquium over just what is meant by that troublesome concept of freedom. The new Russian press law declared the press to be free; and although it guaranteed journalists access to official information, it indicated access might not always be easy to gain because it set up an appeal procedure whenever access was denied. Moreover, it defined not only the *rights* of journalists but also their *duties*. Newspersons were not, for instance, allowed to publish articles that instigated class, national, or religious intolerance. Furthermore, they were obliged to register with the government before going into business and to guarantee a right to reply to anyone whose honor or pride they had defamed. Americans were disturbed, declaring that under the First Amendment and other legal language in the United States, limits were placed on *government*, not on journalists. The rights and responsbilities of journalists, the American participants said, were primarily a matter of professional judgment and business decision making. The Russians disagreed, noting the Russian legal system was based on the Napoleonic code rather than on English common-law precedents.[30]

The essence of this dispute goes back deep into history and involves the difference between positive and negative liberty. American civil liberties derive almost entirely from the concept of negative liberty articulated by John Locke. The Bill of Rights protects individual citizens *from* oppressive rules and regulations handed down by the government. Congress is barred, for instance, from writing laws abridging the freedom of speech or of the press; it may not create a national religious establishment; it may not force a person to testify against himself or herself; it denies the government the authority to unreasonably search or seize an individual's private property. These civil liberties do not obligate the citizen in any way. The individual may be responsible or irresponsible so long as he or she does not break the law. Negative liberty is the foundation stone on which the market belief system rests. The balance wheel safeguards individual rights over those of society, the collective. On the other hand, the communitarian belief system protects the rights of the collective against destructive behavior by individuals. Following the concept of positive liberty, citizens are bound by certain prescribed duties and obligations. They must use their freedom *for a purpose*, in the imagery of Rousseau to carry out the "General Will" that always operates for the benefit of collective society.[31] Zechariah Chafee, one of the leading American First Amendment scholars, had reservations about the negative-liberty concept, arguing that freedom from something was not enough, that "it should also be freedom for something." Chafee said freedom meant courage, that it was not merely security: "We must do more than remove the discouragements to open discussion. We must exert ourselves to supply active encouragements."[32]

Etzioni's communitarian movement spoke also of an agenda with something for everyone that flowed logically from "the ethic of political obligation." The reviewer Edward Schwartz, president of the Institute for the Study of Civic Values in Philadelphia, saw as the weakest link of Etzioni's work his emphasis on obligations above rights, duty above freedom.[33] On the other hand, the Harvard law professor Mary Ann Glendon assailed the U.S. emphasis on rights as damaging to social justice "because they tend to be presented as absolute, individual, and independent of any necessary relation to responsibilities."[34] Glendon, promoting the ideals of communitarianism, called attention to the fact that U.S. political documents such as the Bill of Rights contain no language similar to the Universal Declaration of Human Rights statement that "everyone has duties to the community."[35] Glendon deplored the widespread veneration of certain U.S. rights ("the right to do whatever I want" or "the right to life" or "the right to choose" or even "animal rights") at the cost of genuine political discourse that could lead to benefits for the community. Presumably, this covers also such clichés as "the public's right to know." Unhappily, she said, "cliché-ridden" political language in the United States "takes the individual as the basic social unit [and] treats all individuals as presumptively strangers to one another."[36]

The Soviet press until glasnost adhered closely to Lenin's model of his own form of communitarianism. In that form, the party-dominated media represented the most efficient and desirable of instruments available for influencing community organs of administration. Surveys showed it was the newspaper above all that could present to the authorities "requests, remarks, suggestions, and demands of the population."[37] Certainly, the Soviet public wrote letters to the editor of publications at an astonishing rate. The letter department of *Pravda*, the official party organ, claimed no fewer than forty-five staffers were needed to sift through the letters and choose which to publish. The government organ *Izvestia* said, in what was no doubt somewhat of an overstatement, it published one-fourth of the letters it received.

Even under Stalin and Brezhnev, the Soviet people were avid readers of newspapers; increasingly, they became enthusiastic viewers of television. Studies of Soviet readers and viewers showed them to be remarkably similar to those in America: the more highly educated the viewer, the fewer hours were devoted to television watching and the greater the interest in news and cultural programming; the less educated, the greater was the interest in quiz shows and human-interest programs. Rural housewives are heavy daytime viewers. And, just as does the television audience in capitalist countries, the Soviet viewers said they would like to see more programming devoted to entertainment and relaxation. On the collapse of the Soviet regime, they got exactly this. Newspapers and television turned increasingly to the entertainment features already common in the West.[38]

The Soviet newspapers were limited in number of pages. *Pravda*, with its daily circulation of 11 million readers, consisted of only six pages, and these followed a rigid form. Page one regularly presented an editorial, official news from the leadership of the Communist party, several brief news items foreign and domestic, and some material about the state of the economy. The second page supplied stories about the Communist party itself. Page three carried domestic news, letters to the editor, and often the results of Soviet-style investigative reporting. Page four carried stories continued from the first page, as well as some foreign news, usually about developments in the communist world. Foreign news stories were on page five. The back page contained a potpourri of sports, human interest, humor, radio and television schedules, practical information about medicine, and other miscellany. Few photographs were published, and there were no articles about crime, except in unusual circumstances; rarely were there stories about celebrities or film stars.

Before the fall of the Soviet Union, the content of the Soviet press was so different from the regular content of capitalist newspapers that visitors from the capitalist world invariably found *Pravda* and the other Soviet newspapers dull. By contrast, Soviet visitors to the United States condemned American newspapers as sensationalistic and lacking in material that served readers' needs.

Interestingly, Russian readers tended to find their newspapers objective. The capitalist formula—presenting "both sides" of an issue—was not considered of value in the Marxist-Leninist model, where only one objective reality existed. It was seen as counterproductive to present opposing, "erroneous" views of reality. In the Soviet model, objectivity was associated with truth rather than with fairness.

The element of the Marxist model with the greatest impact on the new nations of Africa and Asia was the letters-to-the-editor phenomenon, which Hudec called "participation by the popular masses in progressive journalistic activities."[39] Success of the press in the capitalist world has also been dependent on appeal to the popular masses. In both capitalist and Marxist systems, the press stirred the masses to perceive political, economic, social, and even cultural issues in a framework of conflict, of us versus them. The collapse of the Soviet Union altered the us and the them. The press shifted, at least temporarily, from an ideological conflict between the United States and the Soviet Union to a series of bitter ethnic, religious, and nationalistic conflicts among the former Soviet republics.

When the old-line communists who had hung on to their own power base in the Russian Parliament sought unsuccessfully to oust Yeltsin in October 1993, the president issued an emergency decree dissolving Parliament and suspending all political parties and all opposition newspapers. Two days later, he lifted the ban on many newspapers, acknowledging that his reaction to the revolutionary movement had been "excessive." But less than a week after that, he announced a permanent ban of thirteen newspapers and the television program "600 Seconds," blaming them "to a great extent" for destabilizing the political scene and promoting revolt.[40] Democracy and a free press had not taken a firm foothold in Russia.

The challenges for the new media of Russia and Eastern Europe were magnified by financial woes, the end of which were not in sight as the twenty-first century approached. *Pravda,* once the rock-solid instrument of the Soviet Communist party, was so hamstrung in the new economy it was forced to suspend publication in early 1992. It was back on the newsstands a month later, but only after accepting loan guarantees in the West that allowed it to publish three times a week. Before the year was out, a majority share was acquired by *Akadymos,* a small Greek publishing concern whose owner, Yannis Yannikos, was connected to the Greek

Communist party.[41] After the October uprising, Yeltsin ordered *Pravda* to change its name, but the paper's chief editor, Gennedy Seleznev, refused.[42] *Izvestia,* the first Russian newspaper to accept advertisements, was also in a financial bind. *The New York Times* moved into the Russian market by launching a joint venture with *The Moscow News; The Times* provided a weekly insert supported by advertising revenues from both American and Russian firms.[43]

The continuing instability of the former Soviet empire left the future of the Eastern news media uncertain. Western investors such as Rupert Murdoch and *The Times* watched the unraveling of economies and political systems uneasily. Yeltsin's enemies forced the dismissal of Yegor Yakovlev, his outspoken chief of television services, late in 1992 on the ground he was slanting the news about the ethnic quarrels disrupting the country. The dismissal of Yakovlev, who in the Gorbachev era had made *The Moscow News* the most outspoken force for a free press in the country, made editors nervous across the country. Yakovlev complained that Yeltsin had compromised his principles by placing his own interests ahead of freedom of speech.[44] A month later, Yeltsin created his own propaganda agency aimed at guaranteeing "the timely and broad dissemination of accurate and truthful information about the course of reform in Russia" and to increase the role of the press "in elucidating state policy."[45] The new agency sounded uncomfortably like a Soviet "ministry of truth."

The abortive revolt against Yeltsin and the elections at the end of 1993 further damaged confidence in both the stability of post-Soviet society and the dedication of the new Russian press to the principles underlying the traditional concepts of a democratic press. When opposition political parties preaching xenophobia and savage nationalism registered major election victories, Moscow's more liberal newspapers muttered darkly about the rise of a new fascism. Similar warnings came from abroad, especially about the use of television for inflammatory tirades by the nationalist candidate, Vladimir Zhirinovsky.[46]

It ought not to have come as a surprise to anyone that the Russian press presented a far-from-objective portrait of Yeltsin, Zhirinovsky, or any of the other political participants. The Russian press had not displayed dispassionate and impartial reporting under the czars or the communist rulers either. In post-Soviet society, the Russian press was, in the words of one American journalist, "alive with opinion." Serious Russian journalists of all political persuasions spoke proudly of inserting their opinions in news stories. Only hacks, they said, wrote objective stories.[47]

It wasn't easy, however, to recognize *whose* opinions were being reported. Journalists were not being manipulated so much by clever spin doctors as by hard cash. The slant taken in the stories was regularly for sale. Outright bribery was widespread. A question put by a Russian journalist to visiting American reporters seemed to sum up the pattern of control by the powerful in the new Russia. "What do you do," the journalist asked, "when a candidate offers you money to write favorably about his campaign?" It was not an academic question. It described journalistic life in a new market state where journalists were being paid $40 to $45 a month.

NOTES

1. Adam B. Ulam, *The Bolsheviks: The Intellectual and Political History of the Triumph of Communism in Russia* (New York: Macmillan, 1965), 154-58, 466-70. See also Robert Conquest, *V. I. Lenin* (New York: Viking, 1972).

2. *Lenin About the Press*, compiled by G. A. Golovanova, L. P. Yevseyeva, and R. P. Ovsepyan (Prague: International Organization of Journalists, 1972), 71 (italics added). The issue of *Iskra* was published in vol. 4, May 1901.

3. Vladimir Ilyich Lenin, "The Freedom of the Press," in *Rabochy Put* 11 (September 28, 1917), reprinted in *Lenin About the Press*, 185-89, hereafter cited as Lenin.

4. Lenin, 187. The careful observer will note the similarity between Lenin's 1917 criticism of "the capitalists" and the 1990s criticism in the United States and Europe of the concept of "political correctness." Neither Left nor Right has exclusive claim to moral justification.

5. Lenin, 188.

6. Lenin, 188-89 (italics in original).

7. Vladimír Hudec, *Journalism: Substance, Social Functions, Development* (Prague: International Organization of Journalists, 1978), 48.

8. The goals were not original with Lenin; he credited them to the German socialist leader Wilhelm Liebknecht. "*Studieren, propagandieren, organisieren,*" Liebknecht demanded of a press organ that would serve socialist revolutionaries—"Learn, propagandize, organize," Hudec, 45. See also Rosa Luxemburg, *Reform or Revolution* (New York: Arrow Press, 1937).

9. Yassen Zassursky, interview with the author, Moscow School of Journalism, May 4, 1980.

10. Zassursky. All his quotes in this paragraph and the following two paragraphs are from this interview.

11. Hudec, *Journalism*, 47.

12. Hudec, 45.

13. Hudec.

14. For a discussion of these concepts, see Robert Heilbroner, "Reflections After Communism," *The New Yorker*, September 10, 1990, 91-100.

15. Director Vitaly Ignatenko spoke at a forum at Sochi, Russia, in February 1992. A report of the proceedings, titled "Building a Free Media in the Commonwealth of Independent States," was prepared by Peggy L. Cuciti and Marshall Kaplan, dean of the Center for International Public Administration and Policy, Graduate School of Public Affairs, University of Colorado at Denver. The meeting was designated the Second ASPEN International Forum. Hereafter cited as Report.

16. See the Appendix for further information about Svetlana Starodomskaya.

17. I am indebted to the Soviet scholar Elisabeth Schillinger for this useful construction.

18. Brian McNair, "Glasnost and Restructuring in the Soviet Media," *Media Culture and Society*, 11 (1989), 327-49. Much has been written about the history of the Soviet press. For an excellent overview of the development of television, see Ellen Mickiewicz, *Split Signals: Television and Politics Life in the Soviet Union* (New York: Oxford University Press, 1988).

19. *New York Times*, January 20, 1990; *Washington Post*, December 26, 1990.

20. David Remnick, "Letter from Moscow," *The New Yorker*, March 23, 1992, 65–87, ref. 73. The editor he spoke of launched *Nezavisimaya Gazeta* in December 1990.

21. Letter to the author from Henrikas Yushkiavitshus, Assistant Director-General for Communication, Information and Informatics, Unesco, March 13, 1992. Also included in the material from Yushkiavitshus is the content of an interview conducted in Paris the previous year.

22. For a discussion of these press laws, see Report, 8–13.

23. Celestine Bohlen, "Few Russian Newspapers Thrive in New Climate of Freedom," *New York Times*, January 26, 1993.

24. Bohlen.

25. Report, 13, 18.

26. Report, 47–50.

27. Letter from Yushkiavitshus.

28. John Morton, "Building a Free Press in the Ex-USSR," *Washington Journalism Review* (May 1992): 52. Morton, who was a member of the U.S. delegation, said most of the American delegates were appalled to learn the new press law imposed restrictions on who might launch media enterprises.

29. Letter from Yushkiavitshus.

30. Report, 14–15.

31. Isaiah Berlin, "Two Concepts of Liberty," in his *Four Essays on Liberty* (New York: Oxford University Press, 1969), 118–72. The essay was delivered as the inaugural lecture at Oxford University, October 31, 1958. For a concise summary of the philosophical import, see J. Herbert Altschull, *From Milton to McLuhan: The Ideas Behind American Journalism* (White Plains, NY: Longman, 1990), 88–90.

32. Zechariah Chafee, Jr., *Free Speech in the United States* (New York: Atheneum, 1969) 136–39, 559–66, original publication year: 1941. For a fascinating account of the development of free-press law in the United States, see Anthony Lewis, *Make No Law: The Sullivan Case and the First Amendment* (New York: Random House, 1991).

33. Edward Schwartz, "A Chorus of Many Voices," *New York Times Book Review*, April 11, 1993, 10.

34. Mary Ann Glendon, *Rights Talk: The Impoverishment of Political Discourse* (New York: Free Press, 1991), 12.

35. Universal Declaration of Human Rights, Article 29, adopted, New York, December 10, 1948, reprinted in Kaarle Nordenstreng, et. al., *New Information and Communication Order: A Source Book* (Prague: International Organization of Journalists, 1986), 125.

36. Glendon, *Rights Talk*, 172.

37. Ellen P. Mickiewicz, *Media and the Russian Public* (New York: Praeger, 1981).

38. *Inter Nationes*, a German government-news and cultural-feature service, September 8, 1991, reported that new reading habits in the East were threatening the future of sophisticated journals. Similar reports flowed from throughout Western Europe, condemning the cultural fare on television in Russia and its former client states. In Moscow, Vitaly Tretyakov, founder of the successful *Nezavisimmaya Gazeta*, created a tabloid frankly aimed at "the low-brow reader." See Remnick, "Letter from Moscow," 86.

39. Hudec, *Journalism*, 45.

40. "Yeltsin to Press Ahead with Elections," *Baltimore Sun,* October 7, 1993; Steven Erlanger, "Yeltsin Facing Major Job of Reshaping Government," *New York Times*, October 10, 1993; Craig R. Whitney, "Permanent Ban for 13 Russian Newspapers," *New York Times*, October 15, 1993.

41. "A Greek Publisher Says It Controls *Pravda*," *New York Times*, August 24, 1992. A company spokesperson announced the firm had acquired 55 percent of *Pravda*'s shares, with the remainder in Russian hands. For a review of progress and potential throughout the Eastern bloc, see *Cries for Freedom: The Struggle for Independent Media in the Soviet Union and East Europe* (Arlington, VA: Freedom Forum, 1992). The chairman of The Freedom Forum is Allen H. Neuharth, publisher of *USA Today*.

42. Whitney, "Permanent Ban."

43. "Russian-Language Edition of the *Times* Begins Today," *New York Times*, April 28, 1992. New York editors selected 90 percent of the content, editors of *The Moscow News* the remaining 10 percent. The Russians received half of American advertising revenues and all the Russian revenues.

44. Celestine Bohlen, "Minister of Information Is Dismissed by Yeltsin," *New York Times*, November 26, 1992.

45. "Yeltsin Forms Agency to Oversee Media," *Baltimore Sun*, December 27, 1992. The article was reprinted from *The Los Angeles Times*.

46. Serge Schmemann, "Russian Election Result: Shattering of New Image," *New York Times*, December 15, 1993.

47. Susan King, "In Russia, News for Sale," *Washington Post*, December 18, 1993.

Chapter
13

The Advancing Press:
The Old Order Changes

THE PRESS: A SHORTCUT TO DEVELOPMENT?

The naming of things is one of the most critical aspects of human behavior. What we call something determines to a large extent what and how we think of it. A classic example is the term *Third World*. Or *underdeveloped nations*. Or *developing nations*. Whichever of these terms we choose, there is an implication of inferiority. What we are discussing is not even second best; it is third. The image suggested is of something less important than the first or second world, something still striving for a status not yet within its reach.

But what name *can* be applied to these geographical and political units? Are they not objectively less developed than the powerful nations of the world? Yes, the level of their industrial, commercial, and political sophistication is below that of the great nations of the world. And yet by identifying them as underdeveloped or developing, we are in danger of expressing not merely a technological reality but also a value judgment. Nevertheless, the categorization is so thorough and so widespread the affected countries themselves employ the terms *Third World* and *developing nations*, though they have generally rejected the term *underdeveloped* as going too far. Accordingly, and with strong reservations, we will accept *Third World* as the operative term but make it synonymous with *advancing nations*, a less value laden term.

The United Nations (UN) came into existence in 1945 with a membership of fifty countries, nearly all the original members coming from the American continent and Europe. By 1990, the membership had more than tripled and was still increasing. Virtually all the new countries that had joined the UN were former colonies of Africa and Asia. The industrial world, those with market and planned economies alike, had seen to it their preeminent position would not be upset within the UN, no matter how many new nation-states appeared; the principal powers had assured no substantive action could be taken by the UN without the unanimous agreement of the five great powers that had survived World War II—the United States, the Soviet Union, Britain, France, and China. The regime of Chiang Kai-shek, the original "China" in the UN, was replaced as a member in 1971 by the People's Republic of China, which then received the veto right originally assigned to the Chiang government. In 1991, the old Soviet seat was awarded to the new federation of Russia.

How should we label these new countries? How should we define their press systems? The affected countries identified themselves in 1964 as the Group of 77, at once an objective description of the number of countries that joined forces in an attempt to avoid the values contained in such verbal symbols as Third World. The shortcut G-77 has also come to stand for the less developed countries, although there are now well over 100 members of G-77. No designation seems entirely satisfactory; most are somehow demeaning. As used here, the word *advancing* characterizes not only the press systems of these nation-states but also their economies. *Advancing* is a synonym of sorts for *developing*, but it lacks some of the stigma associated with whatever has so far failed to develop. Anyone—individual, institution, or nation—may advance. Even the top-seeded player in a tennis tournament must advance from round to round. Any newspaper or radio station may advance; it may acquire a larger audience or may progress in terms of its moral judgments. Of equal importance, it is clear that those who advance must not necessarily do so through win-or-lose competition, although that is possible, as in the example of the tennis player. But individuals or nations may also advance together. They may advance quite as nicely through cooperation as through competition. In fact, groups that find themselves discriminated against are more likely to advance through joining forces with others on the bottom in order to approach more closely to the top. So let us speak of the press of these advancing countries as the advancing press.

To advance is clearly what the nations of the world must do if they are to provide the kind of economic and political environment under which their citizens might enjoy the prosperity, freedom, and justice a democratic society is meant to offer. They have a long way to go. The World Bank says per-capita income in the G-77 nations actually declined in 1989 and 1990, and under the most optimistic of predictions, only modest gains could be expected in the next decade. To be "really competitive," the Bank's chief economist, Larry Summers, says, they must demonstrate striking advances in transportation networks, marketing expertise, and telecommunications systems.[1] The industrialized nations are heavily to blame for the continuing primitive state in the advancing nations. Summers says that if the United States, Europe, and Japan were to reduce their trade barriers, the G-77 countries could increase their exports by as much as $50 billion a year. Richard J. Barnet, senior fellow at the Institute for Studies in Washington, D.C., agrees. Only structural changes in the world economy can reverse the process of impoverishment in sub-Saharan Africa, he says.[2] Those structural changes would involve a massive degree of help in promoting democratic systems in the poorly developed lands. Otherwise, Barnet says, he fears more civil wars, greater disease, a mounting number of refugees, and dramatic spoliation of the global environment.

Of what does the ideology, the belief system, of an advancing press consist? Is there, in fact, such an ideology? Or are the affected nation-states so different from one another we cannot reasonably speak of an advancing press? There is, of course, no such thing as *the* advancing press, even as there are no such things as *the* market press or *the* communitarian press. Differences abound in all three structures. Still, we may with confidence identify models of all three structures. In the market model, the belief system embraces the theology of the First Amendment, the code of objectivity, the idea that an independent press stands as a protection for the people against abuses of power and, above all, as the centerpiece of the democratic assumption. The communitarian model corresponds in substantial degree to the collective belief system that was codified in Lenin's three roles, but it is also fortified by its own code of objectivity and by specifically assigning to the press the critical function of education in the service of the community. The *ideology* of the

The radio challenges the chaos of many cultures and many languages: getting out the news in the village of Anuradjapura, India.

SOURCE: Unesco/C. A. Arnaldo

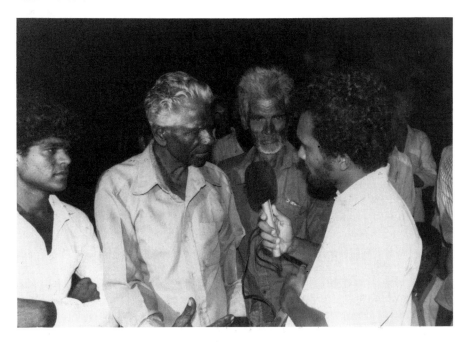

advancing press is derived from two sources. One is *acquired*—learned from the models of the market and the socialist press; the other is *indigenous*—rooted in the history and the culture of the new nation-states. The first is frankly imitative, the second is natural.

The press *systems* in the advancing world seem to be entirely acquired. In fact, the press in the contemporary sense of that word does not seem to have existed in the advancing world before the colonial conquerors arrived and imposed their own press systems. Certainly, there were no mass media in the mountains of South America or in the bush and savanna country of Africa or in the rice fields of Asia before the appearance of the Spanish, the Portuguese, the British, and the French. The communication patterns predating the colonial conquerors were primitive and local, devoted almost entirely to the daily needs of the people. News, as we understand the term, did not exist. Thus, all the press institutions of the advancing world are acquired institutions, learned first from the colonial powers and later from the United States and the Soviet Union. The important messages dispatched in Africa and Asia were similar to those circulated in ancient Rome, in the ecclesiastical social order of the medieval world, and among the merchants of Venice—all were exchanged not among the people but among the elite, the leaders of church, state, and commerce. For the ordinary people, the mechanism of communication was not the written word; it was the drum and the smoke signal and above all the spoken word, relayed in tales, song, and ritual chants.

Obviously, the structures of the press that developed among the scores of new nation-states differed from one another in the same ways their political, economic, social, and cultural structures differed. But in a very important way, these structures were also similar—they were without exception acquired. It could not be surprising that among the new nation-states the expressed goals were to be free, to be objective, to educate, and to serve as an arm of the public in safeguarding against the abuses of power. Each one of these goals, it is to be remembered, was a learned goal; none of them arose from the indigenous information systems or from the beliefs that naturally grew up around those systems. It is mere quibbling to overemphasize the differences among the media in the advancing world. The essential similarity lies in the fact that these media are universally derived from the industrialized nations of the world.

Political change is almost inevitably linked with startling shifts in science and technology. So it was that a revolution in communications accompanied the collapse of the colonial order, the shock of two disastrous world wars, and the emergence of deadly new power blocs. The advancing nations emerged together with the computer—and, interestingly, with the "science" of communications. A new press concept, identified as "development journalism," was at hand.

The driving force behind development journalism was the wildly attractive concept of nation building. The new African political entities south of the Sahara were carved out of British and French colonial holdings, many of them artificial creations with a variety of hostile ethnic groupings and a multiplicity of languages. The leaders of the new geographical units faced a serious challenge: to make nations out of the disparate elements. The idea of using the mass media as a tool to build—

or develop—a whole out of the parts came naturally to these leaders and to the western theorists advising them.[3] There was no agreement, however, about *how* the media were to be used—as instruments to bring about a growth of democratic institutions or as weapons to further a thirst for personal power.

The concept of development journalism, in whatever guise, was from the beginning expressed in idealistic, even utopian, terms. Two years before his country achieved independence, Kenya's minister of economic planning and development, Tom Mboya, gave voice to the dream that was inspiring those who envisioned the media as a driving force in building democratic nations in Africa. Yet he also issued a stern warning. It was critical, he told a 1962 gathering of journalists in Paris, that development journalism serve the cause of nation building. For African reporters and editors to be conscious of their role in the building of nations was, Mboya said, crucial. Moreover, the African journalists had to be informative, critical, and educational; they had to be permitted to operate in freedom. But they couldn't do it alone; in nation building, they had to join forces with their leaders. At the height of the Cold War, facing pressure from the power blocs of the north, Mboya cautioned the African press to "learn to treat Africa in her own context on the basis of her people's emotions and not in the East-West context or on the basis of foreign interests." And, he added, with prescience: "These things it must do, or face the charge of traitor."[4] Many editors and reporters were to face that charge, and freedom of the press was to be no more evident in the advancing world than it was in the industrialized nations.

To the leaders of the new nations of Africa and Asia, it seemed merely obvious the press promised a kind of shortcut to development. The press folklore that had gained sway over more than two centuries assured them of the power of the press to influence and to persuade. What more useful instruments could be imagined than newspapers and radio to spread the word of political freedom, nationhood, and the opportunity to assume an honored place at the table of world society? Such an assumption was inevitable, for the leaders of the new nations had themselves been schooled in the folklore of the capitalist states; their ideas derived from those of Britain, France, Belgium, Holland, and the political giant that was spawned by those ideas, the United States. Belief was universal in the power of the press and its companion in education, the schools, to raise a citizenry dedicated to the principles of democracy and social justice. The leaders of the advancing nations found support in an army of development researchers who saw the press as central in the process they identified as nation building. Neither the leaders nor the scholars paid more than scant attention to the desires and wishes of the residents of the advancing world who lived outside the urban centers in the "periphery," the power-ridden rural reaches where indigenous religious and nonverbal practices continued to flourish.[5]

The concept of development journalism is difficult to define precisely, for it has arisen in many forms. In fact, since the idea of development carries with it an aura of inferiority, we speak here instead of *the belief system of advancing journalism*, a set of ideas woven from the cloth from which most—if not all—of the costumes worn by "development journalism" have been fabricated. These ideas (or rather these articles of faith) include belief in the press as a unifying force; belief in

The medium is the message man: Marshall
McLuhan, University of Toronto professor,
tells students of his dream of a global village.
SOURCE: University of Toronto

the press as an instrument of social justice and a device for beneficial social change;
and belief the press is properly an instrument of two-way communication, with
equal importance assigned to the writer and the reader, to the broadcaster and the
listener. Sadly, the practice in much of the developing world has been far from the
articles of faith. Muzzling and misuse of the press are widespread.

Although the theorists and leaders who preached the cause of development
journalism borrowed extensively from the belief systems that had grown up in capitalist and socialist societies, they introduced modifications of major proportions.
The extent of these modifications may have gone unnoticed since the new nations
were instantly drawn into the political, economic, and cultural conflicts that were
already dividing the world. The threads that made up the cloth of development
journalism were never free of politics. To some, especially in Asia, it was mandatory
that reporters and editors in the newly independent states be themselves independent, free of political constraints; to others, especially in Africa, it was critical for
journalists to ally themselves with the political forces seeking to build unified
nations of sectional, ethnic, and linguistic components. The goal was unrealistic in
both cases because the press is never independent or free of political and economic
constraints. Moreover, the press is powerless to create a unity in a void.

In Asia, where the British had established a flourishing press system construct-ed on the British model, the term *development press* was used to define a press free of political direction, whose first duty was to report news *about* economic development. The Press Foundation of Asia, created in 1967 by Asian newspapers and the Ford Foundation, promoted a development press "based on professional-ism, objectivity, and total independence from any government or bureaucratic con-trol and influence,"[6] a statement that might have been made by any U.S. or British press executive. By contrast, the influential president of Ghana, Kwame Nkrumah, told a group of African journalists in 1963 it was their duty to "help establish a pro-gressive political and economic system" to free people from want and poverty, to educate them and even inspire them to "work for equality and the universality of men's rights everywhere." Nkrumah, following Lenin's dictum, portrayed the African newspaper as "a collective educator—a weapon, first and foremost, to over-throw colonialism and imperialism, and to assist total African independence and unity."[7] The journalists he addressed then specifically rejected the idea that the press ought to be nonpolitical; they announced it as their obligation to show the nonpolitical atttiude was nothing more than "imperialist politics." Nkrumah later

The nonaligned lead the advancing nations: Five powerful men refuse to play lapdog to the mighty United States and Soviet Union. From left, Jawaharlal Nehru of India, Kwame Nkrumah of Ghana, Gamal Abdel Nasser of Egypt, Sukarno of Indonesia, and Josef Broz Tito of Yugoslavia.

SOURCE: UPI/Bettmann

tumbled from power, accused (as were so many of his colleagues) of himself sub-verting the principles of a revolution of freedom by building a dictatorial regime in which all liberties were suppressed, including freedom of the press. However, the ideas Nkrumah expressed have by no means been repudiated.

The sounding board for discussions about the behavior and role of the press was to become concentrated inside Unesco—the United Nations Educational, Scientific, and Cultural Organization—and various other international bodies, as well as among journalism and communications researchers in both the industrial-ized and the advancing world. We will turn later to a detailed discussion of Unesco's role. In that organization, discussions dealt first with the idea of the flow of information and later, increasingly, with technological developments and the relationship between journalism—the reporting of news—and other forms of com-munication. The schools of journalism that sprang up in the new nation-states and in the former colonial societies of Latin America placed greater stress on research and communications models than did U.S. schools, where the primary emphasis remained on the training of reporters, editors, and photographers. Those who were charged with operating the newspapers and radio stations in the advancing world rushed off to the United States in ever-increasing numbers to study what came to be called "the nuts and bolts" of journalism. And they returned to their newspapers and radio stations to put into practice the techniques they had learned from the Americans, as well as those they had observed among the British and French news-papers that had long circulated in the colonies.

In the socialist world, the breakup of colonial empires and the creation of new nation-states were viewed as fulfilling the predictions of Marx, Lenin, and other socialist theorists, who had seen the imperialist capitalist world collapsing under the weight of its internal contradictions. To Marxist analysts, the new, rev-olutionary societies required a press system in the image of the Leninist model. Nation building fit comfortably into the model of collective organization. Just as in the capitalist countries researchers found an exciting new subject for study, so did theorists in Marxist lands and indeed socialist theorists in capitalist nations. To them, the operative term was *cultural imperialism.* Now that the capitalists had surrendered direct political control of their colonies, they were, it was said, moving into a more subtle sphere of domination. With the help of newspapers, especially television and advertising, capitalists were seeking to subject their for-mer colonies to a different kind of exploitation. They were attempting to blot out the native histories of the new nation-states, to destroy their cultures and their traditions, and replace them with the mechanized consumer found in industrial-ized lands. It was a different form of exploitation of the proletariat, and its spear-head was the press and the information industry. Despite the fall of the Soviet empire and the disappearance of Marxist-Leninist training programs, the concept of cultural imperialism remains today as widely discussed as ever. Indeed, it was not necessary for socialist analysts to impose the concept on the advancing world. The same idea had already occurred to many Africans, Asians, and Latin Americans. Nkrumah was not alone in voicing a fear of inroads by Western ideo-

OUR SHRINKING GLOBE

SOURCE: Robert Grossman, *The Nation*

logues and journalists. Similar expressions came from other leaders and the socialist thinkers in the advancing world.

THE "TWIN AGENTS" OF PROGRESS

Contempt for cultural penetration by the United States, Britain, and the rest of the capitalist world is universal throughout Africa. At a conference of journalists in the Nigerian city of Ibadan (which I was privileged to attend), Bode Oyewole, a leading radio newsman and an official of the Nigerian Union of Journalists, said the mission of the journalist was to educate "the society of which he is an integral part. The journalist is a mass educator. His role is as important, if not more so, than the role of the classroom teacher."[8]

He rejected cultural penetration of TV entertainment programs while applauding capitalist values of news production. Yet Oyewole and his fellow journalists at Ibadan, like editors and reporters all over the advancing world, did not seem to recognize the inconsistency of their position. Few U.S. journalists would have endorsed this comment by Oyewole:

> So long as the journalist is aware of his responsibilities towards the community—principally that of helping development—so long as he realizes that his freedom has bearing on what is good for the society and as such is not freedom without limits, then the traditional mistrust will be dissolved, and government and journalism will become twin agents of socioeconomic progress.

The linkage of freedom and responsibility is a familiar theme in discussions of journalism, but in the older capitalist nations, the need for limits on freedom is rarely mentioned, and scarcely ever are journalists and governments regarded as twin agents of anything, let alone socioeconomic progress. The idea of the press as an instrument of progress dates back to the earliest days of the modern news media. The business of the press was *information*; if progress occurred, that was all to the good, but the role of the news was to inform, not to act as an agent of social or economic change. The proper business of the press, in Oyewole's view, was not just to provide information but to provide it within a context that promoted socioeconomic progress, and that could occur only under lasting peace. If stories emphasize conflicts rather than aim at resolving them, they do not promote lasting peace, which he said was the ultimate goal of humankind. Lasting peace requires good communications among peoples: "Messages must be clear and precise, not ambiguous and not censored or 'doctored,' if we are to avoid the conflicts which give rise to misunderstanding."[9]

Bode Oyewole's comments are typical among journalists and press students throughout the advancing world. An examination of the press of advancing countries will turn up many similar observations and hopes; Oyewole's remarks are especially well put. At the conclusion of the Ibadan meeting, I pointed out to one Nigerian journalist that many—perhaps most—U.S. journalists would have scoffed at Oyewole's statements about twin agents as naïve, would have urged instead devotion to facts, to integrity, to truth, rather than to unrealistic demands for the press to operate as an agent for socioeconomic progress. "Why," he asked, "should we be like you? What have your ethics and morality brought the world beside injustice, cruelty, and war?" It was not an easy question to deal with, although he might have spoken also of the positive contributions of the United States in terms of political freedom and social justice.

The very term *development journalism* has come under severe criticism, attacked as a smoke screen allowing dictators to subject their press to iron controls and strict censorship. This criticism grew in large measure out of the special case of the Philippines, in which the idea of development journalism was first broached. By 1973, a Department of Development Communications had been established at the University of the Philippines at Los Baños, where development journalism was revised in name and concept to "development support communications." Under the ideal expressed in the revised nomenclature, the media were to be simply instruments of development. The plans for development were to be created by government agencies, and the press was to assist in the accomplishment of the announced goals. The first chairwoman of the university department at Los Baños, Nora Quebral, said her program was aimed at rescuing the public from poverty through economic growth "that makes possible greater social equality and the larger fulfillment of human potential."[10]

Philippine journalists, during the regime of the authoritarian President Ferdinand Marcos, were denied the right to criticize the government, its policies, or any member of the Marcos family. Repression, in the name of development, has for many years been a way of life in many parts of the advancing world in Asia, Africa, and Latin America. This reality, however, has not diminished the appeal of development journalism. Narinder Aggarwala, an executive in the United Nations Development Program, argued it was an aberration for development journalism to be converted into a tool for repression of the news media; instead, development journalism properly should be likened to the practice in the industrialized world of "investigative journalism." The duty of a journalist reporting on development, Aggarwala wrote, is to examine each development project "critically" and report "the differences between its impact on people as claimed by government officials, and as it actually is.[11] Such a definition would seem to reduce development journalism to the status of ordinary journalism as (at least in theory) it is practiced in all parts of the world.

Much of the difficulty of modernizing and upgrading the press of the advancing world is, of course, financial. But that is not the only problem. In fact, there are many social and cultural factors posing roadblocks. For one thing, some segments of advancing-world society simply reject the goals of development journalism. Strong supporters of traditional as opposed to modern values simply prefer an oral culture. They disapprove of any use of the media to improve education and literacy. Norwegian researcher Helge Rønning has pointed out that the campaign for restructuring and modernizing the media originated to a large extent with white colonists, since the structure of advancing-world media follows the model inherited from the colonial period, even though media ownership patterns have changed a great deal. Moreover, she said, many advancing-world residents remember well that traditional and oral cultural factors played a significant role in the colonial countries' struggle for liberation.[12] Modernization may actually work against integration of society and thus interfere with nation building, since it tends to fragment social groups. In a traditional culture, the term *modernization* implies acceptance of the values of the white society of Europe and the United States, where the individual takes precedence over the community and communication patterns devalue traditional ideas and practices. Rønning's studies were concentrated in the new nation of Zimbabwe, but her findings are applicable to most of Africa and indeed throughout the advancing world. Even in Zimbabwe, where government control has been less rigorously exercised than in other countries, journalists tend to censor themselves out of fear, a practice not unknown in the capitalist world, where self-censorship based on concern about potential displeasure of advertisers is not unknown.

Despite a continuing campaign for financial assistance from the industrialized countries, concern about "cultural imperialism" runs deep in the hearts of the new class of media magnates throughout the advancing world. So it is not only the traditionalists who are concerned about the potential loss of language, cultural, religious, and even linguistic customs. Recent criticism has been directed especially against giant transnational corporations, which use modern merchandising and advertising messages to help create a consumer society in the advancing world, in effect selling their belief systems along with their products.

The penetration of an alien consumer society may be generally accepted, though it is difficult to find any officials in Africa or Asia who publicly endorse this particular form of cultural invasion. Rather, they suffer in relative silence, hoping to gain from the transnationals the benefits of trade and technology they consider mandatory for their economic development. The irony is supreme. Government officials who in their hearts despise the products and norms of their former colonial masters not only find themselves accepting their dissemination but also often crack down harshly on those who protest in public. Hundreds of Asian and African editors have suffered as a result, and more than a handful have been flung into prison, tortured, or killed for their protests.

Jerry Domatob, a prominent Nigerian educator, has viewed the media of sub-Saharan Africa as instruments of "neo-colonialism," which he said has replaced "the epoch of force and gunboat diplomacy" but continues the power relationships established during the colonial era. Despite new ownership of the media in Africa and despite "isolated incidents" of opposition to cultural imperialism, Domatob said, "sub-Saharan Africa's media are supportive rather than antagonistic of neo-colonialism." According to Domatob, "the media foster neo-colonialism through training, advertising, news, technology, etc."[13] Cees Hamelink, an authority on Third World media, has spoken of "global cultural synchronization," under which transnational media empires, especially through the transmission of televised entertainment programs, destroy local social inventiveness and cultural creativity or at the very least throw them into confusion.[14] The communications scholars Everett Rogers and Arvid Singhal have noted that such programs "contribute almost nothing toward the development goals of Third World nations." Indeed, they say, the broadcast content is actually antidevelopment, since "advertising and entertainment programs . . . depict urban life as attractive and thus encourage over-urbanization."[15]

The ideal of free expression has been endorsed everywhere throughout the former colonial world, but it is more honored today in the breach than in the practice. Like Thomas Jefferson and all the American presidents who have followed him, the leaders of the new countries of Africa and Asia have preached the cause of a free and open society before taking office yet have found themselves compelled to condemn a hostile press and even to move to suppress it upon taking office. If a truly independent press has not appeared in the industrialized world, it would be ludicrous to expect one to arise in the advancing world. There, as everywhere, newspapers and broadcasting outlets are agents. In the immediate postwar years—the late 1940s and early 1950s—they were mainly agents of the foes of colonial power who wished to drive out the British and French. In the early 1960s, in the euphoria of liberation, they were agents of the newly enfranchised leadership celebrating the end of colonial rule. In the late 1960s and early 1970s, as reaction set in, the press became agents of the military leaders who took power in an attempt to preserve order. By the 1980s, the new nation-states were progressing in different directions: In some of them, the press had been included as a partner of government and the commercial and industrial interests and was permitted a substantial degree of latitude; self-censorship had become a widespread if uncomfortable practice. In some African and Asian states, the press operated under rigid direction, and, as in Marcos's Philippines, the media were forced to accept and even propagandize for official political and economic norms. In some countries, censorship was firm and unbending. In others, such as India, self-censorship was for the most part considered adequate, although for a time President Indira Gandhi found that practice not to her liking and reimposed firm rules of censorship.

Whatever the specific rules at the particular time in the advancing world, the press acquiesced in and promoted the norms of the political and economic leadership. In the few countries that pursued a Marxist course—for instance, Cuba, Tanzania, Ethiopia, and Vietnam—the norms involved vigorous criticism of the consumer society and the values exported by the transnationals. In the overwhelming majority of countries, however, the accepted value system was that of capitalism, and only limited criticism of this system appeared in newspapers or on radio and television. Still, even among the majoritarian press, there often appeared defense of traditional cultural values and criticism of the importation of alien ideas. Such criticism was even more widespread in private gatherings of journalists and editors.

At the Ibadan conference, Olufolaji Ajibola Fadeyibi, a lecturer in the faculty of social sciences at the University of Lagos, drew the heaviest applause with a speech complaining that Ibadan radio and television stations were presenting too many TV programs produced in Britain and the United States. He zeroed in on a British disco program with a "London Soho background; sleazy foreground and many ill-fated misled Nigerian youths wriggling and contorting to foreign (precisely American) music—in between frequent swigs at beer bottles right on camera." To knowing laughter and ringing applause, he went on to ask: "In what way does this program educate our children, reflect our cultural heritage, and promote national unity?"[16] Fadeyibi reserved his corker for his finale:

> The conclusion is obvious. There is no need for us to perpetuate a situation as well as condemn it at the same time. If the Western nations won't talk about us, play our music and enlighten their audiences about our culture, then we have no business talking about them, playing their music and showing "Kojak." By so doing, we'll be putting an end to our cultural genocide and communication neocolonialism. To expect the Western nations to facilitate the bidirectional flow of information is to expect a river to flow backwards. Surely no flow is better than free flow.[17]

It was in Nigeria, the most populous country in Africa, that the dream of a new country unified by reason, dispassionate leadership, and a healing, cooperative press would founder most spectacularly. Cooperation was the ideal, but it didn't work that way. Tribal strains led to bitter and brutal civil war shortly after Nigerian independence was gained in 1960. A shaky unification was ultimately achieved, however, and a succession of national governments went about the business of forging a federal system that would strengthen the national identity of Nigeria and enable it to play a leading role in international society. The press remained central in this effort, even though it was evident early on that the dream of nation building through the pages of newspapers and the voice of radio was a chimera. Intertribal, interracial, and interreligious strains imposed painful frustrations on the emerging press ideology of the new nation-states.

The road to a flourishing press system throughout the Third World has been rocky. Journalists and editors have had to find new pathways through those rocks, discarding along the way as best they could the colonial heritage that had taught them all they knew about the press. In Nigeria, the first newspapers were introduced by missionaries a century before independence, and the dozens of broadsheets that were born and died throughout that century inevitably followed the British model. So it was even after 1960. In the decade that preceded independence, when the Nigerian press openly agitated for an end to colonial rule, it was still following the procedures and practices of the London newspapers. Imitation may be the sincerest form of flattery, yet it is also self-demeaning. To adopt the colonial model was to accept a position of cultural inferiority. However, to do so was also to be realistic; there were no other models.

NOTES

1. Steven Greenhouse, "Third World Economies Shrink Again," *New York Times*, April 16, 1992.
2. Richard Barnet, "But What About Africa?" *Harper's,* May 1990, 41–51.
3. Among the earlier studies was the influential collection of articles edited by Lucien Pye, *Communication and Political Development* (Princeton, NJ: Princeton University Press, 1964). Also noteworthy are Daniel Lerner, *Passing of Traditional Society* (New York: Macmillan, 1958); Wilbur Schramm, *Mass Media and National Development* (Stanford, CA: Stanford University Press, 1964); Everett Rogers and L. Svenning, *Modernization Among Peasants: The Impact of Communication* (New York: Holt, Rinehart & Winston, 1969); Everett Rogers and Floyd Shoemaker, *Communication of Innovations* (New York: Macmillan, 1971); and George Gerbner, ed., *Mass Media Policies in Changing Cultures* (New York: Wiley, 1977).
4. Quoted in Frank Barton, *The Press in Africa* (Zurich: International Press Institute, 1969), 172.
5. Majid Tehranian, "Communication and Revolution in the Islamic World: An Essay in Interpretation," *Asian Journal of Communication* 1, 1 (1990): 18.
6. Press Foundation of Asia, declaration of principles.

7. Kwame Nkrumah, *The African Journalism* (Dar es Salaam: Tanzania Publishers, 1965). This is primarily a reproduction of Nkrumah's speech, together with commentary and reports of the actions of the assembled journalists.

8. Much of the material in the African section of this chapter is derived from personal experience, attendance at journalism conferences in Nigeria and Tanzania, and private conversations with journalists and journalism scholars in these and other African countries.

9. Bode Oyewole, address at journalism symposium in Ibadan, Nigeria, April 12, 1980.

10. Nora C. Quebral, *Development Communication* (Laguna: University of Philippines at Los Baños, 1988); and "Development Communication: Where Does It Stand Today?" *Media Asia* 3, 4 (1975).

11. Narinder K. Aggarwala, "What Is Development News?" *Journal of Communication* 29 (1979): 2.

12. Helge Rønning, "The Structure of the Media in Zimbabwe: A Survey of Developments and Problems," *Third World Publications*, 47 (1989): 9.

13. Jerry K. Domatob, "Sub-Saharan Africa's Media and Neocolonialism," *Africa Media Review*, 3, 1 (1988): 149–73.

14. Cees Hamelink, *Cultural Autonomy in Global Communications* (New York: Norwood, 1983).

15. Everett M. Rogers and L. Arvid Singhal, "Television Soap Operas for Development in India," paper presented at the Annenberg School of Communications, University of Southern California, University Park, 1987. Cited in Domatob, "Sub-Saharan Africa's Media," 166.

16. Olufolaji Ajibola Fadeyibi, "Free Flow of Information in Broadcasting: Nigeria's Cornucopia or Pandora's Box," speech delivered at the Ibadan conference, April 12, 1980.

17. Fadeyibi.

Chapter
14

The Advancing Press:
Africa, Asia, and Iran

AFRICA EAST AND WEST

In late spring 1991, delegates from thirty-eight African countries gathered in Windhoek, the capital of Namibia in Africa's southwestern corner, to announce a brave new program aimed at creating an independent, pluralistic, and free press across Africa.[1] The delegates, echoing journalists in the former Soviet Union and elsewhere among the poorer countries, argued for a press free of government or monopoly control while at the same time recognizing the difficulty of arriving at such a state without the infusion of large sums of capital from the market countries. Their report was sobering. It noted "welcome changes" as some countries moved toward multiparty democracies but called attention also to the repression of journalists, editors, and publishers in many other countries—repression by murder, arrest, detention, and censorship. The complaints were similar to those expressed at the Russian colloquium previously discussed: restrictions on newsprint, licensing controls, and access to news sources. "In some countries," the declaration said, "one-party States control the totality of information."[2]

The Windhoek meeting involved only print journalists, though the delegates called on the United Nations and its cultural arm Unesco to summon the same type of seminar for journalists and managers of African radio and television services. If nongovernmental control of newspapers and magazines were difficult to imagine, independent and pluralistic broadcasting media seemed utopian, for the infrastructure required to support a thriving television system is so costly. Still, the African journalists were determined to push for what they considered true freedom, not only from dictatorial controls at home but also from cultural imperialism from abroad. Among the optimistic methods proposed were "twinning" arrangements between African publishers and those from the industrialized world, but such arrangements with African media were less attractive to Western and Japanese firms than were deals with entrepreneurs from Eastern Europe and the former Soviet Union.

Westerners saw greater opportunities for profit in the Northern Hemisphere. A *Wall Street Journal* analysis showed rising interest by transnational corporations and individual investors in industrially developing lands, yet the interest tended to be located where profitability seemed most likely. The countries at the bottom of the list were the have-not lands of sub-Saharan Africa, whose share of direct foreign investment had been sliced in half during the 1980s, from 1.5 percent of the world total to 0.7 percent. Their share was even less than that of the poorest and riskiest investment countries of Asia: India, Pakistan, and Vietnam.[3] Additionally, the fall of the Soviet Union had brought about a sea change in geopolitical strategies around the globe. Once Western governments had backed investments in Africa in order to build up allies against a perceived Soviet threat; now such political motivations were no longer operative. One Kenyan political scientist noted that the disappearance of aged African despots had offered the United States an opportunity to promote democracy in Africa but observed it was difficult to find countries "democratic enough to merit especially generous amounts of the $800 million available for foreign aid to Africa."[4]

The most treasured "freedom" for African journalists is the freedom to criticize their government or any individual or organization protected by it. Governments and the economic power behind them justify repression of seditious libel in the name of national unity and the spirit of development. The case of Cameroon, a francophone country on Africa's west coast, is instructive. In recent years, political changes have permitted greater freedom from government controls than had been the case after the end of French colonial rule in 1960, even though repressive press laws nonetheless continued to be enforced. Freedom of expression could be enjoyed by the citizens of Cameroon, President Paul Blya said, "but they must not misuse it." Cameroon's minister of information and culture put it this way: "Government must insure that the press does not indulge in gratuitous provocation of legitimate authority and the entire national community or contribute to intoxication and disinformation."[5] There is only one daily newspaper published in the country of 10 million. Radio is owned and operated by the government. Under the press laws ostensibly written for use during war or national emergency, no newspaper may be published without a license from the Ministry of Territorial Administration.

Commercial control of the mass media remains restricted throughout Africa, and the degree of press freedom as that term is defined by Western analysts is low everywhere. Perhaps surprisingly, a 1989 survey by Freedom House rated the press of South Africa in the days of apartheid as having the highest level of freedom in Africa, a score of two where one was the highest and six the lowest.[6] Despite receiving the relatively high rating, the South African written press, all of it run by whites, was pressured by the government into self-censorship, subject as it was to economic pressures. Broadcasting in South Africa is a virtual government monopoly.[7] Open criticism of governments has been unacceptable throughout sub-Saharan Africa. Cameroon and the other formerly French colonies in Africa received the lowest rating (4.88); Nigeria and the other former British holdings in West Africa followed with 3.75, and those in East Africa rated 4.4.[8]

In the 1980s, as the economies of the former French colonies of West Africa slumped and as age and lassitude dimmed the heroic aura of their leaders, a new breed of journalists emerged to clamor for a competitive free press. The heart of the movement lay in the Ivory Coast, where in 1990 a group of dissatisfied state media journalists launched *La Voie* (*The Path*) under Atta Koffi, with his brother assuming command of the long-standing Abidjan daily *Fraternité Matin* (*Morning Brotherhood*). They began publishing articles opposing the policies of President Félix Houphouët-Boigny, long revered as the Philosopher King of the Ivory Coast, whose "Thought of the Day" had been bannered across the front page of *Fraternité Matin* for years.[9] Actually, a free opposition press had always been legal in the Ivory Coast, but the government had up until then always thrown up unscalable legal and financial barriers. The official goals were the same ones followed by all African newspapers: to pursue the cause of national unity, to lend fervent support to the leader, and to avoid animosities among the country's ethnic groups; more than fifty existed in the Ivory Coast. The freest elections in the history of the country followed; similar elections took place in neighboring Mali, Ghana, Congo, and Burkina Faso.

However, genuine democracy remained elusive. The national debt continued to rise. Cocoa and coffee farmers found it no easier to earn a living. The old elites continued to control the economy, and the old habits of blind partisanship remained intact. "In a sense," said editor Atta Koffi of *La Voie*, "each of us has to learn the craft all over again, to stop being someone else's tool. But no one imagined how hard that would be."[10]

Among the former British colonies in East Africa, Tanzania was for many years the chief bastion of socialism under the leadership of its influential president, Julius K. Nyerere. No African leader has been more consistently outspoken in voicing fear of inroads by market ideologists and journalists than Nyerere, whose insistence on modernization from within exerted a powerful influence on leaders in Africa and in other parts of the advancing world.

During a 1980 visit to Tanzania, I found a depressingly poverty-ridden press system that sought to make up for its technological and financial shortcomings with enthusiasm and energy. There were only two daily newspapers in a country of 18 million, both located in the capital city of Dar-es-Salaam and with the most modest of circulations. The English-language *Daily News* had a circulation of 90,000, the Swahili-language *Uhuru* one of 100,000. Nevertheless, the editors of those papers saw a bright journalistic future as the literacy rate climbed. Nyerere claimed to have raised the level of literacy from 15 percent to 70 percent over a twenty-year period. "Our role is to inform and to entertain. It is important for our country to develop sophisticated newspaper readers," said Wilson Bukholi, the editor of *Uhuru*.[11] To him, as to Nyerere, the most effective method of avoiding cultural imperialism was to generate a discriminating public that could recognize efforts to foist an alien culture on it.

Nyerere placed severe censorship restrictions on radio and television, but newspaper censorship was prohibited by law. It was nevertheless clear that news was suppressed on a regular basis. Like editors everywhere, Tanzanian editors were skillful readers of cues and clues from Nyerere and his aides as to what kind of news would be pleasing to the leadership. On a number of occasions, Nyerere chided editors for censoring information. What they needed, all those in Tanzania associated with the press believed, was a homegrown training program to upgrade the quality of journalists and perhaps to stiffen their backbones a bit. Yet here also reality frustrated hope. In Dar-es-Salaam, a small coterie of enthusiastic young men sought to build a school of journalism in a rickety building donated by the Salvation Army. Nearly half the thirty-one students had not seen a typewriter before enrolling. Next to raising money to operate the school, the chief ambition of the directors was to go to a U.S. school of journalism to learn better how to train their students.

With the end of colonialism, students from the Third World began flooding into journalism schools in the United States; as long as the Soviet Union survived, many others went to Moscow to study Marxist-Leninist interpretations of the press. What once was referred to as "a battle for men's minds" was for a generation waged among journalists of the advancing nations. The belief system that had become widespread through the advancing world pleased neither U.S. nor Soviet theorists. On the one hand, it endorsed the goals of objectivity, fairness, and balance so dear to U.S. press thinkers; on the other hand, it set great store on the role of the press as organizer of public opinion, the political instrument prized by Soviet analysts. Moreover, the belief system of Third World journalists was passionately rooted in the conviction that the press must lead a fight against racism, militarism, and antagonism among nations. Where the press philosophies of the market and socialist systems embraced conflict, the operative word in the ideology of the advancing press system was *cooperation*. This was true even in the new "free" press of the Ivory Coast in West Africa.

Nyerere surrendered the presidency in 1985 but remained the chief theorist of the Tanzanian Revolutionary Party. By 1992, with his country, like most of the nations of Africa, plunging ever deeper into economic disarray, Nyerere called for a shift in policy away from socialism and toward the triumphant market ideology. "We must," Nyerere told a party congress, "admit our previous mistakes and start afresh."[12] Opposition parties were to be permitted in the next election. President Ali Hassan Mwinyi, Nyerere's successor, described the move to political pluralism as in line with changes in the rest of the world. The Tanzanian Revolutionary Party, which had once dismissed television as a capitalist luxury aimed at "propagating alien culture and social norms" in the Third World, now recognized that TV could play an important role in economic development so long as it was charted along lines acceptable to Tanzanian authorities, not entrepreneurs from abroad.[13] Here, too, absence of financial resources was a critical problem. Tanzania lacked the skilled engineers and technicians required to operate and maintain a TV system, and government coffers were too sparse to provide the pay that might attract good engineers from abroad. And there was an even more disturbing likelihood: The public probably couldn't afford TV sets.

While broadcast media in sub-Saharan Africa have made modest advances in numbers of outlets and in technological development, they have nonetheless lagged far behind the levels attained even in other less industrialized lands since they are plagued by economic constraints, inefficient planning, inadequate roads, lack of coordination, and a generally low priority on the agenda of governments.[14] The United Nations General Assembly declared the years 1978–87 the Transport and Communications Decade in Africa. Among specific targets were one telephone and twenty TV sets per hundred inhabitants and one post office to serve 3,000 to 6,000 people. The will is there but limited resources, international indebtedness, and increasing worldwide patent protection remain critical roadblocks. The goal is still far away.

Adjoining Tanzania along the east African coast is the country of Kenya, a land of 25 million that remains embroiled in bitter ethnic warfare threatening the continuance of what was long viewed as the most modern and democratic country in Africa. Unlike socialist Tanzania, it welcomed private enterprise and, until recently, received relatively generous commercial and industrial support from market countries and their media. Africa's first daily newspaper, *The East African Standard*, appeared in the capital city of Nairobi in 1910. Today, Kenya boasts three dailies—two published in English, one in Swahili.[15]

The task of building viable nations with healthy economies is formidable. Even a generation after Kenya achieved its independence, its annual per-capita income stood at a mere $330, and Kenya was considered a "middle-income country in Africa." Sixty percent of the population of Nairobi lived in slums, typically with no electricity and but a single water source for as many as 200 families.[16] All of Africa needs intensive care; of her 650 million people, roughly 280 million are poor by anyone's standards. The gross national product of sub-Saharan Africa, with the fastest-growing birth rate in the world, totals that of Belgium; the entire continent accounts for a mere 3 percent of world trade. Richard Barnet, a senior fellow at the Institute for Policy Studies in Washington, D.C., said only a structural overhaul of the global economy could permit Kenya and most other countries of the advancing world, especially in sub-Saharan Africa, to escape the trap in which they find themselves.[17] A renewed flow of money to the developing world, unlikely under conditions created by the fall of the Soviet empire, could, as *The Wall Street Journal* reported, mean rising standards of living in Africa with "foreigners selling everything from tractors to toilet tissue."[18] But transnational corporations and small entrepreneurs are especially conservative about investing in what they consider "political hotspots." Still, sales of news and entertainment programs in advancing nations offer a powerful potential for profit. Kenya enjoys the advantage of having its

Catching up on the news in Mali.

SOURCE: Unesco/Alexis N. Vorontzoff

population's professional skills rated the highest in black Africa; but with the possible disadvantage of a fast-growing population that experts predict will double every eighteen years. What is required, Barnet said, is the building of democratic institutions and a mass media compatible with local culture and traditions.[19]

Absolom Mutere, a Kenyan commentator, took Barnet's argument one step further. He called for a clearly articulated national communication policy established by both governmental policymakers and "social actors," a group he said would lead the Kenyan media to self-reliance.[20] Key elements were less government control and greater use of native resources. Regional cooperation in East Africa, Mutere said, ought to replace dependence on the economic might of major powers and their African cohorts. Independence in Kenya, as in most African countries, brought political authority into the hands of Africans, but industry and agriculture remained in the hands of Europeans. It was time, Mutere said, to keep the media from becoming "more market" in order to avoid opening the door wider to outside capitalist interests and making Kenyans even more dependent on advanced technology from abroad.

What Mutere feared, however, seemed to be happening in the TV industry. Until 1989, Kenya's radio and television service was a branch of the Ministry of Information, with its tiny advertising revenues going into the national treasury. In that year, the Kenya Broadcasting Corporation (KBC) became quasi-independent, free to keep its advertising revenues and licensing fees. More dramatically, the government authorized an astonishingly ambitious second TV system patterned after Ted Turner's CNN, including plans for a sixty-story building that would be the largest in Africa. It was placed under the control of the only legal political party in the country, the KANU (Kenya African National Union), and the party's official newspaper, *The Kenya Times*.[21] Interestingly, the new channel was a joint venture with 40 percent of its ownership acquired by Robert Maxwell, the British-Australian transnational magnate who was to die three years later under mysterious circumstances.

A viable television system supported by advertising seemed at best a remote possibility. Reliable statistics on the number of TV sets in the country were impossible to gather, but it was unlikely there were more than 400,000, and power supply was not adequate to run them all. Most did not receive over-the-air programs in any case, even though they were able to play videocassettes smuggled into the country. Many of these cassettes were of poor technical quality with subtitles that were extraordinarily difficult to read. In any case, KBC's efforts to encourage local talent and native programming made little progress, despite assistance from German and Japanese organizations. The potential for profit was simply too limited.

At first, KBC and its predecessor permitted only African commercials, yet it found the financial losses too painful and authorized foreign-made spots, on which the government levied a 50-percent surcharge. Even at a rate of about $100 for an advertising slot, takers were few; rates were tripled, but money remained a serious problem. In any case, the role of television turned into a hot political issue in a country already torn by ethnic rivalries and quarrels over cultural imperialism.[22]

Ethnic rivalries grew more bitter and more violent. Native and foreign authorities cautioned that the outbursts might lead to civil war, a tragedy that had occurred elsewhere in Africa but not yet in Kenya.[23] Attacks by the minority

Kalenjin tribe, from whose ranks President Daniel Arap Moi stemmed, were apparently motivated by fears the majority tribal group, the Kikuyu, were seeking to return to power. The attacks resulted in an unknown number of deaths. Western and church leaders estimated the death toll at a hundred times the figures given by the government. Tens of thousands were made homeless; reading the newspapers or listening to radio or television offered few clues to the reality of the situation. The communitarian belief system, strong among the various ethnic groupings, did not carry over into national politics.

In the generation following the end of colonialism in Africa, the industrial world persistently transplanted its cultural norms to the new countries, where they found little opposition and frequently outright acceptance of the norms. In Nigeria, for example, the traditional page 3 feature in the London popular press—a photograph of a beautiful, bare-breasted woman—was still appearing on page 3 of the newspaper in the capital of Lagos thirty years after independence; and in Lagos most of the pictures were of white women. Such is a particularly blatant acceptance of an alien culture. Most other examples are less showy and more significant.

Much news reporting in Nigeria is sensationalized, although the excesses are usually deplored by serious journalists, as in the United States. At a conference of African journalists and educators in the city of Jos, a U.S.-trained university lecturer argued that what Nigeria and all of Africa needed was an African media policy, one that was not borrowed from the capitalist countries. "A nation whose media [are] dominated from outside is not a nation," said the lecturer, referring not only to technological but also to ideological domination.[24] Demands for media policies of any sort tend to ring hollow in the ears of journalists and scholars in the capitalist world. A policy to them smacks of control from without because the adoption of policies requires the drafting and approval of laws and regulations that must inevitably be enforced by government. Western journalists point to the imposition of censorship and harsh restrictions by leaders of countries with press policies throughout the advancing world.

The Jos conference was, perhaps surprisingly, much like a gathering of journalism practitioners and scholars in the market or socialist world. Broad ideological concord was clear among the participants. Without exception, the sophisticated journalists and professors, many educated in England or the United States, stood firmly behind the official policy of the Nigerian national radio and television network that linked the nineteen state broadcasting systems. The policy aimed at preserving the country's cultural traditions, no matter how primitive in modern eyes. Everywhere in Nigeria TV programming featured colorfully costumed native singers and dancers chanting in local languages and dancing to the beat of ceremonial drums. There was an occasional "Starsky and Hutch"; but, compared to the capitalist world, including Latin America, very little of the comedy or dramatic programming viewed in the United States could be found. English may be the common language of Nigeria—the news programs are broadcast in English—but cultural preservation is measured in terms of African languages. In some states, efforts were intensifying to add more programs in Hausa or Yoruba or Ibo and to concentrate on traditional African themes.

Although permissible under press laws, attacking the government in print or on the air was fraught with peril. When *African Concord*, a weekly magazine, published a series of reports criticizing the military government in power in 1992 for, among other things, failing to halt inflation, the government sent armed police to occupy the magazine's offices in defiance of a court order against intervention. The government said the move was made because it had ample evidence the magazine had begun "to undermine national security." The editor Sully Aby remarked laconically, "When governments are in trouble, they try to muzzle the press." However, he added, "the complexity of the country makes it difficult to box the press in. The government can try to muzzle the press, but the press always wins in the end."[25]

Political turmoil has been a part of the Nigerian scene ever since the country achieved independence from Britain in 1960. Democratic elections in June 1993 were swiftly annulled when the military seized power once again and promptly banned all opposition political activity. However, the new leader, General Sani Abacha, was careful to avoid an open assault on the news media. In fact, he lifted bans on outlawed news organizations. But he said pointedly they had better be careful about what they reported. Still, some of the remarkably independent press of Nigeria responded sharply. *Newswatch*, a national news weekly, condemned Abacha's "lust for power," and *The Guardian*, a Nigerian daily, said the "unwarranted" military seizure of power "wiped out the gains, admittedly modest, of Nigeria's transition to democratic rule."[26]

Efforts at democratic government have marked Nigerian history. Following their brutal civil war, which broke out shortly after the country won its independence, military authorities inevitably thwarted elections and reclaimed power. Oil drilling had made Nigeria a relatively prosperous country during the 1970s, but when the oil boom collapsed and prices tumbled, the Nigerian economy slumped badly. Some degree of press independence has existed from the very beginning. The thirty daily and weekly newspapers, together with the fifty magazines, have been generally regarded as the freest from government control in Africa. Yet there has always been the threat of a crackdown. An unknown number of journalists has been jailed or worse when they went too far. African editors have spoken privately and sometimes publicly of the effectiveness of self-censorship in reporting sensitive topics.[27] Unlike the editor of *African Concord*, one Nigerian scholar, Olumuyiwa Ayodele, said reporters learn that to keep their jobs, they have to become sycophants and apologists for power.[28] A reporter or editor who is interested in job security, he said, learns quickly that he or she had better follow policy. Virtually all broadcast organizations and most newspapers throughout sub-Saharan Africa are owned to at least some extent by state or federal governments, which are dependent on the wielders of economic power.[29] According to practicing journalists, African newspeople are more subject to sycophancy than those in other places because of the especially high racial, ethnic, social, and religious tensions across the continent.

Conflict is inevitable between the lofty goals of the ideology endorsed by so many African journalists and scholars and the harsh realities that bedevil an advancing press system. The optimistic Windhoek Declaration took careful notice of the economic and political pressures and called not only for financial support from outside but also for further steps in Africa toward the growth of multiparty democracies that "provide the climate in which an independent and pluralistic press can emerge."[30] The lofty goal was a noble one. To reach the goal will be murderously difficult.

ASIA AND THE MONEY MEN

The first thing to be said about the news media in Asia is that, on the whole, they are far less poverty-ridden than those in Africa. For one thing, much of Asia has been free of the colonial control of Great Britain and France, including, of course, the two most powerful countries on the Asian continent, China and Japan. Australia and New Zealand have been for many years independent commonwealths associated only loosely with the British homeland. Even among the former British colonies of southern Asia, opportunities for wealth far outstripped those of the African colonies. However, it is still true that, with certain exceptions, we are speaking of the media of the advancing world. For all practical purposes, we can identify Australia, New Zealand, and Japan as part of the family of Western nations, rooted firmly in market economics and the political institutions that developed under capitalism. For the second half of the twentieth century, China has been a major component of the communitarian world, and since the fall of the Soviet Union, it has been the most powerful remaining practitioner of Marxist ideology. Vietnam, a long-time French colony, is also a component of the Marxist world. In this chapter, our concentration is on the lands of Southeast Asia: Malaysia and Singapore, former British colonies; Indonesia, for centuries a Dutch colony; and the Philippines, long under Spanish rule but in the twentieth century under U.S. domination.

Greater wealth is concentrated in each of these four lands than in any of the excolonies of sub-Saharan Africa, but nearly all that wealth is to be found in the metropolitan capitals of Singapore, Jakarta, Manila, and, to a lesser degree, Kuala Lumpur, each with a population of more than a million. The rural regions of these countries remain largely undeveloped industrially; illiteracy is widespread, and communications are sharply limited. English-language media circulate widely among the educated urban classes. Concerns about "cultural imperialism" are as widespread in Asia as they are in Africa. Suspicions of insidious foreign influence are universal and have been a factor in the controls, both direct and indirect, exercised over the news media. In Singapore and Malaysia, for instance, the governments agreed mutually to ban each other's newspapers, viewing them as potential inciters of rebellion.[31] The forces of political and economic power, deeply worried about their countries' dependence on news and entertainment from foreign sources, have worked to develop their own news agencies and to limit the import of foreign films.[32]

The new nations of Asia, like those of Africa, have been faced with the challenge of nation building made difficult by numerous diverse ethnic groups and languages. On the 13,500 islands that make up the Republic of Indonesia, no fewer than 500 separate dialects are spoken among the three major ethnic groups of Malay, Chinese, and Irianese. The capital, Jakarta, is the most densely populated city on earth, and many among its 8 million residents cannot read the language of the others.[33] In Malaysia, the 16 million people are 59 percent native Bumiputra, 32 percent Chinese, and 8 percent Indian. But it doesn't stop there. The Bumiputras are divided into at least six different ethnic and linguistic groups. The Chinese are similarly diverse.[34] English-language publications such as *The Asian Wall Street Journal* and *The International Herald-Tribune* have bridged the gap among the well-educated, though the rural masses do not read English, if they are at all literate. Ethnic rivalries are fierce, and often bloody. In Malaysia, the minority Chinese resent the political clout of the Bumiputras, who in turn feel themselves economically exploited by the wealthier Chinese. The government has responded in part by setting up a media quota system under which ethnic Malays receive four of every five jobs on the government-controlled RTM (Radio Television Malaysia) and the national news agency, Bernama.[35] In an effort to promote a unified nation with Malay as its national language, the Malaysian government launched a "Love Our Language" movement in 1987, flooding the radio airwaves with unity songs and discouraging Chinese-language publications. At the same time, a quasi-private TV station was created in the hope of stopping the videocassettes in either English or Chinese that had been flooding—many illegally—into the country.[36]

It was at the University of the Philippines at Los Baños, as we have noted, that development journalism was given a great boost beginning in the 1970s. Scholars, journalists, and a number of political leaders enthusiastically promoted the news media as instruments of development. Print and broadcast journalists were to work with government agencies to build strong unified nations economically sound and free of poverty in order to promote the fulfillment of human potential.

Among the most active cheerleaders in the cause of development journalism were the leading media scholars of the 1960s and early 1970s, men like Wilbur Schramm, Daniel Lerner, and Lucien Pye, each of whom argued, reasonably enough according to market theory, that exposure to information would inevitably result in modernization, which was assumed to be of benefit to everybody.[37] But experience proved things do not work out in the real world as comfortably as they do in theory. Marxist analysts argued that not only did the mass media turn out to be inefficient as agents of development but also they actually worked, as Lenin had maintained, in the interests of the propertied classes rather than those of workers and peasants; indeed, they reinforced the power of the holders of wealth and political office.[38] Non-Marxist scholars like William Hachten held that the modernization theorists had "unintentionally provided a rationale for autocratic press controls."[39]

An intriguing study by Richard Shafer turned up disappointing evidence that the efforts of highly motivated journalists for newspapers in the rural Philippines actually led to the direct opposite of what they had hoped to accomplish. Rather than serving as agents for change and development, Shafer reported, Third World journalists were "likely to serve as agents of the status quo and an impediment to change and development."[40] Shafer based his conclusion on a study of a representative number of journalists in rural areas in both the northern and the southern areas of the Philippines. Most of them, he said, started out quite optimistic that development journalism would lead to better lives and greater power for the people but ended up convinced that too many roadblocks had been put in their way and that they were in fact "victims of political and economic circumstances beyond their control."[41]

The survey was conducted at a time of severe media oppression under the martial law imposed by the Marcos regime in the 1980s. Those bitter days for journalists came to an end with the ousting of Marcos and the rise to power in 1986 of Corazón Aquino, who ordered an end to censorship and restraints on the press. Many journalists had defied the Marcos-imposed censorship and justifiably claimed credit for playing a major role in his overthrow. However, holders of power everywhere rarely sit by idly under attacks in the news media. Twenty-six journalists were murdered from 1965 to the time Marcos was ousted, but in the next four years no fewer than thirty-two more were killed, many of them crusading provincial editors and radio reporters.[42] It became prudent for the others to censor themselves and play along with power. Mainstream press analysts pictured press freedom at a very high level under the post-Marcos governments. Some were not so sure, although all sides agreed nevertheless that the Philippine news media were *partners* of government and not *adversaries*. A commentator drawing on the views of mainstream editors and government officials said the Philippine press "stands as watchdog of the government on the people's behalf—not necessarily an adversary (unless the government is abusive), but ally and partner in the cause of democracy."[43] On the other hand, a dissident Philippine journalist said reporters in his country (and India as well) were "tools of vested interests," who were forced into corrupt practices by economic rather than political pressure. This journalist, Adlai Amor, former training director of the Press Foundation of Asia, said one way of keeping journalists in line was by holding their salaries so low they became easy prey for bribes to slant stories favorably to the donors.[44] The average monthly salary for Manila journalists, Amor wrote, was $71; according to a survey by a research institute, a family of five needed a minimum income of $306 to meet its basic needs. The bribery practices came to be known as "envelopmental journalism," a kind of bitter pun calling attention to the bribes that came to reporters in unmarked white envelopes.

Press suppression was general under three centuries of Spanish rule in the Philippines. In the final years of that rule, revolutionary underground newspapers fired an independence movement that drove the Spanish from power in 1898. It was the time of the Spanish-American War, and the United States moved in, occupying the islands for nearly a decade and then arranging a protectorate that lasted until the Japanese occupation during World War II. Under U.S. control, what came to be known as "Big Business Journalism" came to the islands.[45] Fortunes were made in the newspaper business (although the journalists themselves were poorly paid). During the Marcos regime, media magnates either allied themselves with the dictator or were driven out of business until revolutionary fervor returned again in the 1980s. At first, under the Aquino government dozens of new newspapers emerged, but only briefly. The logic of economics prevailed, and soon newspapers were once more in the hands of the wealthy families that had owned them prior to World War II.[46] Filipino was decreed the official language, yet the twelve largest daily newspapers were printed in English. The American cultural influence was unmistakable. Ninety-five percent of music played on the radio came from the West, primarily from the United States. Fears of cultural imperialism through the media emerged again, boosted by the rise of multimedia conglomerates. And Aquino and her successor, Fidel Ramos, remained committed to the goal of nation building. As the twentieth century neared its close, the Philippines remained in the roster of advancing countries, far from experiencing economic well-being, far from being a unified nation.

The same can be said of the heavily populated Indonesian archipelago south of the Philippines. Journalists were on the firing line there, too, in the struggle for independence from Dutch colonial rule after the Japanese were deposed at the end of World War II. For at least a score of years thereafter, Indonesian newspapers were little more than propaganda instruments for the many political parties vying for control. The government unabashedly earmarked the media as the agents of modernization. It was under the one-party rule of President Sukarno that Indonesia launched the most dramatic effort in the advancing world to promote political and economic objectives through the media. In 1959, Sukarno officially designated the press "a tool of the revolution" in setting up a system he named "Guided Democracy." During his one-man rule, which lasted until 1965, Sukarno maintained iron control of the media under the banner of his own brand of socialism, issuing a series of decrees aimed at creating a frankly propagandistic press utterly free of outside influences.[47] Sukarno's plans included building new training institutes for journalists and locally controlled paper mills. Newspapers remained under private ownership, but their content was "guided" by government officials. After Sukarno was ousted, new press regulations abolished the guided-press structure and installed what the new leader, General Suharto, called a free-press system. However, this rightist system followed much the same lines as the previous leftist model, and the press, although technically free, was forced in self-defense to suppress any information contrary to the philosophy of the Suharto regime.[48]

Suharto's rules required the news media, broadcast as well as print, to operate under an official five-point "ideology" known as *Pancasila*. The word means literally "five principles," and the first article of the Indonesian Journalists Association's code of ethics decrees that the Indonesian journalist "shall be faithful to *Pancasila*." Edward Janner Sinaga, Indonesia's director general for press and graphics, made it clear that Indonesia and its press were officially embarking on a "third way" that rejected both the "liberal and individualistic philosophy" of the West and the "totalitarian Communist philosophy" preached by Moscow and Beijing.[49] Pursuing this doctrine, Indonesia took over leadership of a Third World movement that proudly identified itself as the Nonaligned Nations. Even after the fall of the Soviet Union, Indonesia and a number of allies continued to promote the cause of the Nonaligned Nations.

The five principles of *Pancasila* are directed at achieving a national unity through belief in God, a just and civilized society, democracy, and social justice for citizens.[50] Missing from that list was individual freedom. Four public questions were designated as taboo. Reporters were "consistently reminded" they were to avoid writing stories that "tendentiously or sensationally" dealt with ethnic issues, religion, race, or conflicts between groups. The goal was clearly national unity, for the wrong kind of treatment about those four topics might, Sinaga said, "inflame a situation leading to chaos and political instability."[51] Sinaga set out one of the critical ingredients in advancing world-press philosophy:

> One of the main principles of the *Pancasila* Press System is the importance of freedom and responsibility. Thus freedom is interwoven or intertwined with responsibility. Freedom alone, without responsibility, could result in anarchy. Responsibility alone, without freedom, could lead to totalitarianism, and this is against *Pancasila* philosophy.[52]

Like newspaper publishers in Eastern Europe and throughout the Third World, Indonesian publishers must have a license from the government in order to print. A number of laws govern the issuance of licenses, one of which assures journalists they are eligible to own at least 20 percent of shares in the ninety-four daily newspapers and other publications. We are speaking here, Sinaga says, about a "third major press system" that stands between a Western system of "practically absolute freedom of the press" and a totalitarian system where the press is "a mere tool of the government."[53]

Television, which under the doctrine of development journalism holds great potential for bridging cultural, ethnic, and linguistic gaps, has become a booming industry in Indonesia. It launched a domestic communications satellite in 1956; today, national television programs can be viewed in the capitals of all twenty-seven Indonesian provinces. Two networks operate in Indonesia, one owned by the government, one by private commercial interests. Both operate under *Pancasila*, one by direct order, the other by self-censorship. Five channels (one government-owned, the other four in private hands) are on the air in the Philippines. There, too, the official policy is freedom, but again few producers are willing to risk airing programs the holders of power might perceive as running counter to national unity and development or as not stressing sufficiently Philippine culture and history.[54] Mushrooming chances for profit are too tempting to take risks.

If the potential for profit is substantial in Indonesia and the Philippines, it is monumental in the Southeast Asian peninsula that includes both Malaysia and Singapore, a city-state of 2.5 million covering an area smaller than that of New York City, jutting into the Indian Ocean at the southern tip of the Malay peninsula. From its settlement by the British in the early nineteenth century, Singapore was targeted as a port and transshipment center from West to East and from East to West. Today, Singapore is the second-busiest port in the world, handling nearly 200 million tons of cargo per year. It is also a fixture in the information-society world that is dominated by giant transnational corporations. These conglomerates are engaged in manufacturing, servicing, and shipping state-of-the-art telecommunications equipment and data systems. It may be off-target to speak of Singapore as an advancing country, with its per-capita income of more than $8,000, but it is also true the overwhelming share of Singapore's wealth comes from giant foreign corporations that could, if conditions in Singapore ceased to be favorable, decide to relocate their operations. In 1985, for instance, AT&T (American Telephone and Telegraph) moved its residential telephone-manufacturing operations from Shreveport, Louisiana, to Singapore, where wages were less than one-fourth those paid in Shreveport.[55] This deal meant for Singapore a $30-million capital transfer; not long afterward, the Singapore government awarded AT&T a $41-million contract for a digital-switching project.[56] General Electric is the biggest private employer. All told, transnational corporations have invested some $7 billion in the economy of Singapore.

During the years of Cold War rivalry between the United States and the Soviet Union, Western propaganda often turned to Singapore as a role model to prove the virtues of forward-looking, free-trade capitalist policies and a disciplined labor force. In fact, Singapore was often cited as illustrating a "Third World miracle."[57] In reality, however, the economy of Singapore was propped up not only because of its geographical advantages but also through government ownership of industry and heavy regulations. As one Indonesian writer commented, Singapore's achievement was "the result more of the Long Arm of state intervention than . . . the Invisible Hand of the Free Market."[58]

The Malaysian economy is not doing as well as that of Singapore, but it, too, enjoys the benefits that go with lavish transnational financial operations. Still, in both countries fears of cultural imperialism remain strong. Singapore, worried about "cultural pollution," has banned construction of dishes to provide direct satellite transmission of foreign news and entertainment programs, and all motion pictures and videocassettes are reviewed by censors in an effort to prevent political destabilization or ethnic tension. The government-owned Singapore Broadcasting Company promotes a "speak Mandarin policy" just as Malaysia promotes a "Love Our Language" movement out of fear that Chinese-language media might damage the indigenous culture.

As journalism has become increasingly profitable on the Malay peninsula, the development journalism theory of using the news media to build democracy has declined, in true capitalist fashion. The more profitable the media, the less interest there is in using them as vehicles for social and political change. Polemics must take a back seat to entertainment programs, and news reports grow increasingly sensational in character. Big-business journalism is in full sway. Government controls have not been lifted, but, as John Lent, a leading authority in Asian media, put it, "less noisy forms of control are preferred."[59]

Still, governments do crack down forcefully when they see their interests threatened. The government of Lee Kuan Yew—who ran Singapore with an iron fist for thirty-one years (1959-90) under a Sukarno-like Guided Democracy policy, readily censored newspapers, cut the circulation of foreign papers, imprisoned indigenous journalists, expelled foreign newspeople, and occasionally even killed feared dissidents.[60] Lee's successor, Goh Chok Tong, challenged Merrill Lynch for allegedly leaking information to a business publication in 1992, imposing a chill on reporters that *The New York Times* predicted would bring "new censorship and second-guessing among news organizations, which are not known here for aggressive reporting of domestic affairs."[61] Malaysia, which like Indonesia has established a national ideology (called *Rukunegara*), imposed official censorship in order to head off any repetition of the ethnic riots that shook the country in the early 1970s.[61] The Malaysian government has authorized TV3, a private television operation, and has spoken of privatizing some of its media holdings, including Bernama, its new agency, but it was unlikely this move would lead to public criticism of the government or its policies. Mainstream media have been as reluctant in Malaysia as those in Singapore to oppose official policy or speak against the goals of national unity and the preservation of indigenous cultural values.[63]

Singapore boasts one of the mightiest media conglomerates on earth, Singapore Press Holdings (SPH), an enterprise worth more than $2 billion. It owns *The Straits Times*, a daily founded in 1845, and a host of other publications in Singapore and elsewhere. Moreover, SPH is deeply involved with transnationals. It has a 50-percent share in Matra, the largest book publisher and periodical distributor in France, as well as 10 percent of *The Asian Wall Street Journal*, which is published by Dow-Jones, which in turn owns 3 percent of *The Straits Times* and 20 percent of Times Business Publications, both part of SPH. Through Matra, the SPH holdings include a diversified network of industrial and commercial enterprises. SPH also has a share in publications in Thailand, Hong Kong, New Zealand, Australia, Tahiti, and even Britain, where it owns a 30-percent share of the Marshall Cavendish book publishing house.[64] Not to be outdone, Malaysia, which regularly challenges Singapore as a regional media and information distributor, is in unofficial control of a giant collection of media operations, including Bernama; *The New Straits Times* (in which Singapore's *Straits Times* owns 20 percent); and a number of other business and industrial groups, among them the Fleet Group, whose directors are associated with the ruling government coalition. In theory, the government has no direct control of the news media in Malaysia, although in practice, the media support the government without question.

It is not at all clear what impact development journalism has had on the indigenous population living on the "periphery" in all the countries of Southeast Asia. Old cultural habits and old ideologies die hard no matter how powerfully they are assailed by wealth and the forces of modernization. We turn now to the ancient land of Iran, where modern ideas of development journalism have collided in dramatic form with the old ways.

IRAN AND THE NEW MINIMEDIA

Unlike the other nation-states we have been discussing under the rubric of advancing states, Iran is an old country. It dates back to biblical days, when as Persia it was a mighty power in the civilized world. Nevertheless, Iran has been front and center in discussions about the Third World and especially about the

Western or capitalist idea of development and modernization. Yet, as scholar Edward W. Said has argued, *modernization* may simply be a code word for the maintenance of Western control over what have been seen as underdeveloped nations. In the popular mind in many of those "underdeveloped" countries, Said has said, modernization is connected with "foolish spending, unnecessary gadgetry and armaments, corrupt rulers, and brutal United States intervention in the affairs of small, weak countries." He was responding to statements by U.S. government leaders and academics that modernization theory was "the ideological answer to a world of increasing revolutionary upheaval and continued reaction among traditional ruling elites."[65]

Said's argument was that in the market world, modernization and its parallel concept, development journalism, were rhetorical devices to be circulated as a move to strengthen the power position of capitalist nations in Cold War struggles against the Soviet Union. Smaller countries, especially those in the ancient lands of the Middle East and along the Persian Gulf, were in his view pawns in a power struggle. Market theorists, he wrote, believed their religion Islam exists in "a kind of timeless childhood, shielded from true development by an archaic set of superstitions, prevented by its strange priests and scribes from moving out of the Middle Ages into the modern world."

Traditional culture and religion play a key role. Another Iranian-American scholar, Majid Tehranian, has said the intellectual base of modernization theory lies in both Marx and Freud, who anticipated that the rational discourse of science and technology would ultimately replace religion as central to human existence. However, it hasn't done so. Although modernization has brought many material benefits to urban groups, it has done little for those on the "periphery" who live in a twilight of poverty afflicted by a dearth of material benefits and the shame that goes with backwardness. According to Majid Tehranian, an authority on Iran, people of the periphery have managed to defend themselves mainly by clinging to "the primordial ideologies of nationalism and religion."[66] The instrument of resistance against modernization and the technological marvels of their news media has been, ironically, new forms of media, as modern in scope as they could be—the "minimedia"—the sneaked-in audio and video cassettes as well as transistor radios, copying machines, and personal computers that could not be kept out by even the most watchful security guards.

Bazaars, mosques, and *doreh* were the most popular of Iranian meeting places where news, ideas, and rumors could be shared. The *doreh* is a kind of social club where for many generations professors, students, merchants, and journalists have gathered to talk and pass to one another tales and stories of what was taking place behind the doors in the corridors of power.[67] It was in those places, at public gatherings uncontrolled by the security police, where the oral culture was preserved and smuggled audio tapes could be heard. Adherents of communitarianism are all foes of modernization and the fruit of modern high-tech media; they gathered at the thousands of *doreh* and bazaars and the country's 100,000 mosques and holy places to plot opposition to the most widely-held beliefs in the market world:

belief in the power of the nation-state and in the wondrous opportunities afforded by the products of advanced technology.[68]

Western secularism was alien to communitarian Islamic tradition. Modernization, so widely esteemed among market nations, failed to make major inroads among the general populace in Iran and other Islamic nations because it was unable to elaborate a coherent doctrine that could unite the spiritual and social values at the heart of Islamic beliefs.[69] Power-seeking modern leaders armed with the military and economic might promised by modern technology and supported by market political leaders did their best to suppress traditional values, relying heavily on the big media under their control, but in the end they were unable to conquer the mini-media of the opposition that were used for maximum political and cultural advantage.

Over the centuries, periods of Persian autonomy in the ancient land had alternated with rule by Greeks, Turks, and Mongols. The first Persian-language newspaper, *Akhbar*, appeared in 1837, and it and the papers that followed took on a political and educational function. In the nineteenth century, as British and Russian empires vied for influence, it became a habit for Iranian artists and writers to mark time in Paris, where they joined a society of intellectuals intoxicated by the air of Western liberalism. These Western-educated elites began publishing newspapers in exile, though following a 1911 revolution, many returned home to find themselves in conflict with spokesmen for the traditional Islamic culture holding forth in the mosques rather than the cafés that dominated the French cultural scene. A period of relative press independence followed. During World War I, when Iran assumed a position of strategic significance, the British military moved in to establish a protectorate. Three years after the end of that war, a military coup installed Reza Khan as shah in charge of a new Iranian monarchy. He was forced from power during World War II after collaborating with the Nazis; his son, Reza Shah Pahlavi, succeeded him and, bolstered by his oil economy and solid Western support, introduced many Western, market-oriented ideas.

A fierce opposition movement swept Premier Mohammed Mossadegh to power in 1953, almost toppling the shah. Mossadegh was a colorful figure whose behavior, which was considered eccentric in the West, antagonized the Western-educated Iranian elite and the U.S. and British supporters and bankrollers. Inside Iran, the anti-modernization public applauded his public weeping and his speeches in the *Majles* (Parliament) given from his bed, which he had carried into the chamber. Mossadegh supporters revered him as a skillful spin doctor and manipulator of the press and public opinion. But after he nationalized Iran's rich oil resources, U.S. and British intervention returned the shah to the throne. Nevertheless, Mossadegh had tapped into the country's traditional hatred of foreign ideas of modernization; and his ideas, nurtured by embittered cultural and religious traditionalists, sparked a determined struggle in exile under the leadership of a religious elder, the Ayatollah Khomeini. Mossadegh was captured and kept in prison until his death in 1967.

The news media, not surprisingly, became a critical battleground in the struggle between the shah and the ayatollah. Under the first shah, the media had already lost

A victim of the minimedia, "The Shah Is Leaving": The Ayatollah Khomeini, director of the Xerocratic revolution, reviews headline in Portchartrain, France, announcing the Shah of Iran is out.

SOURCE: UPI/Bettmann

whatever autonomy they had exercised earlier. Censorship had forced opposition papers into exile. Radio was a government monopoly. After Mossadegh's fall, the shah established a national radio-television network and encouraged the growth of newspapers that supported his regime and his determined efforts at modernization. Legal opposition was forcibly ended.

The shah controlled only the formal channel of communications, the Big Media print and broadcast media; he never gained control of the informal channels operating out of the mosques and bazaars under the supervision of the country's religious leaders. In Teheran alone, no fewer than 90,000 clerics were active, each preaching against modernization. Perhaps ironically, it was television with its secular Western-style news programs and entertainment shows that was the enemy. A television serial called "Dear Uncle Napoleon" produced a political uproar by poking fun at religious symbols and nationalism.[70] Police had to quell riots in the street after an explicit sexual act was shown on the air.

The "indigenous traditional information system" remained, however. It had survived a decade or more "of vigorous importation of Western culture and on the crest of a wave of oil prosperity."[71] The counterattack directed by Khomeini and his allies made use of both channels of communication. He had available the traditional channel for reaching people through mosques and religious associations. But the channel of modern media was also available through a kind of "Cassette and

Xerocratic Revolution." Relying on the oral culture of ancient Iranian communitarianism, Khomeini sent message after message to Teheran by telephone and audio tapes; in Teheran, his cohorts copied these messages by the thousands, even photocopying some in government offices; they moved them along through the informal networks to mosques, bazaars, and *doreh*, where news and ideas had circulated freely for generations. Journalists have long been *doreh* members along with professionals, merchants, and students. Dependence on the traditional media of the oral culture stamped the messages with a special aura of credibility. Furthermore, the messages excited the Ayatollah's followers because they frustrated the Shah's vast body of spies and censors.[72] Tehranian noted the irony of multiplying the power of traditional channels with readily accessible inexpensive modern media, cassettes and photocopies, to spread the message of antimodernism.[73]

In fact, once Khomeini had installed his Islamic revolution, he began employing modern media to integrate his country culturally. He dictated a radical change in the content of big media. He banned almost all Western television imports; one show that was allowed was "Little House on the Prairie," which featured tales of morality and religious consciousness in the traditional American West. He ordered sex and violence removed from domestic productions and even shifted the attire of TV announcers from coat and tie to revolutionary fatigues.[74]

As American University's Hamid Mowlana points out, the Islamic community is linked by revelation, not information.[75] It is united by invisible as well as visible bonds. Tehranian said modernization theorists failed because they neglected the need for cultural continuity. They overemphasized "the universal aspects of the transition to modern society," he said, "and underestimated the uniqueness and resilience of cultural traditions in the processes of social change."[76] To reject the idea that information is good is to deny the very essence of modernization and progress. Small wonder the "power" of the big media failed to conquer Iranian communitarianism. Iranian traditionalists observe correctly that information and knowledge are not value-free but transmit, on purpose or not, ethical and moral imperatives. The Islamic theory of *tawhid*, the unity of God, human beings, and the universe, is not receptive to the secular scientific method that is the heart of the Western concept of modernity. It is not that Islam is opposed to science; after all, in the Middle Ages it was Islamic scholars who were at the forefront of scholarship in medicine, mathematics, geography, history, and the arts. Mowlana notes that "what is known as a dark age of the medieval period of Western history was a golden age in the Islamic community."[77] The difference between Western and Islamic science is the difference that divides the ideologies of the market and the community, the individual and the collective. Western culture is rooted in the study of humankind only, Islamic culture in the study of the universe.

Backed by Iran's oil wealth and the deeply committed support of the United States and Britain, the shah poured tremendous resources into his campaign to bring Western modernization to Iran. With all the country's political institutions and the physical instruments of power under his control, the shah and his Western supporters were convinced they could turn the country around and make it receptive to the modern world. Above all, he had complete control over the news media.

Obviously, it wasn't enough to enable the shah to hang on to power. As Khomeini's messages were fed by minimedia to the faithful in Teheran and through the Iranian countryside from his exile base in Paris, the shah fought back with the techniques of modernism: police surveillance and repression and personal exhortations on television. The consummate irony was that the modern technology enabling him to deliver his message in person over television boomeranged badly. Before he went on the air, the Western-educated shah (whose face was unknown to the multitudes) basked in the image created for him by history and which he could himself promote—as the King of Kings, the Shadow of God, the Light of the Aryans. Constant TV appearances stole the mystery and made him vulnerable to the ayatollah and his minimedia.[78]

We will turn our attention to the role of the media in Peru in the next chapter; meanwhile, it is useful to compare media power in Iran and Peru. In both places, one where the cultural tradition is Islamic, one where it is Roman Catholic, attempts by the wielders of political power operating out of modern cities have encountered fierce resistance from the "periphery." Khomeini's minimedia, like the underground communications mechanisms of Peruvian revolutionaries, tried to reestablish the broken links of the fragmented lives of individuals in the high-tech capitalist culture through a larger, collective, cosmic dogma.[79]

The Islamic leadership in contemporary Iran has by no means discarded the modern big media. Instead, they have converted them to their own cause, making them official propagators of Islamic culture.[80] They have banned commercial advertising and American sitcoms; they have required censors to check all program content to make sure it is compatible with the tenets of Islam. "Entertainment and information are recognized as social items and not as neutral manufactured commodities."[81] Khomeini made the point graphically in his last will and testament (made public after his 1988 death), declaring that the glorification of commercial products on Western television produced pessimism in the Iranian public and "Western-style freedom that is condemned in Islam's view and by reason and intellect . . . degenerates the youth."[82]

Nothing illustrates more vividly the vast gulf that can stretch between market and communitarian media belief systems.

NOTES

1. "Declaration of Windhoek," adopted May 3, 1991, by sixty-three delegates. See *Final Report Seminar on Promoting an Independent and Pluralistic African Press* (Paris: United Nations Educational, Social, and Cultural Organization, 1991), cited hereafter as Windhoek.

2. Windhoek, 26.

3. Bernard Wysocki, Jr., "Returning to the Third World: Emerging Nations Revive as Investment Hot Spots, But the Risks Are Hard to Assess," *Wall Street Journal World*

Business Report, September 20, 1991, R1-2. The leading candidates for investment were listed as Southeast Asia (especially Malaysia), Latin America, Eastern Europe, and the former Soviet Union.

4. Jane Perlez, "Stranded by Superpowers, Africa Seeks an Identity," *New York Times*, May 17, 1992. See also article by Michael Chege, "Remembering Africa," in *Foreign Affairs* 71,1 (1992): 146-163.

5. Francis Berg Nyamnjoh, "How to Kill an Undeveloped Press: Lessons from Cameroon," *Gazette: An International Journal for Mass Communication Studies* 46, 1 (1990): 57-75.

6. John C. Merrill, ed., *Global Journalism: Survey of International Communication*, 2nd ed. (White Plains, NY: Longman, 1991), 192. The section on Africa by L. John Martin appears on pp. 155-204. The data on press freedom were compiled from R. D. Gastil, *Freedom in the World* (New York: Freedom House, 1989), and *Country Data Papers: Africa* (Washington, D.C.: United States Information Agency, 1989).

7. Anthony C. Giffard, "The Role of the Media in a Changing South Africa," *International Journal for Mass Communication Studies* 45, 3 (1990).

8. Merrill, *Global Journalism*, 192.

9. Howard French, "Old Habits Are Hard to Break," *Columbia Journalism Review* (July/August 1993): 46-47.

10. French, 47.

11. Wilson Bukholi, interview with the author, Dar-es-Salaam, Tanzania, 1980.

12. "A Father of African Socialism Now Sires Shift to Capitalism," *New York Times*, February 19, 1992. The article was an AP dispatch from Dar-es-Salaam.

13. Ludovick A. Ngatara, "TV for Tanzania," *Intermedia* 18,1 (1990): 38-40.

14. Charles Aloo, "Development of Telecommunications Infrastructure in Africa: Network Evolution, Present Status and Future Development," *Africa Media Review* 2,3 (1988): 19-34. See also Aloo's note about still-unfulfilled plans for a regional African satellite system on p. 28.

15. Merrill, *Global Journalism*, 165-66.

16. Richard J. Barnet, "But What About Africa?" *Harper's*, May 1990: 43-51.

17. Barnet, 48.

18. Wysocki, "Returning to the Third World," R1-10. The data were based on research conducted by the Economic Intelligence Unit, a subsidiary of the Economist Group, London, and International Business Communication, Ltd., London.

19. Barnet, "But What About Africa?" 50.

20. Absolom Mutere, "An Analysis of Communication Policies in Kenya," *African Media Review* 3, 1 (1988): 46-63.

21. Rex Winsbury, "TV in Kenya," *Intermedia* 18, 1 (1990): 35-37.

22. Winsbury.

23. Jane Perlez, "Kenya, a Land That Thrives, Is Now Caught Up in Fear of Ethnic Civil War," *New York Times*, May 5, 1992.

24. From personal notes taken by the author at the Jos conference, April 8-11, 1980.

25. Karl Maier, "Nigerian Military Stops Presses of Critical Magazine Publisher," *Washington Post*, April 21, 1992.

26. "Nigeria's Latest Military Rule Bans Political Activity," Associated Press dispatch printed in *New York Times*, November 18, 1993; Kenneth B. Noble, "First Signs of Resistance to Nigeria Coup Appear," *New York Times*, November 24, 1993.

27. Maier, "Nigerian Military." The author can confirm this fact through a number of interviews and conversations with Nigerian journalisms who cannot be identified by name.

28. Olumuyiwa Ayodele, "Objectivity, Sycophancy and the Media Reality in Nigeria," *Africa Media Review* 3,1 (1988): 106-20.

29. Ayodele, 114. See also Jerry K. Domatob, "Sub-Saharan Africa's Media and Neocolonialism," *Africa Media Review* 3,1 (1988): 149-73; John Osakue, "Domestic Financing of Communication in Developing Countries: A Preliminary Investigation of the Nigerian Case," *Africa Media Review* 2, 3 (1988): 123-33; and Chris Okwudishu, "Patterns of Ownership and Accessibility to Information and Media Facilities in Democratizing the Media in Nigeria," *Africa Media Review* 3,1 (1988): 121-33.

30. Windhoek, 26.

31. Lee Kuan Yew, "Singapore and the Foreign Press," in Achal Mehra, ed., *Press Systems in ASEAN States* (Singapore: Asian Mass Communication Research and Information Centre, 1989), 117-24.

32. John A. Lent, "Mass Communication in Asia and the Pacific: Recent Trends and Developments," *Media Asia* 16, 1 (1989): 16-24.

33. S. K. Ishadi, "Towards the Information Revolution Era," *Media Asia* 16, 1 (1989): 42.

34. John A. Lent, "The Development of Multicultural Stability in ASEAN: The Role of the Mass Media," *Journal of Asian Pacific Communication* 1, 1 (1990): 45-59. See also Syed Arabi Idid, "Malaysia," in Mehra, *Press Systems in ASEAN States*, 42.

35. John A. Lent, "Government Policies Reshape Malaysia's Diverse Media," *Journalism Quarterly* 52, 4 (Winter 1975): 667.

36. Lent, "Development of Multicultural Stability," 53. See also Douglas A. Boyd, Joseph D. Straubhaar, and John A. Lent, *Videocassette Recorders in the Third World* (White Plains, NY: Longman, 1989), 103.

37. See, for instance, Wilbur D. Schramm, *Mass Media and National Development* (Stanford, CA: Stanford University Press, 1964); Lucien Pye, *Communication and Political Development* (Princeton, NJ: Princeton University Press, 1964); and Daniel Lerner, *Passing of Traditional Society* (New York: Macmillan, 1958).

38. Armand Mattelart, *Multinational Corporations and the Control of Culture: The Ideological Apparatus of Imperialism* (Brighton, England: Sussex Harvester Press, 1981), quoted in Richard Shafer, "Provincial Journalists in Third World Development: A Philippine Case Study," *Media Asia* 17, 3 (1990): 125-26.

39. William A. Hachten, *The World News Prism: Changing Media of International Communication,* 3rd ed., (Ames: Iowa State University Press, 1992), 129.

40. Shafer, "Provincial Journalists," 129.

41. Shafer, 128.

42. Adolf J. Amor, "Bribes and Bullets," in *World Media Journal* (New York: Gannett Foundation Media Center, 1990), 77. It remains difficult to identify all the perpetrators; some may have been members of the communist revolutionary movement.

43. Doreen G. Fernandez, "Philippines," in Mehra, *Press Systems in ASEAN States*, 81-82. Much of her information, she says, came from the publisher of *The Philippine Daily Inquirer* and a number of government officials.

44. Amor, "Bribes and Bullets," 74–76.

45. See Fernandez, "Philippines," 57–84, for an excellent brief summary of Philippine press history.

46. Anne Cooper Chen and Anju Grover Chaudhary, "Asia and the Pacific," in Merrill, *Global Journalism*, 223–24: "There are no government owned newspapers. Yet the newspapers tend to practice self-censorship, and journalists are inclined to be protective of the government in power."

47. Oey Hong Lee, *Indonesian Government and Press During Guided Democracy* (Zug, Switzerland: Inter Documentation, 1971). See also John A. Lent, ed., *The Asian Newspaper's Reluctant Revolution* (Ames: Iowa State University Press, 1971).

48. The grumbling acceptance of Suharto's rules were made clear to me in private conversations with Indonesian journalists at meetings held safely beyond the country's borders.

49. Edward Janner Sinaga, "Indonesia," in Mehra, *Press Systems in ASEAN States*, 33.

50. Sinaga, 27–39.

51. Sinaga, 34.

52. Sinaga, 35.

53. Sinaga, 38.

54. Chen and Chaudhary, "Asia and the Pacific," 236–38.

55. Gerald Sussman, "The 'Tiger' from Lion City: Singapore's Niche in the New International Division of Communication and Information," in Gerald Sussman and John A. Lent, eds., *Transnational Communications: Wiring the Third World* (Newbury Park, CA: Sage, 1991), 298.

56. *Asian Wall Street Journal*, November 3–4, 1986.

57. See, for instance, L. Wallerstein, *The Politics of the World Economy* (London: Cambridge University Press). See also Sussman, "The 'Tiger' from Lion City," 280–85.

58. L. Y. C. Lim, "Singapore's Success: The Myth of the Free Market," *Asian Survey* 752–64.

59. Lent, "Mass Communication," 19.

60. Sussman, "The 'Tiger' from Lion City," 299–300.

61. Philip Shenon, "Singapore Inquiry into the Press Entangles Merrill Lynch," *New York Times,* August 31, 1992.

62. Syed Arabi Idid and Latiffah Pawanteh, "Media, Ethnicity, and National Unity: A Malaysian Report," in Mehra, *Press Systems in ASEAN States*, 72–85; Sussman, "The 'Tiger' from Lion City," 299.

63. Idid and Pawanteh, 50–55.

64. John A. Lent, "Transnational Linkages of Singaporean and Malaysian Print Culture," *Southeast Asia Business* 14 (1987): 23.

65. Edward W. Said, *Covering Islam: How the Media and the Experts Determine How We See the Rest of the World* (New York: Pantheon, 1981), 27–29. Said's further commentary continues in the next paragraph.

66. Majid Tehranian, "Communication and Revolution in the Islamic World: An Essay in Interpretation," *Asian Journal of Communication* 1, 1 (1990): 12.

67. Hamid Mowlana, "Technology versus Tradition: Communication in the Iranian Revolution," *Journal of Communication* (Summer 1979): 110.

68. Mowlana, 109.

69. Hamid Mowlana, "The New Global Order and Political Ecology," *Media Culture & Society* 15, 1 (January 1993): 17-18.

70. Tehranian, "Communication and Revolution," 25-27.

71. Anthony Smith, *Geopolitics*, 59.

72. Mowlana, "Technology versus Tradition," 111.

73. Tehranian, "Communication and Revolution," 26-27.

74. Tehranian, 28.

75. Mowlana, "New Global Order," 12-13.

76. Tehranian, "Communication and Revolution," 19.

77. Mowlana, "New Global Order," 14.

78. Mowlana, "Technology versus Tradition," 111.

79. Tehranian, "Communication and Revolution," 16-18. See also Beniger, *Control Revolution*, and C. Geertz, *The Interpretation of Cultures* (New York: Basic Books, 1973).

80. Hamid Mowlana, "The Islamization of Iranian Television," *Inter Media* 17, 5 (October/November 1989): 38.

81. Mowlana, "Islamization."

82. "Imam Khomeini's Last Will and Testament," cited in Mowlana, 39.

Chapter
15

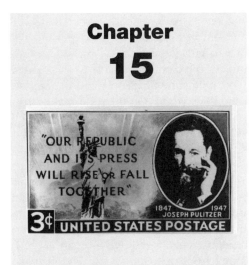

"OUR REPUBLIC AND ITS PRESS WILL RISE OR FALL TOGETHER"

1847 1947
JOSEPH PULITZER

3¢ UNITED STATES POSTAGE

The Advancing Press: Peru

A REVOLUTIONARY PRESS EXPERIMENT

Few countries have led a more troubled existence in the last half of the twentieth century than Peru, a mountainous land of 22 million that lies along the northwest coast of South America and was once the center of the proud Inca empire. It has been forced to cope not only with poverty and exploitation but also with revolution, repression, assassinations, disappearances, drugs, terror, and civil war. Yet there has always been ample room for idealism and quixotic aspirations. In this environment, the story of its remarkable press experiment is sobering though instructive.

As the century drew to a close, Peru found itself the pivotal point of a turbulent mix of violence and anarchy, destruction and hope. Commentators everywhere described the setting as one of mystery, fertile ground for holders and seekers of power eager to use information and misinformation to gain their ends. What was truth and what was distortion, intended or otherwise? It was a life-and-death struggle. Each side sought to manage the news: The rebels set up clandestine newspapers; the authorities shut them down. There were not only two sides; they were many sides, although each side sought to portray itself as virtue incarnate against *the* wicked enemy. We will turn our attention later to the revolutionary movement, *Sendero Luminoso* (Shining Path) and its struggle against the existing Peruvian government; however, first let us review some essential historical background and examine the remarkable but unsuccessful press experiment that was launched in 1968 and has continued to intrigue journalists and editors from the Third World. They see in this experiment the elements of a press policy that might one day contribute to greater understanding among people and nations and help bring about a more peaceful and harmonious world. On the other hand, newspaper publishers in all parts of the Western Hemisphere continue to condemn the Peruvian experiment as one of the most invidious attacks on press freedom in the twentieth century. The truth is more complex.

The Peruvian press developed in a fashion similar to the press throughout Latin America. Peru is one of a score of nation-states that ousted the Spanish in the early nineteenth century after 300 years of harsh colonial rule. Spanish conquistadores subjugated most of Latin America south of the Rio Grande as well as the southwestern part of what is now the United States in the fifteenth and sixteenth centuries. The largest country, Brazil, was colonized by Portugal. These Latin conquerors represented a different breed from the English and Dutch who journeyed to North America. Instead of putting down roots and building a homeland, the Spanish concerned themselves almost entirely with military conquest and expropriation of mineral wealth and labor. Those colonists who stayed behind in the New World did not resemble the yeoman farmers and merchants of North America; rather, they carved out great baronies and lived like grandees. The native Indians became their servants, as did the black slaves they imported from Africa. The grandees made little effort to integrate their servants; they did not educate them or even instruct them in the Spanish language. The feudal society resembled the social order in the Spain the conquerors had left behind; power resided only in the colonial barons and in the Catholic church. Colonial control was total, and it endured until a wave of nineteenth-century revolutions swept through the hemisphere. In country after country the lesser soldiery, assisted by liberal elements of the Church and the few frustrated merchants and intellectuals who inhabited the larger cities, rose up against the grandees and drove them out.

The Spanish rulers were expelled from Peru in 1824. The feudal structure, however, remained largely intact. The rulers who succeeded the conquistadores comported themselves in much the same way as the Spanish before them. They owned the banks, the mines, the great plantations, and the newspapers. The pattern was largely the same throughout Latin America, although in a number of countries, Brazil and Argentina foremost among them, industrial growth weakened the feudal structure more than was the case in Peru.[1] In Peru, illiteracy was high, especially among the descendants of the Incas, the Quechua-speaking Indians who made up half the population and who could not read the Spanish-language papers published in Lima, the capital, or the few regional papers that appeared in the early twentieth century.

Missionaries published a few information sheets in the seventeenth and eighteenth centuries, and a few dailies began to appear in Latin America in 1790, but the first publication to resemble a standard newspaper was the *Gazeta de Caracas,* which appeared in the capital of Venezuela on October 24, 1808.[2]

It was not a true Latin American product since it was published by two print-ers from the United States, Mathew Gallagher and James Lamb. Thus, from the very beginning, the Latin American press was influenced by U.S. newspapers. At the out-set, as with the *Gazeta de Caracas*, newspapers served as agents of the royal gover-nors, yet as revolutionary fervor increased and more publications appeared, they divided into pro-Spanish and pro-liberation instruments, much as did the U.S. press in the revolutionary years.[3] Within a decade or two of the achievement of indepen-dence, however, the Latin American press had settled into the usually comfortable stance of the press—defender of the status quo.

The newspaper industry that arose in nineteenth-century Peru was a mirror of the larger feudal social order. The dominant newspaper then as now was *El Comercio*, the oldest continuously published major daily in Latin America. It was established in 1839 by the Miró Quesadas, one of Peru's most powerful families for a century and a half. As time passed, others among the baronial families acquired newspapers. *La Prensa*, launched in 1905, became the platform for the Beltrán family; *La Crónica*, founded in 1912, passed from the Larco Herrera family to that of the Prados; *Expreso*, a morning paper begun in 1960, and its companion, the afternoon *Extra*, became the publications of the Ulloa family. Each of these families was a powerful force in Peru. Their newspapers, all situated in Lima, were only divi-sions of their banking, commercial, and industrial empires. At the time the Peruvian press experiment was undertaken, the public—at least those elements of the public that paid attention to such things—correctly perceived the country's press as repre-sentative of economic and political power. Pedro Beltrán, the publisher of *La Prensa*, for instance, served as prime minister. Four presidents of the country were members of the Prado family, owners of *La Crónica*. No fewer than forty-five employees of *El Comercio* were members of the Miró Quesada family, whose staunch support of capitalism paralleled that of the government of President Fernando Belaúnde Terry, the man who preceded and succeeded the generals who led the Peruvian press experiment.

Belaúnde Terry headed a mildly democratic government, one far more liberal than the dictatorial regimes that had dominated Peruvian life until the mid-twentieth century. Stability in ruling regimes was as unfamiliar in Peru as it was throughout South America, where palace revolutions occurred with monotonous regularity. Bolivia experienced more than sixty revolutions in the nineteenth centu-ry. Venezuela counted fifty. By 1950, Honduras had undergone 115 changes of gov-ernment in its 125 years of existence. Anarchy, it can be said, was a way of life in Latin America, but these exchanges in rulership scarcely affected the existence of the people; the press seemed equally unperturbed. The Miró Quesadas and the Ulloas conducted business as usual whichever politician ran the country.

While U.S. journalists were promoting the value system of progressivism and endorsing the code of objectivity and political disinterest, their fellows in Latin America were following their own guiding star. To the Latin journalists as well as to the Latin poets and novelists, the literary scene in the United States was chaotic and formless. They admired U.S. technology and know-how, although they deplored what they saw as cultural poverty, the culture of Mickey Mouse and fast-food chains. Still, belief in freedom of the press was as strong among Latin American journalists as among American and European newspersons. Journalists everywhere preach the cause of freedom and demand for themselves the rights and benefits of free expression. However, their definitions of these terms are often so different that the dispassionate observer can see little room for conjoining their thoughts. Journalist Georgie Anne Geyer called attention to one central difference in the viewpoints of journalists in North and South America. In the Latin world, she wrote, "truth seldom stands alone and objectivity does not exist. Everything serves a point of view." Every newspaper, she said, was the vehicle for a political movement, every writer an advocate. Geyer quoted Clemente Marroquín Rojas, a salty Guatemalan journalist who for a time served as his country's vice president, as telling her: "The difference in our ideas of freedom of the press is that you think of it as freedom of information. We think of it as freedom of conscience—you cannot say things that would hurt the country."[4]

The similarity between the views of Marroquín Rojas and those of Kwame Nkrumah and Tom Mboya is readily apparent. The kind of freedom admired throughout the Third World differs sharply from the freedom revered in the United States and Europe. Even India's Jawaharlal Nehru, one of the most passionate defenders of liberty, rejected the critical article of faith in libertarian doctrine that holds the right to free expression ought to be unlimited. Words alone may produce grave international situations, Nehru said, and states must therefore be "armed with the authority to deal with" dangerous language in the press. "We cannot," he said, "imperil the safety of the whole nation in the name of some fancied freedom which puts an end to all freedom." At the same time, Nehru rejected as "dangerous" the suppression of thought, for this might, "besides suppressing a particularly good thing, produce many kinds of evil which stunt the growth of a social group."[5]

The ultimate freedom to Nehru—and to Marroquín Rojas and the majority of the journalists of Latin American, as well as Africa and Asia—is freedom of conscience. *Information is of less importance than thought and the expression of opinion.* It is in this light the press revolution in Peru must be viewed.

In a coup on October 3, 1968, General Juan Velasco Alvarado wrested power from President Belaúnde Terry. In keeping with Peruvian tradition, the coup was bloodless. What was different was that Velasco and the "band of revolutionary colonels" who joined him in the takeover were military leaders of a different stripe.[6] Unlike the aristocratic generals who regularly seized control throughout Latin America, Velasco was an enemy of the feudal barony—and for good reason. He was the son of a street sweeper, a *cholo*, a man of mixed Indian and Spanish blood, part of a social class scorned by the feudal powers. Included among those holders of powers were the owners of the Lima press. Velasco and his cohorts, most of them also *cholos*, had used the army as a form of upward mobility since it was the military and the Church that offered the greatest opportunity for social advancement. The "band of revolutionary colonels" was determined to modernize Peru and shatter the country's social order. It was not entirely clear at the outset, but there was nothing pseudo-revolutionary about the Velasco takeover. Ulloa's *Expreso-Extra* saw the danger to its own position at once and spoke up in opposition; also opposed, but to a lesser degree, was Beltrán's *La Prensa*. For the first year, however, the leading Lima daily, *El Comercio*, supported the regime. In the words of the analyst Robert Pierce, "From its head offices of marble, velvet and gilt went forth editorials calling for restructuring of the government."[7] Pierce's account, in which he gave voice to a somewhat grudging support of Velasco's aims but also assailed much of what Velasco attempted, was one of the most thorough accounts of the Peruvian experience by a North American. U.S. press reports were generally antagonistic, many fiercely so. A score of years later, the *World Press Encyclopedia* wrote that the Peruvian press had "reached its nadir" under the rule of the generals; they had "virtually destroyed every vestige of press freedom."[8] Accounts far friendlier to the experiment were written in the Third World. The most detailed was written from the inside by Carlos Ortega, who assisted in the development of the Peruvian plan; Juan Gargurevich, a Peruvian who lamented the failure of the experiment; and Raquel Salinas, a Chilean who provided a careful account of a noble though lost cause.[9]

The history of the Peruvian adventure is complex and cannot be related in detail here. The plan itself developed slowly over a period of seven years and came to an end with the overthrow of the Velasco regime on August 19, 1975.[10] Velasco himself died two years later. The intellectuals and theoreticians who worked for and with the Velasco regime characterized their movement as one of "revolutionary humanism," drawing equally on nondogmatic and nontotalitarian socialist thought and the heritage of libertarian thought. Moreover, they said, they were "inspired by Christian thought." Thus, they specifically rejected both capitalism and communism and all dogmatisms, "refusing violence as a system." Three "final objectives" were identified: (a) "a participatory political system grounded in the masses," (b) "a pluralist economic system based on a priority sector of social ownership," and (c) "a social system upheld by a combination of components and moral values stressing justice, freedom, work, participation, solidarity, creativity, integrity, and respect for human dignity." In this lofty vision, the role of the press was crucial. Many of Velasco's men looked on themselves primarily as press theorists. A few were journalists but none was a working professional, a fact that engendered contempt among the greater share of Peru's reporters, editors, and publishers.

Velasco's men insisted they launched their revolution with a full-blown press plan in mind but invoked it by degrees rather than imposed it at once. Velasco's foes, on the other hand, maintained there never was a clear plan and measures were put into force as expedients in response to rising criticism. Whichever view is correct, it is nonetheless clear the program did possess a rationale, a philosophical lodestone. Both the print and the broadcast press would free themselves of the domination of the grandees and come under the direction of working journalists and the important interest groups among the public at large. To some degree, this program was reminiscent of syndicalism and the corporate structure popular with Mussolini and other social engineers in the 1920s. Differences were critical, especially in the internationalist demand for cooperation among nations and "for the construction of a real community of free and sovereign countries based on equality."

The Velasco regime's initial press decree, the Statute on Freedom of the Press, imposed a number of limits on freedom of expression, law, truth, moral considerations, national security, and the honor of individuals and families. At the same time, the decree denied the regime the right to censor except in time of war. The order also placed severe limitations on foreign participation in press ownership and on absentee ownership. Actually, the Peruvian decree differed only slightly from a similar order issued in Chile by the liberal regime of Eduardo Frei. The Latin American press and its allies among U.S. publishers generally accepted the Chilean orders without complaint, but across the hemisphere the response to the Velasco order was sharp and fierce.

The Peruvian decree, issued on December 30, 1969, provoked a war of words between the government and the entire Peruvian press. During the next five years, as new orders and decrees flowed regularly from the presidential palace in Lima, opposition increased. So bitter were the attacks from Ulloa's *Expreso* and *Extra* that Velasco expropriated them in March 1970 and converted them into public utilities, handing over their direction to union groups sympathetic to him. Not surprisingly, the Ulloa newspapers then became staunch supporters of the regime. Velasco characterized *Expreso* as "a sort of bulldog that I pushed against the big dailies." The Inter-American Press Association (IAPA), a group of publishers in North and South America, took up the gauntlet from its Miami headquarters and drummed out a steady tattoo of condemnation of the Peruvian experiment. When the Peruvian "Inca Plan" culminated in 1974 with the expropriation of the rest of the country's major dailies, the IAPA criticism rose to a crescendo. It must have given Velasco, the son of a street sweeper, infinite pleasure to respond like this to the IAPA attack: "The organization of owners of newspapers in the continent should know now that today their opinion matters very little in Peru and that their members no longer give orders here."[11]

Nationalization of newspapers and radio and television stations was not an end in itself, however. That came when the news media were declared "social property" belonging to the people. For radio and television, as well as other elements in the telecommunications system—telephones, telexes, and the infant computer industry—control was vested in the government itself so programming might be slanted for "adequate humanistic, cultural, and social training to back up the educational reform and the structural changes required by the development of the country."[12] Although important changes had appeared in the daily newspapers by the time the experiment ended, little had been accomplished in broadcasting, the result, according to Velasco's men, of inadequate time to train radio and television staffers and insufficient opportunity to raise funds for training and developing indigenous production teams to produce programming that rivaled imports from the United States and other industrialized countries. The governments of West Germany and France provided money and training for Peruvian broadcasters, and Velasco's men maintained they were well on their way to remodeling the industry when the ax fell on them. Another unfulfilled goal of the Peruvian reformers was to extend the broadcasting industry from Lima, where all the important radio and television facilities were located, into the countryside as part of a campaign for national integration, much like those that are so intensely desired in Africa.

Under the social property provisions of the Inca Plan, the major dailies were taken away from their owners and turned over to those sectors of the population that could be organized into coherent interest groups (or "sectors"). These were charged with publishing newspapers to interest and inform their readers and at the same time to keep watch on the government to see it stayed on course in its campaign for revolutionary humanism. The plan guaranteed all private citizens and organizations access to the pages of the newspaper no matter what their ideological orientation. None could doubt that the intellectuals who created the Inca Plan were dreamers. Their vision was of a press that was no longer the voice of minority interests or foreign ownership. The same spirit of revolution was abroad on the land, where a number of radical political movements were awakening from slumber.

On two crucial points, Velasco's men made fatal misjudgments. In the first place, they assumed their new "Peruvian press" run by workers rather than grandees would automatically support all their goals. When the journalists failed to live up to those expectations, the planners found their skins to be thinner than they had imagined and began to issue restrictive directives. An even more serious miscalculation was the belief in the reality of the organized sectors—or communities—to which they entrusted direction of the newspapers. In truth, these communities were not organized at all. There had been at best wishful thinking. One day they might have become coherent units, but in 1974 they were not.

Velasco's planners also ignored the traditions of the newspapers. *El Comercio*, whose readership was primarily urban and sophisticated, was assigned to a social community of peasants. *La Prensa*, which catered to agricultural interests, was turned over to industrial workers. And *Ojo*, a paper with a heavy dose of sex and violence, was given over to cultural and fine-arts workers. To Pierce, these designations were made "with either malicious humor or profound stupidity."[13] Ortega admitted the error and blamed insufficient study of the prior readership.[14] The plan was, as one new editor said, filled with "creative audacity" but sadly lacking in practicality. Capitalist analysts have written off the plan as at best a pie-in-the-sky project run by amateur theorists who weren't living in the real world. Although there is certainly some truth in that assessment, it is also true that in the countries of the Third World, Velsaco's experiment became the subject of intense interest and analysis. In these circles, rather than discarding the experiment, the question being asked was, "What went wrong?" or "Why can't it work?"

Others, among them Kurian and the IAPA, condemned the plan as little more than an attempt to solidify authoritarian power by silencing opposition in the press.[15] When the last of the Velasco-induced press regulations were lifted by the Belaúnde Terry regime in 1980, the IAPA saluted the action as "the most auspicious event for the freedom of the press in the hemisphere in the last years."[16] Not only did Belaúnde Terry abolish the old rules, but he also appointed as his prime minister Manuel Ulloa, the owner of *Expreso* and *Extra*, the first papers expropriated by Velasco.

The newspapers were returned to their former owners and directed not to revile the government and to foreswear "the sensationalist, alienating, and venal line which [had] characterized their reporting [and had made them] twisters of the truth, and instigators of disunity among Peruvians." The Left-leaning intellectuals who had been serving as editors of the paper under Velasco were ousted and replaced by conservative journalists. More than 100 staffers were fired.

What could not be known by the journalists of the advancing countries who had watched the experiment with interest was whether it was an aberration, a freakish interlude in the history of the press, or whether it might have been something of greater significance, an augury of what was to come if only the experiment were more skillfully executed. To be sure, nothing worked out as the planners anticipated; and the Velasco regime found itself behaving in ways that were not altogether dissimilar from those engaged in by the grandees of the press before the takeover. Confronted with opposition and resistance by the publishers and many among their staffs, they fired dozens of staffers. Needing support for their ideas from the press and finding little, they began issuing directives about how information was to be interpreted. They did not seize recalcitrant publishers and editors and fling them into jail—that would have been going too far—but they did exile some of them, especially those with foreign connections. Some foreign correspondents were expelled; some were taken into custody briefly. Rather than invoke censorship, the Velasco regime populated the papers with staffers sympathetic to its revolution, though circulation declined so sharply the government was forced to pump in cash to keep the newspapers afloat. Most serious of all, the public sectors to which control of the papers was handed were themselves so weak and poorly organized they were unable to carry out the role assigned to them. Theory was frustrated, as it so often is, by practicality. The question that remained was this: "Was the failure inevitable?"

THE *SENDERO LUMINOSO* AND THE NEWS

The specific programs set in motion by Velasco's planners may have died with the end of their experiment in communal control, yet their legacy is certainly one that would have horrified the bright young men who dreamed of a peaceful land of social, economic, and political justice. Not that the guerrilla movement that named itself *Sendero Luminoso* (Shining Path) claimed descent from the Velasco movement, but it too, aimed at undoing the rule of wealthy landowners and their political cohorts. Terror and deadly violence marked the struggle between the guerrillas and the authorities. Control of information was crucial for both sides, and the role of the news media once again became a critical element in a life-and-death contest.[17]

It is unclear exactly how the tragedy of Peru will play itself out; in any case, a discussion of the profound ramifications of the tragedy is beyond the scope of this book. Our primary concern here is with the role of information and the news media in these events. It is useful to point out how extraordinarily difficult it is for anyone to provide a sound and trustworthy determination of the rights and wrongs

Revolution in the Andes: Three female revolutionaries of the Shining Path (aged 12–15) set their own agenda in the Peruvian mountains southeast of Lima.

SOURCE: Reuters/Bettmann

of the bloody events that have marked the remarkable growth or even the history of the *Sendero* movement. What can be said is that the *Sendero*'s aims and tactics and those of other rebellious left-wing groups were far more bloody and disruptive than those of Velasco's men. Most Western journalists and many scholars believe the *Sendero Luminoso* was primarily a movement of anarchic Andean peasants and

Maoist intellectuals. Just how deeply involved these peasants were at the beginning of the *Sendero* movement is uncertain, but probably not extensively. In any case, the deepest concern about Latin America in the West following the collapse of the Soviet empire was over traffic in drugs, especially cocaine, and it can come as no surprise that much of the information circulated to Western readers and viewers linked the revolutionaries to the drug traffic.

In fact, the activists of *Sendero* and other revolutionary groups have claimed to be foes of the drug culture, even though they found in it two advantages they have carefully nurtured to support their cause. First, in the drug trade there was money to be gained for weapons and other instruments of both terror and communications. This was so because the *Sendero* controlled the intermountain low valleys of Peru where peasant farmers produced the coca leaves that are the raw material of cocaine and its crack derivative. They were able to run a highly sophisticated protection racket, under which the peasants paid the *Sendero* for protection or faced dire consequences.[18] Second, the revolutionaries were convinced, reasonably enough, the drug trade could sap the wealth and the will of the United States, the most powerful defender of the capitalist institutions so despised by the journalists and intellectuals who founded the *Sendero* movement.[19] Combating the drug trade, the Peruvian revolutionaries believed, would damage the American economy.

In early 1992, the United States increased its military aid to Peru by $10 million as the first stage of a policy to help the military fight drug traffickers and the *Sendero* rebels who Washington officials said were involved in the cocaine trade.[20] With the collapse of the Soviet Union, U.S. drug-enforcement agents began to work more zealously than before with the Peruvian police and military in seeking to eradicate drugs and maintain search helicopters. Later that year, after Peruvian President Alberto K. Fujimori declared a national emergency, dissolved the Peruvian Congress, and assumed dictatorial powers, the United States halted its aid program. Fujimori, who had studied mathematics as a graduate student at the University of Wisconsin, brought a greater degree of stability to the government under his stringent one-man rule, and by 1994 the United States appeared ready to resume assistance whenever Fujimori was able to give assurances his government was no longer violating human rights.

In some ways, rank-and-file *Sendero* members seemed to resemble Velasco's planners; many were optimistic dreamers, romantics, and naïve utopians. The American journalist Tina Rosenberg, who gained access to a number of young *senderistas*, found that they saw themselves as pursuing a "people's war," compelled to murder and assassination in order to wrest power away from the "fascist genocidal government."[21] Other rebellious movements gained, including APRA (*Alianza Popular Revolucionaria Americana*), whose left wing split from the main body to launch bloody guerrilla warfare in the jungles of northern Peru. The mainstream APRA, now composed of moderate leftists, won Peru's presidency in 1975 under Alán García Pérez.[22] A third faction, the Tupac Amaru Revolutionary Movement (MRTA), celebrated the ideas of the Cuban revolutionary, Che Guevara. The *Sendero Luminoso*, which revered the ideas of China's Mao Zedong, fought with them all, challenging them as "revisionists," even as they assaulted the "fascists" on the right.[23] Violence became endemic during this period, and the police and the military were as fierce and murderous as the rebels. The toll in lives and fortune was enormous.

The story of the Peruvian civil war achieved at best sporadic treatment in the U.S. press, but when Lima police seized Abimael Guzmán Reynoso, the leader of the Shining Path movement, on September 12, 1992, the U.S. news media jumped at the opportunity to report on and analyze the Peruvian drama. Previous stories about the war had been few, nearly all concentrating on reports of how many people had died or "disappeared" since the violence began. The arrest of Guzmán had a special appeal. A videotape of the reclusive leader could be shown. The television networks, which had pretty much ignored the story, presented the tape and not much else, a sentence or two on the evening news programs, all the stories making sure to label Guzmán a Maoist. The longer newspaper and newsmagazine accounts made much of the Maoist label yet didn't bother to explain what that meant. All the stories were derogatory, describing him in such terms as "murderous ideologue" or "a man known for his ruthless executions" or "the most fanatical Latin America guerrilla leader."[24] "NBC Nightly News" used seven of its thirty-four words to note that Guzmán had been captured with his second in command, a woman.[25]

Bolstered by the capture of Guzmán, Fujimori won a series of close elections, bringing with them a new Congress and a new constitution. Foreign investors saw in a revived Peruvian economy an opportunity for big returns and moved in to buy up TV stations, mines, fishing companies, and airlines. Governments that are stable and authoritarian are usually more attractive to investors than struggling democracies. Leonard Harris, general manager of the Newmont Mining Company, one of the major investors, said his firm was moving into boom times. "The day Guzmán was caught, the country was different." Newmont, which invested $37 million in a gold mine, was producing a million dollars' worth of gold bullion before the end of 1993.[26] The Mexican global network Televisa bought a $22-million controlling interest in a TV channel in Peru. Maintenance of a strong, supportive media was high on Fujimori's list of policy objectives. He went so far as to invite a *New York Times* correspondent to his office along with a delegation of visiting U.S. congresspeople to boast of a decline in guerrilla violence and a drop in the high Peruvian inflation rate. Fujimori said the jailed Guzmán was now "pleading for peace talks."[27]

Human rights organizations remained doubtful about Fujimori's claims of halting the slayings of suspected *Sendero* militants. He himself spoke with pride about his authoritarian rule: "The person who manages the state is me," he said. Ricardo V. Luna, Peru's ambassador to the United States, wrote in *The New York Times* that "crimes committed by individuals in the performance of official duties are sanctioned according to law."[28] Meanwhile, *Istoe*, a newsweekly in nearby Brazil, accused Fujimori of trying to persuade other Latin American countries "to follow Peru's example [so that] traditional democracies will end up in the garbage heap." Informed that in a recent opinion survey 43 percent of Brazilians said democracy was not "fundamental," Fujimori said people in unstable countries are tired of

The first appearance of the captured Maoist revolutionary: Abimael Guzmán Reynoso is shown for the first time on global television.

SOURCE: AP/Wide World

manipulation by politicians and "look at Fujimori as a man who broke the establishment with one blow."[29]

During the first decade of the insurrections, at least 3,300 persons were killed, according to a government report.[30] Amnesty International, which had for years been reporting gross violations of human rights in Peru, said it had documented more than 4,000 "disappearances," blaming these on government security forces.[31]

The organization had, of course, also deplored the terror campaign of the *Sendero* and other revolutionary groups. Figures on the number of those killed in the civil war varied widely, ranging usually from 22,000 to more than 27,000. Nearly all the news stories in Western publications failed to quote any named sources for the figure total. Few mentioned that Amnesty International's reports had blamed the police and military for most of the deaths and disappearances. One headline claimed, "Shining Path Guerrillas Killed 26,000 Since '80," but the story quoted experts as saying it was the *war* that had cost that number of deaths.[32]

Why did the news reports in the United States and throughout the Western world, Peru included, rejoice over the capture of Guzmán? Alan Brinkley, a history professor at Columbia University who studied media reports of the 1992 Clinton-Bush election campaign, offers one explanation that seems to apply. Brinkley acknowledged that right-wing critics were correct when they attacked the U.S. news media for slanting their reporting of the Republican national convention in Houston. There, the news media subjected right-wing speakers to fierce criticism. Brinkley said American journalists saw these speakers as out of the political mainstream as they charged the Left with invoking cultural wars and expressing strident antifeminism, ideas that he said are not "part of the acceptable range of political discourse." Since journalists are not prepared for such ideas, Brinkley said, they have "difficulty in dealing with ideas that they consider extreme."[33] The same might be said about coverage of radical *leftist* ideas as personified by Guzmán and the *Sendero Luminoso*.

The spin from the government officials, academics, and journalists who served as sources was that the capture of Guzmán was a victory for Fujimori and the forces of good. In all cases, Guzmán was described as a power-hungry and bloodthirsty leftist fanatic. Although most of the stories pointed to the widespread poverty in the country, none of them suggested Guzmán and the Shining Path may have had a wide public following or a serious program in mind.

People identified as extremists, whether of the Right or the Left, are rarely given balanced treatment in mainstream news media anywhere. Reporters and editors are men and women of the center, committed to the values of moderates. We find among mainstream journalists few if any bound to objectivity, balance, or fairness when writing about people and movements of the extreme Left or extreme Right. This is not to suggest the U.S. press *means* to be unfair or to turn out slanted news stories. The point is that it is extremely difficult to be fair. The beliefs and attitudes journalists carry around with them were forged long before they became journalists. After all, they were born babies, not journalists, and all the intellectual and emotional baggage they carry around with them is impossible to deposit in the storage locker. Whatever the merits of the opposing forces may be, it is clear the question of "community power" is at the heart of all interpretations of the foundation of the troubles. It is worth making a slight detour to trace the role of "community" as it has developed in Peru. Students of other developing societies will notice unmistakeable parallels, although local differences, some substantial, are inevitable. Let us begin with an examination of social organization in Peru before the arrival of the European invaders who shattered the local native traditions.

José Carlos Mariátegui, an influential journalist-revolutionary who inspired Velasco's planners as well as all twentieth-century reformist leftist groups in Peru, labeled that pre-Columbian social organization "Inca communism" but carefully distinguished it from modern communism. Rather, he wrote, it was rooted in the *ayllu*, a pre-Incan Quechuan word that stands for a group of related Indian families that make up a "community."[34] The Spanish conquerors, Mariátegui said, did their best to destroy the *ayllu*, as did the wealthy landowners who succeeded them. But, he maintained, "the communist spirit" survived, with its characteristic respect for the family and its tradition of working together. It was feudal *individualism* that was the enemy of the Quechuan, who, according to Mariátegui, "never felt less free than when he was alone."[35] Each of the twentieth-century Peruvian reformist movements, whether moderate or radical, has stressed solidarity and cooperativeness over the individual, group freedom over individual freedom—the essence of the communitarian belief system.

Some, perhaps most, of the analysts of the unhappy state of affairs in beleaguered Peru have identified the *Sendero* movement as rooted in what the influential U.S. political scientist David Scott Palmer spoke of as "Inca messianism."[36] The connotation in this widely accepted analysis, one that has been spread far and wide throughout the world, is that the movement is fanatical and irrational, based on an unrealistic "primitive communism" lacking any political goals. Other commentators raised serious doubts about Palmer's analysis.[37] In a perceptive commentary on the *Sendero* scholarship, the analysts Deborah Poole and Geraldo Renique suggested this analysis fits the need of Western academics and governments for uncomplicated explanations that can satisfy puzzled readers and policymakers looking for answers to complex political and cultural questions. Palmer's analysis, they hold, is, among other things, "a response to the market demand for handy conceptual tool kits which can be applied to complex Third World political scenarios."[38] The reference applies with even greater force to the reports of journalists both inside and outside Peru, faced as they are with time and space considerations as well as their own cultural perceptions of a movement that seems to defy rational explanations in a market-society world view. The opportunity for media managers to feed simple explanations to busy journalists is enormous.

The greatest interest of Western governments and readers in Andean countries is with drug traffic. It isn't, therefore, surprising that a new term arose to offer a dramatic, shortcut explanation of a complex question: *narcoterrorism*. This terrifying word links the *senderistas* with drug barons in a way that stirs interest and frightens readers. Here we see sensationalism at work. I am not suggesting the term is a deliberate invention designed to sensationalize the story of Peru (the violent events are sensational enough in themselves) but rather to demonstrate how belief systems so often dictate the interpretations placed on events. As demonstrated by President Reagan's reference to the Soviet Union as the "evil empire," it is not difficult in a market society to see the devil in a communitarian society (and vice versa). One of the leading spokeswomen for the concept of narcoterrorism, Gabriela Tarazona-Sevillano, who has appeared as a visiting scholar at the Hoover Institute at Stanford University, describes the *senderistas* as irrational barbarians.[39] Colleagues claimed they were using the drug trade to work for unification of the entire "Andean nation" in a reign of terror designed to unite the Quechuan nation in a new socialist state.[40] As the Soviet Union was falling, Tarazona disciple Rachel Ehrenfeld saw in Peru, the center of narcoterrorism, a linkage of terrorism, the drug trade, and "the Marxist-Leninist allies" of the Soviet Union in a "deadly symbiosis that tears at the vitals of Western civilization." Rosenberg's portrait of rank-and-file *Sendero* members depicted them as rather ordinary, certainly not barbarians, although prepared to engage in violence and terror in the belief they were responding to violence and terror directed against *them*. Researcher Ronald Berg's conversations with revolutionaries and peasants in the mountain district of Andahuayla showed that even the nonrevolutionary peasants expressed "passive support" for the *Sendero,* viewing them as friendlier and more committed to sound economic change than the military and police.[41]

Amnesty International's frequent reports on Peru demonstrate the ferocity of both *Sendero* terrorists and the government's security forces. According to Amnesty, the *Sendero* has committed widespread atrocities, including holding mock trials and then executing "peasants accused of collaborating with the authorities, members of religious orders, welfare and development workers, and municipal mayors." At the same time, its reports say, the military and police have caused thousands of disappearances and imposed "extrajudicial executions" on thousands of others.[42] The story of Peru is indeed a sad one.

To tell that story, the Peruvian media have found themselves very much in the middle. More than a few journalists have been killed trying to report the story. In fact, one of the ugliest events to play a role in the struggle for public opinion was the 1983 murder of eight journalists.[43] This lamentable event took place in Uchuraccay, a small community in the highland province of Ayacucho, where the *Sendero* movement was first noticed. The journalists, writers, and photographers for the liberal and left-wing newspapers and magazines that had flourished under Velasco had gone to the region to look into the veracity of government reports about atrocities committed against peasants. When their bodies were found, they were without eyes or tongues. The Belaúnde government chose a commission headed by the conservative writer-politician José Vargas Llosa to investigate. The commission's report, which Vargas Llosa described for foreign readers in an article in *The New York Times Sunday Magazine,* blamed the murders on the peasants. He spoke of the peasants as Indians of a violent and archaic culture driven to desperation in their mountainous isolation; besides, he said, the peasants had mistaken the journalists for guerrillas. According to Vargas Llosa, Velasco left a legacy of violence that had muted the democratic spirit and muzzled the press. Further judicial investigations indicated, however, the Vargas Llosa report had been a coverup and "the army had been complicitous if not directly responsible for the killings." Articles in leftist publications pointed out that many of the witnesses to the killings were "disappeared" or murdered during the course of the trial.

What was written in the press and what could be seen on television was a large determinant in the images of Peru both inside and outside the country. Journalists who dug for the truth behind official pronouncements were literally in deadly danger. In the years that followed the massacre at Uchuraccay, many journalists were to die, some under equally grisly circumstances. It was, as already noted, a grim opportunity for media managers. One Peruvian writer, Javier Díaz Canseco, claimed the military engineered the massacre. Not long afterward, the counterinsurgency forces guaranteed their own image would dominate; they barred journalists from the region.[44] According to independent analysts, much of the information reported from the embattled regions was concentrated in the moderate-rightist magazine *Caretas,* which was sympathetic to the government. The ownership of *Caretas* was, as is so often the case in Peru, a family matter. Among the owners were Vargas Llosa and former President Belaúnde. Many Peruvian journalists and nearly all Western reporters relied heavily on the accounts in *Caretas.* As always in such situations, truth became a casualty. With information controlled both by *Sendero* strategists and government imagemakers, it was next to impossible to ferret out the real from the unreal. Moreover, as the journalist Tina Rosenberg observed with vivid imagery, the victims of Peruvian massacres were poor, brown, illiterate Quechuan villagers who lived in places where few journalists went or were allowed to go. "Their widows," she wrote, "do not issue press releases. . . . They are usually too terrified even to give their accounts to a local investigator in the unlikely event there is one. . . . If they do try to protest, their echo does not travel far; the wall between Peru's Indians and the typical newspaper reader is insurmountable."[45]

THE REPORTER IS "A REPORTER . . . NOT A POLITICIAN"

Of the many objections to the Peruvian experiment raised by publishers in both North and South America, perhaps the most important was to its frankly political coloration. The "news" was to be presented in such a way as to educate and instruct the readers toward the specifically described ends of "revolutionary humanism." In this, Velasco's men were pursuing ends not markedly different from those espoused by Nkrumah and Nyerere or even Greeley and Pulitzer. Those American publishers, however, lived in a different time frame, before market press ideologues had firmly embraced the apolitical value system. Exporting the apolitical value system to the Third World was clearly of major importance to the press of the industrialized countries and also the political and economic forces that exercised power in those nations. The Cold War programs of capitalist and socialist nations had for more than a generation pushed for Third World support for a press ideology sympathetic to their political and economic goals.

The puzzlement of Third World journalists over the contradictions between the objectivity model of the capitalist media, whose technology and skills they much admired, and the political model of the communitarian media, which was more to their ideological liking, is illustrated in a booklet by Frank Barton, who directed the Africa Program of the International Press Institute (IPI) in the 1960s. His trainees, Barton reported, were tormented by "the clash of loyalties between journalism and what might be called the African idea." The IPI, an association of publishers from capitalist and Third World nations, endorses with ferocity the American model in which journalists observe and report what they see and are told but avoid with painstaking patience the expression of their own political views. A major training manual supplied to African journalists by the IPI makes the point graphically: "A Reporter is just that—a reporter. He is not a writer. . . . And most important of all, he is not a politician."[46] Peter Golding, a British researcher calls attention to the pervasive guilt that afflicts advancing-nation journalists when they are indoctrinated into the creed of objective reporting as it is preached in European and American media.[47]

The BBC and French broadcasting (and newspaper) models have been a strong influence in Asia and Africa, but in Latin America the primary influence has inevitably been the U.S. model. Consequently, advertising has been of far greater significance to the mass media of Latin America than to those of Asia and Africa or even those of Western Europe. Radio and television broadcasting, more advanced in Latin America than in Asia and Africa, is almost entirely financed by advertising. It was partly to eliminate the influence of advertisers that the Velasco experiment was conducted in Peru.

To the supporters of the capitalist press system, the prevalence of advertising as a financing agent frees the mass media from direct control by the government.

Seeking the attention of the people of the advancing nations: In remote Bhutan, a young woman runs the radio station sending electronic messages to the people.
SOURCE: Unesco/C. A. Arnaldo

Yet even where advertising pays the freight for broadcasting, governments assert control, usually indirectly (as in Western Europe and Japan and even in the United States) but sometimes directly and forcefully (as is usual in Africa and Asia and often in Latin America). The relationship of advertising to government control has varied in different parts of the capitalist world, although the political and economic interests of the advertisers and the governments have been sufficiently congruent that they have almost always operated in comfortable harmony. In the commercial arena, governments and advertisers are partners in control. Consensus works for the mutual benefit of governments and commercial interests. In Latin America, where palace revolutions have been common, the printing and broadcast of commercial notices have continued without interruption from one government to the next. Where presentation of news is financed by commercial interests seeking profits, tyrannical governments usually can go right on operating without fear of a media challenge to their control.

In Peru, of course, commercial interests lost their control of the daily press under Velasco; advertising of commercial products and services continued on radio and television even after these media were placed under direct government control. The Velasco regime imposed numerous restrictions on the freedom of action of journalists; and the lifting of those restrictions by the successor Belaúnde Terry government drew applause from the Peruvian journalists employed by the post-Velasco newspapers. "We now have complete freedom of the press," an editorial writer for *El Comercio* exulted two years after Belaúnde's election. Yet, under questioning, he acknowledged the freedom was not in fact complete. It was permissible to make any kind of comment on foreign affairs—even communist journalists were accorded that privilege—but it was not acceptable to discuss certain aspects of the political or economic situation in Peru.[48] However, such restrictions did not disturb the editorial writer. Why should they desire to offend their readers? *El Comercio*, after all, supported the president and his prime minister, the owner of *Expreso* and *Extra*.

Governments everywhere have restricted the freedom of action of editors and publishers when vital interests were considered threatened. Sometimes repression has been harsh. History is full of tales of martyred journalists who have gone to their deaths defending their right to speak their minds; and governments have fallen because of public anger over restrictive press policies. Belief in freedom of expression seems to be deeply held everywhere. In the Third World, however, self-restraints have often been imposed by the journalists themselves in order to ensure a unified social and political order.

That tyrants have made use of this belief to manipulate the press to their own ends is well known. Third World mass media that suffer repression and official terror at the hands of dictatorial regimes receive a lot of sympathy and support throughout the capitalist world. But supinely climbing into bed with those regimes solidifies the contempt for the advancing nations' press often expressed in the West. To media analysts in the United States and Western Europe, press aspirations in the Third World—as, for example, in Peru—have been hypocritical. A developmental press has come to be equated with one in which the government exercises tight control and prevents freedom of expression in the name of noble ends. The Indonesian press provides a clear illustration. Journalists from the advancing nations sometimes share the view of the West, especially when their governments engage in unexpected acts of repression. Certainly, belief in the goals of Nehru and other democratic statesmen was shaken during the censorship imposed by Indira Gandhi in 1975. It was not in India alone that the advancing press was affected; if censorship could be imposed in the most modern press system in the advancing world, who was exempt? Even after the "emergency" censorship was lifted two years later, advancing-world press ideologues spoke of the future with the most cautious optimism, as did the delegates to the African colloquium at Windhoek and the Russian colloquium at Sochi.

Despite the censorship, many Indian journalists sneaked into their news columns words, phrases, and even sentences and paragraphs that escaped the attention of the censors and conveyed concealed meanings to knowledgeable readers. In this, they were following the practice Karl Marx employed to outwit the Prussian censors more than a century earlier. The capacity to convey hidden and double-meaning phrases seems to be one journalists master in all parts of the world. Freedom to say what they want may be denied journalists; but, as Marx pointed out, so long as the press and the public share an interest in the communication of information, that information will emerge in one form or another.

Such communication was raised to an art form in Brazil, the largest and most powerful country in South America, during the scores of years it spent under dictatorial military control. Military censors appeared in the newsrooms of Brazilian newspapers to make sure no information unacceptable to the government was printed. When the papers were finally locked up ready for printing, the censors read through the editions, accepting some articles and rejecting others. In addition to attempting to sneak in unwanted material, hostile editors sought to hit back at the censors. In the early years of censorship, editors printed their papers with columns of white space clearly indicating censored material. When the government cracked down on that practice, the editors responded by filling censored columns on the front page with recipes and advice to the lovelorn. The most original ploy used in Brazil was conceived by the humor magazine *Pasquim*, which found a way to criticize the government without appearing to do so. In condemning the Brazilian military, it simply substituted for *Brazilian* the word *Greek*. In the takeover of Greece by right-wing military leaders in the late 1960s, *Pasquim* found a suitable target for attack. It regularly published articles charging the "Greek military government" with violations against democratic principles, human decency, and press freedom. Its readers were well aware that *Greek* was a code word for *Brazilian*, but it took the authorities a year or more to figure it out. The publication was ultimately suspended and its editors thrown into prison and tortured, but they had made their point, and to them that may have been reward enough.

Brazilian censorship was never carried out well. No more than ninety censors were ever employed at one time, a number scarcely adequate to police the entire press. However, penalties were severe; and, for the most part, the editors were careful to avoid antagonizing the leaders. They played it safe, as so many advancing-nation journalists do, by censoring themselves. The majority of the Brazilian press did not push too hard. Among other factors, the editors were unnerved by the erratic nature of the censorship program; they didn't know when they would be censored and when they would be able to get away with incautious reports. In 1977, the government lifted the "state of siege" and replaced it with a "state of emergency." Direct censorship was relaxed, but the restrictions were by no means lifted. The military leaders had become more skillful; whenever they found a publication straying, they called in the publisher for drinks and dinner and a friendly word about subversive comments stealing onto pages. In the name of social responsibility, they said, such practices had to stop. The publishers, powers in Brazil like their colleagues in Peru and throughout the hemisphere, then took over the censorship role themselves. Hostile working journalists nevertheless kept pushing: "I always go one step past the limits," one Brazilian editor confided. "Not too far, but I am always trying." It was a matter of how "social responsibility" was defined.[49]

NOTES

1. The relative backwardness of Peru can be attributed in part to the difficulty of building roads through the mountains. The railroad network developed in Peru in the mid-nineteenth century was superior to that in other sections of the continent, however, and by the later years of the century, more information was flowing from the capital of Lima into the hinterlands than from other capital cities in Latin America.

2. What was probably the first daily newspaper in Latin America appeared in Peru in 1790 in the form of the short-lived *El Diario de Lima*, founded by a Spaniard. It was followed a year later by the biweekly *El Mercurio Peruano*, established by a group of liberal Peruvian intellectuals as a literary forum. It later served as an instrument for political independence.

3. Gonzalo Soruco, "Press Development in Venezuela and the Lippmann Model," unpublished paper presented at annual convention of Association for Education in Journalism, Boston, 1980.

4. Georgie Anne Geyer, *The New Latins: Fateful Change in South and Central America* (Garden City, NY: Doubleday, 1970), 57.

5. Donald Eugene Smith, *Nehru and Democracy: The Political Thought of an Asian Democrat* (Bombay: Orient Longman, 1985), p. 138.

6. Geyer, *New Latins*, 261.

7. Robert Pierce, *Keeping the Flame: Media and Government in America* (New York: Hastings, 1979), 119–45. Pierce makes a strong effort to treat the topic objectively but seems to be plagued by a sense of "us vs. them" polarization, and fails to see the critical nuances involved.

8. George Thomas Kurian, "Peru," in *World Press Encyclopedia*, vol. 2 (New York: Facts on File, 1982), 735–39. Kurian, demonstrating the passion of the foes of the Peruvian experiment, saw the Velasco years as "a case study of survival" for the Peruvian press, and added: "In a bitter decade-long confrontation with an authoritative regime, [the press] proved its essential indestructibility. Where the press is threatened, the Peruvian experience should be an encouraging lesson."

9. Carlos Ortega, *Communication Policies in Peru* (Paris: Unesco, 1977). The account of the press role in the Velasco Experiment draws primarily from Ortega's history. See also Juan Gargurevich, *Introduction a la historia de los medios de communicación en el Peru* (Lima: Editorial Horizonte, 1977); Raquel Salinas, "Development Theories and Communication Models: A Critical Approach," unpublished paper presented at a conference of the International Association of Mass Communications Research (IAMCR), 1980.

10. The overthrow of Velasco was accomplished by General Francisco Morales Bermúdez, who had served as prime minister and had assumed increasing powers after Velasco's health declined.

11. Ortega, *Communication Policies in Peru*, 23.

12. Ortega.

13. Pierce, *Keeping the Flame*, 127.

14. Ortega.

15. Kurian, "Peru," 738, summarized this view in an ironic passage: "The crowning rationale was the time-honored definition of the press as a public service. What could be better than that such a public service should be controlled by that most public of all institutions, the government itself? Velasco went further and claimed that freedom of expression never existed in Peru and therefore hardly needed to be taken away. Freedom of the press, he said, was only freedom for the businessmen and families that owned it."

16. Pierce, *Keeping the Flame*, 133.

17. Susan C. Bourque and Kay B. Warren, "Democracy Without Hope: The Cultural Politics of Terror in Peru," *Latin American Research Review* 23 (1988): 7-34, refs. 17-25.

18. Deborah Poole and Geraldo Renique, "The New Chroniclers of Peru: U.S. Scholars and Their 'Shining Path' of Peasant Rebellion," *Bulletin of Latin American Research* 10, 2 (1991): 133-91, ref. 172. The authors quote Raul Gonzáles, "Coca y subversión en el Huallaga," *Quehacer* 48 (1990): 58-72, as an authoritative account of the *Sendero* and the drug trade.

19. Many of the ideas of the Peruvian left (revolutionaries, democrats, and activists alike) derived from the writings of José Carlos Mariátegui, the essence of whose writings can be found in *Seven Interpretive Essays on Peruvian Reality*, trans. Marjory Urquidi (Austin: University of Texas Press, 1971).

20. Clifford Krauss, "In Shift, U.S. Will Aid Peru's Army Against Drugs and Rebels," *New York Times*, January 25, 1992.

21. Tina Rosenberg, *Children of Cain: Violence and the Violent in Latin America* (New York: William Morrow, 1991), 143-215, ref. 154.

22. Peter Klaren, *Modernization, Dislocation and Aprismo: Origin of the Peruvian Aprista Party, 1830-1932* (Austin: University of Texas Press, 1973).

23. For an insightful review of the growth of the post-Velasco left in Peru, see Ronald H. Berg, "Sendero Luminoso and the Peasants of Andahuaylas," *Journal of Interamericans Studies and World Affairs* (1986): 165-96. The literature in the field is extensive. See, for instance, the influential work of David Scott Palmer, ed., *The Shining Path of Peru* (New York: St. Martin's, 1992), and Cynthia McClintock, "Why Peasants Rebel: The Case of Peru's Sendero Luminoso," *World Politics* 37 (1984): 48-84.

24. J. Herbert Altschull, "Fairness, Truth and the Makers of Image," *Media Studies Journal* (Fall 1982): 7-8.

25. Altschull, "Fairness," 8.

26. Nathaniel C. Nash, "No Longer a Pariah, Peru Is Being Recast As Business Magnet," *New York Times*, November 2, 1993.

27. James Brooke, "Dictator? President? Or General Manager of Peru?" *New York Times*, November 25, 1993.

28. Richard V. Luna, letter to editor, *New York Times*, September 4, 1993.

29. Brooke, "Dictator?"

30. *New York Times*, January 12, 1992, reported this figure as announced by a commission in the Peruvian Senate. It is unlikely the exact number of victims will ever be known. Statistics vary depending on the sources.

31. *Peru: Summary of Amnesty International's Concerns Since 1983* (London: Amnesty International, February 1992).

32. *The Evening Sun*, Baltimore, September 14, 1992.

33. J. Herbert Altshull, "Fairness, Truth, and the Makers of Image," in Media Studies Journal (Fall 1992), 6.

34. Mariátegui, *Seven Interpretive Essays*, 75.

35. Mariátegui, 57-58.

36. Poole and Renique, "New Chronicles of Peru," 138. It is difficult to know which Palmer book or article is referred to.

37. Steve J. Stern, ed., *Resistance, Rebellion and Consciousness in the Andean Peasant World, 18th to 20th Centuries* (Madison: University of Wisconsin Press, 1987). See especially chapter 7.

38. Poole and Renique, "New Chronicles of Peru," 165.

39. Gabriela Tarazona-Sevillano with John B. Reuter, *Sendero Luminoso and the Threat of Narcoterrorism* (New York: Praeger, 1990). The foreword is by David E. Long of the U.S. Coast Guard Academy.

40. Gordon H. McCormick, "The Shining Path and Peruvian Terrorism," in David Rappaport, ed., *Inside Terrorist Organizations* (New York: Columbia University Press, 1988), 109-26.

41. Berg, "Sendero Luminoso," 165-96.

42. "Peru," *Amnesty International Annual Report*, 1992, 213-16. See also frequent "Urgent Actions" publications from Amnesty International, all of which deplore violations of human rights by governmental authorities. These reports also cite the murder of thousands of "defenseless civilians" by the *Sendero* and a smaller number of additional killings by Tupac Amaru.

43. Many accounts of this event are available. See, for instance, José Vargas Llosa, "Inquest in the Andes," *New York Times Sunday Magazine*, July 31, 1983, 18-23; Cynthia McClintock, "Why Peasants Rebel," 48-84; Bourque and Warren, "Democracy Without Hope," 21-22; Poole and Renique, "New Chroniclers of Peru," 138, 179. Some of the cited sources seem bizarre. For instance, McClintock cites the right-wing mercenary magazine *Soldier of Fortune* for estimates of the *Sendero*'s strength and organizational culture.

44. Javier Díaz Canseco, *Democracia, militarizacion y derechos humanos en el Perú, 1980-84* (Lima: Servicios Populares [SERPO] y Asociación Pro Derechos Humanos, 1985), cited in Bourque and Warren, 22.

45. Rosenberg, *Children of Cain*, 202.

46. Frank Barton, *The Press in Africa* (Zurich: International Press Institute, 1969).

47. Peter Golding, "Media Professionalism," 301.

48. Conversation with a Peruvian journalist who would not authorize the use of his name, Berlin, 1982.

49. Conversation with the author, Berlin, 1982.

PART V:

FREE FLOW AND BALANCE IN THEORY AND PRACTICE

Chapter

16

"OUR REPUBLIC
AND ITS PRESS
WILL RISE OR FALL
TOGETHER"

1847   1947
JOSEPH PULITZER

3¢ UNITED STATES POSTAGE

The World Challenge
for Fairness in Expression

THE QUARREL OVER "FREE FLOW OF INFORMATION"

News and opinion reporting has rarely descended to a lower level than it did in
dealing with the story of "a new international information order" during the last
quarter of the twentieth century. No other story illustrates more clearly the linkage
between news and politics. It is filled with overtones and undertones of racism,
colonialism, ideology, and power politics. It is shot through with the perhaps insurmountable difficulty of squaring emotional realities and concrete reality. The setting
for this lugubrious portrait of journalism was, ironically, an international organization that had been created with the hope of encouraging a global brotherhood and
sisterhood for the peoples of the earth. The role of the news media in striving for
the French Revolution's goal of fraternity was considered central by the organization's founders. The moral doctrine advanced in every resolution and every policy
developed by the organization was the doctrine of brotherhood through social
responsibility. What happened? How did the world press fall so short of achieving
its dreams of moral grandeur? How was its reporting so barren, so incorrect, and so
inclined to deepen rather than bridge the rifts between races, between nations, and
between ideologies? How did the news media go so wrong? This book attempts to
answer that question.

The organization referred to here is Unesco (United Nations Educational, Scientific, and Cultural Organization). It was inside Unesco, one of the subsidiary institutions established under the United Nations in the years following World War II, that the concept of a new world information order surfaced in the 1960s. The story of how this concept arose, flowered, and died was examined at length in an earlier version of this book.[1] The details of these events will not be repeated here. Our desire is to place the broad lines of the story in focus and to stress what is to be learned from these events about Unesco; about world organizations in general; and about the relationship between news media and political forces in the real world, where human beings are driven more by passions than by rational thought. So bitter were the confrontations inside Unesco, so subversive were the news stories about the proposed new information order, that the United States and, later, Great Britain withdrew from membership, plunging the organization into financial disarray.

Theoretical and philosophical questions about the nature of a mass press and about the flow of information had grown more and more emotionally charged with the breakup of the old colonial empires, the establishment of the United Nations, and the growth of interest in information as a tool of development in new nations. These questions took on an increasingly political coloration; and, ironically, it was inside the cultural arm of the UN that the politics of news exploded.

In creating the UN in 1944 and 1945, the founders anticipated that the critical political issues facing the nations of the world would be hotly debated inside the Security Council and the General Assembly. But they believed also that the UN family, especially Unesco, would win universal support for weaving patterns of global cooperation to help resolve the challenges that face all humankind. Interestingly, despite periodic outbursts of acrimonious debate among politicians and journalists, the Unesco organization itself has remained united in its vision of the news media as instruments to bring about an age of global cooperation.

Unesco is mainly involved in scientific, literary, artistic, and educational matters; news and other communication issues occupy less than 7 percent of the organization's attention.[2] Officials at its Paris headquarters tend to feel dismay and sometimes anger over what they correctly believe to be misrepresentation in the press, especially in the United States, about the organization's mission.

Proposals for a "new international information order" follow more than a decade of discussions aimed at increasing the free flow of information around the world; at the same time, the so-called less-developed countries campaigned to redistribute the world's wealth under the banner of a "new *economic* order." The flow of information had been recognized as a significant topic for the United Nations from its inception. Members of the international organization, without notable exception, have endorsed and promoted the philosophy of a free press, although the definition of *free press* may well be less than universal. Of all the statements of principle by the UN, none is more sweeping than a 1948 declaration asserting the rights of each individual in the world to *know*, to *impart*, and to *discuss*. Each of these is an element in a doctrine of free expression, but each is also capable of being interpreted in many ways, and lamentably also of being distorted consciously or unconsciously. The heart of the declaration's goals is contained in Article 19, which says: "Everyone has the right to freedom of opinion and expression; this right includes freedom to hold opinions without interference and to seek, receive and impart information and ideas through any media and regardless of frontiers."[3]

For a quarter of a century, Unesco sought ways to implement the goal set forth in Article 19; many hundreds of conferences were held, bringing together scholars, journalists, government officials, and media authorities. At its biennial conferences, Unesco has adopted many resolutions, virtually all of them with the objective, stated or implied, of raising levels of information in all parts of the world to increase knowledge and understanding and to help prevent war and expand the rights of individuals, groups, and nations.

Despite a steady increase in the number of news outlets around the world and a steady rise in the literacy rate, the communication of news is not today a salient factor in the lives of most inhabitants of the planet. Unesco has set a minimum standard of "adequate communications," yet much of the world is nowhere near its target. In 1961, Unesco proposed that for each 100 inhabitants of a country, the minimum standard be at least ten copies of daily newspapers, five radio receivers, and two television sets, a standard that remained unchanged more than 30 years later. In 1961, it was estimated it would take Asia at least until 1992 and Africa until 2035 to reach that goal.[4]

Despite the gains in the number of mass-media outlets in the new nation-states, the industrialized countries of North America and Europe, together with Japan, continue to dominate the field. For example, in 1989, the total consumption of newsprint in the world amounted to 32,100,000 metric tons; of that total nearly half—14,300,000 metric tons—was consumed in the United States and Canada. Consumption in Europe, including the Soviet Union, was 8,300,000 metric tons. Of the total world consumption, the industrialized nations accounted for 85 percent. Per-capita consumption of newsprint in Africa actually declined 0.3 percent between 1970 and 1990; in Asia the figure was up 0.7 percent. The industrial countries increased their share of the world newsprint supply by 4.4 percent.[5]

The accompanying graphs and tables approximate reality but cannot be taken as absolute. They are based on figures reported to Unesco by the member governments and illustrate a comparison over a protracted period. Comparisons are frustrated not only by the different statistical methods used in various countries but also by the fact that in some years certain countries did not report at all. Nevertheless, the statistics taken as a whole illustrate the nature of the imbalances and point to two of them: the gap between technological advances in the northern and southern hemispheres and the continuing chasm between present reality and Unesco's goals.

Unesco itself is an intergovernmental organization and cannot act on its own. Like all other international bodies associated with the United Nations, including the UN itself, Unesco provides a platform for discussion and recommendations. It is meant to be, as Director General Federico Mayor has said, "the intellectual component of the United Nations system."[6] Unesco may take certain actions, but only if those actions are approved by its member nations. One of the chief sources of misunderstanding that has dogged the efforts of Unesco staffers has been criticism of the organization for proposals and recommendations made by outside

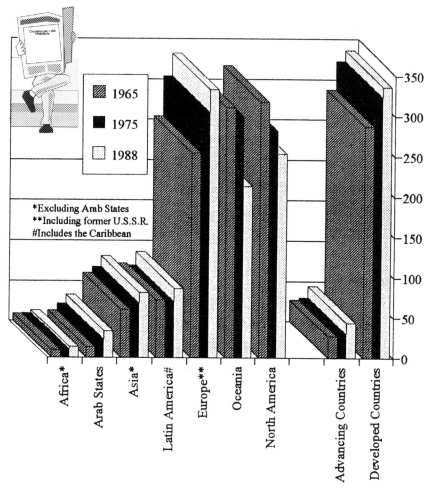

Daily newspaper circulation per 1,000 inhabitants.

SOURCE: Peter Shayotovich

participants in conferences and meetings conducted under its auspices. Such participants are, of course, not Unesco offiicials, and their statements do not represent Unesco policy.

The genesis of the Unesco discussions about free flow of information came, like so many ideological issues, from concrete events, in this case primarily World War II and the ensuing power struggle between the United States and the Soviet Union. One of the earliest statements of the issue derived from Nazi Germany's co-opting of the press and other communications facilities for use as instruments of propaganda without which, some felt, Hitler and his Fascist regime might never have been able to rise to power. Many journalists and the U.S. government argued that only a society with access to the "free flow of information" can be free. In the years that followed the victory over Germany, the free-flow issue became a central part of the Cold War.

TABLE 16.1   Daily Newspapers—Estimated Circulation (in millions)

	Estimated Circulation		
	1965	*1975*	*1988*
Africa*	2	3	6
Asia*	70	90	150
Arab States	1	3	7
Europe**	170	220	332
Latin America†	20	20	40
North America	70	70	70
Oceania	5	6	5
Developed Countries	290	360	410
Advancing Countries	40	60	120
World	330	420	530
	Circulation per 1000 Inhabitants		
Africa*	9	10	13
Asia*	60	68	81
Arab States	13	22	33
Europe**	254	304	332
Latin America*	72	70	86
North America	317	281	253
Oceania	310	299	213
Developed Countries	287	323	336
Advancing Countries	27	30	44
World	128	133	132

*Excluding Arab States
**Including the former U.S.S.R.
†Includes the Caribbean
SOURCE: This table is drawn from summaries provided by the Section of Statistics on Culture and Communication, Division of Statistics, 1989-1992, Unesco, Paris.

There was little new in these discussions. The subject of freedom of expression was at the heart of the troubles of Socrates and Galileo and of Milton and Voltaire. It was an issue of great importance to the Founding Fathers of the United States and in the drafting of the First Amendment. Now, however, these discussions became global and were cast in the context of nation-states. The free flow of information was, as the U.S. State Department asserted, "an integral part of our foreign policy."

The new nation-states of Asia and Africa, convinced they had been denied free flow of information by their former colonial masters, found in the arguments for free-flow doctrine a vehicle to use against those same countries and their domination of the means of communication. It is doubtful the new nation-states needed the coaching, yet they got it nonetheless. As early as 1944, before World War II had ended, the directors of the American Society of Newspaper Editors issued a statement endorsing government policies that would remove all barriers—political, legal, or economic—to the free flow of information. In 1945, while the war was still

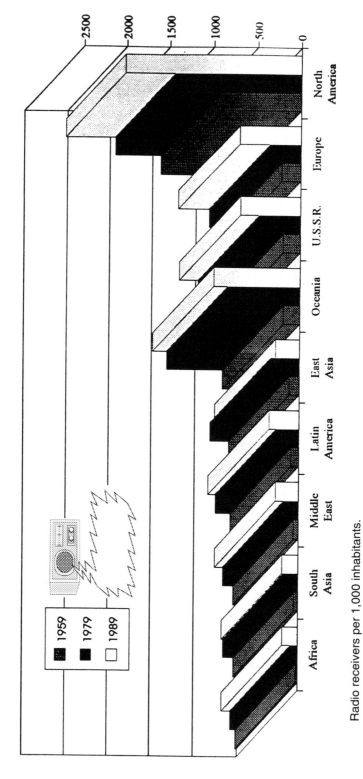

Radio receivers per 1,000 inhabitants.

SOURCE: Peter Shayotovich

TABLE 16.2   Total Radio Receivers (in millions)

	1959	1979	1989
Africa	4	35	105
North America	177	476	551
Latin America	18	105	146
East Asia	16	90	353
South Asia	8	38	159
Middle East	—	29	53
Europe	91	209	337
Oceania	3	19	26
U.S.S.R.	41	126	194
World	358	1127	1932
Receivers per 1,000 Inhabitants			
Africa	18	80	177
North America	903	1437	2016
Latin America	89	259	342
East Asia	113	326	274
South Asia	46	167	182
Middle East	53	172	263
Europe	216	352	701
Oceania	186	823	984
U.S.S.R.	194	473	686
World	159	448	375

SOURCE: This table is drawn from summaries provided by the Section of Statistics on Culture and Communication, Division of Statistics, 1989-1992, Unesco, Paris.

going on, a delegation of American editors, joining with representatives of the two major U.S. news agencies, traveled to twenty-two countries to carry tidings of the free-flow doctrine. A conference of Western Hemisphere leaders in the spring of 1945 endorsed the free-flow doctrine, and when Unesco was created, its constitution, largely composed by U.S. representatives, called for the promotion of "the unrestricted pursuit of objective truth, and . . . the free exchange of ideas and knowledge."[7] As new nation-states were created, they, too, enthusiastically endorsed the free-flow doctrine, but they meant something quite different from what the United States and its allies had in mind.

The difference from the outset was essentially economic. Few can doubt the honesty and good intentions of both sides in the dispute about free flow over the years. Each side has perceived the world in such different ways, so locked into its own ideological stance it has seemed incapable of comprehending the other side's point of view. Although all parties believed in the intrinsic value of free exchange of information, free flow to the United States and its industrialized allies meant their

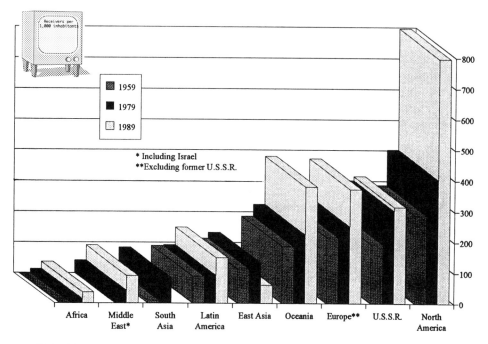

Television receivers per 1,000 inhabitants.

SOURCE: Peter Shayotovich

own continued domination of the channels of communications, while to the advancing countries it meant an end to that domination. Free flow is, like democracy and the people's right to know, a term so emotionally charged it has lost its value in international dialogue.

The United States and the Soviet Union dominated discussions of the free-flow issue from Unesco's first general conference in 1946 as they jockeyed for power and influence among the new nations. In the early years, Moscow had little influence over the proceedings, and the new nations had none. Western European countries gave solid backing to the U.S. campaign against the Soviet stifling of free expression, but they pointed also to the commercial advantages that free flow had for U.S. information media interested in marketing their wares abroad. Blinded by the folklore of the press, U.S. journalists failed to note the inextricable linkage of free expression and free exploitation of markets.

With the destruction of the Western colonial empires, the mathematics of international organizations changed, and the Western powers found they could no longer maintain their powerful base in international bodies. Military power continued to rest with the United States and its allies, though it was only through diplomatic pressure and the exercise of its veto right in the Security Council that the United States could guarantee the imposition of its will on the advancing world in Unesco and elsewhere.

TABLE 16.3   Total Television Receivers (in millions)

	1959	1979	1989
Africa	0.4	3.3	21
North America	56.2	151	217
Latin America	18	37	69
East Asia	18	37	128
South Asia	7.5	42	60
Middle East*	—	9	21
Europe**	91	127	184
Oceania	3	6.6	10
U.S.S.R.	40.8	80	106
World	234	593	797
TV Receivers per 1,000 Inhabitants			
Africa	0.2	14	36
North America	287	403	796
Latin America	89	92	149
East Asia	113	133	60†
South Asia	9	84	—
Middle East*	—	42	90
Europe**	216	252	372
Oceania	186	225	379
U.S.S.R.	194	303	315
World	39	213	148

*Including Israel
**Excluding the former U.S.S.R.
†Combined Asia listing
SOURCE: This table is drawn from summaries provided by the Section of Statistics on Culture and Communication, Division of Statistics, 1989-1992, Unesco, Paris.

The Soviets at first lost ground psychologically, for the new nations enthusiastically supported the American ideal of freedom of expession; it seemed to them a promise that they could for the first time in their history speak freely in global exchanges. Despite the fact the Soviet Union was no friend of a free flow of information, the Soviets found a way to benefit: They condemned the Americans as hypocritical for using free-flow to impose cultural imperialism and win lucrative markets for U.S. products. The accusation drew a warm response in the Third World.

At the 1970 Unesco general conference, advancing-world delegates introduced a new and startling demand: for "a more balanced flow of information." This challenge to the free-flow doctrine, which had been simmering for years, was based on assertions by Africans and Asians that the news media in the richer half of the world, operating under the free-flow doctrine, were leading a drive to dominate world opinion. The charge was that free flow did not really mean free flow because Third World countries did not have the financial resources to compete freely with the Western media. To the developing world, free flow meant flow in only one

Turmoil over the "new world information and communication order": "Free
flow" and "balanced flow" collide at Unesco in Paris, where angry words
were what flowed the most.

SOURCE: Unesco/Domenique Roger

direction: from North to South. As a result, it was alleged, the mighty industrialized
nations were spreading "moral and political pollution."[8]

The role of the news media had now become the most dramatic issue on the
world's intellectual stage. In the United States, however, it was not seen as a crucial
one. In fact, most American commentators, both official and press, saw the dispute
as part of the ideological struggle between the United States and the Soviet Union.
They did not recognize the intensity of feelings on the subject in the Third World,
where it reached the very heart of the conflict between the old colonial order and a
new world of free and equal nations. The charge of cultural or media imperialism
became a battle cry. Nations identifying themselves as "nonaligned" called on the
Third World to free itself from dependence on industrialized countries for both
manufactured goods and information, arguing that such dependence was a legacy
of the colonial past.[9]

Western nations and those in the Soviet bloc went along cautiously with Third
World proposals for change. As early as 1970, Unesco delegates adopted by acclama-
tion a resolution affirming "the inadmissibility of using information media for propaganda on behalf of war, racialism, and hatred among nations."[10] Some speakers went
so far as to call on Unesco to create a code of conduct that would encourage the
media to promote accord rather than discord among nations. Unesco proposed no
such code either at that session or at any subsequent conference, although accusations flew back and forth on the subject of such a code for many years.

In supporting the idea of a code, a number of delegates, mainly from advancing-
world and Marxist countries, argued that only such a clearly defined code could
guarantee unbiased and objective reporting. Western delegates countered that free
flow can be achieved only where governments impose no restraints in the form of

codes or otherwise. Others took the position that the main obstacles to free flow were not governments but rather lack of basic materials, such as paper. Still others held that imbalance in news flow resulted from the fact that the industrialized lands could afford to send correspondents abroad and advancing-world nations could not.

At a 1976 conference of nonaligned nations, a movement began that would set up a new international news agency, or "pool," backed by Unesco to enable the advancing nations to challenge the power of the capitalist news agencies. It was at that conference in Colombo, Sri Lanka, that the term *new world information order* first achieved wide circulation. Interestingly, it was linked with a proposal for a

The man in the middle: Former Director-General Amadou Mahter M'Bow, the central figure in the Unesco dispute that caused the United States and Britain to withdraw.

SOURCE: Unesco

new world *economic* order, a restructuring of the economies of the world that was considered a prerequisite for balancing the flow of information.

Two months later in Nairobi, Unesco delegates approved the idea of an international news pool. Mustapha Masmoudi of Tunisia, the early leader in the campaign for a new world communication order, argued for the pool on the ground that the U.S. giants the Associated Press and United Press International were presenting a distorted picture of the advancing world, concentrating on the "negative aspects" of the poorer countries. Only a pooled Third World agency could provide balance, he said. In the end, he won adoption of a general call for a "more balanced and diversified exchange of news." The word *balance* had now entered the official international language. The United States and its allies went along reluctantly with the resolution for two reasons: to avoid further acrimony in its dealings with Third World delegates and to prevent endorsement of a stronger assault on its free-flow position by the Soviet Union, which was at no cost to itself gleefully seeking to deepen the rift between the capitalist and the advancing countries. The Russian draft would have condemned both the Western news agencies and governments: "States are responsible for the activities in the international sphere of all mass media under their jurisdiction."[11] The conference ended indecisively with the delegates tabling action for two years.

The name calling in the dramatic confrontations in Nairobi had at last attracted the attention of the world press, and Unesco suddenly began to appear on the front pages of the world's great newspapers. Interest grew with the adoption of a resolution calling on Director-General Amadou Mahtar M'Bow of Senegal, the first African to head an arm of the United Nations, to appoint a commission to review the problems of contemporary society as seen against the backdrop of technological progress and the development of international relations. In due course, M'Bow chose a representative sixteen-member commission under the chair of Sean MacBride, an Irish statesman and journalist who had won both the Nobel Peace Prize and the Lenin Peace Prize.[12] As one might expect when the arena of conflict involved the press itself, press interest in a new world information order was running high when Unesco met in 1978 in Paris. Characteristically, the capitalist media presented the issue as a threat to democratic freedoms while the Marxist press applauded it as a challenge to capitalist exploitation. Western governments and news media approached the meeting with trepidation.[13] U.S. newspapers, among them *The Christian Science Monitor*, insisted it was not new rules that would ease "the manifest shortcomings" of news-gathering in the Third World but rather technical assistance and Western training for journalists.[14] Unesco itself came under heavy attack. The executive director of the American Newspaper Publishers Association demanded defeat of a Soviet declaration that only the power of national governments could enforce press freedom and "a democratic role for the press." *The Seattle Times* (November 12, 1978) headlined an article: "Unesco Declaration Threatens Press Freedom." Press freedom figured in the rhetoric of both sides, but the name calling grew ferocious. Finally, as happens in so many international organizations, Unesco came up with a compromise that satisfied both the United States and the Soviet Union. Under the compromise, which was the handiwork of Director-General M'Bow, the Soviet plan was set aside and replaced by an eleven-point resolution *The Guardian* proclaimed a "world charter for a free press."[15]

Joyous Third World delegates cheered the resolution as formal adoption of a new information order. It went nowhere near that far. However, it did link together clearly the concept of free flow and the concept of balanced flow calling for "a free flow and a wider and better-balanced dissemination of information." It went beyond that in support of the stance of the advancing countries. It assigned a *political* function to the news media by urging them to work to preserve peace, to further human rights, and to aid in eliminating prejudice and misunderstanding between individuals and nations. It also called on nation-states to guarantee freedom of information and demanded the news media allow the public to participate "in the elaboration of information."[16] In other words, Unesco was asking the news media to let the people decide what was news.

The members of the U.S. delegation were delighted with the outcome. They described the declaration as "a triumph for the spirit of international cooperation, goodwill, and common sense." The statement was less a comment on the actual contents of the declaration than a sigh of relief that the Soviet resolution, which had been before Unesco in one form or another for eight years, had not been approved. As Jim Browning of *The Christian Science Monitor* noted soberly, the price of the American "triumph" was agreement to ante up several million dollars to help improve communications in the Third World. But, he wrote, echoing other Western journalists, that the United States had succeeded in undoing the "de facto alliance" between Moscow and the advancing nations. Browning nevertheless drew attention to the fact that diplomats for the United States and its allies privately scoffed at the Third World governments as being largely authoritarian and ineffective and not really interested in a free flow of information. The new nation-states got the denunciation message, too.

NEWS AGENCIES AND "CULTURAL IMPERIALISM"

The words *balance* and *imbalance* play a decisive role in any discussion of the flow of information. A generation after the words had been introduced, no definition had yet been found that could be accepted in all parts of the world. In fact, those words were still enflaming passions at Unesco meetings in the 1990s. Central to any examination of balance is the role played by news agencies, which unquestionably distribute the greatest share of news about what is taking place in the advancing world. Moreover, no examination of news agencies makes sense without placing it in an economic context. Indeed, pressure for an international information order came only after the advancing nation-states had proposed a new international *economic* order under which there would be a major redistribution of wealth.

Statistical evidence has for a long time confirmed the second-class—or even lower—status of the new nations. As early as 1964, new nation-states organized themselves into a single pressure group, the Group of 77 (G-77), designed to reshape the face of international trade and production. A decade later, this pressure group, swollen to 120 members, demanded a new international economic order that would correct the imbalances in economic power that were the heritage of colonialism.[17] Noting at the time that less-developed countries accounted for only 7 percent of the world's industrial production, the G-77 countries set a target of 25 percent by the end of the twentieth century. In the fall of 1974, the UN General Assembly adopted a far-ranging "Charter of the Economic Rights and Duties of States," which, while failing to include all the demands embodied in the proposed new international economic order, came very close to it. Article 31 of the charter imposed on all nations "a duty to contribute to the balanced expansion of the world economy."[18] The industrialized nations did not, however, agree to transfer resources to the new nation-states by *multilateral* agreements. The United States in particular insisted on maintaining a unilateral assistance program so it could specifically target its aid to countries of which it approved and deny its aid to others. Disagreement on this issue has been a major sticking point in all discussions of a new international information order.

Attempts by the advancing countries to correct the global imbalance both in economic power and in control over information are two parts of the same struggle; they are inseparable. Believing that information is power, many Third World nations view the news agencies as enormously significant in adding to the power imbalance in both economics and information. The news agencies are seen as primary instruments of propaganda, presenting false pictures of the new nation-states and discouraging investment and aid—ultimately keeping the Third World in a state of subservience. This is a powerful indictment and requires close examination.

The charge of media imperialism has a sound historical basis. It holds it is through the news agencies, the spearhead of all the mass media, that economic control is maintained. The news agencies established in nineteenth-century Europe were frankly commercial enterprises.[19] European agency journalists fanned out through the colonial world to fill the demand for information about what was going on in regions that offered the promise of healthy financial rewards to enterprising businessmen.[20] In order to prevent cutthroat competition, Britain, France, and Germany carved up the world into spheres of influence under the 1869 Agency Alliance Treaty. Running about as emissaries of "the civilized world," the intrepid agency correspondents and their fellows who worked for the great imperial newspapers, chief among them *The Times* of London, found a limitless source of magnificent drama to report. They discovered wars and pitched battles, exotic religions and strange customs, jungles and mountains, savages and heathens, disease and revolution. The mass audiences that emerged in the nineteenth century ate up these reports with relish and developed an appetite for more and more spectacular and sensational news reports. No force of socialization in the colonies was more powerful than the news agencies. Their impact on the perceptions of native citizens about the outside world remains a major influence today and is indeed one of the factors in the complaints lodged against media imperialism.

It is a source of consummate irony that the most widely publicized challenge to media imperialism directed against the European news agencies was lodged by none other than what has now become the very symbol of media imperialism, the Associated Press. The United States was a minor power in 1869 when the Agency Alliance Treaty was signed, and in 1893 the AP agreed to join the European cartel, thus receiving the right to distribute the dispatches of the European agencies in the United States. It was not, however, permitted to operate its own news service outside the U.S. confines. Recalling the situation years later, Kent Cooper, longtime general manager of the AP, said it was "shocking" that Havas, a government-subsidized French news agency, could deny the Associated Press the right to send news to and from South America. "I resented the fact that the Associated Press submitted to such degrading news repression," Cooper wrote.[21]

By the time the debates were taking place within Unesco, however, it was the AP that was presenting its version of the news throughout the advancing world and the fledgling news agencies of those countries that lacked the money needed to present news about their countries to the rest of the world.[22] Cooper's blast at Reuters, accusing it of sending no reports that cast credit on America, sounded astonishingly similar to the words spoken about the AP in the advancing world half a century later. It was Reuters, he said, that decided what news was sent from America, and it told nothing but news "about the Indians on the war path in the West, lynchings in the South and bizarre crimes in the North."[23] Unlike Reuters, the AP was not an open instrument of U.S. imperialism; the agency proclaimed itself from its early years as an objective news-gathering and news-reporting service. Such was and remains the folklore that envelops the Associated Press. Yet its journalists were socialized into the U.S. belief system as thoroughly as were the journalists for Reuters and Havas in the nineteenth century. Journalists tend to follow the flag.

The rapid growth of the U.S. news agencies that followed Cooper's successful challenge propelled them into the forefront of the business of news. By the time the colonial world was breaking up in the 1950s, the Associated Press and United Press International (a merger of Scripps Howard's UP and Hearst's INS) had joined the British and French agencies as the dominant forces in international news. The stereotypes that filled the brains of men and women everywhere were the stereotypes transmitted around the globe by the Big Four. They were the most visible bits of information about the outside world reaching the literate elites of the advancing nations. They did not like what they read. To them, the pictures of their world were inaccurate and condescending, drawn by an arrogant band of men afflicted with the narrow horizons of the ethnocentric and who, wittingly or unwittingly, carried out the bidding of their wealthy, greedy masters. Unsurprisingly, the number-one target of the press reformers in the advancing world were the Big Four capitalist news agencies. To these four the Soviet TASS was sometimes added, but its circulation in the Third World was limited, and it was far less visible.

Press perceptions in East and West have been heavily dependent on Cold War attitudes. Throughout most of Unesco's history, the Western community of journalists was openly hostile to Unesco-sponsored meetings on the press, seeing them as orchestrated from the Kremlin in an attempt to win friends among the new nation-states and to weaken the power of the capitalist nations in the Third World. Organizations of editors and publishers condemned not only attacks on a free press but also Unesco itself.[24] The International Press Institute and Freedom House, a self-selected group of journalism authorities who monitor threats to "press freedom," often defended the news agencies as disinterested, objective reporters of events taking place in the advancing world.[25] Later, as the Soviet empire was collapsing, much of the Western hostility was directed at what were seen as undemocratic governments in the advancing world.

Still, by the time Unesco met in 1978, a shift had taken place. The inadequacies of the four news agencies were more generally observed and accepted. Yes, it was said, the news agencies *had* been deficient in their reporting of events in the new nation-states. Too many stories had been filed about wars and revolutions, pestilence and famine, earthquakes and murders.[26] Journalists who toiled for the news agencies should devote more time and space to slowly evolving trends and to the realities behind the appearances, even to "development news." Moreover, journalists ought to be writing and broadcasting more than they had about the daily lives of the unknown millions who resided in the advancing world. Yes, there were weaknesses, but there were also strengths. The news-agency journalists sometimes risked their lives to report news from around the world. These journalists were professionals well-equipped to help train the young reporters of the advancing world in the techniques of sound journalism. Technology and training—these were the answers to the challenges raised at Unesco. As for the charge of media imperialism, that was rejected. Indeed, as researcher Oliver Boyd-Barrett chronicled, emphasis on media imperialism began to retreat in the 1980s.[27]

The parties to the dispute over the news agencies have never agreed on the exact nature of their differences. On the one hand, the dispute is economic, related to the part the news agencies play in opening up markets for manufactured goods. On this point, little agreement has emerged. To their capitalist defenders, news agencies are instruments of information, not economic expansion. They seek to ferret out the facts and present those facts to readers and viewers in a manner that will interest and educate them, following the traditional folklore of the press. To their opponents, the information function of the news agencies is a smoke screen to mask their real function, which they say is to popularize capitalist lifestyles in the Third World as a means to awaken the desire to buy and consume the products of that capitalist world; in short, they are the vanguard of the advertisers. For the most part, the agency defenders have paid little attention to this side of the dispute.

On another level, the dispute is ideological. Critics accuse the agencies of biased reporting. They hold that the pictures the agencies portray are false, the result of rigidity in the belief systems of the journalists themselves, who are seen as so blinded by adoration of everything new and modern they are unable to recognize the worth of the traditional, of the products of an alien social order. Many who condemn the news agencies argue that part of this capitalist ideology is openly racist. What is white is good and modern; what is black (or brown or yellow) is poor and outdated. It is often seen also as rooted in Christianity to the point that the worth of other religious convictions, especially those of Islam, is not acknowledged. Apologists for the news agencies deny these allegations, arguing that the lodestars of agency journalists are truth and objectivity. Little progress has been made in resolving these ideological differences, but at least they are not discussed with such volatility as in the past.

On yet another level, the dispute is professional, involving the definition of news. To critics in the advancing countries, news-agency obsession with the dramatic and the conflictual gives the news reported a character so distorted it bears little relationship to reality. The sensationalism that marked the reports of nineteenth-century agencies remains typical of journalism of the late twentieth century covering events in Africa and Asia and even Latin America. The slow-unfolding patterns of life in the Third World do not make news. The emphasis is on action and conflict, on spot news. The important developments, critics say, are in the trends and not in spot news. The processes of development are ignored. To this charge, the journalists of the industrialized world tend to plead guilty. However, they argue that in quest of the dramatic and conflictual they are not acting out of prejudice against the advancing world but rather are following the market and giving the readers what they want. Moreover, emphasis on dramatic and conflictual reporting is as prevalent in their own countries as it is in reports from the Third World.

The gap between attackers and defenders of the news agencies remains substantial. This is not to say the journalists of the advancing countries pay no attention to drama and conflict. In fact, their eye for the dramatic is quite as keen as that of any American or Western European. The difference is that the attention of advancing-world journalists is less intensely focused on the dramatic and conflictual than that of their counterparts in the industrialized countries. Nor is it correct to say the United States and Western Europe have no journalists interested in trends and slow development, but far fewer of those analytical journalists can be found among the news agencies than among the quality newspapers. Although no one knows the exact percentage of world news distributed by the news agencies, it is clear that most of the information provided by the media about the world at large comes from the Big Four news agencies. While the large newspapers, newsmagazines, television, and radio do base some journalists in foreign countries, their numbers are insignificant when compared with the number of reporters stationed abroad by the news agencies.

Of all the discomfort generated in the advancing world by the omnipresence of the news agencies, none was more painful than the fact that most of the news those countries received about one another came from those same Big Four news agencies. This was true in part for historical reasons, yet even more because few news agencies in the new nation-states had either the financial resources or the technological organization to send correspondents to other countries. As a result, the usual practice has been for national news agencies throughout the advancing world to sign contracts with one or more of the Big Four agencies and simply redistribute AP or Reuters news reports over their own national facilities. A news item from Chad would, for instance, be reported by Agence France Presse; distributed to Senegal, Cameroon, and the Ivory Coast; and then appear in the newspapers of those countries. Most countries now have national news agencies, but few among them report foreign news directly.[28] One of Unesco's goals has been the development of local news agencies, and important steps have been taken in this direction, especially in the development of PANA (Pan-African News Agency), though such fledgling outfits are nowhere near competitive on the international scene. Launched in 1979, PANA serves forty-three countries in sub-Saharan Africa from its headquarters in Dakar, Senegal, transmitting in English, French, Arabic, and Portuguese. Plans for expansion of PANA hinge very much on available financial resources. So far, adequate funding has been slow in arriving.

In this situation, Third World critics of imbalance in the flow of news often turn to the remarks of the AP's Kent Cooper, whose complaint in the early twentieth century stressed that "Americans want to look through their own eyes, not throught the British eyes," was directed at the then news monopoly enjoyed by Reuters. India's D. R. Mankekar, who served as the first coordinating head of the pool of nonaligned news agencies, put it this way: "All that nonaligned countries are asking for is that they too want to look at the world through their own eyes instead of through the eyes of the Western news media."[29]

The News Agencies Pool of Non-Aligned Countries marks a major effort to correct the imbalance perceived by critics of the Big Four. Established in January 1975, it followed by a decade the creation of the privately financed Inter Press Service (IPS). Although neither of these agencies commands much attention (or respect) in the industrialized world, they have grown in both quality and prestige in the advancing world. In fact, PANA represents but one move to develop thriving regional news agencies; others gained strength in the Caribbean, Africa, Asia, and the Middle East. In all cases, the rationale for these agencies has been rooted in the desire to crack the monopolistic position of the Western agencies. Each of the new agencies has been portrayed as serving the cause of a new international information order.

The pool is not really a news agency, at least not in the sense the Associated Press is an agency. It has no budget, no board of directors, and not even a headquarters. Transmissions are paid for by the sender of the news report. In the beginning, all the pool's transmissions were delivered over the facilities of its distribution centers in Cuba, India, Tunisia, Indonesia, Iraq, Mexico, Vietnam, and North Korea. Originally its distribution was handled by Tanjug, the news agency of former Yugoslavia. The original membership of twenty-six has increased to ninety; the members are satisfied the pool is here to stay, and it will increase in both size and quality. Meeting in Jakarta in 1978, the members agreed they had already proved the pool was not "a caprice of the moment," and served the long-term needs of the nonaligned movement for an alternative source of news about the happenings in the advancing nations.[30]

Critics have attacked the news-agency pool as being little more than a propaganda instrument for Third World governments, which may send out press releases over the pool network. Others, especially in the industrialized world, have argued that the quality of the writing is so turgid few newspapers or broadcasters are using the material dispatched. Certainly, the kind of news disseminated differs markedly from the kind of news sent out by the Western agencies. Little interest is displayed in spot-news developments; much attention is paid to news of economic development, social change, trade, and commerce. Moreover, the articles tend to be longer than the concise, punchy Western reports. Newspapers in the United States and the other industrialized countries consider the output of the pool "nonnews." The issue is one of definition. The pool countries maintain that much of what the Western agencies report is not news either, but rather sensationalism or come-ons for the economic benefit of the capitalist nations. Although the pool has expanded, it is by no means replacing the Western agencies as a news source for newspapers and broadcasters of the Third World. My travels in different advancing nations and conversations with practicing journalists have turned up little enthusiasm for the kind of product being turned out by the pool countries. These attitudes may merely reflect the power of the press folklore of the industrialized world.

In any case, the press of the capitalist countries seems to react with uncontained glee to evidence, purported or otherwise, that the news practices of the pool countries and of the advancing world in general are dull and uninteresting. One incident is enough to illustrate the point. In the fall of 1981, Ben Mkapa, a former editor of *The Daily News* in Dar-es-Salaam and at that time Tanzania's minister of information, spoke at the opening ceremonies for his country's new national school of journalism. In that address, he urged the students to make their reports first factual and second interesting. Poor newspapers, he said, were inaccurate and dull. In due course, German newspapers received a report of Mkapa's address, in which he was quoted as saying, "With only a few exceptions, the newspapers of Africa are deadly dull, so boring they drive the audience to tune in the BBC."[31] The writer Ernst-Otto Maetzke of the the *Frankfurter Allgemeine Zeitung* used Mkapa's speech as a springboard to attack not only the quality of the African and socialist press but also the new world information order. Acknowledging there was something to be said for improving the press, Maetzke argued, however, that only authoritarian regimes could benefit from new information rules, which, he said, would merely enable repressive governments to maintain their monopoly over information and result in "a threatening boredom. . . . The people in the developing countries would scarcely notice."[32]

The only national news agency to mount a serious challenge to the supremacy of the Big Four in the Third World was TASS, the Soviet news agency. The collapse of the Soviet empire changed all this. In any case, even in their heyday, the Russians could not really compete successfully. In their challenge to the West, Third World editors read through the TASS dispatches often as a check on the reliability of the AP and AFP, but only rarely were those reports printed without revision; they were often ignored altogether. As one Tanzanian editor observed, "When a TASS report crosses my desk and I read something about American imperialism, I throw it on the floor." He said the U.S. news agencies were more factual, even though their reports were often propaganda. It was there all right, he said, "but you have to discover it."[33]

The IPS has achieved some success, especially in Latin America, its chief base of operations for most of its existence. In the late 1970s, it began to extend itself actively into Asia and Africa and forged links with thirty advancing-world national agencies. By the 1980s, IPS had become the sixth-largest world agency, exceeded in scope only by the Big Four transnationals and TASS. It began as a cooperative of Latin American journalists eager for social reform but soon abandoned its political activism in favor of what its director general, Italy's Roberto Savio, called "alternative journalism." Its approach was horizontal rather than vertical; in other words, it rejected the traditional concept shared by the transnationals and TASS that news properly flows vertically from top to bottom, journalist to reader. Instead, Savio proposed "a horizontal process—the exchange of information between individuals, between social groups, and between nations."[34]

The researcher Al Hester, who made a thorough study of the content of IPS reports, concluded that IPS was "a truly alternative type of press agency, basically serving Third World countries and with content mainly about or affecting the Third World."[35] More than three-fifths of the content of IPS stories studied were grouped under economics and business (27 percent), foreign relations (20 percent), and domestic government politics (14 percent). Hester found almost no coverage of disasters, sports, or celebrities.

Savio was somewhat of a missionary. He described himself as a utopian dreaming of a democratic world free of hunger and scarcity. Some of his experiences were, however, disturbing to him. He found that conventional definitions of news had been so deeply ingrained in journalists the world over that even IPS writers had trouble switching from emphasis on "spot news" to reports on trends. In other words, he told an international gathering, "they must be 'sexy.'"[36] For there to be a genuine new information order, in Savio's view, correction of imbalance in the flow of news was not enough and improvements in the infrastructure would not do the job. The most important change had to be in the *content* of newspapers and broadcasts. And for the content to change, the gatekeepers—the editors who decide what to publish and what to slap on the dead hook—must be prepared to change their definition of news. The conventional criteria, Savio said, have little to do with the special problems of the advancing world or with "the basic questions which concern mankind today, such as hunger, population, resources, environment, social structures, or culture."[37] IPS has pretty largely abandoned its original plan to operate as a formal news agency, committing itself frankly to aiding in the process of development of the less industrialized nations of the world. Its network covers 91 countries and distributes material to 840 media and nonmedia organizations around the world. Its content is not sexy.

An even more offbeat agency developed in the late twentieth century: the Gemini News Service, operating out of London. This nonprofit organization aimed to bring about changes in the conventional pattern of international reporting. Some 130 correspondents from 50 countries file stories and articles emphasizing environmental, cultural, health, and educational issues. Its most unusual thrust has been to send its correspondents into remote Third World villages for two-month stays, enabling them to send out periodic features called "View from the Village." Not surprisingly, Gemini reaches only about 150 magazines around the globe.[38]

NOTES

1. J. Herbert Altschull, *Agents of Power: The Role of the News Media in Human Affairs* (White Plains, NY: Longman, 1984), 207–51. For an excellent historical account, see C. Anthony Giffard, *Unesco and the Media* (White Plains, NY: Longman, 1989).

2. J. Herbert Altschull and Hemant Shah, "How the World Press Reported Unesco's 22nd General Conference," unpublished report commissioned by Unesco, 1984. Table 2 of the report shows that the Unesco communication programs received 7% of the total budget. By contrast, education received 37.9%, natural sciences 24.8%, culture 11.2%, and social and human sciences 9.7%. The communication category included other communication elements as well as news.

3. "Universal Declaration of Human Rights," adopted December 10, 1948, reprinted in Kaarle Nordenstreng, Enrique Gonzales Manet, and Wolfgang Kleinwächter, eds., *New International Information and Communication Order: Sourcebook* (Prague: International Organization of Journalists, 1986), 121–25. Article 19 appears on p. 123.

4. My (cq) von Euler, Unesco researcher in the Free Flow Section, letter to the author, February 14, 1992.

5. *World Communication Report* (Paris: Unesco, 1991), Table 6.3.

6. Interview in *The Unesco Courier*, November 1991, 48.

7. Herbert I. Schiller, "Genesis of the Free Flow of Information Principles," *Instant Research on Peace and Violence* (1975): 162–83. Schiller's article in the Tampere, Finland, journal is perhaps the best single work on the history and development of the free-flow concept. The great majority of the sources cited in the article are government documents. Another useful historical monograph is Roger Heacock, *Unesco and the Media* (Geneva: Institut Universitaire des Hautes Études Internationales, 1977). Heacock examines U.S. and Latin American newspaper coverage of Unesco activities in the information and communication areas during 1974–1976.

8. That description was first given by Mustapha Masmoudi, Tunisian delegate to Unesco and one of the leading spokespeople for the concept of the new international communication order. For a detailed look at his views, see Mustapha Masmoudi, "The New World Information Order," in Jim Richstad and Michael H. Anderson, eds., *Crisis in International News: Policies and Prospects* (New York: Columbia University Press, 1981), 77–96.

9. Key meetings of the Symposium of Non-Aligned Countries on Communication, a group given impetus in North Africa, were held in Algeria, Tunisia, and Sri Lanka from 1973 to 1976 as the dispute inside Unesco was heating up.

10. See the biennial report of the proceedings of the 16th General Conference of Unesco, Paris, 1970.

11. See the proceedings of the 16th General Conference, Nairobi, Kenya, 1976.

12. Masmoudi was among the members, as were delegates from the United States, the Soviet Union, and other nations from market, Marxist, and advancing countries.

13. Western media did go out of their way to condemn the Soviet proposal. Lord McGregor, a British sociology professor who had served for three years as chairman of a royal commission on the press, called it "monstrous" in a speech to a convention of Japanese editors. He said that what was needed was practical assistance, not ideological declarations.

14. "Keep World Press Free," *Christian Science Monitor*, October 24, 1978.

15. "World Charter for Free Press," *Guardian*, December 3, 1978. The "world charter" was approved by 144 delegates, with only China and Switzerland voting in opposition.

16. "Universal Declaration of Human Rights," 225–29. The official title of the declaration was "Declaration on Fundamental Principles Concerning the Contribution of the Mass Media to Strenghtening Peace and International Understanding, to the Promotion of Human Rights and to Countering Racialism, Apartheid and Incitement to War."

17. The G-77 group was created at the 1964 meeting of UNCTAD (United Nations Conference on Trade and Development). The demand for a new international economic order was made at a special session of the United Nations in the spring of 1974.

18. "Universal Declaration of Human Rights," 168–76. The charter was adopted by the UN General Assembly on December 12, 1974.

19. The leading agencies were the Havas (later Agence France Presse) agency founded by Charles Havas in France; Reuters, founded by Paul Julius Reuter in England; and the Wolff agency, created by Bernhard Wolff in Germany.

20. Anthony Smith, *Geopolitics*, 68–116, provides a useful and interesting historical account of the rise and development of European news agencies.

21. Kent Cooper, *Barriers Down* (New York: Farrar & Rinehart, 1942), 12. See also Kent Cooper, *Kent Cooper and the Associated Press* (New York: Random House, 1959), and Oliver Gramling, *AP: The Story of News* (New York: Scribner's, 1938).

22. The European cartel was broken in 1934, the result of the inexhaustible efforts of Cooper, who acted with the open assistance of the U.S. government. See Smith, *Geopolitics*, 44.

23. Cooper, *Barriers Down*, 43. With a flamboyant touch, Cooper declared that Reuters had done more for England than her "great navy, which ruled the seas, or its shipping, which then led in carrying on the commerce of the world." Those who spoke of media imperialism in the 1970s and 1980s relied on similar language to condemn the news reports of the AP.

24. A statement published by the IAPA (Inter-American Press Association), 1976, argued that press freedom was being challenged in Latin America not merely by restrictive measures by some governments but also by threats from "a world organization where authoritarian governments consistently outvote Western democracies."

25. See A. H. Raskin "U.S. News Coverage of the Belgrade Unesco Conference," *Journal of Communication* 31, 4 (Autumn 1981), 164–74.

26. See, for example, Morton Rosenblum, *Coups and Earthquakes: Reporting the World for America* (New York: Harper & Row), 1979.

27. Oliver Boyd-Barrett, "Western News Agencies and the 'Media Imperialism' Debate: What Kind of Data-Base?" *Journal of International Affairs* 35, 2 (Fall/Winter, 1981–82): 247–60. Casting doubt on the traditional charge by Third World critics that the major Western news agencies practiced media imperialism, Boyd-Barrett held that advancing-nation governments were able to control the activities of those news agencies within their own borders. In that same issue, which is devoted entirely to the information-order issue, can be found interesting articles by such diverse thinkers as Unesco's Doudou Diene and the U.S. critic Leonard R. Sussman of Freedom House. The articles provide a reasonably clear statement of opposing points of view on the issue. For updated material, see Oliver Boyd-Barrett, *Contra-Flow in Global News* (London: Easton, 1992).

28. By 1988, thirty-five countries in sub-Saharan Africa had news agencies; twenty-five national agencies were operating in Asia and the Pacific; almost all countries in Latin America had their own news agencies; many operated as well in the Arab states and the Caribbean. The news staffs of all these agencies are limited, although in some cases, they are quite capable of shipping direct reports from foreign countries to agency members. The main staple of their news diet remains the output of the Western news agencies. See *World Communication Report,* 139–41.

29. Cited in Anthony Smith, *Geopolitics*, 108.

30. *World Communication Report*, 137–38.

31. *Frankfurter Allgemeine Zeitung* (FAZ), July 15, 1982.

32. FAZ.

33. Ulli Mwambutukulu, managing editor of *The Daily News*, interview with the author, Dar-es-Salaam, August 11, 1980. Echoing the sentiments of many African editors, he wished fervently the United States and the Soviet Union would quit attacking each other in their news agencies. "If they fight," he said, "we'll be the ones to be hurt."

34. Roberto Savio, interview with the author, Paris, October 24, 1980.

35. Al Hester, telephone interview with the author, Bloomington, In., June 29, 1982.

36. Savio, speech at an international conference, the Netherlands, summer 1982.

37. Savio speech.

38. *World Communication Report*, 138.

Chapter
17

The Attempt to Find
a World Information Order

THE MACBRIDE COMMISSION
AND THE DECLARATION OF TALLOIRES

The most important document to come out of the years of debate about the press at Unesco was the report of the sixteen-member MacBride Commission, which made public its findings and recommendations during the twenty-first General Conference at Belgrade in October 1980.[1] Perhaps most remarkable and encouraging was that this disparate group of individuals coming from a multitude of backgrounds, social and economic systems, and ideological roots was able to agree on a single document aimed at "a new more just and more efficient world information and communication order."[2] To be sure, there was no total agreement. The 312 pages of the MacBride Commission report contained many footnotes in which particular members took issue with statements in the text. For the most part, however, these differences were predictable and dealt with matters of degree. However, some differences were fundamental.[3] For example, Elie Abel of the United States criticized a call to limit media concentration and monopolies, reduce the impact of advertising on editorial policy, and circumscribe actions of transnationals. In an apparent reference to the practices of the then Soviet Union, Abel said it was "a travesty to speak of measures against concentration and monopolization in countries where the media are themselves established as state monopolies." As for advertising, Abel acknowledged it was appropriate to study the influence of advertisers on editorial policy but said a sweeping demand to reject advertising altogether was "a symptom of ideological prejudice."[4]

Canada's Betty Zimmerman, the only commission member with a primarily TV background, took issue with some sweeping criticisms of television. The commission rejected as exaggerated an argument that television was anticultural yet found that in trying to appeal to the widest possible audience, commercial TV programs "all too often lack content of the highest quality."[5] Zimmerman chided the commission for a proposal that the "power" of the media be used for constructive purposes. Speaking of the press as a powerful socializing agent (along with church, family, associations, and schools), the commission noted that while some news stories had helped curb environmental pollution, others—in certain unnamed countries—had had negative results. Some critics, the report observed, accused the news media of creating a climate of fear that has led to government repression.

If the media have the power to spread fear, the commission asked, "why should they not exercise this same power in order to free men from distrust and fear and to assert their unshakable opposition to all forms of war and violence, and to all recourse to force in international relations?"[6] It is a question of great significance, one that lies at the heart of the perception of the role of the news media in differing belief systems. Zimmerman called the idea that the media ought to be *used* for any purpose, however valuable, "an unacceptable concept."[7]

Ideology and folklore often interfere with understanding the realities of the power of the press. To Canada's Zimmerman, using the media is an unacceptable concept. Yet history demonstrates that the press, dating back to its origin, has always been used, and individuals and groups in power have always sought to manipulate the press into serving their particular causes. That the news media are powerful instruments cannot be doubted; what is in dispute is *how* that power is exercised and *who* does the exercising.

To call attention to specific areas in which some members took exception is not to point to fundamental disagreement; rather, it is to place stress on the remarkable accomplishment of Sean MacBride and his fellow commission members in producing their report. Of course, several compromises were reached, and humankind is far from putting into practice many if any of the commission's eighty-two recommendations. However, there does exist now a basic document with which authorities from all parts of the world were at least at one time in essential accord. In a section of that document to which no objections were raised, the commission members specifically linked the proposed new information order to the calls for a new world economic order.[8]

Reporting of the issues involved in the new economic order has, the commission said, contained "many misrepresentations." Later, the reporting of the findings and recommendations of the MacBride Commission were themselves to be misrepresented in the press. News reports about the Unesco meetings contained—as the commission had said reports of the new economic order contained—"too much rhetoric on one side, too many prejudices on the other, too many blunt assertions and simplistic interpretations."[9] The commission reduced to a single paragraph the "fundamental arguments" for a new information order:

> The disparity between North and South is not a mere matter of time-lag. Thus, it cannot be expected that the developing countries will catch up through being given financial and technical assistance by the developed. In reality, the disparities are becoming greater and more serious. This points to needs which go beyond the need for assistance: the elimination of unjust and oppressive structures, the revision of the present division of labor, the building of a new international economic order. Communication reflects the disparities which characterize the entire international scene and therefore stands in need of equally far-reaching changes.[10]

Efforts to respond to the commission's findings by offering infusions of money and technical aid are inadequate. More is demanded. The commission proposed that the "more" demanded fit into three clusters: first, acknowledgment that communications is a personal right, belonging democratically to all individuals, not only to journalists and governments and not only to those who exercise political and economic power; second, that the imbalance in the flow of news and information around the world be remedied; and, third, that the content of the news be revised to help achieve human rights for all people and to reduce violence and the threat of war.

The commission cited with enthusiasm a comment by Luis Ramiro Beltrán, a Mexican researcher, that it was necessary to build "a new concept of communication" that was "humanized, nonelitist, democratic, and nonmercantile." What often passed as communication, Beltrán said, was "little more than a dominating monologue." For communication to take place, a dialogue was necessary between communicator and audience, Beltrán's message was similar to that of Roberto Savio and the Inter Press Service in calling for a horizontal rather than a vertical pattern of communication. The commission said it was aware the implications of this proposal were utopian but argued that a new relationship between journalist and audience was conceivable if greater prominence were given to the idea of citizen involvement. The aim was to create more democratic relationships by integrating the citizen into the decision-making processes of public affairs. In a nice bit of phrase making, the commission suggested a change in the distribution of roles "in which the media give and the public takes."[11]

The second cluster of proposals also dealt with the direction of information, although in this situation the concern is over the passage of news and other intelligence from one part of the world to another. This is the "free flow" issue that was introduced into the United Nations by the United States at its inception but returned later to haunt the Americans. The commission stated, simply and correctly, that recognition of imbalances in the flow of information was no longer a controversial issue. It is recognized everywhere that information flows from North to South, from the industrialized nations to the advancing nations.[12] In his opening remarks to the commission, MacBride argued the entire world shared the blame for the imbalance in the flow of information, not merely the press of the industrialized world. In the new nation-states, there were many examples of elites repressing information so that the masses were not brought into the news process. But the main problem, he said, was that information all too often seemed to flow only from top to bottom. The commission concluded that the primary factor in the imbalance was an economic one. It minced no words: "Seen broadly, the one-way flow in communication is basically a reflection of the world's dominant political and economic structures which tend to maintain or reinforce the dependence of poorer countries on the richer."[13] It was not only an imbalance in news about which the commission complained but also an imbalance in the flow of all kinds of information, especially through instruments of advanced technology. To the members of the commission, transnationals were exerting a positive influence in extending "facilities for cultural development," but they were also having the negative effect of promoting "alien attitudes across cultural frontiers," thus practicing cultural imperialism through their control of "communication infrastructures, news circulation, cultural products, educational software, books, films, equipment, and training." The effect, according to the commission, was "to impose uniformity of taste, style, and content."[14]

The third cluster of recommendations dealt with the content of news pages and broadcast news programs. Distortion occurs, the commission wrote, primarily when "inaccuracies replace authentic facts; or when a slanted interpretation is woven into the news report, for example through the use of pejorative adjectives and stereotypes."[15] After sifting through various definitions of what makes news, the commission concluded that the differences are not as great as they first appeared and that most journalists tend to agree that "good news is as worthy and interesting as bad news, provided it is authentic and significant." Expanding this perspective, the commission found the role of the communicator included not only "objective reporting of 'hard' news" but also commentaries and analysis that might "play a vital role in the worldwide struggle to promote human progress."[16] News, then, must be redefined. As the commission argued, the proper role of the journalist is that of activist, not disinterested bystander. The mass media have the power to help strengthen peace, international security, and cooperation and lessen international tensions. The press has a duty "to mobilize public opinion in favor of disarmament and of ending the arms race." In the last three of its eighty-two recommendations, the commission declared that new communications policies around the world should center on "the contribution of the mass media to strengthening peace and international understanding, to the promotion of human rights, and to countering racialism, apartheid, and incitement to war." Moreover, "a new world information and communication order requires and must become the instrument for peaceful cooperation among nations."[17]

In overdramatizing disagreements between East and West, the commission said, the press was raising tensions around the world, not lessening them. In a passage epic in its scope, the commission asserted: "The dangers of war are heightened by intolerance, national chauvinism, and a failure to understand varying points of view. This should never be forgotten by those who have responsibilities in the media. Above all national and political interests, there is the supreme interest of all humanity in peace."[18]

The findings and recommendations of the MacBride Commission were vague and capable of differing interpretations, but this was the price forced on the sixteen members if they were to reach agreement. Even so, it was a remarkable accomplishment. That the members were willing to pay the price was testimonial to their interest in international harmony. Whatever the political differences dividing the commission members, whatever their fears of losing political or economic ground to other nations or economic forces, these differences and fears were overcome in the final document.

Even though few publications on the press have been so carefully thought out, so profound in scope and insight, the report received a bad press in the United States, even though the U.S. delegation to Unesco was quite pleased. It had succeeded in preventing Unesco from adopting any international code of ethics or any resolution to require licensing of journalists. The commission had recommended in clear and unmistakable language the belief that journalists should have free access to all news sources. Moreover, the delegates had given unanimous approval to the establishment of a new agency to be known as IPDC (International Program for the Development of Communication), an agency the United States had itself proposed in order to emphasize assistance grants and the financing of training of advancing-world journalists as a mechanism for righting the global imbalance.[19] That there *was* a global imbalance no one questioned. Nor did anyone doubt the need for efforts to rectify the imbalance, which can be seen most clearly perhaps in the sharp division between the illiteracy rates in the northern and southern hemispheres. Figure 17.1 and Table 17.1 show how great that division remains more than a decade after the commission's report. The IPDC has tried to help, but it has had to work with limited resources and only token support from most of the industrialized world. The story of the hostility of the market nations' press to a world information order aimed at correcting the imbalance offers a partial explanation.

What went wrong? Why did the U.S. press report critically on the proceedings of the General Conference while it was in progress and then condemn Unesco with such overt hostility at the end of the meeting? In most of the rest of the world, the reports were not unfriendly.[20] The National News Council, although concerned about the course of events at the Unesco conference, was disturbed by complaints that the U.S. press had reported the conference in a biased and distorted manner. So it directed its staff to make a thorough study of the coverage of the Unesco conference by the U.S. press.

The findings of the News Council study are revealing.[21] In virtual unanimity, the American press reported and commented on the Unesco proceedings with unmasked antagonism, concentrating on fear that foreign authoritarians and bureaucrats were seeking to damage, if not destroy, freedom of the press as it had been experienced in the United States for more than two centuries. The News Council study showed that the single article most widely used in the American press was an AP report on October 21, 1980 that appeared in different versions in morning and

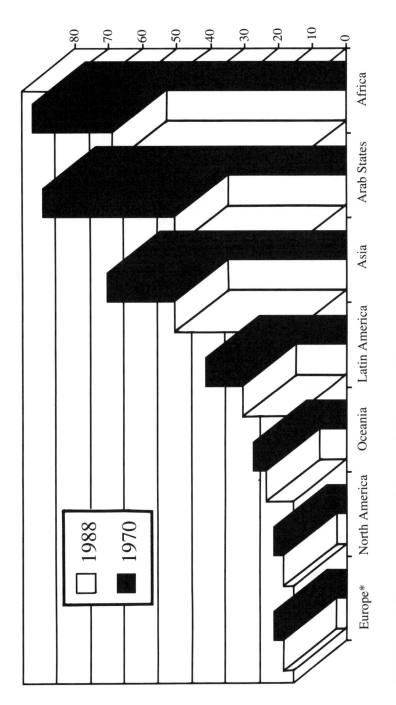

FIGURE 17.1 Illiteracy rate—population aged 15 years or older.

SOURCE: Peter Shayotovich

321

TABLE 17.1   Illiteracy Rate (in percentages), Population Aged 15 Years and Older

	1970	1988
Africa	77	53
Asia	55	35
Arab States	74	49
Europe*	6	3
Latin America	26	15
North America	6	3
Oceania	12	8

*Including the former U.S.S.R.
SOURCE: This table is drawn from summaries provided by the Section of Statistics on Culture and Communication, Division of Statistics, 1989–92, Unesco, Paris.

afternoon papers. In the afternoon-paper article, the lead paragraph ran: "Communist and Third World nations used their majority in Unesco to pass resolutions aimed at getting more control over international news reporting." Typical of the headlines prompted by that article was one reading "Unesco Votes to Muzzle Press" in *The Independent-Record* of Helena, Montana. So intense was the concentration on the discussion of news at the conference that not a single article appeared in any of the newspapers studied by the National News Council on any topic of discussion at Unesco other than news policies. The approval of IPDC went "almost unreported."[22] Leonard Sussman, executive director of Freedom House, which opposed the campaign for a new information order, found the U.S. reporting unbalanced, with 60 percent of American articles unfavorable to Unesco.[23]

Unfavorable coverage did not arise from animosity to Unesco and the proposed information order, according to Stan Swinton, head of world services for the Associated Press, but rather from the fact that none of the other Unesco activities was even newsworthy. Were it not for the controversy over the new international information order, Swinton said, "nobody from the press would be there at all. It's like a safe landing at an airport."[24]

The irony is noteworthy. It was this very question of news judgment that underlay much of the MacBride Commission report and much of the discussion of the new international information order. It was the search for spot news, for the dramatic and the conflictual, that marked the U.S. press coverage of the Unesco proceedings, just as it has always marked press coverage in the United States and throughout the capitalist world. Among the dangers of the existing information order, the MacBride Commission reported, was precisely this concentration on the immediate and the dramatic. What was overlooked were the great political, economic, and social issues.

News reports and commentary in the French press were generally similar to those in the U.S. news media, although the French wrote a good deal more about the establishment of the IPDC, and a number of French newspapers, mainly those on the political left, did react favorably to Unesco. What seemed to disturb mainline French newspapers was fear that Unesco had become too politicized. Director-

General M'Bow had commented at a news conference that "every intergovernmental organization is a political organization par excellence"[25] not an especially remarkable observation, but one that upset U.S. editors as it did the French. Complaints on this score are astonishing, because it is unthinkable that those who represent their governments in international bodies would not reflect the views of the political leaders who sent them there in the first place.

One of the most important elements separating press ideologies from one another is the matter of politicization. To the Third World and communitarian societies, the role played by the press is inevitably seen as political, while among capitalist nations, it is not. The Western news media are expected, as Raskin wrote, to operate in "the spirit of detachment."

The MacBride Commission report was never formally voted on—and that is probably a good thing. Any call for a formal vote would have produced a great deal of rhetoric from all sides, and the commission's findings and recommendations would have been lost in airy verbiage. Instead, the delegates voted to circulate the report to their governments as well as to journalists, scholars, and the general public and to take the recommendations into consideration later. Without saying so specifically, the delegates in effect approved a new order under this resolution: "The General Conference expresses the wish that Unesco demonstrate its willingness in its short and medium-term activities to contribute to the delineation, broadening, and application of the concept of a new world information order."[26]

By 1980, global discussion of information policy was once again embroiled in a burning conflict as bitter as any of those that had preceded it. The dispute itself was much ado about very little, but it served as a launching pad for soaring flights of oratory and even launched threats by the U.S. Congress to withdraw from Unesco, threats that would be carried out by President Reagan not long afterward. The quarrel was over codes of ethics and the protection of journalists; it arose at a conference at Unesco's Paris headquarters, where Pierre Gaborit, a little-known French political scientist, proposed that journalists be licensed in order to guarantee they adhere to a system of "generally accepted" ethics for the profession. Rumors circulated claiming that Unesco itself was behind the proposal and that it was designed to interfere with freedom of the press. The MacBride Commission had explored and rejected the idea of licensing journalists, which had been introduced as part of a plan to provide protection for reporters who otherwise might be placed under life-threatening risks. The commission had also turned down the imposition of formal codes of ethics, despite extensive support among the advancing countries on the ground that no agreement on any such code was possible. The commission did say, however, that an international code was desirable if one could be worked out, recommending that it be voluntary and self-enforced. Canada's Zimmerman protested that professional journalists opposed any kind of formal codes, even if they were voluntary. In the face of this division, the commission had sought to follow a cautious middle course.

Unesco itself did not then approve, nor did it ever approve, the licensing of journalists or the institution of a code of ethics. The meeting at which the French professor offered his own proposal was one of many Unesco meetings and miniconferences where experts air their points of view. Reporters are usually invited to but rarely attend such meetings. This meeting, however, was well attended since journalists and officials of journalism organizations flocked to Paris not only to listen to the professor but also to deliver themselves of speeches opposing any licensing plans. Unesco aides, led by Director-General M'Bow, insisted that any proposals for licensing journalists did not reflect the views of Unesco. The denials of M'Bow and his associates, however, did not satisfy the complainants. A UPI report spoke of "Unesco's touchiness" and maintained that Third World delegates were trying to sneak through a plan on the quiet.[27]

Shortly afterward, in May 1992, U.S.-led media organizations adopted what came to be known as the Talloires Declaration of the "Voices of Freedom."[28] The gathering at the French resort town drew sixty organizations to one of the most distinguished assemblages ever of journalism societies, scholars, and officials interested in the press. Unesco officials were invited to attend, and M'Bow himself spoke to the participants. His address was moderate in tone, but when questioned by journalists, he reacted with anger. Although the Declaration of Talloires was essentially affirmative in tone, hostility between the press theorists of the capitalist world and those of the advancing world was in no way assuaged.

Questioners complained to M'Bow that Unesco favored government controls over the press, that it operated in secret, and that it was being manipulated by the Soviet Union. The director-general angrily denied those charges and replied the press was delivering a distorted image of Unesco.[29] The line certainly appeared to be drawn by the Declaration of Talloires. Yet, ironically, there was little in the declaration that differed in spirit from the report and recommendations published by the MacBride Commission. The declaration supported "the free flow of information and ideas," opposed any international code of ethics, and rejected any plan to license journalists or to provide any formal system for protecting journalists. None of these recommendations was inconsistent with the MacBride report. Indeed, both the MacBride Commission report and the Talloires Declaration endorsed the Universal Declaration of Human Rights and the Unesco constitution.

The essential differences were once again economic. The Talloires declaration specifically endorsed advertising as both a service to consumers and a provider of financial support for "a strong and self-supporting press." No press can be independent, the declaration asserted, "without financial independence." Moreover, the declaration said, the sensible approach to correcting the imbalance in the world of information was through "practical solutions," specifically "improving technological progress, increasing professional interchanges and equipment transfers, reducing communication tariffs, producing cheaper newsprint, and eliminating other barriers to the development of news media capabilities."[30] The split between the have nations of the capitalist world and the Third World have-nots was manifest in the division over the importance of advertising. To the advancing countries, as evidenced in the MacBride report, advertising represented a threat to the free flow of information; to the industrialized nations, advertising provided the underpinning for an independent press free of government controls.

THE PERILOUS PUSH
FOR INTERNATIONAL COOPERATION

One of the arguments underlying this book is that the press has never operated as an independent actor and that it has never been free from the direction of power, whether of governments or of economic forces. The division between capitalist and Third World countries turns out, on close examination, to be ephemeral. Each side loudly proclaims its mission as it marches under the ideological banner of a free flow of information; yet in neither case is the declared mission of the press what it seems. Skimmed milk, as W. S. Gilbert observed wisely, masquerades as cream.

In any case, the Talloires Declaration turned out to be enormously popular with the press and with representatives of the U.S. government. As was to be expected, the Soviet Union condemned the declaration.[31] The advancing nations and Unesco officials expressed less concern over the declaration itself than over the attacks on Unesco that marked the Talloires meeting. Herve Bourges of France, then press spokesperson for M'Bow and author of *Decoloniser l'information*, complained that certain elements of the U.S., British, and French press had turned their "war machine" against Unesco. M'Bow, who in his speech at Talloires had said he welcomed the dialogue, was no longer as sure. Editorials in U.S. newspapers vigorously applauded the Declaration of Talloires. So did the outpourings of columns by such writers as Carl Rowan and John Roche. *Stars and Stripes* headlined the Roche column, "Unesco Tries to Muzzle the Press." U.S. officials joined in criticizing the activities at Unesco, although their comments were more reasoned and less inflammatory than some of the headlines.[32]

The pace of criticism of Unesco increased. The International Federation of Newspaper Publishers (FIEJ), an association of newspaper owners from twenty-five countries led by the United States, endorsed the Declaration of Talloires and called on Unesco to "abandon attempts at regulating news content and formulating rules for the press." The organization urged Third World nations to agree to practical solutions for their problems, meaning acceptance of direct assistance and journalism-training programs. In keeping with the dominant American belief system, the publishers feared communitarian ideas meant putting the interests of governments above those of individuals. In a comment that might have been written by John Stuart Mill, the publishers expressed their belief that "the state exists for the individual."[33]

In a *Wall Street Journal* article, Leonard R. Sussman, executive director of Freedom House, applauded the Talloires Declaration for its "free-press counterattack" against actions taken at Unesco meetings where "free-press advocates have taken beatings in the last six years."[34] He warned that in creating the IPDC, its new mechanism for providing assistance to Third World countries, Unesco was writing "shorthand for institutionalized trouble" because the IPDC might be used to channel funds only to countries with repressive press policies. Countries with controlled presses held a majority of votes in Unesco and on IPDC's thirty-five-member council; moreover, according to Sussman, censorship, either before or after publication, was practiced in 57 percent of African countries, 53 percent of Asian lands, and 38 percent of Latin American nations.[35]

U.S. government officials kept up the attack. Elliot Abrams, assistant secretary of state for international organization affairs, went before the House Foreign Affairs Committee to condemn Unesco, which he said sponsored the meeting where the licensing plan was discussed. The plan, he said, assaulted the free-press values Unesco was "mandated to defend." Three months later, Congress approved a bill that threatened the viability of Unesco.[36] The measure expressed the will of Congress that U.S. contributions to Unesco never be used for any projects that would license journalists, impose mandatory codes of ethics, or restrict the free flow of information. A tough amendment offered by Representative Robin L. Beard, a Tennessee Republican, vowed to cut off its annual $12-million contribution to Unesco if it went forward with any of those plans. Unesco did none of those things. Still, President Reagan quickly signed the measure into law.[37]

The power of the folklore of the press was evident in the House debate. Representative Clarence E. Miller, an Ohio Republican, condemned Unesco and all UN bodies for trying to control information. The idea of a new world information order, Miller said, was clearly a Soviet initiative to build an alliance with Third World nations to control information "the way it is controlled in their own countries." Only one House member, Representative Mervyn M. Dymally, a California Democrat, spoke against the Beard amendment, pointing out that Unesco had taken no action to censor the press or license journalists so there was no need to respond "hysterically to what we perceive as censorship." Despite Dymally's intervention, 372 House members voted for the Beard amendment and only 19 opposed it.[38]

The debate illustrated clearly the distance between market and Marxist perceptions of the role of the press. To the overwhelming majority of the congressional delegation and the market-oriented journalists, the Marxist press was an instrument or tool of the State or of the Communist party. At the same time, to the majority of the members of the Communist party and the communitarian journalistic community, the market press was an instrument or tool of the capitalists. In the face of this diametrical division, the task of anyone who sought some kind of international accord on the role of the press turned out to be Herculean.

Even though the measure became law, Unesco does not have the power to enforce codes of ethics or licensing arrangements. The United States has vigorously rejected the notion that any agreement or convention adopted by any agency of the United Nations is binding. So, in fact, did the Soviet Union and most of the world's industrialized powers, with the notable exception of France, which is given historically to sweeping moral declarations of principle. Only the advancing nations have sought to rewrite international law to make regulations adopted by intergovernmental bodies binding on all nations. In any case, neither the United Nations nor any of its subagencies can enforce any Unesco rules or regulations. The debate in Congress was political as well as symbolic. To Americans, symbolic actions have a long and honored tradition, dating back to the Boston Tea Party. Refusal to participate in the 1980 Olympic Games was in this tradition, as have been various embargoes. As with all these symbolic acts, the desire was to hoist a warning flag.

The misunderstanding of the American press and the Reagan State Department about the work of Unesco was quite remarkable. The entire news coverage of the Belgrade General Conference was distorted. Nearly every story about the six-week meeting dealt with something other than the main focus of the organization.

Two years later, the world information order was still attracting the attention of the news media. American and Western European papers gave scarcely any mention at all to the educational, cultural, and scientific issues before the twenty-second General Conference in Paris. The tone of the debate over the information order was gentler, although once again advancing nations asked for curbs on the power of the Big Four news agencies, urging that technological advances go to help the new

Director of the new line at Unesco: Henrykas Yushkiavitsus, Unesco assistant director-general, who dreams of a world united by communications and information.

SOURCE: Unesco/Michel Claude

nation-states and not subject them to Western domination. The United States and its allies continued to insist on the principle of free flow of information and to express the suspicion that the new information order was aimed at restricting freedom of movement by news media and transnationals. The Soviet Union accused the capitalist nations of hypocrisy. Nothing new took place. Unesco's role in all aspects of communication, the information order being but a part of it, took up only 7 percent of the Unesco budget but nearly 70 percent of the news reports in the Western nations. Education, the main focus of Unesco's work, commanded 40 percent of its budget but only 15 percent of the Western news coverage.[39] Another indication of the overriding interest of the press in stories about drama and conflict at the expense of substantive news can be found in a tabulation of the number of mentions of individual countries among the 161 attending the conference. The United States was mentioned most often, naturally enough; the host country, France, was second; the Soviet Union third. But fourth was the tiny island country of Grenada. It figured not at all in any of the issues before the conference, but shortly before the conference began the island had been invaded by U.S. troops. It was, therefore, mentioned from time to time by speakers addressing the conference on other subjects.[40]

The mood at the Paris conference was actually one of accommodation, even among U.S. delegates. Nevertheless, a month after it ended, Secretary of State George Shultz announced the United States was withdrawing from Unesco at the end of 1984—on the grounds that issues before Unesco were being "extraneously politicized," that it was mismanaging its funds, and that it was showing "hostility to free-market and free-press concepts." Britain and Singapore followed the United States out, but efforts to pull Japan and West Germany with them failed. With a third of its budget gone, Unesco found itself forced to rein itself in. The only thing left of the new world information order was the funding agency, the IPDC.

The U.S. congressional debate took place after the first meeting of the IPDC Council in June 1981. The council has met regularly since and become a critical adjunct to Unesco even though its fund-raising efforts have been hampered by political differences. To limit IPDC funds is to reduce its capacity to provide the kind of assistance that might enable the Third World to catch up with the industrialized nations and remedy the imbalance in communications. From the start, the United States worried the IPDC would operate not as a purely dispassionate mechanism for assistance but would serve instead as an ideological or politicized battleground. In fact, the United States tried to force the IPDC to operate separately from Unesco. It sought unsuccessfully to get the MacBride Commission to agree. Instead, the commission approved over opposition of U.S., French, and Canadian members a recommendation that the IPDC be created "within the framework of Unesco."[41] Its purpose was to mobilize support within the industrialized world for direct financial assistance to be provided mainly on a multilateral basis. The funds were to go to develop and strengthen communications infrastructures; improve information-delivery systems among news agencies, press, cinema, radio, and television; provide professional training for journalists and communications planners; and facilitate transfer of technology for press instruments, satellites, and data banks.[42] The central issue was whether the money given to the IPDC by either governments or private interests should go into one large collection pot or whether the assistance was to be earmarked for use only for specific purposes decreed by the donor. The United States wanted the money to help only countries whose press it considered to be free. As Clifford H. Block, director of research and development for the Agency for International Development, put it in 1980, it was "simply unacceptable" for his government to fund any IPDC project that might be ideologically contentious. Any effort to promote a project of this kind would threaten U.S. support for the IPDC concept. Block saw bilateral funding as the way out of the impasse.[43]

In the end, the United States had its way, although only in part. Delegates to the second IPDC Council meeting in 1982 adopted a compromise under which the organization agreed not to exclude any source of finance. Although the language did not suit some Third World countries, it provided the vehicle to get the IPDC moving and to avoid—for the time being at least—a walkout by the United States. Two different forms of funding were possible: one through IPDC funds-in-trust for projects selected by the council, the other to a Special Account, an umbrella for contributions from government and private sources and for bilateral assistance, the latter often involving political strings.

When the delegates left their second meeting, they seemed on the whole pleased with the spirit of cooperation, even though they deplored the minimal $741,000 in funding made available to the IPDC. Some advancing-nation delegates let it be known they were not abandoning their efforts to organize the IPDC as a multilateral program to try to prevent industrialized countries from maintaining imperial power by tying ideological strings to aid money. Although U.S. delegates praised the meeting as marking "a welcome reduction" in ideological posturing, the tough resolution by the U.S. Congress followed seven months later, and it wasn't long afterward the Reagan administration announced its withdrawal from the intergovernmental organization. Kaarle Nordenstreng of Finland, a leading international journalism scholar, found nothing surprising in the reluctance of the United States to endorse a multilateral assistance program. "Why?" he asked ironically, "should they pay for music that does not follow their tune?"[44]

The opposing viewpoints were expressed clearly and with some asperity. José Mayobré Machado, a member of Venezuela's Unesco delegation, rejected "paternalistic advice" from industrialized countries that might want to make advancing nations "the repository, at a very high price, of all the technology you have discarded as obsolete." Rather than being classified ideologically, he said Third World countries wished "an honest, intelligent, mutually respectful cooperation on an equal and equitable basis." At the same time, Leonard Sussman of Freedom House urged the United States and its partners supporting "free-press" concepts to state openly and publicly they would provide communication-technology assistance only to Third World countries "that accept as a fundamental commitment the expansion of the free flow of information worldwide."[45]

Five years later, Sussman blamed inadequate press coverage and challenges by "some governments" for the U.S. withdrawal. He clearly had the "ideologues" in the United States in mind. As for the press, Sussman said, it "repeatedly covered Unesco as though it was about to install press censorship—an impossibility." When the

Reagan administration added "politicization, financial extravagance and maladministration to the charges against Unesco, the American press was amply conditioned to believe only the negatives."[46] The analyst C. Anthony Giffard correctly placed much of the responsibility for the public's failure to learn what had actually happened inside Unreco on "the laziness of reporters, editorial writers and columnists to do their own research rather than rely on handouts from interested parties. Partly it was due to the well-documented tendency for reporters to rely on government spokesmen, rather than seek out a range of alternative views."[47]

After the withdrawal of the United States and Britain, media interest faded quickly. News about Unesco all but disappeared from TV news shows, although an occasional item appeared in major newspapers.[48] Press interest picked up in 1987 when, after a bitter fight in the fifty-one-member Executive Board, M'Bow lost his bid for a third term as director-general and was replaced by Federico Mayor Zaragoza of Spain, a former deputy to M'Bow. Third World delegates accused Western members of racism. A Pakistani who also sought the position spoke out

A plea for the return of the Anglo-Saxons: Federico Mayor Zaragoza of Spain, Unesco's new director-general, appeals to the United States and Britain to return to the organization they rejected angrily in 1984.

SOURCE: Freedom Forum

against "the ideology of supremacy of the white man."[49] The flurry of press interest that accompanied the election of Mayor quickly tapered off again to zero.

Mayor promptly launched a campaign to induce the United States, Britain, and Singapore to rejoin the international organization, asserting that the internal reforms had altered the organizations and complaints were no longer justified. The American Society of Newspaper Editors changed directions and endorsed reentry. A British commission found that creation of a new performance-appraisal system, improvements in recruiting, and introduction of management training for top-level officials had altered the equation, and England seemed prepared to rejoin if the United States did also. All these appeals fell on deaf ears during the Bush administration. Mayor, re-elected director-general in 1993, was still working on the United States as this book went to press, hoping and expecting the Clinton administration would reverse the decision to withdraw. Clinton's State Department recommended rejoining in 1994, but suggested the move be delayed by a few years for financial reasons.[50]

Supporters of the concept of New World Information and Communication Order (NWICO) remained quiet but privately deplored the bowing to pressure from the Western powers. They were biding their time, hoping that changes in the international landscape would sooner or later bring the concept to the fore once again. Meanwhile, they concentrated their efforts on work "in the field," even with limited funding, and on the surviving Unesco institution, the IPDC. Andri Isaksson of Iceland, Unesco delegate to the United Nations, said simply, "The Third World sees Unesco as a place for intellectual dialogue on the basis of equality."[51]

Various resolutions affirming "free flow" and "balanced flow" were introduced; they were never defeated but swept under the rug while Unesco struggled to preserve its own existence in the face of the loss of one-third of the organization's funding. A 1989 resolution remained in force encouraging "the free flow of information at the international as well as the national level and the promotion of a wider and better-balanced dissemination of information without any obstacle to freedom of expression." Abandoning the overt fight for NWICO brought no resolution of international communication problems. "The irony is that even though we gave up on NWICO, the problems are still there," observed a Unesco spokesperson who requested anonymity. "The most dreadful today are overcommercialization of the media, violence, and ethical questions."[52] Mayor elected to try to work through existing organizations of journalists and strengthen the IPDC. The Windhoek conference has been the most ambitious of the seminars to date. The meeting aimed at promoting "an independent and pluralistic African press" led to new funding from the IPDC and the International Federation of Newspaper Publishers.[53]

In fact, the thirty-five-member IPDC Council agreed to make it "a prority concern to orient its projects on the basis of freedom of the press and pluralism and independence of the media." From its outset, the council gave the greater share of its limited funding to regional news agencies and regional broadcasting organizations, which the council hoped might one day rival the Big Four. The chief beneficiary of the first awards was PANA; other agency awards went to Arab, Caribbean, trans-Pacific, and Latin American agencies. In that first year, the funding approved was a modest $910,000, but $3.4 million in additional pledges came in also. By 1992, the IPDC had approved more than 350 Special Fund projects at a cost of some $15 million. Eighty-three news-agency projects were under way, as were 100 more involving installation of radio and television stations, printing presses, newspapers, and publishing houses. In addition, the IPDC had overseen 160 programs to train journalists, technicians, and producers and awarded 900 training fellowships.[54]

It takes voluntary contributions from member states to finance new projects authorized by the IPDC Council. In 1991, all twenty-four approved projects received some financing, but these moved only a small distance toward upgrading Third World media to the level of genuine competitors of the media in industrialized countries. The total outlay from the Special Account for 1992 was $2,304,000, though that was only one-fifth of the $10,706,000 requested. Even so, it was an improvement over the less-than-a-million figure of the first year.

What the future holds for the IPDC and Unesco was far from clear. The task facing Unesco remained enormous. "Perhaps we shouldn't have retreated so far," a Unesco spokeswoman told me in 1993, "but the Reagan and Bush people were so recalcitrant. They simply hated Unesco and everything it stands for." Even before Bush left office, however, American editors were switching sides and urging the United States to rejoin Unesco. The ASNE applauded Mayor's recognition of "the essential role of an independent press in countries around the world" and endorsed his program to streamline and reorganize Unesco.[55]

NOTES

1. The MacBride Commission's report appeared in book form under the title *Many Voices, One World. Towards a New More Just and More Efficient World Information and Communication Order* (London: Kagan Press, 1980), hereafter identified as MacBride. Of the sixteen members of the commission, eight represented the Third World. Marxist representatives included Sergei Losev, director general of TASS, the Soviet news agency. MacBride was one of six representatives from capitalist countries. Most members had journalism connections.

2. MacBride, title page.

3. For a review of those differences, see J. Herbert Altschull, *Agents of Power: The Role of the News Media in Human Affairs* (White Plains, NY: Longman, 1984), 231–33.

4. MacBride, 266.

5. MacBride, 177.

6. MacBride.

7. See MacBride, 177, for Zimmerman's comment: "The Report is accusing the media of exercising too much power, while at the same time advocating the exertion of power for other (valuable) purposes. In both cases, however, the situation is being viewed from the standpoint of using the media, which is an unacceptable concept."

8. MacBride, 192–93.

9. MacBride, 132.

10. MacBride.

11. MacBride, 200.

12. MacBride, 142. U.S. member Elie Abel said thoughtful journalists and students of communications had acknowledged that the one-way flow of information must be changed "for the benefit of all nations, developed and developing alike."

13. MacBride, 148.

14. MacBride.

15. MacBride, 158.

16. The commission cited 1979 observations by Zbigniew Brzezinski, then foreign policy adviser to President Carter, about the "philosophy of news" in the United States, which he said failed to present information in a systematic, thoughtful manner. The emphasis was on whatever was new, on disparate facts that were not related to one another, and were not interconnected: "It's very difficult to convey this kind of perspective in the context of an approach to reality which in America focuses very much on hard individual facts and is less interested in broad historical sweep." MacBride, 157.

17. MacBride, 271-72.

18. MacBride, 271. See also the heading "Towards International Understanding," 268.

19. MacBride, 270.

20. The Soviet Union expressed modest disagreement with some of the recommendations but generally applauded the result. Most responses in the advancing world were enthusiastic. Among the capitalist nations allied with the United States, the press tended to report the conference with approval.

21. A. H. Raskin, "U.S. News Coverage of the Belgrade Unesco Conference," *Journal of Communication* 31, 4 (Autumn 1981): 164-74. The issue included a number of other articles supporting (or criticizing, in part) Raskin's findings. See especially Colleen Roach, "French Press Coverage of the Belgrade Unesco Conference," 175-87. See also John Massee, "Unesco Defends MacBride Report," *Editor and Publisher* 114 (1981): 42-52.

22. For further details of the reports in U.S. newspapers, see Altschull, *Agents of Power*, 238-39.

23. Leonard R. Sussman, "Opposing Assaults on the World's Free Press," *Wall Street Journal*, June 16, 1981.

24. Quoted in Raskin, "U.S. News Coverage." A former assistant editor of the editorial page of *The New York Times*, Raskin blamed the selection process for the unbalanced reporting. By finding newsworthy only those stories that seemed to fulfill the fears expressed so unanimously on the editorial pages of the U.S. press, the journalists systematically excluded opposing viewpoints. This procedure, Raskin wrote, was "inconsistent with the spirit of detachment that is invariably set forth as the touchstone of sound news judgment." Other questions in this section from same source.

25. Roach, "French Press Coverage."

26. Proceedings of the twentieth General Conference, Paris, October 1980.

27. For a full account of the Gaborit story, see the first edition of this book, pp. 240-42. As for the meeting itself, Third World representatives expressed anger over the presence of "gate-crashing" Western groups. Frank Campbell, information minister of Guyana, replied that no arguments were needed, rather discussions on how to resolve differences

of opinion, that Unesco "is merely the facilitator, not some kind of bogeyman trying to rob people of their freedom." Leonard H. Marks, secretary treasurer of the World Press Freedom Committee and a former director of the U.S. Information Agency, said he would be opposed to any new information order if that meant "government or Unesco control over the media, reporters' access, their freedom to cover what they want to cover, and censorship of their stories."

28. The Declaration of Talloires, which has been widely reprinted, appeared originally in the *Journal of Communication* 31, 4 (Autumn 1981): 113-15. See Universal Declaration of Human Rights, 368-70.

29. *The New York Times* applauded the declaration as "the first time Western and other free newspapers and broadcasting networks took a united stand against the campaign by Soviet bloc and Third World countries to give Unesco the authority to regulate the flow of news and information." A news report filed by the information arm of the U.S. State Department said the declaration "was seen as a major move against the establishment of a so-called 'New World Information Order' involving arbitrary restrictions on the media, which is under consideration in Unesco." See *Journal of Communications* 32, 3 (Summer 1982): 54-95, for articles by Kaarle Nordenstreng, Clifford H. Block, and Colleen Roach offering differing perspectives.

30. The Declaration of Talloires.

31. Yuri Kornilov, a TASS analyst, portrayed the declaration as a fraud and accused the capitalist news media of waging "psychological war against sovereign states" under the guise of supporting free flow of information.

32. Sarah Goddard Power, a former aide to President Carter, "Freedom of World Press in Danger," *Press Woman*, wrote of a "communications revolution" damaging to traditional ideas of press freedom.

33. At its Madrid meeting, the FIEJ held that the ultimate definition of a press "does not lie in actions of government or international bodies, but in the professionalism, vigor, and courage of individual newspapermen, freely accepting their duties and serving the community, and thereby the individual, by free and open reporting."

34. Leonard R. Sussman, "Opposing Assaults."

35. According to Sussman's report, preventive detention of journalism was the practice in 51 percent of Africa, 89 percent of Asia, and 38 percent of Latin America.

36. Abrams set forth his position in a statement to the committee on July 9, 1981, stating that the United States would retain its Unesco membership "as long as there is any hope of returning Unesco to its mandated responsibility."

37. *Congressional Record*, September 17, 1982. Beard read into the record a letter from President Reagan supporting his proposal and endorsing the Declaration of Talloires. A dozen House members rose to join Beard in a series of ringing speeches endorsing the American concept of a free press, the First Amendment, and even speeches by Thomas Jefferson.

38. Representative Ralph Regula, an Ohio Republican, said in the House debate that "an open press and an open flow of information . . . is fundamental to our nation." Many speakers openly condemned Unesco. Representative Edward J. Derwinski, an Illinois Republican, said Unesco's goal was "muzzling of the press." To Representative Jerry Lewis, a California Republican, it was necessary to move against "those in world bodies such as the UN who would undermine free speech." Representative Gerald B. Solomon, a New York Republican, applauding the U.S. press as a watchdog "checking abuses and

rooting out corruption," asserted there was nothing Communist leaders fear more than a free press. Solomon said he feared "the United States might be put in the position of tacitly approving this suppression. To think that Unesco—an arm of the United Nations—would ever consider some sort of journalistic licensing. It is outrageous."

39. J. Herbert Altschull and Hemant Shah, "How the World Press Reported Unesco's 22nd General Conference," unpublished Unesco document, May, 1984, 40.

40. Altschull and Shah, 15.

41. The recommendation was the seventy-eighth of eighty-two adopted.

42. MacBride, 270-71.

43. Block said, "U.S. funds can go to those projects that are fully consistent with its views, as a nation, of the central importance of freedom of information to a society." "Promising Aid at Acapulco; A U.S. View," *Journal of Communication*, 32, 3 (Summer, 1982): 69-70.

44. Kaarle Nordenstreng, "U.S. Policy and the Third World: A Critique," *Journal of Communication*, 32, 3 (Autumn 1981): 154-59.

45. José A. Mayobré-Machado, "The New World Information and Communication Order: Common Approaches to a Mutual Problem," address, Southern Illinois University, Carbondale, Ill., April 5, 1980.

46. Leonard R. Sussman, "Who Did in Unesco?" foreword in C. Anthony Giffard, *Unesco and the Media* (White Plains, NY: Longman, 1989), xi-xvi.

47. Giffard, 273.

48. Giffard, 223.

49. Giffard, 234.

50. Steven Greenhouse, "Rejoining Unesco Suggested to U.S.," *The New York Times*, February 19, 1994.

51. Andri Isaksson, interview with the author, New York, January 6, 1991.

52. Interview with the author, New York, March 12, 1993.

53. "Report of the Representative of the Director-General on Activities Achieved Since the 12th Session of the Council," Unesco, Paris, February 17, 1992.

54. Report by Eduardo Portella, Deputy Director-General for the IPDC, at the thirteenth session of the IPDC Council, Paris, February 17-24, 1992.

55. "Newspaper Editor Group No Longer Opposes U.S. Membership in Unesco," Associated Press dispatch, Washington, D.C., April 5, 1992.

Chapter
18

Learning and Training
for a Free and Balanced Press

THE EDUCATION OF JOURNALISTS

The challenge to gain and hang on to freedom and fairness in the news media remains elusive. The struggle in Unesco must be viewed in the context of the education of journalists; the turnings and twistings of scholarly research about the news media; the ethical values that are increasingly drawing the attention of the public at large; and the amazing changes that advances in technology are bringing about in education, research, and ethical values.

The school of journalism with an emphasis on practical training is an American invention; it has not established a strong foothold in other nations with market economies. In Western Europe even today, little support is evidenced for practical journalism at institutions of higher learning. Attempts to follow the U.S. model of "nuts-and-bolts" training in the Third World have been frustrated by economic and political pressures. There, too, the European model, which relies on on-the-job training, serves as a counterweight. The difference on the two sides of the Atlantic can be attributed in large measure to the difference in the financial structure of the press. In the United States, where advertising revenues have long represented the chief financial support of the press, political "independence" was early seen as a virtue. Because advertisers are not eager to publish their notices in press vehicles that represent opposing political viewpoints, they are more likely to pour their revenues into the coffers of political independents or those supporting their own views. In Europe, the news media are far more partisan than in the United States and have traditionally adopted open political stands, often serving as outright instruments of political parties. European governments regularly challenge, and even threaten, news media that attack them and their powerful economic interests. Similarly, reacting against criticism of themselves or their interest in pro-government media, German political and economic elites have lent strong support to a campaign to "privatize" German television.[1]

Organs of the opposition in Germany and elsewhere were less interested in maximizing advertising revenue than in political persuasion. The publishers, in these cases, sought to recruit staff members whose politics they shared rather than those who possessed the skills of writing, editing, layout design, and headline writing, which could be taught on the job. In Great Britain, as in Germany and France, publishers have long been inclined to recruit staff members from university programs in economics, politics, or even Latin and Greek. Few European universities publish student newspapers; Oxford students are among the few who have put out their own paper. The American influence has been greater in Latin America and the Far East than in Europe, and a number of university journalism programs have developed in Asia and South America; an increasing number are appearing also in Africa and the Middle East; but in all these cases, training is more likely to stress journalism history and philosophy, theory, and methodology rather than the practical skills.

The earliest-known program of journalism instruction at a university occurred in England in the mid-nineteenth century. By today's standards, these were curious patterns of instruction. Some schools, such as the University of Birmingham, tried in the nineteenth and early twentieth centuries to make journalism training stick; but it was an off-and-on proposition never providing much hands-on practice. More intriguing was the "training" at Balliol College at Oxford University, which became a place for aspiring young newsmen (never, of course, newswomen). Only elite and daring young men considered journalism a career in the 1850s, when Balliol became famous as a springboard for journalists. The idea was that young men would learn the world at the feet of distinguished scholars in the classics. They would chat with the great men as they took their afternoon constitutionals, walking along the banks of canals, commenting during pauses among the showy, splashy colors of spring flowers about the subtleties of international politics. That was all they needed, it was said, to make a distinguished name for themselves on Fleet Street or in India's sunny climes.

After most of these young men died in the trenches in World War I, the plebeian University of London began journalism training in the 1920s. However, the training was not markedly practical. The students did take one seminar in "Practical Journalism," styled somewhat after the American model; however, that instruction was lost in a sea of required courses in English literature, politics, principles of criticism, and a course titled "Economic and Social Structure of Today"—a far remove from the American model. Despite the University of London program, a Royal

Commission on the Press, active in the years after World War II at the same time as the Hutchins Commission, condemned British journalism education for not providing enough training in writing and editing.[2]

The developing of journalists in France followed a similar pattern. As a result, the eyes of aspiring young journalists in the Asian and African colonies of both Britain and France were turned to London and Paris as guideposts, at least during the colonial era and in the early years of independence. Later, they turned to both the United States and the former Soviet Union as models.

Although journalism education did not begin in the United States, it was out of the special political and economic climate of the United States that it arose and flourished and from where it was exported to all parts of the world, where it underwent local transformation in response to differences in political, economic, and even social involvement.

In the United States, schools of journalism appeared as the ideas of progressivism and populism were at their zenith, especially in the Midwest, where the movement for journalism schools began. In the early twentieth century, the Whig interpretation of history was universal: Every day and in every way, things were getting better. Still, while capitalism was certainly morally superior to the oligarchies of Europe and the communism of Soviet Russia, there was always room for improvement and progress; and the press marched in the vanguard of the preachers of improvement and progress. The word that went forth from the journalism schools was that the press was destined to help lead the way to a bright tomorrow in which unlimited years of progress lay ahead. The muckrakers were the heroes, and the code of the watchdog was holy writ. Thus, the students who emerged from journalism schools were automatically tub-thumpers for progress and watchdoggery. They also championed financing newspapers and magazines by advertisements and not by government; advertisers were seen as uninterested in political issues and unlikely to seek to exercise control over content. If advertisers ever tried to do so, they were to be spanked sharply and reminded of who ran the papers and what the mission of the press was. The standard was to keep the advertiser and the business manager in the boardroom, not in the newsroom; it was a standard given clear expression by no less a figure than Joseph Pulitzer, the patron saint of schools of journalism.

After World War I, the Western allies and Germany joined forces in attempting to conquer the Bolshevik revolutionaries. In Russia, they were unsuccessful; on the other hand, they were stunningly victorious in overcoming the Marxist movements that had sprung up in their own countries. By the mid-1920s, Marxist doctrine as modified and applied by Lenin had become a way of life in the Soviet Union; and the Soviet press had put into practice the theories enunciated by Lenin. The Soviet press had become the principal cheerleader for the policies and practices of the Soviet leaders and their carefully planned economy. At the same time, the American press, without benefit of Leninist dogma, had become the principal cheerleader for the policies and practices of the powerful of America and their by now well-established economic system. What had begun as laissez-faire had evolved into a system of free enterprise and on into the modern corporate industrial state. The capitalist belief system as it developed in the United States differed from that of Western Europe in important detail. It took several decades for the press ideology that germinated in the United States to take firm root in the remainder of the industrialized capitalist world.

In post–World War I America, the good life was available for the taking. Americans needed no new consciousness, no Communist party in order to achieve the good life. Indeed, they needed no party at all; they could do it alone. What had beckoned millions of European immigrants in the nineteenth century was for native-born Americans as well a land of unlimited opportunity.

It was at this time that journalism first became an academic discipline in American colleges and universities. Joseph Pulitzer offered to endow a journalism program at Columbia University in 1903, but it took a while for the details to be worked out, and his Graduate School of Journalism did not open its doors until 1912. The first journalism school in actual operation, therefore, was at the University of Missouri, where Walter Williams, a veteran newspaper editor backed by publishers, was installed as dean in 1908. Williams's curriculum was dominated by practical studies—reporting, feature writing, and advertising—and the course of study was centered on practical experience gained in working for the newspaper

Pioneer in journalism education: Walter Williams, first dean of the University of Missouri School of Journalism, introduced academic training for newspersons in 1908.

SOURCE: Western Historical Manuscript Collection, Columbia, MO

published by the students.[3] At the rival University of Wisconsin, Dean Willard Bleyer, a professor of English, followed a somewhat different path. His department did not establish a student newspaper and emphasized instead a program of general education, particularly in writing and the social sciences that, as reported in a history of the university, was viewed as "of greater usefulness in developing journalists than preoccupation with artisan training."[4]

Disputes over which is more valuable for journalists, practical training or general knowledge, have not ceased to this day. Even so, little difference between the two approaches can be found with regard to the basic ideological underpinnings of journalism. It is important to take note of the time when these journalism schools were established. Both the Missouri and the Wisconsin approaches saw the world through the prism of capitalism and progressivism.

Students trained at schools of journalism in the 1920s and 1930s were taught within a belief system that was perhaps as rigidly ideological in its orientation as the system taught to students at journalism schools in the Soviet Union. In later years, as journalism programs expanded to almost every college and university in the United States, some of the teachers and professors who took over were less committed to progressive and laissez-faire dogmas. However, their numbers have been small, and the prevailing belief system holds sway today much as it did in 1912 or 1921.

Schools and departments of journalism have grown from modest beginnings into major institutions. Hundreds of thousands of young men and women are enrolled in these programs, available in the majority of U.S. colleges and universities and thousands of secondary schools as well. Children learn about newspapers and broadcasting stations from their first year in school; they are encouraged to write articles for school newspapers when they are just learning to write. As part of their general education, they acquire information about the free press and its significance in democratic life. By the time young men and women accept employment as journalists, they have had twelve or fourteen years of association with press folklore in their schools; and they have also been socialized by the press itself, rarely modest in its reporting about its own power, significance, and value. Not much of this barrage of material is likely to be cynical; the folklore of the press is believed—as is all dogma—with little challenge. On the limited occasions when it is challenged and questioned, ready answers are available. In the modern industrial state every citizen has an "opinion" about the press and is rarely reluctant to express it. Many of those who condemn the practices of the press act not out of hatred for the institution but out of love for it and a desire to "restore" the press to the honored place it occupied before it became dishonest and corrupt. Americans have a weak sense of history, and folklore finds fertile ground among those who know little of the past.

Within U.S. journalism schools, the excesses of the sensationalistic tabloids that have sprung into prominence came under sharp attack. Serious journalists, those who would graduate from the schools, were to eschew sensationalism and practice instead the code of objectivity, which they saw as the appropriate counter to sensationalistic tabloids. They dreamed of countering the excesses of sensationalism and following the model of Pulitzer, who promoted truth and accuracy (at least in his later years) above sensation and profit. This was also the period in which news agencies or wire services attained greater prominence and preached a form of political fence sitting in the name of objectivity.

In the early years of journalism education, the newspaper industry itself was ambivalent about the wisdom of such training at institutions of higher learning. Some editors liked to recruit their staffs from journalism schools, but more were suspicious of college-trained reporters. Many editors preferred those who had studied, as the saying went, "in the school of hard knocks," drawing on experience over education. The model reporter, the hero of dozens of movies and novels, came out of the stage classic *The Front Page*; he was the hard-drinking, hard-loving cynic with a heart of gold, the ink-stained cousin of the range heroes of the Wild West.[5]

Still, with the passage of time, more and more publishers recruited their staffs from schools of journalism. Whatever the appeal of tradition and the resistance to book learning, the publishers were unable to resist the economic advantages available to them in the journalism schools. These advantages were significant. By recruiting staffs from the journalism schools, publishers could eliminate the considerable cost of on-the-job training. They demanded college and university graduates who were skilled in writing and reportorial techniques, knew how to write headlines, understood the principles of advertising and subscription sales, and were already socialized into the belief systems of the publishers themselves. Who could resist such a financial bonanza? Here were staffs trained for the most part at public expense, reporters who could be relied on to accept and advance the political, social, and economic environment in which they operated. It was the best possible mechanism of social control: adherence to the familiar, cost-effective status quo—and at virtually no cost. It was the taxpayer who footed the bill for this education, because the leading schools of journalism were situated at state colleges and universities supported by public funding. At the private colleges and universities, the expense was borne by students or their families in the form of tuition or endowment funds. In neither case was the cost paid by the press industry. In recent years, many newspapers and broadcasting outlets have reduced their costs even further through internship programs, often without salaries for the student interns, who are compensated instead with academic credit.

Although U.S. schools of journalism are essentially training grounds in the capitalist ideology of the press, the news media are frequently subjected to critical examination in classrooms and research projects. Students are regularly assigned to evaluate press performance, often to examine whether a newspaper or especially a television news outlet has lived up to the ideological expectations of the student or professor. This practice is not universally applauded by media officials, who argue passionately that journalism schools ought to concentrate on training students in newswriting, editing, and electronic skills. Press theorists of a conservative bent tend to follow the lead of such critics as Spiro Agnew, the former vice president, who in 1969 stirred the wrath of the press community by attacking the leading national dailies, *The New York Times* and *The Washington Post,* and the three TV networks, arguing that the journalists who worked for those news media were members of an eastern, liberal establishment whose views did not represent those of Middle America.

Sharp attacks on the media and their alleged independent power continue to fly from both Left and Right, most vigorously from the most conservative wing of the Republican party. The attacks reached a peak in the 1992 presidential election campaign, when all the major candidates devoted many hours to attacking the news media and even individual journalists. The issue of "media bashing" by politicians had entered the journalism education curriculum. As early as 1977, a group of conservative publications set up in Washington, D.C., a National Journalism Center training program for student interns within a context of "traditional values." The conservative columnist M. Stanton Evans, director of the center, said "too many journalists have been taught that capitalism is evil or that America is imperialist and that journalism should be used as a method of advancing political ideas."[6] For some media critics in the United States, the traditional educative role of the journalism schools is not conservative or traditional enough. Dispassionate observers are astonished to hear that. Conventions and meetings of journalism professors and graduate students devote themselves, to a remarkable extent, to programs and research within a framework of preserving and strengthening the belief system that includes devotion to the principle of objectivity and to traditional press values.

In recent years, the European press seems to have been moving closer to the American journalistic mystique embodied in the First Amendment and to the American press style as well, with its emphasis on short paragraphs and sentences and on sharp, conflict-ridden phrasing—and even to its method of training journalists. For instance, German newspapers are beginning to read like American ones, and German universities and institutes are increasing their journalism course offerings to the point of providing training in writing and editing skills. Adoption of the American model has been slower in other European countries, but the ideological and pedagogical movement has been flowing from West to East; and party-oriented newspapers are giving way to a press ostensibly "objective" and free of partisan posturing.

Publishers as well as writers throughout Europe have for generations clung to a belief that writing nonfiction is a talent that cannot really be learned in school. That belief is eroding, even though newspapers and radio and television organizations are still far more likely to opt for on-the-job training than for training in university settings. A training institute in Munich opened its doors in 1958, but enrollment is rigorously controlled, with only 45 individuals a year surviving the first competition for admission.[7]

While American-style journalism education has never been wholly accepted as appropriately academic in Western Europe, most major European universities now provide some lectures and/or seminars in communications. The emphasis remains primarily on research, however, with only limited university training provided in basic skills. As far back as 1909, the German sociologist Karl Bücher called for university training of journalists; however, his emphasis was on what he called "the science of press research."[8] In France, Belgium, Holland, Austria, Denmark, Norway, Sweden, and Finland, the same pattern obtains: schools or institutes of journalism with heavy concentration on research in linguistics and the social sciences. In Finland, for example, university education in journalism and communications began in 1925 following the model pioneered by Bücher; but not until 1980 were efforts made to reorganize the training along American lines. Courses are offered today in news writing and editing, yet the heavy emphasis remains on social-science techniques.

Throughout Western Europe, training in basic skills continues to be confined primarily to private schools and polytechnic institutes. England, like Germany, has been increasing its training programs in journalism skills at polytechnic institutes. Two German universities have been experimenting with seminars on writing skills. To a U.S. journalism professor, it seemed more than mildly strange to offer, as one university did, a "seminar" requiring each student to prepare but one story in a semester. More common in German universities are seminars on communications within faculties of philosophy, psychology, or pedagogy.

From the time the Soviet Union took control over Eastern Europe after World War II, journalism education there adhered to the Leninist program. The important institutes for journalism training at universities in Prague and East Berlin drew thousands of journalists from Eastern Europe as well as the Third World. The collapse of the Soviet empire brought an end to education in the Marxist-Leninist model. Practicing and would-be journalists began clamoring for American-style training. "We don't know the techniques of how to be tough but not rude or how to be a watchdog," American visitors were told by Karol Jakubowicz, deputy director of international relations for Polish Radio and TV.[9] Similar comments came from reporters and editors from Czechoslovakia, Hungary, and the former Soviet zone in Berlin. With financial help from the New York Times Foundation and the Knight Foundation, an institute called the Prague Center opened in Prague in 1991 aimed at providing hands-on training for journalists and media managers; at the same time, plans were launched to create foundations whose members will buy shares in the central printing plant.

The School of Journalism at the Moscow State University somehow managed to bridge the gap between old and new. Yasen N. Zassursky remained as dean but shifted from the ideological strictures of Marxism-Leninism to American-style pragmatism. Away with fixation on politics and economics, he demanded; more emphasis on everyday life. For Russian papers, he said, splitting sharply from his own earlier stance under the old Communist regime, revenues from advertising were demanded. Readers' concerns that had been "unjustifiably ignored" needed to be taken into account. Zassursky said, "Take, for example, subjects like domestic affairs, family matters and health. And what about theater, cinema, education and sport? Here we are always being hammered by politics. It dominates everything."[10]

The future direction of journalism education in the industrialized world seemed not altogether clear as the twenty-first century approached. Would there be more specific hands-on training or would there be further emphasis on scholarly research? How would the opportunities and restrictions that grew out of the rapid changes in technology play themselves out? It was not unlikely the rift between academics and practitioners would deepen rather than narrow.

INTERNATIONAL INFLUENCES ON THIRD WORLD TRAINING

Outside the industrialized nations of the West, Japan, and the major cities of the former Soviet Union, it has been radio above all other media that has influenced the definition of news and the training of journalists. And the model, not only for radio but for newspapers and television as well, has been the British Broadcasting Corporation (BBC). It stands even today as a model for "good" journalism not only in Britain's former colonies but almost everywhere. For the market world, the training of journalists from the advancing world has been a matter of major importance. For the British and the French, this kind of training was for years a staple of foreign policy. In this particular game, the United States and the former Soviet Union were newcomers, though their economic and military might cast them into dominant positions. Still, of all the press instruments in the industrialized world, the most powerful in the transfer of ideology has continued to be the BBC. It has not only accomplished a remarkable job in public relations but also for more than half a century has been running its own journalism education program.

Over the years, the BBC raised studied indifference to the level of art. BBC chieftains and staffers took pride in their dispassionate treatment of the most dramatic and shocking news events; in this, they consciously pursued the goal of public-service broadcasting. It was not their mission to influence the audience to one position or another but simply to lay out for their listeners the "facts" and coolly rational explanations of the meaning of those facts.

All around the planet, BBC newscasters established a reputation as the most thorough and most objective of all reporters of international news, certainly among broadcasters if not among all journalists. In the former British colonies of Asia and Africa, the reputation has been especially exalted, since in the revolutionary days in which the colonial powers were ousted, the BBC studiously avoided any kind of overt bias in its broadcasts. Moreover, the BBC standards were reinforced in the advancing world by training and education. With positive support from the British government, the BBC in 1951 began providing training courses for broadcast journalists from the advancing world. In the decades that followed, nearly 1,000 broadcasters have attended the BBC courses, at least half from Africa. In 1965, television training was added to the program; the journalists who attended these TV courses then returned to their native lands prepared to reinforce the already popular BBC model. Even before the training courses were initiated in London, the BBC had been dispatching experts throughout the British Empire to assist those who were starting radio enterprises.

In the francophone colonial empire, the French conducted similar programs, bringing African broadcasters to Paris for training. The French Office of Radio Cooperation (*l'Office de Cooperation Radiophonique*) went the British one better, taking direct charge of developing television in France's African territories and ultimately merging the new groups into the homeland French radio and television system. The French model is not unpopular in former French territories, but it has never enjoyed the immense prestige of the BBC. For one thing, it was not unknown in Africa that French broadcasting was far more tightly controlled by the government in Paris than was the BBC in London. Hence, the public-service image of the BBC has never been matched by the French broadcasting system. The reputation of the BBC is high not only in Britain's former colonies but also in Western Europe, Japan, the United States, and even China and the countries once dominated by the Soviet Union. One might say that over the years the BBC has been Britain's most valuable export—for the BBC has exported not only a particular style of broadcasting but also a set of political and cultural values that have taken root all over the world.

Despite its public-service image and appearance of disinterest, the BBC has been no more capable of objective treatment of news than has any other medium of communication. For the most part, BBC journalists inhabit an upper-middle-class social order with the values of that socioeconomic order; they are just as likely to view the people of the advancing world as children to be led by the hand and socialized into polite society as are any other members of their class. Try as hard as they might, these journalists have been unable to convince many people in the advancing world they do not hold them in some form of contempt. The result is confusion. For although the BBC style is profoundly respected, the content of the news programs is often denounced.

Moreover, those African and Asian broadcast journalists who have studied in the United States have been exposed to a quite different model, that of commercial broadcasting. Few American radio or television journalists pattern themselves on the men and women of the BBC. To present the news in a cool, dispassionate manner is anathema. Conventional wisdom holds that audiences will switch dials to competitor stations if the news is not presented in a dramatic fashion. To many journalism students and practitioners from the advancing world, the American style seems more suitable since it can be adapted more easily to political ends. On the other hand, the commercialization of American television dismays many journalists of the advancing world, who, following the BBC model with which they have long been familiar, concern themselves primarily with "serious" news and not gossip or frivolous information. What does fascinate and excite the students and journalists from the advancing world is the technical quality of American broadcasting (and of newspapers as well). To be able to make use of the technological innovations in their homeland would enable them, most are convinced, not only to provide more interesting broadcasts but also to bring greater stores of information to their audiences and thus ultimately assist mightily in the modernization of their nation.

Technology does not come without a price. That price is the system of values accompanying the technology. And the value system imparted in the United States is identical in all major aspects to the value system imparted in the BBC and French training courses. It is the value system of the professional. Whatever else may characterize a professional, it is certain that he or she operates within the belief system in which the profession has achieved status—meaning the status quo. Whether pursuing the traditional public-service stance of the BBC or the dramatic public-interest posture of the American broadcasters, the professional carries out the role of observer rather than that of participant and, with few exceptions, makes a fetish of avoiding direct political pronouncements or even political involvement. As two British researchers pointed out correctly, professionalism not only props up the status quo but also favors proficiency over ideology and the pragmatic over the utopian.[11] Ideology is rejected even as it is being disseminated. And the grand dreams of the utopian journalists are ridiculed even as they are being given expression in the capitalist framework that has glorified the utopian image of a free press shining as a beacon of human liberty. Social control is at the heart of the status quo, and the new governments of advancing countries all aim for political stability in a social order they attempt to drive into political equilibrium in a newly constituted status quo. This pattern is found in the new countries structured along both authoritarian and or democratic lines.

Media technology and media value systems represent important ideological weapons. The former Soviet Union and its East European allies, notably Czechoslovakia and East Germany, sought under their communist regimes to export their technology and value systems. Journalists from the advancing world were often provided full financing to study at the schools of journalism in Moscow, Prague, and East Berlin. And Soviet journalism instructors regularly traveled to Africa and Asia to aid—and to convert—journalists of the advancing world to their ideological orientation. In the case neither of the capitalist nations nor of the socialist nations was the effort successful. Instead, the advancing world developed a press belief system of its own. It is far too early, however, to speak of that belief system as one of permanence. The efforts of the powerful nations of the industrialized world to dominate and ultimately undo an ideology for the advancing world continue—and with increasing determination.

It is important to keep in mind that the fall of the great colonial empires, from Britain and France to the Soviet Union, was accompanied by a phenomenal explosion of new technologies. The developing media in the new nations have often been more committed to expanding their technical skills than to questions of truth, free expression, and moral values. Nowhere is this development more evident than in South Asia, where strides in technology and commercial benefit have outstripped questions of professional behavior. It was in Asia, as pointed out earlier, that the idea of "development journalism" had its impetus. Institutes in the Philippines, India, and Singapore led the way, and it was chiefly from those institutes that the drive for a New World Information and Communication Order gained force. The compelling goal among the new entrepreneurs was profit, and it was soon apparent that only through derailing dissident forces that the dominant political and econom-

Marsden Epworth (left) learns about journalism life in Indonesia:
U.S. reporter on the job in Jakarta

SOURCE: Marsden Epworth

ic forces could exercise social control. Journalism education provided the means of social control. Marsden Epworth, who put in two years as a journalist in Indonesia, made the point graphically. If journalists "can read and write," Epworth wrote, "and if they can tell what news bolsters the regime and what news does not, they've got a job."[12] In other words, being educated in the system and recognizing the need for self-censorship guaranteed the journalist could find work. If a journalist tried to operate outside the system, he or she was effectively disqualified from the field. Direct censorship was not necessary.[13]

I am well aware of the pattern. As a teacher in foreign journalist-education programs at Indiana University and at a special school in Berlin, I had many occasions to chat informally with journalists from all parts of the advancing world. They were careful to protect their own identities, but there was just about universal agreement that students in journalism-education programs in their own countries learned quickly their viability was linked to their political and economic reliability. Promote the status quo, they learned, and they had an economic future. It was far safer, and potentially most profitable, to drink in technological skills than it was to concern yourself with the moral dictates of free expression. Hence, all the journalism schools in Asia, Africa, and Latin America laid heavy weight on communications research, where what was learned was not likely to pose political or economic challenges to the wielders of power.

Academic programs in communications have mushroomed in Asia; by the mid-1980s, the region counted no fewer than 250 such programs, all of them strong on research and weak on practical training. Some newspapers, such as *The Times of India*, created their own in-service programs. In addition, radio and television organizations followed the British model, offering training to prospective employes. Together with research techniques and communication skills, these programs provided subtle training in how to get along in a job. The best way, of course, was to avoid rocking the boat. One of the most striking examples of what could happen took place in 1980 when the Malaysian government shut down the seventeen-year-old newspaper *Tamil Malar* for publishing an article implying the Moslem practice of polygamy could spread venereal disease. The government revoked the publisher's license, charging that the article was insulting to Islam.[14]

Malaysia, incidentally, has developed one of the strongest education programs for journalists in the advancing world. By the late 1980s, nearly 1,000 students were enrolled in programs at five universities and colleges. And Singapore set up, with the help of Germany's Friedrich-Ebert Institute, the most prestigious communications research center in Asia, where many conferences draw scholars from the West as well as the Asian lands.[15] Despite the number of such institutes throughout the region, many working journalists are without college education or any special journalistic training. Prospective journalists from all over Asia frequently journey to the United States to study at American colleges. Many, although initially determined to return home as newspersons or educators, change their minds and return to the United States.

Similar tales can be told about the training of African journalists, although it must be said that journalism education in Africa is nowhere near so advanced as it is in Asia. One of the main challenges posed by the 1991 Windhoek Declaration was put to the United Nations and Unesco, demanding as "a matter of urgency" that steps be taken to upgrade the training of journalists and managers of journalism-education institutes.[16] Not only that. Delegates from thirty-eight countries also demanded removal of economic barriers to training institutes, news-media outlets, newsprint quotas, and printing and typesetting equipment, all of which stifle establishment of an independent press.

Unesco and other nongovernmental organizations promptly set up limited budgets to help push forward some of the proposals set forth at Windhoek. The most ambitious provided a budget of $6 million to create three regional training programs—in Benin, Senegal and Zimbabwe—to develop a cadre of qualified professionals who would head up a plan for developing the necessary infrastructure to produce "an independent press in Africa."[17] Other programs, underwritten by journalists' federations in the industrialized world, would provide for enlightening exchanges among journalists in various countries to help the causes of antigovernment dissidents.

On-the-scene journalism education in sub-Saharan Africa began when Kwame Nkrumah opened the Ghana Institute of Journalism in 1957, but progress has been slow, and although schools have appeared in countries throughout the region, few if any of them can be described as adequate.[18] In these pages, reference has been made to schools in both eastern and western Africa, but neither visiting Western educators nor African journalists have found these underfinanced institutions to be of outstanding value. As in Asia, the heaviest concentration has been on communications research and new technologies. Education in writing and editing is severely limited. In addition to pressures from governments that have no interest in training political dissidents, journalism education is faced with serious problems of language. Dozens, even hundreds, of languages are spoken in each country, so the most common languages for the literate classes remain English and French. Only elite Africans are able to read either of these languages, and even they resist the "cultural imperialism" that inevitably accompanies the use of a foreign tongue. Furthermore, would-be journalists and would-be scholarly researchers continue to find greater financial opportunity with universities and journalism organizations in the West. The brain drain on African journalists remains extensive.

Television has been growing slowly, but as the twentieth century nears its end, the primary means of reaching citizens in African remained the radio. Even there, the linguistic problem has been troublesome. Some broadcasts in native languages have been accomplished, yet here, too, the main languages for radio broadcasts continue to be English and French. Most African governments have been making serious efforts to expand radio coverage, often assisted by Unesco's IPDC. But, as always, there has not been enough money to go around.

The heritage of British colonialism remains a further roadblock in the development of journalism education in Africa. Britain has never welcomed the idea of teaching journalism skills in universities, and many African journalists have inherited what Professor L. John Martin of the University of Maryland speaks of as "prejudice against formal academic training in journalism."[19] These are the seasoned reporters who have worked their way up from "tea boy" (the equivalent of the American gofer copy boy) to editor. Many of the leading old-line African editors were in fact educated in Britain and served their journalism apprenticeship in that country. More recently, it is the American university that has attracted African journalists, many signing on with healthy scholarships awarded by their own governments or sometimes by the American universities themselves. But, as in the case of American-trained Asian journalists, many of them decide to remain in the United States, further slowing the pace of development at African colleges and institutes.

The U.S. pattern of journalism education has influenced training in Latin America for many years, although there has always been heavy concentration on questions of communication research. Much of Latin American research has been Marxist in tone, fired by a desire among Latin scholars to dispute the unwritten assumption in communication research in all market economies that "democratic" news media are part and parcel of a free-market economy. A number of Marxist scholars in Mexico, for instance, see the social-control function of news media in the United States as working for a competitive economic advantage over Latin America. In this view, the U.S. media serve by and large as agents of another form of cultural imperialism that works for the financial well-being of U.S. media organizations and as salespeople of instruments of new technology, especially computer software.

The market economy has been so successful in the United States that it has offered journalists, most of whom ardently support the system, substantial rewards in terms of money and prestige. The same is true to some extent in Latin

America, but there one finds far less tolerance of press criticism of institutions of power. In Latin America, as we have seen in the case of Peru, vast, almost unbridgeable differences remain between the holders of power and the have-not peasants and workers, from whose ranks journalists often emerge. U.S. journalists have by and large joined—or been co-opted into—the ranks of the powerful, so that only in small, relatively powerless newspapers and magazines does one find active dissent from the market system. In Latin America, however, dissident journalists remain an important threat to the holders of economic power. One method of controlling dissident journalists has, appropriately, been pay scales. As recently as 1986, for example, the beginning salary for reporters in Mexico was a mere $120 per month. To make ends meet, it was quite necessary for working journalists to take on a second or even a third job. Politicians moved in to offer jobs to the financially desperate reporters, but only, of course, if they turned out news reports satisfying the wishes of their employers.[20] Latin American academics have, accordingly, been among the most zealous of those urging a new world information order at Unesco.

Journalism education itself has made remarkable advances throughout Latin America. Between 1950 and 1985, the number of journalism programs there rose from 7 to 200. The most prestigious institute was actually founded with Unesco funds. CIESPAL (International Centre of Advanced Studies in Journalism), operating out of Quito, Ecuador, has become one of the leading journalism research centers in the hemisphere. Practical training, however, continues to be limited, both there and at institutions of higher learning.

One of the more interesting aspects of journalism education south of the border has been the controversy over *colegio* laws that have been adopted in a dozen countries. Under these laws, which were written in the 1980s, only those who received a journalism *colegatura*, meaning a degree from an officially accredited university, were permitted to practice their trade. You can get an argument almost everywhere about the impact of these laws. One side argues that the laws were written in order to guarantee illiberal governments legal authority to manipulate the press to their own advantage. The other side says the laws were designed to upgrade the salaries and prestige of journalists and even to protect them from unwanted governtment presssures. The American educator Mary Gardner, among others, has complained that these laws allow despotic governments to keep firm control not only over employment practices but also over the content of news stories.[21] Under *colegio* laws, native reporters have been chastised and foreign correspondents expelled. Still, delegates to Unesco conferences tend to support the laws on the ground they tend to upgrade the quality of journalism education, and many Latin journalists endorse them because they guarantee higher salaries.

The great majority of nineteenth- and twentieth-century Latin-American writers have found that only a journalism career offered them a chance to survive financially while trying to create literature.[22] Like Mariátegui, they tended to avoid political topics for fear of government reprisals, contenting themselves with writing "chronicles" on what were ostensibly nonpolitical questions. However, like Marx, they often managed to sneak in cryptic commentary whose dissident messages were clear only to those prepared to read the messages hidden between the lines. There are no easy answers to complex problems.

NOTES

1. For instance, an outpouring of official protests followed the recent nationwide airing over a government-supported TV network of a program exposing the World War II use of slave labor at an Auschwitz plant operated by Daimler-Benz, now the largest corporation in the country.

2. Patrick Brogan, *Spiked: The Short Life and Death of the National News Council* (New York: Priority Press, 1985), 104–108.

3. Sara Lockwood Williams, *Twenty Years for Journalism: A Complete History of the School of Journalism of the University of Missouri* (Columbia, MO: Stephens, 1930).

4. Merle Curti and Vernon Carstenen, *The University of Wisconsin*, vol. 2 (Madison: University of Wisconsin Press, 1949).

5. Ben Hecht and Charles MacArthur, *The Front Page* (New York: Macmillan, 1927).

6. *Columbia Journalism Review*. January/February/1981, 6.

7. Kaarle Nordenstreng, ed., *Reports on Journalism Education in Europe* (Tampere, Finland: University of Tampere Department of Journalism and Mass Communication, 1990). See the section on Germany by Jürgen Wilke.

8. Karl Bücher, "The Genesis of Journalism," in *Industrial Revolution* (New York: Henry Holt, 1901), 215–43.

9. Brian J. Buchanan, *Cries for Freedom: The Struggle for Independent Media in the Soviet Union and East Europe* (Arlington, VA: The Freedom Forum, 1991). The American delegation, under the chairmanship of Allen H. Neuharth, head of the Gannett chain, spent ten days in August 1991 visiting Eastern Europe and eliciting the views of journalists there.

10. Interview with Zassursky, *Pravda*, January 18, 1992, reprinted in Peggy L. Cuciti and Marshall Kaplan, *Building a Free Media in the Commonwealth of Independent States* (Denver: Graduate School of Public Affairs, University of Colorado, 1992), 46.

11. Jay G. Blumber and Michael Gurevich, "Journalists' Orientation to Political Institutions: The Case of Parliamentary Broadcasting," in Peter Golding et al. (eds.) *Communicating Politics: Mass Communication and the Political Process* (Leicester, England: Leicester University Press, 1986).

12. Marsden Epworth, "Why Chernobyl Was a Nonstory and Other Tales of Indonesian Journalism," *Columbia Journalism Review* (September/October 1988): 42.

13. John A. Lent, "Mass Communication in Asia and the Pacific: Recent Trends and Developments," *Media Asia* 16 (1989): 23–24.

14. John A. Lent, "Restructuring of Mass Media in Malaysia and Singapore—Pounding in the Coffin Nails," *Bulletin of Concerned Asian Scholars* 16, 4 (1984): 32.

15. Anne Cooper Chen and Anju Grover Chaudhary, eds., "Asia and the Pacific," in John C. Merrill, ed., *Global Journalism: Survey of International Communication* (White Plains,

NY: Longman, 1991), 205-66. The reader interested in additional details about journalism education throughout the advancing world is directed to Merrill's book and its extensive bibliography.

16. *Final Report: Seminar on Promoting an Independent and Pluralistic African Press* (Paris: Unesco, 1991), 27.

17. "Follow-Up of Windhoek," mimeographed document provided by Unesco and circulated at the close of the Windhoek Conference, 1991.

18. L. John Martin, "Africa," in Merrill, *Global Journalism*, 155-204.

19. Martin, 204.

20. Michael B. Salwen, Bruce Garrison, and Robert T. Buckman, "Latin America," in Merrill, *Global Journalism*, 267-310.

21. Salwen, Garrison and Buckman.

22. Among them was the distinguished writer Mario Vargas Llosa, whose *Aunt Julia and the Scriptwriter* (New York: Farrar, Straus, & Giroux, 1982) is a portrait of the tough life of Latin-American journalists.

Chapter

19

Ethics and the Explosion of Knowledge

COMMUNICATION RESEARCH: A VARIETY OF PARADIGMS

The twin tracks of journalism education can be symbolized by Walter Williams's plan at the University of Missouri and Willard Bleyer's model at the University of Wisconsin. In both cases, however, journalism education found its scholarly home in a new discipline which emerged as "mass communication." We have seen how the Wisconsin model fit comfortably into the development in Europe of scientific studies of sociology, psychology, and political science. The Missouri model was more suitable as a division of the humanities rather than as one of the social sciences. Time has blurred the edges of this distinction, but the division still continues today.

In the mid-twentieth century, the division was often portrayed as a collision between the Green Eyeshades and the Chi Squares. The Eyeshades were a shortcut symbol for the gritty, no-nonsense, hard-boiled copy editor who insisted on clean, well-written copy; dispassionate, objective reporting and editing; and a dedication to the human animal and the human condition—hence one of the humanities. The Chi Square stood for a statistical measurement that served as an instrument for finding answers to complex sociological problems in communication, such as how and why individuals and groups communicate with one another; it scorned the humanities and identified itself as one of the social sciences. Its ultimate aim was to analyze empirically collected data in order to predict the course of human and social behavior and how the mass media affect ideas and behavior. In the early days of the rift, the face-off was fierce, as it was in other disciplines. Today, the two tracks move forward in uneasy harmony. Among practitioners, however, much of what is taught and learned in schools of mass communication is regarded as unnecessary and harmful to the actual work of the news media.

The rise of communication research is part of what we call the communication revolution, the explosion of knowledge; this "revolution" came simultaneously with the collapse of the European order. The advancing nations rose alongside the computer. The study of both interpersonal and mass communication has been the most striking new area for social research in the postwar world. In particular, communication research spearheaded analysis of modernization and the impact of new technology on human life everywhere. In all corners of the world, theorists plunged with abandon into the arenas of cybernetics, data flow, and computer models. A literature that did not exist as recently as 1945 has grown into one of the most voluminous anywhere. The search for answers intrigued scholars and laypeople, spawning even the "science" of futurology. Empirical studies without end have collected data about the way information travels from person to person and from nation to nation as well as about how to predict the future.

It is not within the scope of this book to explore all the avenues of social-science research in the field of mass communication or interpersonal communication. Clear differences persist between interpersonal and mass communication, although sometimes the two overlap. Our concern here is with *mass* communication—more specifically with the communication of *news*, information that human beings either want or need in order to carry out their function as citizens of a community, a nation, a universe. We have seen how difficult it has become to distinguish news from entertainment. This, too, is a topic that interests many researchers.

The question of the power of the media is central in media resesearch. In the early days of communication studies, it was widely assumed the media exerted an enormous impact on ideas, values, and behavior. The idea of an all-powerful media gave rise to a number of colorful catch phrases, such as the "Magic Bullet theory" and the "Hypodermic Needle theory." But *theory* is far too grand a term to apply to these and other concepts of mass communication. Today's scholars are almost universally skeptical; academic publications are filled with *calls* for a theory; many articles identify themselves as steps *toward* a theory. To avoid the pitfall of "theory," researchers have turned to "paradigms"—and these are in fact hypotheses or quasi-theories.[1] These paradigms deal with the interaction of media, society, and individuals; cover the media, the audiences they address, and the relationships between them. Some of the prominent paradigms under discussion include the cognitive, the evolutionary, the interdependent, the structural functional, and the symbolic interactive. Each paradigm has its own supporters, and each represents an earnest effort to find a way to integrate the data collected in half a century of research.

Our concern here is with the question of media power, and the explanations and analyses set forth in this book take issue with much of the paradigmatic work in the field. A diminishing number of authorities cling to the Magic Bullet theory, which holds that a media report has a direct impact on each audience member, forgetting that audience members interact. Many still contend that the mass media dictate most of the opinions and attitudes held by the public. The agenda-setting idea holds that the media may not tell us what to think but what to think about. Other paradigms see the media as exerting less a *direct* impact on ideas than a partial impact, but that even this must be corroborated by other factors. Still others hold that the power and influence of the media are continuing to gain strength with advances in technology and the increasing complexity of the modern world. Different audiences for news reports, it is argued, use the media for different purposes: some to gain better understanding of the world around them, some to learn what is for sale in the marketplace, and some simply for entertainment. Many scholars lament polluting "news" with too heavy a dose of "entertainment." Others are much kinder to the entertainment role and see it as a form of useful play. Melvin De Fleur and Sandra Ball-Rokeach argue that "by removing entertainment from the realm of information, we diminish the role of play in personal and social life."[2] William Stephenson goes further; he takes the position that the capacity of an audience to choose its own individual entertainment safeguards it from the social control that might otherwise be exercised over it by the media or the forces behind the media.[3]

A model espoused by De Fleur and Ball-Rokeach marked a promising attempt to integrate all the theories under the mantle of one paradigm in which society, the individual, and the mass media are dependent on one another. It attempted to build a theory describing the processes and the effects of this dependency. Moreover, it applauded a sociological model in which a network of checks and balances maintains equilibrium among media, government, and other sociopolitical segments as each tries to increase its own power at the expense of the others.[4]

There is a fundamental difference between the concept of media power described in this book and that found in current research paradigms. It is argued here that there is no balance of power among society, individuals, and the mass media. The holders of power are in ultimate control over available resources.[5] In a coup, it isn't the media that silence governments; it is governments that muzzle the media. Here we come close to what mass-media scholars sometimes describe as the "control paradigm." However, power is not shared equally. In a confrontation between the holders of political and economic power and the media, it is the media that must yield, even though on most matters the media are allowed considerable latitude. It is in the interest of the holders of power to grant that latitude so long as the perimeters of acceptable dissent are not bridged. To some degree, this theoretical approach resembles Marx's concept of the *Überbau*, or superstructure, though the approach parts company with Marx in many other areas.

Journalism education has been under attack for years. Criticism has taken many forms and is often contradictory partly because the field has not always been easy to define. There was a time when journalism education, whether it followed the Missouri or the Wisconsin model, meant precisely training and preparing of students who aspired to the life of newspeople. That relatively straightforward characterization began to crumble after World War II, when schools started admitting students who wanted to prepare for careers in advertising or public relations or perhaps public-opinion studies or media management. Still later, the schools began training students who were not really interested in any kind of career associated with journalism but wanted training in how to become more sophisticated "consumers" of the news product. All these were part of preparing *undergraduates* for the degree of bachelor of arts or science. Professors of journalism were not considered scholars. Few had master's degrees; almost none was a doctor of philosophy. Academics in other fields scoffed, objecting to "trade-school students" being considered proper inhabitants of "higher education." In order to elevate the field into a "discipline," many professors and researchers switched loyalty from journalism to communication. This switch came simultaneously with mounting awareness of the use of propaganda in warfare and the development of opinion research. It was a short step to recognition that there are many different aspects of communication. In fact, everything is communication—without the transmission of information between individuals, there would be no civilization.

Scholars began seeking and earning advanced degrees in *mass* communication; soon it became a discipline of its own, accorded the kind of academic recognition that had never been granted to journalism. Communication departments sprang up in universities from one end of the country to the other. In these departments, journalism was only part of the academic program. The division between Green Eyeshades and Chi Squares deepened. Editors, who had become comfortable in seeking out and hiring journalism-school graduates, were now responding with displeasure to schools that concentrated on studies of statistics and other research skills.

However, not all the criticism was directed at jargon-filled programs in mass communication. There was equal condemnation of U.S. journalism schools for focusing too narrowly on basic writing and editing skills and not dedicating sufficient attention to the substance of the stories graduates would deal with on the job. In a survey of newspaper editors as far back as 1974, the editors found students trained in other "professional" schools were far better educated than those in journalism schools.[6] Three years later, delegates to a symposium of publishers agreed that journalism schools were doing such a poor job that "most of the talent turned out by the J-schools today is unfit for newspaper use."[7] Many of the publishers wanted the schools to hire fewer academically trained professors and, as the California publisher who keynoted the session demanded, more of the "pros who can show the students how it is really done."[8]

These are harsh criticisms indeed, and leading American journalism schools have worked hard in the last several decades to provide their graduates with the kind of training most desired by editors and publishers. Many schools have downplayed the nuts-and-bolts training and required their graduates to devote as much time to studying a nonjournalism academic specialty as to studying journalism skills. Many require double majors. Even so, the criticism continues. Carolyn Lewis, onetime associate dean of the prestigious Columbia University Graduate School of Journalism, wrote in 1986 that she had found most university programs in journalism to be "merely trade schools," whereas, they ought to have been "training young

Editor assails journalism schools: Charlie Peters, editor-in-chief of *Washington Monthly*, says even the best journalism schools do not teach students "how to think."

SOURCE: *Washington Monthly*

people to think critically and evaluate information." Charlie Peters, editor-in-chief of *The Washington Monthly*, continued in the same sharply critical vein, suggesting that a year of law school would do prospective journalists more good than a journalism school. "A good law school," he wrote, "teaches you how to think, which, alas, even the best journalism schools and undergraduate colleges usually fail to do."[9] While the drumbeat of criticism continued, American journalism education has retained substantial support among the country's editors. Indeed, 40 percent of the journalists on staffs of newspapers, magazines, and broadcast organizations are graduates of journalism programs.[10] Edmund Lambeth, who has written frequently about the ethics of journalism, suggested that the disparity in the views about journalism education arises in part because it is often compared with other professions, such as law and medicine. Journalism, he wrote, was actually "a craft with professional responsibilities."[11] In any case, despite the complaints, enrollment in journalism schools, in 1992, remained high. Nearly 150,000 students were enrolled in 360 U.S. schools, most of them in undergraduate programs. Master's programs are offered at 161 institutions, doctorates at 32.[12]

Some of these doctorates are in journalism, but most are in mass communication. This fact caused the other half of the paradox of journalism education: While, on the one hand, some editors said too much time is spent in basic-skills courses, others complained too *little* time was devoted to skills and too much to sociological studies in mass communication—that is, to "numbers crunching." Among the new communication scholars there was an overriding concern with the hardware of communication. It was this concern that often divided communication researchers from journalism researchers. The studies of many communication scholars tended to pay only limited attention to newspapers and broadcasting outlets, dealing with broader areas of communication almost as if the news media did not exist, as if global communication were imaginable without the news media. On the other hand, many in journalism doctoral programs, inspired by widely publicized debates in international forums, have collected mountains of data as they sought to learn whether news reports around the world give balanced information about international events.

How ironic it is that, although the avowed goal of communication scholars has been to build theories of communication, their research has often been so narrow that understanding has been muddled rather than enhanced. Borrowing from the "truth trees" of philosophers, the stimulus-response diagrams of psychologists, and the mathematical models of physicists, communication scholars adopted the arrow as their universal symbol. Some arrows ran in straight lines; some were curved; some even bent back on themselves. These scholars sought to describe the flow of communication from source (stimulus) to receiver (response) with elaborate cross-arrowed mechanisms illustrating single or multiloop feedback systems. The arrows had the fortuitous characteristic of impressing fellow scholars with the rigor behind the graphic design yet do lamentably little to resolve the crucial international (and domestic) ills that grew from faulty communication.

If the arrow symbolized the work of the communication scholars, the table of contents typified the efforts of journalism researchers. They prepared and published towering piles of books, monographs, and scholarly papers recording and comparing the contents of newspapers and items on the evening-news reports as they assessed whether the media presented balanced reports about the "news." However, a mere tabulation of content told little about balance. And, even if it did, that information would be of limited utility in attacking the real challenges that face contemporary journalism.

And that brings us back to the intimate linkage of the computer, the symbol of the communication revolution, and the emergence of the advancing states. In advancing states, many political leaders sought to gain and hold power by leaping from traditional forms of communication to the high-technology patterns of the modern world, where nation building was more important than adherence to the free-press model of earlier years. While the numbers of arrows and tables of contents multiplied in libraries and research centers, the attention of journalists, public officials, and many researchers in the advancing world were directed to a different question: how to harmonize the press systems those nation-states acquired from the industrialized nations with the traditional patterns of information in their pasts. It was in the framework of this question that an ideology of the advancing world appeared. In Iran and other Islamic and communitarian societies, the public and traditional leaders did not view high technology as a good thing. The information society revered in market nations ran "contrary to the basic conceptions of the Islamic community and a number of the principal tenets of Islam," researcher Hamid Mowlana wrote.[13] The resurgence of the oral culture and the revolutionary political movements were reactions against Western high-tech modernization. Meanwhile, in

An optimist about the future of the media: David Bartlett, president of the Radio and Television News Directors Association, is convinced high-tech growth brings more knowledge and harmony.

SOURCE: RTNDA

the West, the pace of technological growth was so swift that the very nature of mass communication is changing. Journalism schools have struggled to adapt their curricula to the demands of the new technologies, but the challenge may be too great. That is certainly the viewpoint of the men and women who deal with the production of computerized news. Officials of the RTNDA (Radio and Television News Directors Association) said they were convinced the current ways in which news is reported and disseminated may well vanish like the dodo within a decade or two. Their objection to journalism education was that it was not training students for the complex world of contemporary telecommunication, let alone for the world of the twenty-first century. David Bartlett, the RTNDA president, said the shift from analog to digital technology was making it possible for the flow of information to be identical for all media and for all news consumers as well.[14] The digital bit-stream distribution system, Bartlett said, would soon make obsolete the traditional methods of news dissemination from central news-gathering locations, such as newspapers and television stations. Standard television networks would vanish; so would newspapers and magazines that stubbornly stuck to the old methods.

In this view, technology would introduce a flood of information along the bit-stream flow, which would be available at blinding speed to anyone with the appropriate receiver. The news-*gathering* function of journalists would, Bartlett said, "change very little, although most of their work [would] be on local or regional stories," while the leading national and international stories would be classified and analyzed by the remaining news agencies. The Associated Press, for instance, was already "on the cutting edge of technology." Kent Cooper's old news-gathering agency was already feeding audio signals and video images to its members and might well soon become a leading bit-stream operator. The AP, he said, intends to be as ubiquitous in the high-tech world as it had long been in the news-*distribution* business. He did not envisage the demise of newspapers. While in the high-tech world just down the pike, the distribution function of newspapers would be gone, he said, the news-gathering function would expand, a phenomenon that would benefit newspapers, which had far larger news-gathering staffs than television. Besides, he said, newspapers were portable, and "the people want their news to be portable."

The director of the Knight-Ridder newspaper chain's Information Design Laboratory, Roger F. Fidler, saw a bright future for newspapers. He said that although printing and delivery systems of the daily press were on the way out, the new opportunities for news gathering and packaging would more than make up for the decline in dailies. Appearing at the 1993 ASNE convention, Fidler envisaged the newspaper of the future as a notebook-size electronic "tablet" on which the customer could read his or her daily paper continually updated with the latest information, watch news videos, consult the newspaper library, or order advertisers' products.[15]

Bartlett rejected as nonsense the idea that in the new high-tech world, control of the news media will fall into fewer and fewer hands. "It's the opposite," he said. Instead of concentration of ownership, he predicted a broader fragmentation into more localized news operations. Globalization and synergy would continue along the path carved by Ted Turner, Rupert Murdoch, and the Time Warner magnates, according to Bartlett, but local control would reassert itself to meet the public demand, assertions by Bagdikian and his colleagues not withstanding.

Our response to these differences of opinion depends in large measure on our views about high technology. Will it work for the good of humankind, as Bartlett and most other market ideologues on the cutting edge of modern communication developments believe? Or will it lead to the shattering of moral values, as held by most communitarians, who see the destruction of oral and community patterns of communication? Or will there be a compromise?

And what is to become of reporters and editors in such a world? They will, Bartlett predicted, become "software managers" rather than distributors of news, men and women who direct the flow of information along the bit-stream transmission belt. Bartlett says optimistically that more jobs will be available in the future for gatherers of news, and, moreover, the vast outpouring of information would bring about an explosion in public demand for explanatory and analytical news reports fed along the bit-stream flow to consumers; they could then decide for themselves what to punch up on their home or office electronic receivers. Journalism education that did not keep pace with the newest technological developments was, Bartlett said, of little benefit to media news organizations. Professors of journalism and news directors continue to debate the point heatedly, but neither side has been satisfied with the stance of the other. The topic has remained open.

Another view of technological progress.
SOURCE: Mike Lane, *Evening Sun*

THE ETHICS OF JOURNALISM

In all the disputes about journalism education, whether between educators and dedicated humanists or between educators and committed technologists, one topic has retained a central position: ethics. What is moral? What *ought* to be done? When Pulitzer and Williams and Bleyer dreamt their dreams about the training and education of journalists, their concern was with the product. How best to *get* the news, write it, edit it, and distribute it. While some—like the early Horace Greeley and Lincoln Steffens—professed adherence to socialism, no one in the mainstream rejected a market economy. Although they may have had their own ideas about morality, the question was not central to them. Today, however, all journalism programs examine the moral and ethical implications of the news business.

No journalistic exposé in modern times has had a greater impact on the field than the Watergate-affair reports that appeared in *The Washington Post* in 1972 and 1973 under the bylines of Carl Bernstein and Robert Woodward. Adulation for Bernstein and Woodward was unmatched in the history of the news media, for it was their reports that were widely credited with bringing about the Nixon administration's downfall and changing the course of human history. Hundreds, perhaps thousands, of young men and women rushed into journalism-education classes at U.S. colleges and universities, stoked by a missionary zeal to equal the Bernstein-Woodward exploits and make their mark on American history. Belief in the power of journalism mounted, as did enthusiasm for investigative journalism. There was also increasing interest in the question of journalism ethics.

Because the power of journalism seemed almost overwhelming, the proper training of future journalists now appeared to require an examination of the responsibilities that accompany such power in order to avoid its abuse. The Hutchins Commission had sounded warnings about the potential for abuse a generation earlier. Now those warnings emerged as a call to arms in journalism faculties across the country and around the world. It was not, however, only in the faculties of journalism that anxiety arose about the relationship of power to responsibility. Media audiences were anxious as well. So indeed were other university faculties. The questions about social responsibility or accountability the Hutchins Commission had raised in regard to journalism were being asked also about other fields. Questions about ethics among lawyers, doctors, businesspeople, and even academics appeared everywhere. What was ethical behavior? And how was it to be safeguarded?

The applause for Bernstein and Woodward has not ceased, even though journalism students of the 1980s and 1990s have been less visionary than their brothers and sisters a decade earlier, frequently presenting the face of cynicism rather than that of idealism, more committed to making money than making waves. Nagging questions have been raised about the Watergate exposé. The ethicist Sissela Bok, one of the most profound analysts of moral behavior in the land, observed that, though the public was indebted to the two newspapermen, it was also true their behavior in digging out the story was not uniformly ethical; they had engaged in deceptive tactics, lying to persons they interviewed, collecting information by misrepresenting themselves as others, and luring grand-jury members to violate their oaths of confidentiality. What troubled Sissela Bok most about their book *All the President's Men* was less the lies and deception than "the absence of any acknowledgement of a moral dilemma."[16]

Bok, deeply disturbed about the glib ways in which we justify our lies, was equally concerned about the impact made on youthful minds by elevating ends above means, as when Bernstein and Woodward rationalized their deceptive behavior by convincing themselves that breaking ethical imperatives was justified in order to expose the Watergate break-in and the abuse of presidential power. Might it not have been possible, she asked, to expose the dirt *without* the lies and deceptions?

It had now become fashionable for investigative reporters to seek out the counterfeit and knavery around them and to find such high-sounding justifications as "the public's right to know" for their own guile and deceit. It became an easy matter for readers and viewers to take it for granted that journalistic standards included lying and misrepresentation. Bok wrote that the results are severe "in terms of risks to the personal professional standards of those directly involved, the public view of the profession, and to many within it or about to enter it."[17]

As noted earlier, discussions of journalism ethics are not new. So long as books, pamphlets, and articles have been written, readers have challenged the morality of writers. All writers have values, whether they acknowledge them or not; however "professional" the writer, he or she cannot set words to paper without allowing his or her socioeconomic position, education, and experiences to intrude on the information imparted. It has been this question of "objectivity" that has been the most enduring element in courses on ethics in journalism schools. It is moral, would-be journalists have been taught, to "keep yourself out of the story," to "let the facts speak for themselves." As faith in complete objectivity has declined, the instruction has concentrated on *balance* or *fairness*, as if those words represented something really different from *objectivity*. Since the Hutchins Commission report, the issue of social responsibility has appeared as a central topic in courses on ethics.

In other words, throughout most of the existence of journalism schools, the subject of ethics has often appeared to be quite as pragmatic as the subject of news judgment or of what makes a good lead. Books on journalistic ethics today are filled with practical questions, based on real or hypothetical cases in which the student is asked to decide what is right and what is wrong in decision making on specific journalistic questions. In a field so pragmatic, it is not strange the discussions have involved actual decision making more than philosophical principles. Though that practice has been changing in some institutions, the emphasis has remained heavily on "real-life cases."[18]

To Plato and the ancient Greeks, the study of moral philosophy was essential to realizing one's own potential and achieving the good life. To Aristotle, absolute good seemed to be beyond us, but he believed virtue lay in the *search* for good. The quest was personal. An unbridgeable gulf spreads between our personal ethics and professional ethics.[19] It was, for instance, deemed perfectly proper under the generally accepted standards of the media industry for Bernstein and Woodward to dissemble in order to get to the facts of the Watergate story. Ethically, they could have been said to have sacrificed their own values for the greater good of the human community. Put another way: Professionally, it was acceptable to lie, but personally, lying cannot be considered moral behavior. The dilemma is a ferocious one for aspiring young journalists. And it isn't easy for the experienced. Experienced editors have compiled formal codes of ethics and standards of professional conduct, yet it is a mistake to accept those as a moral philosophy. In journalism, as in all crafts and occupations, standards of professional conduct inevitably masquerade as moral philosophy.

Clifford Christians, who has reflected on and written about journalism ethics for many years, continues to urge contemporary media to develop "a sincere sense of social responsibility and a genuine concern for the citizenry," while at the same time acknowledging that "only the individual is an authentic moral agent."[20] Impersonal organizations can, he writes, have corporate obligations and can "in a sense" be held accountable for their behavior, but in the end, he acknowledges, "guilt finally rests upon individuals."[21] Dilemmas abound. The question of corporate obligations grows even thornier when the media are held to include, as Christians says, news, advertising, public relations, and entertainment. In most American universities, courses in ethics cover all these media, even though it is all too apparent that in a capitalist society, the ultimate goal of all commercial behavior is profit. Ethical considerations can, and often are, taken into account in these media, but lip service is always rendered while corners are always cut, for it is clear that once a business ceases to make profit, it must very likely either bend the moral codes or fail to survive.

Often, moral dilemmas are more vivid in fiction than in fact. It is more comfortable to sit in a library or before a screen and judge moral questions at a distance, away from the pressures that come with pursuit of enhanced prestige, a high salary, or a competitive edge. The immoral bad guys of journalism can be spotted easily enough in novels and films; some outstanding films have centered on the ethics of journalism. The viewer of *Citizen Kane* can with impunity condemn the dishonest journalism of the character based on publisher William Randolph Hearst, but it takes moral fortitude for a reporter to denounce his or her own publisher or editor who distorts information for political or economic advantage. Literature is filled with stories about the real cost attached to strict adherence to moral codes. Don Quixote is not alone in paying the price; in fact, Cervantes portrays the Don as a fool for his naïveté. Playwright Paddy Chayefsky's editor-hero in *Network*, a man who refuses to sanction a dishonest news show, loses his job. Heinrich Böll, the distinguished German novelist, depicts the most immoral of tabloid journalists as a highly successful practitioner in *The Lost Honor of Katharina Blum*. The director Federico Fellini's *La Dolce Vita* offers a tragedy that results from the presence of swarms of sensation-seeking photographers—the Italians have a word for them, *papparazzi*, which has come to stand for these amoral vultures. Dozens, perhaps hundreds, of disillusioned ex-journalists, who were fearful about speaking up while on the job, turn out novels and screenplays that expose unethical journalistic practices. None are more laden with indignation than the stories about the practices of war correspondents.[21]

What leads reporters, doctors, lawyers, engineers, and other "professionals" to engage in practices they would condemn in private life? Fame? Greed? Power? Who can resist the beckoning allure of those sirens?[22] The literature is filled with illustrations of those who failed to resist; it does not devote much time or space to those who did. Why not explore the similarities and differences between personal morality and professional ethics in schools of journalism? There is no more appropriate place to conduct this kind of exploration. Some experienced and world-weary editors and reporters may scoff at these studies as utopian and illusory, but it is certainly true that little time is spent on moral philosophy in newsrooms. This is not to say journalists are immoral or unethical; it is to say rather that newsrooms are busy places where deadlines must be met. In newsrooms and at bars and coffee shops after work, journalists regularly talk about ethics and often enough condemn their own behavior.

The search for justice was always central to Plato and Aristotle in their quest for the virtuous life. Whatever else justice may demand, it always demands fairness. It was this question of media fairness that dominated the fierce attacks on the news media during the 1992 U.S. presidential-election campaign. It was as that campaign swung into gear that Larry Sabato's eye-catching phrase, *feeding frenzy*, was introduced. The attack on the media, with President Bush in the forefront (he campaigned under the slogan "Annoy the media"), pinpointed another unanswerable question: To what does *the media* refer? They are words that slide easily off the tongue, all-purpose words, including within their scope all the news items, advertisements, talk shows, and entertainment programs on TV screens, on radio, in newspapers and magazines, sometimes in popular songs, in political columns, in letters to the editor, and even recipes.[23]

Adding the word *news* to the phrase narrows the field a bit, one of the reasons I have concentrated in this book on the *news* media. But even *news media* can be defined in different ways, raising a question that is also highly suitable for discussion in schools of journalism. I prefer to define that term as narrowly as possible, so journalists can be separated out from those whose primary emphasis, in what I have spoken of as the central tension inside the news media, is on the private-profit side rather than the public-interest side.

In either case, bashing of "the media" reached a remarkable level during the 1992 election campaign. Seymour Lipset, a long-time analyst of public policy, said the heavy assault on the media was a reflection of the increasing "oppositional role" the news media had taken on itself. "Today's media," Lipset wrote, "feel morally and professionally bound to expose everybody." So much so, Lipset maintained, that only "bad news is news."[24] Sabato, of course, went a step further, likening journalists to a pack of bloodthirsty piranhas moving in for the kill whenever a politician is in trouble. However, it wasn't only academics who were worried about feeding frenzies. In July, as the presidential contest was just heating up, a headline in *U.S. News & World Report* spoke of "curbing attack-dog journalism." In the article, then editor-at-large David Gergen challenged journalists to ask whether they were contributing to something "dangerously loose in our politics," a public distemper fueled by "our relentless assaults on every crack and flaw in a candidate's past and our willful refusal to explore any shine in the armor."[25]

At that time, the campaign was still focused on a story that had jumped onto the nation's front pages after the *Star*, a supermarket tabloid, printed an article in which one Gennifer Flowers was quoted as saying she had once had an affair with the then Democratic candidate, Bill Clinton. The tabloid had paid her about $150,000 for her revelations. In the past, the mainstream media wouldn't have touched the story, but this time they gobbled it up. Not long afterward, however, the anchorpeople who had converted the unconfirmed story into a sizzling example of attack-dog journalism were having second thoughts. Five of them appeared on a television special (on C-Span) to wonder publicly whether they had lost their way.[26] They all agreed that their fixation on scandal had crippled their coverage of the campaign. Tom Brokaw of NBC wondered aloud whether they might have made it "unbearable" for candidates to enter the public arena. Peter Jennings of ABC said campaign coverage had started well but had been "derailed" by preoccupation with scandal. Jim Lehrer of PBS acknowledged that television was losing its credibility. "We're in really serious trouble," he said. Dan Rather of CBS was equally contemplative. The only alternative note was struck by Bernard Shaw of CNN, who said the media were "duty bound" to report Flowers's allegation and it was the public's responsibility to sort through the various reports to check their accuracy.[27]

Furthermore, technology advances have made it possible to report news live and as it is happening. The capability to air events instantaneously has exerted a powerful negative impact on ethical standards. There is no time to check the accuracy of information or to place events in historical context when news stories are being aired live. There is also no time to evaluate the morality of a story when driven by the intense competitive pressure to be first.

From the very beginning, one motive above all others has lured young men and women into journalism: the desire to make their own mark on the course of history, to work in the service of the people, providing for them the information they need to carry out their lives. To perform a useful and helpful service is to act in an altruistic manner, and many reporters and editors have thought of themselves as benevolent altruists, a bit selfless, ethically pure, acting in the common good, and more deeply devoted to public service than to personal gain. Indeed, journalism has not, until modern times, been a source of wealth. Reporters have struggled through tough times economically and consoled themselves with the righteousness of their calling. Studies of the belief system of journalists have illustrated this point clearly. The surge of students into journalism schools following the Bernstein-Woodward investigation of the Watergate-scandal was molded from this enduring pattern. It was a chance for an idealistic quest to locate wrongdoing and bring the culprits to justice. Not surprisingly, journalism has always attracted the young. The average age of journalists has for years been lower than the average age in other "professions."[28]

But idealism is a Janus with a second face: disillusion and despair when it turns out the lofty aspirations cannot be attained on this imperfect earth. And disillusion has indeed set in. More than 20 percent of 1,400 full-time American journalists surveyed in 1992 said they planned to leave journalism within five years; this was double the number who had said they would leave ten years earlier.[29] This data, the authors of the study said, meant "a serious problem of retention [in journalism] may be just over the horizon." The chief reasons cited for the desire to get out were both pay and "the need for a different challenge." The level of job satisfaction had fallen sharply, and the most disgruntled were "the most experienced and altruistic persons."[30] For 61 percent of those surveyed, helping people was rated as a "very important" aspect of news work. This study confirmed earlier findings that newspersons were more inclined to "burn out" at an early age, shifting into other occupations—government work or advertising or especially teaching.[31] Another study showed that in the burnout rate in the 1990s, the newsroom manager was the "villain in the newspaper newsroom." Morale was low, the study showed, in part because managers didn't know when their staffers were discouraged or frustrated by such workplace conditions as "stress, salaries, changing individual goals and perceptions." Several respondents blamed managers' imperviousness to staffers' needs on "corporate preoccupation with journalism-as-profit."[32]

Disappointment about certain reporting practices played a major role in job dissatisfaction, particularly among the older, experienced journalists and those most dedicated to public service. On the other hand, more respondents were ready to engage in what used to be thought of as questionable practices—for example, making unauthorized use of confidential documents or even of such personal documents as letters or photographs. Sixty-three percent endorsed the use of hidden microphones or cameras, and 28 percent agreed with the use of actors in re-creating or dramatizing certain events. Here we see illustrated once again the central tension between the drive for public service and the drive for private profit that marks the news business. The profitable and successful history of "60 Minutes" has attracted followers throughout the news industry. Interestingly, there was a fall over the past decade in the number of journalists, especially in television, who believed it was "extremely important" that the news media provide entertainment. It is likely the survey respondents were agonizing, however internally, over the bottomless fissure that yawns between institutional standards and private morality.

It is painful to face up to the reality of moral decision making, especially when one is dealing with *applied* ethics. We can deal with abstract concepts easily enough, for there are no costs there in adhering to the loftiest ethical standards. But it is a grave matter to maintain a moral stance that endangers our financial well-being or our personal freedom. Kant demanded that we risk all in accepting absolute rules for right behavior. The followers of Mohandas Gandhi and Martin Luther King, Jr., subjected themselves to beatings and imprisonment, even death. Most of us slide by our toughest decisions, usually by the simple expedient of not facing them at all. We find alternative ways of expressing goodness. Sometimes we find them in slogans, such as "freedom of the press" or "the public's right to know." More often, we find them in law. It is not painful to abide by what is legal. But what if what is *legal* is not *right*? Schools of journalism frequently escape the thorniest choices by means of a course in "law and ethics." Such courses are comforting, for they sidestep moral questions by substituting legal questions.

We turn next to the question of *money*, since, as someone once said, it is the root of all evil.[33] And good and evil are what ethics are all about.

NOTES

1. An excellent description of *paradigm* as used in the context of mass-communication research can be found in Melvin L. De Fleur and Sandra Ball-Rokeach, *Theories of Mass Communication*, 4th ed. (White Plains, NY: Longman, 1982), 14: "In communication science today, the term *paradigm* combines the idea of a model for comparison with the more complex idea of a set of assumptions of the nature of some aspect of social or psychological reality."

2. De Fleur and Ball-Rokeach, 304.

3. William Stephenson, *The Play Theory of Mass Communication* (Chicago: University of Chicago Press, 1967), 2-3.

4. De Fleur and Ball-Rokeach, *Theories of Mass Communication*, 5th ed., (White Plains, NY: Longman 1989), 319.

5. The term *resources*, as used here, refers not only to money but also to the social beliefs that undergird the wielders of power.

6. John L. Hulteng, "What Editors and Journalism Educators Expect from Journalism Education," *News Research Bulletin* (Arlington, VA: American Newspaper Publishers Association), September 16, 1971.

7. Jim Scott, "Editors Give Journalism Education Failing Grade," *Editor & Publisher*, November 2, 1984, 10.

8. The publisher in this case was Ronald H. Einstoss, publisher designate of the Visalia, Calif., *Times-Delta*.

9. Charlie Peters, "But I'd Really Rather You Didn't Go At All," *The Washington Monthly* 18, 4 (May 1986): 54.

10. David H. Weaver and G. Cleveland Wilhoit, *The American Journalist: A Portrait of U.S. Newspeople and Their Work*, 2nd ed. (Bloomington: Indiana University Press, 1986), 56.

11. Edmund Lambeth, *Committed Journalism: An Ethic for the Profession* (Bloomington: Indiana University Press, 1986), 83. For further discussion of journalism as a profession, see J. Herbert Altschull, *Milton to McLuhan*, 297-98. See also Fred Bales, "Newspaper Editors' Evaluations of Professional Programs," *Journalism Educator* 47, 3 (Autumn 1992): 37-42.

12. Lee Becker and Gerald M. Kosicki, "Annual Census of Enrollment Records Fewer Undergrads," *Journalism Educator* 48, 3 (Autumn 1993): 55-65.

13. Hamid Mowlana, "The New Global Order and Cultural Ecology," *Media, Culture & Society* 15, 1 (January 1993): 12-13.

14. David Bartlett, interviews with the author, San Antonio, Texas, September 26, 1992, and Washington, D.C., March 23, 1993. The citations from Bartlett in the next two paragraphs are from the same interviews.

15. James Bock, "Editors Ponder Future of Newspapering," *Evening Sun*, Baltimore, March 31, 1993.

16. Sissela Bok, *Lying: Moral Choice in Public and Private Life* (New York: Vintage, 1978), 129.

17. Bok.

18. See, for instance, Louis A. Day, *Ethics in Mass Communications: Cases and Controversies* (Belmont, CA: Wadsworth, 1991).

19. Altschull, *Milton to McLuhan*, esp. 25–29 and 357–64.

20. Clifford Christians, Kim B. Rotzoll, and Mark Fackler, *Media Ethics: Cases and Moral Reasoning*, 3rd ed. (White Plains, NY: Longman, 1991), 22–25.

21. See, for instance, Philip Caputo, *DelCorso's Gallery* (New York: Harper Collins, 1983), which deals with journalistic practices in Vietnam and Lebanon.

22. Consider the case of Janet Cooke, a *Washington Post* reporter who first won a Pulitzer Prize for a story about an eight-year-old heroin addict but later was fired and forced to give up the award when it was discovered the story was manufactured. For a brief review of the case, see Altschull, *Milton to McLuhan*, 361–62.

23. J. Herbert Altschull, "Fairness, Truth, and the Makers of Image," *Media Studies Journal* (Fall 1992): 2.

24. "Political Ethics and Voter Unease? Interview with Seymour Martin Lipset," *The Public Perspective: A Roper Center Review of Public Opinion and Polling* (Storrs, CT: The Roper Center, July/August 1992), 10.

25. David Gergen, "Curbing Attack-Dog Journalism," *U.S. News & World Report*, July 6, 1992, 76.

26. For printed accounts of the broadcast, see Marvin Kalb, "Too Much Talk, Not Enough Action: A TV Veteran Tells the Networks How to Clean Up Their Act," *Washington Journalism Review*, July 1992, 33–34, and "The Talk of the Town," *The New Yorker*, August 24, 1992, 19–20.

27. Kalb.

28. John N. C. Johnstone, Edward J. Slawski, and William W. Bowman, *The News People: A Sociological Portrait of American Journalists and Their Work* (Urbana: University of Illinois Press, 1976).

29. David H. Weaver and G. Cleveland Wilhoit, "The American Journalist in the 1990s: A Preliminary Report" (Arlington, VA: The Freedom Forum World Center, 1992), 14. See also Weaver and Wilhoit, "Journalists—Who Are They, Really?" *Media Studies Journal* (Fall 1992): 69–79.

30. Weaver and Wilhoit, "American Journalist in the 1990s," 11.

31. Johnstone, Slawski, and Bowman, *News People*.

32. Ted Pease and J. Frazier Smith, "The Newsroom Barometer: Job Satisfaction & the Impact of Racial Diversity at U.S. Daily Newspapers," Ohio Monograph Series No. 1, July 1991, 33–34.

33. George Bernard Shaw, in his usual ironic vein, wrote that "*lack* of money is the root of all evil." See his *Maxim for Revolutionists*. The epigram appears in the Bible in a letter from the apostle Paul, drawing on an older Greek saying; see I Timothy 6:10. Paul continues (6:11): "But thou, O man of God, flee these things; and follow after righteousness, godliness, faith, love, patience, and meekness."

PART VI

PAYMASTERS AND PIPERS:
THE SYMPHONY OF THE PRESS

Chapter
20

"OUR REPUBLIC AND ITS PRESS WILL RISE OR FALL TOGETHER"

1847 1947
JOSEPH PULITZER

3¢ UNITED STATES POSTAGE

The Lords of the Global Village

THE BOUNDARIES OF JOURNALISTIC AUTONOMY

Among the most remarkable aspects of the folklore of the press is the absence of references to money. The mythology casts the press as Athena, sprung full-born from the brow of the people. The authors of *Four Theories of the Press* mention the financing of the press only in passing and ignore the question of profit.[1] In the reports of the Hutchins Commission and the British Royal Commission, money took the form of an ominous cloud threatening to divert the press from the duty assigned it by the people, who are perhaps the representatives of Zeus. Even more startling is the cavalier treatment accorded by working journalists to the influence of money on their livelihood. To be sure, they are concerned about their own incomes and expense accounts and are cognizant of the costs of publishing and broadcasting. Yet, until quite recently, little attention has been given to the connection between those details of financing and the news product they deliver. It is as if journalists, whose daily lives are dedicated to close observation, have blinded their senses to the realities of their calling. Advertisers are often held in contempt; they and their kind are not welcome in the newsroom, and many reporters and editors would cheerfully go to prison rather than allow their news judgment to be influenced by the crass commercial world of advertisers. Journalists are willing—more than willing—to let it go at that. Beyond the surface of reality many journalists are

not prepared to go. Or, rather, beyond the surface of reality journalists do not permit themselves to go—for in the shadows beyond lies the fear that the truth would
surely explode the comforting folklore of press independence.

Such, at least, is the pattern of journalistic life in the United States and, in varying degree, throughout the capitalist world. In the former Soviet Union, the financing of the press was a matter of no greater concern among socialist journalists. The
part of Zeus in the Soviet Union was taken not by the people but by the Communist
party serving as vanguard of the people. If pressures were brought on Soviet journalists, they came not from the sellers of commercial notices but from party func-
tionaries. In other words, the press mythology in the lands of the Superpowers (and
their allies as well) held and continues to hold that it is from politicians the pressure for conformity comes, not from the moneyed interests.

The reality, on the other hand, is that the content of the press is directly corre-
lated with the interests of those who finance the press. The press is the piper, and
the tune the piper plays is composed by those who pay him or her. This is so even

The press as piper.
SOURCE: Library of Congress

though the identity of the paymaster is not always known; in fact, it is in the pay-master's interests to maintain the lowest sort of profile, for to do so contributes to the maintenance of the folklore.

The image of the press as piper is a perfectly natural one. It occurred to Johann Amos Komenský, a Moravian churchman and educator, as early as the first years of the seventeenth century, only a short time after newspapers made their appearance in Europe. Komenský—or Comenius, as he called himself—was one of the most distinguished writers of his era, although his work has received only limited attention outside Eastern Europe and Western educational circles.[2] Complete translations of Comenius's writings are rare. His *Labyrinth of the World*, for instance, is best known in English in a 1901 translation by Count Lützow.[3] The *Labyrinth,* which appeared in 1623, bears some resemblance to John Bunyan's *Pilgrim's Progress*, and indeed Comenius sent his Pilgrim into the world to study workers and their behavior. Chapter 22 found the Pilgrim in the company of journalists. Count Lützow, recognizing how primitive was the state of journalism at the time, used the word *newsmen*, but Vladimír Hudec, dean of the journalism school at the University of Prague, spoke of the workers as journal-ists.[4] In the marketplace of a city, the Pilgrim noticed these journalisms piping

And who will pay the piper? Johann Amos Komenský envisioned the press as piper early in the seventeenth century, soon after the appearance of the first newspapers.

SOURCE: Bettmann

melodies into the ears of bystanders. When the piping was pleasing, the audience rejoiced, and when it was doleful, the people were sad. The pipes were provided by "vendors" whom Comenius did not otherwise describe; from our vantage point three and a half centuries later, we can identify them as paymasters. Comenius was intrigued by the fact that those who heard the piper could be exulted by the sound or plunged into terrible grief, as "men allowed themselves to be deceived by every gust of wind." Even back in the seventeenth century, he perceived with rare prescience an important fact of life in the universe of the press: To be a journalist is risky business. From all sides, the Pilgrim observed, the journalists found accusations falling on their shoulders, especially from those who did not listen carefully to what was being piped around them. "I see here . . . that it was not safe for all to use these whistles. For as these sounds appeared different to different ears, disputes and scuffles arose," the Pilgrim concluded; the victims of these scuffles were most likely to be the journalists themselves.[5] Many writers, Shakespeare among them, have called attention to the danger of being the bearer of unwelcome news. It was a situation that distressed MacBride as well.

The tolerance of the paymaster for behavior he or she considers unsuitable is inevitably limited, as was that of William Congreve's character Sir Sampson Legend, who introduced the piper-paying metaphor into the English language in *Love for Love*. Sir Sampson announces that as a father he possesses both authority and arbitrary power and will cut off his son without money in retaliation for the son's lack of subservience to the father's wishes and his offensive behavior. "I warrant you," Sir Sampson says, "if he danced till Doomsday, he thought I was to pay the Piper."[6] That, in 1695, was the promise of an early paymaster. The threat of punishment for offenses has not been modified over the past 300 years. Such is the case despite the fact that the faces of both piper and paymaster have changed drastically in that time frame. Few pipers work for a single paymaster any longer. Among journalists, the employer today is likely to be a syndicate or conglomerate.

The relationship between the piper and the paymaster, as noted earlier, takes four different forms: official, commercial, interest, and informal. The press cannot, however, be forced into a national classification system; there is too much overlapping for that. The degree of political autonomy differs from one publication to another. The mistake is to equate levels of political autonomy with freedom. No newspaper, magazine, or broadcasting outlet exceeds the boundaries of autonomy acceptable to the paymasters. The boundaries are not carved in stone; rather, they are flexible, and in every place on earth the boundaries have changed over time. Models that quantify the dynamic are inevitably flawed, as are those that tag the measuring sticks with national labels. The imperfect best we can do is to deal in degrees. The political system in a country derives from the economic power structure. Its press reflects at any given time the ends of those who manage the economy. Those ends may be openly stated or may be concealed. When the ends are openly stated, the press is likely to be subjected to a large measure of official control, and when they are concealed, the press is likely to be directed through either commercial channels or informal arrangements. In all cases, interest groups, those that support the objectives of power, and the dissidents who oppose those ends use the press for their own differing purposes.

In the former Soviet Union, the identity of the paymaster was supremely clear: The Communist party made the ultimate decisions about how money was spent. No doubt existed in any mind that newspapers, magazines, and broadcasting outlets were required to operate within the boundaries fixed by the party. Journalism students in the Soviet orbit were instructed to present information "objectively" and work for the benefit of society. To present contrary information was to serve reactionary interests and was thus unacceptable. The piper carried out the goals of the paymaster, the tunes played in the interests of the paymaster. Not surprisingly, Marxist schools of journalism failed to examine the financing of the Soviet press but taught that capitalist journalists served the interests of their paymasters. They dismissed Western notions of fairness and balance as mere pretenses and held that objectivity was possible only under the banner of Marxism-Leninism.

Statistical data on the financing of the Soviet press were difficult if not impossible to obtain. Very likely no one knew the cost of conducting the Soviet press system. Take, for example, the case of *Pravda*, the official party newspaper that collapsed financially as soon as the Soviet Union fell apart. The word may ring strangely in this context; but, according to Soviet authorities, *Pravda* operated at a profit. With a circulation of 11 million, the newspaper sold for 3 kopecks, or about 5 U.S. cents. Soviet officials said newsprint for the six-page paper ran to less than 1 kopeck per issue. With a staff of only 200 to be paid, subscriptions produced more revenue than it cost to publish the paper. According to Soviet estimates, any newspaper with a circulation in excess of 10,000 was a profit-making venture. In line with these estimates, Soviet officials said they had to subsidize only the tiniest of papers. Radio and television were fully subsidized since they were operated by civil servants. No one listed newspapers and magazines as state-run enterprises. Missing from this curious financial accounting were all capital expenses. The cost of equipment was simply not counted; nor were the costs of the buildings housing the newspapers or the costs of maintenance of equipment and buildings. Even distribution costs were budgeted under other headings. By these standards, almost every newspaper on earth would be a profitable enterprise. The most agonizing challenge for those news organizations in the post-Soviet world has been to build up a new network of paymasters.

The Soviet accounting system, of course, was not designed especially for newspapers. Capital costs were not included in any budget reckonings. The vertical system was highly compartmentalized; work units did not communicate with one another, only with authorities above. Whatever the cost of producing newspapers, when they appeared on the streets their content was not displeasing to the managers of the papers or to their superiors in the Kremlin, who footed the bill for the capital outlays under whatever budget heading they were hidden.

The party was not the only paymaster in the Soviet Union. *Izvestia*, with a circulation equal to that of *Pravda*, was financed by the Council of Ministers, *Trud* by the trade unions, and *The Literary Gazette* by cultural organizations. Various interest groups were prominent as financiers of the pipers whose tunes were sung in the pages of the papers. In the tightly controlled Soviet society, the identity of the paymasters was not publicized; still, they profited personally from their positions in money as well as power. To this extent, they were financing a kind of commercial venture. Informal arrangements also existed. For a long time, for instance, the son-in-law of Party Chairman Nikita Khrushchev held the position of *Pravda*'s chief editor. Thus, in one form or another, all the patterns of relationships between piper and paymaster could be found in the Soviet Union. The same is true in the United States, although the emphases are different. While the most obvious relationship in the former Soviet Union was official, in the United States the commercial pattern is most evident. Exceptions are permitted—a modest dissident press has continued to persist with limited resources and power—but the overriding concern of U.S. press paymasters is with profit; and the measure of profit is revenue from commercial notices. As in the Soviet Union, it is extraordinarily difficult to find out how much it costs to produce a newspaper. It is impossible to determine the extent of profits, but some inferences can be drawn.

Eighty percent of the income of U.S. dailies comes from advertising, which occupies somewhat more than 60 percent of the space. Despite the ups and downs of the economy, revenue from advertising has been steadily increasing and even with declining readership, investment in the news media remains a sound business venture. When profits decline, the newspapers or broadcasting outlets can still be sold for financial gain to the rising number of combines and conglomerates in the field. Although profit is the goal of the industry, it is always represented as a means and not as an end. The phrase "a sound financial basis" often appears as a euphemism for profit because it suggests a more altruistic purpose than the acquisition of money.[7]

Massive infusions of money from advertisers are mandatory if the news media are to maintain a viable economic posture. The vital interests of both publishers and advertisers lie in healthy, profitable print and broadcast media. While completely accurate figures are not available, it is clear the rate of profitability of both television and newspapers is much higher than that of industry as a whole; some analysts say it is more than twice as high. At a conservative estimate, before-tax profits were running at more than 20 percent per year for both newspapers and television. Clearly, the interests of advertisers coincide with those of the owners of the print and broadcast media. Whatever furthers the goals and values of the system that provides profit to both is good, and whatever puts that system at risk is bad. This same simple truth underlies the structure of the commercial mass-media system and ideology.

As the content of the Soviet press reflected *official* goals and values, so the content of the U.S. press reflects *commercial* goals and values. Censorship is unnecessary in either case. Only in the rarest of circumstances are challenges raised to basic goals and values. Three factors contribute to the absence of challenges in the United States. First, there is the *educational system* under which the journalists learn to adopt those goals and values as their own. Second, the *hiring process* weeds out nearly all those who might be likely to raise challenges. Finally, those rebels who make it through the first two screening processes undergo *pressure to conform*—either from their colleagues or from their own wish to rise up the ladder. Desirable assignments and promotions go to those who make the minimum of waves. A few independent thinkers survive, tolerated as illustrations of the "true independence" of the media. Others give up the battle and move into different professions, as statistical evidence demonstrates.

Most journalists in the United States, China, Nigeria, and everywhere else are true believers. If they are the products of the journalism schools in market or socialist systems, they tend to endorse and promote the goals and values they have learned. If they are from the advancing nations, they are more likely to be dissidents, free thinkers, or perhaps learned supporters of either market or communitarian goals and values. Third World journalists continually experience conflicts between their cultural heritage and the modern educational systems they encounter. In their puzzlement, they are often more inclined to search than merely to accept. Moreover, peer pressures in the more fluid places of work in the advancing countries are less persistent than those in news offices in the industrialized world. In the newer nation-states, informal and interest patterns of relationships are more prevalent than official or commercial ones.

In the revolutionary period in the Third World, groups committed to overthrowing the colonial powers discovered they had a most excellent tool at hand. The press, especially in Africa, followed the U.S. model—the pages of many colonial papers became rallying points for opposition to British rule and later to active support for rebellion. The African revolutionaries represented a particular interest group. The financial resources they poured into their newspapers were meant to bring specific results: the end of colonial rule and their own ascent to power. Once entrenched in power, they anticipated that a press no longer under their direct control would still continue to support their goals and values. However, when these leaders ceased to be the paymasters, the pipers no longer played the tunes they expected. The repression that followed was inevitable. Another avenue beyond repression was open to them, however. It was a far more fruitful road to travel than repression, because journalists everywhere react with hostility to censorship, rigid official directives, and direct pressures from commercial forces. The approach that many of the advancing-world leaders adopted was an informal one enormously effective and difficult to trace. It was the hidden subsidy. Such subsidies have been common throughout the history of the press. In many cases, subsidies have represented the difference between profit and loss for owners of publications. As an example, the withdrawal of special low-cost mailing privileges to U.S. magazines in the 1970s forced so many closures and mergers that the face of the magazine industry was permanently altered. Printing subsidies still represent major sources of revenue in U.S. newspapers. Those designated to publish official notices can be assured of guaranteed advertising revenue that is denied to those without such designations. Usually the nature of the subsidies has been masked, like the profit-and-loss statements of newspaper owners.

Public-disclosure laws in the capitalist countries forced newspaper owners to use their imaginations to cloud their statements; they lumped some of their profits into other categories, such as reinvestment in new equipment or, increasingly, as newspapers have expanded into other financial activities, into diversified enterprises. Many have found their way into giant multimedia conglomerates.

Before World War II, most newspaper enterprises were family owned, and publishers refused to report information about their profitability. They said the public was not interested; however, at the same time, they demanded public disclosure of the financial activities of the government and other corporations. With the decline of competition and the growth of chain ownership, many newspapers went public and began offering shares on the stock exchanges. The 432,000-member work force employed in the newspaper industry in 1992 was the largest among those in manufacturing industries in the United States. By 1993, circulation of the newspapers owned by the six leading chains totaled 20 million, or 40 percent of the total daily circulation in the country.[8] The Hutchins Commission expressed concern about the concentration of press ownership as early as 1947. By 1994, no fewer than 130 chains were active in the newspaper industry. All told, three of five daily newspapers were owned by conglomerates, four of five television stations, and more than a third of radio stations. At the start of the 1990s, the Gannett chain, the largest in the field and publisher of *USA Today*, owned eighty-three daily newspapers, more than fifty weeklies or other nondaily publications, ten television stations, and fifteen radio properties in major markets, as well as the largest outdoor advertising group in North America, the Lou Harris polling organization, satellites, and motion-picture production units.[9] In 1993, for the first time, *USA Today* operated at a profit, although Gannett declined to provide figures for its separate units. Gannett itself made a net profit of $398 million in 1993, double its profits of the previous year. Circulation of Gannett dailies was well over 6 million. *USA Today* accounted for nearly 2 million of that total. The mere existence of chains and conglomerates does not necessarily mean a decline in diversity of opinion. All along, the news media have tended to support the basic values of the political and economic system and have reflected the ideology of the paymasters.

No one knows exactly how profitable newspapers are, and though the newspaper industry in the United States has been shrinking, the newspapers that survive are doing very well.[10] E. F. Hutton, the market analyst, offered newspapers as one of the most lucrative investment opportunities available, noting the chief reason was that they sold access. "Advertisers buy access to potential purchasers of their products, providing newspapers with 70 to 80 percent of their revenues," a spokesperson observed. "Readers pay for access to news, information, advertising, and entertainment arranged in a convenient, predictable, and cheap package."[11] Since no new purveyors of access other than cable TV arrived in the consumer capitalist society, advertising rates rose steadily for both newspapers and broadcasters. They rendered themselves even more attractive by becoming diversified communication complexes.

The direct relationship between advertising and the viability of newspapers that marks the U.S. press scene is not the usual pattern in the Third World. There, the usual pattern of relationships between the piper and the paymaster is often informal; families and friends play an important part. Only those persons with substantial resources have been able to purchase controlling or total interest in newspapers, and those persons have inevitably had powerful friends or relatives in high positions in government. Even with initial capital, these owners have continued to need some form of subsidy to remain afloat, and they have naturally turned to their friends and relatives for help. The scenario frequently runs something like the following.

The brother-in-law of publisher A in a certain country has held sway in the capital as finance minister. Because newsprint allotments were fixed by the finance ministry, the brother-in-law could count on regular shipments so long as his relative remained in power. Thus, it was no surprise his newspaper served as an unofficial voice for the government and its financial interests. The content of his paper reflected the goals and values of the government. The position of power over information held by the government in this situation was unassailable. Not only was it able to ensure favorable news reports in the brother-in-law's paper, but it could bring other owners either into line or into bankruptcy by assigning or withholding shipments of newsprint. None of these transactions was reduced to writing, so there was no way to check up. The head of government himself might not be aware of the newsprint arrangements, and the finance minister, if he himself sought power, could use his control of newsprint as a device to help him gain public support for a bid to overthrow the head of government. Informal arrangements exist in all nations, always operating to the end of ensuring the content of newspapers and broadcasting outlets does not stray far beyond the boundaries acceptable to those of the paymasters. This truth does not reflect on the integrity of the overwhelming majority of pipers. The point is that the interests of the pipers and those of their paymasters are generally in harmony.

Despite the high profitability of newspapers in the United States and among some allies, it grew increasingly difficult in most places to operate newspapers without government subsidies. For a number of years, Sweden has provided direct government support to its press. In other capitalist countries, the support has been less direct. In Africa, subventions were mandatory if a newspaper was to survive. In relatively prosperous Nigeria, it cost nearly 20 kobo (about 55 U.S. cents) to publish each copy of *The Daily Times* of Lagos, the country's most efficient newspaper. In order merely to break even, the paper required a subsidy of nearly 5 kobo (14 cents) per copy. The other Nigerian papers needed far greater subsidies, perhaps as much as 2 naira (a little over $5) a copy. Press freedom exists officially in Nigeria, but as Segun Osoba, general manager of *The Sketch* in Ibadan, commented: "Once you ask for subventions, you are controlled." *The Sketch* was operating the 1980s without subsidies but was steadily losing money and had to go to interest groups for support. To provide sound information to Nigeria's millions, Osoba said, the country needed another forty newspapers, but "anyone would be crazy to start a paper today."[12] The remark might be amended to add, "unless one could be assured of adequate subsidies." For along with the rising cost of salaries were even larger increases in the cost of raw materials, ink, and newsprint.

TRANSNATIONALS, CONGLOMERATES, AND MEDIA MOGULS

The word *revolution* is overworked, so much so it may well have lost useful meaning. In any case, it rarely carries the image of anything so soul-wrenching and bloody as the French upheaval in the dying days of the eighteenth century or anything so shattering as the Bolshevik uprising of 1917. Writers have discovered a plethora of "revolutions" in the scientific breakthroughs that led to computer technology, but few current uses of the word would be permissible under T. S. Eliot's conception of a revolution as meaning to murder and create.[13] A partial listing of key innovative technologies includes such phenomena as electromagnetics, computer graphics, speech synthesis, voice recognition, data-base management, data encryption, satellite television, artificial intelligence, fiber optics, digital bit streams, interactive media, and other ramifications of the computer revolution. We have arrived at the realm of the information society.

These developments have been greeted variously with enthusiasm and despair. Prophets of heaven and hell have multiplied in number with the multiplication of microminiaturization devices. Our specific interests are with the impact of modern technology on the news media and on how they are financed. Certainly, the forms in which media are delivered have already changed dramatically. Newspapers may be delivered to homes electronically. Video data menus systems enable audiences to select what they wish to read by punching a series of buttons on home computers. Other systems for packaging and delivering news and advertising are being added and subtracted daily, especially in the industrialized lands of the West and Japan. Costs have grown to astronomical proportions so that only the wealthiest and most powerful international corporations are able to compete. Experts say that U.S. firms alone will have invested well over a trillion dollars in computer and telecommunication technology by the end of the twentieth century.[14] Japan, Britain, France, and Germany will pour in additional trillions. Few among these firms operate entirely within national boundaries any longer. A new paymaster has risen: the transnational corporation; and few if any governments can compete with it. Power to restrain media transnationals rests more with audiences than it does with governments. If no one pays attention to the media product, the media are as good as out of business. It is imperative then for these global media moguls, as it has been for all news operators of the past, that they tell interesting stories in the most financially efficient manner. Journalists are never independent of their audiences, yet those audiences have so far, at least, been easily maneuvered by the management skills of the paymasters. Entertainment has been the most important weapon in the hands of the paymasters.[15]

Our perception of transnationals inevitably colors our attitudes about their impact on the content of news and on the transmission of news, information and advertising around the world. To some, transnationals are cold, inhuman instruments for maximizing profits; to others, they are agencies for promoting international accord by cutting through national pride and prejudice. For transnationals, each of these roles is possible. How in the end they will affect humankind is not yet known. That they will grow in power and influence is certain.

The one overriding reality of the rapid growth of computers, electronics and miniaturization technology has been the emergence of a synergized information industry. *Synergy* is a medical term describing the cooperative working together of different body organs to perform complex movements or the combined action of two or more drugs whose effect is greater than that of the sum of the component drugs.[16] In the world of the mass media, synergy allows the use of different media controlled by the same corporation to promote the same idea, product, celebrity, or politician in other media.[17] Each of the new global giants tries to gain control of as many different media as possible—newspapers, news agencies, syndicates, magazines, radio and television stations, networks, book publishers, motion-picture companies, cable outlets, cable systems, satellite channels, recordings, videocassettes, chains of movie houses, and as many further media as can be located.

Although the big investors applauded the concept of synergy as a technique for bringing more and more useful information to the public, some critics of the new media giants scoffed at venerating the idea of synergy. Lewis Lapham, the editor of *Harper's* magazine, saw *synergy* as simply another word for *monopoly*. The men who were seizing control of the media conglomerates were, he said, latter-day incarnations of Cornelius Vanderbilt, J. P. Morgan, John D. Rockefeller, and the other nineteenth-century robber barons. The combinations and recombinations of their companies, Lapham wrote acidly, "served the interests of a very small number of individuals, none of them known for their love of free speech."[18]

In January 1986, in the midst of the era of unlimited corporate acquisitions, Capital Cities, operator of a score of middle-market TV and radio facilities, took over the powerful ABC Television Network, then in its thirty-second year, for $3.5 billion. At the time, its total sales came to a fourth of those of the network.[19] When Capital Cities/ABC, Inc., emerged, its holdings were vast. Within five years it was operating the ABC TV and radio networks, plus eight TV stations and twenty-one radio stations. It also was running a successful cable-TV business; its holdings included ESPN, 38 percent of A&E, and 33 percent of Lifetime. But that was only the beginning. It was also distributing programs for cable TV; publishing such newspapers as the *Kansas City Star*, *Fort Worth Star-Telegram*, and *Oakland Press*; producing shopping guides, business and other specialized periodicals, books, and records; providing research services; and distributing information from data bases.[20] By 1994, Capital Cities had become the third-largest communication company in the world, with annual earnings of $5 billion.[21]

The giant corporation was making its presence felt in the foreign marketplace with investments in TV-program production and distribution in France, Spain, Germany, England, Japan, and other countries. CBS and NBC struggled to keep up with ABC by moving into foreign markets and diversifying. NBC purchased Super Channel, a TV service seen in 30 million homes, and began airing its own top-rated shows; it also launched a 24-hour news service in Latin America and planned a business-news operation in Asia.[22] Capital Cities/ABC put out a magazine in Europe called *Fashion Life*, the first pan-European fashion lifestyle publication. Further European enterprises included foreign editions of *Supermarket News, Women's Wear Daily,* and *Children's Business.* Capital Cities reached out into yet other fields. As a result of the presentation over its cable-TV operation of Sunday telecasts on medical and health-related programs, the corporation developed a new business called Healthlink, providing monthly videotape service to the offices of 8,000 doctors. Its publishing ventures included the journals put out by Fairchild Publications on financial services, metalworking news, multichannel news, cablevision, electronic news, and energy-user news. Capital Cities was active in religious publications as well: Its Word, Incorporated, was the largest American publisher of inspirational books.

In order to cash in even further on its expanding synergization, the communication colossus split into five semiautonomous divisions: the network; the broadcast station group; the publishing division; the cable and international broadcast group (linking Capital Cities to the BBC); and a multimedia division, which planned to expand in the "interactive, pay-per-view and video-on-demand areas," as well as in the VCR and high-definition television industries.[23] John Tinker, a media analyst for Forman, Seitz, said ABC hoped to ride the new technologies into the creation of more programming to meet the demand of the increasing roster of channels. "They do not want to be caught on the distribution side," he said.[24]

The move abroad by U.S.-controlled conglomerates raised renewed concerns about American cultural imperialism, concerns that Michael Solomon of Warner Brothers dismissed grandly as "bullshit." Solomon said, "All that people in television care about is ratings and profit." In fact, he went on, most people in other countries "totally welcome the Americans."[25] Jan Mojto, managing director of the Kirch group, Germany's most prolific producer of television programming, agreed that he did not fear U.S. programming was taking over and controlling the world, but he added a troubling cautionary note. He does worry about the loss of "national culture" in the face of U.S. imposition of its own way of life as "a kind of universal culture." Those worries, he said, showed a very European attitude, to which there was a ready answer: "compete."[26] The European Community continued to block export of U.S. television fare, an effort that posed a continuing threat to international trade.

The head men at a number of the multimedia giants are so well known their names are almost household words. Not so of Capital Cities; its ownership and management are known mainly to people in the field. Ben Bagdikian has given a useful name to this small coterie of multimedia giants: "Lords of the Global Village." These moguls have their own political agenda: to uphold at all costs the status quo. "All resist economic changes that do not support their financial interests," Bagdikian said. "Together they exert a homogenizing power over ideas, culture and commerce that affects populations larger than any in history." Never before, he wrote, has any group commanded "so much power to shape the information on which so

The new media moguls: Journalism scholar Ben Bagdikian coined a new name for the giants of media globalism.

SOURCE: Robert Grossman, *Nation*

A trio of Lords of the global village: Three men who built mighty news and entertainment empires in the age of information. From left—Rupert Murdoch, Robert Maxwell, and Jean-Luc Lagardère.

SOURCE: Robert Grossman, *Nation*

many people depend to make decisions about everything from whom to vote for to what to eat."[27] The road taken by the media Lords was often a rocky one, and more than a few overreached themselves, borrowing beyond their ability to repay. These magnates fell by the wayside. A case can be made that Bagdikian overstates the extent of their power; for the most part, the organizations they direct move ahead under whatever management.[28] Even so, however, no one can deny the power potential of the Lords. The idea of a global village was broached in 1962 by the Canadian literary scholar Marshall McLuhan, who envisaged a brave new paradise gained through the agency of modern electronics. McLuhan's imagery was religious—he saw electronics technology as promising "a Pentecostal condition of universal understanding and unity."[29] To McLuhan, the magic of high-tech would create a global village that reconstructed *the communal world of the ancient village*. To Bagdikian, the global media oligopoly, invisible to the consumer, did no such thing. It stood for personal profit and cared little for universal understanding and unity.[30]

The power of the Lords and the lesser corporate giants in the new global village is greater than that of past media owners. Moreover, their economic stake has risen. Third World media people maintain that dominant news media like the American TV networks, CNN, and international conglomerates like Rupert Murdoch's News Corporation are increasing the flow of distortion and prejudice through the international news system. Similar complaints are addressed against the news agencies and the handful of newspapers and magazines that make up the international press. Further, it is argued in the advancing countries that the real aim of these practices is to provide additional markets for the products of information transnationals and that journalists are willing or unwitting tools in carrying out these objectives.

The Lord to attract the widest public attention was Robert Maxwell, whose bizarre death at sea in November 1991 came as his empire, which was really a house of cards, was collapsing all around him. He may have believed his own boast that his media empire would make him prime minister of Britain, or he may have been one of the wiliest crooks of the century. In whatever case, banks across

The mysterious media magnate, Robert Maxwell, who exploded onto the scene and disappeared just as quickly after a bizarre suicide.

SOURCE: UPI/Bettmann

Europe bought into his claim that he was creating an immensely profitable media organization and loaned him vast sums of money. Examiners trying to piece the whole complicated puzzle together said that on his death, misguided banks found themselves with hundreds of millions of dollars of worthless loans and with dozens of foundering newspaper, television, cable, and publishing companies. An accounting firm estimated that the banks, suppliers, employees, and other creditors of the private companies owned by Maxwell and his family would lose more than $1.5 billion.[31]

Maxwell was a wheeler and dealer from the beginning. He was born Jan Ludvik Hoch in 1923 Czechoslovakia. His mother and father died in Nazi death camps, but he managed to escape to England, where by the time he was twenty-eight he had scratched up enough to launch the first of his media enterprises, a scientific journal called the Pergamon Press. He sold out at a handsome profit two years later, though the purchaser, a U.S. company, shortly afterward complained to the City of London corporate-watchdog committee that Maxwell had misled them about the worth of the company. The commission agreed and issued a reprimand affirming that his reports to his stockholders betrayed "a reckless and unjustified optimism"[32]

That would have finished a less flamboyant person. Maxwell bounced back with a vengeance. Twenty years later, this man who was the very model of the boundlessly optimistic entrepreneur of the 1980s returned to challenge Murdoch in a ferocious battle of conglomerate giants, each seeking to become chieftain of the Lords of the global village. The two men were not at all alike. Where Maxwell, a man of Falstaffian appetite, was dedicated to the Left and sometimes extolled the leaders of the Communist governments of Eastern Europe, Murdoch was a staunch conservative less interested in the perks of power and more driven by a desire for wealth. So committed to profit building was Murdoch that he walked away from his early political liberalism and even surrendered his Australian citizenship to become an American so that he would be unrestrained in acquiring television property in the United States.[33]

At the time of his death, Maxwell owned in totality or in part the London *Daily Mirror* and five other British newspapers; the New York *Daily News*; newspapers in Israel and Hungary, Germany, and Kenya; Macmillan Publishing Company; McGraw-Hill School Publishing; Berlitz International; television operations in Britain, France, and Spain; encyclopedias; airline guides; various business-publishing groups; and a variety of others.[34] His much-publicized purchase of the ailing New York tabloid came after a five-month strike of *Daily News* workers and a devastating collapse in circulation. At the time, he was hailed as a flamboyant rescuer. At his death less than a year later, the newspaper was in bankruptcy and its future uncertain.[35] His insurer, Lloyd's of London, pronounced his mysterious death at sea a suicide. To complete the involved bankruptcy proceedings took years. A New York investor, Mortimer D. Zuckerman, bought the bankrupt *Daily News* for $17 million in 1992.[36] Maxwell's 1984 claim that in ten years his would be one of only ten global corporations of communication seemed a hollow boast.

Murdoch, on the other hand, had come closer to achieving his goal, which he had announced as "the creation of the world's first global television, publishing and entertainment operation."[37] Murdoch also overborrowed, but he moved with far greater caution than Maxwell. Still, in 1987 he bought New York's liberal afternoon tabloid, *The Post*, and turned it into a racy conservative paper. However, financial troubles forced him to sell it a year later. He wasn't finished, though, and after *The Post* had gone bankrupt, he repurchased it in 1993.[38]

His concentration, however, was really on television and international dealings. The centerpiece of his international empire was the News Corporation, a British conglomerate featuring Sky Television, a satellite service offering European viewers four different channels devoted to entertainment, movies, sports, and news. His Sky Two news venture was in direct competition with CNN. With his four-channel operation, Murdoch was convinced he could change Britain's viewing habits. "We don't deal in market share," he said. "We *create* markets."[39]

But Sky was only one part of his $7-billion media empire, which ranked behind only Time Warner; it sprawled across four continents. In the United States its most visible product was the Fox Corporation, which challenged the three older networks for TV supremacy. By the end of 1993, Murdoch's property included the Fox movie studio; an Australian airline; two newspapers and twenty-seven magazines in the United States, Britain, and Australia; and a major book publisher in the United States; five national newspapers in Britain, including *The Times* and *The Sun*; and more than one hundred Australian newspapers with 60 percent of the country's total circulation.[40] He was in the market for more, launching a new magazine division in the United States and expanding into Asia, where for half a billion dollars he took command of Star-TV, that continent's pioneer television service. His determination to bring Fox entertainment shows like "The Simpsons" to Asia ran into a fierce cultural backlash. China and Singapore banned private ownership of satellite dishes, threatening the profitability of Star-TV.[41] When the ban was announced, Chinese citizens already owned several million dishes.

Murdoch's reputation, far more than Maxwell's, was that of a marauding mogul prepared to bust unions and serve up trash to the public. Serious journalists regularly blast Murdoch for lowering the quality of newspapers. Bagdikian, for instance, wrote that Murdoch perfected "prurient journalism . . . a mix of lurid crime tales under souped-up headlines and pinups with their bare breasts pushing out of page three."[42] More recently, Murdoch seemed to tone down his sensationalism, and his concern, he was wont to say, was in entertainment and profits.

Synergy opened for the fiercely competitive Murdoch the road to potential financial bonanzas, one of which could result if the BBC declined as a rival to his Sky TV satellite operation. Sky was financed by advertising, while the BBC's basic source of income was the license fees British TV owners must pay. Murdoch's three daily newspapers, drew readers from quite different socioeconomic groups, campaigned editorially for abolishing the BBC's license fees, making survival of the public broadcasting service dependent on advertising.[43] Anthony Smith raised a question of morality, asking whether it was proper for media enterprises to use the influence of one of their parts to pursue the interests of another. Bagdikian pointed to Murdoch's frequent intervention in the editorial stands of his papers when his financial interests were at stake. The idea that media owners did not intervene in the content of news, he wrote, is "a parochial myth that permeates all the media."[44]

The Lords of the global village enjoy a unique opportunity to influence the course of public policy. With some exceptions, Maxwell was among them, they deny they are interested in causes. Because their global ventures are, they say, bottom-line affairs, they are not much interested in the content of their newspapers, movies, or television and cable presentations, just so long as they make money. Murdoch and his aides say so directly. Joe Roth, chairman of the Fox movie studio, says Murdoch doesn't interfere in questions of politics or taste, only when major financial risks are involved.[45] Similar comments come from Japanese entrepreneurs who have moved into the American and global entertainment business in force.

In 1989, the Sony Corporation, which already owned CBS Records, paid $5 billion to take over Columbia Pictures. A year later, the Matushita Electric Industrial Company put up some $7 billion to acquire MCA Inc., the owner of Universal Studios, a major record company, a publishing house, theme parks, and large amounts of Los Angeles real estate. Both deals were arranged by Noio Ohga, Sony's president. The MCA takeover followed shortly after Ohga had invited Akio Tanii, president of Matushita, to dinner. *The New York Times* wrote that "history may record it as Japan's back-to-the-future rendition of the days when Louis B. Mayer dined with Samuel Goldwyn."[46] As a result of the two deals, Ohga and Tanii gained control of one-fourth of the American movie market. U.S. movie moguls were retreating before the financial clout of overseas corporate leaders. Murdoch was already in firm control of 20th-Century Fox.

Matushita's Tanii was extraordinarily active in the global marketplace, creating a computer division to challenge IBM and pursuing foreign deals in industrial equipment and semiconductors. But it was only when he acquired MCA that he entered the software business, following conventional wisdom that synergy required control of a combination of hardware and software businesses. Matushita's operations include eighty-seven Japanese companies and nearly as many abroad, making Sony and Matushita strong forces in consumer electronics products. The Japanese acquisitions naturally brought anxiety in Hollywood, amid fear that Japanese ownership might stifle creative impulses. Matushita executives refused to discuss that issue, yet Sony's Ohga said he was not interested in interfering with the "software," by which he meant movies, music, and TV programs. It was profits to which he was devoted. Criticism of Japanese penetration of corporate media in the United States was widespread. Noting that Japan's Global News Network had taken on Ted Turner's CNN around the world, the best-selling novelist Michael Crichton wrote that "if past history is any guide, . . . kiss the American media goodbye."[47]

Sony's acquisition of CBS Records and Columbia Pictures represented what Smith called "the most daring demarche in 20th-century cultural history."[48] That description rose from Sony's avowed goal to achieve "global localizing."[49] Following the pattern begun by IBM, Sony presented itself as a local company in the fourteen countries where it researched and manufactured (actually, 70 percent of Sony's sales were outside Japan). When Murdoch, by contrast, placed his name securely on the Star-TV enterprise, the Chinese and Singapore governments reacted angrily. Sony's pattern of operation obviously made it difficult for national governments to impose rigid regulations on its activities or those of other cautious transnationals, for there was no way in which governments could be totally in control of transborder transmission of information. This represented a significant loss of national sovereignty, which was troublesome to governments. As a result, multinationals have exerted pressure to prevent any restrictions on data flow. Officials made their case simply: If they couldn't "move information," they said, they would be forced out of business. Some countries, led by Sweden in 1973, adopted comprehensive laws designed to protect data flow.[50] Any move to regulate the flow of data in certain countries is obviously a major threat to the profitability of the transnationals. The argument may turn out to be academic, however, since logistical difficulties may very well prevent any national control over transborder data flow. Censorship becomes impossible when information can be freely sent from computer to computer across borders.[51]

Sovereignty of the global village is becoming a crowded affair. In the next chapter, we will turn to the largest of all media enterprises, Time Warner. It is important also to recognize the power of the Germans, French, Italians, Canadians, and other Australians seeking success on the field of play. The house of Bertelsmann A. G. in Gutersloh, Germany, has quietly assumed a dominant position in book and magazine publishing and the record industry, as well as in the allied entertainment world. The company's founder, Reinhard Möhn, took an entirely different (and cleverly decentralized) approach from Maxwell and Murdoch, encouraging his many subsidiaries to retain their own names. As a result, few buyers of Bantam and Doubleday books are aware they are purchasing Bertelsmann products. The same can be said of buyers of RCA and Ariola recordings. Bertelsmann's annual sales come to $7 billion annually, only a third of it in Germany. The company has also become a leader among multinationals bidding for new outlets in the former Soviet empire.[52] It has one marked advantage over other international conglomerates in that it is wholly privately owned. This makes Bertelsmann impervious to hostile takeovers.

The threats of government interference and of overextending themselves remain the chief problems for the media magnates. Like Maxwell, the French giant Hachette S. A., the largest publisher of magazines in the world, ran into serious trouble because of stretching its resources too thin. In 1992, its head man, long touted as a chieftain among the Lords, Jean-Luc Lagardère, was forced to merge his interests with the giant Matra defense group. Lagardère blamed his troubles on the failure of his private television channel, Le Cinq, which was unable to overcome the powerful political forces that backed the existing channels. Rightist Premier Jacques Chirac sold off France's most popular operation, TF1, to the construction giant Bouygues S. A. in a sweetheart deal while state-owned channels continued to receive guaranteed financing. Le Cinq couldn't meet the competition and went bankrupt earlier in the same year, costing Lagardère and his partners some $700 million. Lagardère vowed to fight back, hoping the merger would put Hachette-Matra on a sound financial footing, but without the benefits of synergy, since Matra's holdings were not in media or entertainment.[53]

Among the losing partners in the operation of Le Cinq was the renowned Italian media tycoon Silvio Berlusconi, who had for years been seeking to challenge the other Lords on the international front yet who had been stymied by political forces in his own country. Berlusconi was highly successful inside Italy, where by 1984 he had gained control of all the private TV channels, wresting command of several from major publishers who had entered the field. He ran afoul of the courts, however, which held nationwide private television ownership illegal. However, unlike Lagardère, he had strong friends in high places, and within a week, Premier Bettino Craxi had reversed the ruling and Berlusconi was once again in total control. Within three years, his firm was earning annual sales of $8 billion, largely through movies and made-for-TV films. Striving to go international, he acquired control of a German subsidiary, Fininvest, which owned 45 percent of a Munich cable operation. Changes were brewing in Italy, where courts may end his empire. Smith observed the Berlusconi case showed clearly that media buccaneers could keep going only so long as their political support held up in the hostile, competitive world that makes up today's global village.[54]

The dedication of communication conglomerates and transnationals to the marketplace is complete. The overriding commitment to profit of communication empires and their news media strengthen their position as agents of power. These organizations need not concern themselves much with partisan politics. Neither Rupert Murdoch nor Ted Turner nor Matushita nor Bertelsmann must get involved in contests between candidates for public office, so long as those candidates stand firm for the market economy. As Roth said, they enter the creative picture only when financial risks are at stake. The media do the job for the moguls.

NOTES

1. Fred S. Siebert, Theodore Peterson, and Wilbur Schramm, *Four Theories of the Press* (Urbana: University of Illinois Press, 1956).

2. In 1956, Unesco, recognizing the internationalism in Comenius's vision, decided to publish a volume of excerpts of his work and commissioned Jean Piaget, the Swiss educator, to write a preface. See Piaget's *On Education* (New York: Teachers College Press, Columbia University, 1957).

3. Count Lützow, *The Labyrinth of the World and the Paradise of the Heart* (London: Swan Sonnenschein, 1901).

4. Vladimír Hudec, *Journalism, Substance, Social Functions, Development* (Prague: International Organization of Journalists, 1978). Hudec used the English word *piper* as translation of Comenius's term; Count Lützow seemed unsettled as to whether the key word should be *piper* or *whistler*, but the effect is the same.

5. Since Comenius believed, as Piaget wrote, that educators should "teach all things to all men and from all points of view," (*On Education*, 7), he qualifies as a kind of patron saint of this book. Comenius was born in 1592 and died in 1670; it was in his lifetime that a press first appeared in Europe.

6. William Congreve, *Complete Plays*, ed. Hubert Davis (Chicago: University of Chicago Press, n.d.). The passage from the play originally performed in 1695 is from Act 2, Scene 1.

7. Newspaper Association of America, *Facts, 1982*, spoke of newspapers as serving as a watchdog, "a beacon in a murky world as a marketing voice for goods and services, as a source of entertainment, as a flagger of the important and the unpredictable—and as a source of the common knowledge that fashions common interests. To do that job newspapers must remain strong and independently free institutions—not only by exercising their right to express diverse views freely and openly but also by maintaining a viable economic posture." In the 1992 edition of *Facts*, the NAA dropped references to economic viability, stating that as the world and newspapers were changing, its goal was "to ensure that newspapers are just as vibrant and compelling today and tomorrow as they have always been, to inject vision and energy into an industry that continues to be a pillar of democracy and a force for change."

8. These figures were provided by the research bureau of the *American Journalism Review*, February 2, 1994.

9. *The Wall Street Journal*, January 28, 1994.

10. Patrick O'Donnell, "The Business of Newspapers: An Essay for Investors," *Institutional Industry Review*, February 12, 1982.

11. O'Donnell.

12. Segun Osoba, interview with the author, Ibadan, Nigeria, April 14, 1980.

13. T. S. Eliot, *The Idea of a Christian Society* (Harcourt Brace, 1940), 14–16. Eliot's views on revolution were set forth in three lectures at Corpus Christi College, Cambridge, 1937, reprinted in this volume and in a radio talk on BBC, February 1937.

14. The prediction was made by J. N. Pelton, *Global Talk* (Aalphen aan der Rijn, the Netherlands: Sijthoff and Nordhoff, 1981), 265. Pelton spoke as an executive of the International Telecommunications Satellite Organization (INTELSAT).

15. Attractive packaging of the news remains an important weapon for transnational moguls. The techniques of skillful packaging concern Bagdikian, for, as he correctly reports in *The Media Monopoly*, the brilliant packaging often conceals the tarnished products within. A similar point is made by Edward S. Herman and Noam Chomsky in *Manufacturing Consent: The Political Economy of the Mass Media* (New York: Pantheon, 1988), 1–36. For an interesting discussion of audiences, see Herbert J. Gans, *Deciding What's News: A Study of CBS Evening News, NBC Nightly News, Newsweek and Time* (New York: Vintage, 1980), 281–85.

16. *Webster's New Twentieth-Century Unabridged Dictionary*, 2nd ed. (Cleveland: World, 1972), 1851.

17. Bagdikian, *Media Monopoly*, 242–43. See also Joseph Turow, *Media Systems in Society: Understanding Industries, Strategy, and Power* (White Plains, NY: Longman, 1992), 235–57. Turow writes: "When the TV production division of Disney promotes the company's theme parks and they drum up business for the record and video division, which, in turn, promotes the book division, which, in a circular action abets the TV division's programming, that is synergy" (235).

18. Lewis H. Lapham, "Robber Barons Redux," *Harper's*, January 1994, 7.

19. *International Directory of Company Histories*, vol. 2 (Chicago: St. James Press, 1990), 131.

20. Capital Cities/ABC, Inc., *Annual report*, 1990, 12. Additional material in this chapter comes from the same report, pp. 14–15.

21. Ken Auletta, "TV's New Gold Rush," *The New Yorker*, December 13, 1993, 81.

22. William W. Stevenson, "Foreign Horizons Lure U.S. Broadcast Networks," *New York Times*, November 15, 1993.

23. Elizabeth Kolbert, "High-Level Promotions at ABC," *New York Times*, July 22, 1993.

24. Kolbert.

25. Auletta, "TV's New Gold Rush," 88.

26. Auletta, 87.

27. Ben H. Bagdikian, "Cornering Hearts and Mind: The Lords of the Global Village," *The Nation*, June 12, 1989, 807, cited hereafter as "Lords."

28. For a discussion of the relative power in today's world exercised by powerful men and powerful organizations, see John Kenneth Galbraith, *The Anatomy of Power* (Boston: Houghton Mifflin, 1983).

29. Marshall McLuhan, *The Gutenberg Galaxy: The Making of Typographical Man* (Toronto: University of Toronto Press, 1962), 272. See also Marshall McLuhan,

Understanding Media: The Extensions of Man (New York: McGraw-Hill, 1964), and J. Herbert Altschull, *Milton to McLuhan*, 337–43.

30. For a thorough examination of the financial aspects, see William H. Melody, "The Information Society: The Transnational Economic Context and Its Implications," in Gerald A. Sussman and John A. Lent, eds., *Transnational Communications* (Newbury Park, CA: Sage, 1991), 27–41. The entire book deals with the implications of transnational communications for Third World nations.

31. Articles in *The New York Times* provide an excellent source for information about Maxwell's death and the unraveling of the story of the financial losses. See, among others, Roger Cohen, "Charming the Big Bankers Out of Billions," December 20, 1991; Steven Prokesch, "Estimates Rise for Maxwell Family Debts," December 12, 1991; Craig R. Whitney, "Lloyd's Concludes Maxwell Was Suicide and Won't Pay," February 22, 1992, 37; and Steven Prokesch, "Maxwell's Sons Arrested on Charges of Fraud," June 19, 1992. For additional material on Maxwell's career, see, among others, Peter Thompson and Anthony Delano, *Maxwell: A Portrait of Power* (New York: Bantam, 1988); Bill Hoffman, "Born Again," *Washington Journalism Review* (May 1991): 25–29 and "Robert Maxwell," *The Nation*, June 12, 1989, 814.

32. *The New York Times.*

33. Murdoch's career is presented in some detail in a full-length biography by William Shawcross, *Murdoch* (New York: Simon & Schuster, 1992).

34. "Turmoil for Maxwell Means Anxiety at the Daily News," *New York Times*, December 4, 1991.

35. Kate McKenna and Diane Bart, "The Daily News: Too Tough to Die?" *Washington Journalism Review* (March 1992): 27.

36. For details on the bankruptcy proceedings, see William Glaberson, "A Swan Song for Maxwell Newspapers," *New York Times*, July 12, 1993.

37. Roger Cohen, "Rupert Murdoch's Biggest Gamble, *New York Times Magazine*, October 21, 1990, 311ff.

38. Martin Gottlieb, "Staff Cheers As Murdoch Reclaims *Post*," *New York Times*, March 30, 1993.

39. Roger Cohen, "Rupert Murdoch's Biggest Gamble: The Media Mogul Is Reaching for the Sky As He Bets Heavily on TV and Inches Away from Print," *New York Times Magazine*, October 21, 1990, 64.

40. Cohen, 31.

41. Auletta, "TV's New Gold Rush," 87; William Shenon, "Star TV Extends Murdoch's Reach," *New York Times*, August 22, 1993.

42. Ben Bagdikian, "Murdoch," *The Nation*, June 12, 1989, 806. Bagdikian writes that after purchasing the august *Times* in 1981, Murdoch put out a memo demanding more sex. "The next day, *The Times* carried the headline 'How I Sold Myself to a Sex Club.' "

43. Anthony Smith, *The Age of Behemoths: Globalization of Mass Media Forms* (New York: Priority Press, 1991), 18–19. The survey was conducted by the Broadcasting Research Unit, London, in 1989. The three papers owned by Murdoch's News Corporation were *The Times*, a "quality" paper; *The Sun*, a "popular" paper; and *Today*, aimed at a middle-income readership. All three have taken similar editorial stands on media issues.

44. Bagdikian, *Media Monopoly*, 40–41.

45. Bernard Weintraub, "Rupert Murdoch, in Hollywood, Learns the Value of 'No,' " *New York Times*, July 21, 1992.

46. David E. Sanger, "Tanii-san Goes Fishing in Hollywood," *New York Times*, March 25, 1990.

47. Michael Crichton, *Rising Sun* (New York: Ballantine, 1992), 233. Crichton was especially critical of what he called "crazy American regulations" that he said made it easier for foreign firms such as Matushita to buy out American companies (231).

48. Smith, *Age of Behemoths*, 36–37.

49. "Sony Starts to Peddle Dreams," *Financial Times*, September 29, 1989.

50. Similar laws have been enacted in Germany, France, Denmark, and Austria. In many other countries, such legislation is pending.

51. Smith says nationhood itself is at risk: "There is no longer such a thing as national autonomy without control over data flow." *The Geopolitics of Information*, 127–128.

52. Bagdikian, "Lords," 810; Smith, *Age of Behemoths*, 37–39. Bertelsmann has 42,000 employees in twenty five countries. In addition to its publishing and records business, Bertelsmann puts out *Stern*, a popular German weekly magazine, as well as video, radio, and TV operations. Its book club reaches 22 million members in twenty-two countries.

53. Roger Cohen, "Hachette Announces a Merger," *New York Times*, May 6, 1992; Alan Riding, "The Shakeout Begins in French TV Stations," *New York Times*, January 13, 1992; Bagdikian, "Lords," 818. Hachette's magazine empire remained in good shape, however. The company signed a deal with Ford Motor Company in the same year, under which Ford agreed to pay $10 million for media packaging in eighty-four Hachette publications. A similar, even richer deal was in the works with General Motors Corporation. See "Hachette Signs Ford in Global Media Deal," *Advertising Age*, February 10, 1992.

54. Smith, *Age of Behemoths*, 30–34. "Political skill and a healthy address book," Smith wrote in 1991, "are a constant invisible ingredient in Berlusconi's successes (lapses in these areas account for his failures)" (32). Others who have been seeking success among the Lords include Conrad M. Black, a Canadian press mogul whose holdings include *The Daily Telegraph* of London, and the John Fairfax Group of Australia, whose newspaper and television networks were struggling to keep pace with Murdoch's. See Alex S. Jones, "A Press Lord from Canada Is Building a Global Empire," *New York Times*, April 6, 1992; Steven Erlander, "Australia News Group Facing Tough Times, *New York Times*, February 17, 1991.

Chapter
21

"OUR REPUBLIC
AND ITS PRESS
WILL RISE OR FALL
TOGETHER"

1847   1947
JOSEPH PULITZER

3¢ UNITED STATES POSTAGE

Whither the Information Society?

THE TIME WARNER STORY

The march toward an international information society is relentless; it has been going on for nearly a century. The German sociologist Ferdinand Tönnies foresaw it in 1922. He who controls the press controls the world, he said, or at the very least controls public opinion around the world.[1] Like a number of U.S. sociologists of his era, Tönnies feared that where newspapers were wholly in the hands of capitalists, the public's interests would largely be ignored. In a more optimistic vein, however, he predicted the press would ultimately emerge as a liberalizing force. It was so international that "its ultimate aim [was] to abolish the multiplicity of states and substitute for it a single world market." Tönnies's world market was to be ruled by "thinkers, scholars and writers."[2] Anticipating McLuhan, he saw the press leading the world away from a tightly knit xenophobic set of communities toward a global society without boundaries. Power in such a social order would be global rather than parochial or merely national. To Tönnies, the press was an instrument of public opinion; and public opinion was a kind of faith, religious in character and generally intolerant of anyone else's moral precepts. Only a press that was financed by circulation alone, free of advertising and not in the control of paymasters of any kind, could be expected to be free of propaganda and psychological pressures.

Transnational control of the press would, in his view, be something for the entire world to fear.

The news media play a pivotal role for transnationals and governments jockeying for position. Management of the news media's ideological content is critical as financial stakes increase and the numbers of paymasters shrink. (See Table 21.1.) Conglomerates and group owners are replacing single owners and families as the owners of the news media even as transnational corporations wrest financial power from the families and partners who once controlled the wealth of capitalist countries. Maintenance of the status quo and a peaceful social order have always been important for the owners of the press and the commercial enterprises whose advertising financed those owners. For the faceless managers of the transnationals, maintenance of the social order is even more critical. Their interests can no longer tolerate bitter strife between capitalist countries. As Tönnies foresaw, the demands of a global market require an international press preaching the kind of social order in which transnationals may flourish.

TABLE 21.1 Top U.S. Media Companies: 1990 Revenue by Industry (millions)

Company and Location of U.S. Headquarters	Newspaper	Magazine	Broadcast	Cable TV	Other
Capital Cities/ABC, New York	$524.2	$367.2	$3,842.0	$442.0	—
Time Warner, New York	—	$1,947.8	—	$3,017.0	—
Gannett Company, Arlington, VA	$2,775.2	—	$396.7	—	$271.4
CBS, Inc., New York	—	—	$3,261.2	—	—
General Electric Company, Fairfield, CT	—	—	$3,202.9	$33.1	—
Advance Publications, Newark, NJ	$1,787.0	$845.0	—	$397.6	—
Telecommunications, Inc., Denver, CO	—	—	—	$2,942.0	—
Times Mirror Company, Los Angeles	$2,066.0	$313.4	$104.5	$371.3	—
News Corporation, New York	$174.4	$707.3	$834.8	—	$517.9
Hearst Corporation, New York	$715.0	$1,022.0	$289.6	—	$111.0
Knight-Ridder, Miami	$1,992.1	—	—	$114.0	—
New York Times Company, New York	$1,358.3	$340.0	$69.0	—	$9.5
Cox Enterprises, Atlanta	744.8	—	$419.1	$547.0	—
Tribune Company, Chicago	$1,196.7	—	$506.3	—	—
Thomson Corporation, New York	$654.0	$750.0	—	—	—
Washington Post Company, Washington	$691.0	$340.2	$179.4	$145.5	—
Viacom International, New York	—	—	$164.0	$1,173.5	—
E. W. Scripps, Cincinnati	$784.6	—	$235.9	$199.4	—
Turner Broadcasting System, Atlanta	—	—	—	$1,069.1	—
Dow Jones and Company, New York	$983.7	—	—	—	—

SOURCE: *Adversiting Age*, January 6, 1992, p. S-3, "100 Leading Media Companies." Copyright © 1992, Crain Communications, Inc. Chart: Jeff Pruzan.

Even though news media account for only a small portion of the information disseminated around the world, global paymasters survey warily what is written in the printed press and aired on radio and television. They are well aware that the only forces with the potential to limit their freedom of operation are national governments. The leaders of those governments pay close attention to the news media. To manage the content of the media is of vital interest to both transnationals and national governments. International organizations and agencies like Unesco also play an important part in this pattern of relationships, and even though these organizations have no troops, by generating a great deal of publicity they can influence both transnationals and national governments. Control of "news" and the contents of data bases are equally necessary, for they may store unlimited volumes of intelligence that computers can pass to one another in optical twinklings.

In a world of shrinking bases of power, the interests of advertisers. press owners, and individual journalists grow ever closer to those of one another. Media chains are international; global news agencies operate subsidiary units everywhere; TV companies send signals to many countries, often in multiple languages. The news media, telecommunication, and information industries are inextricably joined. Students of the press in both advancing and capitalist countries who fear the power of concentrated technological and industrial power are demanding some measure of international regulation. It is not only cultural imperialism that is feared but also *mind control* and the kind of psychological pressures for conformity envisaged by Tönnies two generations ago and by many present-day scholars. Media scholar Herbert Schiller says the United States has incurred the animosity of the rest of the world "as the foremost source of global communication pollution."[3] He wants government to switch course and insure equal access for all to the "information superhighway," although conservative operators believe the marketplace will guarantee the competition that opens up all the on-ramps anyone might need.[4]

Among the most spectacular of all media mergers to date, one must have set Henry R. Luce spinning in his grave. It linked in one vast conglomerate the newsmagazine empire that Luce founded in 1923 and Warner Communications Inc., a hodgepodge created out of an earlier merger between a Hollywood movie studio and a New York auto-rental firm. Luce's grandson, Henry R. Luce III, was a member of the Time Inc. board that approved a $14-million deal fulfilling what Time's chairman called its "manifest destiny." The media and entertainment holdings of the new corporation, Time Warner Inc., dwarfed those of all others, joining *Time* and its fellow magazines with such diverse enterprises as the Warner Music Group, the world's largest record company; DC Comics, the biggest group of comic books in the world; several cable channels, including Home Box Office; a major book-publishing house; movie studios; and even a 7.5-percent investment in Ted Turner's broadcasting company.[5] Nearly half of Time Warner's operations were international in scope.

Before the man chiefly responsible for the development of this global giant, Steven J. Ross, died in December 1992, he was able to gaze out on an enterprise one critic said was "capable of stirring the minds and emotions of more people than any commercial enterprise on earth."[6] Ross and Time Warner came under severe criticism for some of the products of that enterprise: Oliver J. Stone's controversial film *J.F.K.*, singer Madonna's highly publicized soft-porn book *Sex* (which *Time* itself called "trashy" and "Madonna's masterpiece of media manipulation"), and rapper Ice-T's single "Cop Killer" (which brought on a national protest and a boy- cott of the company's products). Time Warner was forced to withdraw from the market the album containing the song, but not until it had sold 330,000 copies.[7] The writer Richard Clurman expressed a fear heard in many media offices: that Time Warner's profits might have been on "a collision course" with its principles.

Like Maxwell and Murdoch, Ross was an adventurous wheeler-dealer, his rags- to-riches story the most spectacular of all. Born to a working-class Brooklyn family in 1927, he earned his first pay at eight by lugging sacks of groceries for a nickel each. In 1990, he received a salary of $78.2 million, the most any executive had yet

Sex and the image media of the 1990s: Pop star Madonna
staged a photo-op to plug her aluminum-jacketed sex-fantasy
book, produced by Time Warner at $49.95 a copy.

SOURCE: AP/Wide World

received.[8] Along the way, he bought and sold one property after another. Among those he sold off was MTV, the pop-music TV channel, this to another major player among the media moguls, Sumner Redstone, Chairman of Viacom, Inc. Some of Ross's deals paid off, some did not. His Atari video-game operation was a disaster, costing him a billion dollars. That loss gave Murdoch a shot at the Warner business, and he tried to buy in at a low rate. Ross frustrated that effort, however, by selling off a chunk of Warner holdings.[9]

How *Time* has changed: What once was the modest dream of newsman Henry R. Luce becomes part of the biggest media empire and finds new things to feature.

SOURCE: Copyright 1993 Time, Inc.

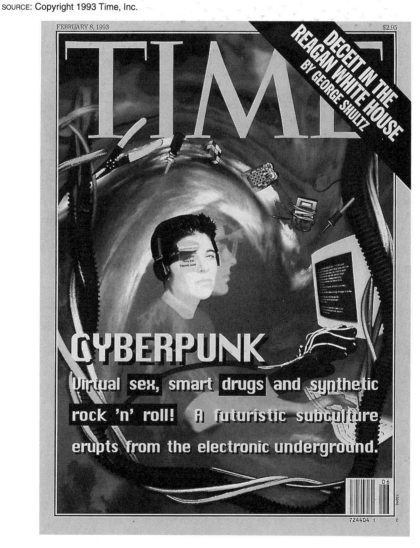

The maneuvering that brought about the merger of Warner and Time makes for an intriguing tale of Byzantine corporate deal making that is difficult for the uninitiated to sort out. The full story may never be told. Connie Bruck's recounting of the deal, with its many players all looking for power and profits, is fascinating reading for the interested. In the end, Nicholas Nicholas, the president of Time, Inc., and one of the leading movers and shakers pushing for the merger, was ousted and replaced by Gerald M. Levin, who then succeeded Ross as head man of the merged conglomerate. Nicholas saw the merger deal as a step toward the journalistic vision of Henry R. Luce. Before his removal as head of *Time*, Nicholas said he was convinced Luce would have been "ecstatic if he saw the company today."[10] *Time* staffers were far less enthusiastic, particularly at a time when 650 magazine employees had just been laid off; they believed journalism was bound to suffer as the organization moved ever more deeply into the field of entertainment. Levin sought to mollify them. He told a group of *Time* staffers that "journalism is at the core of Time Warner" and indicated the departure of Nicholas reflected its dedication to journalism. Heartened, union officials tried to have the layoffs rescinded, but Levin declined. He did, however, win a favorable response from Time newspersons by urging everyone to trust and respect "and, finally, love [one another]—in the unconditional sense. *Agape*, I think it's called."[11]

Yet Levin had been the *Time* leader in the move toward the merger; it was he who had spoken of the merger as manifest destiny. That comment was made in an internal memorandum in which Levin depicted the restructured Time Inc. as an "entertainment oriented company." His goal for a merger was linkage not only with Warner but also with Ted Turner.[12]

It was not at all clear at the outset the merger would be a financial success. The combined earnings of Time and Warner did not grow; warring board members sought different avenues. Nicholas wanted to sell off some of the merged corporation's assets, to "weed the garden," as he phrased it. He particularly promoted sale of some cable systems, but Ross was committed to cable as a device to deepen global operations. In fact, Ross saw cable as the bedrock of a global communication system. His vision of the global corporation was not as a huge monolith but rather as the parent of many smaller companies, each of which would "operate autonomously [and] retain the national identity and cultural orientation of the country in which it operates." He made this comment in the featured address at the Edinburgh International Television Festival in August 1990.[13] It was not a new position for him. He had been a sharp vocal critic of the sale of Columbia Pictures to Sony and of MCA to Matushita. Ross did have his eyes on global expansion, particularly in Asia, but only by selling minority interests while maintaining American ownership and control. Nicholas was worried about partnerships with Japanese companies, fearful they might take over altogether. Ross was prepared to bring in Japanese partners but only as minority interests.

In the end, faced with a serious financial shortfall, Ross worked out a complex billion-dollar deal with two Japanese giants, Toshiba and C. Itoh, which acquired 12.5 percent of a new division called Time Warner Entertainment. The deal, one of the biggest of Ross's many deals, reduced the Time Warner debt, nearly $9 billion at the time of the merger, to less than a billion dollars.[14] Ross said sales in Japan, increasingly important as an entertainment market, could quadruple over five years. Time Warner stock jumped $3.25 per share on the New York Stock Exchange the next day to a level of $89.50. The media mogul also set up a local company in Japan, TWE Japan, owned 50 percent by Time Warner and 25 percent by each of the Japanese firms. Ross's vision included a network of similar organizations, such as HBO Olé in South America, a Time Warner Cable joint venture in Sweden, another with HBO in Hungary, and a Warner Brothers movie-theater joint venture in Japan. In none of these cases would the foreign partner put up capital for an equity stake in Time Warner or its key businesses. Long a spokesman for the concept of synergy, Ross pushed his plan around the world, although he carefully kept control in his own hands.

Before Ross's death, his conglomerate had achieved promising levels of profit. The corporation had turned losses into gains and managed to pay off one-fourth of the $11-billion debt Ross had incurred. It would be foolhardy, however, to suggest the giant media complex was out of the woods. Although it was attracting additional capital from abroad, its stock had not gained substantially, and securities analysts were still waiting nervously for it to make its big move on the market.[15]

The English analyst Anthony Smith was, like the American writer Richard Clurman, alarmed that the Time Warner media monster seemed to be threatening the survival of media pluralism in the United States. When it merged with Time Inc., Warner controlled a startling 14 percent of the national total of 66 hours a week of prime-time TV programming. Smith, long worried that communication media were "shaping the general culture" in the United States, had no recommendations, however, about what to do about "the Age of Behemoths."[16]

Levin was by no means prepared to stop expanding. He forged a deal with U.S. West, one of the seven "Baby Bells" that had been formed after antitrust rules broke up "Ma Bell," forcing a reorganization of AT&T, the American Telephone and Telegraph Co. This deal cleared the way for direct delivery of information and entertainment programming directly to consumers over an upgraded cable system. U.S. West agreed to invest $2.5 billion in Time Warner as part of the deal. Three weeks later, Time Warner signed on with three other firms that planned to service interactive and multimedia computer software to homes over cable.[17] Future plans called for even further expansion: Time Warner was to join forces with Tele-Communications Inc. (TCI), the largest cable-TV company, and Microsoft Corporation, the largest software company, in an enterprise called Cablesoft, an ambitious venture that management consultants described as "the gateway for popular culture."[18]

Then, abruptly, late in 1993 a new player entered the field, sending Time Warner, Redstone, Turner, Murdoch, Capital Cities/ABC, and other media moguls scrambling to regroup and forge new alliances. The new player was the Bell Atlantic Corporation, another one of seven "Baby Bells" that has been formed after antitrust rules broke up "Ma Bell," forcing a reorganization of AT&T. Relaxed FCC rules permitted the Baby Bells to compete for a dominant role on the information superhighway with television, cable, and video-production companies.

The announcement of a $33-billion merger between Bell Atlantic and TCI sent shock waves rumbling through the nation's financial markets and indeed across the pages of newspapers and magazines. Malone laid it on the line by envisioning a powerful box on top of each home-TV set joining all the streams of information that flow separately into the home: telephone calls, television shows, video rentals, newspapers, and even books. "It will," Malone said, "allow us to control all the communications needs of a household with one device."[19] Raymond W. Smith, the chairman of Bell Atlantic, shared the vision. His image in the communications industry, however, was far less flamboyant than that of Malone, long labeled by critics as "Darth Vader," the prince of darkness, especially after he cut 20,000 jobs from his payroll.

The analyst Jolie Solomon wrote that the merger created "a new breed of communications company that will shape our economy and our culture." She described Malone and Smith as risk takers betting that eased regulations would allow them to combine all their assets, a move to give them the delivery system, the cable channels and the programming on those channels. Telephone lines would be "enhanced" with video and cable networks permitting two-way communication and bringing to fruition the industry's vision of an interactive future.[20]

But the deal didn't last. Five months after it was announced, Malone and Smith abruptly called off what would have been the largest corporate merger in history. Officially, they blamed a new FCC ruling that cut cable television prices by 7 percent, but the planned merger had already encountered severe problems. For one thing, the flock of investors they had been expecting did not materialize. To the contrary, Bell Atlantic stock tumbled rather than rose sharply, as had been expected. It looked as if the move had been too daring and risky for the market; prospects for a financial killing had faded, and Malone decided he wanted out. There were other deals to be made; it seemed now that it would take longer to build an information superhighway than the earlier hype had indicated.[21]

FCC Chairman Reed E. Hundt offered no apologies for the rate increase. Instead, he spoke of protecting the public against "unreasonably high, unfair, monopolistic prices" for cable service. He predicted "the national information infrastructure is going to be a magnet for investment."[22]

Interestingly, in all the talk about two-way communication, interactive media, and new information futures, there was virtually no mention of the news function of the media. The emphasis was always on entertainment. Walter Isaacson, assistant manager editor of *Time* and a spokesman for Time Warner, told TV news executives that unless those in the news community did some broad rethinking, they faced a real threat they would be "squeezed out" along the information highway. The differences between broadcast news and newspapers had to be eliminated. "Rather," he said, "our interest is in the news business itself," meaning a business where the medium ceased to be a factor and only the message mattered.[23] Vincent Grosso, an AT&T project director, went a step further. "Everything has to be entertainment," he told the newspeople, "an integration of information and entertainment. The news viewer becomes a technical director." And Chris Lee of Bell Atlantic information services put in the final word. "The battle is over," he said.

"There is no threat. This is a tremendous opportunity. You either join or you roll over."[24] The financial press reported the events reverently. The editor Lewis Lapham observed perceptively that it touched its stories with "the bloom of awe," portraying the media moguls as entrepreneurs and visionaries like the Vanderbilts, Morgans, and Rockefellers of the nineteenth century. Reporters, Lapham wrote, saw the press as "dazed by the wonders of technology and the splendor of money."[25]

Interaction between viewers and what appeared on their screens was clearly inevitable. Viewers could retrieve what they wanted, and in some experiments this was already happening—for example, in Bell Atlantic's fledgling Stargazer program, where subscribers in Arlington, Virginia, were shopping by video at a mall in Littleton, Colorado. Lee said viewers had created their own interactive network.[26] What remained to be seen, however, was how journalists would interact. If viewers could choose whatever they wanted from the bin on their screens, what role was there for the journalistic gatekeeper?

In any case, newspapers, striving not to be squeezed out of the news business altogether, scrapped their long-time opposition to admitting telephone companies into the news business. A number began quietly working out deals with the Baby Bells, figuring it was time to team up with the telephone companies before they found other allies—which, as the TCI deal made clear, they did later on.[27] In England, TCI and U.S. West, another Baby Bell, ran a combined cable-television service, TeleWest.

Time Warner was ready to act to preserve its turf. It created a joint venture with other leading cable companies to compete directly with the phone companies for a variety of local telecommunications services. Curiously, one of its partners in this deal was Malone's TCI, which had already announced plans to merge with Bell Atlantic.[28] TCI was not the only cable company to place itself in competition with itself, since most of the other cable enterprises also had ties to a Bell company. Time Warner, as has been noted, had earlier formed a $2.5-billion joint venture with U.S. West.

On the same day Bell Atlantic announced plans to add 1.5 million homes a year to its fiber-optic network, allowing nearly 9 million homes in its territory to tap into advanced video and electronic services by 2000. Bell Atlantic's Raymond Smith said his company had now gained "the edge in what will be a highly competitive communications and entertainment marketplace."[29]

The array of competitors for key positions on this so-called information superhighway was bewildering, and their interlocking relationships with one another even more so. Untangling the complicated set of relations demanded the most intricate of road maps. Small wonder the U.S. government was looking into allegations of monopolistic practices. All the Lords were aiming at broad synergy and convergence of their companies with others. But some of the Lords were accusing others of trying to corner the market on the superhighway. One of the complainants was Viacom's Redstone, who was particularly vociferous in condemning the planned TCI-Bell Atlantic merger. Joining the FCC and the Justice Department, a Senate committee moved in. Howard Metzenbaum, an Ohio Democrat, warned that "monopolists" like Malone and Smith were seeking to gain "excessive market power."[30] The extent of Malone's entanglements along the highway certainly looked like it. In addition to his control over TCI, the country's largest cable enterprise, Malone owned the biggest outside stake in Ted Turner's broadcasting company; he also was involved in joint ventures with Time Warner and Rupert Murdoch's Twentieth Century Fox, enjoyed an expanding relationship with Barry Diller of QVC Inc., and was in contact with Sony and MCA about joint contracts. Malone, the most active of the Lords, acknowledged that he was playing "hardball" in the market; moreover, he said he wanted a piece of everyone's business." Everyone on the highway Malone said, was both a friend and an enemy; no one was either.[31]

During the noninterventionist years of the Reagan and Bush administrations, the government stayed away from the jockeying of the media giants, but in 1993, when Bill Clinton assumed the presidency, the government's presence began to be felt. The point man for the White House was Vice-President Al Gore, who helped develop an administration White Paper declaring it the government's role to keep the highway democratic and to protect both privacy rights and intellectual-property rights. Gore pledged minimal regulation; he said he intended to "prevent someone from taking advantage or unfairly bludgeoning valuable competition." His model was the telephone dial tone, which anyone could get.[32]

Even as Malone and Smith were entrenching themselves in the field, other Lords and would-be Lords battled for dominant positions particularly in a struggle that had Wall Street and the financial press stumbling over themselves for superlatives. Taking place late in 1993 and early in 1994, it was the most bizarre episode of wheeling and dealing over communication empires yet. Some of the biggest names in the field squabbled in public and private over a merger with Paramount communications Inc., the largest remaining U.S. motion picture enterprise. The Lords jousting in the fiscal lists were among the most daring and hard-nosed of all. In the end, the price Paramount stockholders exacted from the successful antagonist was well in excess of what the entire Paramount operation was said to be worth.[33] The dream, or perhaps the competitive impulse, was stronger than the price.

Paramount's holdings were not only in movies but also in sports, TV shows, and books, but it lacked cable channels and was weak in distribution of movies and television programs. Paramount's chairman, Martin S. Davis, who had been beaten by Time Inc. when he went after a 1989 merger with Warner and now faced declining profits, cast about for a good fit. When he found two zealous applicants, he opened up one of the most dramatic and bitter battles in American financial history, rivaling the jockeying for money and power among the nineteenth-century robber barons.

The contenders this time were two little-known outfits: Viacom Inc., operator of the enormously successful MTV, a cable channel featuring video programs of the varied forms of popular music, and QVC Network Inc., a cable shopping channel and the nation's leading interactive television company. In September 1993, Paramount's Davis offered a deal to billionaire Sumner M. Redstone, Viacom's chairman, who had for a long time nursed a yen to challenge Lords Murdoch and Turner. Redstone was thrilled: "We will be No. 1," he said. "We're creating a colossus."[34]

Paramount stockholders originally approved the friendly takeover but were forced to reconsider when a rival offer came from QVC, tendered by its chairman, Barry Diller. Financial interests were of course at stake, but the challenge was personal as well, adding to the bitterness with which the takeover struggle was waged. Diller had served for decades as chairman and chief executive of Paramount until he was eased out in 1984, convinced that Davis was the man behind his ouster. Moreover, Diller thirsted as much as Redstone to assume leadership of the Lords of the global village. The word *visionary* hovered around Diller as it did around Turner. The producer Howard Rosenman said this: "Barry is a visionary, like William Paley or David Sarnoff. He's putting together this grand design."[35]

Like lookers-on at the craps table, other companies placed their wagers on the high-rollers. The bidding soared into astronomical figures. In the biggest preliminary deal, Redstone acquired Blockbuster Entertainment for $8.4 billion. This deal, which was operative however Viacom's bid for Paramount fared, joined together Viacom's cable channels and broadcast-television programs with video-rental stores across the country. By early 1994, both Viacom and QVC were offering enormous sums of money as well as stock trades.[36] The most zealous numbers crunchers were unable to decide the extent of the total offer since so much hinged on the time period when stock exchanges were scheduled.[37]

Redstone won in the end, but it cost him dearly. The complex offer accepted by Paramount was worth about $9.7 billion in cash and securities. The merged Viacom-Paramount became after Time Warner the nation's second-largest media conglomerate, including MTV, Blockbuster Video, Paramount Pictures, a number of cable television stations, Simon & Schuster, the book publisher, and even the New York Knicks professional basketball team and New York Rangers hockey team. By the time the deal was consummated, however, Redstone's Viacom had slipped to only a third of its value at the start.[38] Redstone cheered his victory, but Diller was already in the market for other collaborators, including perhaps Time Warner. Meanwhile, Malone was courting AT&T and other telephone companies.[39] Bell Atlantic was also still moving ahead with technology for "telecommuting," which promised desktop video conferencing, and movies-by-phone.[40] The lure remained of linking cable with the telephone companies' skill in switching technology. As Bell Atlantic's Smith put it, the superhighway's target was to get the computer to speak, the TV to listen, and the telephone to show the pictures.[41]

And the content? Well, the media magnets weren't talking very much about that. But then the worries of communication transnationals about possible laws to limit their freedom of mobility was real and urgent. *Business International,* a transnational research and promotion company, told its clients in an internal message the barriers some governments were putting up against "the free and timely flow of data" were motivated by genuine concern for safeguarding privacy, but that in other advancing countries, leaders were "bent on protecting nascent sensitive local industry in the computer hardware and software fields,"[42] obviously an unacceptable form of behavior for transnationals. The move to regulate the data flow in certain countries was a major threat to the profitability of transnationals. Anthony Smith was convinced efforts to control transborder data flow would fail because of the logistical difficulties. In fact, he said, it may very well be the nation as we know it is itself doomed, at least those without the technological know-how to maintain autonomy over the flow of information across their borders. Censorship becomes impossible if information can be freely sent from computer to computer across borders. As Smith observed: "There is no longer such a thing as national autonomy without control over data flow and informatics."[43] What was at stake, Smith noted perceptively, was nationhood itself.

Media watchdogs remained worried about the interlocking nature of the new media alliances. Some feared a threat to the privacy of individuals. Congressional antitrust watchers planned to examine the implications. In any case, to some, the move toward giantism threatened the Lords of the global village with an ailment Maryann Keller, an automotive analyst who studied the decline of the auto giant General Motors, described as "the disease of bigness."[44]

The information society had clearly arrived. Although some viewed it with alarm, others argued with persuasive force that the interests of telecommunication transnationals were much closer to those of humankind everywhere than are those of national companies, which continue to profit from the production and sale of weapons. Wars and international violence are anathema to the media transnationals. Their profits can be maximized only in a state of international harmony where the chief values of individuals are consumption and the good life. Unfortunately, cooperation among these conglomerates is limited largely to those societies that are already heavily industrialized and share the market goals and values of the corporations. Despite startling strides in Asia, Third World countries remain far behind in telecommunication technology. In fact, the thrust of discussions in international settings tends to join the technology links between the market nation-states and Russia in a contest against those of advancing nations—in the shortcut terminology, of North versus South.

Many scholars worry the information spread by transnationals pours into data bases and fails to pass through the conventional channels of the press. They deplore control of telecommunication technology by the transnationals, especially those with headquarters in the United States, and fear the marketing skills that ensure vast profits to the transnationals able to sell their hardware in the Third World. Through control of replacement parts and the software needed to operate the machines, transnationals can see to it that the technical gear is used only in pursuit of their ideological goals, chiefly the maintenance of the capitalist system and the largest possible volume of laissez-faire outside the direction of government—national, regional, or international. Entertainment notwithstanding, transnationals are not likely to ignore the news content of the media, recognizing the key role played by news, which, however tainted, remained a crucial connecting medium in the survival of the capitalist social and economic order.

THE CHOICE: GOSSIP OR ANALYSIS?

It is not the purpose of this book to predict the future. It is rather to call attention to the past and the present and to raise questions about the future. The subject is news—how news is perceived in all parts of the world. The content of the news reflects the belief system of those who finance the press. This relationship will continue no matter what form or forms the news media take in the next century. This is not meant to be a prediction; rather, it is a statement about the nature of news.

It is well to keep in mind that reporters and editors have never ceased to buck the system. Dissent is permitted and in some circumstances even encouraged, just so long as it does not go beyond the perimeters of acceptable beliefs. In the capitalist world in particular, dissent and social protest have long been acceptable behavior—provided, again, that no one goes so far as to threaten what is perceived to be in the vital interests of the paymasters. It is even acceptable for one organ of the press to attack another as a puppet of power. Print and electronic media criticize one another all the time. In France, *Le Monde* has for years accused *Le Figaro* and other rightist newspapers of serving as mouthpieces for industry and commerce. In Germany, the *Frankfurter Rundschau* deposes in the same manner about *Die Welt*. And, of course, the compliment is returned. In Britain and the United States, as it was in the Soviet Union, criticism in the press is regularly directed against corruption, mistakes in judgment, heartlessness, and inefficiency. Reporters for the major dailies and the television networks seek out these deficiencies in public and private behavior as a matter of course. "Pure" journalists also have taken to calling attention to "impure" behavior by colleagues. For instance, when an NBC documentary set out to test the safety of gas tanks in a General Motors truck by showing pictures of a truck exploding when struck by another vehicle, the producers helped the explosion along by secretly slipping in some incidendiary devices.[41] The other networks and newspapers piously reported and editorialized on the deception. Similar condemnation of the tabloid *Star* followed its publication during the 1992 election campaign of a story alleging Bill Clinton's infidelity. The slurs at the *Star* did not, however, prevent the more serious news media from repeating the undocumented allegation.

Nothing gratifies the individual journalist more than unloading a challenge to power, even as Don Quixote rejoiced in tilting at windmills. There is built into journalism the *possibility* of inducing change and helping to create a world that is more just and more peaceful. It is this possibility that has fired and contines to fire the imagination of journalists everywhere on earth. Political and especially economic reality, however, severely circumscribes these possibilities. To make sure of a substantial measure of satisfaction among journalists, it is almost always necessary for power to permit a limited volume of success to its critics. The achievement of these successes is growing less likely, for in much of the press the volume of news about the *essence* of major public issues and *substantive* public questions is lessening—even, it might be added, as the casting of judgments is increasing. The news media have, in fact, grown so judgmental that the volume of opinion in print and on the air seems to have equaled the volume of factual reporting. This process has speeded up ever since journalists gained celebrity status and began appearing on TV talk shows and flooding the market with "insider" books. The elusive goal of "objectivity," which once ranked high among journalistic standards, is rarely invoked anymore.

What has been occurring slowly, so slowly it has attracted little attention, is that the press has been losing its character as an instrument of substantive information. The decline of competition in the newspaper industry has been widely noted and universally deplored. Daily newspapers in direct competition with one another exist in fewer than 5 percent of U.S. cities. Television stations add another dimension to the competition, but competition in terms of news reporting and diversity of opinion between newspapers and television is more illusory than real. Few individuals acquire TV sets for the purpose of watching reports of the news, and many individuals buy newspapers primarily for reasons other than to read the news. With 1,750 daily newspapers; thousands of magazines, weeklies, and radio stations; a thousand commercial television channels; and cable and satellite transmissions around the clock, the *appearance* of diversity is certainly present. However, what diversity exists is about people and institutions, not about structure, or essences, or the basic belief system of American citizens. In the United States, for instance, as the journalism scholar Robert McChesney has pointed out, there is among the news media no fundamental criticism of capitalism. This is so, he has said, because of the capitalist basis of the mass media themselves: "The corporate media are in an ideal position to control the public perception, or lack thereof, of any posssible debate regarding the control and structure of the mass media."[46]

This is not to suggest that some other political or economic philosophy is superior; it is rather to point out *the absence of expression* of diverse points of view. Bagdikian put it another way:

> The lords of the global village have their own political agenda. All resist economic changes that do not support their own financial interests. Together, they exert a homogenizing power over ideas, culture and commerce that affects populations larger than any in history. Neither Caesar nor Hitler, Franklin Roosevelt nor any Pope, has commanded as much power to shape the information on which so many people depend to make decisions about everything from whom to vote for to what to eat.[47]

Anthony Smith has been equally alarmed. The appearance of more news organizations was supposed to help reconcile opposing viewpoints by permitting so many ideas to be brought to public attention. Instead, Smith wrote, the media seemed to be turning into "instruments of homogenization." The dynamics of an unrestrained market cleared the way for bringing diverse thoughts to the public, but it didn't work out that way. As Smith put it, "In a multi-channel society in which providers of information are not even obliged to reflect the main debates of the day, it is easy to avoid the conflict of ideas." Thus, "behind the diversities there are new homogeneities in information and entertainment."[48] The RTNDA's David Bartlett acknowledged that while the greater number of news organizations in "the hot format in the 21st century" will produce a greater variety of news programs, they will be "aimed at much narrower audiences."[49] Smith's point was that fragmented audiences meant fragmented information—lots of *bits* of news but little by way of ideas or clarification or genuine diversity. In fact, the impression that competing media ensure the presentation of diversity of views turns out on examination to be an illusion. Studies show the news reports on mainstream media are painfully similar. The biggest difference in TV-network news reports is found in the identity of the anchorpersons delivering the news, not in the reports themselves.

The quickest and cheapest instrument for learning the news remains the radio. Home computers and interactive cable may soon become the media of choice in this role, but they are not likely for a long time to come—if ever—to perform precisely the same function as newspapers and television news reports.

What are those functions? Why do people watch television? Why do they read newspapers? Many studies have been conducted on these questions. They demonstrate, not surprisingly, that people expend time, money, and energy in order to satisfy their own desires or needs. And news clearly represents only a small portion of those needs; otherwise, the content of newspapers and television programming would be far more heavily devoted to news than it is. The greatest share of the content is, of course, advertising. Beyond that, the words and pictures of newspapers and television address themselves to a wide variety of information, not much of it news as it is usually conceived. As we have seen, what we speak of as news is really entertainment. Television and radio talk shows masquerade as news but present virtually none of it. These programs are minidramas that give the hosts the opportunity to spread their opinons before thousands and even millions whether or not what they say is gibberish. All TV "programs" are fictive; watching television is rather like reading an illustrated novel. In newspapers, the fare is more diverse: comic strips; sports pages; recipes; columns on gardening, health, and bridge; advice to the lovelorn and to the stamp collector; stock-market citations; and the Dow-Jones Index. None of this is news as far as the news industry is concerned. All of this material is more than acceptable to the paymasters, since it tends to sell apples and leave the apple cart right side up.

The content of newspapers and magazines shifted when television usurped the very essence of the journalist's raison d'être: being there first with the news. Losing the advantage of immediacy meant the print press could no longer compete on traditional grounds. How could it? Radio and TV tell people what happens the moment it does. There had to be a turn in the road; and, all too often, that turn was to gossip. Gossip has always been there, just as news analysis has always been there. Until the arrival of television, the reporting of news came first. Gossip publications like the supermarket tabloids sprang up everywhere. *USA Today* converted simplicity into vast sales. The news stories themselves changed shape. Reporters abandoned the traditional "who, what, when, where" leads for discursive approaches that dealt with complexities by focusing on single individuals. Stories about poverty became tales of how one poor family lives in an urban or rural slum. Gossipy stories about politicians told more about their private lives than where they stood on public questions. Readers were given more information about "people" and about "celebrities" than about events of great political, economic, or social significance. In this environment, it cannot be surprising that the greatest audience for a TV interview came when talk-show host Oprah Winfrey spoke for an hour and a half with pop singer Michael Jackson at his California ranch. A total of 90 million people watched.[50] In sum, the news media increased their reportage of gossip as a substitute for "hard news." Gossip is no more likely to upset apple carts than are commercial notices about undergarments or horoscope columns.

In the past in Western Europe, newspapers tended to serve as open party organs or at least as apologists for particular political movements, but this pattern has been changing. Newspapers, especially those outside the capital cities, have been turning their attention increasingly to problems of local and regional interest, and as a result they have been attracting more advertising as well as readership. The greatest circulations in Europe by far are enjoyed by the boulevard press, such as Germany's *Bild Zeitung*, the flagship publication of the Springer press empire. Like its fellow papers in Britain, France, Italy, and elsewhere, even now in Russia, it makes no pretense of reporting news. Instead, these papers, like the *Star* and *The National Enquirer* in the United States, publish large doses of reports about the private lives of celebrities and about exotic crimes. That little of what appeared in these periodicals was accurate seemed not to disturb the readers. It is stretching the word to its outer limits to describe these publications as newspapers. The traditional press noticed that the number of such publications was increasing and that their circulations remain high. Significantly, the traditional press began copying their success story.

Just as the traditional press coopted the underground press movement in the United States, it seeks to co-opt the boulevard press. Characteristically, the Luce publications, perhaps as a forerunner to joining the Warner entertainment complex, jumped on the boulevard bandwagon and achieved success, in terms of both advertising and circulation, in its magazine *People*. Newspapers, among them even *The New York Times*, began publishing special sections on celebrities. Gossip, which had always been a factor in the news, has now become perhaps its most valuable staple. This development is particularly cheering to those in power, who fear the possibility of disaffection among their pipers in the press. News media that devote large amounts of their precious space to gossip and trivia are less likely to pursue challenges to power than those with large "newsholes."

There is another side to these developments. Confronted through the rise of radio and television with the recognition they no longer had the capability to present information first, U.S. newspapers undertook a role somewhat different from the one they played traditionally. They began to produce longer stories, concerning themselves less with timeliness and more with in-depth treatment of complex issues. In short, they began to set aside their long-held admiration for the code of objectivity and to produce analytical and interpretive reports, often at considerable length. In this, they were following a practice long pursued by the leading European newspapers; moreover, they were responding to complaints issued by the underground press and the new journalists. Such an approach represented the precise opposite to that taken by the boulevard press and posed a substantial threat to power. The bitter attacks on the press begun during the Nixon administration have continued without cease. The public has joined in, wildly cheering President Bush's "Annoy the Media—Elect Bush" placards in 1992. This development can be explained to a large degree by the shift in emphasis on the part of newspapers and television, which had learned that an occasional exposé or in-depth documentary could produce a high level of public interest, greater sales, and higher ratings among the powerful.

Even so, this kind of reporting represents only a small portion of newspaper and television content. The "serious" press does engage in analytical journalism, though the emphasis is usually on personalities rather than on complex public issues. Here, we encounter once again news as entertainment. The smaller provincial press, both print and broadcast, is generally content to rake in the profits without spreading the muck. Censorship is not required. Self-censorship is adequate to do the job. And, as we have seen, hiring practices as well as pressures from colleagues and ambition join together in ensuring that the bulk of the U.S. news media pushes the apple cart along its appointed highway.

The media plunge into gossip about the private lives of celebrities led in 1992 all the way to the startling story in *USA Today* that the prominent tennis star Arthur Ashe was suffering from AIDS. Ashe had maintained his privacy for many months; journalists who knew him had declined to report the event on the ground that Ashe's privacy ought to be respected. The violation of Ashe's privacy brought on a great deal of soul searching among journalists; many among them depolored the publication of the story. *The New York Times* published a lengthy article that maintained it was not easy for editors "to reconcile the twin American passions for both information—including quantities of gossip—and privacy." Not easy, perhaps, but appeal to "the public's right to know" won out over privacy then as it almost always has. *The Times*'s conclusion was laconic: "At mainstream publications, what is considered legitimate news has expanded in recent years."[51] Ashe's death a year later brought an unusual outpouring of laudatory obituaries. His illness, as was pointed out in all the press articles, was caused by transmission of contaminated blood.

The journalist Janet Malcolm charged journalists with an offense far more serious than invasion of privacy. First, she charged best-selling writer Joseph McGinniss, author of *Fatal Vision*, with deliberately deceiving the subject of his book, convicted murderer Dr. Jeffrey MacDonald, into thinking that McGinniss believed in his innocence—a device to trick him into speaking freely. Then she went way beyond that legitimate complaint to condemn journalists in general as treacherous and unworthy folk who earn their bread by confession and end up in "a state of moral anarchy." In fact, she puzzled over why the subjects of journalistic articles are crazy enough to "trust in the good intention of journalists."[52] She exaggerated, of course, in extrapolating from a single, lamentable case to the broad world of journalism, but she was on target in calling attention to the sharp increase in the pages of newspapers, magazines, and books of dramatic confessional-type stories, a development that paralleled the rise of gossip about celebrities.

Although it used to be said the American people believed everything they saw in print, polls and letters to the editor in the 1990s show a disaffection with the press. People might read the gossip avidly, but they seemed to have less confidence that what they read was true. Some observations by writers quoted by Malcolm show why. Among those who testified on behalf of McGinniss when he was brought to trial on charges of misrepresentation were William F. Buckley, Jr., the columnist, television personality, and novelist, and Joseph Wambaugh, the policeman-turned-author who has written a number of best-sellers. Buckley and Wambaugh made it clear they considered it quite ethical to deceive their interview subjects in order to get them to talk. Wambaugh told the jury he didn't believe in telling his subject "a lie" but would tell him an "untruth." Buckley said it ought not to shock anyone ethically if the journalist "gives an impression intending to disarm the person he's writing about."[53] The journalistic venture into gossip and confession plunges reporters into a moral quagmire. Malcolm spoke of journalists as facing a "baffling and unfortunate occupational hazard." As journalists descend deeper into the world of gossip, that hazard will intensify; and it is at least possible that as a result lawmakers will take another look at the First Amendment guarantee of free expression on public questions. It is doubtful the Founding Fathers meant to include gossip among public questions.

The rapid growth of technology speeded up the pace of change in the mass media, and even though the stakes were higher, the choice remained between analysis and gossip, between contribution to public understanding and contribution to public entertainment. It was not a new choice: The Romans dealt with bread and circuses; the MacBride Commission tried to find a way in which the media could work to eliminate war and hatred, recognizing that when the media succumbed to the pressures exerted by conflicts among communities, nations, and belief systems, tomorrow was likely to be a scary place. Delegates to a conference assessing telecommunication in the year 2000 agreed the "old media" were not likely to wither and die. Instead, the "new media" had a chance "to benefit the world information need and not the world information power."[54] To move in this direction would require a change in emphasis on profits and a dedication to cooperate with those struggling to achieve information equality. Researcher Kenneth Edwards noted after a thorough examination of the growth of electronic news-delivery systems that they offered "new opportunities for international cooperation through vastly improved communication." Their chief backers, Edwards said, saw new news-delivery systems as "a medium promoting understanding and peace."[55]

To the management researcher Roy Eales, choosing to opt for analysis and public understanding would signify hope for the future. However, he cautioned business, governments, and the news media to try to understand one another a little better. The pressure to get out the news makes the media "a natural adversary" of business and government, Eales wrote, but the media would be serving the public interest if they conquered their "ignorance" of business affairs and their "search for the sensational" everywhere. At the same time, he criticized business because it "does not always transmit a straight message."[56] No doubt he, like many other critics, failed to recognize the symbiotic relationship between news media and their sources. Despite the hostility between media and sources, they have an identical goal: survival in a decent world.

That goal was the goal of the MacBride Commission. It is also the clearly expressed aspiration of the Third World ideologues. Perhaps we might detect it in the ideologies of the market and communitarian societies if our vision were but strong enough to see it. Sadly, only Supereyes, with his X-ray sight, can penetrate the dark, menacing clouds that obscure the vision. In those clouds lurk conflict and confrontation, and not far off in the distance we can hear the ominous thunder of martial music. The music salutes the quest either for the maximization of profit or for the bearing of witness to historical destiny. And it is the leaders of the parades who are the paymasters of the press. While Lenin's answer may have been exposed as inadequate and threatening, his question remains—to trouble us as it did the world at the turn of the twentieth century: "What is to be done?"

NOTES

1. Ferdinand Tönnies, *Community and Association* (London: Routledge and Paul, 1955). For an interesting examination of Tönnies's career, see Hanno Hardt, *Social Theories of the Press: Early German and American Perspectives* (Beverly Hills, CA: Sage), 236.

2. Tönnies, cited in Hardt, *Social Theories*, 172-73.

3. Ken Auletta, "Under the Wire," *The New Yorker,* January 17, 1994, 50. See also Herbert Schiller, *Mass Communication and American Empire* (New York: Augustus Kelley, 1969). Schiller writes of "traumatic anxiety in international communication-cultural circles" resulting from the technology that permits direct transmission via satellites of U.S. television programs. See also the work of Ben Bagdikian, Noam Chomsky, Jeremy Tunstall, Cees Hamelink, and Kaarle Nordenstreng, among others.

4. Connie Bruck, "The World of Business: Strategic Alliances," *The New Yorker*, July 6, 1992, 41 hereafter cited as Bruck. She is quoting Gerald M. Levin.

5. Roger Cohen, "A $78-Million Year: Steve Ross Defends His Paycheck," *New York Times Magazine*, March 22, 1992, 28-31 ff. See also Anthony Smith, *The Age of Behemoths: The Globalization of Mass Media Firms* (New York: Twentieth Century Fund, 1991), 24-26, and Bruck.

6. Richard M. Clurman, "Pushing All the Hot Buttons," *New York Times*, November 29, 1992. See Clurman's book expanding on the same theme, *To the End of Time: The Seduction and Conquest of a Media Empire* (New York: Simon & Schuster, 1992).

7. Clurman, "Pushing All the Hot Buttons."

8. Cohen, "78-Million Year," 30-31.

9. The sale of 20 percent of Warner holdings was to Chris-Craft Industries, a New York–based conglomerate headed by an investor named Herbert J. Siegel. It turned out to be a good deal for Siegel. He received a payoff as part of the Time Warner merger that netted him more than a billion dollars for his five-year investment. See Roger Cohen, "The Creator of Time Warner, Steven J. Ross, Is Dead at 65," *New York Times*, December 21, 1992.

10. Cohen, "$78-Million Year," 66.

11. Bruck, "The World of Business," 54-55.

12. Bruck, 41.

13. Bruck, 47.

14. Geraldine Fabrikant, "Toshiba and Itoh Agree to Time Warner Deal," *New York Times*, October 30, 1991.

15. Fabrikant, "Toshiba and Itoh."

16. Anthony Smith, *The Age of Behemoths,* 11.

17. Lawrence M. Fisher, "Interactive TV Alliance Is Formed," *New York Times,* June 7, 1993; Geraldine Fabrikant, "U.S. West Will Buy Into Time Warner," *New York Times,* May 17, 1993. The new alliance linked Time Warner with Kaleida Labs. Inc., Motorola Inc., and Scientific-Atlanta Inc. Kaleida, a joint venture of IBM and Apple, arranged to supply its multimedia software for new devices placed on top of TV sets.

18. John Markoff, "Microsoft and 2 Cable Giants Close to an Alliance," *New York Times,* June 13, 1993.

19. John Markoff, "A Phone-Cable Vehicle for the Data Superhighway," *New York Times,* October 14, 1993. See also Allen R. Myerson, "Casting the Star Roles at Bell Atlantic," *New York Times,* October 26, 1993.

20. Jolie Solomon, "Big Brother's Holding Company," *Newsweek,* October 25, 1993, 40.

21. Floyd Norris, "Malone Knows Cable Has a Rocky Future," *New York Times,* February 27, 1994. See also "FCC Blamed as Bell, TCI Cancel Merger," *Los Angeles Times,* February 24, 1994.

22. Edmund L. Andrews, "Collapse of a Giant Deal: Economics Slows the Merger of Phones and Cable TV," *New York Times,* February 24, 1994. The TCI-Atlantic Bell deal was not the only such plan to collapse. Cox Enterprises and Southwestern Bell called off their plan six weeks later. See Geraldine Fabrikant, "$4.9 Billion Cable Deal Called Off," *New York Times,* April 6, 1994.

23. Walter Isaacson was speaking at a panel session at the annual convention of the Radio and Television News Directors Association, Miami, October 1, 1993.

24. Grosso and Lee also spoke at the RTNDA session (see note 21).

25. Lewis H. Lapham, "Robber Barons Redux," *Harper's,* January 1994, 10.

26. Lee. See also Solomon, "Big Brother's Holding Company," 41 (See note 20).

27. William Glaberson, "The Baby Bells Are Finding an Unlikely Ally in the Information-Services War: Newspapers," *New York Times,* July 5, 1993. Cox Enterprises Inc., which owned *The Atlanta Journal and Constitution* and other papers, was a leader in the movement, setting up a joint venture with the Bell South Corporation, another of the seven Baby Bells to deliver Yellow Pages information by telephone and computer in the Southeast. Other deals were in the works.

28. John Markoff, "Cable Companies in Venture to Rival Phone Companies," *New York Times,* December 2, 1993. In this challenge to Bell Atlantic, Time Warner and TCI said they would work with the Teleport Communications Group, a fiber-optics company based in Staten Island. As part of the deal, Time Warner said it would acquire a 16.67-percent stake in Teleport.

29. Michael Dresser, "Bell Posts Its Itinerary on Information Highway," *Baltimore Sun,* December 2, 1993.

30. Ken Auletta, "Under the Wire," 51.

31. Ken Auletta, "John Malone: Flying Solo," *The New Yorker,* February 7, 1994, 67.

32. Auletta, "Under the Wire," 49–50.

33. Susan Antilla, "Is Paramount Really Worth That Price?" *New York Times,* November 7, 1993.

34. Michael Meyer et al., "Hollywood Square-Off," *Newsweek*, September 27, 1993. See also Geraldine Fabrikant, "Sumner Redstone Lands the Big One," *New York Times*, September 13, 1993. Together, Paramount and Viacom enjoyed a market value of $16 billion.

35. Bernard Weintraub, "What's Driving Diller to Play for Paramount?" *New York Times*, September 21, 1993.

36. Geraldine Fabrikant, "Newhouse and Cox Join QVC in Hostile Bid for Paramount," *New York Times*, October 18, 1993, and "Bell South Said to Be Joining QVC's Bid for Paramount," *New York Times*, November 5, 1993. Advance Publications Inc., the Newhouse family's media mammoth, backed the QVC bid with $500 million; so did Cox Enterprises, of Atlanta. Not long afterward, Bell South got into the picture with a $2-billion contribution.

37. Viacom's bid had reached the astronomical level of $105 a share for 50.1 percent of Paramount with the balance of its offer involving an exchange of stock. Diller's offer stood at $92 a share for 51 percent of the stock and its balance also involving a stock exchange.

38. Geraldine Fabrikant, "Viacom Is Winner Over QVC in Fight to Get Paramount," *New York Times*, February 16, 1994. The worth of Viacom was given as $6.8 billion when the bidding war began in September 1993; by the following February, the figure was down to $2.85 billion.

39. Edmund L. Andrews, "With Merger a Failure, an Industry Seeks a Leader," *New York Times*, February 26, 1994.

40. Michael Dresser, "Bell Atlantic's Disappointment Brief," *The Sun*, Baltimore MD, March 16, 1994.

41. Ken Auletta, "John Malone: Flying Solo," 63.

42. "Transborder Data Flow," *Business International* newsletter, 1982.

43. Smith, *Geopolitics*, 128, 142.

44. Jolie Solomon, "Big Brother's Holding Company," 45.

45. The NBC show, "Dateline NBC," aired on November 17, 1992.

46. Robert W. McChesney, "Off Limits: An Inquiry into the Lack of a Debate over the Ownership, Structure and Control of the Mass Media in U.S. Political Life," *Communication* 13, 1 (1992): 9, 14, 16.

47. Bagdikian, "Lords," 807.

48. Smith, *Age of Behemoths*, 18–20.

49. David Bartlett, address to the annual convention of the Public Relations Society of America, Kansas City, Mo., November 12, 1992.

50. When Oprah Winfrey's interview of Michael Jackson was aired on February 10, 1993, a total of 36.4 percent of households were tuned in (*Facts on File*, February 1993).

51. Alex S. Jones, "News Media Torn Two Ways in Debate on Privacy," *New York Times*, April 26, 1992.

52. Janet Malcolm, *The Journalist and the Murderer* (New York: Knopf, 1990), 3–4.

53. Malcolm, 53. *Journalist and the Murderer*, 53. There was no jury verdict in the case because McGinniss paid Dr. Jeffrey MacDonald $325,000 to settle his suit out of court. The jury was clearly offended by McGinniss's deception. Floyd Abrams, the prominent constitutional lawyer, said in an appearance on Buckley's TV show "Firing Line"

(September 18, 1967) that in his experience ordinary citizens find it "very offensive" when a journalist misleads people (Malcolm, 111).

54. Kenneth Edwards, "Delivering Information to the Home Electronically," in Michael Emery and Ted Curtis Smythe, eds., *Readings in Mass Communication: Concepts and Issues in the Mass Media*, 5th ed. (Dubuque, IA: William C. Brown, 1983), 268-86.

55. Edwards, "Delivering Information," 283.

56. Roy Eales, "Multinationals and the Media: Time to Lift the Veil," *Multinational Business* 2 (1990): 29-30.

Chapter

22

Politics, Power, and Perceptions

A SYMPHONIC CLASSIFICATION SYSTEM

The roles assigned to the press can be compared to the movements of a global symphony with many themes, melodies, and variations. One perhaps surprising truth that emerges from an examination of the news media in all societies and all countries is their similarities are often as great as their differences. In a real sense, we can speak of the news media of the world as a single unit, as a symphony is a single unit composed of a variety of themes and melodies. A symphony does not have to be harmonious; in fact, it can be anything but—filled with dissonance and discordant notes. We might be tempted to speak not of a symphony of the press but of a cacophony of the press. Still, with all the dissonance and discord, there is a fundamental unity. Like a Wagnerian opera, a leitmotiv runs through the structures and the ideologies of the news media of the world. The unifying element is agreement on the role of the media as educator.

In this symphony of the press, we can identify three movements, each containing a basic theme, though also numerous variations on that theme. A number of possible names can be given to these movements, and since the names given to things inevitably shape our perceptions of them, it is crucial that we approach the names with a great deal of caution. We might, for instance, simply give them numerical identity—as first, second, and third. There is some comfort and famil-

418

iarity in this numerical identification. After all, the three movements parallel the political designations that were dominant for most of the twentieth century: the First, Second, and Third Worlds. Or we might use identifications that are equally familiar, substituting *market* for *First*, *Marxist* for *Second*, and *developing* for *Third*. Or we might apply equally familiar geographical names: Western, Eastern, and Southern. Our difficulties clearly increase if we attempt to impose value-laden terms on any of the three movements. Words such as *democratic, libertarian, communist*, and *authoritarian* hinder understanding. *Socialist* is also a troublesome term. After all, it has been used to stand for the monstrous regime of the Third Reich. So, in fact, is *revolutionary*, a term that sometimes stands for what is good and sometimes for what is evil. In the classification scheme outlined in these pages, I have chosen to use identifications that are economic in scope but subject to critical modification by late-century developments. This terminology is used in the full realization it possesses the fragility of all nomenclature. We can, however, compensate for this fragility by recognizing the richness of the many melody *variations* in each movement. The themes in the movements by no means limit themselves to matters of economics. Each movement embraces all the realities of the environments in which the news media exist: historical, political, social, cultural, and—importantly—psychological. With all these qualifications in mind, let us identify the movements of the symphony of the press as *market, communitarian*, and *advancing*.

This is not meant to be an absolute classification structure. Variations in degree in the real world generate a good many exceptions. Still, we cannot abandon the classification system because it is not perfect. To do so would be to yield to the fallacy of false dichotomous questions wherein groupings are either mutually exclusive or collectively exhaustive.[1] Either/or questions are common in all literature, even in historical scholarship. Consider such titles as "What Is History, Fact or Fiction?" and "Plato, Democrat or Totalitarian?" Ambiguity is familiar enough in the real world. Prince William of Orange used as his motto a Latin phrase that translates into "I didn't steal; I received." The historian David Hackett Fischer suggests wryly that maybe William was a receiver of stolen goods, even if they were stolen in a noble cause.[2] Market is not inseparable from communitarian, nor is advancing exclusively different from either.

Reference was made at the beginning of this book to a perceptive comment of Pierre Sarrazin, a thoughtful Canadian movie director whose films have explored the similarities and differences between Americans and Canadians, people with a common cultural heritage who have lived in peace for hundreds of years despite an undefended border that stretches 3,000 miles from the Atlantic to the Pacific.[3] In Sarrazin's view, the social belief system of Canadians is closer to the communitarian model than is that of Americans. Allowing for the many exceptions to the rule, Sarrazin says that in Canada, "on the other side of the border, the defining interest is the communal life." As has been illustrated again and again, "the defining interest" of Americans has been the *individual*, the centerpiece of capitalist, or market, ideology. Canada, Sarrazin says, "represents a compromise between American capitalism and socialism."[4]

One of the fruits of America's worship of the individual, the "lone rider" in Ray Stannard Baker's imagery, has been an intense antipathy to government control or direction of the lives of individuals. Any suggestion of government direction of the news media in the United States has met with passionate opposition. We have seen that even a program as well meaning as television's Fairness Doctrine was unable to withstand the pressure from the TV industry, whose market economic interests were hampered by required adherence to the doctrine. The industry's appeal to the public did not stress the economic advantages but turned rather to the more useful spin that emphasized the individual freedom promised under an open, competitive market.

In each of the three movements, the press is assigned a central role in the social order: to educate the people so they can carry out their own individual roles in society. However, the ends of education are far from identical in the three movements. In the market movement, the education of the people is designed to help them vote wisely so that the social order will be safeguarded. There is some uneasiness in the United States over describing the press as a means of education; the preferred word is *information*, for *education* can imply propaganda, which remains a dirty word. But this seems to be mere quibbling since information is of little use unless it increases its audience's level of education. Aside from the United States, the market countries are little inclined to draw distinctions between information and education.

In Marxist countries, the press was frankly an instrument of propaganda in accordance with the theories of Marx and Lenin. Those theories disintegrated in the former Soviet orbit with the collapse of communist rule in the Soviet Union. Despite the death of the U.S.S.R., however, many elements of Leninist doctrine survived, especially its emphasis on *collective* action. Moreover, communism itself persists in China, Cuba, and indeed the former Soviet empire. It is an *"ism"* that will not die easily, if indeed it ever will. Marxist doctrine, especially emphasis on the media as a promoter of group consciousness, remains strong in many places, even in the United States, where it is not generally recognized as a Marxist concept. As for education and information, here, too, there is much quibbling over words— even in the former U.S.S.R., it was the education of the people that was viewed as the ultimate goal so they might behave wisely and thereby safeguard the social order. As we have seen, the media everywhere serve as agents of social control, however that term may be defined. We must note also that the three roles Lenin assigned to the press are in essence all educative, just as Marx's image of the press was as an instrument that went beyond the Prussian censors to educate the people about their communal identity.

Of the three movements, the third is the most open and direct about the press as an instrument of education. The press model throughout the Third World is as an instrument both to help safeguard the social order and to educate the people to change that social order where necessary. In fact, it is at this point the third movement brings a decisive change in the pace of the symphony: Although education in the first and second movements has an essentially static character (that is, of preserving a form of the status quo), in the third movement its character is dynamic, dedicated to change. Nevertheless, the leitmotiv of the press as an instrument of education unifies the symphony. The least sophisticated of observers can recognize this fundamental unity, even though this recognition has all too often been concealed from those blinded by ideological rigidity. Thus, an American editor could always dismiss the Soviet news media as propaganda arms of the Communist party, or a Soviet editor could dismiss the American media as tools of Wall Street; and both could dismiss the advancing press as childlike, ethnic, and xenophobic. For their part, advancing-world editors could scoff at the Soviet and the American press as devices of colonial exploiters. The level of global understanding will certainly be raised if editors acknowledge the similarities in the press everywhere.

Not surprisingly, recognition of these similarities has always been far more likely among journalists who have spent time with one another than among those reporters, editors, and scholars who merely theorize about the press from afar. Journalists who fraternize with their colleagues often develop a sense of camaraderie transcending social, political, and national differences. Among journalists, foreign correspondents represent but a small percentage; many who answer to the name of foreign correspondent are themselves itinerants who flit back and forth from place to place and spend much of their time at their home base. Thus, the opportunity for developing strong cross-national social contacts has been limited. When those contacts are developed, however, journalists discover the similarity in their thinking and find a remarkable degree of agreement that the best journalism occurs when the reporter is not burdened by restrictions—political, economic, or otherwise. As for those who pontificate from afar or even from an isolated nearness, it is not surprising they fail to detect the similarities in both theory and practice. Discussions at international gatherings are inevitably bedeviled by this failure. Editors have often given voice to the most sweeping condemnations of journalists from other countries, proclaiming them propagandists or puppets or profiteers without ever having so much as chased down a news story in the places under attack. Delegates to international gatherings of journalists or educators have frequently issued impassioned pronunciamentos about one another without ever having so much as read a newspaper or a book published in the other's country. Such meetings have often merely strengthened ideological purity and increased discord.

I have attempted en route to this point to sketch the background for the classification system offered here by likening it to a symphony. Inside the movements of the symphony, variations on themes are sometimes striking. In the market movement, for instance, there are important structural variations. Radio and television in the United States are organized in a fashion quite different from the broadcasting industries of Western Europe and Japan. In the United States, financing of broadcasting is accomplished almost entirely by advertising, whereas in most other capitalist countries, advertising plays a limited role. Tax revenues and public funding provide a great deal of the resources for broadcasting in Western Europe and Japan. Important differences occur in the broadcasting content of capitalist countries, but the root similarity remains. All these countries—some to a greater, some to a lesser degree—practice capitalism. Some countries have more state-owned industries than others, yet modern capitalism has adapted to acceptance of a measure of state ownership. What unites all capitalist countries, whatever the level of socialist enterprises permitted, is their belief systems and a common hostility to a communitarian or tribal system, especially to a Marxist social order.

Yet it may have been communitarian impulses that allowed the humanistic spirit to survive during the long suppression of individual freedom in the Soviet Union and the countries of Eastern Europe. The journalist-politician Vaclav Havel, who led Czechoslovakia in its drive to return to its old democratic traditions, said those traditions survived because they had lain dormant "somewhere in the subconscious of our nations and were passed on from one generation to another."[5] The main carriers of these traditions were the communities of civil society and mutual aid, such as the Solidarity movement in Poland.[6] Havel, who served as president of Czechoslovakia, lived to witness his country split in two: into a Czech Republic committed to market values and a Slovak Republic still clinging to the vestiges of Lenin's ideological orientation. Subsequently, Havel was chosen president of the new Czech Republic. He remained convinced the fall of the Soviet Union meant the end of a major era in human history because it showed we can no longer believe in an absolute or scientific answer to all problems. The Soviet communist experiment, Havel declared, illustrated that science was not enough and man was not "the pinnacle of everything," that he could not grasp and rationally direct "everything that exists."[7] The resolution, Havel was suggesting, did not lie in new technologies or in *any* system, however scientific. In a sense, he was advocating a new form of communitarianism. So, indeed, was Mikhail Gorbachev, the former Soviet leader, who declared that "the idea of socialism lives on" despite the collapse of "the Stalinist model" in the Soviet Union. There was a place for market economies in Gorbachev's concept of "a new socialism" where "democracy and humanitarianism should naturally have pride of place."[8] Exactly how the role of the media will be defined in the still-unsettled land that was once the chief standard-bearer of a communitarian press ideology remained to be determined. Despite the heights on which the market was riding, it was clear enough as the twenty-first century approached that the communitarian movement of the symphony of the press continued to command a robust group of adherents.

The first movement of the symphony encompasses variations in the market's level of hostility to a communitarian belief system. While certain capitalist countries have adapted to certain aspects of Marxism, their basic belief systems remain intact. The press remains an instrument to safeguard the market social order. Although the ideological boundaries beyond which the press may not go are not identical among the capitalist countries or even inside an individual country at different time periods, the boundaries exist. In the end, the paymasters see to it those boundaries are not violated.

Each of the three movements of the press symphony is filled with a variety of melodies, which sometimes clash; there is no shortage of discord in any of the movements. The French reader will likely differ in important detail from the Dutch reader, the Belgian TV viewer from the Norwegian. Still, all these readers and viewers approach the topic from a common perspective, one rooted in a common belief system. Discord notwithstanding, the broad sweep of the first movement of the symphony is heard throughout the industrialized capitalist world, in Japan as in Denmark and Canada. The same kind of broad sweep can be detected in each of the other two movements.

Throughout Eastern Europe, Marxist nations sought different roads to socialism. And while communism has been replaced by market considerations throughout the former Soviet empire, it retains substantial numbers of devotees. Lithuania, released from Soviet control, at first gleefully adopted a fiercely anti-communist government yet not long afterward voted it out in favor of a regime friendly to Russia. Czechoslovakia, as we have seen, split into two countries, one looking to the West, the other to the East. Yugoslavia disintegrated, and no one could tell where it would turn ideologically. The fall of Marxist East Germany and its reunification with the affluent market economy of West Germany was seen at first as a decisive victory for capitalism in the middle of Europe, but inequality of job opportunities and bitter racial hostilities posed a new threat for market institutions. Advice poured in from Western news organizations urging the new media of the East to replace Marxist press doctrine with capitalist practices. Political and economic realities made that hard to accomplish.

The latitude for criticism of the social order has varied from place to place and from time to time. In the Third World, the variations in the movements are many, often following the leitmotiv of the communitarian movement; others approach that of the market movement. Some insist on tight central control of the press; others permit considerable scope for individual decisions about what is news. These variations are rich indeed, presenting a texture as far-ranging as a symphony by Mahler. And yet the fundamental unity remains. That unity can encourage us to hope for a reconciliation that could be of service to all of us, whichever movement of the symphony we may be hearing.

PURPOSES AND ARTICLES OF FAITH

Although the differences among the movements of the press symphony can be seen most easily by assigning them national characteristics, *we should keep in mind that these differences are not peculiarly national.* Differences have always existed inside countries as well as between them. Believers in the Marxist folklore can be found today in Kenya and the United States, in Venezuela and the Philippines. Believers in the market folklore can be found in North Korea and Cuba, in China and Vietnam. Believers in the communitarian folklore can be found in Germany, Iran, Russia, Japan, and Peru. Still, while presenting the three movements in national terms may be somewhat of a distortion, such imagery offers a convenient passage to comprehension of the reality of the universe of the press.

Let us examine first the perceptions of the purposes of journalism in the three movements. Why does journalism exist? What is its mission? It is apparent that under whatever political, economic, or social system, the mission of the press is seen as pursuit of truth under the banner of social responsibility. Moreover, this pursuit is to be undertaken by means of informing or educating the people who consume the news media. On these fundamentals, agreement is universal, yet these terms are defined in different ways in different places and among different people in the same places. Crucial differences exist among the three models. In the communitarian and the advancing world, one of the purposes assigned to the press is political; in the market countries, the reverse is true. There, the press is to be above politics, to present information impartially, without taking sides. On this point, however, the defenders of the market melody are deceiving themselves. *There is no way the press can be above politics.*

As Aristotle observed long ago, human beings are by nature political animals. They exist in society. To live outside the social order is to be less than a human being. By virtue of their humanity alone, journalists are political creatures. In carrying out their trade, journalists attain political importance far above that of most men and women. Everything journalists write is related to the social and political order they inhabit. To take sides for a certain political point of view is to be clearly political. *To take no side is also to be political, for if we do not oppose the status quo, we are giving it our tacit support.* There can be no impartiality about what exists. Either you are for it and are a political supporter, or you are against it and are a political antagonist. To take no position is also to support that which exists. The folklore of the press in capitalist countries, especially in the United States, overlooks this fundamental truth. Only one who imagines journalists can be free of this essential element of their humanness can condemn the activities of Unesco on the ground they have been politicized.

When they pause to consider the nature of humankind, journalists may recognize the political quality of the work they perform. But too few of them take time off from their busy schedules of reporting and editing the news to undertake this kind of reflection. On a number of occasions I have attended workshops and colloquia bringing together reporters and editors, some of them leaders in the field, and concerned academics for reflection on some of the burning philosophical and ethical challenges facing journalists. Again and again the reporters and editors stated, often in some surprise, that the occasion had marked one of the very few times they had been able to pause and think about these problems. On the job, they were too busy *doing*. That left little time for *thinking*.

It is not only busyness but also the dogmas inherent in folklore that inevitably limit our capacity for independent analysis. So it is with the dogmas in the folklore of the press in the market nations, especially the United States. Thus, many otherwise reasonable individuals inside and outside the world of journalism are able to state with utter conviction that reporters and editors are above politics and are impartial observers and chroniclers.[9] Those who observe the U.S. press scene from vantage points in the communitarian and advancing worlds are able to see more clearly and can recognize that the debate over politicization of the press is, in fact, a nondebate. The press is, simply, a political institution.

Part of the problem involves definitions. When it is said in the United States that the press is above politics, what is often meant is that the press is above *partisan* politics. The press in this imagery does assume a kind of political character, serving an AWA role as adversary, watchdog, and agenda setter. But this political character is considered to be nonpartisan, neither Democratic nor Republican, neither liberal nor conservative, neither pro-civil rights nor anti-civil rights, and neither pro- nor anti-abortion rights. In short, the kind of political role seen for the press in the U.S. construction is that of objective fact finder and dispassionate channel of information.

It is true the typical American journalist perceives this to be his highest calling: to get the facts and lay out those facts for the reader, who may or may not act on those facts, as he or she sees fit.[10] It is not recognized that in this quest the journalist is an agent for the way things are. *Objectivity is a mechanism for ensuring the status quo*, an instrument to guarantee the preservation of institutions and the social order. It permits criticism of individuals but not of the fundamental political, economic, or social system. The state of impartiality is, in fact, defensive of the system. That in this model the press retains the potential to challenge the social order is the element that poses a threat to those who exercise power. Inasmuch as the press fails to live up to its potential, it is carrying out the political role desired of it by those in power. *To the extent the press endorses the idea that it is above politics, it is serving the needs of power.*

In the Marxist perception of the purposes of the press, the news media lend their unswerving support to the doctrines of Marxism-Leninism. To fail in this support is to fail to serve the people; if the failure is severe enough, it can be called treason, a betrayal of the people. Lenin's charge to the press went unchallenged in the Soviet Union, and even though Lenin's dramatic call to arms vanished in the Soviet collapse, the ideas behind his words remain intact wherever the melodies of the communitarian movement are heard. In the former Soviet bloc—as well as in a number of advancing countries such as Peru and Iran—the many who adhere to communitarian ideas reject the market. As political scientist Benjamin Barber has noted, markets are enemies of parochialism, isolation, and fractiousness.[11] In particular, the communitarian culture rejects "homogenization" or "Americanization" of the mass media, whether we speak of films or television or the printed word. It is well, in this context, to keep in mind that the movements of the symphony are never national in character. We are not speaking of countries but of cultures and belief systems. Barber scoffs at both the market and the communitarian cultures; he is convinced neither "is remotely democratic in impulse," but he is speaking of absolutes. He fears the society of "McWorld," an integrated, uniform society that mesmerizes the social order "into one commercially homogenous global network" dominated by transnational corporations; however, he fears it less than "Jihad," which he characterizes as "a threatening Lebanonization of national states in which culture is pitted against culture, people against people, tribe against tribe."[12]

Although the age of globalization of which Bagdikian and many others have cautioned is at hand, at the same time the contemporary world is fragmenting into ever smaller, warring bits. The future role of the news media is uncertain. In any case, the centerpiece of Lenin's belief system remains that it is the purpose of the press to operate as a collective organizer, to mold attitudes and alter behavior especially in rejecting what communitarian theorists view as the iniquities of individualistic capitalism. Russia and the countries in what used to be the Soviet bloc have publicly endorsed the idea of a market economy, but their perception of a market economy remains communitarian, as reflected in the work of Solidarity in Poland, rather than ruggedly individualistic. The fierce dogma of Leninism has retreated; it is no longer impossible to imagine a harmonious resolution of the dissonance between the first two movements, as both Havel and Gorbachev have demanded. Yet the gulf is still wide, and the clash between the belief that the press is the servant of the community and that the press is the servant of the individual has by no means been resolved.

Is it the role of the media to control communitarian behavior or individual behavior? Governments may deny it, but it is inevitably their expectation that the news media will play their role as agents of social control and support the government in carrying out its domestic and especially its foreign policies. Those in the news media who would like to see a more independent role must recognize that the achievement of this goal, unlikely as it is, can be gained only when media representatives are fully aware of the actual nature of the problem. Nations and cultures in the Third World are drawn to the market model in the hope that competition, productivity, and foreign assistance can help them move toward financial security. Most countries of South America have been notably attracted in this direction; so have Kenya, Nigeria, Singapore, the Philippines, Costa Rica, and Mexico. However, a powerful magnet has also been pulling the developing countries toward a collective, communitarian, culturally pure model. The civil war in Peru is clear demonstration of this attraction; so are the culturally divided movements in India, Pakistan, Iran, and Egypt, even in certain industrialized lands like Ireland and the former republics of the Soviet Union. Shifts and changes can be expected as the dynamics of economic imperatives ebb and flow.

In all three movements of the symphony, the press is assigned responsibility for serving the people. This service is described in different terms. Believers in the market system of economics add that the news media must support that system; the communitarian media, as the Marxist-Leninist media, are meant to support collectivist doctrine. In the market image, the press is seen as operating outside the control of government, as a watchdog or even as a kind of adversary of the government. In the communitarian image, the press is the creature of the government (or the party) endorsing its actions and seeking to persuade its readers and viewers to the same kind of endorsement. Among the advancing nations, however, the image is different: It is of news media that serve as partners of government, of (as in the words of Bode Oyewolo of Nigeria) "twin agents of socioeconomic progress." Neither market nor communitarian theorists view the purpose of the press in these terms. In the market model, the press reports *about* change; it is not an agent *of* change. In the communitarian model, the press supports change when that is the desire of the people as reflected in the Communist party and in the government; it is not itself an agent of change. Of course, it needs to be kept in mind that these are *perceptions* of the purpose of the press. As with all institutions, the practice is quite different from the theory.

The three movements of the symphony of the press are systemic—they include elements of the political structure and environments, economic forces, and

TABLE 22.1 Articles of Faith

Market Nations	Communitarian Nations	Advancing Nations
The press is free of outside interference.	The press transforms and educates people to class and cultural consciousness.	The press is a unifying and not a divisive force.
The press serves the public's right to know.	The press provides for the objective needs of the people.	The press is a device for beneficial social change.
The press reports fairly and objectively.	The press reports objectively about the realities of experience.	The press is meant to be used for two-way exchanges between journalists and readers.

the paymasters of the press but also the other ingredients of life, both public and private. This combination includes the aesthetic components of the human experience—literature, architecture, painting, sculpture, and theater; the scientific components; and all the social institutions—the churches, the schools, the universities. The ideology of a sociopolitical system is made up of all these ingredients, inseparable one from another except as units of operational description. Inasmuch as the press is part of this unity, we cannot withdraw it from the system for independent examination unless it is with acceptance of the fact that our aim is to understand the role of the press inside the unity. We are halting the motion of the system, suspending it in space so we can understand its components. Thus, the three-movement taxonomy outlined here is fictional, a suspension in space of that which is always in motion. It is a static representation of the dynamic and hence itself illusory. Still, insofar as it contributes to understanding of the system as a whole, it serves a distinctly useful end.

Articles of faith (see Table 22.1) are irrational, not arrived at by reason, often held with the passion shown by true believers. An article of faith is not subject to critical analysis. We believe or do not believe; we are of the faith or are outsiders, infidels. Much of the acrimony that has marked international discussions of the press, whether at Unesco or elsewhere, has grown out of conflicting articles of faith, out of charges and accusations by true believers and apostates who adhere passionately to their articles of faith and those who counter that such beliefs are spurious. For example, journalists and press theorists from industrialized capitalist countries argue with inflexible fervor that their press is free of outside interference, that no government body or advertising agency tells the press what to write or how to construct its news reports. To this, journalists and press theorists of communitarian and advancing societies reply, "Nonsense, it just isn't so." In such a collision of words, there is no compromise.

At the same time, journalists and press theorists in Marxist and communitarian societies argue their newspapers are educational instruments that help rid their readers of false consciousness of what is going on in the world. These newspapers serve the "true interests of their readers" by pointing to the deceits and hypocrisies of capitalist or advancing-world officials who mislead the people and subvert the true interests of the working class. To this, the journalists and press theorists of the market and advancing lands reply, "Nonsense, it just isn't so. The communitarian press is presenting mere propaganda and not serving the true interests of its readers." Compromise seems unlikely.

When Third World journalists and press theorists argue their news media serve their readers' interests by avoiding the kind of divisive reporting characteristic of the news media in market and communitarian societies, the response in both individualistic and collectivist lands is once again, "Nonsense. It just isn't so. Your reports are very much divisive. You attack your neighbor quite as fiercely as we attack each other." The difficulty of accommodating opposing articles of faith may never be minimized.

Every article of faith in the symphony of the press is subject to violent attack. Outside the market countries, for example, we are not likely to find many who agree that the news media of the capitalist countries seek to learn the truth and present that truth to their readers. It is far more likely the capitalist media will be criticized for concealing the truth from their readers as they work mainly to turn profits for their owners. The communitarian article of faith that the press facilitates effective change is rejected outside the communitarian sphere. There, it is argued that the only kind of change the communitarian press is interested in is change that will work to help the hierarchy maintain its sway over the people and not to help the people for whose benefit the press is supposed to be working. Advancing-world ideologues who see the press as an instrument of social justice are ridiculed in other parts of the world by those who point to diatribes of hate that have appeared in the Third World press. Any claim of objectivity in one movement of the symphony is mocked in the others.

Among the articles of faith, none is more intriguing than the Third World belief that the press is meant to be used for two-way exchanges, not as devices for the one-way flow of information from the top down, from journalists to readers. Proper journalism, according to this article of faith, is participatory. The readers and viewers are meant to be more than vacuum cleaners sweeping up the information pushed at them by journalists. Instead, they are meant to participate in deciding what news is sent out into the general flow of information. The flow of news, in this image, is horizontal, not vertical. This article of faith is absent from the market and communitarian movements of the symphony. The subject of participatory journalism is a difficult one for both market and communitarian theorists, for they do not wish to be seen as journalistic elitists. They do not perceive themselves as journalistic elitists. It is an article of faith in the market movement that the news media serve the public's right to know; it is their raison d'être. If they did not serve the public, they would not be able in the United States to assert their special status under the First Amendment. Their constitutional freedom is predicated on the concept of service to the public. Yet they maintain the right to be sole judges of what constitutes news. By so defining the news, they isolate themselves from their readers, who are left, in a sense, to take the news or leave it.

In the market model, the news media remain subject to the same laws of the market as all other institutions. The marketplace offers consumers a choice: to buy or not to buy. They may or may not purchase the newspaper or watch the TV news show or switch channels. In this sense, they vote with their dollars. If they approve of what appears in the news media, they will pay the bill; if theu don't, they will refuse to pay. In market imagery, readers and viewers are the actual paymasters, not the owners of the newspaper or broadcasting outlet. Such, however, is not the reality of the press world in market economies. The essence of Adam Smith's invisible hand is that it guarantees the powerful will limit their selfish desires in order to market their products successfully. They must serve the interests of the people or suffer the financial consequences. Smith envisioned a social order devoted to virtue, not vice; he did not foresee the rise of monopolies and oligopolies or transnational corporations. He did not imagine the growth of great press empires and information conglomerates. Against such entrenched financial power, the individual reader or viewer voting with his or her few dollars has little or no clout. The public's right to know is a euphemism for the right of the press to tell the public what it wants the public to know. (See Table 22.2.)

Journalists, including owners of the news media and their reporters and editors, are for the most part true believers in the doctrine of the public's right to know. To the extent that this fraternity and sorority can be characterized as monolithic, it can be said the serious American press is convinced it is operating in the interests of the public, who have a right to know what is going on in order to carry out their duties as citizens and fulfill the democratic assumption. This conviction is self-delusional, but it is a cardinal article of faith of the market movement.

The communitarian articles of faith hold that the news media in communitarian society serve the needs and the interests of the masses. In the United States, emphasis is placed in part on letters to the editor as a mechanism for participation of the masses. The marketplace provides the interaction. If readers react negatively to the content of a newspaper, they will cease to buy it, and the newspaper must then modify its behavior in order to survive. In both East and West, then, the image of the press is of an instrument that responds to the wants and needs of the reader.

TABLE 22.2 Purposes of Journalism

Market Nations	Communitarian Nations	Advancing Nations
To seek truth.	To search for truth.	To serve truth.
To be socially responsible.	To be socially responsible.	To be socially responsible.
To inform (or educate) neither politically nor culturally.	To educate the people and enlist allies politically and culturally.	To educate politically and culturally.
To serve the people impartially; to support capitalist doctrine.	To serve the people by demanding support for correct doctrine.	To serve the people by seeking, in partnership with government, change for beneficial purposes.
To serve as a watchdog of government.	To mold views and behavior.	To serve as an instrument of peace.

It is in this sense that readers participate in the formulation of news. Despite this imagery, it is clear that in most market and communitarian societies, the news travels in a vertical direction—from the journalist who decides what is "news" to the reader who is a simple receiver of news.

Among advancing nations, efforts have been undertaken to bring about a more horizontal pattern. For two decades, the Unesco researchers Roland Schreyer of Switzerland and Babacar Fall of Senegal have been generating in the rural reaches of Africa a "rural press" to serve readers' real needs, by operating not in the traditional way as an agent of power, but as what Schreyer called "an instrument of dialogue." Schreyer, who died in 1989, worked on the scene in Africa to assist unlettered Africans to expand their learning of what they needed to know to create a better life for themselves. "The readers are not interested in political debates," Schreyer said at one time, "but in subjects such as culture and marketing of their products, education, improvement of sanitary conditions, etc."[13]

To Schreyer, the newspaper was the most useful device available to humankind for achieving genuine dialogue. "With the newspaper is born dialogue, the possibility of reply," he said. Schreyer began his work in 1972 in the remote, landlocked African country of Mali, whose skimpy population of seven million was extended across 465,000 square miles and whose chief city, Bamako, was peopled by only 450,000 persons. Working with officials of the Mali Ministry of Information, Schreyer established a monthly newspaper, *Kibaru*, printed in the Bambara language. Its aims at the outset were to supply general information to the public and to further rural development. Over the years, *Kibaru* broadened its scope to provide news of current events and also to seek to raise living standards and increase civic consciousness. None among the staff—which included an editor-in-chief, two subeditors, and a newswriter—was a formally trained journalist, but each went through a brief period of training by instructors who were themselves only modestly trained. *Kibaru* began as a four-page mimeographed publication and expanded over the years into a printed, offset publication of eight to ten pages. Circulation rose from 5,000 to 12,500, and the paper attracted an ever-widening string of letters and other communications from readers.

From the outset, the effort in Mali was to involve readers, to convince them that *Kibaru* was their paper and not a government propaganda device. To reinforce this conviction, Schreyer and his colleagues introduced the concepts of a council of editors and a network of what Schreyer identified as "rural communicators." The council consisted of experts in different subject areas who met regularly to discuss what *Kibaru* readers needed and ought to know. This information was then passed along to the editors, who in turn tracked down the information suggested and produced news items. In this way, the definition of news was supplied by both the journalists and the readers. In fact, the network of rural communicators, none of whom was a staffer but all of whom qualified as stringers, wrote most of the items in the paper.

Schreyer insisted over the opposition of a number of officials that the newspapers be sold for a price and not distributed free. "It is only then," Schreyer said, "that the reader can actually feel that the newspaper is his. We tell them: 'This is your newspaper. You can write us and provide a dialogue, but for us to continue the paper, you must pay. You must be the owner.'" In the context of our theory, such a practice converts the reader from being a mere consumer to being a paymaster.

Rural press systems have been established in sixteen African countries. Schreyer and his colleagues moved also to develop rural press outlets in Asia and Latin America. Circulation of these papers, most monthlies but some weeklies, varied from a bare 500 to the thriving agricultural newspaper *Terre et Progrès* of the Ivory Coast with a circulation of 60,000. Although Schreyer saw a good beginning in Mali and several other countries, he acknowledged that successes were outnumbered by failures. Schreyer, Fall, and their colleagues urged greater investment in a rural press by national and international bodies, journalism research institutes, and reporters and editors themselves. Pay scales for the reporters and editors remained meager, and available research at journalism schools was channeled primarily into urban news centers. Moreover, some governments sought to convert their rural press into instruments of propaganda to boost the images of national leaders. Still, Schreyer was convinced the rural press offered an opportunity to develop the kind of dialogue between journalists and readers that could elevate human understanding. He pointed to the heavy volume of letters from readers of the rural press who were finding through them a sense of participation in their own future.

Not all advancing-world ideologues are as enthusiastic about the rural press. They call attention to the fact that the kind of participatory journalism possible in remote rural areas is not feasible in industrialized society or even in the large cities of Africa. However, development theorists have come up with a modification of the rural press concept that shows distinct promise. It is a concept that has sometimes been identified as "community journalism."[14] In this concept, which concurs with the communitarian belief system, the citizen has direct access to the pages of the news media and participates in editorial decision making. Like the rural-press concept, it seeks to carve out a new role for the press, where it serves not as the agent of paymasters or of political power but as the agent of the consumer, the interested and articulate citizen.

Among the great deficiencies in the African press scene is the lack of a thriving system of news agencies on which print and broadcast media can rely for information about Africa's rural reaches and small communities. Both PANA and IPS have been in operation for a number of years, but their mission is to distribute news and not to build up news-gathering organizations. In 1984, Fall, then a journalism professor at the University of Dakar,[15] undertook an ambitious program with the acronym WANAD (West African News Agencies Development) designed to bypass the training programs offered in the industrialized world and provide for training of Africans on the scene at home. Fall was himself an experienced journalist; he had studied in Montreal and Paris and had been a reporter in Rome, Paris, and Dakar.

The job he set up was formidable. In particular, he had to face the hostility of governments that didn't really want trained journalists snooping around in their affairs. Still, he had the backing of Unesco and of some governments. By 1991, WANAD had opened 336 offices in 16 West African countries. The staffers at those offices received their training at Cotonou, the capital city of Benin, a fortress-like country slightly smaller than Pennsylvania on the Gulf of Guinea. Most of the sixteen countries had only one daily newspaper, but since the Cotonou school began sending out its graduates, a substantial number of dailies, weeklies and monthlies have sprung up across West Africa. Fall recruited his faculty from fourteen countries—including India, Britain, Hungary, and the United States—but most were themselves Africans, graduates of universities with degrees in history, law, and literature.

"They [students and faculty] came to us," Fall said, "because they realized that it was important for Africans to share their information with other Africans." It was a rewarding experience for some of the journalists trained by WANAD, but for more than a few it was disappointing. "Our goal is to prepare professionals who will promote freedom of the press throughout West Africa," Fall said, "but it is a fight." He noted that some ministers of information fired reporters who wrote stories about strikes and violence. "They have to be ready to go to jail, if necessary, to uphold freedom," Fall said. His trainers devoted time to encouraging staffers to refuse to censor themselves in order to avoid trouble with their governments. "We try to be professionals and not censors," Fall said. "Let the government do the censoring."[16] There is no way for the press to be above politics in any of the three movements of the symphony of the press.

In any case, progress is being made. Information is circulating into the countryside in villages and communities that have in the past received no reliable information from beyond their areas. Much of the training has concentrated on environmental issues, a major problem throughout the areas. "There has been too much deforestation on the edges of the desert," Fall said. Trainees were required daily to write feature stories on the environment, many of those researched on the scene, so the trainees could see for themselves the challenges posed to communities in their region.

Distribution was, of course, a problem, as was the reality that so many different languages were spoken, often within the same national borders. Because both radio transmission and telephone service were unreliable, WANAD sent out motorcycle couriers to deliver copy to newspapers and radio stations. Reporters at the 336 offices used whatever transmission facilities were working to get back to their national headquarters, where often the material was translated into several different languages and shipped out by courier. In Mali, for example, a reporter might send in his or her story in French and editors at headquarters would translate it into Pular, Soussou, and Mandinka. Across the border in Guinea, the material might be translated from Mandinka to some other tongue. Whatever the difficulties, however, Fall was convinced the program was working. Funding came from abroad, especially from Germany. "But," Fall said with a grin, "they are not requiring us to buy German equipment."

CAN THE PUBLIC BE PARTICIPANTS IN JOURNALISM?

The Hutchins Commission in 1947 and the MacBride Commission in 1980 each called for greater participation of the public in defining news. Hutchins said the news had to reflect the goals and values of the people. MacBride said it needed to express the people's search for an end to war, racism, and imbalance. The goal in each case would be less use of the news media as agents of social control by wielders of power and greater dedication to the needs and wants of the powerless. As difficult an achievement such a role may be, as foolishly ideal as it may sound, might it not be worth exploring further? In this dream, the news media would serve as instruments *of* the society rather than as instruments for disseminating information *to* or *for* the society. The press, then, could help give citizens a sense of participation in working out their own fates. One of the characteristics of modern society has been the citizens' sense of isolation from the surrounding world and the sense of malaise and powerlessness this has produced. People do not feel they are the captains of their fate. In the United States, for example, participation in elections has been declining for a generation, although there was a slight spurt noticeable in and after the 1992 presidential elections. Still, many people remain convinced their votes do not count, and that, by indirection, *they* don't count for much, either. Under the appropriate circumstances, the news media could provide them with a sense of participation and of importance. The popularity of radio and TV talk shows has illustrated the demand for participation. After all, as the news media are structured, few individuals have personal access to the news pages of their papers or the news broadcasts of their radio and television stations. A participatory journalism structure would offer them that opportunity. A powerless citizenry might sit dispiritedly by as its world drifted from one deadly crisis to another. A positive citizenry who felt it counted would be tempted to intervene. A participatory press could give it that opportunity.

To the argument that those in power would not permit this kind of access and participation, it can be answered that no serious effort has yet been made; the answer cannot be known until the question is asked. It is certainly not likely the news media and their paymasters, locked in their symbiotic embrace, will easily yield their monopolistic control over the definition of news; for them, the stakes in terms of power and prestige are too great. To them, press freedom means their right to judge what is and is not news. To surrender this right to the participating citizen is to change the nature of the institution and to invite, at the very least, anarchy.

Yet change does not have to be total to be productive. A greater degree of public participation in the definition of news is entirely possible, and even modest shifts in power relationships carry the seeds of progress. Several such programs have been attempted, in industrialized market countries as well as in the newer nations. One of the more interesting experiments was undertaken in Finland. TV producers there made an attempt to select the subject matter of some of their news and current-events programs based on the relevance to the audience rather than on the usual basis of drama and conflict. Producers of one such program, *"Tietolaari"* ("Barrel of Knowledge"), invited its audience to write in suggestions about how to resolve local problems. A film unit was then dispatched to the area to work with the people to report their situation. The resulting documentary was aired, followed by a live question-and-answer period between the inhabitants and decision makers with the power to remedy some of the problems. This series has not found a permanent place in Finnish programming, but it demonstrates that citizen participation in defining the news is more than an idle dream. The producer of *"Tietolaari"* gained a more powerful platform from which to launch experiments. He became director-general of Finnish Radio and TV and an active participant in "Euronews," a European challenger to CNN as a global news operation.[17] The Finnish experiment was not unique. A number of broadcasters and newspapers have produced documentaries drawn from human needs, though they have rarely permitted their audiences to assume any means of control over the product. The approach comes close to Schreyer's goal of dialogue through the mass media.

In this form of "community journalism," researcher Frances Berrigan says, ordinary people have access to the media "for information, education, entertainment, when they want access."[18] This is the goal expressed by all press ideologies: The mass media are meant to serve as instruments of education. The difference lies in who decides what is to be taught. Julius Nyerere, the former president of Tanzania, provided a thoughtful definition of education. Its purpose, he said,

> is the liberation of Man from the restraints and limitations of ignorance and dependency. Education has to increase men's physical and mental freedom—to increase their control over themselves, their own lives, and the environment in which they live. The ideas imparted by education or released in the mind through education should therefore be liberating ideas; the skills acquired by education should be liberating skills. Nothing else can properly be called education.[19]

Few will quarrel with the lofty goals set forth by Nyerere. His goal for education might be enunciated also for the press: Its purpose, too, might be to help liberate humankind from ignorance and dependency, to help men and women increase their control over their lives and their environment.

It is ironic that neither the education system nor the press system of Tanzania practices what Nyerere preaches. The ideal remains distant from the reality; the considerations of practical politics and practical economics inevitably take precedence in the real world over the needs of the reader or viewer. It is thus utopian and perhaps counterproductive, because it runs contrary to human nature, to expect the mass media to become communal property working for the needs of everyone.

What is possible, however, is a greater measure of citizen access to the mass media. Here, too, it is utopian and wildly impractical to imagine the mass media can ever provide access to all persons. One of the weaknesses in Schreyer's vision is that it assumes the individual *wants* access to the pages of the newspaper. Most

TABLE 22.3 Views on Press Freedom

Market Nations	Communitarian Nations	Advancing Nations
A free press means journalists are free of all outside control.	A free press means all opinions are published, not only those of the rich and powerful.	A free press means freedom of conscience for journalists.
A free press is one in which the press is not servile to power and not manipulated by power.	A free press is required to counter oppression of legitimate communities.	Press freedom is less important than the viability of the nation.
No national press policy is needed to ensure a free press.	A national press policy is required to guarantee that a free press takes the correct form.	A national press policy is needed to provide legal safe-guards for freedom.

men and women everywhere seem prepared to be mere consumers of news, even as they are quiescent absorbers of education in the schools. Few persons are interested in participating, but even those who care little about participating themselves argue for the principle. And, although broadcast talk shows have been motivated largely by the desire for profit and thus serve more as entertainment than news programs, they do present a new horizon for contemplation. How might these be developed toward the Finnish model?

The gatekeeper role of the mass media is what is at issue here. In all press belief systems, decisions about what constitutes news are made by journalists. We have seen, however, that journalists are subject to manipulation by the wielders of power about what constitutes news. In the symbiotic relationship between journalists and the sources of their news, the odd one out is the reading and viewing public. Steps in the direction of increasing the level of citizen participation in the definition of news would surely make of the press a stronger instrument of education than it has ever been before.

In every social order, free expression is glorified. (See Table 22.3.) No nation publicly opposes the ideal of free expression. Few segments of society—national, domestic, or cross-national—argue against laws or regulations to promote the idea that anyone has the right to say or write what he or she wants, provided such expression does not cause injury to anyone else. In all social orders, important restrictions are placed on the right of free expression. In the United States, for example, it is unlawful to shout "Fire!" falsely in a crowded theater. Politically correct movements inhibit some forms of expression. In China, it is illegal to voice public criticism of elected officials; in India, it is against the law to endorse racism. In no country does freedom of expression include the right to call for the overthrow of the government by force and violence. The key problem, as with most philosophical questions, is one of definition.

In capitalist countries, emphasis is placed on freedom of information. What ought to be guaranteed, it is held, is the right for us to send out whatever information we wish. The theory is that the information receiver will be able to make wise decisions based on that information. Such a belief is at the heart of the democratic assumption. On closer inspection, it can be seen that the theory is incomplete. To make decisions, the consumer needs more than just what is provided by the press. He or she also needs the intelligence and the background knowledge required to place this information in a context that will facilitate decision making. Without intelligence and education, the information will be of no utility to the consumer. In the United States and other market social orders, it is assumed that our freedom to express ourselves in print is part of a broad sociopolitical and economic system that makes provision for public education. Without schools, free expression is largely irrelevant.

On the whole, the systems under which the communitarian and advancing press operate also include devotion to public education and public health. In much of the Third World and a substantial number of communitarian societies, inadequate financial resources mean also inadequate schools and medical facilities. To the underprivileged people there, freedom of expression is a luxury far less significant than the availability of schools. Not surprisingly in those social orders, there is far less devotion to abstract principles of free expression than among those in the United States and its allies. And while in all parts of the world the free flow of information is recognized as a universal goal, outside the capitalist world, it is of itself not usually considered a matter of urgency.

Moreover, as we have seen, the citizenry of communitarian and advancing societies doubt that the press of the United States and its allies is actually free of outside controls. Inevitably, as the MacBride Commission argued, the content of the press in the capitalist world is influenced (if not directed) by the commercial forces spearheaded by advertising agencies and transnational corporations.

Lenin's assertion that in the capitalist world a free press meant only freedom for the rich continues to be accepted as fundamental truth in most communitarian and advancing cultures, as well as among many dissident individuals and groups in the capitalist world. In the nineteenth century, Marx issued impassioned defenses of a press system of total freedom. Before the Bolsheviks had solidified their power in the Soviet Union, Lenin also strongly supported the idea of total press freedom. In fact, both Marx and Lenin argued that if oppression was to be overcome, it was necessary for a free press to lead the battle as a crucial element in the advance guard of the working class. In the capitalist and advancing societies, those statements by Marx and Lenin have been largely ignored. Critics have pointed instead to the practices of the Soviet press; they have argued, correctly, that the media in Marxist countries were not free.

In the Third World, there is by no means universal agreement on the meaning of freedom of the press or even on exactly what is desirable press behavior. Since many of these societies are not yet completely formed or institutionalized, it is not surprising to find no precise agreement. In fact, it is healthy that agreement is not universal—openness of mind is often barred by the institutions and folklore that have become formalized and encrusted in tradition. For much of the advancing world, a free press is not much concerned with freedom of mere information. It is more important, as the Guatemalan journalist Clemente Marroquín Rojas observed in discussing attitudes in Latin America, that the individual be assured freedom of conscience than that he or she be flooded with information.

Why has so much of the debate about the role of the press revolved around that word *information*? Discussions of the role of the press would surely be of greater profit to all if addressed more to the question of what kind of information is being demanded. Outpourings of words about football games, bank robberies, film stars, fires, fashions, exotic sexual practices, and auto design are of little significance to discussions of anything so lofty as freedom and morality; neither are the pages of advertising in newspapers and magazines or commercial announcements on radio and television.

To the struggling, insecure nations of the Third World, abstract principles of press freedom are less important than the viability of their nations. This stance is often condemned among journalists and press theorists in the capitalist world. According to the U.S. folklore of the press, a free press brings to light the "truth" wherever it finds it, regardless of the consequences of such exposure. Thus, the withholding of news in the advancing world in the name of saving the state from collapse is usually perceived as a transparent defense for keeping the truth from being known. What those critical journalists overlook, however, is their own willingness to withhold information they (and their sources) perceive to be threats to the security of their own state. Lost in the folklore of the watchdog, they fail to recognize the symbiotic nature of the relationship of the press to government in their own society, even though they have no difficulty observing the same phenomenon in another social order.

It is largely to assure that the press plays an institutional role subservient to the legitimate interests of the state that every Third World country endorses the idea of national and international press policies. The Inca Plan in Peru was one such national press policy. National programs different in content but similar in structure have been developed all over the advancing world as, unsurprisingly, they appeared among Marxist nations. Most capitalist countries have looked with suspicion on the construction of formal press policies, and many have openly opposed any formal policies. Still, all countries have in fact adopted press policies, though market nations have called them by other names. Press councils; associations of publishers, editors, journalists, broadcasters, and photographers; and journalism educators all concern themselves with proper behavior for the press—and hence with policy. But to these individuals and groups, they are discussing practices and not policy. To them, policy is something directed by government and hence political. Operating in a belief system that is suspicious of politics and finds direct political intervention in press behavior repugnant, these individuals and groups respond with horror and loathing to proposals that political bodies assume leading roles in dealing with the press. We have seen many illustrations of loathing in these pages.

On the other hand, press theorists of both the communitarian and the advancing social orders see political intervention as natural and potentially beneficial. Communitarian and advancing-world press theorists part company, however, on what kind of government intervention is desirable. The result is a kind of journalistic anarchy. With little agreement on what is, there can be none on what ought to be.

Each side is ever ready to hold forth on abstract principles of journalism, relying on the folklore of its particular social order. Consequently, few journalists or press theorists anywhere have come forward to grapple with concrete problems in the field of journalism. In writing of ethics in general, Sissela Bok suggested that hard ethical choices are avoided in most fields: "Why tackle such choice when there are so many abstract questions of meaning and definition, of classification and structure, which remain to challenge the imagination?"[20] The classification system presented here may serve to remove some of those abstract questions from the field of journalism and clear the way for concrete applications.

NOTES

1. David Hackett Fischer, *Historians' Fallacies: Toward a Logic of Historical Thought* (New York: Harper Torchbooks, 1970), 11. The examples cited are taken from Fischer.
2. Fischer, 12.
3. In 1993, Sarrazin completed work on a film called *La Floride*, which portrays the experiences of a Canadian family that moves to Florida.
4. Pierre Sarrazin, telephone interview with the author, Baltimore, November 30, 1992.
5. Vaclav Havel, "New Year's Day Address," January 2, 1990, cited in Mary Ann Glendon, *Rights Talk: The Impoverishment of Political Discourse* (New York: Free Press, 1991), 180.
6. Glendon, *Rights Talk,* 180-81.
7. Vaclav Havel, "The End of the Modern Era," *New York Times*, March 1, 1992.
8. Mikhail S. Gorbachev, "No Time for Stereotypes," *New York Times*, February 24, 1992.
9. For an interesting analysis of just how political a traditional, "objective" news story can be, see Paul H. Weaver, "The Politics of a News Story," in Harry M. Clor, ed., *The Mass Media and Modern Democracy* (London: Rand McNally, 1974), 85-111.
10. David H. Weaver and G. Cleveland Wilhoit, "The American Journalist in the 1990s," preliminary report, *The Freedom Forum* (Arlington, VA: The Freedom Forum, November 17, 1992), 11.
11. Benjamin R. Barber, "Jihad vs. McWorld," *Atlantic Monthly* (March 1992): 54.
12. Barber, 53.
13. Roland Schreyer, interview with the author, Paris, October 25, 1981. The ensuing citations from Schreyer are from the same interview.
14. See, for instance, Paul Ansah, Cherif Fall, Bernard Chandji Kouleu, and Peter Mwaura, "Rural Journalism in Africa," no. 88 (Paris: Unesco, 1981), and Frances J. Berrigan, "Community Communications: The Role of Community Media in Development," no. 90 (Paris: Unesco, 1981).
15. The institution in Dakar is one of three journalism programs at African universities. It is the only French-language program; the other two, in the English language, are in Accra, Ghana, and Lagos, Nigeria.
16. Babacar Fall, interview with the author, Paris, January 8, 1991. The citations from Fall in the following two paragraphs are from the same interview.
17. Kaarle Nordenstreng, letter to the author, February 9, 1993. See also Berrigan, "Community Communications."

18. Berrigan, "Community Communications."

19. Julius Nyerere, quoted in *Unesco Reports*, no. 87, 1978.

20. Sissela Bok, *Lying: Moral Choice in Public and Private Life* (New York: Vintage, 1978), 11.

Epilogue: The Seven Laws of Journalism

In summary of the truths that have emerged from this study of the role of the press, and from the classification system embodied in the metaphor of the symphony of the press, we offer here seven laws of journalism on which reasonable people might agree. Perhaps by doing so, we may build a foundation for the development of concrete ways for the press to cease serving as a force to divide humankind and to begin serving as a force to help resolve the terrible challenges we face at the dawn of the twenty-first century.

1. In all press systems, the news media are agents of those who exercise political and economic power. Newspapers, magazines, and broadcasting outlets thus are not independent actors, although they have the potential to exercise independent power.
2. The content of the news media always reflects the interests of those who finance the press.
3. All press systems are based on belief in free expression, although free expression is defined in different ways.
4. All press systems endorse the doctrine of social responsibility, proclaim that they serve the needs and interests of the people, and state their willingness to provide access to the people.

5. In each of the three press models, the press of the other models is perceived to be deviant.
6. Schools of journalism transmit ideologies and value systems of the society in which they exist and inevitably assist those in power to maintain their control of the news media.
7. Press practices always differ from press theory.

The contemporary world has been called the Nuclear Age and it has been called the Age of the Information Explosion. The terms refer to the same thing—a world that has been transformed by science and technology. Everything seems possible in a world of instant digital communication. Hitherto unheard-of global giants have occupied strategic positions along an electronic superhighway where words, pictures, and information speed by as fast as light. All of us can now watch the same things and receive the same information; we are driven together into a genuine global village. Yet here we encounter a paradox of unsurpassed dimensions, for at the very same time we are being dismembered into tiny fragments. There are so many sources of information that it is feasible for all of us to look at and listen to different things. We can be a true global community, yet we can be isolated in our own private hermitages. We can all receive the same news; we can all receive different news.

Information is available for all of us, although poor and rich do not enjoy equal access to it. At best, however, information is not knowledge, and it is a fatal error to mistake one for the other. Knowledge may, as has often been said, be power, but true knowledge can arrive only in an orderly, rational, sequential way. B must follow A; it can't come before it. Indeed, too much information can be a detriment (an impediment) to knowledge.

It is troublesome also that the explosion of news and information has not yet lessened the hatred of ethnic groups for one another, nor of nationalities, nor races, nor sexes. Cynicism and alienation have not been expelled from the data superhighway.

This world transformed by science and technology, it is clear, is a world of promise and hope but also of great peril in which there exists a real threat of its extermination. The mushroom clouds carry the seeds of both knowledge and death. The men and women of the press—the merchants of news—are crucial figures in this transformed social order, for it is they who paint the pictures of the world on which decisive human actions are based. To fail to understand this basic but grim truth is to fail to understand the role of the press in the affairs of humankind. The last notes of the symphony of the press are yet to be played.

Three possibilities are available. The press can render it easier for humankind to destroy itself, to the accompaniment of drums and crashing cymbals, in a kind of Wagnerian explosion. Or it can assist in the creation of a global harmony, to a satisfying resolution that resembles those of Vivaldi. Or, finally, it can serve out its days as an uninvolved outsider, subject to the shifting winds of the moment, as a kind of brainless robot awaiting yet not participating in its fate. The immodest hope behind this book is that the press will turn away from its historic role as blind chronicler of conflict and search out a different role, that of conflict resolver. Harmony and global survival rest on the peaceful resolution of conflicts.

The classification system presented here provides little comfort. More conflict than resolution confronts us. The good guys are on "our" side, whoever "we" may be; the bad guys are on the "other" side, whoever "they" may be. The history of the press demonstrates that newspapers and the more modern variations of the press have tended to serve the selfish interests of the paymasters, while at the same time perpetuating the image of a press operating in the service of the consumers of the news. To expect that the news media will make a dramatic U-turn and scoff at the paymasters' wishes is to engage in the wildest kind of utopian fantasies.

Students of conflict tend to agree that most disputes among individuals as well as among nations involve questions of identity, security, and recognition.[1] The needs of each person and of each nation require a feeling of being safe from irrational aggression and a sense of personal or national dignity. If their needs are not met, according to sociologist John Burton, the deprived individual or nation will resort to behavior that is described by those in power as deviant. In this situation, "they" are the bad guys who engage in "deviant" behavior while "we" are the good guys who live by the codes or norms of the prevailing belief system. To understand how people behave and how people think outside the accepted and comfortable ideological system in which they live is imperative for those journalists who would truly inform, educate, or assist in the resolution of problems. Access to the news media must be given to the bad guys as well as the good guys if there is to be genuine understanding. The code of objectivity may not be discarded at the water's edge. Burton speaks of the valuable role in the resolution of conflict that may be played by "third parties," to whom he assigns the role of articulating precisely and dispassionately the issues involved in the conflict and, more important, of assuring that the opposing sides become involved not in confrontation, competition, bargaining, or power, but rather as solvers of problems. The third-party rule is also suggested by Amitai Etzioni in his concept of a communitarian agenda (see chapters 11 and 12).

What stronger role could the press play?

Albert Camus, the existentialist French novelist, essayist, and journalist and winner of the Nobel Prize for literature, spoke of the journalist in heroic terms. "The nobility of our calling," he declared, "will always be rooted in two commitments difficult to observe: refusal to lie about what we know, and resistance to oppression."[2] Strong words. Yet he might have added for the journalist a third commitment: to write and edit in such a way as to help resolve the problems of humankind and not to exacerbate them.

The challenge is even greater today than it was in 1957 when Camus won the award. The new high-tech world had not emerged with its bit-stream flows and its golden tablets. Nor had the astronomical gains in prestige and income yet been made. The challenge is greater, yes—and so are the temptations.

NOTES

1. See John Burton, *War, Deviance, and Terrorism: The Process of Solving Unsolved Social and Political Problems* (New York: St. Martin's, 1979).
2. Albert Camus, address in accepting the Nobel Prize for literature in 1957.

"OUR REPUBLIC AND ITS PRESS WILL RISE OR FALL TOGETHER"

1847 1947
JOSEPH PULITZER

3¢ UNITED STATES POSTAGE

Appendix

THE ABSURDITY OF "SOCIAL RESPONSIBILITY"

The term *social responsibility* is of obscure origin, but it seems to be associated with the philosophy of utilitarianism, which attained a wide following in England and the United States in the nineteenth century and derived many of its ideas from the writings of Jeremy Bentham and John Stuart Mill. The latter, hero of liberals and democratic thinkers for a century and a half, introduced a moral factor into Bentham's principle that virtue consists of whatever brings the greatest pleasure to the greatest number. Bentham, laying out a moral principle widely endorsed in most non-Marxist societies, held that good is determined by its consequences: When an action produces well-being among the public—for example, reduces the level of poverty—it is good. Mill's important addition to Bentham's equation was his insistence that not only the consequences must be good but also the motive of the actor must be good. If not, good may result from evil intentions. Although neither Bentham nor Mill was asserting an original idea (the Greeks had wrestled with similar conceptions two millennia earlier), what they said seemed amazingly applicable to the Anglo-Saxon world of the mid-nineteenth century. It was the incorporation of Mill's concept of moral utilitarianism with the image of the supreme virtue of the General Will enunciated by Jean-Jacques Rousseau that provided the philosophical foundation for the modern doctrine of social responsibility. To Rousseau—who, like Mill, opposed arbitrary power—the voice of the people was supreme, and that voice was heard in the mystical expression of the General Will.

The most significant political contribution of Bentham and the utilitarians was the enactment of Britain's Poor Law in 1834. Passage of that law followed years of campaigning by Bentham and the Whig politicians who were advocating social reform. It was the first assumption by the national government of responsibility for caring for the poor, a practice up to that time entrusted to the church and local relief agencies. Moreover, the Poor Law was a perfect illustration of the execution of the doctrine of social responsibility. In short order, the term was being used throughout the Anglo-Saxon world, in the United States by the abolitionists and the supporters of prison reform and compulsory education, as well as those who demanded laws against the sale of alcoholic beverages. In 1837, a British-born expatriate to the United States, John Bartholomew Gough, electrified temperance workers and foes of poverty and slavery with a lecture at London's Exeter Hall that he titled "Social Responsibilities." Gough's message, which was so well received he was invited to deliver the same tidings for a score of years thereafter, was that each of us is indeed his or her brother's or sister's keeper and is responsible for seeking out the poor and the downtrodden and offering them our help.

Gough's message was of one's *individual* responsibility to society, and this was the essence of Mill's message, though Mill also went beyond a call for assistance by individuals and assigned responsibility to institutions, not the least of which was the press. An unbending advocate of free expression and open discussion, Mill waxed dramatic when speaking of the potential for good in the press. To censure the press, he said, is to revive

> ignorance and imbecility, against which it is the only safeguard. Conceive the horrors of an oriental despotism—from this and worse we are protected only by the press. Carry next the imagination, not to any living example of prosperity and good government, but to the furthest limit of happiness which is compatible with human nature; and behold that which may in time be attained, if the restrictions under which the press still groans, merely for the security of the holders of mischievous power, be removed. Such are the blessings of a free press.[1]

By the time the term *social responsibility* was employed by the Hutchins Commission, it was becoming commonplace in the United States and Britain. The number of books dealing with the concept increases every year. The greatest number are appearing in connection with business practices, especially in marketing and the world of science. The U.S. National Education Association published a slim book in 1963 urging the public and the government to make adequate financial provisions so schools and colleges might continue to teach young people to concern themselves with the country's problems: "The continued health of the American society—perhaps its very survival—demands a high and rising awareness of social responsibility on the part of the people."[2] The literature of business and science as well as journalism demands that these institutions practice their social responsibilities. A journal called *Social Responsibility* appeared in 1975.

And yet the painful reality is that the term *social responsibility* is devoid of meaning. Put another way, it is a term whose content is so vague that almost any meaning can be placed on it. As such it, too, serves the ultimate end of social control in ways that would have horrified Mill and Rousseau. Perhaps this is the reason we cannot find the term *social responsibility* in the *Oxford English Dictionary* or in the *Dictionary of the History of Ideas*. Several pages in the OED are devoted to other compounds with *social*, as are many references in *Notes and Queries for Readers and Writers, Collectors and Librarians*. Indeed, an exhaustive compendium of the ideas of Mill published in *Notes and Queries* contains page after page of compounds with *social*, but not *social responsibility*. We find, on the other hand, valuable references to social morality and social obligation.

Nevertheless, even though the term is meaningless and operates as a mechanism of social control, it has considerable value for working journalists. First, it gives journalists the positive feeling that they are making a contribution to society and that they are working in the public interest, carrying out a public service in the image of the BBC. Second, it allows them to avoid uncertainty about their purpose; as Freud and others have pointed out, feelings of uncertainty and ambiguity are difficult and painful to sustain. Third, it enables journalists to ignore the economic realities of their trade. They can choose to report the conflictual because it is socially responsible to do so, not because in so doing they are pandering to the baser interests of their readers, in gossip as well as in sex and violence. Fourth, it heads off the threat of government intervention, a threat of primary concern to the Hutchins Commission.

What if journalists recognized the masquerade of social responsibility? Would this recognition shatter their self-image? Would it reduce them to cynicism or to blatantly seeking the greatest amount of money, prestige, and power by openly yielding to the basest tastes? Would they quit their jobs and seek other work? All of these things have indeed occurred. Many U.S. journalists abandon their jobs for other employment, in advertising and public relations, as civil servants, as attorneys, as politicians, as teachers, and as professors. A remarkable 1971 study demonstrated that the average age of the working American journalist is three years lower than that of others in professional-type careers, an indication that many newsmen and newswomen grow disillusioned with their work and seek their rewards elsewhere. In this way, some of the most thoughtful and potentially productive journalists make their way out of the trade. It is likely they have discovered the spuriousness of the doctrine of social responsibility. Unquestionably, awareness of how difficult it is to meet the needs of their audience will be accompanied by the pain that grieves all human beings who recognize their impotence in effecting social change. Yet there remains for the individual journalist the possibility of performing important services for the public—and, more significant, the possibility of uniting institutionally with his or her colleagues to help change the course of human history.

Our problem in dealing with the term *social responsibility* is similar to the problem we face with the term *freedom*. Neither can be defined in a universal way.

Each depends entirely on our ethical system, on our set of values. We cannot be responsible for our actions unless we are free. Since journalists are not free, they cannot be responsible, at least in any institutional sense. They may, on the other hand, be free individuals. Certainly they have free choice. They may choose to carry out the orders given by their publishers or they may not. They are free to continue to work or to quit. They are free to choose to go to prison, if that is the punishment. And since they possess these kinds of individual freedom, they act out of their own individual sense of duty.

The English philosopher T. H. Green has made a useful distinction between obligation and duty. Obligation, Green said, may be enforced by law; duty may not. Thus in a situation in which journalists are obliged to report only information that is acceptable to their publisher or government, they are fulfilling their responsibility (obligation) by following orders. On the other hand, if journalists refuse to report only this kind of information because they find it morally repugnant to do so, they are equally fulfilling their responsibility (duty). Responsibility can be defined either as obligation or as duty. It has never been possible to separate legal (obligatory) responsibility from moral duty, and discussions of the ethics of journalism are eternally muddied by the confusion generated by this semantic puzzle. When social responsibility is invoked, it is usually in terms of morals or, in Green's phrasing, duty. The question remains: To whom are we socially responsible, and for what? Assuming that at least in theory we are responsible for the presentation of reasonably accurate information on a variety of subjects, to whom is this responsibility owed? It could not be to ourselves, for then the word *social* would be irrelevant. If it is to a publisher or government, we would be talking principally of our obligation, or legal responsibilities, either through a private contract with an employer or through the implied citizenship contract by which we are affiliated with our government. It seems that the charge is for the responsibility to be owed to "society." And thus it is related to the duty described by Gough in his famous temperance lecture, to the duty to Rousseau's General Will, or to the greatest number, as invoked by Bentham and Mill.

Yet *society* turns out itself to be an absurd concept. It is at best an indefinable abstraction. Consider its relationship to the concept of *state*, a term introduced by political theorists in the nineteenth century and ever since a source of massive confusion, not only in terminology but also in relation to thought. Sometimes it has been used to refer to government, sometimes to nation, and sometimes to society. All three—*government*, *nation*, and *society*—are vague words. A renowned student of political philosophy has observed that although they are vague, these words are by no means interchangeable. In fact, society seems to incorporate both government and nation. To Green, when we speak of the function of society, we are using a meaningless combination of words.

Still, since journalists have something in mind when they speak of society, it is likely they are referring to the society they know—that is, the men and women of the upper-middle class, literate, articulate, interested in public affairs, those who are well educated and affluent. Michael Novak suggests that because of this affiliation, the working person hates the news media and is jealous of the social benefits that accrue to those who practice the trade.[3] History does indeed indicate that, for the most part, journalists have interpreted their societal responsibility as to their own kind. The coverage of racial minorities in the United States sustains this analysis. Thus the doctrine of social responsibility reaffirms the existing social order while at the same time it provides the cloak of moral rectitude for those who claim to follow the doctrine. As the philosopher John Hobhouse pointed out, any institution that says it serves society may lay claim to a moral dignity and authority it otherwise cannot justify. This is not to say the institution of the press lacks moral dignity; it is rather to point out that the doctrine of social responsibility offers its practitioners the opportunity to lay claim to moral dignity whether or not it affirms the status quo or operates in the interests of all people.

However, social responsibility can be adapted to refer to the duty to work for the benefit not of a social elite but of those who often suffer at the hands of that social elite. For the advancing world, the only kind of social responsibility that counts is directed to the benefit of the underclass, especially in the liberated colonies. In similar vein, Louis Finkelstein, chancellor of the Jewish Theological Seminary in New York, has proposed in his *Social Responsibility in an Age of Revolution* that the doctrine of social responsibility be directed toward "all those who are lacking essential needs and a sense of self-worth." He adds: "The disprivileged of this country and of the world need self-respect; they need to believe in themselves. If we cannot help all men everywhere to recapture their sense of human dignity and individual worth, our failure may have consequences impossible to predict."[4]

To set one's bearings on this course, Finkelstein says, is the responsibility of the privileged. Surely, the privileged include the men and women who engage in the practice of journalism. In the Third World, it is taken as a matter of fact that the responsibility of the journalist is precisely to work to help people develop a sense of human dignity and individual worth. To this end, Third World journalists have proposed a new world information order. That order is frankly political, in that it follows a policy for journalists enunciated by the Mahatma Gandhi in his role as editor of an English-language newspaper, *Young India*, when in 1919 he began his campaign for Indian independence. The policy of *Young India*, he wrote in its first issue, was not only to draw attention to "injustices to individuals," but also to devote its attention to constructive "'Satyagraha,' . . . civil resistance where resistance becomes a duty to remove a persistent and degrading injustice."[5] Not everyone will agree about what constitutes such an injustice, but journalists who overlook "a persistent and degrading injustice" in pursuit of an ephemeral role free of politics are hardly carrying out a role that can be praised as moral or responsible.

SVETLANA STARODOMSKAYA'S COMMENTS ON THE SOVIET CODE

Svetlana Starodomskaya was a distinguished TV journalist at the height of the stern rule of Leonid Brezhnev (see chapter 12). I interviewed her on a visit to Moscow in May 1980.

Were she and her fellow Russian journalists content, she was asked, to follow the Soviet code, to work in accordance with Marxist-Leninist guidelines? On the whole, the answer seemed to be yes. Starodomskaya suggested her own "four theories" of the responsibility of the Soviet journalist: "First, you please yourself: that you have done the best work you know how. Second, you please your friends, the people you know, those who are in your circle. Third, you please and inform your viewers. And, fourth, you please your government, your society, your political system."[6]

What happens when conflicts develop among those four groups? "You hope there are none," she said, "but you must try most of all to please yourself." The admonition sounded much like Polonius's advice to Laertes in *Hamlet*: "To thine own self be true." It is a dilemma faced by journalists everywhere, in all political systems, then and now. Indeed, many Russian journalists seemed at that time more concerned with technical journalistic problems than with ideological issues.

Restraints were, of course, fewer in pluralist capitalist nations, such as the United States, than they were in the Soviet Union. One American reporter who had worked for years in the Soviet Union recalled a trip he had taken with a Soviet reporter who condemned American practices and also the high cost of living and the lack of adequate housing in the Soviet Union. The American asked the Russian why he did not attack in print what he condemned orally. After many vodkas, the Russian journalist broke down in a fit of weeping, insisting all the time that he had not been trained to criticize social developments in the Soviet Union.

WILL IRWIN'S VIEW OF 1911 ADVERTISING

No journalistic campaign against the influence of advertising was waged more fiercely than that of the early twentieth-century muckrakers. The most dramatic assault came in Will Irwin's 1911 series in *Collier's* magazine. The "system" of advertising had been, Irwin wrote, "the main handicap on American journalism in its quest for truth." He gave this account:

Slowly at first, then with increasing momentum, advertisers learned their power. Indeed, in certain quarters, the advertising solicitors helped to teach them. For the less conscientious and solidly run newspapers began offering comforts and immunities as a bonus to attract customers. Advertisers got into the way of asking for special privileges; often, in communities where the newspapers were timid and mushy, for every privilege, even to dictating policies. The extent of their demands varied with the local custom of their communities. But finally, in cities like Philadelphia and Boston, an impossible state of affairs confronted even that publisher who cared more to be an editor than a money-maker. The system had grown so set that he must make concession or fail. For if he did not, his rival would get "the business." And without the "business," he could not pay the high editorial salaries, the press bureau fees, the telegraph tolls, the heavy wages to mechanics, which first-class journalism demands. So must he cheapen product, lose circulation, and fade away.[7]

CHARLES DICKENS'S COMMENTS ON THE AMERICAN PRESS

British novelist Charles Dickens was one of the most colorful critics of the American press. On a visit to the United States in 1842, he even seemed to anticipate the modern tabloid media:

> While that Press has its evil eye in every appointment in the state, from a president to a postman, while, with ribald slander for its only stock in trade, it is the standard literature of an enormous class, who must find their reading in newspaper, or they will not read at all; so long must its odium be upon the country's head, and so long must the evil it works, be plainly visible in the Republic.[8]

The reader who would pursue with interest Dickens's further reflections on the American press is directed to the novel *Martin Chuzzewit*, which Dickens published in 1844; in it he presents one of the more entertaining (if exaggerated) views of the American press—raucous, uninhibited, gossipy, slanderous, and uninformed on any but the most trivial of subjects. However hyperbolic his presentation, Dickens perceived correctly the profitable nature of the penny press, with its open appeal to the common man and his fascination with backstairs gossip.

NOTES

1. John Stuart Mill, "Law of Libel and Liberty of the Press," in G. L. Williams, ed., *John Stuart Mill on Politics and Society* (Hassock, England: Harvester Press, 1975), 169.
2. *Social Responsibility in a Free Society* (Washington: Educational Policies Commission, NEA, 1963).
3. Michael Novak, "Why the Working Man Hates the Media," in John C. Merrill and Ralph D. Barney, eds., *Ethics and the Press*: Readings in Mass Morality (New York, Hastings House, 1975), 108–17. Novak's essay appeared originally in (MORE), New York, October, 1974.
4. Louis Finkelstein, *Social Responsibility in an Age of Reason* (New York: Jewish Theological Seminary, 1971), 4.
5. Mohandas Gandhi, *The Collected Writings of Mahatma Gandhi* (New Delhi: Navajivan Trust, 1971), v. 8:386–87.
6. Svetlana Starodomskaya, interview with the author, Moscow, May 11, 1980. The subsequent citations from the Russian journalist are also from that interview.
7. Will Irwin, *The American Newspaper* (Ames: Iowa State University Press, 1969, a reprint of the fifteen essays printed in *Collier's* in 1911).
8. Charles Dickens, *American Notes for General Circulation* (Baltimore: Penguin Books, 1972), 287.

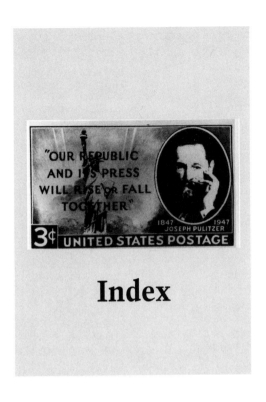

Index

ABC, 104, 124, 170, 383
Abel, Elie, 316-317
Abrams, Elliot, 326
Accountability, 141, 362
Adams, John, 9
Adams, John Quincy, 15
Adams, Samuel Hopkins, 31
Advancing nations. *See also* Development journalism
  and advertising, 316-317, 324
  defined, 227-228
  education of journalists, 304, 308, 337, 344-350, 431
  and international news systems, 386
  paymaster relationships, 381
  press model, 419, 420, 424, 426-427, 428, 429, 435-436, 437
  revolutionary period, 379
  schools of journalism, 234, 245
  and technology, 407
Advertising
  and advancing nations, 316-317, 324
  and capitalist model, 214-215
  and convergent selectivity, 50
  and development of American press, 17-18, 86-88, 449
  government control, 284
  and journalism schools, 338

  and journalists, 373
  Kenya television, 248
  Latin America, 283-284
  patent medicine, 26, 27, 31
  Russia, 212
Advertising agencies, retrenchment, 98
Advertising revenues, 336-337, 378, 380
  cable television's share, 110
  decline, 97
  and growth of American press, 28, 90-92
  television's share, 102-103, 104
  top U.S media companies, 397
African-Americans, employed by media, 181-184
African Concord, 250
Agence France Presse, 309
Agenda-setting function, 149-150
Aggarwala, Narinder, 145, 237
Agnew, Spiro, 69, 143, 147, 341
Ailes, Roger, 174
Akadymos, 222
Akhbar, 259
Alianza Popular Revolucionaria Americana, 276
Alienation (Marx), 203-204
All the President's Men, 363
American Newspaper Publishers Association, 95, 304
American Society of Newspaper Editors, 94-95, 181-182, 297, 331, 360

American Telephone and Telegraph. *See* AT&T
Amnesty International, 278-279, 281
Amor, Adlai, 253
Anderson, Jack, 108
Anekdota, 199
Annenberg, Walter, 148
Aquino, Corazón, 253, 254
Aristotle, 6, 363, 424
Arnett, Peter, 114-115
Ashe, Arthur, 412
The Asian Wall Street Journal, 252, 257
Asner, Edward, 75-76
Associated Press (AP), 64-66, 304, 307, 309, 360.
    See also News agencies
Association for Education in Journalism and Mass
    Communication, 111
AT&T, 256, 402, 406
Atwater, Lee, 164
Ayodele, Olumuyiwa, 250

Bad Tendency guideline, 11, 199-200
Bagdikian, Ben, 92, 94, 123, 128, 131, 384, 386,
    389, 409
Baker, Ray Stannard, 34, 37, 38-39, 420
Ball-Rokeach, Sandra, 355
Barber, Benjamin, 425
Barnet, Richard J., 229, 246, 248
Barrett, Marvin, 71
Bartlett, David, 125, 126, 360, 361, 409
Barton, Frank, 282-283
BBC (British Broadcasting Corporation), 117, 124,
    283, 344-345, 389
Beard, Robin L., 326
Beasley, Maureen, 185
Belaúnde Terry, Fernando, 269, 270, 273, 281,
    282, 284
Bell Atlantic Corporation, 402-403, 404, 406
Beltrán, Luis Ramiro, 318
Beltrán, Pedro, 269
Bennett, James Gordon, 15, 24
Bennett, W. Lance, 128
Bentham, Jeremy, 444, 445
Berents, Kenneth T., 95
Berg, Ronald, 281
Berlusconi, Silvio, 391
Bernays, Edward, 88
Bernstein, Carl, 158, 159, 362-364
Berrigan, Frances, 434
Bertelsmann, A. G., 390-391
Bild Zeitung, 142, 411
Bill of Rights, 7, 9, 220, 221
Bismarck, Otto von, 35-36, 47
Bleyer, Willard, 340
Block, Clifford H., 329
Blockbuster Entertainment, 406
Bode, Ken, 170
Bogart, Leo, 168
Bok, Sissela, 362-363, 438
Bolivia, 269
Bolshevik Revolution, 46, 338

Bonafede, Dom, 175
The Boston Globe, 182
Boulevard press, 411
Bourges, Herve, 325
Boyd-Barrett, Oliver, 308
The Brass Check, 28, 37-38
Brazil, 285-286
Breed, Warren, 64
Brezhnev, Leonid, 217
Bribery
    Philippines, 253
    Russia, 223
Brinkley, Alan, 279
Brinkley, David, 67
Broder, David, 142
Brogan, Patrick, 142, 143
Brokaw, Tom, 366
Browning, Jim, 305
Bruck, Connie, 401
Bryant, William Cullen, 22-23
Bücher, Karl, 342-343
Buckley, William F., Jr., 413
Bukholi, Wilson, 245
Burton, John, 442
Bush, George
    and imagemakers, 159, 160, 161, 162, 163-165
    Iran-Contra affair, 171, 174-175
    media, attacks, 365
    news management, 51
    and pollsters, 170
    Unesco, opposes, 331, 332
Business International, 406

Cable News Network (CNN), 104, 109-118, 388,
    390
Cadell, Patrick, 168
Cameroon, 243, 244
Camus, Albert, 442
Canseco, Javier Díaz, 282
Capital Cities, 124, 383-384
Capitalism, xviii, 54-55, 81-82, 85, 86, 88, 89,
    103, 248-251, 278-279, 339, 421-422. *See
    also* Market society
    in advancing nations, 239, 311
    and democracy, 55
    and ecology, 216
    and freedom, 55
    and free press, 8, 408
    Marx on, 202, 204-206
    media acceptance, 409
    and news agencies, 308
    and schools of journalism, 340, 341
    television journalists as agents of, 103
Caretas, 282
Carmichael, Stokely, 181, 183
Carter, Betsy, 98
Carter, Hodding, 125, 128
Carter, Jimmy, 159, 160, 168
Carville, James, 165
Casey, William, 171

Castle Rock Entertainment, 116
Castro, Fidel, 68
Cater, Douglass, 70, 149
CBS, 104, 113, 127, 170, 174, 383
Celebrities, news of, 410–411, 412
Censorship, 378, 379, 412
  advancing nations, 249
  Africa, 432
  Brazil, 285–286
  Chile, 272
  and computers, 390, 407
  Gulf War, 161–162
  India, 239, 285
  Indonesia, 254–255
  Iran, 260, 262
  Malaysia, 257
  Nigeria, 250
  Peru, 272
  Philippines, 253
  Prussian and Marx, 199–201, 205
  Russia, 219, 222
  Singapore, 256–257
  Tanzania, 245
  Zimbabwe, 237
Chafee, Zechariah, 220
Charles X (France), 11, 12, 13–14, 47
Chile, 272
China, 47
  United Nations, 228
Chirac, Jacques, 391
Chomsky, Noam, 76
Christians, Clifford, 364
The Christian Science Monitor, 304, 305
Churchill, Winston, 140
Circulation. *See also* Newspaper readership
  and advertisers, 30, 90
  newspaper chains, 380
  rural press, 431
  worldwide, 296–297
Citizen Kane, 364
Clinton, Bill, 109, 155, 158, 165, 366, 405, 408
Clinton, Hillary Rodham, 185
Clinton-Bush election campaign, 279
Clurman, Richard, 399, 402
CNN. *See* Cable News Network (CNN)
Coaxial cables, 103, 110
Cohen, Bernard C., 149
Cohen, Richard, 127
Collectivist theory, 55–58
Collier's, 31
Columbia Pictures, 389, 390
Columbia University, school of journalism, 140,
  339
El Comercio (Peru), 269, 271, 273, 284
Commodities, newspapers as, 23
Common Man, Age of, 15
Communication research, 353–358
Communitarianism
  and advancing nations, 282
  Etzioni's movement, 220–221

in Iran, 261
in Kenya, 249
and modernization, 258–259
in Peru, 280
press model, 419, 420, 421, 424, 425–429, 431,
  435–436
in Soviet Union, 195–196, 197–198, 215, 216,
  217, 422
and Talloires Declaration, 325, 326
Community, duties to, 221, 229
Community journalism, 431, 434
Community power, 279–280
Computer and communication revolution, 354, 358
Computers and censorship, 390, 407
Conglomerates, *see* Media, 384–392, 397–406
Congreve, William, 376
Converse, Philip E., 166–167
Coolidge, Calvin, 36
Cooper, Kent, 66, 307, 310, 360
Craft, Christine, 184
Crane, Stephen, 17
Craxi, Bettino, 391
Credibility, 141, 142
La Crónica (Peru), 269
Cultural imperialism
  in advancing nations, 234–235, 238
  in Africa, 349
  in Asia, 251
  and conglomerates, 384
  and free-flow doctrine, 301
  in Philippines, 254
  in Singapore and Malaysia, 256
  in Tanzania, 245
  and transnationals, 319
Czech Republic, 124, 422

Daily Mirror (London), 388
Daily News (New York), 388
Daily News (Tanzania), 244
The Daily Times (Lagos), 381
Dana, Charles, 202
Daniels, Derek, 69–70
Davis, Haydn, 142
Davis, Martin S., 405
Day, Benjamin, 21–22
Deaver, Michael, 124, 126, 127
De Fleur, Melvin, 355
Democracy
  and capitalism, 55
  and media, 5
Democratic assumption, 6–7, 139–140
Desmond, Robert, 139
de Tocqueville, Alexis, 29, 46
Development journalism, 229–237, 252, 258
  Asia, 346
  and government control, 284–285
  Malaysia, 256
  and sensationalism, 309
Dewey, Thomas E., 167
Diamond, Edwin, 128, 130

Dickens, Charles, 29, 450
Diller, Barry, 406
Docudrama, 122
Domatob, Jerry, 238
Doreh (social club Iran), 258-259, 261
Dowd, Maureen, 185
Drug trade (Peru), 276, 280-281
Dukakis, Michael, 161, 163-164, 169, 170
Dulles, John Foster, 83
Dye, Thomas R., 71
Dymally, Mervyn M., 326

Eales, Roy, 413
The East African Standard (Nairobi), 246
Economic and Philosophical Manuscripts (Marx),
  203
Education of journalists, 332, 355-358. *See also*
  Schools of journalism, U.S.
  advancing nations, 304, 308, 337, 344-350,
    431
  England, 337-338
  European model, 336, 342-343
  France, 338
  Soviet Union, 343
  U.S. model, 336, 338, 343
Edwards, Kenneth, 413
Ehrenfeld, Rachel, 281
Eisenhower, Dwight, 69
Ellul, Jacques, 149, 155
Emporia Gazette, 31
Engels, Friedrich, 198, 202, 204
England
  education of journalists, 337-338
  Poor Law, 445
English Bill of Rights, 7, 9
English press
  advertising in, 26-27
  government control, 103
  human interest stories in, 22
  as model, 47
  and political struggles, 48
  press council, 142, 143
Enlightenment philosophers, 7, 56
Entertainment, news as, 58, 122-131, 165, 355,
  367, 382, 403, 410, 412
Entman, Robert, 159, 186
Epstein, Edward Jay, 64, 75
Epworth, Marsden, 347
Erhard, Ludwig, 89
ESPN, 112
Ethics, media, 362-368
Etzioni, Amitai, 196, 205, 220-221, 442
Europe
  education of journalists, 336, 338, 342-343
  government control of media, 47, 103
  politics and press, 337
  sensationalism in newspapers, 411
  and U.S. model, 342
European Community, 384
Evans, M. Stanton, 342

Expreso/Extra (Peru), 269, 270, 272, 273

Fadeyibi, Olufolaji Ajibola, 239
Fairchild Publications, 384
Fairness Doctrine, 107-109, 420
Falklands Islands, 76
Fall, Babacar, 430, 431, 432
Fashion Life, 384
Fatal Vision, 412
Federal Communications Commission (FCC),
  105-109, 111
Fiber-optic systems, 103, 110, 404
Fidler, Robert F., 360
Le Figaro, 408
Finkelstein, Louis, 448
Finland, 433-434
First Amendment, 3, 8-9, 10, 69, 107, 137, 155,
  220, 229, 297, 413, 428
Fischer, David Hackett, 419
Ford Foundation, 233
Forrest, Wilber, 139
Fourier, Charles, 202
Four Theories of the Press, 140, 188, 373
Fox Broadcasting, 104, 111, 388
France
  education of journalists, 338
  freedom of press battles, 11-14, 47
  information/education distinction, 59
  and Unesco, 322-323
Frankel, Max, 184-185
Franklin, Benjamin, 7-8, 27
Franklin, James, 7
Fraternité Matin, 244
A Free and Responsible Press, 138
Freedom House, 52, 243-244, 308, 322, 325, 329
Free flow of information, 296, 297-298, 299-306,
  327-328
  vs. balanced flow, 304-306, 318-319
Free press, 408, 435-436, 437
  and capitalism, 8
  definition, 294-295
  Marx on, 201, 436
  support for, 5-6
Frei, Eduardo, 272
Friedan, Betty, 185
Fromm, Erich, 204
Fujimori, Alberto K., 276, 277, 279

Gaborit, Pierre, 323
Galbraith, Kenneth, 77
Gallagher, Matthew, 269
Gallagher, Wes, 66
Gallup, George H., 166
Gandhi, Indira, 239, 285
Gandhi, Mahatma, 448
Gannett newspaper chain, 380
Gans, Herbert J., 64, 128-129
García Pérez, Alán, 276
Gardner, Mary, 350
Gargurevich, Juan, 271

Gazeta de Caracas, 268
Gemini News Service, 312
Gerbner, George, 129
Gergen, David, 127, 155, 365
The German Ideology, 205
German press, 342
Geyer, Georgie Anne, 270
Ghana Institute of Journalism, 348
Ghorbanifar, Manucher, 171
"Giantism" age of, 141
Giffard, C. Anthony, 330
Gilliam, Dorothy, 182
Gitlin, Todd, 130, 131
Gladstone, William E., 36
Glasnost, 216-221
"Glass ceiling," 183, 184
Glendon, Mary Ann, 221
Global News Network (Japan), 390
Global village, 116, 384, 386
Gobright, Lawrence, 65
Goh Chok Tong, 256-257
Golding, Peter, 283
Goldman, Peter, 174
Goldwater, Barry, 69
Gollin, Albert E., 93, 94, 97
Gorbachev, Mikhail, 54, 217, 422, 426
Gordon, Thomas, 24
Gore, Al, 405
Gough, John Bartholomew, 445
Government control
    and advertising, 284
    Cameroon, 243
    and development press, 284-285
    opposed in U.S., 420
Government Printing Office, 32
Gramling, Oliver, 64-65
Gray, Herman, 187
Greeley, Horace, 16, 24, 31, 92, 202, 214
Green, T. H., 447
Greenberg, Stan, 165
Grenada, 328
Grosso, Vincent, 403
Group journalism, 83
The Guardian, 250, 305
Gulf War, 114-115, 118, 158, 161-162
Guzmán Reynoso, Abimael, 277, 279

Hachette, S. A., 391
Hachten, William, 76, 252
Hadden, Briton, 81, 83
Hall, Jane, 126
Hallin, Daniel C., 157-158
Hamelink, Cees, 238
Hamilton, Alexander, 155
Harris, Leonard, 277
Harris, Louis, 168
Hart, Gary, 158
Havel, Václav, 124, 422, 426
Healthlink, 384
Hearst, William Randolph, 17, 29-30, 364

Hegel, Georg W. F., 203
Heisenberg, Werner, 63
Herman, Edward, 76
Hess, Moses, 198
Hester, Al, 312
Hewitt, Don, 72, 74
Hill, Anita, 187
Hill, William, 69-70
Hilliard, William A., 182
Hobhouse, John, 448
Hofstadter, Richard, 29
Holmes, Oliver Wendell, 6, 7, 88
Home Box Office (HBO), 111, 112, 113, 402
Honduras, 269
Houphouët-Boigny, Felix, 244
House critic (press), 143
Hudec, Vladimír, 198, 213-214, 215, 222, 375
Human-interest stories, 22, 30, 98, 124
Hundt, Reed E., 106, 403
Hungary, newspapers in, 218
Hutchins, Robert, 70-71, 138
Hutchins Commission, 75, 138-139, 141-142,
    154, 173, 362, 373, 380, 433, 445, 446

Ideology, press, 58-59
Illiteracy, 320, 321-322
Imagemaking, 153, 158-165
Inca Plan, 272-273, 437
Index Expurgatorius, 31
India, 270, 285
Individual, rights of, 220
Individual, welfare of, 55-58
Indonesia, 251-252, 254-255
Indonesian Journalists Association, 254
Industrial Revolution, 14, 50
Information, primary and secondary, 215
Information superhighway, 117, 404, 441
Ingersoll, Bruce, 74
Institute for Public Opinion, 166
Interactive television, 117, 404
Inter-American Press Association (IAPA), 272, 273
International Centre of Advanced Studies in
    Journalism, 350
International Federation of Newspaper Publishers,
    325, 331
The International Herald-Tribune, 252
International news pool, 304
International Press Institute, 282-283, 308
International Program for the Development of
    Communication (IPDC), 320, 322, 325,
    328, 329, 331, 332
Inter Press Service (IPS), 310, 311-312, 318, 431
Investigative journalists, 147, 148, 362-363
Iran, 257-262, 359
Iran-Contra affair, 171-174
Irwin, Christopher, 117
Irwin, Will, 28, 31, 141, 449
Isaacson, Walter, 403
Isaksson, Andri, 331
Iskra, 211

Istoe, 277
Ivory Coast, 244
Izvestia, 123, 221, 223, 377

Jackson, Andrew, 15, 24, 32-33
Jayaweera, Neville, 188-189
Jefferson, Thomas, 10, 11-13, 32, 48, 211
Jennings, Peter, 74, 170, 366
Johnson, Kirk, 182
Johnson, Lyndon, 69, 77
Journalism Quarterly, 139
Journalists. *See also* Education of journalists
  dissatisfaction of, 366-367, 446
  investigative, 147, 148, 362-363
  licenses, 320, 323-324, 326
  pay scales (Latin America), 350

Katz, Jon, 74
Keller, Maryann, 407
Kelly, Michael, 155
Kempe, Frederick, 71
Kenya, 246-249
Kenya African National Unity, 248
Kenya Broadcasting Corporation, 248
The Kenya Times, 248
Kerensky, Alexander, 212
Kerner Commission, 181, 182
Khomeini, Ayatollah, 68, 259-262
Kibaru, 430
King, Rodney, 186, 188
The Kingdom and the Power, 26
Kirkpatrick, Jeane, 76
Kochman, Thomas, 184
Koestler, Arthur, 206
Koffi, Atta, 244
Komensky, Johann Amos, 375-376
Korsch, Karl, 204
Kovach, Bill, 95
Kurtz, Howard, 185, 188

Labyrinth of the World, 375-376
Lafayette, Marquis de, 11-12
Lagardère, Jean-Luc, 391
Lamb, James, 269
Lambeth, Edmund, 357
Landon, Alfred E., 167
Language and social control, 50-51, 227-229
Lapham, Lewis, 383, 404
Latin America
  advertising, 283-284
  journalist pay scales, 350
  Marxism, 349
  press, 47
Law of Justice and Love (France), 12-13
Le Cinq (French television), 391
Lee, Alfred McClung, 28-29
Lee, Chris, 403-404
Lee Kuan Yew, 256
Leggett, William, 23
Lehrer, Jim, 366

Lenin, Vladimir Ilyich, 196, 206, 414
  on free press, 436
  on Marx, 204
  on role of press, 205, 209-212, 214, 215, 221,
    338, 420, 425
Leninism, 197
Lent, John, 256
Lerner, Daniel, 252
Letters to the editor
  Africa, 431
  Soviet Union, 221, 222
Levin, Gerald M., 401, 402
Levy, H. Phillip, 142
Lewis, Carolyn, 356
Licenses
  Indonesia, 255
  journalists, 320, 323-324, 326
  publications in Russia, 218
  radio and television, 107, 109
Lippmann, Walter, 36, 77, 88
Lipset, Seymour, 365
The Literary Digest, 167
The Literary Gazette, 378
Locke, John, 220
"The Lone Rider," 34
The Los Angeles Times, 94, 97, 187
Luce, Henry R., 81-85, 111, 123, 138
Luce, Henry R., III, 398
Luna, Ricardo V., 277

MacBride, Sean, 304, 317
MacBride Commission, 316-320, 322-324, 328,
    413-414, 433
McCarthy, Joseph, 64, 106
McChesney, Robert, 409
McClure's, 37
MacDonald, Jeffrey, 412
McGinniss, Joseph, 412-413
McGovern, George, 159
McGowan, William, 182, 187
McGrath, Judy, 96
Machado, José Mayobré, 329
McLuhan, Marshall, 86, 90, 116, 386
Madison, James, 9, 10, 12-13, 32
Maetzke, Ernst-Otto, 311
Magazines, advertising revenue, 97-98
Malaysia, 251, 252, 255-257, 348
Malcolm, Janet, 412, 413
Mali, 430, 432
Malone, John (TCI), 403, 404, 405, 406
Management of news, 32-33, 49-51, 126-127
Manifest Destiny, 16
Manipulation of press, 152-153, 217, 317, 435. *See
    also* Power, media as agents of
Manipulation of public opinion, 215
Mao Zedong, 276-277
Marcos, Ferdinand, 237, 239, 253
Mariátegui, José Carlos, 280, 350
"Marketplace of ideas," 6
Market society, press model, 419, 420, 421, 422,

424, 426–427, 428–429, 435–436. *See also*
    Capitalism
Marroquín Rojas, Clemente, 270, 436
Martin, L. John, 349
Martin Chuzzelwit, 450
Marx, Karl, 35, 36, 89, 195–206, 351
    on censorship, 48, 285
    collective defined, 57
    on free press, 201, 436
    on religion, 127
Marxism, 209, 210
    on advancing nations, 234
    on development journalism, 252
    in Latin America, 349
    on role of press, 215, 326, 338, 420, 425
Masmoudi, Mustapha, 304
Mathews, Tom, 174
Matra, 257, 391
Matushita Electric Industrial Studios, 389
Maxwell, Robert, 114, 248, 386–388
Mayflower Compact, 57
Mayor Zaragoza, Federico, 295, 330, 331
M'Bow, Amadow Mahtar, 304, 305, 323, 324, 330
Mboya, Tom, 231, 270
MCA Inc., 389, 390
Media, *see* Journalists
    agenda-setting function, 149–150
    as agents of power, 5, 13–14, 128, 155, 325,
        398, 440
    and democracy, 5
    conglomerates, 111–118, 382–392, 396–414
    coverage of
        minorities, 181–187
    distinguished from press, 5
    as pleasure, 50
    power of, 70–77, 354–355
    and urban centers, 14
Media imperialism, 306, 308
Media Research Center, 75, 76
Mediated journalism, 157–158
Meese, Edward, 172
Merrill Lynch, 256–257
Metzenbaum, Howard, 404–405
Mexico, war with, 16
Microsoft Corporation, 402
Mill, James, 48
Mill, John Stuart, 51, 325, 444, 445
Miller, Clarence, 326
Milton, John, 6, 7, 88
The Minneapolis Star-Tribune, 97
Minority affairs, coverage, 180–181, 186–188
Minority employment, media, 181–186
Minow, Newton, 105, 108
Mkapa, Ben, 311
Modernization and Iran, 258–259, 260, 261
Möhn, Reinhard, 391
Moi, Daniel Arap, 249
Mojto, Jan, 384
Le Monde, 408
The Moscow News, 223

Moscow State University School of Journalism,
    211, 343
Moskovsky Komsomolets, 218
Mossadegh, Mohammed, 259, 260
Mowlana, Hamid, 261, 359
Moynihan, Daniel Patrick, 147
MTV, cable-TV channel, 405
Muckrakers, 34–39, 141, 338, 449
Mungo, Ray, 147
Murdoch, Rupert, 104, 218, 223, 388–389, 390,
    400
Murrow, Edward R., 106, 107
Muskie, Edmund, 159
Mutere, Absolom, 248

Narcoterrorism, 280–281
National Association of Black Journalists, 182
National Education Association, 445
National Gay and Lesbian Journalists Association,
    182
The National Journal, 175
National Journalism Center, 342
National News Council, 122, 142, 143, 320, 322
Nation building
    and development journalism, 230–231
    Philippines, 254
    and technology, 358–359
Nazi Germany, 11, 116, 296
NBC, 104, 117, 158, 170, 383
Nehru, Jawaharlal, 270, 285
Neue Rheinische Zeitung, 35, 198, 199, 200–201
Neuharth, Al, 94
New Deal, 89, 137–138
New Englander, 16
New international economic order, 294, 304,
    305–306, 317
New international information order, 293, 294,
    303–304, 305–306, 310, 311, 317–318, 322,
    323, 326, 327, 350
New Line Cinema Corporation, 116
Newmont Mining Company, 277
New Republic, 94
News agencies, 306–312, 327–328, 341, 386. *See
    also* Associated Press (AP); United Press
    International (UPI)
News Agencies Pool of Non-Aligned Countries,
    310–311
News management, 32–33, 49–51, 126–127, 144,
    156–170
    and spindoctors, 159–170
    for patterns, 52–53
Newspaper Advertising Bureau, 93
Newspaper Association of America, 182
Newspaper chains, 380
Newspaper readership, 92–97
    African-American, 187
    Soviet, 221
Newspapers
    circulation, 30, 90, 296–297, 380, 431
    competition, decline of, 409

subsidies, 381
tabloids, 124
Newsprint
   discovery of, 30
   per-capita consumption, 295
The New Straits Times (Malaysia), 257
Newswatch (Nigeria), 250
Newsweek, 85, 182
New world economic order. *See* New international
   economic order
New World Information and Communication
   Order, 331, 346
New world information order. *See* New
   international information order
The New York Evening Post, 22-23
The New York Herald, 24, 26
The New York Morning News, 16
The New York Sun, 21-22, 27
The New York Times, 26, 31, 94, 139, 158, 182,
   223, 341, 411, 412
The New York Tribune, 24, 202
New York Woman, 98
New York World, 28
Nicholas, Nicholas, 401
Nigeria, 240, 244, 249-250, 381
Nigerian Union of Journalists, 235
Nixon, Richard
   press, relationship with, 69, 71, 143, 155
   and Watergate affair, 13-14, 33, 67-68, 158,
      159, 176, 362
Nkrumah, Kwame, 233-234, 270, 348
Nonaligned nations, 254, 302, 303, 310
Nordenstreng, Kaarle, 329
Noriega, Manuel, 161
North, Oliver L., 171-172
Novak, Michael, 447-448
Nyerere, Julius K., 244-245, 434

Objectivism, 214
Objectivity, 10, 173, 408
   in advancing nations, 245, 282
   in Asia, 233
   in Europe, 342
   in penny press, 24
   Soviet model, 222
   and *status quo*, 425
Objectivity, code of, 62-70, 165, 205, 229, 411,
   442
   in journalism schools, 340-341, 363
Ochs, Adolph, 24-26, 31
L'Office de Cooperation Radiophonique, 345
Ogonyok, 218-219
O'Heffernan, Patrick, 155
Ohga, Noio, 389-390
Ojo, 273
Olasky, Marvin, 75
Ombudsman, 143-144
Ortega, Carlos, 271, 273
Osheyack, Dan, 99
Osoba, Segun, 381

O'Sullivan, John L, 16
Owen, Robert, 202
Oxford University, 337
Oyewole, Bode, 235-236, 426

"Pack" journalism, 158
Page, Clarence, 186
Paletz, David, 159
Palmer, David Scott, 280
Pan-African News Agency (PANA), 310, 431
Panama, 161
Pancasila, 254-255
Paramount Communications Inc., 104, 405-406
Parenti, Michael, 122
Participatory journalism, 428, 429-430, 433-434
Pasquim, 285
Patent-medicine advertising, 26, 27, 31
Patriotism, 162-163
Paymasters, *see* Capitalism, piper
   relationship patterns with news content, 52-53,
      376
   relationship with pipers, 376-380
Pease, Ted, 187, 188
Pennsylvania Gazette, 8
Penny press, 21-22
   advertising, 26
   and department stores, 27
   mass audience, 23
   and yellow press, 30
People, 85, 411
Pergamon Press, 387
Perot, Ross, 165
Persian Gulf War. *See* Gulf War
Peru, 262, 267-282, 284
   feudal society, 268
   government control of media, 272-273
   illiteracy, 268
   press, role of, 271
Peters, Charlie, 357
Peterson, Theodore, 140
Peyronnet, Charles Ignace de, 12
The Philadelphia Inquirer, 183
Philippines, 236-237, 239, 252-254
Philosophical Notebooks (Lenin), 210
Pierce, Robert, 271
Pike, Sid, 112
Pinkney, David, 13
Piper, image of press as, 375-376
The Pittsburgh Gazette, 27
Plato, 363
Poindexter, John M., 171
Political goals and press, 31-32
Politicians, criticism of media by, 341-342, 365
Politics, point-of-purchase, 98-99
Polling, 166-170
Poole, Deborah, 280
Postal rates, 32
Postman, Neil, 128
The Post (New York), 388
Power, media as agents of, 5, 13-14, 128, 155,

325, 398, 440
Power of media, *see* Presidents and the press, spin-doctors, xi-xiii, 70-77, 137-143, 147-149, 354-356, 362, 354-355
and agenda setting, 149-150, 169-172
as lacking independence, xxiii-xxiv, 70, 155-159, 201, 324-325
in election campaigns, 155-170
vis à vis political and economic power, 233-234, 238-240, 250-251, 252-257, 269-271
Prague Center, 343
Pravda, 123, 212, 218, 221-222, 377, 378
La Prensa (Peru), 269, 271, 273
Presidents and the press, 67-70, 108-109, 126-127, 138, 143, 147, 153-176
Press agents, 31
Press councils, 141-143, 437
Press Foundation of Asia, 233
Proctor & Gamble, 98
Profit motive, 8, 105, 155-156, 162, 364, 367, 378. *See also* Capitalism
Propaganda
  role of press (Marxism), 215, 420
  sociological, 149, 155
Public expectations of the press, 59-60
Public opinion
  and the elite, 145
  manipulation of, 215
  press, role of, 245, 319
  shaped by holders of power, 155, 396
Public-opinion polling, 166-170
Public policy and the press, *see* News management, Power of media, Presidents and the press, Social control, xi
Public's right to know, 412, 429
Pulitzer, Joseph, 15, 17, 28, 29-30, 31, 93, 140, 338, 339, 340-341
Pye, Lucien, 252

Quebral, Nora, 237
QVC Network Inc., 405-406

Rader, Daniel, 13
Radio
  Africa, 349
  and social control, 102
Radio and Television News Directors Association, 126, 157, 360
Radio receivers, worldwide, 298-299
Radio Television Malaysia, 252
Ramos, Fidel, 254
Rather, Dan, 106, 107, 170, 174-175, 366
Rattner, Steven, 93-94
Reagan, Ronald, 126, 168, 280
  economic policies, 89, 164
  Fairness Doctrine, opposes, 108, 109
  and imagemakers, 159, 160-161, 162, 164
  Iran-Contra affair, 171-172, 174
  news management, 51, 126-127

Unesco, opposes, 323, 326, 327, 329, 330, 332
Reasoner, Harry, 72
Redstone, Sumner M., 400, 404, 405-406
Reed, John, 88
Renique, Geraldo, 280
Reno, Janet, 130
"Reptile fund," 35-36, 47
Reuters, 307, 309, 310
Revolutionary press, 145-147
Reynolds, Barbara, 185
Reza Khan, 259
Reza Shah Pahlavi, 259, 260, 261-262
Richmond Enquirer, 12
Roche, John, 325
Rockefeller, John D., 37
Rogers, Everett, 238
Rønning, Helge, 237
Roosevelt, Franklin D., 89, 90, 138, 154, 158, 167
Roosevelt, Theodore, 34, 37, 38
Roosevelt University, 182
Rosen, Jay, 75
Rosenberg, Tina, 276, 282
Rosenman, Howard, 406
Ross, Steven J., 398-402
Rosten, Leo, 23
Roth, Joe, 389
Rousseau, Jean-Jacques, 57, 202, 444-445
Royer-Collard, Pierre-Paul, 12
Ruge, Arnold, 199
Rukunegara, 257
Rural press (Africa), 430-431
Russia, 46, 48, 123, 338. *See also* Soviet Union

Sabato, Larry, 149, 158, 173, 365
Said, Edward W., 258
Salinas, Raquel, 271
San Diego Tribune, 97
Sarrazin, Pierre, 57-58, 419
Savio, Robert, 312, 318
Schiller, Herbert, 398
Schonfeld, Reese, 112
Schools of journalism, U.S., 58, 339-341, 356-358, 360, 441. *See also* Education of journalists
Schramm, Wilbur, 140, 252
Schreyer, Roland, 430-431, 434
Schudson, Michael, 62-63
Schwartz, Edward, 221
Schwartz, Leland, 117
Scientific method, 63, 261
Sears, Roebuck, 99
The Seattle Times, 304
Sedition Act, 9
Seleznev, Gennedy, 223
Sendero Luminoso (Shining Path), 274-282
Sensationalism, 29-30, 124, 138, 142, 309, 311, 340-341, 411. *See also* Yellow press
Shafer, Martin, 116
Shafer, Richard, 252-253
Shaw, Bernard, 366
Shriver, Donald W., 125-126

Shultz, George, 328
Siebert, Fred S., 140
Sierra, Rob, 186
Simpson, Carole, 184
Sinaga, Edward Janner, 254, 255
Sinclair, Upton, 28, 31, 37-38, 88, 141
Singapore, 251, 255-257
Singapore Press Holdings, 257
Singhal, Arvid, 238
"60 Minutes," 72-75, 113, 367
The Sketch (Ibadan), 381
Sky Television, 388, 389
Smith, Adam, 429
Smith, Anthony, 147, 389, 390, 391, 402, 406, 409
Smith, Frazier, 187, 188
Smith, Raymond W., 403, 404, 405, 406
Smith, Roger, 129
Social contract, 56-57
Social control, xiii
    in advancing nations, 346
    and government, 34-38, 55-57
    and news management, 33, 49-51
    and the press, 11, 22, 26, 69, 420
    radio and television, 102
    views of Marx and Lenin, 202-205
Social Darwinism, 26, 34, 36
Social responsibility, doctrine of, 70, 137-140,
        144, 148, 152, 173, 180, 188, 212, 362,
        363, 364, 423, 440, 444-448
Society, welfare of, 55-58
Sociological propaganda, 149, 155
Solomon, Jolie, 403
Solomon, Michael, 384
Sony Corporation, 389-390
South Africa, 244
Soviet Empire, fall of, 47, 103, 114, 140, 214, 216,
        217, 311, 343, 422, 423
Soviet Union
    and collectivist theory, 55
    and communitarianism, 195-196, 197-198, 215,
        216, 217, 422
    education of journalists, 343
    financing of press, 374
    objectivity and Marxism-Leninism, 377
    power structure and the media, 54
    and social responsibility, 144
    subsidies, radio and television, 377
    and Unesco, 300-301, 307-308, 325
Spanish-American War, 17, 30, 253
Spin doctors, 155, 156-157, 158, 279
Stalin, 217
Star, 366, 408
Starodomskaya, Svetlana, 217, 448-449
Stars and Stripes, 325
Star-TV, 389, 390
Statute on Freedom of the Press (Peru), 272
Steele, Audrey, 104
Steffens, Lincoln, 31, 37, 88
Stephenson, William, 50, 355
Stevenson, Adlai, 69

Stone, Vernon A., 186
The Straits Times (Singapore), 257
Sukarno, 254
Sulzberger, Arthur Ochs, Jr., 182, 187
Summers, Larry, 228
Sussman, Leonard R., 322, 325, 329
Swinton, Stan, 322
Syndicalism, 271
Synergy, 383
The Syracuse News-Journal, 96
Syracuse Peace Council, 108-109

Tabloid newspapers, Europe, 124
Tabloid television, 125-126, 130
Talese, Gay, 26
Talloires Declaration, 324, 325
Tamil Malar, 348
Tanii, Akio, 389-390
Tanjug, 310
Tanzania, 244-246, 434
Tanzanian Revolutionary Party, 245
Tarazona-Sevillano, Gabriela, 280-281
Tarbell, Ida, 37
TASS, 212, 307, 311, 312
Tawhid (Islamic theory), 261
Technology, 358-361, 382, 441
    in advancing nations, 407
    and live news, 366
    and the press, 51, 361
    and television, 103, 109-110, 117, 130, 345-346
Tehranian, Majid, 258, 261
TeleCommunications Inc. (TCI), 114, 402-403,
        404-405
Televisa (Mexico), 277
Television
    advertising revenues, 102-103, 104
    hours watched, 4
    Indonesia, 255
    interactive, 117, 404
    local news programs, 105
    niche programming, 104
    Nigeria programming, 249
    profits, arguments for, 106
    rating systems, 107
    and social control, 102
    tabloid television, 125-126, 130
    Tanzania, role in, 245-246
    and violence and crime, 129-130
Television receivers, worldwide, 300-301
Television stations, profits, 104
TeleWest, 404
Telstar, 110
Terre et Progrès, 431
Thatcher, Margaret, 169
Third World. *See* Advancing nations; Development
        journalism
Thomas, Clarence, 158, 187
Thorburn, David, 74-75
Tietolaari, 433-434
Time, 81-85, 98, 111, 123

The Times (London), 306
The Times of India, 347
Time Warner Inc., 114, 116-117, 398-402, 404
Tinker, John, 384
Tönnies, Ferdinand, 145, 396, 398
Transnational corporations, 246, 382-392, 397
  in Africa, 243
  and cultural imperialism, 319
  and data flow, 406-407
  fostering consumer society, 238
  in Singapore, 255-256, 257
Trud, 377-378
Truman, Harry S., 167
Tuchman, Gaye, 64
Tudesq, A. J., 13
Tupac Amaru Revolutionary Movement, 276
Turner, Robert Edward (Ted) III, 104, 111-118, 401
"20/20" (ABC), 72

Überbau (Marx), 201-202, 203, 204-205, 206, 355
Uburu, 244, 245
Ulloa, Manuel, 273
Underground press, 145-147
  Philippines, 253
Unesco, 234, 294, 295-296
  attacks on, 325-327
  and code of conduct, 302-303, 323-324, 326
  free-flow doctrine, 299-305, 318-319, 328
  and international news pool, 304
  and journalism education, 350
  and licenses, 320, 323-324, 326
  and local news agencies, 310
  and Soviet Union, 307-308
  standards of communication, 295
  and U.S. press, 322
  U.S. rejection, 326-330
United Nations, 228, 294, 295
United Press International (UPI), 66, 304, 307. *See also* News agencies
Universal Declaration of Human Rights, 221, 324
University of Birmingham, 337
University of London, 337
University of Missouri, 339-340, 353
University of Wisconsin, 340, 353
Urban centers and media, 14, 22
U.S. News & World Report, 185, 365
USA Today, 94, 380, 410

Vanocur, Sandor, 158
Vargas Llosa, José, 281, 282
Velasco Alvarado, Juan, 270, 271, 272, 273, 274, 284

Venezuela, 268, 269
Viacom-Paramount, 406
Videocassette recorders (VCRs), 117-118
Videocassettes, 252
Vietnam War, 176
Villèle, Jean Baptiste de, 11, 12, 13
La Voie, 244

Wallace, Mike, 74
Wallach, John, 171
Wambaugh, Joseph, 413
Warner Brothers, 104
Washington, D.C., journalists in, 153-154
The Washington Post, 94, 143, 341, 362
"Watchdog" press, 34-35, 148-149, 338
Watergate affair, 13-14, 33, 67-68, 158, 159, 176, 362, 364
WCTG-TV, Atlanta, 112
Weaver, David, 130
Weber, Max, 50-51, 145
Werner, Larry, 97
West African News Agencies Development (WANAD), 431-432
WGN, Chicago, 186
White, William Allen, 31
Wilhoit, G. Cleveland, 130
Williams, Walter, 339-340
Wilson, Woodrow, 83
Windhoek (Namibia) conference, 242-243, 250-251, 285, 331, 348
Winthrop, John, 16
Wirthlin, Richard B., 160, 168, 169, 170
WLBT-TV, Jackson, Mississippi, 107
Wolff, Perry, 72
Wolff, Robert Paul, 68
Women, employed by media, 184-185
Woodward, Robert, 158, 159, 362-364
World Press Encyclopedia, 271
World Service Television, 117

Yakoviev, Yegor, 223
Yannikos, Yannis, 222
Yellow press, 17, 30, 37-39. *See also* Sensationalism
Yeltsin, Boris, 218, 219, 222, 224
Young India, 448

Zassursky, Yasen N., 214-215, 343
Zenger, John Peter, 7
Zhirinovsky, Vladimir, 223
Zimbabwe, 237
Zimmerman, Betty, 317, 323
Zuckerman, Mortimer D., 388